Human Behavior in the Social Environment

Human Behavior in the Social Environment

Theories for Social Work Practice

Bruce A. Thyer
Catherine N. Dulmus
Karen M. Sowers

JOHN WILEY & SONS, INC.

Library of Congress Cataloging-in-Publication Data:

Thyer, Bruce A.
  Human behavior in the social environment : theories for social work practice / Bruce A. Thyer, Catherine N. Dulmus, Karen M. Sowers.
    p. cm.
    Includes bibliographical references and index.
  ISBN 978-1-118-17694-8 (pbk.)
  ISBN 978-1-118-26488-1 (ebk.)
  ISBN 978-1-118-24016-8 (ebk.)
  ISBN 978-1-118-22725-1 (ebk.)
  1. Social service. 2. Human behavior. I. Dulmus, Catherine N. II. Sowers, Karen M. (Karen Marlaine) III. Title.
  HV40.T51377 2012
  150.1023'36132—dc23
                                                                                          2012008111

Printed in the United States of America
V10004440_090718

This work is respectfully dedicated to those numerous social work researchers, practitioners, and academics who have contributed toward developing the empirical foundations of the human services.

Contents

Preface   xiii

Acknowledgments   xxix

About the Editors   xxxi

Contributors   xxxiii

Chapter 1   **Human Behavior and the Social Environment:
           Exploring Conceptual Foundations   1**
           *Susan I. Stone, Yolanda Anyon, Stephanie Berzin, Sarah
           Taylor, and Michael J. Austin*

           Scholarly and Professional Dilemmas Related to Human Behavior
              and the Social Environment   2
           Development of the Human Behavior and Social Environment
              Construct   7
           A Selection of Frameworks That Address Linkages Between Human
              Behavior and the Social Environment   14
           Life Course Approach: An Application   17
           The Social Environment: Key Concepts   28
           Frameworks for Linking Knowledge to Practice   36
           Conclusion   38
           Key Terms   39
           Review Questions for Critical Thinking   39
           Online Resources   40
           References   41

Chapter 2   **Respondent Learning Theory   47**
           Bruce A. Thyer

           Respondent Learning Processes   49
           Naturally Occurring Examples of Respondent Learning in Real
              Life   56
           Experimental Examples of Respondent Learning   59
           Examples of Respondent Learning of Psychosocial Problems   62
           Using Respondent Learning in Social Work Practice   67
           Creating Conditioned Reactions   69

Philosophical Foundations of Respondent Learning   71
Key Terms   74
Review Questions for Critical Thinking   75
Online Resources   75
References   75

Chapter 3

Operant Learning Theory   83

Stephen E. Wong

Historical and Conceptual Origins   83
Basic Theoretical Principles   85
Advanced Theoretical Principles   96
Recent Theoretical Developments   98
Relevance to Social Work Practice   103
Critiques of the Operant Learning Approach   111
Key Terms   112
Review Questions for Critical Thinking   112
Online Resources   113
References   114

Chapter 4

Cognitive-Behavioral Theory 125

Paula S. Nurius and Rebecca J. Macy

Relevance to Contemporary Practitioners 125
Overview of Cognitive-Behavioral Theory 126
Historical and Conceptual Origins 128
Basic Theoretical Principles 132
Advanced Theoretical Principles 140
Recent Theoretical Developments 144
Relevance to Social Work Practice 146
Evidence-Based Foundations 154
Critiques of This Approach 155
Key Terms 157
Review Questions for Critical Thinking 157
Online Resources 158
References 159

Chapter 5

Attachment Theory 165

Michelle Mohr Carney and Phen M. Young

Historical and Conceptual Origins 166
Basic Theoretical Principles 168

Advanced Theoretical Principles 169
Recent Theoretical Developments 171
Relevance to Social Work Practice 173
Critiques of This Approach 182
Key Terms 183
Review Questions for Critical Thinking 183
Online Resources 184
References 184

Chapter 6   **Psychosocial Theory 193**
Roberta R. Greene

Developmental Theory 193
Historical and Conceptual Origins 194
Basic Theoretical Principles 197
Advanced Theoretical Principles 207
Recent Theoretical Developments 210
Relevance to Social Work Practice 212
Evidence-Based Foundations: Erikson on Erikson 214
Critiques of This Approach 215
Key Terms 219
Review Questions for Critical Thinking 219
Online Resources 220
References 220

Chapter 7   **Person-Centered Theory 225**
Michael J. Holosko, Jeffrey Skinner,
and Catherine A. Patterson

Historical and Conceptual Origins 226
Basic Theoretical Principles 233
Advanced Theoretical Principles 239
Recent Theoretical Developments 243
Relevance to Social Work 244
Assessment 246
Intervention 248
Evidence-Based Foundations 251
Critiques of This Approach 254
Key Terms 257
Review Questions for Critical Thinking 258
Online Resources 258
References 259

Chapter 8   **Genetic Theory 263**
Laura J. Pankow

    The Eukaryotic Cell 266
    Chromosomes 268
    Reproduction 270
    Mitosis 271
    Mendelian Genetics 273
    The Process of Meiosis 275
    Pedigrees 277
    DNA and RNA 278
    The Genetics of Gender 281
    The Human Genome Project 285
    Conclusion 291
    Key Terms 292
    Review Questions for Critical Thinking 292
    Online Resources 292
    References 294

Chapter 9   **Ecosystems Theory 297**
Mark A. Mattaini and Kristen Huffman-Gottschling

    The Ecosystems Perspective in Social Work 298
    The Conceptual Roots of the Ecosystems Perspective 300
    Evaluating the Ecosystems Perspective 311
    Returning to the Science 314
    Mapping Practice 316
    Conclusion 318
    Key Terms 319
    Review Questions for Critical Thinking 319
    Online Resources 320
    References 320

Chapter 10   **Small Group Theory 327**
Lorraine Moya Salas, Dominique Roe-Sepowitz,
*   and Craig Winston LeCroy*

    Definitions 329
    History and Conceptual Origins 330
    Basic Theoretical Principles 339
    Advanced Theoretical Principles 344

Recent Theoretical Developments 350
Relevance to Social Work Practice 353
Evidence-Based Foundations 359
Critiques of This Approach 361
Key Terms 362
Review Questions for Critical Thinking 363
Online Resources 363
References 364

Chapter 11   **Family Systems Theory 369**
Martha Morrison Dore

Historical and Conceptual Origins 369
Basic Theoretical Principles 377
Advanced Theoretical Principles 379
Recent Theoretical Developments 383
Relevance to Social Work Practice 385
Evidence-Based Foundations 396
Critiques of This Theory 398
Key Terms 401
Review Questions for Critical Thinking 401
Online Resources 401
References 402

Chapter 12   **Organizational Theory 411**
John E. Tropman and Emily J. Nicklett

Organizational Behavior 411
Historical and Conceptual Origins 414
Basic Theoretical Principles 422
Advanced Theoretical Principles 426
Recent Theoretical Developments 432
Relevance to Social Work Practice 442
Overall Social Work Demographics 443
Evidence-Based Foundations 451
Critiques of This Approach 452
Conclusion 452
Key Terms 453
Review Questions for Critical Thinking 453
Online Resources 453
References 454

Chapter 13   **The Potentially Harmful Effects of Theory in Social Work 459**
Bruce A. Thyer
Some Harmful Effects of Bad Theory 461
Where Can We Go From Here? 476
Conclusion 481
Key Terms 482
Review Questions for Critical Thinking 482
Online Resources 483
References 484

Author Index 489
Subject Index 499

Preface

This book is designed as a foundation for understanding human behavior in the social environment for undergraduate and graduate students in social work programs. The text provides an overview of some of the major theories used to guide social work practice with individuals, families, small groups, and organizations. This book addresses the Council on Social Work Education (CSWE, 2008) required competencies for accreditation. Specifically, the book addresses the following required accreditation competencies:

- Educational Policy 2.1.3—Apply critical thinking to inform and communicate professional judgments
- Educational Policy 2.1.7—Apply knowledge of human behavior and the social environment
- Educational Policy 2.1.9—Respond to the contexts that shape practice

Each chapter begins with an overarching question or issue that the particular theory attempts to address, and concludes with definitions of some of the key terms related to that approach, some discussion questions, and references to websites that can provide additional information about that given theory and its originators. PowerPoint slides that illustrate the major points of the chapter and multiple choice questions are provided for instructors at the book companion site at www.wiley.com.

From the beginnings of the professionalization of social work, our discipline has been concerned with the possible applications of valid social and behavioral science theory to the world of practice. As we transitioned from a paraprofessional and apprenticeship model of training to a university-based academic or professional school model, behavioral science theory increasingly became an important component of our curriculum (see Bruno, 1936). We draw on theory for a variety of purposes: to understand normative individual human development across the life span; to understand the etiology and maintenance of dysfunctional behavior, including so-called mental disorders; to assess clients; to provide guidance in the development and application of social work intervention; to help us understand how intervention may work; and to extend these individualistic applications of theory to ever-larger systems of human functioning—family life, the dynamics of couples, the interaction of small groups, the behavior of organizations and communities, and the behavior of even more complex systems.

We have drawn from an increasingly diverse array of theory. Early adoption of simple classical conditioning theory (e.g., Mateer, 1918;

Rovee-Collier, 1986) and psychoanalytic theory gave way to more complex and encompassing derivatives, such as operant learning theory, ego psychology, and attachment theory. The disciplines of mathematics and cybernetics gave us general systems theory, which saw widespread endorsement in the 1970s. Client-centered theory and cognitive-behavioral theory also arose in the 1970s and 1980s, as well as myriad other approaches. Some older readers will remember transactional analysis, and neurolinguistic programming, and the contemporary avant-garde among social worker theorists are busy bringing us their interpretations of chaos and complexity theory, as well as perspectives rich in complex mathematics (as was general systems theory), but fortunately absent such challenging aspects in their social work translations. Each new edition of Frank Turner's 1974 classic text *Social Work Treatment: Interlocking Theoretical Approaches* grew plumper as more and more chapters were included that addressed the newest theoretical orientations. His latest edition (Turner, 2011) contains separate chapters on 36 theories now said to inform social work practice. In comparison, the second edition (Turner, 1979) included only 19 distinct theories. Thus the range of theories applicable to our field has almost doubled in about 30 years!

Practically speaking, a major stimulus for social work education's current focus on theory rests in the prior accrediting standards of the Council on Social Work Education (CSWE; 2003), which clearly stipulated the educational competencies that students be taught:

> *Social workers apply theories and knowledge from the liberal arts to understand biological, social, cultural, psychology, and spiritual development....*
> *Social workers ... utilize conceptual frameworks to guide the process of assessment, intervention, and evaluation; and ... critique and apply knowledge to understand person and environment. (Educational Policy 2.1.7)*

> *[U]se theoretical frameworks supported by empirical evidence to understand and support individual development and behavior across the life span and the interactions among individuals and between individuals and families, groups, organizations, and communities.*

The CSWE's (2004) *Educational Policies and Accreditation Standards* (EPAS) document went on to say that required

> *[C]ontent includes empirically based theories and knowledge that focus on the interactions between and among individuals, groups, societies, and economic systems. It includes theories and knowledge of biological, sociological, cultural, psychological, and spiritual development across the life span; the range of social systems in which people live (individual, family, group, organizational, and community); and the ways social systems promote or deter people in maintaining or achieving health and well-being. (p. 9)*

This was quite an ambitious undertaking, especially given the brief time in which students have to earn their BSW or MSW degree. But for the student grumpily scratching her head, asking, "Why do I have to learn all this theory?" the short answer is that the CSWE said that it must be taught, as it is seen as an essential component of the BSW and MSW programs of study.

The situation has changed recently with the newest edition of the EPAS (CSWE, 2008), which contains only four brief mentions of theory, and no longer indicates that students should be taught empirically supported theories. Most current social work programs were accredited under the prior EPAS competencies, but as the cycle of reaccreditation rolls on, it remains to be seen if content on social work theory actually diminishes in the curriculum.

There are other reasons why our field has stressed training in theoretical content. Charlotte Towle (1964, p. vii) implied one function that is seldom explicitly articulated: "Certainly a profession does not come of age *until it develops its own theory*" (italics added). As far back as 1915, Abraham Flexner (1915/2001) concluded that social work was not a true profession, in part because of its lack of a solid foundation of indigenous theory; to some extent we have been trying to remedy this embarrassing deficiency ever since. It must be admitted that for the past 90 or so years, our preoccupation with theory, mostly borrowed and little new, has been stimulated by our sense that our discipline is somehow less than fully developed due to our theoretical inadequacies.

The view that possession of a strong theory or theories is crucial to the legitimacy of a discipline is widespread within the scientific community. For example, Simonton (2006, pp. 98, 104) contends, "In the absence of some theoretical framework, there is no way of separating critical findings from trivial results," and "the most scientific of the sciences tend to be the most theoretical. Or more precisely, the hard disciplines possess strong theories that provide a consensus on what are the key concepts and questions that underlie scientific research."

By incorporating theory legitimately into social work education, practice, and research, our claim to being a genuine profession and science-based discipline is seen as enhanced. Sometimes, however, our use of theory in these areas is spurious, misguided, uninformed, and harmful, more akin to the workings of what Feynman (1974) called a *cargo-cult science*, a discipline with the outward appearance of being science-based but lacking any true understanding of what is going on as the researchers go through the motions of investigation.

What Is a Theory?

It is always helpful when addressing a complex subject to begin by defining fundamental terms. Since the subject matter of this volume is theories of *Human Behavior in the Social Environment*, let us begin with the concept of *theory*. Turning to *The Social Work Dictionary*, we find theory defined as:

> *A group of related hypotheses, concepts, and constructs, based on facts and observations, that attempts to explain a particular phenomenon.*

> (Barker, 2003, p. 434)

Theory consists of an interlocking set of hypotheses that are logically related, and it seeks to explain the inter-relationships among empirical generalizations.

(Tripodi, Fellin, & Meyer, 1969, p. 13)

Theories are sets of concepts and constructs that describe and explain natural phenomena.

(Tolson, Reid, & Garvin, 1994, p. 21)

So theories are first and foremost efforts to *explain* something, and hence the focus of this book is on some selected theoretical orientations that try to explain the phenomena of human behavior as it develops and is influenced by our social environment, across our life span. Some theories are genuinely comprehensive and provide accounts of human development from birth through death; others are more limited in scope, addressing a circumscribed range of phenomena, such as cognitive development, moral reasoning, psychosexual development, or juvenile delinquency.

A theory is not a model of practice. Theories explain, *whereas models provide direction to practitioners on what they are* to do, *to wit:*

A theory consists essentially of definitions and propositions; it defines, explains, and it predicts, but it does not direct. In contrast a model prescribes what the practitioner is to do.

(Reid, 1978, p. 12)

[A] practice model, which consists of prescriptive statements or directives about how intervention should *be conducted.*

(Tolson et al., 1994, p. 23, emphasis in original)

A model is derived from a theory but it is put together differently.... A model is an analog of a theory, built to solve a problem. It has outcomes. It is a problem-solving device, while a theory may be said to be a hypothesis-generating system.

(Loeb, 1959, p. 4)

Task-centered practice and empirical clinical practice are two practice models indigenous to social work, whereas solution-focused treatment is a more interdisciplinary model.

A theory is also not a *perspective on practice.*

[The ecosystems perspective] is not a model, with prescriptions for addressing cases; it does not draw from a particular theory of personality; it does not specify treatment outcomes. It is often misunderstood as being a treatment model.

(Meyer, 1988, p. 275)

The ecosystems idea is a perspective, or a way of looking. It is not a practice model and hence does not tell one what to do. It only directs one's vision toward the complex variables in cases.... Once a practitioner has done this, his or her

choice of interventions will be guided by the practice theories, knowledge and
values the practitioner has.

(Meyer, 1995, p. 19)

This ecosystems approach, so widely endorsed within social work, is one example of a perspective on practice, as are the strengths perspective and the person-in-environment perspective.

One's preferred social work theory is not the same as one's philosophy, with the latter being defined as "a discipline that attempts to understand the first principles of all knowledge based primarily on reason and logic, and covering such topics as theology, metaphysics, epistemology, ethics, politics, history, and aesthetics" (Corsini, 2002, p. 720).

Another way of distinguishing behavioral science theory from philosophy is by the former's reliance on empirical observations. For example:

Social scientific theory addresses what is, not what should be. Theory should not
be confused with philosophy or belief.

(Rubin & Babbie, 1997, p. 56)

Theories, models, and systems must fit the facts. Again, that criterion is what
separates science from natural philosophy.

(Simonton, 2006, pp. 98–99)

Thus, while theories and philosophies share the common element of trying to explain things, theories primarily rely on facts and empirical observations, whereas philosophy places a far greater emphasis on logical reasoning, sometimes irrespective of how philosophically derived conclusions correspond with external reality. This traditional distinction between theory and philosophy may be eroding, however, with the rise of the subfield known as *experimental philosophy*, the use of empirical experiments to test philosophical hypotheses (Nichols, 2011).

Most of the chapters in this volume clearly relate to highly complex theories, not to practice perspectives, models, or the philosophical underpinnings of professional social work. Although these domains are of considerable significance to our field, a strong case may be made that these are considerably different topics; hence, they are not addressed here.

Selected Philosophical Assumptions of Social Work Theory

Both early and contemporary efforts to locate existing theory that could be applied to social work issues and to develop indigenous theory, created by and for social workers themselves, were motivated by a set of explicit and implicit philosophical assumptions. Quite separate from our discipline's religious, ethical, or value-based foundations, there resides an underlying philosophy shared by most social workers who are concerned with theory, and these views can be broadly labeled our *philosophy of science*. An embrace of a scientific philosophy, as an orientation to conceptualizing social issues and interpersonal problems and in the design and conduct of social work research, is what distinguishes truly professional social work from other forms of altruistic helping. This has moved us from the church, temple, synagogue, community organization, and settlement house into the academy and the university-based nature of contemporary social work education.

The social work historian John Graham (1992, p. 304) described how one charitable agency in Toronto made this transition in the early part of the 20th century, a transitional experience shared by many social service programs in North America:

> *Professional social work ... had been firmly installed at* The Haven, *and the last vestiges of the benevolent philanthropy of the nineteenth century were abandoned. A growing sense of professional identity moreover demanded a strict delineation between the social worker and the social agency volunteer. Differentiating the former from the latter was a* scientific knowledge base and specialized skills *which were the social worker's alone. (emphasis added)*

This shift to a more scientific orientation was given a great shove forward by the critical appraisal of Abraham Flexner (1915/2001) regarding the primitive state of social work education about 90 years ago, an impetus similar to the one he gave medical education (Flexner, 1910), but with less far-reaching results for social work. However, the language and perspectives of science were not totally alien to the profession of social work in the pre-Flexner era. An early article published in the influential journal *The Charities Review* was titled "A Scientific Basis for Charity" (Wayland, 1894), and a paper presented at the 1889 meeting of the National Conference of Charities and Corrections was titled *Scientific Charity*. A rough outline of U.S. social work organizations with an avowed interest in empirical research and dedicated to promoting a more scientific orientation within the discipline follows:

Science-Friendly Social Service Professional Organizations in the United States

American Social Science Association (ASSA, 1865 to 1909)

—From the ASSA emerged an affiliated organization, the

Conference of Charities (1879 to 1884)

—Which itself evolved into the

National Conference of Charities and Corrections (1884 to 1917)

—Which changed into the

National Conference on Social Work (1917 to 1957)

—Which transmogrified into the

National Conference on Social Welfare (1957 to 1980s, when it expired)

—See also the independent but contemporaneous

Social Work Research Group (1949 to 1956)

—Which was one of the six organizations that merged to form the current

National Association of Social Workers (1956 to present)

—But maintained a recognizable identity as the

NASW's Research Section (1956 to 1963)

—Which changed to the

NASW's Council on Social Work Research (1963 to middle 1960s, when it quietly lapsed, apparently unmourned)

—See also the independent contemporary organization called the

Society for Social Work and Research (1994 to present, www.sswr.org)

—Which arose due to the lack of attention given to research issues by the NASW. The SSWR is now a thriving and vibrant international research organization, with membership open to all social workers.

Note our earliest beginnings in the middle of the 1800s (see Haskell, 1997) in the organization called the American Social Science Association, a lineage that can be traced, with some fits and starts, up to the present.

What is meant by this concept called research? One common definition is deceptively simple: "systematic procedures used in seeking facts or principles" (Barker, 2003, p. 368). The definition of "scientific method" is more informative:

> [A] set of rigorous procedures used in social and physical research to obtain and interpret facts. The procedures include defining the problem, operationally stating in advance the method for measuring the problem, defining in advance the criteria to be used to reject hypotheses, using measurement instruments that have validity and reliability, observing and measuring all the cases or a representative sample of those cases, presenting for public scrutiny the findings and the methods used in accumulating them in such detail as to permit replication, and limiting any conclusions to those elements that are supported by the findings. (p. 383)

There are a handful of points to be expanded on in this definition, but one worth pointing out is in the first sentence, the clear statement that scientific methods can be applied to both the physical sciences *and* the social sciences. This assumption is the hallmark of the philosophy of science called *positivism*, established by August Comte in the early 19th century. Interestingly, the original label he used to describe the science of human affairs was *social physics*, reflecting his view that the same methods used to study the natural world could be fruitfully applied to study people and their behavior. Understandably, perhaps, social physics never really caught on as a disciplinary title and it was eventually superseded by the now more familiar Comtean term, *sociology*.

Theory, undeniably, is an integral component of the scientific research enterprise, and when social work adopted a more scientific orientation, theory, perforce, came along as an important part of the package. Scientific theories rest on a bedrock of philosophical foundations, and some of these are briefly outlined:

Some selected philosophical assumptions of scientific theories of human behavior

- An acceptance of:
  - *Determinism*: The assumption that all phenomena, including psychosocial ones, have physical causes (as opposed to purely supernatural or metaphysical causes) that are potentially amenable to scientific investigation.
  - *Empiricism*: A preference to rely on evidence gathered systematically through observation or experiment and capable of being replicated (e.g., reproduced and verified) by others, using satisfactory standards of evidence.
  - *Operationalism*: The view that concepts or variables used in scientific research must be definable in terms of identifiable and repeatable operations that can be reliably replicated by others.
  - *Pragmatism*: The view that the meaning of the truth of anything (e.g., a theory) resides in its consequences in action.
  - *Parsimony*: A preference to seriously consider the simpler of the available and adequate explanations of a phenomenon prior to accepting a more complex account. This does *not* imply that the simplest answer is always right.
  - *Positivism*: The belief that valid knowledge about the objective aspects of the world can be arrived at via scientific inquiry.
  - *Progressivism*: The belief that society can be gradually improved through the application of scientific methods and expertise.
  - *Rationalism*: The belief that reason and logic are useful tools for scientific inquiry and that, ultimately, truthful or valid accounts of human behavior will be rational or logically understandable. This is not to say that human beings always behave in a rational or logical manner.
  - *Realism*: The point of view that the world has an independent existence apart from the perceptions of the observer. This does not deny the idea that some aspects of our world are socially constructed, but merely asserts that much of it is not a social construction.
  - *Scientific skepticism*: The point of view that all scientific claims (e.g., social work intervention X helps clients) should be considered of doubtful validity until substantiated by credible empirical data. The more unusual the claim, the greater the amount of evidence is needed to support it. Scientific skepticism represents the attitude of *doubting claims,* not of *denying* them.
- A denial of:
  - *Anecdotalism*: The belief that anecdotes, by themselves, can constitute credible empirical evidence.

- *Circular reasoning*: An explanation for human behavior in which causes and effects cannot be distinguished from each other. A circular explanation provides a superficial but logically untenable causal accounting.
- *Dualism*: The doctrine that the world consists of two different aspects, material matter and immaterial mind. If the mind exists at all, a scientific account places its origin in the brain, arising from physical processes.
- *Metaphysics*: Explanations involving supernatural, incorporeal, or immaterial entities or factors. This does not deny the possible reality of these influences, only that they cannot be invoked in a proper scientific account of some phenomena.
- *Nihilism*: The doctrine that all values are baseless and that nothing is known or can be learned. Also known as *radical or Pyrrhonian skepticism*.
- *Reification*: Attributing reality status to an abstract or hypothetical construct, in the absence of credible evidence of the existence of that construct.
- *Scientism*: The assumption that the research methods used in the natural sciences can and should be applied to *all* aspects of human affairs (including moral and ethical issues) and provide definitive guidance thereto.
- *Teleology*: The assumption that humanity, as a species, is striving toward some future goal (e.g., a state of advanced intelligence, spiritual perfection).

The views articulated here can be seen as axiomatic, incapable of definitive proof or of repudiation. In some deep philosophical sense, the assumption of realism cannot be conclusively proven. We might simply exist as a brain in a vat of chemicals, with our world merely a complex and lucid dream, as in the movie *The Matrix*. Similar caveats might be made for the other positions put forward in this list. They are axiomatic, not provable, but be that as it may, these views do form the foundations of contemporary scientific theorizing about human behavior and development across the life span, and virtually all of the perspectives represented in this volume subscribe to a large degree to these views. Legitimate discussion of the merits of these views, or the lack thereof, is also a part of the discourse called philosophy of science, and sincere people of goodwill and keen intellect take issue with some of these axioms all the time. But the existence of debate should not overshadow the fact that these philosophical assumptions remain widely accepted by those scientists who focus on the development of scientific theories of human behavior across the life span.

The distinguished social work educator and theorist Frank Bruno (1936, pp. 192–193) summarized this mainstream scientific orientation in social work:

> Social work holds as its primary axiom that knowledge of human behavior can be acquired and interpreted by the senses and that inferences drawn from

such knowledge can be tested by the principles of logic. The difference between the social work of the present and all of the preceding ages is the assumption that human behavior can be understood and is determined by causes that can be explained. We may not at present have a mastery of the methods of understanding human behavior, but any scientific approach to behavior presupposed that it is not in its nature incomprehensible by sensory perceptions and inference therefrom. It follows from such a theory that understanding is the first step in the direction of control and that the various forms of human misery are susceptible not only of amelioration, which our predecessors attempted, but also of prevention or even of elimination, when once their nature is understood.

Some Characteristics of Good Theories

Scientifically oriented theories themselves should possess a number of desirable characteristics in order for them to provide the greatest utility for social work. Obviously, and understandably, these characteristics are closely related to some of the philosophical assumptions undergirding mainstream science outlined earlier. Here are a few of the features characteristic of a genuinely viable theory of human development across the life span and capable of guiding social work practice.

They Are Comprehensive

The theory should provide an explanation for a wide array of human phenomena across the life span. A theory that is focused only on infant and toddler development is not as potentially useful as one whose propositions extend through adolescence. In turn, a theory for human development extending from infancy through senescence is potentially more valuable than one encompassing a more limited span of human existence. Moreover, a good theory should address many different phenomena. One explaining language development only is not as useful as one that accounts for language as well as cognitive development, juvenile delinquency, and so on. Even more challenging is the task of accounting not only for the behavior of individuals, but also for the social interactions we call a family, a small group, an organization, or an even larger entity, and to do so while utilizing a similar set of explanatory or causal factors across all these foci of human activity. Are the principles governing one's economic behavior fundamentally different from those that may account for one's political activities? Or our marital interactions? A theory that explains only family behavioral development but not small group processes is less satisfactory in a scientific sense than one that addresses both aspects of our functioning. And if it can explain both aspects using the *same set of causal mechanisms*, then such a theory is superior to one that relies on one set of principles to account for behavior in one sphere, but invokes a different set of principles to explain actions in another area of human activity.

They Are Cross-Cultural

A theory's origins should not reside in one narrow cultural milieu or cultural background, nor should it be limited to explaining human development for only one or a small number of groups (e.g., people of European ancestry, people of African origins, Hispanics). The database of a good theory should encompass processes and issues that cut across cultures, races, and ethnicities, invoking explanatory mechanisms of broad applicability that are not specific to one group. A good theory will explain those differences that do appear to exist between different groups of people. The book *Black Rage*, authored by two African American psychiatrists, exemplifies the viewpoint that theoretical principles should apply across groups:

> There is nothing reported in the literature or in the experience of any clinician known to the authors that suggests that black people function differently psychologically from anyone else. Black men's mental functioning is governed by the same rules as that of any other group of men. Psychological principles understood first in the study of white men are true no matter what the man's color.... While the experiences of black people in this country are unique, the principles of psychological functioning are by definition universal.
>
> (Grier & Cobbs, 1968, p. 129, emphasis in original)

A bit earlier, similar views were reported in the book *Black Like Me*, a wonderful example of qualitative inquiry undertaken by a White man who disguised himself and passed as a Black man for several months while traveling in the Deep South: "If you want to know about the sexual morals of the Negro—his practices and ideals—it's no mystery. These are human matters, and the Negro is the same human as the white man" (Griffin, 1960, p. 89).

They Are Heuristic

A good theory is one whose propositions yield testable hypotheses capable of being falsified via scientific analysis (e.g., via descriptive study, correlational investigations, experimentation). Moreover, the really good theories are those that not only produce testable, directional, and specific hypotheses, but are those that induce researchers to actually conduct research testing that theory. In other words, theories that tend to produce more good research are generally seen as superior to those that do not. Theories that only stimulate lots of talk or writing, in the absence of generating new empirical research, are less valuable scientifically in applied fields such as social work.

They Are Falsifiable

A good theory is one capable of being proved incorrect or false. The more specific and directional the hypotheses (e.g., predictions) a theory yields, the more testable it is. In general, when the results of a study are in the direction predicted by a hypothesis derived from some theory of human development, the most we can claim is that the theory was supported or corroborated. Only rarely can we assert that the theory has been proven to be true. The reason is that although Theory A may have predicted Outcome Z from a given study, and Z is obtained, it is possible that Theory B,

Theory C, ... Theory n might all have predicted Outcome Z. Thus the same study could be said to support *all* theories predicting Outcome Z, not just Theory A. However, if Theory A predicts Outcome Z (but not Outcome Y), and Outcome Y is found, then it is legitimate to claim that Theory A has been weakened or perhaps even, depending on the magnitude of the evidence, disconfirmed. In sum, the results of scientific research tend to shout *No!* rather loudly, but only whisper *yes*. And even then hesitantly. The more Theory A is corroborated by research results, the more it can be said to have survived efforts to falsify it, and our confidence in its validity grows. But this is tempered by the knowledge that a new study, better designed and more comprehensive in scope, may topple Theory A in favor of some new perspective that accounts for all of the phenomena explained by Theory A, as well as a whole lot more, and perhaps reconciles some problems present in A's account.

They Are Rational

A good theory is one that generates propositions that do not contradict each other, and its derivative propositions, concepts, hypotheses, predictions, and laws should all conform to the principles of scientific reasoning and logic. Requiring that a theory be rational does not assure that the conclusions derived from that theory will be empirically valid, but it is almost a certainty that illogical conclusions cannot be true. And all valid conclusions or observations about the world have the potential (at least) of being rationally explicable. As noted by social work educator Norman Polansky (1975, p. 20), "If deductions made 'logically' from theory do not fit what we observe about our world, we are quite justified in questioning the system of logic—as well as the theory."

They Are Parsimonious

A good theory is parsimonious, meaning that it adequately explains a large proportion of human phenomena using the fewest number of theoretical principles. Abstractly, a theory that uses five major principles to explain some aspect of human development, and does a good job doing so, is to be preferred over one that needs 20 major theoretical principles to explain the same thing. Corsini (2002, p. 696) defines parsimony as "explaining a phenomenon in the simplest manner and with the fewest terms, in keeping hypotheses and explanations simple," but I would add here the important caveat that these simple explanations must provide a *sufficient* account. A mere preference for simplicity is not what parsimony is all about—otherwise we could explain everything by saying that God did it! But science deals with naturalistic accounts, not supernatural ones. An elegantly simple theory that failed to provide an adequate explanation would not conform to this principle of parsimony.

More than 100 years ago, the distinguished psychologist Lloyd Morgan (1894, p. 54) extended this preference for parsimony in psychological theorizing a bit further, in postulating what became known as Morgan's canon of parsimony: "In no case may we interpret an action as the outcome of the exercise of a higher psychical faculty, if it can be interpreted as the outcome of one which stands lower in the psychological scale." Colloquially, this preference for parsimonious accounts is expressed in the dictum "When you hear hoofbeats, think horses, not zebras." If a person's delusional ravings are accompanied a high fever or preceded by the recent ingestion of hallucinogenic drugs, a competent psychiatrist is more likely to ascribe the bizarre speech to the fever or drugs, rather than assume the person has experienced a so-called psychotic break requiring immediate treatment with powerful antipsychotic drugs.

Polansky (1975, p. 27) also addressed this principle in his early research textbook:

> If a theory is to simplify life, it should fit the rule of parsimony. Parsimony in theory means that one should add propositions grudgingly. The same thought is imbedded in the principle called "Occam's razor": "That entities should not be multiplied beyond necessity." … Before proposing a new concept or a new law, one asks: Cannot this discovery be explained by theory already in existence? Is there not an existing law which might be modified to embrace not only the new finding but also what is previously known? Occam's razor prunes toward the magnificent terseness and pyramidal shape which are the marks of parsimonious theory.

They Are Practical

A good theory for social work practice first and foremost should be generative of genuinely effective methods of psychosocial intervention. A theory that does not provide guidance on how to assess and intervene with clients is, quite literally, a useless theory, a theory without uses. Apart from producing assessment and treatment methods, evaluative research should demonstrate that these interventions really do help clients improve their lives! A theory that yields methods of assessment and intervention that properly designed investigations reveal to not be effective is similarly a useless theory. Perhaps even more damaging, because it provides a patina of respectability (after all, it does convey clear applications to practice, which is a characteristic of a good theory), the theory and its ineffective practices may persist for many decades as a widely accepted approach to social care, absent any real impacts on improving the human condition at the individual or macro levels. Most damaging of all are theories that yield interventions that are actively harmful to clients. This all too common circumstance, the consequences of harmful theories, is further discussed in the final chapter of this volume.

I invite the reader to examine the following chapters on human behavior theory in light of the philosophical principles described in these prefatory remarks. Other writers have devised various formal rating scales by which social work theories can be critically evaluated (see Dixon et al., 1992), but I will not burden the reader with such a task. Instead, periodically ask yourself a few simple questions about each chapter after you read it, questions such as:

- Does this theory cover a wide range of developmental phenomena across the life span?
- Does this theory embrace human behavior at the micro, mezzo, and macro levels?
- Does this theory make sense, logically, and is it consistent with my own lived experience?
- Is this theory composed of a limited number of fundamental principles, or it is more complex than it needs to be to do a good job of explaining things?
- Has this theory generated any assessment or intervention methods for social work practice?
- If it has, have these methods been critically examined and tested via research studies?
- If it has, have these methods been shown to be genuinely helpful in improving clients' lives?

If you do this you may find yourself appraising some of these approaches more favorably than others. This is a good thing: to get interested in a particular theoretical orientation and to be inspired to learn more about it, especially the evidentiary foundations of the approach. In time you may find yourself actually using legitimate theory in your own practice as a professional social worker to help you conceptualize client problems, to assist in your assessment process, and to deliver interventions. This integration of theory and practice is one of the hallmarks of a fully developed professional, and it is toward this end that we and the other authors contributing to this volume dedicate this work. But please, be discriminating in your personal adoption of theory, as an awful lot of it out there is inaccurate or useless, if not actively harmful.

Bruce A. Thyer
Catherine N. Dulmus
Karen M. Sowers

References

Barker, R. (Ed.). (2003). *The social work dictionary* (5th ed.). Washington, DC: National Association of Social Workers Press.

Bruno, F. (1936). *The theory of social work*. New York, NY: Heath.

Corsini, R. (Ed.). (2002). *The dictionary of psychology*. New York, NY: Brunner-Routledge.

Council on Social Work Education. (2003). *Handbook of accreditation standards and procedures* (5th ed.). Washington, DC: Author.

Council on Social Work Education. (2004). *Educational policy and accreditation standards*. Alexandria, VA: Author.

Council on Social Work Education. (2008). *Educational policy and accreditation standards*. Alexandria, VA: Author. Available from www.cswe.org/File.aspx?id=13780

Dixon, D., Holzhalb, C., Kelly, T., Leslie, D., Sutphen, R., & Kilpatrick, A. (1992). Adequacy of social work practice: An evaluative framework. *Journal of Applied Social Sciences, 19*(2), 129–135.

Feynman, R. P. (1974, June). Cargo cult science. *Engineering and Science,* 10–13.

Flexner, A. (1910). *Medical education in the United States and Canada*. New York, NY: Carnegie Foundation for the Advancement of Teaching.

Flexner, A. (2001). Is social work a profession? *Research on Social Work Practice, 11*, 152–165. (Original work published 1915)

Graham, J. R. (1992). The Haven, 1878–1930: A Toronto charity's transition from a religious to a professional ethos. *Histoire Sociale, 25*, 283–306.

Grier, W. H., & Cobbs, P. M. (1968). *Black rage*. New York, NY: Bantam.

Griffin, J. H. (1960). *Black like me*. New York, NY: Signet.

Haskell, T. L. (1997). *The emergence of professional social science: The American Social Science Association*. Urbana, IL: University of Illinois Press.

Loeb, M. B. (1959). The backdrop for social research: Theory-making and model-building. In L. S. Kogan (Ed.), *Social science theory and social work research* (pp. 3–15). New York, NY: National Association of Social Workers Press.

Mateer, F. (1918). *Child behavior: A critical and experimental study of young children by the method of conditioned reflexes*. Boston, MA: Badger.

Meyer, C. (1988). The ecosystems perspective. In R. Dorfman (Ed.), *Paradigms of clinical social work* (pp. 275–294). New York, NY: Brunner/Mazel.

Meyer, C. (1995). The ecosystems perspective: Implications for practice. In C. Meyer & M. A. Mattaini (Eds.), *The foundations of social work practice* (pp. 16–27). Washington, DC: National Association of Social Workers Press.

Morgan, C. L. (1894). *An introduction to comparative psychology*. London, UK: Scott.

Nichols, S. (2011). Experimental philosophy and the problem of free will. *Science, 331*, 1401–1403.

Polansky, N. (1975). Theory construction and the scientific method. In N. Polansky (Ed.), *Social work research: Methods for the helping professions* (pp. 18–37). Chicago, IL: University of Chicago Press.

Reid, W. J. (1978). *The task centered system*. New York, NY: Columbia University Press.

Rovee-Collier, C. (1986). The rise and fall of infant classical conditioning research: Its promise for the study of early development. In L. P. Lipsitt & C. Rovee-Collier (Eds.), *Advances in infancy research* (pp. 139–159). Norwood, NJ: Ablex.

Rubin, A., & Babbie, E. (1997). *Research methods for social work* (3rd ed.). Pacific Grove, CA: Brooks/Cole.

Simonton, D. K. (2006). Scientific status of disciplines, individuals and ideas: Empirical analyses of the potential impact of theory. *Review of General Psychology, 10*, 98–112.

Tolson, E., Reid, W. J., & Garvin, C. (1994). *Generalist practice: A task centered approach*. New York, NY: Columbia University Press.

Towle, C. (1964). Preface. In F. Hollis (Ed.), *Casework: A psychosocial therapy* (pp. 1–4). New York, NY: Random House.

Tripodi, T., Fellin, P., & Meyer, H. J. (1969). *The assessment of social research.* Itasca, IL: Peacock Press.

Turner, F. J. (Ed.). (1974). *Social work treatment: Interlocking theoretical approaches.* New York, NY: Free Press.

Turner, F. J. (Ed.). (1979). *Social work treatment: Interlocking theoretical approaches* (2nd edition). New York, NY: Free Press.

Turner, F. J. (Ed.). (2011). *Social work treatment: Interlocking theoretical approaches* (5th edition). New York, NY: Oxford.

Wayland, H. L. (1894). A scientific basis for charity. *The Charities Review: A Journal of Practical Sociology, 3,* 263–275.

Acknowledgments

The editors gratefully acknowledge the helpful support and assistance of the exceptionally capable and patient editorial staff with John Wiley & Sons, including Rachel Livsey and Amanda Orenstein.

About the Editors

Bruce A. Thyer, PhD, LCSW, is professor and former dean of the College of Social Work at Florida State University. He received his MSW from the University of Georgia in 1978 and his PhD in social work and psychology from the University of Michigan in 1982. He is a member of the National Academies of Practice—Social Work, and a Fellow of the American Psychological Association (Divisions 12—Clinical, and 25—Behavior Analysis). He is the founding and current editor of the bimonthly journal *Research on Social Work Practice*, which was established in 1991 and is one of social work's mostly widely subscribed-to and cited journals. He has published extensively in the areas of social work theory, evaluation research, behavior analysis, and evidence-based practice.

Catherine N. Dulmus, PhD, is associate professor, associate dean for research, and director of the Buffalo Center for Social Research at the University at Buffalo and research director at Hillside Family of Agencies in Rochester, New York. She received her baccalaureate degree in social work from Buffalo State College in 1989, the master's degree in social work from University at Buffalo in 1991 and a doctoral degree in social welfare from University at Buffalo in 1999. As a researcher with interests that include community-based research, child and adolescent mental health, evidence-based practice, and university-community partnerships Dr. Dulmus' recent contributions have focused on fostering interdependent collaborations among practitioners, researchers, schools, and agencies critical in the advancement and dissemination of new and meaningful knowledge. She has authored or coauthored several journal articles and books and has presented her research nationally and internationally. Prior to obtaining the PhD, her social work practice background encompassed almost a decade of experience in the fields of mental health and school social work.

Karen M. Sowers, PhD, is professor and dean of the College of Social Work at the University of Tennessee, Knoxville. She is the University of Tennessee Beaman Professor for Outstanding Research and Service. Dr. Sowers received her baccalaureate degree in sociology from the University of Central Florida, and her master's degree and PhD degree in social work from Florida State University. Dr. Sowers serves on several local, national, and international boards. Dr. Sowers is nationally known for her research and scholarship in the areas of international practice, juvenile justice, child welfare, cultural diversity and culturally effective intervention strategies for social work practice, evidence-based social work practice, and social work education.

Contributors

Yolanda Anyon, PhD
School of Social Welfare
University of California at Berkeley
Berkeley, California

Michael J. Austin, PhD
School of Social Welfare
University of California at Berkeley
Berkeley, California

Stephanie Berzin, PhD
Graduate School of Social Work
Boston College
Chestnut Hill, Massachusetts

Michelle Mohr Carney, PhD
School of Social Work
University of Georgia
Athens, Georgia

Martha Morrison Dore, PhD
The Guidance Center
Cambridge, Massachusetts

Roberta R. Greene, PhD
School of Social Work
University of Texas at Austin
Austin, Texas

Michael J. Holosko, PhD
School of Social Work
University of Georgia
Athens, Georgia

Kristen Huffman-Gottschling, MSW
Jane Addams College of Social Work
University of Illinois at Chicago
Chicago, Illinois

Craig Winston LeCroy, PhD
School of Social Work—Tucson Component
Arizona State University
Tucson, Arizona

Rebecca J. Macy, PhD
School of Social Work
University of North Carolina
Chapel Hill, North Carolina

Mark A. Mattaini, DSW
Jane Addams College of Social Work

University of Illinois at Chicago
Chicago, Illinois

Emily Nicklett, PhD
School of Social Work
University of Michigan
Ann Arbor, Michigan

Paula S. Nurius, PhD
School of Social Work
University of Washington
Seattle, Washington

Laura J. Pankow, PhD
Private Practice
South Bend, Indiana

Catherine A. Patterson, MSW
School of Social Work
University of Georgia
Athens, Georgia

Dominique Roe-Sepowitz, PhD
School of Social Work
Arizona State University
Phoenix, Arizona

Lorraine Moya Salas, PhD
School of Social Work
Arizona State University
Phoenix, Arizona

Jeffrey Skinner, MSSW
School of Social Work

University of Georgia
Athens, Georgia

Susan I. Stone, PhD
School of Social Welfare
University of California
at Berkeley
Berkeley, California

Sarah Taylor, PhD
Department of Social Work
California State University at East Bay
Hayward, California

Bruce A. Thyer, PhD
College of Social Work
Florida State University
Tallahassee, Florida

John E. Tropman, PhD
School of Social Work
University of Michigan
Ann Arbor, Michigan

Stephen E. Wong, PhD
School of Social Work
Florida International University
Miami, Florida

Phen M. Young, MSW
School of Social Work
University of Georgia
Athens, Georgia

Chapter 1
Human Behavior and the Social Environment

Exploring Conceptual Foundations

Susan I. Stone, Yolanda Anyon, Stephanie Berzin, Sarah Taylor, and Michael J. Austin

> How might the construct known as *human behavior and the social environment* be conceptualized, and what are some critical issues associated with defining it?

Social and behavioral science theories represent a key source of knowledge for social work practice. One core function of social work scholarship is to select, synthesize, and translate this knowledge for specific use within the profession, including research, practice, and social work education. Because these theories have been generated for purposes that are often loosely related to goals and needs of the social work profession, a complex set of factors shape the "borrowing" process, including assessments of fit between theories and professional values, their evidentiary base, and their applicability and transportability to practice.

There is surprisingly little social work literature explicitly addressing theory selection, synthesis, and translation in terms of constructs related to human behavior and development, environmental influences, and their interrelationship (Kondrat, 1992; Zaparanick & Wodarski, 2004). Indirect evidence related to theory *selection* can be culled from research on the HB&SE (human behavior and the social environment) curriculum and related Council on Social Work Education (CSWE) standards. Content analyses of HB&SE syllabi indicate considerable heterogeneity in theoretical approaches utilized as well as overrepresentation of explanatory theory related to human behavior and development relative to theories related to the social environment (Taylor, Austin, & Mulroy, 2004; Taylor, Mulroy, & Austin, 2004). The most recent CSWE standards (2008) call for the selection of "theories and knowledge from the liberal arts to understand biological, social, cultural, psychological, and spiritual development" (p. 6).

This volume summarizes explanatory theories that are (a) related to human behavior and development in the social environment and

(b) can be used to inform social work practice. It represents, in many ways, an important attempt at selection, synthesis (summarizing core theoretical content, assessments of the evidentiary bases of theories), and translation (assessments of applicability to practice) of key concepts that help bring theoretical depth and breadth to the person-in-environment perspective that has historically been central to the social work profession (Cornell, 2006) Although an introductory chapter to a volume such as this might attempt to classify, compare, and/or integrate the various theories presented (e.g., see Robbins, Chatterjee, & Canda, 2009), our overarching aim will be different. Because social work scholars regularly identify and describe theories of potential utility for the profession (e.g., see Green & McDermott, 2010, for a recent example), such an approach seems premature as we are skeptical that there is shared understanding and definitions of cross-cutting dimensions along which theories might be compared. Instead, our goal is to complement the theories summarized in this volume by describing key scholarly and professional dilemmas related to theorizing about human behavior and the social environment (Bloom & Klein, 1996) that we believe are important to consider prior to comparative endeavors.

Specifically, the chapter approaches constructs related to human behavior and the social environment from multiple perspectives: historical, conceptual, and empirical. It is designed to generate discussion of the critical issues that emerge from the utilization of social and behavioral science.

The chapter is organized around the following question: How might the HB&SE construct be conceptualized, and what are some critical issues associated with defining it? To address this question, the following sections include: (a) a discussion of the role of theory in social work research and practice, especially as it relates to the HB&SE knowledge base as well as enduring tensions related to the uses of theory; (b) key highlights of the historical evolution of the HB&SE curriculum as reflected in curriculum standards developed by CSWE and related debates; (c) a presentation of selected frameworks that link human behavior with the social environment in alternative ways and may assist in the translation of HB&SE knowledge into practice; and (d) conclusions and implications for further critical reflection and dialogue.

Scholarly and Professional Dilemmas Related to Human Behavior and the Social Environment

A hallmark of the social work profession is its long-standing contextualist orientation (Weick, 1999), in which so-called person-environment perspectives serve as core components of the social work knowledge base (Cornell, 2006). At the same time, there has been considerable debate about specific elaboration of the relationship between human development, behavior, and the social environment (e.g., Bloom & Klein, 1996). We briefly sketch these debates as they relate to four overarching themes:

(1) development of the social work knowledge base, (2) the utility of middle range (domain-specific) theory, (3) appropriate specification of units of analysis (individual, group, community, etc.), and (4) the nature of the relationship between persons and their environments.

Development of the Social Work Knowledge Base

Goldstein (1990) uses a three-part model of explicit and implicit theories, accumulated research, and practice-related experiences and information (e.g., skills, practice, wisdom) to characterize the knowledge base of social work. This model suggests that optimal knowledge development occurs when there is a seamless interconnection between theory, research, and practice. Given that there are a variety of factors relevant to understanding the nature of linkages between theory, research, and practice, we note those that relate to knowledge development in the social sciences in general, as well as those that appear to be uniquely germane to the social work profession.

Theory–Research Linkages
Philosophers of science generally agree that formal theory building and testing is uneven and nonlinear, often serendipitous, related to historical and social contextual factors, and dependent on methodological innovation (Committee on Scientific Principles in Education Research, 2001). Because public support for research also influences the extent to and speed with which theory is developed, limited support for social work research represents an important constraint.

Different mechanisms underlie the linkages between theory, research, and practice, and it is important to underscore key differences between basic and applied research processes. For example, strategies used to test formal theory (theory-research links) may, at times, be quite distinct from those used to assess the efficacy and effectiveness of practice (research-practice links; see Fraser & Gallinsky, 2010; Pedhazur & Schmelkin, 1991).

Theory–Practice Linkages
Because formal theories are necessarily abstract, a complex set of steps may be necessary to link theoretical concepts to practice techniques and principles (Van De Ven & Johnson, 2006). Because the social work profession generally borrows formal theories from other social science disciplines, it is also reasonable to expect some degree of mismatch between available theory and practice applications. For these reasons, scholars from other helping professions (e.g., education and nursing) argue for the development and use of middle range (also referred to as domain-specific) theory because of its potential translatability into practice (Committee on Scientific Principles in Education Research, 2001; Liehr & Smith, 1999; McKenna, 1997). According to Merton (1968, p. 39), middle range theories are "intermediate to the minor working hypotheses

evolved in abundance during the day-by-day routine of research, and the all-inclusive speculations comprising a master conceptual scheme."

Due to the heterogeneity of goals related to theory, research, and practice, the development of the social work knowledge base is complex. Some scholars find little use for the theory–research–practice model and argue that theoretical and empirical knowledge are essentially incompatible or, at best, loosely coupled with practice knowledge (Goldstein, 1990; Weick, 1999). More recently, Thyer (2001) documented fundamental misunderstandings about research processes unique to formal theory testing and a tendency toward the overvaluation of theory building in relationship to other research endeavors that support the development of social work practice.

It is notable that these sources of tension within social work stand in marked contrast to recent appraisals of knowledge development within the professions of education and nursing. In general, these appraisals reflect a shared understanding of (a) the current state of the relevant knowledge base, (b) the types of theory building and integration necessary to further the profession, (c) critical areas for research, and (d) strategies that focus on particularly promising midrange theories that promote linkages to practice (Committee on Scientific Principles in Education Research, 2001; McKenna, 1997; Van De Ven & Johnson, 2006).

The lack of consensus about the conceptual foundation of the relationship between human behavior and the social environment provides critical contextual backdrop of this chapter. Each chapter in this volume traces the development of a particular middle range theory in relationship to empirical support and applicability to practice. This approach to explicating an array of explanatory theories raises larger sets of questions about their salience for knowledge development and utilization. For example, is there a common knowledge base related to human behavior and the social environment? If there is, to what extent do we agree, as a profession, that our current theoretical coverage is complete?

The Utility of Middle Range Theory

Middle range theory may be particularly amenable to translation into practice principles (Committee on Scientific Principles in Education Research, 2001; McKenna, 1997), given that constructs are often quite tightly coupled with empirical findings. A key limitation of middle range theory is that it is generally designed to explain narrow attributes (e.g., single domains or dimensions) of more complex phenomena. Relatedly, these theories are often overlapping. In this volume, for example, there are multiple conceptualizations of human development as well as how and what levels of the social environment shape behavior.

Turner (1990) argues that social work needs a diverse set of theoretical accounts to capture the complex and ever-changing nature of persons, the settings in which they are embedded, and the realities of practice, but this position poses several dilemmas. From the perspective of the social sciences, a proliferation of theory suggests the need for pruning and/or synthesis (Merton, 1968). Synthesis and integration clearly are complex processes — especially in relation to the concepts underlying human behavior and the social environment. Drawing on the work of the philosopher David Pepper, Goldhaber (2000) argues that alternative conceptualizations of human development (genetic, psychodynamic) emerge from different explanatory mechanisms or "root metaphors" that make them fundamentally incompatible and, in some respects, virtually incomparable. A more pluralistic perspective (Cowan, 1988) suggests that alternative conceptualizations are essential to explain different domains of functioning or subgroups of persons. In this case, the key task would be to match particular theories with appropriate subdomains of individual functioning or subgroups of persons.

Reliance on middle range theory, moreover, can limit one's capacity to conceptualize the attributes of both persons and environments simultaneously. For example, how do psychodynamic theories incorporate concepts related to the social environment? It is important to note that scholars have variously critiqued the social work knowledge base for being too individually focused (Mulroy & Austin, 2004) or too environmentally focused (Han, 2010), as well as for not attending adequately to the nature of transactions between the person and the environment (Kondrat, 2002). Indeed, this volume reflects this tension, including only a few chapters on explanatory theory (e.g., organizational theory) explicitly focused on the social environment as the primary focus of analysis.

In summary, there are two underlying issues here. The first is the extent to which multiple theoretical accounts are understood, managed, and organized. The second is consideration of the costs and benefits of utilizing particular middle range theories, especially in terms of considering which attributes of persons and/or environments are brought to the forefront, which are left in the background, and which are not included in the account.

Issues Related to Levels of Analysis

Consideration of multiple levels of analysis (e.g., individual, family, group, community, organization) raises several theoretical and methodological issues. Social work's long-standing focus on contextualized accounts of human behavior suggests at least two levels of analysis: person and environment. There are multiple levels of analysis within persons (e.g., genetic, psychological) and environments (e.g., families, groups, organizations, macrosocial forces). A rich literature documents the theoretical and methodological dilemmas associated with accurate specification of units of analysis, how best to characterize the nature of relationships between and among varying units of analysis. Various sources of potential aggregation and disaggregation bias (Cicchetti & Dawson, 2002; Edward, 1979) are important to consider in the study of HB&SE wherein attributions of causal leverage are erroneously pinpointed to person or environmental levels of influence. Alternative conceptions of poverty reduction strategies, for example, may best be understood as a reflection of different levels of analysis (e.g., individual versus cultural versus structural accounts of poverty; Popple & Leighninger, 2002).

Specifying the process of selecting multiple units of analysis is highly salient to social work knowledge development. On the one hand, these processes are very relevant to maximizing ecological validity (the extent to which theories and related empirical findings reflect real world conditions) and external validity (the extent to which theories and related empirical findings reflect particular populations of interest). In essence, better specification of these processes aid in evaluating the extent to which a particular explanatory theory is universal or relevant only to individuals or subgroups of individuals (Runyan, 1988). Unit sensitivity is also critical to identifying and, in the end, selecting appropriate points of intervention.

Characterizing the Nature of the Relationship Between Persons and Their Environments

It should not be surprising that tensions exist when conceptualizing the complex nature and consequences of interactions between humans and their social environments. For example, Wakefield's (1996a, 1996b) critique of the ecosystemic perspective and subsequent interchanges with Alex Gitterman (1996) capture the central theoretical challenges inherent in this endeavor, namely, the need for frameworks that can capture the complexity of person-environment interaction (Gitterman), and the need to use middle range theory to explain and/or derive practice applications for such social problems as mental illness and domestic violence (Wakefield).

At the minimum, there are multiple ways to conceptualize the nature of human behavior in its environmental context. For example, Messick (1983), writing from the perspective of child psychopathology, argues that there are at least three perspectives needed to understand persons in context: (1) *person as context*, where the attributes of persons themselves shape their behavior and development; (2) *person of context*, where development and behavior are shaped by the settings in which a person is embedded; and (3) *person in context*, which elaborates on the developmental or situational constraints under which a particular behavior or set of behaviors occurs. These considerations are useful in terms of locating the focus of a particular explanatory theory. For example, psychodynamic perspectives generally address the person-as-context, social learning perspectives are particularly salient to understanding the person-in-context, and political–economic theory provides explanations for the choices people make based on the situations in which they find themselves.

In social work and other social sciences, there is growing attention being given to the so-called reciprocal or transactional relationships between persons and their environments, that is, the extent to which both are mutually influential and in what ways. However, there are two important dilemmas here. The first relates to the definition of *reciprocity* and how best to measure and appropriately analyze it (Lewis, 2000). Second, it is unclear how to link individual and small group functioning to larger macro forces (economic, historical) beyond more proximal environmental settings (e.g., families; Stone, 2004). Understanding the nature of these linkages directly parallels the agency-structure debate in sociology, in which there is tension between theory that emphasizes the primacy of individual agency (the extent to which persons possess free will to act) and theory that alternatively stresses the role of social structures in constraining individual action. This theoretical gap may be particularly germane to social work's concern, as there is emphasis on both the primacy of the individual as well as on the ways in which larger institutions and economic forces constrain individual life opportunities in the Code of Ethics of the National Association of Social Workers (NASW, n.d.).

In the remaining sections of this chapter, we trace the evolution of the HB&SE curriculum through periodically updated CSWE standards and ongoing debates about the HB&SE curriculum. In response to these intellectual debates, we present various frameworks to approach them. The first debate relates to the attempt to link human behavior to the social environment. Second, in response to concern about the lack of substantive attention to theories focusing on the larger social environment, we present a framework that delineates key cross-cutting concepts that may be used to assess more macro-oriented theories. Third, we highlight conceptual frameworks that may aid in the translation of HB&SE knowledge into social work practice.

Development of the Human Behavior and Social Environment Construct

In this section we review some of the background pertaining to the construct of human behavior and the social environment, including the role of the accreditation standards of the CSWE, empirical research on the construct, and debates around controversial issues.

General Background

Although courses on human behavior and the social environment have always played a key role in the social work curriculum, they have undergone substantive change over time, from a primary focus on human behavior and development heavily influenced by psychoanalytic theory to a focus informed by ecological perspectives. This expansion reflects a confluence of historical factors and changes in social work scholarship and CSWE standards.

Key historical events of the 1960s and 1970s, including the civil rights movement, the War on Poverty, and the Vietnam War, coincided with the inclusion of varying perspectives on human development (including behavioral and social learning traditions) and theories of race, gender, and political economy. More recently, and related to theoretical and empirical advances in biological and neurobehavioral sciences, content related to genetics and the biological bases of human behavior (Mohan, 1980) as well as critical theoretical perspectives (Nicotera & Kang, 2009; Rossiter, 1996) have been considered as key domains of knowledge.

A simultaneous shift occurred in pedagogical strategy. In the 1970s, nearly 66% of bachelor of social work (BSW)–level HB&SE courses were taught outside of social work departments (e.g., in education, psychology, or sociology; Gibbs, 1986). By the 1980s, fully 90% were being taught within social work departments. Additionally, the focus and titles of HB&SE courses changed over time. The content shifted from psychoanalytic theory to human development across the life span, as well as from one foundation HB&SE course to two courses, one focusing on human behavior and development and the other on the social environment (in many, but not all, social work programs). As a result, titles of foundation courses changed from Human Development or Human Growth and Development to Human Behavior *in* the Social Environment to Human Behavior *and* the Social Environment.

These trends reflect the scope and complexity of the theoretical underpinnings of HB&SE courses. Levande (1987) argued that this expansion created an "add and stir" approach to teaching HB&SE, especially when introducing the diversity-related constructs such as race, gender, ability, and sexual orientation along with an array of social problems.

Council on Social Work Education Standards

In 1969 (revised in 1971), the CSWE outlined the content for courses on human behavior and the social environment. This first set of standards on human behavior emphasized the importance of knowledge related to multiple units of analysis (the individual, group, organizational, institutional, and cultural contexts) that impact human behavior by drawing on theories from the biological, psychological, and social sciences. The CSWE acknowledged that many relevant theories existed for possible curricular inclusion. Irrespective of the wide range of theories and systems of knowledge, students were required to master the relevant content, critically assess the content's application to social work practice, and identify implications for theory development in social work.

In the second accreditation manual (published in 1984), standards continued to require a focus on the individual's interactions with families, groups, organizations, and communities, but changed to reflect an emphasis on how individuals develop over the life span (CSWE, 1984). In addition to reemphasizing the importance of theory from the biological, psychological, and social sciences, the standards called for more attention to the differences between theories, as well as their interrelationships, especially those that could inform the "reciprocal relationship" between human behavior and the social environment (reflecting biological, social, psychological, and cultural systems). A new emphasis was included that called for content on diversity related to ethnic background, race, class, sexual orientation, and culture. The standards continued to emphasize that the curriculum should reflect the goals of individual programs and the ways HB&SE content informs social work practice.

The third set of policies and standards emphasized the need to explicate the values embedded within theories (CSWE, 1994). In addition to requiring content on the interactions among biological, psychological, social, and cultural systems and their reciprocal relationship with human behavior, new standards required attention to the impact of social and economic forces and larger social institutions on individuals and how these systems impact health and well-being. Finally, there was a renewed emphasis on the evaluation of theories and their application to social work practice.

The fourth set of HB&SE accreditation standards (CSWE, 2001, p. 35; amended in 2002) were reduced to the following guidelines:

> Social work education programs provide content on the reciprocal relationships between human behavior and social environments. Content includes empirically based theories and knowledge that focus on the interactions between and among individuals, groups, societies, and economic systems. It includes theories and knowledge of biological, sociological, cultural, psychological, and spiritual development across the life span; the range of social systems in which people live (individual, family, group, organizational, and community); and the ways social systems promote or deter people in maintaining or achieving health and well-being.

The most recent set of requirements notably relax core focus on "reciprocal relationships" and focus on competencies related to this content area. Specifically, they (CSWE, 2008, p. 7) emphasize that:

> Social workers are knowledgeable about human behavior across the life course; the range of social systems in which people live; and the ways social systems promote or deter people in maintaining or achieving health and well-being. Social workers apply theories and knowledge from the liberal arts to understand biological, social, cultural, psychological, and spiritual development. Social workers utilize conceptual frameworks to guide the processes of assessment, intervention, and evaluation; and critique and apply knowledge to understand person and environment.

In summary, over the past several decades, CSWE curriculum standards were refined and changed five times. The standards consistently emphasized theories related to biological, psychological, and social development within multiple contexts (i.e., individual, family, group, organizational, institutional, and cultural). They also emphasized the importance of theory for practice. While these elements remained consistent, key changes included an emphasis on (a) the reciprocal relationship between human behavior and the social environment, (b) life course development, (c) cultural and spiritual dimensions of HB&SE, and (d) the role of social systems in promoting or deterring individual health and well-being. Notably, the CSWE removed, then reintroduced language in the standards related to the roles of students in evaluating and developing theory.

Empirical Perspectives

While HB&SE courses ostensibly reflect the core theoretical knowledge for the profession, there has been very little research on HB&SE content as reflected in course outlines or textbooks or its role in social work education. One way to assess HB&SE content is to review the way courses and the most frequently cited textbooks are structured. Recent research on HB&SE textbooks and course outlines reveals the lack of agreement among social work educators about what constitutes HB&SE (Taylor, Austin, et al., 2004; Taylor, Mulroy, et al., 2004). These two studies consisted of a detailed review of 14 HB&SE textbooks (most frequently used in foundation courses for MSW students) and an analysis of 117 HB&SE course outlines submitted by 60 schools of social work in response to a request sent in 2003.

In both studies, the focal point for analysis was the most current CSWE (2001) curriculum statement on HB&SE content. The studies built on previous research, primarily Brooks (1986) and Farley, Smith, Boyle, and Ronnau (2002). Farley and colleagues evaluated 116 HB&SE course outlines used in 61 MSW programs during the 1998 to 1999 academic year and found that HB&SE courses reflected a lack of agreement about core content and theoretical constructs.

Variation in HB&SE courses in social work programs mirror continuing debates about how social and behavioral science theories should inform social work practice (Brooks, 1986; Farley et al., 2002; Mailick & Vigilante, 1987). The debate focuses primary attention either on the behavior of individuals or on the impact of the social environment on the behavior of individuals and families. Since the "rise and fall" of the psychoanalytic perspective (Mohan, 1980, p. 26), social work educators have searched for ways to include more content on the social environment as well as alternative theoretical constructs, especially as they seek to balance the concepts of pathology with those of well-being. According to Levande (1987, p. 59), this process "can result in HBSE content that is contradictory [and] fragmented."

Based on prior CSWE (2001) standards and a social environment framework discussed later in this section (Mulroy & Austin, 2004), assessment forms were developed and applied to each text and course outline to guide the analysis and ensure consistency of data collected. A summary of factors evaluated in textbooks and course outlines is provided in Table 1.1.

Based on Taylor, Austin, and Mulroy (2004), the majority of HB&SE textbooks and course outlines are organized by stages of the *life cycle*, *systems* of varying sizes, or *theory*. A small but significant number of HB&SE course outlines were described as *combination*, because they covered material in at least two of these areas but were not dominated by any one approach. The characteristics of each of these formats are described next.

The *life cycle* textbooks and outlines are organized by the developmental stages of individuals and/or families from birth through death. Some of the courses and textbooks also include sections on various systems (groups, organizations, and communities), but the majority of the

Table 1.1 **Factors Evaluated in Human Behavior and the Social Environment Textbooks and Course Outlines**

Textbooks	Course Outlines
Structure	Structure
General content	Content
Intended audience	Logical flow
Emphasis on diversity	Emphasis on:
Specific social environment content:	— Reciprocal relationship between human behavior and the social environment
— Social justice	
— Political economy	
— Social problems	— Well-being
— Social policies	— Comparative perspectives
— Collective responses	— Diversity
— Communities	— Theory for practice
— Organizations	
— Groups	

content emphasizes the life cycle. The strengths of this approach include comprehensive coverage of human development, family issues, and the biopsychosocial or ecological perspective and a format in which HB&SE theory seeks to inform social work practice. Analyses also indicated considerably less emphasis on groups, organizations, and communities. Emphasis focused on different ways the individual experiences or is affected by groups, organizations, or communities rather than treating these structures of the social environment as dynamic, interdependent systems in and of themselves.

Systems textbooks and course outlines are structured around the concepts of the social environment, often with one or more separate chapters on individuals, families, groups, organizations, and communities. Many of the systems textbooks and course outlines reviewed in Taylor, Austin, and Mulroy (2004) and Taylor, Mulroy, and Austin (2004) also devote significant attention to the role of social justice issues, social work ethics, and a broad array of social science theories. They provide explicit definitions of the social environment and its structures, with detailed content on groups, organizations, and communities. Individuals are often described as being one type or size of system, and all systems are described as interdependent entities irrespective of how individuals experience them.

Finally, the *theory* textbooks and course outlines provided content on ecological, psychodynamic, cognitive-behavioral, and other theories commonly used in social work. They emphasize comparative perspectives and critical thinking skills needed for evaluating the usefulness of a given theory for social work practice and research. The textbooks and course outlines using this approach to HB&SE varied in their treatment of the social environment, social work ethics, and social problems.

In addition to the variation in the structure of HB&SE textbooks and course outlines, social work programs differ in how many courses are devoted to the teaching of foundation HB&SE courses. Of the 60 schools that submitted 117 course outlines for the study, 58% (35) offer two foundation HB&SE courses, 33% (20) offer one, and the remaining 8% of schools (5) offer three or more. The findings reflect a diverse array of approaches to structuring HB&SE. Of the 35 schools offering two HB&SE courses, 31% (11) devoted one semester to life cycle and the second semester to systems, and 17% (6) presented a combination of life cycle, systems, and theory material over two semesters. Another 11% of schools (4) covered life cycle in the first semester and a combination of theory, systems, and diversity in the second semester. Three schools (9%) focused on systems during the first semester and theory in the second semester. One school presented the life cycle over two semesters, and another school presented systems over two semesters. The remaining 3% (9) taught systems, theory, or life cycle in one semester and diversity, psychopathology, or a combination of topics in the other.

Of the 20 schools requiring only one foundation HB&SE course (several schools sent different versions of the same course outline, thus proportions given are based on the outlines received), 35% (9) focused on the life cycle, 19% (5) emphasized systems, and another 19% (5) presented primarily theories. The remaining outlines (8) reflected a combination of theory, diversity, life cycle, and systems.

In summary, these findings identify at least two central issues for social work scholarship in terms of ways to conceptualize (1) the *integration* of human behavior *and* the social environment and (2) the *nature of the relationship* or wholeness of understanding human behavior *in* the social environment.

Debates Around the Human Behavior and the Social Environment Curriculum

Current research on textbooks and course outlines needs to be placed in historical context. Beginning in the 1920s, debates over the merits of psychoanalytic and behavioral frameworks contributed to controversies about the social and behavioral science foundation of social work practice. Mailick and Vigilante (1987) identified the following HB&SE issues: (a) overemphasis on psychoanalytic theories in the teaching of HB&SE, (b) the need for additional content on diversity and stress and coping, and (c) the limitations of organizing content by developmental stages. A more recent review of the major controversial issues in the field of HB&SE identified tensions related to the purpose, content, conceptualization, and teaching approaches of human behavior and the social environment (as noted in Table 1.2; Bloom & Klein, 1996). We summarize the key issues raised in this review in the following sections.

Table 1.2 Controversial Issues Identified by Bloom and Klein

Topic	Issue	Relevance to the Discussion of Human Behavior and the Social Environment
Purpose	Knowledge expansion and theory assessment	Multiple purposes: theory for practice, theory for policy, theory for understanding the social science perspective, or theory analysis to refine critical thinking skills
Content	Environmental versus individual theories	Theories related to the individual versus the environment continue as major point of contention
	Specialized course content	Tension between the use of a breadth perspective or a depth perspective in conceptualization
	Empirically supported and unsupported theories	Adding content to human behavior and the social environment courses such as religion and spirituality, disabilities, values, genetics and sociobiology, and theories of international development
Conceptualization	Epistemological framework	Distinguishing between what is believed and what is empirically supported
	Strengths perspective	Tension between a wellness or strengths perspective and a pathology or problem focus
	Developmental perspectives	Stage perspectives versus life course perspectives
	Life history	Use of life experience to illustrate key human behavior and the social environment concepts
Teaching	Single courses versus multiple courses versus integrating theory into practice courses	Beyond the structure and curriculum, considering how socially sensitive topics are incorporated, related to race, gender, age, sexual orientation, and disability

Adapted from Bloom, M., & Klein, W. C. (Eds.). (1996). *Controversial issues in human behavior in the social environment*. New York, NY: Prentice-Hall.

Purpose

Educators continue to struggle with the purpose of HB&SE content. Is the purpose to describe explanatory theory in order to understand problems facing client populations or to inform the assessment phases of social work practice? Or is the purpose to promote critical assessment of the theoretical social science foundation of the profession? Gibbs (1996) suggests that learning critical thinking skills is an important part of studying the explanatory theory, because these skills lay the foundation for critical thinking about the intervention theory that underlies social work practice. Others see the potential purposes of HB&SE as including a venue for promoting multiple levels of analysis (micro, mezzo, macro), different lenses, or frames of reference with which to examine behavior in context.

Content

Debates also center on the extent to which emphasis should be placed on individual or environmental theories, as well as the nature of the person–environment relationships in an HB&SE course. The theoretical content thought to be relevant to HB&SE has continued to expand, raising the ongoing need to evaluate theory in terms of its historical context, explicit and implicit values, and breadth and depth of empirical support. Of note, efforts at potential synthesis are ongoing. For example, there has recently been an attempt to synthesize each of these content emphases through Developmental Systems Theory (Greenfield, 2011).

Conceptualization

Aside from debates related to the utility of middle range versus unifying or universal theories and concepts, larger philosophical debates are also apparent. These include the relative merits of adopting strengths versus social problem perspectives and whether neopositivism is a suitable epistemological framework for HB&SE given the proliferation of postmodern (e.g., interpretive, constructionist, and constructivist) paradigms. Similarly, newer life span or life course theories raise serious concern about the utility of stage theories in characterizing developmental processes.

Our brief review of the evolution of HB&SE content from the perspective of CSWE standards, research on texts and course outlines, and debates around the general purpose, scope, and focus of courses provides a context for and explicates the larger tensions embedded in the processes through which social work scholars select, synthesize, and translate social and behavioral science theory for the professions' particular use. The next sections focus on two enduring tensions. The first concerns a search for frameworks that potentially illuminate the multiple ways in which the nature of relationships between persons and their environments can be understood. The second provides a heuristic for conceptualizing larger environmental influences.

A Selection of Frameworks That Address Linkages Between Human Behavior and the Social Environment

In this section, we identify a selected group of explanatory frameworks that explicitly link individual and environmental concepts, albeit in different ways. These frameworks include the life course perspective, social capital theory, cultural understanding of human development, opportunity frameworks, neighborhood effects, and institutional theoretical perspectives. These frameworks are potentially useful in that they highlight mechanisms and processes through which forces in the social environment (and vice versa) shape behavior and development and thus may aid in clarifying potential relationships between HB&SE. In addition, they have the capacity to provide integrative functions as a superstructure for more narrowly constructed middle range theories (Merton, 1968). As an example, we illustrate the potential for integration with life course perspectives.

Life Course Perspectives   *Elder*

Sociological perspectives on the life course may have particular utility in conceptualizing social environmental influences on human development. Indeed, Elder's (1995) life course perspective is increasingly viewed as an important potential explanatory framework for social work (Hutchison, 2005; Stone, 2004). In general, Elder suggests that several overriding principles have central explanatory roles in developmental processes and outcomes. First, individual development is best understood as a trajectory. That is, prior developmental experience influences later development. Second, the timing and sequencing of developmental and social transitions influence persons' life trajectories. Third, agency-related attributes of individuals (their human capital characteristics, meaning-making abilities, and efficacy) influence development. Notably, however, human agency is constrained by the availability, structure, and quality of social opportunity structures. Fourth, according to Elder, immediate relationships represent the key context in which human development is actualized. In Elder's formulation, proximal relationships often mediate larger social forces. Finally, historical time and place shape developmental pathways. In other words, cohort effects are central to the understanding of developmental processes.

A key implication of Elder's (1995) theory is that these factors intersect to create a unique set of "turning points" for any individual life trajectory. In other words, the combination of these influences pinpoint key points of intersection between human behavior and the social environment (person–environment fit) and potential points of intervention. Elder's work is both representative and an extension of the larger sociological life course tradition, which highlights the importance of social role–related transitions. We next describe both Elder's perspective as well as a more general life course framework by Hunt (2005).

Specifically, Elder's (1995) principles include *lives in time and place, human agency and self-regulation, the timing of lives,* and *linked lives. Lives in time and place* refers to the interplay between human development and the larger social context, including both historical time and physical place. *Human agency and self-regulation* refers to the choices people make in their lives. Though Elder acknowledges the social constraints on these choices, he also believes that human decision plays a role in the occurrence and sequencing of life events. Individuals' ability to select and construct their environment impacts their trajectory and indeed represents a key way to conceptualize reciprocity. *Timing of lives* refers to influences of both historical time and the social timing of developmental and social transitions and normative and nonnormative events across the life span. Timing is thought to be as important as, if not more important than, the occurrence of an event. Last, *linked lives* refers to the interdependence of human beings. Relationships across generations, marriage, kin, work, and so on all relate to the social context in which people live. Being embedded in a particular network of relationships has significant consequences for life course development. The life course can be viewed in part through social ties.

Elder's (1995) framework is useful for various reasons. It specifies mechanisms of influence between persons and their environments and, indeed, starts by explicitly including attributes of the social environment (including historical and social forces) as well as social opportunity structures (e.g., institutions, communities). In addition, the framework includes multiple units of analysis from historical time and place to more immediate relationships, such as family interactions. In particular, large or rapid changes are thought to have significant consequences on human behavior and the life course. As a perspective emphasizing transitions and life trajectories, this framework also informs our understanding of the nature of the developmental process and the related social constraints. Ultimately, this perspective provides a key set of principles from which a person and a situation can be assessed. That is, attention to social context, timing, age, and relationships is key in understanding individual behavior.

Although the life course perspective is useful, it has clear limitations. It treats human life trajectories as the primary unit of analysis, leaving less room for understanding groups, neighborhoods, communities, and other social organizations, as well as the ways they combine to create opportunity structures. This framework is also relatively new and complex. Although there is an increasing body of research in support of many of the principles, few studies consider the various perspectives simultaneously; hence, the interrelationships among concepts derived from each principle are not well understood.

Extensions of Life Course Approaches

A second reconceptualization of life course theory is outlined by Hunt (2005). Hunt argues that Elder (1995) does not adequately address so-called postmodern phenomena (e.g., significant transformations of the macrosocial context). This framework focuses on the impact of institutions and processes, including economic, technological, cultural, and political, on human behavior.

This interpretation of the life course reflects the changing postmodern world. Specifically, Hunt (2005) focuses on the impact of the increased life span, changes in age-associated transitions, globalization, technology, consumerism, and individualism.

Hunt (2005) argues that a lengthening life span provides individuals with increased capacity to predict and calculate risks as well as to plan accordingly. This ability to predict future events allows us, in some ways, to control parts of our environment. In addition, these macrosocial changes impact the way people develop and behave. As life expectancy approaches life span potential, human beings begin to deny aging and believe in timelessness. This pursuit of youth and pleasure shapes human behavior. Further, Hunt challenges the notion that, in this context, human development takes place in age-defined stages. He discusses changes in the meaning of marriage, family, and old age. In preindustrial societies, people of the same age behaved the same way and experienced things at the same time. This became less true in industrial societies and is even less true in the postmodern age. Though he acknowledges the role of biology in maintaining particular transitions in the life span, he argues that sociological constructs define the phases in the life course. Further, our perception of biology and its psychological implications are impacted by societal views.

Moreover, Hunt (2005) sees globalization as a key force. As global culture develops, systemic social ties are fundamentally altered. In short, this redefinition of society through the global marketplace influences local culture, which influences the social construction of the life course. Norms that were part of one culture may now transcend into this global culture. As a result, changes in one area bring about changes elsewhere. In no other time have global connections been available. Life course norms, which previously developed in each culture, are now part of this global culture. One of the reasons for these emergent global trends is major technological advances that have been made in recent years. Communication has grown tremendously, and technology has made it possible. Further, advances in medicine and science are, in part, responsible for the growing life span. Accompanying these technological changes is the ability to change our environment in ways that were never possible previously. All of these changes affect human behavior in a way that is unique in the current context. Last, consumerism affects the life course. Hunt argues that our new consumerism and cultural notions of choice strongly affect development. Individuals now enter life stages based on choice rather than inevitability. Stages such as marriage and parenthood have become optional. With these changes, individual development includes a new search for self-identity. Societies no longer define our identity or provide moral guidelines. Individualism also becomes increasingly important in this context. People have fewer ties to social contracts and roles. In short, Hunt argues that each of these aspects of postmodernity has changed the life course dramatically.

As we conceptualize HB&SE, we must consider the influence of these rapid cultural changes in terms of both social structures and individual behavior and development. In short, this work extends Elder's (1995) conceptualization of the life course and encourages the consideration of postmodernity as more than a cohort effect.

Life Course Approach: An Application

At least three attributes of Elder's (1995) theory present challenges for translation. First, life course theory is quite complex, requiring the integration of variable individual developmental trajectories with larger structural forces. Indeed, Hutchison (2003) suggests that the complexity of Elder's framework may interfere with its practical application. Second, predicting the direction of any individual life course trajectory is clearly not an exact science. Patterns within and across individuals generally can be discerned retrospectively, generally through longitudinal methods. Finally, key concepts in Elder's framework are quite broad and need elaboration.

Acknowledging the diversity of individual trajectories and their complex interplay with larger social forces, we employ three general strategies. First, for each life phase, we focus on a single, highly salient life course principle. Second, we identify a set of plausible sources of turning points and of structural constraints. Third, we highlight areas in which current explanatory theories presented in this volume may be particularly applicable (see Table 1.3).

Highlighting Historical Time and Place: Mid- and Late Adulthood

Few would argue that dramatic growth in the aging population, its implications for the economy and the workforce, and its implications for aging policy and practice (Administration on Aging, 2002) represent a key social transformation. Moreover, gerontologists argue that this demographic change will dramatically alter public perceptions and attitudes toward those over 65 and will also dramatically alter service provision to this population. In other words, what is unique about contemporary mid- to late adulthood is that adults are moving into and through this developmental phase at the same time that there are significant demographic shifts. From the life course perspective, these demographic shifts represent a unique historical and situational context that is likely to have marked impacts on the current aging population and uniquely affect their subsequent trajectories relative to past and future cohorts.

These demographic shifts shape the current opportunity structures available to mid- and later adulthood. These generally include the formal Social Security system and social services that may be available to the elderly. Newman (2003) documents how the current formal arrangement of services for aging adults is largely mismatched to the needs of poor and minority aging subpopulations, especially in terms of the provision of health services. Of increasing relevance are existent workforce and workplace structures that may shape the timing of retirement decisions and responsiveness to older employees in the workforce. In addition, a vast majority of elderly living in the community receives key supports from relatives. The nature and quality of family caregiving support structures, as well as additional formal and informal supports to caregivers, represent an interesting set of ties between mid- and late adulthood.

Given this current social context, the period between mid- and late adulthood is associated with a unique set of physiological, biological, psychological, and social transitions. Between mid- and late adulthood there is a general move from peak physical and intellectual functioning to normative decrements in select domains of physiological functioning. For some subpopulations, aging is associated with increasing risk of particular health problems (Newman, 2003). There are also changes in memory and changes in overall rates of encoding and processing of

Table 1.3 **Summary of Life Course Concepts and Application to Developmental Stages**

Principle	Late Life	Midlife	Early Adulthood	Adolescence	School Age	Early Childhood
Time and place	Changing demographics of elderly population; Social Security resources	Women in the middle Entrance of women in the labor force Family-centered policies	Emergent adulthood; few supports when evidence of need for increased mentorship	Emergent adulthood; few supports when evidence of need for increased mentorship	Structure and quality of schooling Child and family supports	Valuation of infants Parent-friendly policies Moms and work
Linked lives	Key others (spouses, children) Caregiving relationships	Familial relationships/ parenting functions	Peer and romantic relationships	Peers, parents, teachers	Parents, teachers, peers	Caregivers
Agency and opportunities	Generative functions Differential access to resources that facilitate healthy aging (structure of work, health system)	Family- and work-related efficacies Structure of work and family supports	Cognitive skills Access to work and educational opportunity	Cognitive capacities Quality of peer, school, neighborhood contexts	Individual abilities valued by schools Parenting environments Classroom environments	Sensitivity and structure of caregiving environment
Timing and transitions	Physical: Cognitive and physical aging Social: Retirement, grandparenting, widowhood	Physical: Menopause Social: Sequencing of work and family time clocks	Physical: Identity consolidation, formal cognitive functioning Social: Leaving home, family formation	Physical: Puberty and key cognitive transitions	Physical: Cognitive change (perspective taking) Social: transition to school	Physical: Rapid physical, cognitive, social growth

information. Aside from this set of physical transitions, key social transitions (generally signaling changes in role) include retirement, widowhood, grandparenthood, and, for some, transitions into caregiving and recipient roles. Aside from these normative transitions associated with aging, Elder's (1995) theory underscores the importance of personal agency in development. Among adults, key agency-related variables include planful competence and efficacy, coping skills, and financial resources (Settersten & Lovegreen, 1998).

Three sets of relationships are relevant to life trajectories at this phase. These include relationships with significant others and relationships with children. Social networks at mid- and later life are populated by family members and a few close friends. Empirical research in the life course tradition generally focuses on the relationship between supportive marital relationships and health and mental health. In other words, the nature and quality of significant relationships represent key developmentally related processes at this time period.

In summary, the application of Elder's (1995) life course perspective to mid- and later adult life features the occurrence (or nonoccurrence), timing, and specific overlap of key social transitions in the current social context of demographic change. It predicts, for example, that simultaneously experiencing retirement, the death of a spouse, and decrements in intellectual functioning will generally place a person at risk for worse outcomes. In addition, it highlights the historical time effects that will likely have salient influence on work (and retirement) trajectories and opportunities (e.g., structure and availability of services) that facilitate healthy aging.

The life course perspective also directs us to two central explanatory theoretical systems. Given work- and family-related social transitions that mark mid- to late life, role theory represents a key explanatory framework for this life stage. Psychosocial theory covers integrity and generative meaning-making strategies that are hypothesized to be particularly salient during this period (Galatzer-Levy & Cohler, 1993). In short, generative meaning-making processes and coping strategies suggest two potential domains from which to approach human behavior processes past midlife.

Adolescence and Early Adulthood: Timing, Agency, and Opportunity

The period of adolescence and early adulthood is distinguished by the intersection of both developmental and social transitions. Aside from changes related to puberty, which is unique to early adolescence, two developmental processes unfold over this life phase. First, there is ongoing cognitive development between adolescence and early adulthood, marked by increasing capacity for foresight, contemplation, and abstract thinking. These changes in cognition form the basis of identity development processes. Adolescence and early adulthood represent a period when identity formation across multiple domains is under way.

As we move from adolescence into early adulthood, we enter and negotiate a series of key social transitions, from school to work, to independent living, to relationship formation (that is increasingly intimacy-based), and to parenthood.

In light of these developmental and social transitions, a key characteristic of early adulthood is that it offers unique opportunities to act as an independent person in increasingly widening, socially defined contexts outside of families. Besharov (1999) identifies differential access to work and educational opportunities by race and class as key opportunity constraints during this time. For adolescents in particular, current research indicates that peer networks (prosociality, academic orientation), junior high and high schools (safety, opportunities for challenge and support), and neighborhood contexts act as salient constraints on optimal adolescent functioning (Eccles & Roeser, 1999).

Finally, developmental theorists argue that young adults currently are experiencing a protraction in the transition to traditional adult roles (Arnett, 2000). In short, timing and sequencing of key transition-to-adulthood markers (from school to work, to independent living, to parenthood) are in flux and generally are taking place over longer periods of time. It is notable that the current historical context is unique in that key socialization units, notably schools, are peer segregated, offering few opportunities for meaningful interactions between adolescents and nonrelated adults. In addition, although there appears to be a greater need for mentorship, few formal structural arrangements are available in this respect.

In summary, adolescence and early adulthood provide important examples of the intersection between the development of individual capacity (in terms of cognitive development, increased independence, and individual identity formation processes) and situational constraints around key social structures, including the structure of the secondary and post-secondary education system and the structure of the workforce. Cognitive theory, psychosocial theory, and role theory are salient explanatory systems at this life stage.

Linked Lives: Infants and Young Children

Given that infancy and early childhood are marked by rapid physical, cognitive, and social growth, the concept of linked lives is perhaps most saliently represented in this period. Parents and key caregivers represent key developmental contexts for infant and young children. Moreover, the sensitivity, structure, and responsiveness of the caregiving environments represent the key social opportunity structure for young children. Environmental forces are almost completely mediated by the qualities of caregiving and caregiver–child relationships (Duncan & Brooks-Gunn, 2000). Of particular relevance to school-age children, the quality of relationships with teachers and peers can generally enhance and optimize the academic and psychosocial trajectories of children. It is notable, however, that the quality of parenting environments generally sets the stage for these relationships (Deater-Decker, 2001).

Behavioral, genetic, attachment, and social learning paradigms provide important explanatory theoretical lenses through which to understand the nature and qualities of these relationships. In short, they specify the key mechanisms by which the principle of linked lives operates by explicating the conditions under which caregiver-child relationships develop and are maintained.

Cultural Understanding of Human Development

Rogoff's (2003) theoretical work is based on the premise that human development is a cultural process. Human behavior, though inherently tied to biological processes, is also bound by culture. Culture is constantly redefined in each place and time, which impacts the individual's particular experience. Individual behavior, in turn, impacts cultural processes in a reciprocal relationship. This framework suggests that human development takes place in a particular culture and that development can be understood only by understanding cultural context.

Although her work is influenced by Vygotsky (1962) and Bronfenbrenner (1979), Rogoff (2003) argues that these theorists treated person and context separately, as separate entities or as one producing the other. She describes the reciprocal relationship between culture and development, explaining that they "mutually create" (p. 37) and "mutually constitute" (p. 51) each other. Human development is the process of people's continued and changing participation in sociocultural activities. As individuals develop through this participation, culture is simultaneously developed as a result.

Rogoff (2003) defines several key concepts for understanding cultural processes and argues that the study of human development is an explicit cross-cultural endeavor. Further, it is important to be aware that culture is not constant; cultures continue to change, as do individuals. Rogoff acknowledges the importance of life transitions tied to both biology and chronological age. However, she believes that the transitions themselves are influenced by culture. Though age defines certain transitions, developmental milestones are culturally defined.

Current explanatory theories of human behavior can be enhanced by such concepts as cultural processes and cultural tools, as well as people's involvement in cultural traditions, institutions, family life, and community practices. These concepts can also inform the client assessment process. In short, the cultural processes and their evolution represent another important approach for understanding the nature of relationships between persons and their environments.

Opportunity Framework

Cloward and Ohlin (1960) argue that traditional approaches to understanding delinquency relied too heavily on individual behavior and delinquent acts. Rather, cultural norms, beliefs, and values promote a set of behaviors that allows delinquency to take place. Extending the work of Durkheim (1997) and Merton (1968), they argue that discrepancies between aspirations and opportunity are in part responsible for leading youth to delinquency. These works discuss the ways in which different opportunity structures, particularly as they relate to institutions, contribute to delinquency.

Because this earlier work could not explain why youth lacking in opportunity choose delinquency rather than other outlets (e.g., alcoholism, suicide), Cloward and Ohlin (1960) include additional concepts related to adverse circumstance (including lack of opportunity), problems of adjustment, and social conformity and norms. Youth have aspirations that go beyond what is readily available given their current circumstances. This causes major problems in adjustment, since frustration results as they are unable to achieve conventional goals. This leads to the formation of delinquent subcultures and other nonconformity. As these subcultures evolve, they create new norms that further influence these youth toward maladaptive behavior.

By theorizing on the reasons for delinquency, Cloward and Ohlin (1960) provide an additional framework for understanding person–environment relationships. Their theory suggests the importance of the relationship between the larger social context, the specific subculture, and the individual's adjustment in this environment. Cloward and Ohlin focus on structural rather than individual forces that create disparities in opportunities.

Social Capital Theory

The concept of social capital represents resources deriving from connections among individuals (Bourdieu, 1985; Coleman, 1988; Putnam, 2000). The social environment is thought to exert influences on human behavior and development through the nature and qualities of these social resources.

Loury (1977) argued that the income disparities between White and Black youth were in part related to their social context. He believed social origin and social position were related to the resources invested in an individual's development. Bourdieu (1985) expanded the definition of social capital to include networks of institutions and group memberships that provide individuals access to resources. Coleman's (1988) definition of social capital relies on the relationships between and among people. He identifies six forms of social capital: (1) obligations and expectations, (2) information, (3) shared norms leading to prosocial behavior, (4) transfers of power to a group member, (5) use of organizations for purposes other than or in addition to what they were originally intended for, and (6) intentional organizations created for the purpose of social capital. In these multiple forms, social capital benefits individual, groups, and the collective good. Putnam (2000), who popularized the notion of social capital, refers to social capital as the connections among individuals. These connections are further defined as social networks, trust, and reciprocity. Putnam also links social capital to civic participation and believes that civic virtue becomes more powerful when it is part of a network of reciprocal social relationships. He sees two types of social capital: (1) that which comes from within-group relationships (i.e., bonding social capital), and (2) that which comes from between-group relationships (i.e., bridging social capital).

These varied definitions and explanations of social capital all suggest that persons and environments intersect through social ties. In this way, social capital is an important framework that bridges concepts of human behavior and the social environment. However, it is limited in its application to understanding human behavior and development. Social capital theory also fails to take into account larger dimensions of the social environment that impact its utility in a particular community. As suggested by Foley and Edwards (1999), most conceptualizations of social capital theory neglect to consider power-related contextual factors, including the availability of economic power, political power, and concrete resources.

Neighborhood Effects

The literature on neighborhood effects outlines the social processes by which communities and individuals interact. Early research into neighborhood effects indicated that neighborhood structures and processes (norms, competition, and socialization) influence individual behaviors (Jencks & Mayer, 1990). Taken as a whole, *epidemic, collective socialization,* and *institutional* models suggested that the negative neighborhood effects operated through several mechanisms: peer influences on behavior, the effect of community adults on children, and the influence of neighborhood institutions, respectively. Reviewing past studies on neighborhood and school socioeconomic status and racial mix, Jencks and Mayer (1990) reported neighborhood effects related to educational attainment, cognitive skills, crime, teenage sexual behavior, and employment.

Research reviewed by Sampson, Morenoff, and Gannon-Rowley (2002) highlights the importance of dynamic processes and institutional mechanisms in neighborhood settings. In their review, they noted four different neighborhood processes that influence individual well-being. The first, *neighborhood ties,* relates to social capital. This construct highlights the importance of neighborhood interactions and social relationships. The second construct, *norms and collective efficacy,* refers to the trust and expectations shared by neighborhood residents. Collective efficacy relates to the willingness to get involved for the collective good, social control, and cohesion. The third effect, *mutual resources,* refers to the availability of resources that address community needs. The presence, quality, and diversity of institutions facilitate a neighborhood's ability to support its members. The fourth neighborhood effect, *routine activities,* refers to how the patterns of land use and locations of community institutions affect daily routines. Each of these contributes to the way neighborhoods influence the individual behavior and outcomes of their members. Though these process effects are evident, structural neighborhood characteristics are still salient in determining outcomes.

Concepts related to neighborhood effects help us understand the different mechanisms through which neighborhoods and communities influence behavior. Importantly, this model pays little attention to individual variation within a specific neighborhood context.

Institutional Theory

Institutional theory emphasizes the role of societal context in understanding individual and organizational behavior (Friedland & Alford, 1991; Thornton & Ocasio, 2008). This approach looks to institutions in the environment as the primary source of organizing principles or logics that govern human behavior, which is often nested within organizations (Friedland & Alford, 1991; Scott & Davis, 2006). From this perspective, institutions are not physical places or even organizations, as the term is commonly employed in everyday language. Instead, the concept of institutions references *social and cultural* structures—norms and relationships that are resilient, durable and resistant to change, such as the institution of marriage (Scott, 2001). Over time, as both process and outcome, institutions "come to take on a rule-like status in social thought" through repeated interpersonal interactions (Meyer & Rowan, 1977, p. 341). Institutions from the environment are then carried into organizations and affect human behavior through "symbolic systems, relational systems, routines and artifacts" (Scott, 2001, p. 76). Thus, institutional theory shifts attention away from formal goals and structures within singular organizations to the prevailing institutions and related logics in the larger social environment that shape individual relationships and organizational practices. This approach emphasizes that the organization and delivery of social services, for example, are not necessarily rational, adaptive or efficient, but are socially constructed and historically situated (DiMaggio & Powell, 1991; Meyer & Rowan, 1977). Therefore, one must consider how ideas about appropriate social work services for particular populations are linked to shifting institutions and institutional logics in the environment (Scott, 2001).

Scott (2001) provides a useful framework for conceptualizing institutions as being supported by three pillars: regulative, normative, and cultural cognitive. The three pillars are symbolic, but they interact with material conditions and human activities to give rise to institutions (Friedland & Alford, 1991; Scott, 2001). Regulative aspects of institutions include rules and laws, enforcement and monitoring systems, and associated rewards and sanctions that explicitly delineate the way things *must* be done (Scott, 2001). They induce organizational and individual behavior using coercive mechanisms of authority, force, fear and shame, and their influence can be observed in governance systems, protocols and required reports to demonstrate compliance (Scott, 2001). In contrast, the normative pillar encompasses values and norms regarding the way things *should* be done, shaping expectations and considerations for suitable behavior for actors in particular roles and circumstances (DiMaggio & Powell, 1991; Scott, 2001). Finally, the cultural cognitive element refers to the way things *are* done; shared understandings, meanings and ways of seeing that are unconscious and taken for granted until they are transgressed (DiMaggio & Powell, 1991; Scott, 2001).

A central function of institutions is creating the symbolic conditions of legitimacy, under which some means and ends are considered appropriate and desirable, while others are rendered invisible or illicit (DiMaggio & Powell, 1991; Friedland & Alford, 1991; Meyer & Rowan, 1977; Scott, 2001). In this way, institutions "control and constrain" certain activities, as they also "support and empower" other types of actions, shaping common understandings of what objectives, roles, and behaviors are legitimate (Scott, 2001, p. 50). Taken-for-granted notions of legitimate activities serve to render inequality natural or justified, preserving privilege and maintaining myths of equality of opportunity, thereby contributing to the reproduction of the social order (Bourdieu, 1977). Still, notions of legitimate activities are often contested across organizations; particularly when agencies are responsible to multiple stakeholders who have different values, goals or norms (Colyvas & Powell, 2006; Scott, 2001).

Institutional logics serve as the primary mechanisms by which institutions influence individual and organizational action, providing a bridge between macro and micro processes (Thornton & Ocasio, 2008). They are historically situated, socially constructed "belief systems and associated practices...that provide the organizing principles" guiding and governing human activity, enabling certain kinds of action and not others (Scott, Ruef, Mendel, & Caronna, 2000, p. 171). Institutional logics are not personal beliefs, but they do inform the taken-for-granted notions of individuals. They are collective ideas and frameworks that emerge from the societal sectors in specific historical periods, available to individuals to elaborate on, often enacted and further developed in organizational fields (Friedland & Alford, 1991; Thornton & Ocasio, 2008). Here, the term organizational field refers to a network "of interdependent organizations operating with common rules, norms, and meaning systems," usually with shared governance and financing structures (Scott & Davis, 2006, p. 118). For example, the logic of program improvement through accountability and assessment of client outcomes has played out in the fields of public education, health services, and social welfare (Feuer, Towne, & Shavelson, 2002; Holmes, Murray, Perron, & Rail, 2006). Institutional logics shape cognition through socially constructed classification systems that give meaning to existing categories of people and their actions (Thornton & Ocasio, 2008). Institutional logics also direct the attention of individuals and organizations by providing them "with a set of rules and conventions—for deciding which problems get attended to, which solutions get considered and which solutions are get linked to which situations" (Thornton & Ocasio, 2008, p. 114).

Institutional theory is a useful framework for understanding human behavior in the social environment, as it specifies mechanisms by which the macro environment shapes both organizational (mezzo) and individual (micro) actions. In particular, it asks that social workers not only consider client behavior and needs in the context of their environment, but also how social work practice and social welfare organizations are influenced by larger societal discourses and norms. However, a common critique of institutional theory is that it tends to overshadow the role of individual agency in creating and mediating social structures, emphasizing top-down (macro to micro), rather than bottom-up processes of change (Burch, 2007). That is to say, the theory tends to be overly mechanical in its view of how social structures are reproduced, with insufficient attention paid to the ways people resist and mobilize against dominant institutions. This concern is tempered by a growing recognition of institutions as probabilistic, rather than deterministic—that they can be reinterpreted in unexpected ways and manipulated by individuals and groups to serve their own interests (DiMaggio & Powell, 1991; Friedland & Alford, 1991; Thornton & Ocasio, 2008). Contradictions and competition between dominant and secondary institutional logics are particularly important sources of change over time, as they are openings for actors to have greater impact on prevailing paradigms (Scott et al., 2000; Thornton & Ocasio, 2008).

Such an understanding of institutions reflects the assumption of embedded agency—that personal motivations, aspirations and values are never fully autonomous or discrete from social context—embraced by institutional theory in recent years (Thornton & Ocasio, 2008). From this perspective, theories emphasizing agency and subjectivity are seen as complementary to, rather than in contradiction with, institutional theory. Institutional theorists do not deny the possibility of individual mobility across social strata, or the power for collective movements to redress historical injustices, but they do highlight the way inequalities are reproduced by organizations and institutions, like schools, despite good intentions and actions on the part of individual agents, such as teachers (Bourdieu & Passeron, 1990). In general, institutional theory accentuates how personal agency is constrained by the historical distribution of resources and capital within a society and the influences of social structures on individual experiences. Given this focus, institutional theorists pay less attention to the ways in which institutions are actively, in present time, produced or modified by people. In no small way, this is a response to the dominance of micro, behavioral, and individually oriented theories that have long dominated the social sciences and social work practice (Bourdieu, 1977).

In conclusion, these explanatory frameworks shed light on alternative ways in which connections between persons and their environments can be conceptualized. Life course perspectives draw attention to the intersection between current historical context, available opportunity structures, and individual agency in patterning life trajectories. The opportunity framework emphasizes the relative match between individual characteristics and aspirations and the current array of opportunity structures. Cultural psychological perspectives involve the local cultural processes needed to understand reciprocity. Both social capital and neighborhood effects frameworks underscore the importance of social relationships for understanding person-environment interaction. Despite these various conceptualizations of reciprocity, each of these frameworks underscores the importance of social relationships (e.g., family, cultural, social, and community networks). Finally, institutional theory reminds us that persons inherently create and are constrained by social processes. However, a key limitation across all the frameworks is the insufficient attention to developmental processes. In addition, questions can be raised about the capacities of these theories to inform practice.

The Social Environment: Key Concepts

Although the previous applications focused on frameworks that potentially can link human behavior and the social environment, this section focuses on conceptualization of the social environment. This approach to the social environment differs from the previous applications in that it does not rely on one specific macro linking theory. Instead, it uses the perspective of systems theory to isolate key concepts that emerge from three bodies of social science theory: group dynamics, community theory, and organizational theory.

These systems theory perspectives include such universal concepts as interactions (e.g., within and between groups), subsystems that are parts of a system (e.g., voluntary and governmental organizations), and functions and patterns (e.g., production and consumption, socialization, social control, social participation, and mutual support in communities). This approach to the social environment reflects very little overlap with the human behavior content. Some exceptions include the concept of stages of development (e.g., life span of a group, organization, or community), leadership behaviors, communications, and conflict. This situation is not ideal but needs more dialogue and instructional planning to foster integration and the identification of key concepts in multiple contexts.

In addition, a systems perspective reflects a strong orientation to the value of theory for practice, especially focusing on concepts relevant for conducting trifocal assessments at the group, organizational, and community level. This trifocal perspective is needed to understand the social environment that impacts clients, staff members, and volunteers (both governing and service delivery). The core concepts that are described in this section are placed in the context of a local community as a way to describe the social environment.

A set of concepts provides a framework for understanding the social environment at the local level (Mulroy & Austin, 2004). Because social policies are often implemented at the local level through city or county government as well as by nonprofit and for-profit provider organizations, it is important to be able to assess this community of organizations. Their interorganizational network may reflect an array of integrated and/or fragmented service delivery relationships. These relationships include contracted services with shared responsibilities for financing and client services, co-located services with shared responsibility for maintaining access to client services, and integrated services with shared responsibility for promoting the availability of client services (e.g., one-stop shopping). All of these relationships call upon an understanding of the local perspective of the social environment, namely, the nature of community at the neighborhood level, the nature of community-based human service organizations, and the dynamics of group behavior that underlie citizen involvement in neighborhoods as well as staff involvement inside and outside human service organizations.

Structure and Process

The two most all-encompassing concepts needed to understand communities, groups, and organizations at the local or neighborhood level are *structure* and *process*. Structure refers, in this context, to the arrangement and mutual relationship of the constituent parts to the whole (Brown, 1993). Process is defined, for this discussion, as a continuous series of actions, events, or changes that are directed toward some end and/or performed in a specific manner (Brown, 1993). In essence, how are community neighborhoods and organizations structured? How do groups of citizens and staff behave among themselves and with each other? These are critical questions for understanding the social environment of community neighborhoods and organizations that seek to meet the needs of their residents or clients. These community organizations can include public schools, neighborhood service centers, places of worship, child-care agencies, senior centers, group homes, women's shelters, and neighborhood health clinics.

Community Neighborhoods

The structure of a neighborhood includes both formal and informal organizations and associations. These may be an informal network of local clergy, an association of neighborhood merchants, a neighborhood after-school program, or a neighborhood substation for the police and fire department. These are all part of the formal and informal structure of a neighborhood community. The concept of structure can be used to identify and assess the processes that underlie a neighborhood's horizontal and vertical relationships (Warren, 1963). For example, the horizontal dimension of process dynamics might include regular neighborhood meetings between the clergy, police, school principals, and service center director. The vertical dimension could include the maintenance of relationships between the neighborhood and the larger community (e.g., city, county, or region). Examples of the vertical dimension are organizational relationships with the county social service and public health departments, school districts, nonprofit organizations serving the region, and city police and fire departments. These horizontal and vertical relationships provide another perspective on the vitality of a neighborhood community.

One of the process concepts applicable to a neighborhood community involves community competence (Fellin, 2001, p. 70), that is, the capacity of the neighborhood residents and service providers to engage in a process of identifying community needs, coordinating services, and/or facilitating problem solving related to community concerns or resolving conflicts.

Community-Based Organizations

Just as for neighborhood communities, the concepts of structure and process can also inform our understanding of organizations. For example, all human service organizations have a service mission or purpose. Within such a mission, they can be characterized as primarily people processing, people sustaining, or people changing (Hasenfeld, 1983, p. 5). *People-processing* organizations are structured to make sure that those who are eligible for benefits (e.g., food stamps, immunizations) are processed in an effective and efficient manner. *People-sustaining* organizations are designed to provide a level of care that is high enough to help individuals and/or families attain self-sufficiency (e.g., group homes, service centers). *People-changing* organizations are structured in a way to provide services that help individuals grow and thrive in their community (e.g., schools, mental health and substance abuse services).

In addition to the structure of the organization influencing its internal processes, organizations must also contend with their external environment. Examples of the environment that have direct bearing on their neighborhood location are accessible bus routes and well-established referral relationships with related organizations. The task environment of an agency can be defined in terms of community involvement (client advisory committees and agency boards of directors), sources of funding (city or county government, United Way), and political support (elected officials, opinion leaders, and philanthropic funds).

Groups in Communities and Organizations

In addition to their impact on the community and organizational dimensions of the social environment, the concepts of structure and process have relevance for understanding groups that operate within the social environment. How are neighborhood groups organized (by blocks or shared concerns)? What are the patterns of communications between neighborhood groups and within groups? Similarly, group process concepts focus on the array of systems and behaviors demonstrated by group members (Patton & Downs, 2003). How are leaders identified? How invested are members in their neighborhood groups? Are the behaviors of group members focused primarily on neighborhood improvement projects or on advocacy efforts focused on city hall?

These same group structure and process concepts can be applied to a neighborhood organization, whether it is the staff of an agency or its board members. How are staff members organized (organization chart, labor-management agreement)? How is the board structured (15 members meeting frequently versus 60 members meeting infrequently, or active use of standing versus ad hoc committees)? In addition to the structural dimensions, it is important to note the process or group dynamics dimensions. What role do staff members play in organizational decision making? Are there regularly scheduled staff meetings? Who leads them? What is the nature of interdisciplinary collaboration (e.g., neighborhood health clinic staffed by many disciplines)? What is the nature of teamwork and problem solving between staff representatives and neighborhood client advisory groups? All these questions illustrate the centrality of understanding group processes inside and outside a human service organization.

As noted in Table 1.3, the concepts of structure and process are primary elements in fostering an understanding of the social environment that includes neighborhood communities, organizations, and groups. These key concepts are also connected to a set of related concepts that elaborate or drill down deeper to understand the complexity of structure and process. For example, central to the concept of structure and process are the concepts of *development, exchange,* and *diversity* (see Figure 1.1). Each of

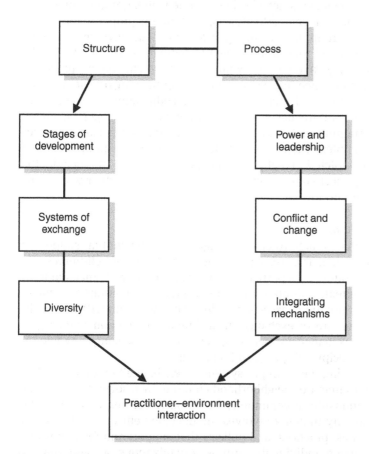

Figure 1.1

The concepts of structure and process in understanding the microsystems of the social environment.

Note. From "Toward a Comprehensive Framework for Understanding the Social Environment: In Search of Theory for Practice," by E. Mulroy and M. Austin, 2004, *Journal of Human Behavior and the Social Environment, 10*(3), pp. 25–59. Copyright 2004 by Haworth Press.

these concepts is described in the next section and illustrated in terms of a group, a community, or an organization.

Elements of Structure

Stages of Development

The term "stages of development" refers to the location of the community, group, and organization along a continuum of time and evolution. Such a continuum is important for understanding the social environment of a community in terms of its stability over time or its changing nature (improving or declining). The same stage of development continuum applies to neighborhood organizations, whether they are new and still finding their way in terms of mission and goals or old and established. The history of an organization is important for understanding its present realities and future opportunities.

The development continuum can be seen most vividly in the evolution of a group (e.g., a citizen's neighborhood crime watch group or an agency staff group working together to develop a funding proposal for a new service). For any group, the beginning or *forming* stage involves clarifying common interests and roles to be played (Tuchman & Jensen, 1977). The *storming* stage may involve the evolution of problem-solving processes (e.g., multiple short meetings versus fewer long meetings). The *norming* stage usually involves the clarification and codification of some rules or guidelines for future behavior (e.g., establishing an agenda, taking minutes, determining voting procedures). The *performing* stage involves the allocation, implementation, and evaluation of different group-identified tasks to be completed. Finally, the *adjourning* stage can include the celebration of project completion or the designation of further work to be done by another group.

Systems of Exchange

Systems of exchange are structures designed to foster mutual support in a social environment that recognizes the central role of self-interest. In essence, collaborators on a particular issue want to know "What's in it for me?" In this context, self-interest is a neutral term (in contrast to some of the negative connotations associated with being self-centered) that seeks to capture the nature of exchange in all human interaction (e.g., I give you money in exchange for services). Systems of exchange involve an arrangement of reciprocal giving and receiving.

When applying the concept "systems of exchange" to understanding the social environment of neighborhood communities, several dimensions emerge in relationship to community building. According to Weil (1996, p. 482), community building involves the development of structures that include "activities, practices, and policies that support and foster positive connections among individuals, groups, organizations, neighborhoods, and geographic and functional communities." In essence, community building involves systems of exchange. For example, engaging members of the community to invest in the improvement of their own neighborhood includes the implicit question "What's in it for me?" The structure might be a neighborhood advisory committee, and the exchange might be the transaction of devoting time to attend or participate in meetings in exchange for a cleaner or safer neighborhood.

Diversity

The concept of diversity has come to acquire many different meanings. Understanding and responding to the diversity of clients when providing human services represents the most prevalent meaning, but there are other meanings with respect to communities, groups, and organizations. When focusing on the neighborhood, diversity can be reflected in the different socioeconomic statuses of the residents (e.g., a blue-collar neighborhood). Diversity can also be seen in the demography of residents who are retired, single, and have young families, as well as the race and ethnicity of a diverse or homogeneous neighborhood. The extent to which neighborhoods are segregated or integrated represents another aspect of communal diversity (Fellin, 2001, p. 152).

Diversity in human service organizations can be viewed from at least three perspectives: the clients served, the staff employed, and the composition of the board of directors. The diversity of client problems or needs requires organizations to develop ways of classifying clients to provide them with the services that meet their needs. In contrast to client diversity, the diversity of staff can be understood, in part, by the organization's commitment to affirmative action (e.g., promoting racial and ethnic diversity) and/or staff development (e.g., promoting career advancement). Clearly, the diversity of staff competence and experience affect career advancement. Other issues of diversity can be seen in the composition of the organization's board of directors with respect to age, sex, race, ethnicity, and sexual orientation.

This discussion of diversity completes the description of the concepts related to structure in Table 1.3. The next section focuses on the process concepts of leadership and power, conflict and change, and integration.

Elements of Process

Power and Leadership

The concepts of power and leadership are complex and can be defined in many different ways. When thinking about both concepts at the neighborhood level, the roles of political and economic power come to mind. Political power may be reflected in the capacity of the neighborhood residents to promote neighborhood improvement (e.g., through the power of a local church) or lobby city hall for changes in the zoning ordinance to promote economic development and job growth in the neighborhood. In contrast, neighborhood leadership might be reflected in the cosmopolitan or local behaviors of neighborhood leaders (Warren, 1963). *Cosmopolitans* are those who have developed networks of relationships beyond the neighborhood with elected officials, business leaders, or leaders of nonprofit organizations. *Locals* are those who have spent most of their time cultivating relationships and coordinating local projects with less emphasis on those outside the neighborhood. Understanding these leadership styles can help explain the use of power at the neighborhood level.

In the context of groups, power can be displayed in terms of expertise, position, and access to rewards and related networks (French & Raven, 1960). Power may be displayed through the concepts of task and process, namely, the ability to help the group stay on task and/or use debriefing sessions to reflect on the dynamics of the group's process. The leadership capacities of group members are essential ingredients for understanding the behaviors of a group. Those group members who practice leadership behaviors are also able to demonstrate followership behaviors (Fiedler, 1967).

Conflict and Change

The concepts of conflict and change are also interconnected. At the neighborhood level, conflicts between renters and landlords can be a source of great tension until there is a change (e.g., housing repairs, rent adjustments). Positive and negative conflicts are important components of the social environment (Coser, 1956). Positive conflict relates to issues that help bind the community together, either in opposition to an external force or as a source for engaging in a dialogue over differences (e.g., mediating property disputes). Negative conflict relates to issues that create such polarization that resolution requires considerable time and energy to resolve.

Conflict and change in most organizations are facts of life. In essence, organizations are in a constant transition from maintaining stability (frequently accompanied by a resistance to change) to fostering improvement and change (Hasenfeld, 1983). Organizations have different capacities to manage change. This capacity is often impacted by the organization's environment (e.g., financial resources and public support). Organizational resistance to change can take many forms and needs to be understood as a critical element of the organization's internal and external environment.

Integrating Mechanisms

Integrating mechanisms can be viewed as networks of relationships that hold communities, groups, and organizations together or as institutionalized processes or procedures that can be used to monitor their health and well-being. In neighborhood communities, such networks include both formal and informal relationships that seek to foster the integration of the individual resident into the larger community. Tenant councils in housing complexes and neighborhood block watch groups serve as integrating mechanisms for a community. They can foster formal and informal relationships over time, as do regular meetings among the clergy whose congregations are located in the same neighborhood.

The use of integrating mechanisms in a group can be seen in the use of feedback processes or debriefing sessions at the end of each meeting to gather the perceptions and concerns of the members. Other integrating mechanisms are brainstorming and problem-solving processes (Patton & Downs, 2003). These processes provide a venue to bring latent group issues to the surface and allow members to voice their concerns through a mechanism adopted by the group. In essence, the integrating mechanisms of the group provide individuals with opportunities to engage in sharing and problem solving.

This discussion of process concepts provides a foundation, along with the previous discussion of structure concepts, for integrating both of these dimensions of the social environment when focusing on the role of the practitioner.

Practitioner–Environment Interaction

Different from the elaboration of the previous concepts related to the social environment, the interaction between practitioners and their environment represents a significantly overlooked dimension of the social environment. The focus here is on the degree to which a practitioner is able to conceptualize his or her role as an influential factor when engaging with neighbor residents, colleagues in a staff meeting, or the supervisor or supervisees in an organizational setting. The interaction is a two-way street whereby the community, group, and organization can also influence the behaviors of the practitioner.

The interaction represents a key element of self-reflective practice (Schon, 1984). The manager as a practitioner in a human service organization can have significant influence over how staff members are treated, issues resolved, funds allocated, and information processed. At the same time, staff members can significantly influence managerial behaviors with respect to the quality of the workplace environment, the management of conflict and change, and the representation of the organization in the larger community. An understanding of the history and customs of the organization can greatly influence a practitioner's effectiveness in working with the internal and external environment of the organizations (Austin, 1996).

The array of concepts relevant to understanding the social environment at the local level is infinite. As a result, choices need to be made. One approach to displaying those choices can be seen in Table 1.4, where the major constructs are identified on the left-hand side and the trifocal view of the local social environment is noted across the top with respect to communities, organizations, and groups. This is only one instructional approach to introducing students to the array of concepts relevant to understanding the social environment at the local level.

Table 1.4 A Trifocal Perspective on Communities, Groups, and Organizations

Major Constructs	Community Concepts	Group Concepts	Organizational Concepts
I. Structures and processes	Community competence Functional/geographic Horizontal/vertical	Communications Member orientation and behaviors	Types (processing, sustaining, changing) Political economy and related organizational theories
II. Stages of development	Urbanization and gentrification Population diversity/immigration	Forming, storming, norming, performing	Evolution of organizational goals and technology
III. Power and leadership	Economic power Political power Locals/cosmopolitans	Task/process orientation Leadership/followership group dynamics	Loosely coupled Sources of control Leadership styles
IV. Systems of exchange	Community building Voluntary organizations and associations Public sector organizations	Problem solving as exchange of views, expertise, resources	General/task environment Power dependence
V. Conflict and change	Positive/negative conflict Change capacity	Norms regarding managing tensions Superordinate goals	Stability/resistance Innovation capacity
VI. Diversity	Socioeconomic stratification Neighborhood integration and segregation	Diversity of members (race, gender, age, sexual orientation)	Client classification Client's organizational career
VII. Integrating mechanisms	Formal and informal networks Client reintegration	Feedback/debriefing Idea generating	Assessing performance Ongoing operations
VIII. Practitioner–environment interaction	Impact of community organizer/enabler on community and vice versa	Impact of group facilitator/leader on group and vice versa	Impact of organization's manager/leader on organization and vice versa

Frameworks for Linking Knowledge to Practice

Although the previous frameworks provide different ways to conceptualize the interaction between HB&SE and the larger social environment, they constitute abstract theoretical concepts that are not easy to apply in every-day social work practice. One approach to utilizing these larger frameworks is to specify conceptual frameworks that operate closer to the realities of practice. The related concepts of risk and resilience and stress and coping cut across most fields of practice (e.g., child welfare, mental health, aging, and physical health). We briefly highlight them in this section.

Risk and Resilience

Fraser, Richman, and Galinsky (1999) define risk as the probability of a negative outcome given a set of individual and environmental circumstances. In short, risk factors may be conceptualized as causing, marking, or correlating a particular negative outcome. Resilience refers to the process of successful adjustment given a particular risk or set of risk factors. Cumulative risk is currently considered to be a better predictor of outcomes than specific risk factors. Both types of risk (specific and cumulative) can lead to individual vulnerability, but they also can be mediated or moderated by other individual or environmental factors. Fraser et al. suggest that resilience can be conceptualized in three ways: occasional success (despite high levels of risk), continuous success (despite prolonged exposure to the risk), and recovery (e.g., from exposure to trauma). Notably, resilient behavior must be understood from the perspective of both individual and environmental characteristics.

Stress and Coping

The concepts of stress and coping are empirical generalizations tied to practice with clients, especially in the fields of practice related to physical health and mental health. The concept of stress has varying definitions; one overarching definition "refers to that quality of experience, produced through a person–environment transaction, that through either over-arousal or under-arousal, results in psychological or physiological distress" (Aldwin, 1994, p. 22). Mason (1975) identified three causes of stress: (1) an internal state or strain, (2) an external event, or (3) an interaction between the person and environment that can lead to positive or negative responses. Internal stresses can be related to both physiological and emotional reactions. External stressors can include traumas, life events, environmental characteristics, hassles of daily life, or relationship issues. Considering stress as a manifestation of the interaction between person and environment draws attention to the fit or mismatch between individual capacities and the demands of a situation. In other words, the concept of stress is inherently "transactional" (Lazarus & Folkman, 1984).

The current conceptualization of stress and coping emerged out of earlier theoretical work in evolutionary theory and behavior adaptation, psychoanalytic concepts, life cycle theories, and case studies of how individuals manage life crises (Moos & Schaefer, 1993). Evolutionary theory proposes that organisms adapt to their environment in order to survive. Psychoanalytic theory suggests that individuals develop in order to promote personal growth. Life cycle theories promote the idea that individuals acquire skills and capacities to negotiate each stage of human development in order to move to the next stage of life. Behavioral adaptation to life crises involves the use of human competence and coping to deal with life transitions and crises. Each of these theories could contribute to a comprehensive framework of stress and coping that features the interactions among environmental systems, individual attributes, and the availability of resources. Life crises can then be interpreted by appraising the stress and coping responses that influence an individual's health and well-being.

Coping strategies, beyond dealing with the daily challenges of life, involve actions for dealing with stressful situations that are rooted in historical and social contexts that create norms for dealing with stress. Coping also involves a learned behavior by which individuals can be taught the skills and mechanisms needed to effectively cope with stress. Resources for coping include a set of personal, attitudinal, and cognitive factors. These include demographic and personality factors, social context (including familial resources), and the interplay of personal and social factors (Moos & Schaefer, 1993). Coping processes can be thought of as both the focus of coping (the person's orientation to the stressor) and the method of coping (the cognitive or behavioral response).

Clearly, these concepts, by themselves, do not constitute explanatory frameworks. However, they provide one way of using the explanatory theories and frameworks covered in this volume to define potential sources of risk and resilience. There are multiple sources of developmental risk and stress and the mechanisms by which risk and stress lead to negative outcomes. There are also multiple sources of resilience and coping strategies. It is notable that both of these concepts indicate the importance of person-environment interactions. The complementary frameworks are suggestive of how particular person–environment interactions and attributes of the social environment may contribute to risk or stress and resilience or coping. As noted earlier, the larger frameworks identify specific social relationships and interactions, as well as environmental opportunity structures, as contexts for understanding risk and stress and resilience and coping.

Conclusion

In this chapter, we have attempted to identify the complexities of utilizing theories from the social and behavioral sciences, a set of conceptual frameworks that may aid in organizing knowledge particularly focused on the social environment side of HB&SE, an array of instructional applications, and a set of suggestions for reframing HB&SE. We noted that there are at least three tasks associated with the process of borrowing knowledge: selection, synthesis (and evaluation), and translation for social work professional use. Dialogue about these three very important and complex processes has received limited attention in the social work literature, especially as they apply to the knowledge base of HB&SE.

As social science and behavioral science knowledge develops over time, our profession will always grapple with how best to manage, organize, and use this information. Although it is unlikely that there will ever be a single metatheoretical framework that covers HB&SE (Turner, 1990), it is important to clarify how we intend to use this knowledge. Messick's (1983) distinction between person as context, person of context, and person in context may be a useful point of departure.

The central goal of this chapter is to offer several alternative frameworks for organizing, synthesizing, and translating knowledge. Three themes cut across our discussion. The first is a need to utilize theoretical accounts that address both human behavior and the social environment, particularly as they aid our understanding of the nature of the interaction between the two. The second is a need to specify key levels of analysis and concepts related to the larger social environment. The third is for a set of concepts that aid in the translation of theory into practice.

If we truly strive to understand the nature of the varying relationships between persons and their environments, there remains considerable conceptual work to be done. We hope that social work scholars continue to not only pose frameworks that help us understand HB&SE, but also offer frameworks for integration (Greenfield, 2011). We are also aware that consideration of multiple levels of analysis complicates the process of describing how theory can inform practice. We attempted to grapple with these translation issues in two ways: (1) by presenting concepts (risk and resilience, stress and coping) that may link complex theoretical accounts back to practice, and (2) through application of the life course perspective to both the life cycle as well as relevant explanatory theory discussed in this volume. The frameworks we presented are clearly not exhaustive. We hope that they aid development of our HB&SE knowledge base by encouraging more discussion about these complexities. We ultimately conclude that the agenda for further dialogue is substantial and needs to be explored annually through special interest groups and faculty development institutes at social work professional conferences, in peer-reviewed journals, and through the wide dissemination of books like this one.

Key Terms

Community competence	Middle range theory	Resilience
Epistemology	Norms	Risk
Institutional logics	Neighborhood effects	Social capital
Level of analysis	Opportunity framework	Stress and coping
Life course perspective	Processes in the social environment	Structures in the social environment
Life cycle		

Review Questions for Critical Thinking

1. What factors contribute to the mismatch between available theory and practice applications in social work?

2. The most recent CSWE standards emphasize that, "Social workers utilize conceptual frameworks to guide the processes of assessment, intervention, and evaluation; and critique and apply knowledge to understand person and environment." How might the frameworks presented in this chapter be used to guide these processes within clinical and macro social work?

3. The life course perspective presents an opportunity to consider person-in-environment through a developmental lens. Can you apply Elder's five principles to how the experience of poverty may differ for different groups of people at particular historical time periods (e.g., men during the Depression, women in the 1970s, and the elderly today)?

4. Identify an "institutional logic" that has influenced the way services are provided in your field placement organization.

5. What are some limitations of relying on middle range theory to conceptualize the relationships between persons and their environment, including the multiple levels of analysis therein?

Online Resources

This website details the life course research being conducted by Glen H. Elder at the Carolina Population Center. Data from the primary life course studies, including the Oakland and Berkeley Studies, the Lewis Terman Study, the Iowa Youth and Families Project, and Add Health, are included.

www.cpc.unc.edu/projects/lifecourse

BetterTogether is an initiative of the Saguaro Seminar on Civic Engagement in America at Harvard University's Kennedy School of Government. It supports research and practice to stimulate dialogue about social capital and its utility for American engagement.

www.bettertogether.org

The World Bank provides a comprehensive definition of social capital and discusses methods for measuring it.

http://web.worldbank.org/WBSITE/EXTERNAL/TOPICS/EXTSOCIAL
DEVELOPMENT/EXTTSOCIALCAPITAL/0,,contentMDK:20185164~
menuPK:418217pagePK:148956~piPK:216618~theSitePK:401015,00
.html

The Social Work Podcast, hosted by Jonathan Singer, PhD, assistant professor, College of Health Professions and Social Work, Temple University, includes interviews with social work scholars and advanced practitioners on social work theory, research and practice.

http://socialworkpodcast.blogspot.com/

The Maternal and Child Health Library at Georgetown University provides a list of resources and information integrating life course theory and maternal and child health.

www.mchlibrary.info/lifecourse/guides.html

The Living Proof Podcast Series highlights the work of social work practitioners and scholars; many of the podcasts are relevant to content related to HB&SE.

www.socialwork.buffalo.edu/podcast

The MacArthur Network on Transitions to Adulthood conducts research on the experience of young adulthood today as it relates to sociocultural issues, time, and place.

http://transitions.s410.sureserver.com

The MacArthur Research Network on an Aging Society focuses on the themes of intergenerational issues, meaningful roles, diversity, and inequality.

www.agingsocietynetwork.org//Research_Network_on_an_Aging_Society.htm

The Project for Public Spaces focuses on building healthy communities and the importance of place in human development and relationships.

www.pps.org

References

Administration on Aging. (2002). *A profile of older Americans*. Washington, DC: U.S. Department of Health and Human Services.

Aldwin, C. M. (1994). *Stress, coping, and development: An integrative perspective*. New York, NY: Guilford Press.

Arnett, J. J. (2000). Emerging adulthood: A theory of development from the late teens through early twenties. *American Psychologist, 55*, 469–480.

Austin, M. J. (1996). Planning for organizational change: Linking the past with the present and future. *Journal of Jewish Communal Service, 73*, 44–52.

Besharov, D. J. (1999). *America's disconnected youth*. Washington, DC: Child Welfare League of America.

Bloom, M., & Klein, W. C. (Eds.). (1996). *Controversial issues in human behavior in the social environment*. New York, NY: Prentice Hall.

Bourdieu, P. (1977). *Outline of a theory of practice*. Cambridge, UK: Cambridge University Press.

Bourdieu, P. (1985). The genesis of the concepts of habitus and field. *Sociocriticism, 2*, 11–24.

Bronfenbrenner, U. (1979). *The ecology of human development*. Cambridge, MA: Harvard University Press.

Brooks, W. (1986). Human behavior/social environment: Past and present, future or folly? *Journal of Social Work Education, 22*, 18–23.

Brown, L. (Ed.). (1993). *The new shorter Oxford English dictionary on historical principles*. Oxford, UK: Clarendon Press.

Burch, P. (2007). Educational policy and practice from the perspective of institutional theory: Crafting a wider lens. *Educational Researcher, 36*, 84–95.

Cicchetti, D., & Dawson, G. (2002). Editorial: Multiple levels of analysis [Special issue]. *Development and Psychopathology, 14*, 417–420.

Cloward, R., & Ohlin, L. (1960). *Delinquency and opportunity*. New York, NY: Free Press.

Coleman, J. S. (1988). Social capital in the creation of human capital. *American Journal of Sociology, 94*(Suppl.), S95–S120.

Colyvas, J., & Powell, W. (2006). Roads to institutionalization. *Research in Organizational Behavior, 21*, 305–353.

Committee on Scientific Principles in Education Research. (2001). *Science, evidence, and inference in education: Report of a workshop*. Bethesda, MD: Author.

Cornell, K. L. (2006). Person-in-situation: History, theory, and new directions for social work practice. *Praxis, 6*, 50–57.

Coser, L. (1956). *The functions of social conflict*. New York, NY: Free Press.

Council on Social Work Education. (1971). *Manual of accrediting standards*. New York, NY: Author.

Council on Social Work Education. (1984). *Handbook of accreditation standards and procedures*. New York, NY: Author.

Council on Social Work Education. (1994). *Handbook of accreditation standards and procedures*. New York, NY: Author.

Council on Social Work Education. (2001). *Handbook of accreditation standards and procedures*. Alexandria, VA: Author.

Council on Social Work Education (2008). *Educational Policy and Accreditation Standards*. Alexandria, VA: Author.

Cowan, P. A. (1988). Developmental psychopathology: A nine-cell map of the territory. *New Directions for Child Development, 39*, 5–29.

Deater-Decker, K. (2001). Annotation: Recent research examining the role of peer relationships in the development of psychopathology. *Journal of Child Psychology and Psychiatry and Allied Disciplines, 42*, 565–579.

DiMaggio, P., & Powell, W. (1991). Introduction. In W. W. Powell & P. J. DiMaggio (Eds.), *The new institutionalism in organizational analysis* (pp. 1–37). Chicago, IL: University of Chicago Press.

Duncan, G. J., & Brooks-Gunn, J. (2000). Family poverty, welfare reform, and child development. *Child Development, 71*, 188–196.

Durkheim, E. (1997). *Suicide*. New York, NY: Free Press.

Eccles, J., & Roeser, R. (1999). School and community influences on human development. In M. Bornstein & M. Lamb (Eds.), *Developmental psychology: An advanced textbook* (4th ed., pp. 503–554). Mahwah, NJ: Erlbaum.

Edward, G. C. (1979). Disaggregation in policy research. *Policy Studies Journal, 7*, 675–683.

Elder, G. H. Jr. (1995). The life course paradigm: Social change and individual development. In P. Moen, G. H. Elder Jr., & K. Luscher (Eds.), *Examining lives in context: Perspectives on the ecology of human development* (pp. 101–139). Washington, DC: American Psychological Association.

Farley, O., Smith, L., Boyle, S., & Ronnau, J. (2002). A review of foundation MSW human behavior courses. *Journal of Human Behavior in the Social Environment, 6*(2), 1–12.

Fellin, P. (2001). *The community and the social worker*. Itasca, IL: Peacock Press.

Feuer, M. J., Towne, L., & Shavelson, R. J. (2002). Scientific culture and educational research. *Educational Researcher, 31*, 4–14.

Fiedler, F. E. (1967). *A theory of leadership effectiveness*. New York, NY: McGraw-Hill.

Foley, M. W., & Edwards, B. (1999). Is it time to disinvest in social capital. *Journal of Public Policy, 19*, 141–173.

Fraser, M., Richman, J., & Galinsky, M. (1999). Risk, protection, and resilience: Towards a conceptual framework for social work practice. *Social Work Research, 23*(3), 131–144.

Fraser, M. W., & Galinsky, M. J. (2010). Steps in intervention research: Designing and developing social programs. *Research on Social Work Practice, 20,* 459–466.

French, J. R. P., & Raven, B. (1960). The bases of social power. In D. Cartwright & A. Zander (Eds.), *Group dynamics* (pp. 607–623). Evanston, IL: Row, Peterson.

Friedland, R., & Alford, R. R. (1991). Bringing society back in: Symbols, practices and institutional contradictions. In W. W. Powell & P. J. DiMaggio (Eds.), *The new institutionalism in organizational analysis* (pp. 164–183). Chicago, IL: University of Chicago Press.

Galatzer-Levy, R. & Cohler, B. (1993). *The essential other: A developmental psychology of the self*. New York, NY: Basic Books.

Gibbs, L. E. (1996). Can critical thinking and HBSE course content be taught concurrently? Yes. In M. Bloom & W. C. Klein (Eds.), *Controversial issues in human behavior in the social environment* (pp. 81–95). Boston, MA: Allyn & Bacon.

Gibbs, P. (1986). HBSE in the undergraduate curriculum: A survey. *Journal of Social Work Education, 22*(2), 46–52.

Gitterman, A. (1996). Ecological perspective: Response to Professor Jerry Wakefield. *Social Service Review, 70*, 472–476.

Goldhaber, D. E. (2000). *Theories of human development: Integrative perspectives*. Mountain View, CA: Mayfield.

Goldstein, H. (1990). The knowledge base of social work practice: Theory, wisdom, analogue, or art? *Families in Society, 71*, 32–43.

Green, D., & McDermott, F. (2010). Social work from inside and between complex systems: Perspectives on person-in-environment for today's social work. *British Journal of Social Work, 40*, 2414–2430.

Greenfield, E. (2011). Developmental systems theory as a conceptual anchor for generalist curriculum on human behavior and the social environment. *Social Work Education, 30*, 529–540.

Han, C. S. (2010). One gay Asian body: A personal narrative for examining human behavior in the social environment. *Journal of Human Behavior in the Social Environment, 20*(1), 74–87.

Hasenfeld, Y. (1983). *Human service organizations*. Upper Saddle River, NJ: Prentice-Hall.

Holmes, D., Murray, S. J., Perron, A., & Rail, G. (2006). Deconstructing the evidence-based discourse in health sciences: Truth, power and fascism. *International Journal of Evidence Based Healthcare, 4*, 180–186.

Hunt, S. (2005). *The life course: A sociological introduction*. London, UK: Palgrave.

Hutchison, E. D. (2003). *Dimensions of human behavior* (2nd ed.). Thousand Oaks, CA: Sage.

Hutchison, E. D. (2005). The life course perspective: A promising approach for bridging the micro and macro worlds for social workers. *Families in Society, 86*, 143–152.

Jencks, C., & Mayer, S. E. (1990). The social consequences of growing up in a poor neighborhood. In L. E. Lynn & M. G. H. McGeary (Eds.), *Inner-city poverty in the United States* (pp. 111–186). Washington, DC: National Academy Press.

Kondrat, M. E. (1992). Reclaiming the practical: Formal and substantive rationality in social work practice. *Social Service Review, 66,* 237–255.

Kondrat, M. E. (2002). Actor-centered social work: Re-visioning "person-in-environment" through a critical theory lens. *Social Work, 47*(4), 435–448.

Lazarus, R., & Folkman, S. (1984). *Stress, appraisal, and coping.* New York, NY: Springer.

Levande, D. (1987). Boundary issues and transformation possibilities in the HBSE curriculum. *Journal of Social Work Education, 23*(3), 59–66.

Lewis, M. (Ed.). (2000). Toward a development of psychopathology: Models, definitions, and prediction. In A. J. Sameroff, M. Lewis, & S. Miller (Eds.), *Handbook of developmental psychology* (2nd ed., pp. 3–21). Dordrecht, The Netherlands: Kluwer Press.

Liehr, P., & Smith, M. (1999). Middle range theory: Spinning research and practice to create knowledge for the new millennium. *Advances in Nursing Science, 21*(4), 81–91.

Loury, G. C. (1977). A dynamic theory of racial income differences. In P. Wallace & A. Lamont (Eds.), *Women, minorities and employment discrimination* (pp. 153–186). New York, NY: Lexington Books.

Mailick, M., & Vigilante, F. (1987). Human behavior and the social environment: A sequence providing the theoretical base for teaching assessment. *Journal of Teaching in Social Work, 1*(2), 33–47.

Mason, J. (1975). A historical view of the stress field. *Journal of Human Stress, 1,* 6–12.

McKenna, H. P. (1997). *Nursing models and theories.* London, UK: Routledge.

Merton, R. K. (1968). *Social theory and social structure.* New York, NY: Free Press.

Messick, S. (1983). Assessment of children. In P. H. Mussen & W. Kessen (Eds.), *Handbook of child psychology: Vol. 1. History, theory, and methods* (4th ed., pp. 477–526). New York, NY: Wiley.

Meyer, J. W., & Rowan, B. (1977). Institutionalized organizations: Formal structure as myth and ceremony. *American Journal of Sociology, 83,* 340–365.

Mohan, B. (1980). Human behavior, social environment, social reconstruction, and social policy: A system of linkages, goals, and priorities. *Journal of Education for Social Work, 16*(2), 26–32.

Moos, R. H., & Schaefer, J. A. (1993). Coping resources and processes: Current concepts and measures. In L. Goldenberger & S. Breznitz (Eds.), *Handbook of stress: Theoretical and clinical aspects* (2nd ed., pp. 234–257). New York, NY: Free Press.

Mulroy, E., & Austin, M. (2004). Towards a comprehensive framework for understanding the social environment: In search of theory for practice. *Journal of Human Behavior and the Social Environment, 10*(3), 25–59.

National Association of Social Workers (n.d.). *Code of Ethics.* Available online at www.socialworkers.org/pubs/code/code.asp.

Newman, K. (2003). *A different shade of gray: Midlife and beyond in the inner city.* New York, NY: New Press.

Nicotera, N., & Kang, H. (2009). Beyond diversity courses: Strategies for integrating critical consciousness across social work curriculum. *Journal of Teaching in Social Work, 29,* 188–203.

Patton, B. R., & Downs, T. M. (2003). *Decision-making group interaction: Achieving quality* (4th ed.). Boston, MA: Allyn & Bacon.

Pedhazur, E. J., & Schmelkin, L. P. (1991). *Measurement, design, and analysis: An integrated approach.* Hillsdale, NJ: Erlbaum.

Popple, P. R., & Leighninger, L. (2002). *Social work, social welfare, and American society* (5th ed.). Boston, MA: Allyn & Bacon.

Putnam, R. (2000). Bowling alone: The collapse and revival of American community. New York, NY: Simon & Schuster.

Robbins, S. P., Chatterjee, P., & Canda, E. R. (2009). *Contemporary human behavior theory: A critical perspective for social work* (2nd ed.). Boston, MA: Allyn & Bacon.

Rogoff, B. (2003). *The cultural nature of human development.* Oxford, UK: Oxford University Press.

Rossiter, A. (1996). A perspective on critical social work. *Journal of Progressive Human Services, 7*(2), 23–41.

Runyan, W. M. (1988). *Psychology and historical interpretation.* New York, NY: Oxford University Press.

Sampson, R. J., Morenoff, J. D., & Gannon-Rowley, T. (2002). Assessing "neighborhood effects": Social processes and new directions in research. *Annual Review of Sociology, 28*, 443–478.

Schon, D. A. (1984). *The reflective practitioner: How professionals think in action.* New York, NY: Basic Books.

Scott, W. R. (2001). *Institutions and organizations* (2nd ed.). Thousand Oaks, CA: Sage.

Scott, W. R., & Davis, G. F. (2006). *Organizations and organizing: Rational, natural, and open system perspectives.* Upper Saddle River, NJ: Pearson Prentice Hall.

Scott, W. R., Ruef, M., Mendel, P. J., & Caronna, C. A. (2000). The changing institutional environment. In W. R. Scott, M. Ruef, P. J. Mendel, & C. A. Caronna (Eds.), *Institutional change and healthcare organizations: From professional dominance to managed care* (pp. 166–235). Chicago, IL: University of Chicago Press.

Settersten, R. A. Jr., & Lovegreen, L. D. (1998). Educational experiences throughout adult life: New hopes or no hope for life-course flexibility? *Research on Aging, 20*, 506–538.

Stone, S. (2004). Reflecting on the social environment dimensions of HB&SE: An HB&SE faculty member as discussant. *Journal of Human Behavior in the Social Environment, 10*(3), 111–118.

Taylor, S., Austin, M., & Mulroy, E. (2004). Evaluating the social environment component of human behavior and the social environment courses through an analysis of course outlines. *Journal of Human Behavior and the Social Environment, 10*(3), 61–84.

Taylor, S., Mulroy, E., & Austin, M. (2004). Social work textbooks on human behavior and the social environment: An analysis of the social environment component. *Journal of Human Behavior and the Social Environment, 10*(3), 85–110.

Thornton, P. H., & Ocasio, W. (2008). Institutional logics. In R. Greenwood, C. Oliver, R. Suddaby, & K. Sahlin-Andersson (Eds.), *The SAGE handbook of organizational institutionalism* (pp. 99–129). London, UK: Sage.

Thyer, B. A. (2001). What is the role of theory in research on social work practice? *Journal of Social Work Education, 37*, 9–25.

Tuchman, B. W., & Jensen, M. A. (1977). Stages of small group development revisited. *Groups and Organizational Studies, 2*, 419–427.

Turner, F. J. (1990). Social work practice theory: A trans-cultural resource for health care. *Social Science and Medicine, 31*(1), 13–17.

Van De Ven, A. H., & Johnson, P. E. (2006). Knowledge for theory and practice. *Academy of Management Review, 31*, 802–821.

Vygotsky, L. (1962). *Thought and language*. Cambridge, MA: MIT Press.

Wakefield, J. C. (1996a). Does social work need the eco-systems perspective? Pt. 1. Is the perspective clinically useful? *Social Service Review, 70*, 1–32.

Wakefield, J. C. (1996b). Does social work need the eco-systems perspective? Pt. 2. Does the perspective save social work from incoherence? *Social Service Review, 70*, 183–213.

Warren, R. (1963). *The community in America*. Chicago, IL: Rand McNally.

Weick, A. (1999). Guilty knowledge. *Families in Society, 80*, 327–332.

Weil, M. (1996). Community building: Building community practice. *Social Work, 41*, 481–499.

Zaparanick, T. L., & Wodarski, J. S. (2004). A curriculum for human behavior in the social environment. *Journal of Human Behavior in the Social Environment, 10*(3), 1–24.

Chapter 2
Respondent Learning Theory

Bruce A. Thyer

> How do the events we have been exposed to in our past influence our current behavior?

Most readers are familiar with the elemental principles of respondent learning theory, also known as *classical conditioning theory*, and tend to associate this approach to understanding human development across the life span with the work in the early 20th century of the Russian physiologist and Nobel laureate Ivan Pavlov. However, as outlined by Gormenzano and Moore (1969), the scientific analysis of so-called reflexive behavior goes back several centuries prior to Pavlov, perhaps beginning in the modern era with the writings of René Descartes in 1660, although many earlier writers, such as Aristotle, at least touched on the topic. Descartes used the term *reflexes* to describe "stereotyped, innate muscular responses following sensory stimulation" (Gormenzano & Moore, 1969, p. 122). In 1751, Whytt asserted that certain forms of nonmuscular bodily reactions, such as pupils contracting when exposed to bright light and salivation, were also reflexive in nature. The Russian physiologist Sechenov undertook a series of empirical studies on reflexes, published in 1863, and he was in turn influential on his compatriots, the young Ivan Pavlov and Vladimir Bekhterev. These authors had a dramatic impact on American psychology, as transmogrified and disseminated by the influential John Watson (1916, 1925). Pavlov's (1927) work, for which he received the Nobel Prize, related in part to how physiological processes could be conditioned. Thus, from the earliest days, it is clear that the school of psychology called *behaviorism* dealt with far more than only the overt, observable actions of animals and people; it also examined inner events, those occurring within the skin, such as one's physiological responses.

Respondent learning theory is one component of the general approach to social work that has been labeled *behaviorism* and has been occasionally mentioned by earlier social work textbooks (e.g., Fischer & Gochros, 1975; Jehu, Hardiker, Yelloly, & Shaw, 1972; Schwartz, 1982, 1983; Schwartz & Goldiamond, 1975; M. Sundel & Sundel, 1975). One of the earliest psychotherapy books describing the applications of respondent learning principles to helping clients solve problems was called *Conditioned Reflex Therapy* and appeared almost 60 years ago (Salter, 1949), so it is clear that this approach to social work theory and intervention has been with us for some time.

Generally, behaviorism proposes that human beings learn, that is to say, change their behavior, in response to environmental experiences through at least three distinct processes: respondent learning, operant learning, and learning via imitation, which is also called *modeling*. It is believed that these three learning mechanisms, combined with one's genetic endowment and relevant biological factors, are responsible for a large proportion of human learning. Behaviorism provides a comprehensive theory of normal human development across the life span, an etiological approach toward understanding what is described as *psychopathology*, and effective approaches toward social work intervention. Indeed, it is one of the few models of social work practice that has applicability across the entire spectrum of social work intervention, micro through macro. One of the earliest textbooks dealing with social work theory was titled, appropriately enough, *The Theory of Social Work* and was written by Frank Bruno in 1936. Bruno provides a very favorable summary of the behavioral perspective as it was then understood. For example:

> Behaviorism may be described as the theory that learning is the association of a new impression with the circumstances present at the time of receiving it. It has several obvious merits. It integrates emotion and intellect in a manner which realistically reproduces actual experience. It is socially acceptable, in the main, as it places such large faith upon capacity to learn, given the right conditions for association....
>
> Behaviorism affords a first class technic.... It is invaluable for the social worker in his efforts to understand the conduct of his clients, because it refers him back to the past experiences in which are to be found the particular circumstances which have determined the attitude of habitual responses of each individual. Thus behaviorism opens up endless possibilities for social work....
>
> It is also of value in treatment, for some of the most interesting work of the behaviorists has been in the field of what is called reconditioning; that is, in the unlearning of the old and the learning of new response patterns....
>
> Its simplicity is a real asset. Such incidents as the dropping of earth upon a coffin, the smelling of certain odors by worshippers in the Catholic Church, the hearing of the national anthem, the reading of certain words—all these under given conditions establish emotional and motor patterns which are powerful and constant, and which can be explained upon the theory of the conditioned reflex. (pp. 197–199)

Behaviorism, and respondent learning theory in particular, may be seen as one of the earliest and clearest explications of the person-in-environment approach that has long characterized social work theory. Given the statements just quoted, and (as described elsewhere in this chapter) noting that behaviorism attempts to explain not only overt, observable actions, but also one's feelings and cognitive processes, it is both misleading and a shame that contemporary accounts of the behavioral perspective perpetuate the notion that it only focuses on overt action. For example, one widely used social work text titled *Understanding Human Behavior in the Social Environment* states: "*Behavioral or learning theories* differ from many other personality theories in one basic way. Instead of focusing on internal motivations, needs and perceptions, they focus on specific observable behaviors" (Zastrow & Kirst-Ashman, 2007, p. 90; italics in original).

It is detrimental to the acceptance of behaviorism that it is erroneously equated with a sole focus on explaining observable behavior, since it is obvious that the domain of social work deals with clients' affective states, thoughts, dreams, aspirations, and other private events. By seeming to exclude such phenomena, as asserted by such secondhand accounts, social work students and practitioners may tend to overlook or dismiss the potential applications of behaviorism to these other important domains. Myers and Thyer (1994) and Thyer (1991a, 2005) provide overviews on how behaviorism has been consistently misrepresented in the social work literature, to the field's disadvantage. Regrettably, the topic of respondent learning theory is given sparse coverage in the human behavior texts most commonly used in social work education, despite the pleadings of a few far-sighted writers urging such inclusion (e.g., Thyer, 1992a, 1992b). In this chapter I try to remedy this omission and look at some of the fundamental concepts and processes of respondent learning theory, followed by illustrations of some naturally occurring examples. I review some aspects of respondent learning as etiologically linked, in a true example of a person-in-environment orientation, to selected psychosocial problems, and how this approach has been used in practice.

Respondent Learning Processes

Unconditioned Stimuli

Unconditioned stimuli are environmental events that our bodies naturally react to in some circumscribed manner. These are present generally from birth and do not have their origins in any specific learning experiences. Most of these unconditioned stimuli are familiar to you, given that you have reacted to them since birth or have witnessed them in others. Brushing a newborn's cheek elicits a reflexive rooting response; sucking results from inserting a nipple or other object into a baby's lips; a puff of air against the eye elicits blinking and tearing; our pupils constrict in bright light and dilate in dim conditions; tapping a knee tendon produces a jerk of the lower leg; a loud noise produces a flinch or startle reaction; a touch to the back of the throat produces coughing or gagging; a sharp pain (being poked, cut, burned, or shocked) causes a sudden withdrawal reaction. Not all of these unconditioned stimuli are equivalently capable of eliciting such reactions across the life span. The Moro reflex is present at birth, appearing as a startled look and sudden extension of the arms and legs when the baby experiences an abrupt loss of support (e.g., being slightly dropped) but disappears after a few months. The Babinski reflex, the extension of the big toe when the sole of the foot is stroked, disappears by the age of 2 years or so. By early childhood the rooting reflex or sucking response associated with nursing has disappeared. By late childhood or early puberty, genital stimulation in both sexes can produce sexual reactions such as erections (in males) and vaginal lubrication (in females), as well as orgasms if the stimulation is sufficiently intense. The acronym UCS is used to designate an unconditioned stimulus, and UCR refers to its associated reaction, or unconditioned response.

Some UCRs are associated with activation of the autonomic nervous system, producing elevations (to varying degrees) in various physiological functions such as heart rate, respiration, muscle tension, and blood flow, and certain hormones (e.g., adrenalin). Other bodily functions are reduced or slow down. For example, blood flow is reduced in the extremities (thus cold hands when frightened), salivation is reduced (thus dry mouth when scared), the digestive movements of our intestines slow down, and our pupils narrow. These autonomic reactions have been referred to as the body's *fight or flight* response. These functional relationships between UCSs and their associated UCRs are common to all human beings. They cut across both sexes and all races, cultures, and ethnic groups and can be considered universal human phenomena. And they go beyond human beings, in that we share such reactions with all other living animals. You can undoubtedly think of examples of dogs and cats displaying UCRs to obvious UCSs, and even single-celled organisms react in their own limited way (e.g., withdrawal) to relevant UCSs (Hennessey, Rucker, & McDiarmid, 1979). It has even been shown that individual human cells can react to UCSs with UCRs. The responsiveness of humans to UCSs is not only present from birth, but is also evident *prenatally*! For example, many pregnant mothers have noted that their fetal baby will jump in response to a loud noise, in a manner similar to a newborn (or for that matter, to an elderly person). Thus is it apparent that we are dealing with a fundamental form of human behavior that functions across our entire life span, and the entire animal kingdom in general.

Conditioned Stimuli

Sometimes neutral events in one's environment are temporally present just prior to one's being exposed to a UCS. Imagine a young naive child being taken to the physician's office for her first vaccination. She sees with curiosity the syringe and needle. They are then plunged into her arm, and the vaccine is injected. The pain from the needle prick and tissue separation of the injection are clearly UCSs to which many children react with fear, flinching, and crying. This can be a potent learning experience indeed! Now, a year later, the child finds herself once again at the pediatrician's office. When the physician enters the examination room and brings out the syringe (if not before), many children become fearful, try to withdraw, and begin crying, even prior to receiving the injection. At this point the previously neutral stimuli, the sight of the physician and the syringe, have become capable of eliciting reactions similar (if not equivalent) to the UCS of the injection itself. These neutral stimuli have become conditioned stimuli (CS), and the reaction to the CS is known as a *conditioned response* (CR). This change in behavior is a learned response and represents one of the simplest forms of learning there is.

Prenatal temporal relationships between unconditioned stimuli and unconditioned responses can be used to establish conditioned stimuli and conditioned responses in fetuses (see Bernard & Sontag, 1947; Kisilevsky & Low, 1998; Kisilevsky & Muir, 1991; Kisilevsky, Muir, & Low, 1992; Ray, 1933). Newborns and very young infants have similar capacities, of course (Kasatkin & Levikova, 1935; D. Wickens & Wickens, 1940). Interestingly, it has been shown that newborns evidence preferences for hearing their mother's voice (a stimulus they had been exposed to during the last part of pregnancy), for a "familiar" story that had been read to the baby prenatally, and for prenatally sung melodies (Cooper & Aslin, 1989; DeCasper & Fifer, 1980; DeCasper, Lecanuet, Busnel, Granier-Deferre, & Maugeais, 1994; DeCasper & Spence, 1986), all clear evidence of some degree of learning *in utero*. These simple functions are the building blocks from which some complex forms of learning can occur, ones that, as we shall see, influence both the everyday, so-called *normal behavior* of you and your social work clients, as well as so-called dysfunctional, abnormal, and pathological behavioral phenomena.

Timing Is Everything!

In respondent learning, as just described, timing is everything—well, if not quite everything, it is certainly very important. Take the following examples:

A. You hear a mild tone, and 5 minutes later a sudden bang, to which you flinch.

B. You hear a mild tone, and half a second later a sudden bang, to which you flinch.

Which arrangement, if repeated, will be more likely to produce a CR to the tone, A or B? If you guessed B, you are obviously correct. The longer the delay between the presentation of the neutral stimulus and the presentation of the UCS, the less likely it is that respondent learning will occur. This functional relationship between time delays and learning varies somewhat according to the duration and intensity of the stimuli being paired, but generally speaking, the interval separating the presentation of the neutral stimulus and the UCS must be very brief indeed (e.g., 1 second or less) for a CR to become easily established.

An exception to this temporal contiguity principle is in learning taste aversions. Nausea is a powerful UCS, and anything paired with nausea is capable of producing aversions (CR), even given a considerable delay between the presentation of the neutral stimulus and the experience of the UCR. When I was a teenager I announced to my stepmother that I thought it would be good for me to experience my first episode of alcohol intoxication at home, where it was safe, rather than at some party with my friends and then have to face driving home. My stepmother smiled at me, sweetly agreed with my assessment of the situation, and promised to arrange things as I asked. A few nights later she brought home a bottle of inexpensive sherry from the local convenience store and invited me to partake of it. Quite excited, I filled a large glass with ice, prepared my notepad and pen, and consumed the entire bottle within 20 minutes. I took careful notes before, during, and after my imbibing, while seated in a reclining chair. The stuff was pretty awful tasting, and I had no idea (at age 16) that the pungent sherry was to be slowly sipped in modest quantities and savored, not guzzled like iced tea on a hot day. I began to experience the early signs of drunkenness, sensations undoubtedly familiar to some readers of this chapter, and continued my introspective notations. After an hour or so I lost my interest in taking notes, which by that time had anyway degenerated into an unreadable scrawl, and instead I developed a keen desire to relocate to the bathroom. I popped the recliner forward and pitched myself onto the living room floor. I could not manage to stand upright but made my way on all fours to the lavatory, trailed by my stepmother cackling with laughter. I was quite sick, experiencing the UCS of alcohol intoxication and the UCR of nausea and vomiting. The room spun and I hung on grimly to the toilet until I had no further contributions to make. Recovering slightly, I made my way to my bed, discovering how the room seemed to rotate around me as I lay there. All in all, it was a powerful learning experience. Unbeknownst to me, however, respondent learning was insidiously at work, without my awareness or consent. The pungent smell and taste of cheap sherry, originally neutral stimuli, through their association with powerful UCS acquired the ability to elicit similar responses. Weeks later, when I had occasion to smell a glass of sherry, I found the odor to be positively nauseating. Through this one experience, technically known as *one-trial learning*, the neutral smell and taste of sherry became a CS, eliciting a CR similar to that evoked by alcohol intoxication, namely nausea. And to this day, some 35-plus years on, I cannot bring myself to drink sherry. Or spirits with a similar smell or taste, such as port. Disgusting stuff!

Anyone who has eaten a bad oyster or suffered a bout of poisoning from some other clearly identifiable food will resonate with this episode. This particular form of respondent learning is called a *conditioned taste aversion* (CTA) and is somewhat special in that the temporal spacing between the presentation of the neutral stimulus and the UCS can be quite distant, several hours in fact, and still have learning occur. Such CTAs occur across all mammalian species and among birds, and their biological adaptive significance is obvious. If after a couple of tastes of a poisonous prey or toxic plant an animal gets sick, that animal will be likely to avoid that type of food in the future, perhaps avoiding a future lethal dose of a harmful food. Members of a species a bit more liable to developing CTAs will be more likely to survive (and reproduce), culminating in the contemporary animal species we see today, with most readily prone to developing CTAs. Some ranchers try to make use of this principle by lacing dead sheep with lithium chloride, an emetic drug that produces severe nausea, in an attempt to condition predatory coyotes so that they develop an aversion to the taste of sheep's flesh. This keeps the living sheep safe from predation without having to kill coyotes.

Respondent Extinction

Respondent extinction occurs when, after the establishment of a CR to CS, the CS is repeatedly presented *alone* with no subsequent pairings with the UCS. For complete respondent extinction to occur, it is important that the UCS never recur in association with the CS. If the UCS always follows the CS, then you can expect the CR to remain in place indefinitely. If it happens 90%, of the time, 70%, 50%, or even 20% or less, the CS will remain capable of evoking a CR virtually indefinitely. If it is randomly associated, it will also remain in place for a long time. For respondent extinction to occur effectively, the CS must be absolutely disconnected from being paired with the UCS. As we see later, the phenomenon of respondent extinction can be extensively used in psychotherapy. Another term for respondent extinction is habituation.

Vicarious Conditioning

Imagine two people, A and B, seated side by side in a laboratory, both connected to instruments that measure their individual bodily reactions, such as galvanic skin response (GSR) and heart rate. Person A is also connected to electrodes that can deliver a mildly painful electric shock. A tone sounds, and a moment later Person A receives a mild but painful shock, producing a flinch and "ooch" exclamation. Person B did not get shocked but observed A's reactions. This occurs over a number of trials. What do you think will happen to hapless person A? Yes, A will develop a CR to the previously neutral tone, perhaps manifested by changes in GSR and heart rate. This makes sense according to the principles of respondent learning. But what about B, who never experienced the pairing of the tone and being shocked? Suppose we disconnect the shock electrodes from A and connect them to person B, and then sound the tone. It is likely that B, who was never shocked following the tone, will *also* display a mild CR to the tone. This phenomenon is called *vicarious conditioning* and illustrates that we ourselves need not *directly* experience associations between neutral stimuli and UCSs in order to develop CRs to these CSs.

Can you think of any possible operations of vicarious respondent learning to daily life?

A soldier in combat lifts his head above the foxhole and is immediately shot, in front of his buddies. Can you see how the buddies would become fearful of peering above the foxhole?

You are watching television and learn of an airplane crash wherein there were no survivors. The photos are vivid and accompanied by images and sounds of weeping relatives. The next day you have a flight out of town.

You are in line for a flu shot and are not particularly anxious. But it appears that the nurse is clumsy, and several times patients in front of you give a loud yelp of pain when injected. Now it is your turn.

You see in a movie a character, someone of your own complexion, who is badly beaten and sexually assaulted by a person of a different color. Later that night, walking down the deserted street to your car, you encounter a person of the same color and sex as the perpetrator portrayed in the movie.

As you might suspect, vicarious conditioning via the observation of the experiences of others is not likely to produce conditioned responses of the same intensity as is directly and personally experiencing associations between neutral stimuli and UCSs. But the effect is nevertheless real and influences our attitudes, beliefs, and bodily reactions to certain stimuli. See Hygge and Dimberg (1983), Hygge and Ohman (1976, 1978), and Kravetz (1974) for some experimental investigations of vicarious respondent learning in people.

Spontaneous Recovery

Sometimes a person can experience respondent extinction so that a CS that previously evoked a CR loses the capacity to evoke that CR. But, at a later time, if the CS is presented again, a diminished version of the CR may recur. This reemergence of a previously extinguished CR is called *spontaneous recovery*, and the CRs that appear with this phenomenon are usually of a considerably lesser magnitude than the CRs prior to extinction. Spontaneous recovery can occur many years after a CR was originally established and then underwent extinction.

Respondent Discrimination

A little girl is toying with a frayed electrical cord and gets a painful shock. Later in life, while changing a lightbulb with wet fingers, she gets another severe shock. As you might imagine, such experiences can make one fearful of handling electrical appliances or wiring. An electrician comes to your home and undertakes some needed repairs on your air conditioner. One of the first things she does is go to the circuit breaker and turn off the power to the air conditioner. Next she opens the electrical box and tests the wires with a circuit breaker to verify that they indeed are not live. At that point, she confidently grasps the electrical wires with no apprehension at all, even though in the past she has received plenty of shocks for touching similarly appearing wires. This process is explained via respondent discrimination. An early experiment examined this process. Bass and Hull (1934) had human subjects acquire a CR to a vibration applied to the skin, a vibration that indicated a mild shock was forthcoming. Some subjects had the vibration applied to the shoulder, others to the calf. In short order, a CS to the previously neutral vibration (on the calf or the shoulder) was established, as measured by GSR when the CS was presented, absent a shock. On later trials the vibration was applied not to the original site, the calf or shoulder, but to other places on the body. There was a clear function between the magnitude of the CR and the distance the CS was applied: The farther away, the smaller the CR. When the vibration was applied to the shoulder, those who were trained using the shoulder site got a strong CR. If the vibration was applied instead to the lower back or calf, the response got less and less, depending on the distance. Apparently the establishment of respondent learning responses is very sensitive to similarities and differences in the nature of the CSs. When they are quite different, the person discriminates these differences, and any CR evoked is weak, or even absent. But try letting the electrician who is working on your air-conditioning unit while holding bare wires hear you snap on the circuit breakers she had turned off, to gain a vivid sense of how well she has developed a discriminated response to electrical wiring.

Sensitization

Sensitization refers to the enhanced learning effects of repeated presentations of a UCS on the establishment of a CR. The first time a UCS is presented, it produces a certain effect. Apart from the salient characteristics of the UCS itself, it is inevitably associated with a situational context during which the learning occurred. When people are placed in a similar situational context, not only will they respond to the original UCS, but they are more likely, or *sensitized*, to respond to other stimuli that are themselves similar to the UCS. Imagine a prisoner of war alone in a room and tied to a chair. The door opens and a man walks in. The prisoner has little initial reaction to this stranger, who then proceeds to abuse the prisoner. The next day, you can readily imagine that when the restrained prisoner sees the same man enter the room, the prisoner will react with extreme fear, physiological arousal, enhanced efforts to escape, and so on. Again the prisoner is abused. The third day, the prisoner is in the now horribly familiar room, the door opens, and a stranger enters. The prisoner will likely have a less severe reaction to this stranger than if the previous torturer had entered, but will also likely have a much more aroused and fearful response to this second stranger than to the first stranger. Quite apart from the first stranger becoming a CR, the second one, a person who had never tortured the prisoner, is something of a CR, eliciting similar, if milder, reactions, whereas, only a few days earlier, meeting a stranger produced little if any fearful response. This enhanced susceptibility to developing CRs to previously benign CSs represents the process of sensitization. It may well account for some of the responses of prisoners of war who have been tortured, who display what has been called *Posttraumatic Stress Disorder* (PTSD; e.g., exaggerated startle response, hypervigilance, suspicion of strangers).

Second-Order Conditioning (or Higher-Order Conditioning)

If, following the establishment of a CS, a second neutral stimulus is paired with the original CS, the second neutral stimulus itself can come to evoke responses similar to those of the first CS_1, and in effect has become a second-order CS, or CS_2. Another neutral stimulus can itself become associated with this second CS, and in turn become a third-order CS, or CS_3, and so on.

Sexual stimulation is a powerful UCS for most people, and neutral stimuli associated with sexual stimulation can quickly become second- or higher order CSs themselves. In turn, neutral stimuli paired with previously established CSs can themselves become CSs. My wife is a powerful CS, having acquired this influence over me through 15 years of being associated with certain UCSs. When she wears a particular perfume while at dinner, one that she reliably has worn on prior evenings that culminated in spousal intimacies, that perfume has become a CS, and I now find it most alluring due to its past associations. This is an example of higher order conditioning, and such chains can be extended through many such pairings. Being beaten by an angry spouse is a UCS, with UCRs of autonomic arousal, fear, and avoidance. If prior episodes of being beaten have been paired with the husband drinking alcohol, the sound of that first beer being cracked open can become a CS. If the husband comes home angry, with a frowning face and irritable demeanor, and these in turn have been paired with his subsequently drinking beer, the frowning face can become a CS. And so on.

Naturally Occurring Examples of Respondent Learning in Real Life

In the best-selling book *Cheaper by the Dozen*, the Gilbreth children related how their father provided instruction in touch-typing:

> *Ern started slowly and then picked up speed, as her fingers jumped instinctively from key to key. Dad stood in back of her, with a pencil in one hand and a diagram in another. Every time she made a mistake, he brought the pencil down on the top of her head. "Stop it, Daddy. That hurts. I can't concentrate knowing that that pencil's about to descend on my head." "It's meant to hurt. Your head has to teach your fingers not to make mistakes." Ern typed along. About every*

fifth word, she'd make a mistake and the pencil would descend with a bong. But the bongs became less and less frequent and finally Dad put the pencil away. "That's fine, Ernie," he said . . . .And some of us recoil today every time we touch the backspace key.

(Gilbreth & Carey, 1948, pp. 58–59)

In this illustration, the pain caused by being hit with a pencil is a UCS, and flinching is the UCR. In the original learning, Ern would make a mistake, hit the backspace key, and get rapped with the pencil (UCS). She would then flinch. Over time, years later, and even in the absence of the threatening pencil, making a typing mistake and hitting the backspace key (CS) causes the conditioned response (CR) of flinching. I would like to thank my son John for bringing this literary example to my attention.

Sometimes, as winter approaches, humidity changes cause a buildup of static electricity so that one receives a mild electric shock on touching the car door handle. In this instance, the static shock is a UCS, and flinching and withdrawal from the source of the pain (the door handle) is a UCR. Each year, after this has happened to me a few times in the winter, I find myself hesitating to grasp the door handle, which has become a CS, eliciting a mild withdrawal reaction as I reach for it (a CR). Now this is relatively easy to overcome, and with a mild effort I can force myself to touch the door, but the effect is real and will be familiar to many readers. Respondent extinction occurs in the spring, when, as the climate becomes more humid, the buildup of static electricity diminishes and the shocks become milder and eventually disappear. Within a few weeks the hesitancy I learned during the winter toward touching the car door handle completely disappears (until next fall!). Technically, I am repeatedly exposed to the CS of touching the handle, *but* the shocks no longer happen (there is no UCS paired with the CS). Soon my CR falls by the wayside. This is an example of respondent extinction.

For one year, while I was serving in the U.S. Army, I lived in a military barracks, with communal showers and toilets on opposite ends of the bathroom. I liked to shower before going to bed, and I enjoyed very hot showers. Shortly after moving into this barracks, late one evening while I was enjoying a leisurely steaming shower, another soldier flushed a toilet from across the bathroom. A moment later my hot shower turned into a scalding inferno as the cold water pressure was cut off for a few moments, diverted to the task of flushing the toilet. I gave a yell of pain and hopped out of the stream of water, literally pushing my way through the shower curtain. A few nights later this occurred again. And again. What do you think happened? Soon I found myself immediately but seemingly involuntarily hopping out of the shower every time I heard the adjacent toilets flush, and thus avoiding getting scalded. I did not, however, develop a hopping or flinching response to the sound of the toilet flush when I was *not* in the shower. For the rest of my assignment to this station, about 1 year, I regularly hopped out of the shower when the toilet was flushed. Fast-forward a couple of years, when I was an MSW student living in an apartment with a roommate. One evening, shortly after moving into this new apartment and while I was enjoying my evening shower, I unexpectedly heard the toilet flush. I gave a yelp of dismay and hopped out of the shower, angrily yelling "Don't do that!" My roommate was astonished at my reaction. Our modern apartment did not have antiquated plumbing that reduced the flow of cold water when the toilets were flushed, and the shower temperature did not change. Nevertheless, to this day, more than 30 years later, I still have a mild flinch if I hear the toilet flush while I am showering. In this illustration, the UCS is painfully hot water, the UCR is flinching and rapidly getting out of the stream of water, the CS is the sound of the toilet being flushed, and the CR is flinching to the sound of the flush.

I absolutely love hot and sour soup, one of my favorite Chinese delicacies. Some years ago I ordered my meal at a terrific Oriental restaurant in Ann Arbor, Michigan, and the waiter brought me my bowl of soup. As he placed it in front of me, even before I tasted it, even before I smelled it, just by looking at it, I found my mouth watering. A lot! I was struck by this response. In this case, hot and sour soup is a UCS. Just about anyone's mouth waters when they taste the combination of vinegar and hot pepper flavorings that go into this recipe. The salivation is a UCR. I have thus, over many years, experienced the following chain: Hot and sour soup comes, is seen, and is then smelled. My mouth responds to the taste (a UCS) of the soup by salivating (a UCR). Nowadays, soup comes, I see it, and I salivate. The mere sight of the soup has become a CS, and salivating to the sight of the soup (not only to its taste) has become a CR. In this response I am just like one of Pavlov's dogs.

My wife, Laura Myers, and I have four children. Laura breast-fed all of them and noticed the following respondent learning process occurring. During the months of breast-feeding, a mother's breasts engorge with milk. What usually happens is that when mothers feed a child, the nipple is presented to the hungry infant, who latches on and begins to suck. This causes the milk to reflexively begin to flow, or "let down." The baby's sucking stimulation is a UCS that produces the UCR of milk flow. Now something else frequently happens. The baby is hungry and begins to cry. Mother hears the crying, picks up the infant, and presents her breast for feeding. The baby latches on, milk lets down, and mother and baby enjoy a nice nursing experience. What Laura found is that after some time had passed after she began nursing, when she heard our infant son John begin to cry, her milk would let down even before she would begin nursing him. In this instance, the temporal pairing of the sound of crying, followed by the baby latching on, resulted in crying becoming a CS, with the reflexive milk flow to the sound of crying being a CR. Previously, crying alone did not result in her milk letting down, but after some pairings, it did. This reflexive let down of breast milk can also be evoked by hearing another baby crying (as in a restaurant) or by watching and hearing a crying baby depicted in a movie. This is respondent learning, pure and simple.

Some years ago I underwent some painful dental work. I heard the high-pitched whine of the air drill, experienced the sound and sensations of the drilling going into my teeth, and moments later, while these stimuli continued, I experienced an abrupt, very severe pain, a pain that continued throughout the drilling process. To this day, when I lie back in the dentist's chair and she activates the drill, I tense with anticipation ....Sound familiar?

Hopping out of the shower, salivating when anticipating soup, breast milk, and tensing while having dental work—all are examples of how we can be affected by respondent learning principles in our everyday lives. Can you think of similar examples in your own life? These naturally occurring examples are interesting and illustrate the processes of respondent conditioning, but it is useful from a scientific sense to see if such operations can be experimentally studied, perhaps even intentionally established and extinguished, in order to learn more about this type of learning. In the next section, we will look at a few such laboratory studies.

Experimental Examples of Respondent Learning

Experimentally Induced Pupillary Constriction

One unconditioned response to an abrupt and loud noise is pupillary constriction. Most persons exhibit this reaction throughout their life. It is an unlearned and durable behavior. Now suppose the following occurred: A person is standing behind you and says the word "Contract" while your pupillary diameter is constantly being measured. What would happen? If you guessed "nothing," you are probably right. And if the person said "Contract" repeatedly, what would happen? Again, very likely nothing. This is because the diameter of your pupil is something you do not have much voluntary control over. Now suppose the hidden person said "Contract" and a second later fired a gun behind you. What would happen to your pupils? Yes, they would contract momentarily. Imagine this happening a number of times: The person says "Contract" and then fires the gun. Then, during one of these trials, the person says "Contract" but *does not* fire the gun. What would your pupils do? Yes, they would contract. At this point, we have established the following operations. The gunshot is a UCS, and pupillary contraction is a UCR to this UCS. After some learning trials, the word "contract" became a CS, and the contraction in reaction to hearing this word has morphed into a CR. See Hudgins (1933) for a description of an experimental demonstration of this phenomenon.

Conditioned Sucking in Newborn Babies

You will recall that mothers can develop conditioned responses to the sounds and sights of unfamiliar babies and experience their milk letting down even though their own baby is not nursing. Psychologists have not neglected infants in their experiments on respondent learning. In one seemingly coldhearted study (Lipsett & Kaye, 1964), newborn babies were presented with hearing a tone, and then a moment later had a pacifier inserted in their mouth (which elicited the sucking reflex). What do you think happened when, after a few trials of this sequence, the tone alone was sounded, but the pacifier was *not* presented? If you guessed that the infants began to suck, even without the pacifier, you would be correct, and obviously well on your way to understanding the topic of this chapter. Let's check on this. In this example, can you identify the UCS, UCR, CS, and CR? Which of these represents the sound of tone *after* it came to elicit the baby's sucking? Are you sure?

Respondent Conditioning of Private Events

Interestingly, respondent conditioning processes are not limited to affecting observable behavior, but they also affect private events—behaviors occurring under the skin, so to speak. The psychologist Neal E. Miller (1955) describes one early series of experiments demonstrating this. He randomly presented subjects in a psychology experiment with a picture of the letter *T* or a picture of the number *4*, and they were asked to say aloud what they saw, *T* or *4*. Whenever the *T* was presented, it was always immediately followed by a brief but painful electric shock. The subject's GSR (a measure of anxiety) was constantly recorded throughout this presentation of a series of initially neutral stimuli. What do you think happened? Yes, after some trials, when they saw the picture of the *T* (originally a neutral stimulus), they developed a strong GSR reaction, evidence that the *T* had become a potent CS. No such GSR reactions were produced by seeing the number *4*, a neutral stimulus never associated with a painful shock. Interestingly, after this CR to the letter *T* was established, N. E. Miller also demonstrated that a similar GSR reaction could be evoked simply by having the subjects *say* the letter *T without* showing it to them. So you have a CR_1 established to seeing the stimulus *T* and a CR_2 to *simply saying it aloud*. N. E. Miller next asked his subjects to randomly *think* (on a cue) of either the letter *T* or the number *4*, without either seeing it or saying it aloud. What do you think happened? Yes, conditioned GSR reactions were evoked by the mere *thought* of the letter *T*, a CR_3, whereas no such reactions occurred when they thought of the number *4*. Thus respondent conditioning affects not only our simple leg twitches and eye blinks but also our visceral (in the literal sense of the word) bodily reactions as well as our *thoughts*.

The comedian Jerry Seinfeld alluded to this process, in a more positive example, in the following shtick:

> *A man is paralyzed mentally by a beautiful woman, and advertisers really take advantage of this. Don't you love those ads where you see the woman in the bikini next to the 32-piece ratchet set? And we'll be looking at the girl in the bikini, and looking at the ratchet set, going "All right, well if she's right next to the ratchet set, and I had that ratchet set…I wonder if that would mean that…I better just buy the ratchet set." (Seinfeld, 1993, p. 53)*

Contemporary advances in neurological research are extending the science behind Seinfeld's anecdotes. Using a sophisticated brain scanning technique called *functional magnetic resonance imaging*, researchers have shown that exposing people to stimuli such as pictures of automobiles can produce differential effects in the brain, with "sexy" sports cars producing more activation in the reward and reinforcement centers of the brain than pictures of plain, vanilla small cars (Erk, Spitzer, Wunderlich, Galley, & Walter, 2002). Similar results are apparent when heterosexual males view pictures of attractive women and when consumers view favored brand names and logos (e.g., Coke versus Pepsi). These emotional reactions mediated by the brain are obviously learned responses acquired during one's lifetime through the contrived pairing via advertising and other experiences of UCSs and some CSs with new, neutral stimuli, so that the new neutral stimuli themselves acquire something of the valence of effect of the established UCSs or CSs. There are reasons why some cars are called *sexy* or *hot*.

Respondent conditioning can cause rather unpleasant reactions. In one classic study by Gale and Jacobson (1970), people were attached to various instruments to measure physiological indicators of anxiety. Then verbal insults were directed toward these persons, and, as you might imagine, they reacted with the mild physiological arousal associated with being frightened or angry. Simple words can cause CRs in normal people. How this comes about is not difficult to envision. A child is told "You are stupid" just before getting smacked by an angry parent. How many trials like this would it take before hearing the word "stupid" would come to elicit an automatic, unpleasant, autonomic response in a child? Not many. Maybe only one, if the smack was severe enough. Insulting someone who speaks only English by calling him a "Dummkopf," a German word for stupid, would produce no such anxious reactions, illustrating how it is not the intrinsic properties of words themselves that evoke responses, but their past associations with good or bad events.

Long chains of CRs can develop. A child is praised by her teacher for her good behavior and then given a delicious treat. Some episodes of this may result in words of praise becoming a positive CS. Later, the teacher breaks out in a big smile, then utters words of praise. The smile can become a positive CS. Ever more subtle cues can come to acquire big significance, as in the ever so slight nod of the head by the taciturn symphony conductor directed to the first violinist who just completed a difficult solo piece during a concerto.

Respondent conditioning processes clearly are significant in accounting for certain forms of muscular activity, but also are involved in the physiological processes mediating observable behavior. Many (but not all) phobic disorders seem to be acquired through respondent conditioning processes, and it has been shown that exposing phobic persons to their anxiety-evoking stimulus (e.g., a dog, cat, snake) can evoke profound neuroendocrine reactions, including elevations in adrenaline, noradrenaline, insulin, cortisol, and growth hormone, as well as blood pressure and heart rate (e.g., Curtis, Nesse, Cameron, Thyer, & Liepman, 1982; Nesse et al.,

1985). These elevations are clearly the types of conditioned responses seen in the processes of respondent learning. Stockhorst (2005) provides a recent overview of how human endocrine functioning can be affected by respondent learning processes. These are not unimportant processes. The conditioned release of insulin or changes in blood sugar levels can profoundly affect the health of diabetics, for example (Fehm-Wolfsdorf, Gnadler, Kern, Klosterhalfen, & Kerner, 1993; Stockhorst et al., 2004), and subjective craving among drug abusers is highly influenced by respondent learning processes (Childress, Ehrman, Rohsenow, Robbins, & O'Brien, 1992).

Here is another recent, fascinating study of respondent learning and private events. Happily married women were subjected to the threat of electric shock under one of three experimental conditions: while holding their husband's hand, while holding a male stranger's hand, or while not holding a hand. The wives heard a tone, then sometimes they were shocked. The experimenters looked for the development and magnitude of CR (fearful anticipation) to the previously neutral tone, as measured by magnetic imagery of the brain. Holding their husband's hand resulted in significantly less of a stress reaction (e.g., a CR) to the threat of electric shock (hearing the tone, CS, previously associated with sometimes being shocked), compared to not holding a hand. Holding a male stranger's hand produced a middle-range effect—better than no hand, but not as comforting as holding onto one's beloved husband. It also turned out that the degree of comfort exerted by the husband's hand varied as a positive function of the reported quality of their marital relationship: The better the reported quality of the marital relationship, the more protective husbandly hand-holding turned out to be (see Coan, Schaefer, & Davidson, 2006, for details on this interesting experiment). Clearly, the processes by which holding one's husband's hand produces more of a comforting response than that of holding a stranger's hand involve respondent learning to some extent. The authors engaged in some fascinating speculation as to the neural mechanisms possibly involved in the protective functions of warm, interpersonal relationships (see also Dalton, Kalin, Grist, & Davidson, 2005).

I have reviewed a few examples of how respondent learning principles exert their influence in our everyday life and how some laboratory experiments can replicate and extend such observations in more controlled settings. I next examine some illustrations of how respondent learning theory may be relevant to our understanding of problematic behavior.

Examples of Respondent Learning of Psychosocial Problems

Learned Social Anxiety

Small children, ages 12 to 24 months, observed their mothers interacting with a stranger under controlled laboratory conditions. Half the time the mothers acted (with prior coaching by the experimenters) in a nonanxious manner, and in the other half of the trials they acted socially anxious, in a manner consistent with what has been called *social phobia*. The children were then exposed to interacting with the same stranger. What do you think occurred? If you guessed that the children exposed to watching their mother act in a socially anxious manner themselves displayed more social anxiety (gaze aversion, crying, frozen posture, avoidance, etc.), you would be exactly correct. The acquisition of clinically significant social anxiety undoubtedly involves multiple elements, including modeling and operant reinforcement, but this study demonstrates the clear relevance of vicarious respondent learning as well, as potentially implicated in the etiology of social phobia (see de Rosnay, Cooper, Tsigaras, & Murray, 2006).

Anticipatory Nausea Among Cancer Chemotherapy Patients

When many patients are diagnosed with certain forms of cancer, one of the common treatment regimens consists of chemotherapy, the intravenous administration of drugs that destroy cancer cells. Cancer chemotherapy usually takes place in outpatient treatment centers. Patients are placed in a treatment room and seated in a comfortable chair or recliner. An intravenous needle is inserted in the patient's arm and a saline drip is established. Soon the toxic anticancer drugs are added to the saline drip, and the patient rests quietly until the prescribed dose is administered. An unfortunate frequent side effect of cancer chemotherapy is the development of severe nausea and often debilitating vomiting, some hours after the chemotherapy session. Later on, a limited percentage of these patients come to experience conditioned or learned nausea upon entered the chemotherapy clinic or the familiar treatment room. In this example, the chemotherapy agents are UCSs, and the nausea and vomiting they elicit are UCRs. By pairing the neutral stimuli of the chemotherapy clinic with the experience of nausea, the sights, sounds, and even smells of the clinic become CSs, which elicit the CRs of nausea. Medically this can be significant if the anticipatory nausea is of such severity as to debilitate the patient, or even render it impossible to administer the chemotherapy (Boynton & Thyer, 1994; Burrish & Carey, 1986). A variety of medical treatments (e.g., antinausea drugs, medicinal marijuana) and psychosocial interventions (relaxation training, distracting stimuli) have been used to help prevent or treat conditioned nausea induced by cancer chemotherapy, with varying degrees of success.

Phobic Disorders

One of the most common categories of so-called mental illness are the anxiety disorders, and among the most common anxiety disorders are *phobias,* severe fear and avoidance evoked by objects or situations that do not reasonably warrant such a reaction. It is fairly well established that respondent learning plays an important etiological role in the establishment and maintenance of phobic disorders, especially specific and social phobias (Mineka & Sutton, 2006), and my own clinical experience bears this out. One of the first clients I ever treated as a clinical social worker was a woman with a severe, disabling fear of dogs, a specific phobia that was clearly established after she was badly bitten on the head and buttocks by a large St. Bernard (see Thyer, 1981). Later, an adult client seen by one of my doctoral students had a severe fear of vaginal penetration, which seemed likely due to a playground accident involving the tearing of her vaginal wall, requiring surgical repairs at age 4 (Vonk & Thyer, 1995). Asserting the role of respondent learning mechanisms involved in phobic disorders does not preclude the importance of other potential etiological factors, such as genetic and environmental risk factors, biological preparedness, parental modeling, instructions, faulty information, and the like. Saying that these processes are important does not necessarily mean that they are all-encompassing. King, Eleonora, and Ollendick (1998) and Field (2006) provide good overviews of the evidence linking respondent learning to the phobic disorders. To give one salient example, systematic assessments of how persons with clinically significant driving-related fears came to acquire their fears revealed that a large majority had origins that could be directly attributed, at least in part, to respondent learning—for example, having been in or observed a vehicular accident (see Taylor & Deane, 1999).

Sexual Paraphilias

Sexual paraphilias are "recurrent, intense sexually arousing fantasies, sexual urges or behaviors generally involving (a) nonhuman objects, (b) the suffering or humiliation of oneself or one's partner, or (c) children or other nonconsenting persons that occur over a period of at least six months" (American Psychiatric Association, 2000, p. 566). Paraphilias can be an essential and recurring feature for some persons' capacity for sexual arousal, while other paraphilias occur episodically. In either case, for the formal diagnosis to be made, the paraphilia must have caused some clinically significant distress or impairment in important areas of functioning for the person. Sexual pleasure related to physical stimulation in general, and the orgasmic experience in particular, is a powerful unconditioned response, initially evoked by physical touch, and then through respondent conditioning processes. It can come to be evoked by a wide array of conditioned stimuli. One's initial sexual encounters, and the stimuli associated with these, are particularly salient learning experiences that can establish enduring patterns of sexual conditioned responses.

For most individuals these are pleasant and harmless associations, for example, a preference for a particular physical appearance in one's partners, type of clothing, hairstyle, perfume, social interactions, and so forth. Some of these responses are culturally determined. In countries with comparatively modest dress codes, the sight of a woman's ankle is erotic indeed, whereas in Japan, the nape of the neck is the height of salaciousness. For some other persons, however, more troubling patterns of sexual responsivity can develop, as in individuals who develop a type of paraphilia called a sexual fetish, a strong erotic response to articles of clothing or to engaging in socially discouraged behaviors, such as exhibitionism, masochism, sadism, or pedophilia. How sexual paraphilias develop is not comprehensively established, but it has long been established that respondent learning experiences play an important role (McGuire, Carlisle, & Young, 1964). For example, in two fascinating studies, male subjects were exposed to a series of photographs, initially to pictures of sexually arousing nude women, followed by a picture of a pair of female boots. Sexual responsiveness was assessed via a device that measured penile diameter (e.g., size of erection). Initially the subjects developed erections to the pictures of the nude women but not to the boots, but by seeing a series of pictures of boots just before the nudes, the participants developed erections to the photographs of the boots alone. These conditioned reactions were also shown to undergo respondent extinction, as well as spontaneous recovery to some extent (Rachman, 1966; Rachman & Hodgson, 1968). Such reactions clearly appear to implicate responding learning principles, and not complicated ones at that, as salient in establishing fetish-like conditioned responses, as well as nonproblematic sexual arousal patterns.

Once established, initial conditioned stimuli that evoke conditioned sexual responses may, through the processes of higher order learning, give rise to a wide and complicated array of reactions through conditioning experiences in real life, or become established and maintained via erotic fantasies, especially those engaged in during masturbation (Aylwin, Reddon, & Burke, 2005). You will recall from earlier in this chapter that private events are themselves apparently subject to the same principles of respondent learning as are overt actions.

Other problems of a sexual nature, such as vaginismus among women—the involuntary, seemingly reflexive contractions of the outer muscles of the vagina, precluding intromission and genital intercourse—may well develop as a consequence of painful or frightening sexual experiences (Shortle & Jewelewicz, 1986), as may male erectile dysfunction associated with performance anxiety. If sexual activity has been associated with prior embarrassing, painful, or unpleasant experiences, the involuntary responses (e.g., anxiety) associated with such reactions can effectively preclude the man's ability to achieve an erection, again a clear illustration of how respondent learning mechanisms are etiologically involved with this disorder.

Racism[*]

Classical learning principles apply not only to simple behaviors, but also to complex behaviors, reactions of our bodies that involve words,

---

[*]Portions of this section on racism originally appeared in Arhin and Thyer (2004).

thinking, and attitudes. For example, if selected words are paired with unpleasant stimuli, soon those words themselves can come to evoke conditioned reactions similar to those caused by the unpleasant stimuli (Gale & Jacobson, 1970; N. E. Miller, 1955). Such emotional reactions can include sentiments such as fear, aversion, and distaste, and in part these emotional reactions are derived from the environmental contexts in which these words occur. Consider the circumstances in which one initially hears words such as *hillbilly, redneck, honky, spic, wetback, wop,* or *nigger.* If the circumstances surrounding exposure to these racially laden words are unpleasant and perhaps associated with strong emotions such as fear or dislike, then the very words themselves may evoke related affective states. Not only affective states but also attitudes seem influenced by respondent learning processes (Doyo, 1971; A. W. Miller, 1966; C. K. Staats & Staats, 1957). Such conditioned emotional states associated with initially neutral words seem to be particularly resistant to extinction (Baeyens, Van den Bergh, & Eelen, 1988). If one is raised in a society, culture, or family where certain words are more likely to be uttered in a pejorative context—said with disdain, disgust, suspicion, or fear—then these negative emotions become inextricably intertwined with the very words associated with them. This can occur at a very young age. For example, Bar-Tal (1996) found that Israeli children as young as 2.5 years rated a photograph of a male figure more negatively when he was verbally identified as an Arab than when the photo was not so labeled. The inculcation of racial prejudice in young, perhaps even preverbal, children may well involve respondent learning processes through exposure to frightening images on television. These portrayals are conditioned stimuli that can come to elicit conditioned responses of fear and avoidance in young children.

Suppose one frequently witnesses real or simulated acts of violence on television, in the newspapers, and in videos and movies, and that a disproportionate share of the perpetrators are African Americans. What not very subtle message by our mass media is being conveyed to the audience of such portrayals? No one is immune to such influences. The Reverend Jesse Jackson once recounted how, walking late one night in Washington, D.C., he heard footsteps behind him. Looking back, he saw that it was a White man, and Reverend Jackson confessed (sadly) that he felt *relieved* to see that it was not a Black man! If someone should have a real-life encounter with a mugger, rapist, or thief, he or she will have experienced these negative associations to salient characteristics connected with the perpetrator, and the perpetrator's *race* can be one of the most conspicuous features noticed. Through the processes of respondent learning, other similar-appearing individuals can come to evoke milder versions of the reactions (such as fear and avoidance) initially associated with the original traumatic act. Even our verbal behavior is affected by respondent conditioning, with a number of experimental studies demonstrating how the very meaning of words (C. K. Staats & Staats, 1957), our attitudes (A. W. Staats & Staats, 1958), and related constructs, such as the prestige associated with certain words (Blandford & Sampson, 1964), can be impacted by such processes.

I hope that it seems evident to you that respondent learning is implicated in much of our normative behavior and is also involved in the acquisition of some psychosocial problems of concern to social workers. Although this is most relevant to practice at the microlevel, mass-media influences and vicarious respondent learning are also important in understanding pervasive social problems such as racism, bigotry, and sexual discrimination.

Using Respondent Learning in Social Work Practice

Using Respondent Extinction

Respondent extinction occurs when a CS is repeatedly presented, without ever being paired with the subsequent presentation of the UCS, in an attempt to unlearn a CR. This approach is usefully employed by social workers and other mental health clinicians in the highly effective psychosocial treatment called *exposure therapy and response prevention* (ETRP). This treatment has been shown to be helpful for use with clients who wish to overcome Specific Phobia, Social Phobia, Agoraphobia, Panic Disorder, Obsessive-Compulsive Disorder (OCD), chronic grief, PTSD (Nathan & Gorman, 2007) — virtually all those conditions in which one or more anxiety- or distress-evoking stimuli can be clearly identified and reproduced in a safe and controlled manner, with full client informed consent. Exposure therapy and response prevention is most effective when used with real-life anxiety-evoking stimuli, but is also beneficial with less direct reconstructions, such as photos, pictures, movies, and drawings of feared situations, and also with troubling thoughts, images, or even nightmares. Over the years, variations of ETRP have been called *systematic desensitization, implosive therapy, covert deconditioning,* or *flooding,* but the more parsimonious and informative term, ETRP, is preferred because it more accurately captures the method.

There is a considerable social work literature describing the process of conducting ETRP, including my own book *Treating Anxiety Disorders* (Thyer, 1987b), as well as a number of other articles and chapters I have authored (e.g., Thyer, 1981, 1983, 1985a, 1985b, 1987a, 1987b, 1988, 1991b, 1992c, 2001, 2002; Thyer, Baum, & Reid, 1988; Thyer & Birsinger, 1994; Vonk & Thyer, 1995). However, a large number of social workers have contributed to this field over the years, including Gail Steketee (1993) and James Troester (2005). Steketee's contributions for several decades in applying respondent extinction techniques as part of multifaceted cognitive-behavioral therapy to treat clients with phobias, PTSD, OCD, and compulsive hoarding are especially praiseworthy.

Another respondent extinction technique is cue exposure, used with clients who are addicted to alcohol or to illicit substances. It has also been successfully used with clients suffering from anorexia, bulimia, and other conditions. In effect, cue exposure involves determining, with the client, what environmental, cognitive, or bodily cues (CSs) evoke a CR, such as fear, craving, or aversion. Those cues are then re-created, ideally in real life, or in imagination if necessary, while the client is encouraged to refrain from leaving the situation or otherwise avoiding the cues. Clients then experience (and to some extent endure) their responses, and maintain this exposure to these CSs, until the CR gradually is reduced. One clinical example is the client who claims that seeing a bottle of liquor causes an uncontrollable craving, or urge to drink, or that other, more subtle cues, such as smoking or certain music, exacerbate the cravings. The social worker may, with proper informed consent, re-create such a situation, remaining with the client, for several hours if need be. A rather wonderful phenomenon usually occurs: Cravings (e.g., fear, urges to avoid, urge to purge) initially increase, increase still further, plateau, and then, with the passage of time, gradually diminish. Such an approach has been used with alcohol and other drug abusers (e.g., Blanken, Franken, Hendriks, Marissen, & Van Den Brink, 2005; Conklin & Tiffany, 2002; Dawe, Rees, Mattick, Sitharthan, & Heather, 2002; de Quiros Aragon, Labrador, & de Arce, 2005), persons suffering from bulimia nervosa (Toro et al., 2003), and those with an addiction to smoking (Lee et al., 2004).

Masturbatory Reconditioning

Masturbatory reconditioning is another respondent learning technique that attempts to help clients unlearn prior (deviant) conditioned responses and learn appropriate ones. This method is always used as part of a multimodal approach to treatment, since by itself it is an incomplete approach to comprehensive intervention. Masturbatory reconditioning is a controversial approach in which voluntary clients masturbate to orgasm while attending to nondeviant stimuli (videos, photographs) and talking aloud about appropriate sexual fantasies. Immediately following orgasm, the stimuli are switched to the client's deviant stimuli (child pornography, for example), and he or she is instructed to continue to masturbate for prolonged periods of time. This is all done privately, at home alone, with instructions from the social worker. These approaches most often are used in the treatment of pedophilia, fetishes, or aggression-related sexual assault. Crolley, Roys, Thyer, and Bordnick (1998) provide one illustration of evaluating outpatient therapy for sex offenders, an approach that involved masturbatory reconditioning. In these approaches, an orgasm is seen as a very powerful UCS, and repeated masturbation and orgasm to deviant stimuli (fantasies, pornography, sex with children, etc.) is seen as maintaining one's deviant arousal (a CR) to conditioned stimuli. By intentionally pairing masturbation to orgasm with appropriate stimuli (e.g., adult pornography, consensual sex), and having the client verbalize aloud nondeviant fantasies while doing so (these can be tape-recorded and later checked for content by the social worker for compliance and to ensure the client is not using deviant fantasies while masturbating), the intent is to create CRs to these more appropriate stimuli. Then, by having the client continue to engage in masturbation to deviant stimuli while in the refractory stage of sexual arousal, during which time masturbation is not pleasurable, it is hoped that the deviant CR to deviant stimuli will be attenuated. This approach makes use of respondent theory (e.g., Hall, Shondrick, & Hirschman, 1993) and what is known about the role of masturbatory fantasies in maintaining one's sexual arousal patterns (e.g., Langevin, Lang, & Curnoe, 1998). This treatment method lacks a strong empirical foundation due to the lack of adequate studies, but it remains a widely employed approach (see Maletzky, 2002).

Creating Conditioned Reactions

Lamaze Training for Pregnant Women

Lamaze training is a method of preparation for natural childbirth without using anesthetics or artificial methods to induce labor or to extract the baby (e.g., Cesarean section, forceps). The Lamaze method was popularized in the West in the early 1950s by a French obstetrician, Ferdinand Lamaze, who learned of its practices in the Soviet Union, where it was an officially endorsed policy. A major part of early Lamaze training consisted of teaching the woman to acquire the skill of patterned breathing so as to enable her to relax during labor, as well as involving the prospective father in childbirth preparation classes, providing massage, and in general to serve as a relaxing conditioned stimulus. By associating certain types of patterned breathing with being relaxed, it was hoped that by reproducing these breathing exercises during labor the mother would be able to be more relaxed during birth, and hence experience less discomfort. Learning to relax on certain cues (a verbal prompt, the onset of a contraction) and the social support provided by the husband all make use of respondent learning principles (see Wideman & Singer, 1984) and illustrate the widespread application of these Pavlovian concepts to the general public and within the field of social work. For example, the distinguished social worker Stanley Witkin used single-subject designs to assess changes experienced by women undergoing Lamaze training, finding these designs to be highly effective as an empirical method of appraising individual responses to intervention (Schuchts & Witkin, 1989).

The Bell and Pad Device to Treat Enuresis

The bell and pad device was developed during the 1930s (Mower, 1938; O. Mower & Mower, 1938) as a behavioral method to treat nocturnal enuresis (bedwetting) that employed respondent learning principles to help establish a conditioned response where one was absent. As most children develop, the normal course of events is that they become continent of urine and feces without too much difficulty. However, some children fail to attain these developmental milestones, or some attain them and then relapse. For children incontinent of urine during nighttime, the bell and pad device is a proven approach to help them acquire the ability to wake up when their bladder is full, rather than urinating while asleep.

The pad is a multilayer blanket consisting of an outer blanket, a layer of thin metal mesh, a middle layer of a blanket, another layer of metal mesh, and a bottom outer layer of blanket. The two layers of mesh are insulated from each other by the middle layer of blanket. The child sleeps on this pad, and when he or she urinates, the initial stream of urine moistens the layers of blanket, completing an electric circuit between the two layers of mesh. These are connected to a bell or alarm, which then sounds, waking the child. At this point the child is to get up, use the toilet, and get back in bed, atop a fresh pad. In the theoretical model of the bell and pad device, the sound of the alarm is a UCS, producing the UCR of waking up. This is an unlearned response, present from birth among all human beings. The sensation of a full bladder in the enuretic child is initially a neutral stimulus; it does not wake the child. However, with repeated episodes of voiding and waking up, the sensation of the full bladder becomes a CS, resulting in the CR of waking up prior to voiding. A large number of studies have demonstrated the efficacy of the bell and pad device as a treatment of enuresis, and social workers have been among those conducting such outcome evaluations (e.g., Morgan & Young, 1972; Turner & Taylor, 1974).

Aversion Therapies

Aversion therapy consists of the conscious and informed use of respondent learning principles to help clients eliminate conditioned responses that have proven to be problematic in their lives. Examples include the elimination of sexual fetishes and craving for alcohol or illicit substances. The social worker Patrick Bordnick and his colleagues (Bordnick, Elkins, Orr, Walters, & Thyer, 2004), for example, conducted a randomized controlled trial of three different forms of aversion therapy as a treatment for cocaine craving among veterans seeking treatment for drug abuse. Here, the client is exposed to cocaine-related stimuli (artificial smokable crack rocks, drug use paraphernalia, music associated with past drug use, etc.) and then presented with various potent aversive unconditioned stimuli, in this case, mild electric shocks, nausea induced by an emetic drug, or aversive imagery (the three active treatment conditions), in an attempt to unlearn prior pleasant associations with these drug-related CRs and to induce an aversion to such stimuli.

Aversion therapies of this nature are appropriate for use as options of last resort, with clients experiencing severe and intractable psychosocial problems that have not been amenable to treatment using other, less intense methods. Nevertheless, they have been subjected to extensive research as potentially effective interventions for persons who suffer from alcohol abuse, drug abuse, and chronic smoking. Studies by J. W. Smith and Frawley (1993) and J. W. Smith, Frawley, and Polissar (1997) are other examples of randomized controlled trials of aversion therapy undertaken by social workers. Respondent learning theory, and the development of conditioned aversions, has long been a part of the treatment picture for persons who abuse substances. Other social workers who have contributed to this vibrant practice-research literature are Butterfield (1975), J. W. Smith (1982), Howard (2001), Howard and Jensen (1990), T. A. Smith and Wolfe (1988), and Timms and Leukefeld (1993).

Respondent learning theory has been immensely productive in terms of its contributions to psychosocial interventions used by social workers and other mental health and health care professionals. I have provided only a brief review of illustrative applications of respondent learning theory to practice. Some are well supported in terms of empirical research, whereas others currently lack a strong evidentiary foundation. Recently researchers have come to consider respondent learning theory as having far greater applications than heretofore thought in our understanding of complex phenomena such as problem solving, the placebo effect, and rule-governed behavior (Turkkan, 1989).

Philosophical Foundations of Respondent Learning

The reader may have noticed the absence of any discussion related to the biological or psychological mechanisms that may give rise to our ability to learn via respondent processes. There are several reasons for this lacuna. The first is that the literature devoted to this topic is very largely speculative, or theoretical, if you prefer. It is also quite large, and doing justice to it is beyond the capacity of a single book chapter, or even a book. I also believe that there is some virtue is presenting as parsimonious a description of empirically established respondent learning processes as possible, eschewing reification, Cartesian dualism and mentalism, circular reasoning, and physiological musings. What I have presented is a purely descriptive, environmentalist approach to some important features of a major form of learning enjoyed by humans that operates across our life span. I have outlined functional relationships between environmental events (e.g., the presentation of stimuli) and their effects on human beings as manifested by behavioral responses. I take the liberal position associated with the discipline of applied behavior analysis: Behavior is whatever a person *does*, irrespective of whether others can witness it. The term *behavior* thus subsumes not only overt or publicly observable actions, but also private events experienced only by the person himself or herself. This includes self-talk, thinking, feelings, dreaming, physiological reactions, cognition, perceptions, and recollections. Quite literally, whatever the body does is grist for the behavior analyst's conceptual framework. This approach, promoted by the psychologist B. F. Skinner, among others, has been labeled *radical behaviorism*, with radical being used in its sense of a complete behaviorism, one that attempts to address *all* human activities, observable or not. This is in contrast to the earlier approach, called *methodological behaviorism*, promoted by the psychologist John

D. Watson, who proclaimed that the subject matter of scientifically oriented psychology must be limited to the analysis of overt actions. This latter approach never really appealed to many folks, especially social workers, who have long been preoccupied with the inner world of clients, and it is a real shame that this distinction is so rarely articulated in our disciplinary literature.

Modern behaviorism, as exemplified in the work of B. F. Skinner and this chapter, does *not* restrict itself to studying the overt actions of people. Behavior analysis *is* interested in the inner lives of people. It is interested in these private events, however, as *phenomena to be explained*, not as causal mechanisms themselves. For the behavior analyst, feelings are something to be explained, but they are unlikely to prove to be useful in explaining behavior itself. For example, a depressed person may act in certain characteristic ways (psychomotor retardation, eats less, sleeps less, cries a lot, etc.) and may express certain characteristic ways of thinking or feeling (e.g., "There is no hope"; "I feel depressed"; "I am thinking of killing myself"). In many conventional accounts, these feelings are said to cause the depressed overt behavior, and this etiological theory leads to psychosocial therapies that devote a great deal of time to having the client recount his or her inner life and to attempt to improve these feelings and thoughts, with the expectation that a resolution of this inner conflict will produce outward, observable improvements. However, for the behavior analyst, the client's inner life of thoughts, feelings, and the like is not the cause of overt behavior, but rather simply behavior worthy of explanation itself. The client's inner life of private events is not the *cause* of depression but the *effect* of whatever is causing the client to generally behave in a dysphoric manner. Something is causing the client to *act* depressed, to *feel* depressed, and to *think* in a depressed manner. These causes may be biological in nature—genetic disorders, the consequences of a medical illness, the result of drugs, and so on—but behavior analytic answers are more often sought in the client's current environment and in the client's recent and distant past experiences. Exposure to an oversupply of aversive events can engender depression, as can a failure to receive sufficient reinforcing experiences. This can arise through a chance concatenation of environmental circumstances (an illness piled atop a job dismissal, combined with a divorce), a steady exposure to low-grade stressors, one really grueling aversive event that eroded morale, or something else. Too much alcohol over too long a time, a severe economic depression, the death of a child, or more subtle factors, such as a client's lack of adequate social skills—these are the potential etiological features assessed by the behavior analyst. The intervention ramifications of this approach are obvious: Work with the client to alleviate future exposure to aversive events; remedy the consequences of past punishing experiences; improve social, educational, or economic skills. These are the environmentalist foci of social work intervention, foci that stand in stark contrast to the mentalist foci of the psychotherapeutically inclined. The reader may judge for himself or herself which perspective is more congruent with social work's historic person-in-environment perspective.

You may also have noted the absence of any reference, or even figures of speech, related to the person's thinking or mind. Any such mentalistic language is purely metaphorical at best, and distracting and misleading at worst, in terms of developing an understanding of the processes of respondent learning. Although respondent conditioning is sometimes called *associative learning*, the associations involved are those occurring between the person and his or her environment. There is no need to invoke any mentalistic language, as in hypothesizing "Bruce's mind associated the pairing of hot and sour soup with salivation, so that he came to salivate to the simple sight of the soup, not merely its taste." It is not Bruce's mind that did the pairing or associating; it was his environment. Using *mentalistic* (as opposed *environmentalistic*) language to try to explain respondent learning processes breaks down when one extrapolates such accounts of respondent learning down the phylogenetic chain (not that there is really such a hierarchy in nature, but it is commonly asserted; see Hodos & Campbell, 1969). For example, if my conditioned salivation is a function of my mind, then the identical phenomenon occurring among Pavlov's dogs needs to be similarly explained as the functioning of the canine mind. But how can such mental mechanism be invoked for organisms of supposedly lesser mental capacity? For example, consider respondent learning in utero by the human baby before birth. Is it reasonable to assert that fetuses of 6 months gestational age have a mind capable of producing the associations our vernacular language invokes to explain respondent learning? What about rats or mice? They too display the capacity for respondent learning. Insects also have this capacity, as do single-celled organisms, animals lacking any sort of brain worthy of saying they have a mind. It seems clear, at least to the behavior analyst, that we need not have recourse to the language of mentalism to try to explain the forms of respondent learning discussed in this chapter. There is a wonderful virtue of the philosophical principle of parsimony in developing explanations. As noted by Wickens (1973, p. 231), "A science should bend every effort toward explaining as broad a range of phenomena as possible with the fewest of principles." This principle has also been expressed by the psychologist Lloyd Morgan (1894, p. 54) in his so-called *Canon of Parsimony:* "In no case may we interpret an action as the outcome of the exercise of a higher psychical faculty, if it can be interpreted as the outcome of one which stands lower in the psychological scale." For example, if a patient has a fear of snakes, with an apparent origin during her teenage years after witnessing the movie *Snakes on a Plane*, it would not make much sense to spend much time exploring the phallic significance of snakes or automatically accepting the hypothesis that the "real" etiology of her snake phobia resides in unconscious memories of being sexually abused. Similarly, if a client is delusional, rule out more parsimonious causal agents (e.g., high fever, drug use) before assuming he is experiencing schizophrenia.

Also supporting a nonmentalistic view is that factors such as memory do not seem essential in the acquisition of respondent learning. This has been established by studies of persons with severe amnesia who can acquire conditioned responses in the absence of any recollection of prior conditioning trials (Gabrieli et al., 1995). Mentalistic conceptions of learning and development almost always ultimately invoke some sort of theory of the homunculus, an inner being who actually sees, reads, perceives, and reacts. The most common homunculus is called the *mind*, but there are others. Think of the scene in the movie *Men in Black* in which a tiny alien is revealed within the head of a man, an alien who was really directing all of the man's actions. The theory of the homunculus is both scientifically and philosophically unsatisfying, since we are left with the question "Well, what is it within the homunculus that is seeing, perceiving, reacting, and so on? Is it yet another little being inside the homunculus? And so on, ad infinitum?" My edited book *The Philosophical Legacy of Behaviorism* (Thyer, 1999) provides a fairly comprehensive overview of how behaviorism addresses major philosophical issues, including free will, determinism, and self-control, for those readers who would like to pursue these topics further.

I close with a quote from a developmental psychology text:

> Students of child development should study respondent learning for a number of reasons. First...respondent learning plays a critical role in helping the child successfully adopt to her environment...the process of respondent learning helps explain the wide variety of emotional responses a child makes to the world. (Novak, 1996, p. 105)

At some point in the future the biological, cellular, and physiological mechanisms of respondent learning will be much better understood than they are at present. Although these are fascinating areas of research, it is not essential for them to be resolved in order for social workers to make use of the empirically established principles of learning outlined in this chapter to aid us in the conceptualization of how everyday life develops across the human life span. We can also use these concepts to understand the emergence of some abnormal and dysfunctional forms of behavior, and, perhaps most importantly, to apply this theory to the world of social work practice to help our clients. Isn't that what theory is all about?

Key Terms

Behaviorism	Respondent discrimination	Sensitization
Conditioned stimuli	Respondent extinction	Spontaneous recovery
Canon of parsimony	Respondent learning	Unconditioned stimuli
Homunculus	Second-order conditioning	Vicarious conditioning
Observational learning		
Reflex		

Review Questions for Critical Thinking

1. Come up with a real-life example of respondent learning in your own life. Identify the unconditioned stimulus, the unconditioned response, the conditioned stimulus, and the conditioned response.

2. Why is "cognition" (i.e., what people "think") typically given little role in explaining conditioned responses?

3. Come up with a plausible example of classical conditioning processes involved in some clinical problem experienced by social work clients. Try to come up with one not used as an example in the chapter.

4. How may media portrayals of various racial groups or ethnic minorities involving respondent learning perpetuate negative stereotypes?

Online Resources

The Pavlovian Society—The Pavlovian Society is dedicated to the scientific study of behavior and promotion of interdisciplinary scientific communication. It recognizes the value of research at the molecular level but encourages members to stress the significance of their scientific observations to the whole functioning organism.

www.pavlovian.org/index.htm

Ivan Pavlov—Wikipedia entry on the life and work of Ivan Pavlov

http://en.wikipedia.org/wiki/Ivan_Pavlov

Classical Conditioning—A YouTube video on classical conditioning, narrated by U.S. psychologist Philip Zimbardo.

www.youtube.com/watch?v = hhqumfpxuzI

Classical Conditioning: Real World Examples—A YouTube video on classical conditioning, illustrating some real-life everyday examples.

www.youtube.com/watch?v = ypCSoVhAyhI

References

American Psychiatric Association. (2000). *Diagnostic and statistical manual of mental disorders* (4th ed., text rev.). Washington, DC: Author.

Arhin, A., & Thyer, B. A. (2004). The causes of racial prejudice: A behavior analytic perspective. In J. L. Chin (Ed.), *The psychology of racial prejudice and discrimination: Vol. I. Racism in America* (pp. 1–19). Westport, CT: Praeger.

Aylwin, A. S., Reddon, J. R., & Burke, A. (2005). Sexual fantasies of adolescent male sex offenders in residential treatment: A descriptive study. *Archives of Sexual Behavior, 34,* 231–239.

Baeyens, F., Van den Bergh, O., & Eelen, P. (1988). Once in contact, always in contact: Evaluative conditioning is resistant to extinction. *Advances in Behaviour Research and Therapy, 10*, 179–199.

Bar-Tal, D. (1996). Development of social categories and stereotyping in early childhood: The case of "the Arab" concept formation, stereotype, and attitudes by Jewish children in Israel. *International Journal of Intercultural Relations, 20*, 341–370.

Bass, M. J., & Hull, C. L. (1934). The irradiation of a tactile conditioned reflex in man. *Journal of Comparative Psychology, 17*, 47–65.

Bernard, J., & Sontag, L. W. (1947). Fetal reactivity to tonal stimulation: A preliminary report. *Journal of Genetic Psychology, 70*, 205–210.

Blandford, D. H., & Sampson, G. L. (1964). Induction of prestige suggestion through classical conditioning. *Journal of Abnormal and Social Psychology, 69*, 332–337.

Blanken, P., Franken, I. H. A., Hendriks, V. M., Marissen, M. A., & Van Den Brink, W. (2005). Cue exposure therapy for opiate dependent clients. *Journal of Substance Abuse, 10*, 97–105.

Bordnick, P. S., Elkins, R. L., Orr, T. E., Walters, P., & Thyer, B. A. (2004). Evaluating the relative effectiveness of three aversion therapies designed to reduce craving among cocaine abusers. *Behavioral Interventions, 19*, 1–24.

Boynton, K. E., & Thyer, B. A. (1994). Behavioral social work in the field of oncology. *Journal of Applied Social Sciences, 18*, 189–197.

Bruno, F. (1936). *The theory of social work*. New York, NY: D. C. Health.

Burrish, T. G., & Carey, M. P. (1986). Conditioned aversive responses in cancer chemotherapy patients: Theoretical and developmental analysis. *Journal of Consulting and Clinical Psychology, 54*, 593–600.

Butterfield, W. H. (1975). Electric shock-hazards in aversive shock conditioning of humans. *Behavioral Engineering, 3*(1), 1–28.

Childress, A. R., Ehrman, R., Rohsenow, D. J., Robbins, S. J., & O'Brien, C. P. (1992). Classically conditioned factors in drug dependence. In J. H. Lowinson, P. Ruiz, R. B. Millman, & J. G. Langrod (Eds.), *Substance abuse: A comprehensive textbook* (pp. 56–69). Baltimore, MD: Williams & Wilkins.

Coan, J. A., Schaefer, H. S., & Davidson, R. J. (2006). Lending a hand: Social regulation of the neural response to threat. *Psychological Science, 17*, 1032–1039.

Conklin, C., & Tiffany, S. T. (2002). Applying extinction research and theory to cue-exposure addiction treatments. *Addiction, 97*, 155–167.

Cooper, R. P., & Aslin, R. N. (1989). The language environment of the young infant: Implications for early perceptual development. *Canadian Journal of Psychology, 43*, 247–265.

Crolley, J., Roys, D., Thyer, B. A., & Bordnick, P. S. (1998). Evaluating outpatient behavior therapy of sex offenders: A pretest-posttest study. *Behavior Modification, 22*, 485–501.

Curtis, G. C., Nesse, R. M., Cameron, O. G., Thyer, B. A., & Liepman, M. (1982). Psychobiology of exposure in vivo. In R. L. DuPont (Ed.), *Phobia: A comprehensive summary of modern treatments* (pp. 117–120). New York, NY: Brunner/Mazel.

Dalton, K. M., Kalin, N. H., Grist, T. M., & Davidson, R. J. (2005). Neural-cardiac coupling in threat evoked anxiety. *Journal of Cognitive Neuroscience, 17*, 969–980.

Dawe, S., Rees, V. W., Mattick, P., Sitharthan, T., & Heather, N. (2002). Efficacy of moderation-oriented cue exposure for problem drinkers: A randomized controlled trial. *Journal of Consulting and Clinical Psychology, 70*, 1045–1050.

DeCasper, A. J., & Fifer, W. P. (1980). Of human bonding: Newborns prefer their mothers' voices. *Science, 208*, 1174–1176.

DeCasper, A. J., Lecanuet, J.-P., Busnel, M.-C., Granier-Deferre, C., & Maugeais, R. (1994). Fetal reactions to recurrent maternal speech. *Infant Behavior and Development, 17*, 159–164.

DeCasper, A. J., & Spence, M. J. (1986). Prenatal maternal speech influences newborns' perceptions of speech sounds. *Infant Behaviour and Development, 9*, 133–150.

de Quiros Aragon, M.-B., Labrador, F. J., & de Arce, F. (2005). Evaluation of a group cue exposure treatment for opiate addicts. *Spanish Journal of Psychology, 8*, 229–237.

de Rosnay, M., Cooper, P. J., Tsigaras, N., & Murray, L. (2006). Transmission of social anxiety from mother to infant: An experimental study using a social referencing norm. *Behaviour Research and Therapy, 44*, 1165–1175.

Doyo, M. C. (1971). Establishing and changing meaning by means of classical conditioning using the paired-associate method. *Philippine Journal of Psychology, 4*, 117–124.

Erk, S., Spitzer, M., Wunderlich, A. P., Galley, L., & Walter, H. (2002). Cultural objects modulate reward circuitry. *NeuroReport, 13*, 2499–2503.

Fehm-Wolfsdorf, G., Gnadler, M., Kern, W., Klosterhalfen, W., & Kerner, W. (1993). Classically conditioned changes of blood glucose level in humans. *Physiology and Behavior, 54*, 155–160.

Field, A. P. (2006). Is conditioning a useful framework for understanding the development and treatment of phobias? *Clinical Psychology Review, 26*, 857–875.

Fischer, J., & Gochros, H. L. (1975). *Planned behavior change: Behavior modification in social work*. New York, NY: Free Press.

Gabrieli, J. D. E., McGlinchey-Berroth, R., Carrillo, M. C., Gluck, M. A., Cermak, L. S., & Disterhof, J. F. (1995). Intact delay-eyeblink classical conditioning in amnesia. *Behavioral Neuroscience, 109*, 819–827.

Gale, E. N., & Jacobson, M. B. (1970). The relationship between social comments as unconditioned stimuli. *Behaviour Research and Therapy, 8*, 301–307.

Gilbreth, F. B., & Carey, E. G. (1948). *Cheaper by the dozen*. New York, NY: Scholastic.

Gormenzano, I., & Moore, J. W. (1969). Classical conditioning. In M. M. Marx (Ed.), *Learning processes* (pp. 121–203). New York, NY: Macmillan.

Hall, G. C., Shondrick, D. D., & Hirschman, R. (1993). Conceptually derived treatments for sexual aggressors. *Professional Psychology: Research and Practices, 24*, 62–69.

Hennessey, T. M., Rucker, W. B., & McDiarmid, C. G. (1979). Classical conditioning in paramecia. *Animal Learning and Behavior, 7*, 417–423.

Hodos, W., & Campbell, C. B. (1969). Scala naturae: Why there is not theory in comparative psychology. *Psychological Review, 76*, 337–350.

Howard, M. O. (2001). Pharmacological aversion treatment of alcohol dependence: Pt. I. Production and prediction of conditioned alcohol aversion. *American Journal of Drug and Alcohol Abuse, 27*, 561–585.

Howard, M. O., & Jensen, J. M. (1990). Chemical aversion treatment of alcohol dependence: Pt. I. Validity of current criticisms. *International Journal of the Addictions, 25*, 1227–1262.

Hudgins, C. V. (1933). Conditioning and voluntary control of the pupillary light reflex. *Journal of General Psychology, 8*, 3–51.

Hygge, S., & Dimberg, U. (1983). Differentiation between vicarious instigation and classical conditioning of electrodermal responses. *Scandinavian Journal of Psychology, 24*(3), 215–222.

Hygge, S., & Ohman, A. (1976). Conditioning of electrodermal responses through vicarious instigation and perceived threat to a performer. *Scandinavian Journal of Psychology, 17*(2), 65–72.

Hygge, S., & Ohman, A. (1978). Modelling processes in the acquisition of fears: Vicarious electrodermal conditioning to fear-relevant stimuli. *Journal of Personality and Social Psychology, 36*, 271–279.

Jehu, D., Hardiker, P., Yelloly, M., & Shaw, M. (1972). *Behavior modification in social work*. New York, NY: Wiley.

Kasatkin, N. I., & Levikova, A. M. (1935). On the development of early conditioned reflexes and differentiations of auditory stimuli in infants. *Journal of Experimental Psychology, 18*, 1–19.

King, N. J., Eleonora, G., & Ollendick, T. H. (1998). Etiology of childhood phobias: Current status of Rachman's three pathways theory. *Behaviour Research and Therapy, 36*, 297–309.

Kisilevsky, B. S., & Low, J. A. (1998). Human fetal behavior: 100 years of study. *Developmental Review, 18*, 1–29.

Kisilevsky, B. S., & Muir, D. W. (1991). Human fetal and subsequent newborn responses to sound and vibration. *Infant Behavior and Development, 14*, 1–26.

Kisilevsky, B. S., Muir, D. W., & Low, J. A. (1992). Maturation of human fetal responses to sound and vibration. *Child Development, 63*, 1497–1508.

Kravetz, D. F. (1974). Heart rate as a minimal cue for the occurrence of vicarious classical conditioning. *Journal of Personality and Social Psychology, 29*, 125–131.

Langevin, R., Lang, R., & Curnoe, S. (1998). The prevalence of sex offenders with deviant fantasies. *Journal of Interpersonal Violence, 13*, 315–327.

Lee, J., Lim, Y., Graham, S., Kim, G., Wiederhold, B. K., Wiederhold, M. D.,... Kim, S. I. (2004). Nicotine craving and cue exposure therapy by using virtual environments. *CyberPsychology and Behavior, 7*, 705–713.

Lipsett, L., & Kaye, H. (1964). Conditioned sucking in the human newborn. *Psychonomic Science, 1*, 29–30.

Maletzky, B. M. (2002). The paraphilias: Research and treatment. In P. E. Nathan & J. M. Gorman (Eds.), *A guide to treatments that work* (pp. 525–557). New York, NY: Oxford University Press.

McGuire, R. J., Carlisle, J. M., & Young, B. G. (1964). Sexual deviations as conditioned behaviour: A hypothesis. *Behaviour Research and Therapy, 2*, 185–190.

Miller, A. W. (1966). Conditioned connotative meaning. *Journal of General Psychology, 50*, 319–328.

Miller, N. E. (1955). Learnable drives and rewards. In S. S. Stevens (Ed.), *Handbook of experimental psychology* (pp. 435–472). New York, NY: Wiley.

Mineka, S., & Sutton, J. (2006). Contemporary learning theory perspectives on the etiology of fears and phobias. In M. G. Craske, D. Hermans, & D. Vansteenwegen (Eds.), *Fear and learning* (pp. 75–97). Washington, DC: American Psychological Association.

Morgan, L. (1894). *An introduction to comparative psychology*. London, UK: Walter Scott.

Morgan, R., & Young, G. (1972). The conditioning treatment of childhood enuresis. *British Journal of Social Work, 2*, 503–509.

Mower, O. H. (1938). Apparatus for the study and treatment of enuresis. *American Journal of Psychology, 51*, 163–166.

Mower, O. H., & Mower, W. M. (1938). Enuresis: A method for its study and treatment. *American Journal of Orthopsychiatry, 8*, 436–459.

Myers, L. L., & Thyer, B. A. (1994). Behavioural therapy: Popular misconceptions. *Scandinavian Journal of Behaviour Therapy, 23*, 18–30.

Nathan, P., & Gorman, J. (Eds.). (2007). *A guide to treatments that work* (3rd ed.). New York, NY: Oxford University Press.

Nesse, R. M., Curtis, G. C., Thyer, B. A., McCann, D. S., Huber-Smith, M. J., & Knopf, R. F. (1985). Endocrine and cardiovascular responses during phobic anxiety. *Psychosomatic Medicine, 47*, 320–332.

Novak, G. (1996). *Developmental psychology: Dynamical systems and behavior analysis*. Reno, NV: Context Press.

Pavlov, I. P. (1927). *Conditioned reflexes*. New York, NY: Dover.

Rachman, S. (1966). Sexual fetishism: An experimental analogue. *Psychological Record, 16*, 293–296.

Rachman, S., & Hodgson, R. J. (1968). Experimentally-induced "sexual fetishism": Replication and development. *Psychological Record, 18*, 25–27.

Ray, W. S. (1933). A preliminary report on fetal conditioning. *Child Development, 3*, 175–177.

Salter, A. (1949). *Conditioned reflex therapy*. New York, NY: Creative Age Press.

Schuchts, R. A., & Witkin, S. L. (1989). Assessing marital change during the transition to parenthood. *Social Casework, 70*, 67–75.

Schwartz, A. (1982). *The behavior therapies: Theory and applications*. New York, NY: Free Press.

Schwartz, A. (1983). Behavioral principles and approaches. In A. Rosenblatt & D. Waldfogel (Eds.), *Handbook of clinical social work* (pp. 202–228). San Francisco, CA: Jossey-Bass.

Schwartz, A., & Goldiamond, I. (1975). *Social casework: A behavioral approach*. New York, NY: Columbia University Press.

Sechenov, I. M. (1965). *Reflexes of the brain* (Translated from the Russian by S. Belsky). Cambridge, MA: MIT Press. (Original work published 1863)

Seinfeld, J. (1993). *SeinLanguage*. New York, NY: Bantam.

Shortle, B., & Jewelewicz, R. (1986). Psychogenic vaginismus. *Medical Aspects of Human Sexuality, 20*(4), 82–87.

Smith, J. W. (1982). Treatment of alcoholism in aversion conditioning hospitals. In E. M. Pattison & E. Kaufman (Eds.), *Encyclopedic handbook of alcoholism* (pp. 874–884). New York, NY: Gardener.

Smith, J. W., & Frawley, P. J. (1993). Treatment outcome of 600 chemically dependent patients treated in a multimodal inpatient program including aversion therapy and pentothal interviews. *Journal of Substance Abuse Treatment, 10*, 359–369.

Smith, J. W., Frawley, P. J., & Polissar, N. L. (1997). Six- and twelve-month abstinence rates in inpatient alcoholics treated with either faradic aversion or chemical aversion compared with matched inpatients from a treatment registry. *Journal of Addictive Diseases, 16*, 5–24.

Smith, T. A., & Wolfe, R. W. (1988). A treatment model for sexual aggression. *Journal of Social Work and Human Sexuality, 7*, 149–164.

Staats, A. W., & Staats, C. K. (1958). Attitudes established by classical conditioning. *Journal of Abnormal and Social Psychology, 57*, 37–40.

Staats, C. K., & Staats, A. W. (1957). Meaning established by classical conditioning. *Journal of Experimental Psychology, 54*, 74–80.

Steketee, G. S. (1993). *Treatment of obsessive compulsive disorder*. New York, NY: Guilford Press.

Stockhorst, U. (2005). Classical conditioning of endocrine effects. *Current Opinion in Psychiatry, 18*, 181–187.

Stockhorst, U., Mahl, N., Krueger, M., Huenig, A., Schottenfeld-Naor, Y., Huebinger, A.,... Scherbaum, W. A. (2004). Classical conditioning and conditionability of insulin and glucose effects in healthy humans. *Physiology and Behavior, 81*, 375–388.

Sundel, M., & Sundel, S. S. (1975). *Behavior modification in the human services*. New York, NY: Wiley.

Taylor, J. E., & Deane, F. P. (1999). Acquisition and severity of driving-related fears. *Behaviour Research and Therapy, 37*, 435–449.

Thyer, B. A. (1981). Prolonged in vivo exposure therapy with a 70-year-old woman. *Journal of Behavior Therapy and Experimental Psychiatry, 12*, 69–71.

Thyer, B. A. (1983). Treating anxiety disorders with exposure therapy. *Social Casework, 64*, 77–82.

Thyer, B. A. (1985a). Audio-taped exposure therapy in a case of obsessional neurosis. *Journal of Behavior Therapy and Experimental Psychiatry, 16*, 271–273.

Thyer, B. A. (1985b). The treatment of phobias in their natural contexts. *Journal of Applied Social Sciences, 9*(1), 73–83.

Thyer, B. A. (1987a). Community-based self-help groups in the treatment of agoraphobia. *Journal of Sociology and Social Welfare, 14*(3), 135–141.

Thyer, B. A. (1987b). *Treating anxiety disorders*. Thousand Oaks, CA: Sage.

Thyer, B. A. (1988). Remorse and guilt in obsessive compulsive disorder: Description and behavioral treatment. *Psychotherapy Patient, 5*(1/2), 95–111.

Thyer, B. A. (1991a). Behavioral social work: It is not what you think. *Arete, 16*(2), 1–9.

Thyer, B. A. (1991b). Diagnosis and treatment of child and adolescent anxiety disorders. *Behavior Modification, 15*, 310–325.

Thyer, B. A. (1992a). A behavioral perspective on human development. In M. Bloom (Ed.), *Changing lives: Studies in human development and professional helping* (pp. 410–418). Columbia, SC: University of South Carolina Press.

Thyer, B. A. (1992b). Should all social workers be well trained in behavioral principles? In E. Gambrill & R. Pruger (Eds.), *Controversial issues in social work* (pp. 79–84, 89–91). New York, NY: Allyn & Bacon.

Thyer, B. A. (1992c). Social learning theory in the treatment of phobic disorders. In C. W. LeCroy (Ed.), *Case studies for social work practice* (pp. 14–21). Chicago, IL: Wadsworth.

Thyer, B. A. (Ed.). (1999). *The philosophical legacy of behaviorism*. Dordrecht, The Netherlands: Kluwer.

Thyer, B. A. (2001). Behavior analysis and therapy for persons with phobias. In H. E. Briggs & K. Corcoran (Eds.), *Social work practice: Treating common client problems* (pp. 148–168). Chicago, IL: Lyceum.

Thyer, B. A. (2002). Treatment plans with social phobia. In A. R. Roberts & G. J. Greene (Eds.), *Social worker's desk reference* (pp. 346–352). New York, NY: Oxford University Press.

Thyer, B. A. (2005). The misfortunes of behavioral social work: Misprized, misread, and misconstrued. In S. A. Kirk (Ed.), *Mental health in the social environment: Critical perspectives* (pp. 330–343). New York, NY: Columbia University Press.

Thyer, B. A., Baum, M., & Reid, L. D. (1988). Exposure techniques in the reduction of fear: A comparative review of the procedure in animals and humans. *Advances in Behaviour Research and Therapy, 10,* 105–127.

Thyer, B. A., & Birsinger, P. (1994). Treatment of clients with anxiety disorders. In D. K. Granvold (Ed.), *Cognitive and behavioral treatment: Methods and applications* (pp. 272–284). Belmont, CA: Brooks/Cole.

Timms, F. M., & Leukefeld, C. G. (Eds.). (1993). *Cocaine treatment: Research and clinical perspectives.* Washington, DC: National Institute of Health.

Toro, J., Cervera, M., Feliu, M. H., Garrigan, N., Jou, M., Martinez, E., & Toro, E. (2003). Cue exposure in the treatment of resistant bulimia nervosa. *International Journal of Eating Disorders, 34,* 227–234.

Troester, J. D. (2005). Experiences with implosive therapy. *Clinical Social Work Journal, 34,* 349–360.

Turkkan, J. S. (1989). Classical conditioning: The new hegemony. *Behavioral and Brain Sciences, 21,* 121–179.

Turner, R., & Taylor, P. (1974). Conditioning treatment of nocturnal enuresis: Preliminary findings. *Behaviour Research and Therapy, 12,* 41–52.

Vonk, M. E., & Thyer, B. A. (1995). Exposure therapy in the treatment of vaginal penetration phobia: A case study. *Journal of Behavior Therapy and Experimental Psychiatry, 29,* 359–363.

Watson, J. (1916). The place of the conditioned reflex in psychology. *Psychological Review, 23,* 89–116.

Watson, J. (1925). *Behaviorism.* New York, NY: Norton.

Whytt, R. (1751). *An essay on the vital and other involuntary motions of animals.* Edinburgh, UK: Hamilton, Balfour & Neill.

Wickens, D. D. (1973). Classical conditioning, as it contributes to the analyses of some basic psychological processes. In F. J. McGuigan & D. B. Lumsden (Eds.), *Contemporary approaches to conditioning and learning* (pp. 213–243). Washington, DC: Winston.

Wickens, D. D., & Wickens, C. (1940). A study of conditioning in the neonate. *Journal of Experimental Psychology, 26,* 94–102.

Wideman, M. V., & Singer, J. E. (1984). The role of psychological mechanisms in preparation for childbirth. *American Psychologist, 39,* 1357–1371.

Zastrow, C., & Kirst-Ashman, K. (2007). *Understanding human behavior and the social environment* (7th ed.). Belmont, CA: Wadsworth.

Chapter 3
Operant Learning Theory

Stephen E. Wong

> What formative experiences in the social and physical world are overlooked while trying to explain human behavior primarily based on internal psychological and neurological processes?

Historical and Conceptual Origins

The earliest studies of operant learning can be traced back to the research of psychologist E. L. Thorndike with cats in puzzle boxes (Kimble, 1961). In Thorndike's experiments, hungry cats had to escape from boxes fastened shut in different ways to obtain food. Thorndike observed that after being placed in the boxes, the cats engaged in various behaviors such as pacing, visually exploring, and scratching at the walls. The animals performed these responses until they accidentally pressed the latch, pulled the string, or did something else that opened the box. On successive trials, the cats spent more time examining and scratching at the latch or the string, while the other responses gradually dropped out. Finally, the animal would perform the correct behavior as soon as it was placed in the box. Thorndike explained the learning of this new behavior with his "law of effect": In situations where responses are followed by events that give satisfaction, those responses become associated with and are more likely to recur in that situation.

B. F. Skinner, another American psychologist, greatly refined the experimental apparatus that permitted the study and conceptualization of operant learning. The "Skinner Box," a chamber with a lever that could be programmed to deliver food following lever presses, provided several improvements over Thorndike's puzzle boxes. One advantage was that the relationship between lever presses and food delivery was arbitrary and could be readily manipulated by the experimenter. This allowed for the study of a wide range of variables, such as the ratio of responses to food deliveries, the time interval between responses that would produce food, and variations in stimuli that signaled the opportunity to earn food and other response-consequence contingencies. A second advantage of Skinner's apparatus was that it permitted the use of response rate as a measure of response strength or response probability. Response rate is a continuous variable that can fluctuate over time, and it is more sensitive to subtle variations in environmental conditions than latency until escape (i.e., from a puzzle box), duration of maze-running, or other early measures of learning. A third advantage of the operant chamber and its measure of response rate was that it allowed the study of histories of reinforcement and other variables that affect learned behavior, such as those influencing extinction and maintenance (Skinner, 1966).

Skinner drew a critical distinction between *operant* behavior, which operated on the environment to change it and which was affected by stimuli that followed it, and *respondent* behavior, an earlier discovered form of learning. Respondent behavior, elucidated by the Russian physiologist Ivan P. Pavlov, involved reflexive responses (e.g., salivation, eye blinks) to certain potent stimuli that preceded the response (e.g., food, bright light, or loud noise). If neutral stimuli (e.g., sound of a bell) were repeatedly presented shortly before these potent stimuli, they could be *conditioned*, and they themselves would elicit a weaker form of the reflexive response. Thus, respondent conditioning was a different form of learning based on antecedent stimuli that triggered anticipatory responses to other antecedent stimuli. In contrast, operant behavior was controlled by both consequent stimuli (such as those producing "satisfaction," mentioned earlier) and antecedent stimuli that were consistently associated with those consequent stimuli (e.g., the sight of the latch, which prompts latch-scratching behavior). In addition, operant behavior was not limited to a relatively small number of phylogenetically determined, reflex-like responses, but instead was a virtually infinite number of behaviors that could be acquired during the individual's lifetime (e.g., speech, operating a computer, driving a car, breakdancing).

Although B. F. Skinner conducted his early research almost exclusively with animals in laboratories, he quickly saw the implications of his work for understanding and improving human behavior. Some of his most influential (Skinner, 1953) and controversial (Skinner, 1948, 1971) writings utilized the laboratory-derived principles of operant learning to analyze complex human behavior in society. Skinner's students and other researchers provided support for these theoretical analyses with successful demonstrations that applied operant principles to ameliorate various psychological and clinical problems. Lindsley and Skinner (1954) and Lindsley (1960) first showed that the behavior of psychotic mental patients could be studied within an operant framework. This paved the way for investigators such as Ayllon and Michael (1959) and Ayllon and Azrin (1965, 1968) to prove that psychotic behavior could be reduced and functional behavior could be increased in chronic mental patients through the use of reinforcement contingencies and structured therapeutic environments, such as the token economy.

In the decades that followed, a sufficient number of psychologists joined to form behaviorally oriented psychology departments at institutions such as Western Michigan University, Drake University, and West Virginia University and a similarly inclined rehabilitation department at Southern Illinois University at Carbondale. An especially visionary and prolific band of psychologists, including Donald Baer, Montrose Wolf, and Todd Risley, established an academic stronghold in the Department of Human Development at the University of Kansas (KU). At KU they recruited other colleagues with operant leanings to join their department; they devised a new methodology for intensive small-n research that they applied to problems in child development, developmental disabilities, family relations, and community organization; they founded the *Journal of Applied Behavior Analysis* in 1968, which became the flagship journal for the expanding field whose name they coined (Baer, Wolf, & Risley, 1968); and they taught generations of doctoral students, many of whom went on to distinguished research and teaching careers.

Behavioral approaches continued to spread to other disciplines, and Edwin J. Thomas and his doctoral students at the University of Michigan were among the first to apply these methods to social work practice in the United States (Reid, 2004). Many of Thomas's early students, including Eileen Gambrill, William Butterfield, Clayton Shorkey, and Martin Sundel, took teaching positions at major universities and further disseminated this approach through their students and their school's program curricula. Course textbooks provided another medium for the transmission of learning principles to newly trained social workers, and numerous books on this subject appeared in print (e.g., Fischer & Gochros, 1977; Gambrill, 1977; Jehu, 1967; Pinkston, Levitt, Green, Linsk, & Rzepnicki, 1982; Rose, 1977; A. Schwartz & Goldiamond, 1975; M. Sundel & Sundel, 1975; Thomas, 1967, 1974; Wodarski & Bagarozzi, 1979; for a more complete list, see Thyer, 1985b).

Basic Theoretical Principles

In this next section we review some basic theoretical principles of operant theory, some of the fundamental ways of learning that help explain much normal and abnormal behavior.

Reinforcement

In the operant learning paradigm, reinforcement is a fundamental process closely related to Thorndike's law of effect. Reinforcement occurs when a behavior is followed by a stimulus that increases the behavior's probability. Certain favorable consequences make responses more likely and strengthen that behavior under similar circumstances. Putting the proper number of coins in a vending machine and pressing a button is reinforced by the delivery of a chilled soft drink. The next time one is thirsty and in proximity of that vending machine, one is more likely to buy a soda from it. Waving at a neighbor across the street and seeing him smile and wave back reinforces the initial behavior of waving. Unfortunately, because reinforcement is merely a biological process, socially undesirable behavior as well as desirable behavior can be reinforced. An adolescent's cruel act of tripping and ridiculing a smaller youth can be reinforced by the laughter of nearby peers.

Reinforcement is often thought to mean the same as reward, but using these terms synonymously is misleading. Rewards, such as achievement awards (e.g., Employee of the Month) or other forms of recognition are often given with the intent of promoting excellence. However, these rewards might not function as reinforcement, in that the performance of workers might not improve after receiving the reward. These employees could already have been working at a high level because they were well trained and derived satisfaction from doing their job well or from receiving good annual evaluations. They might place little value on a piece of paper that they are supposed to frame and hang on their wall. Reinforcement is defined solely by the effect of the consequent stimulus in increasing the probability of the behavior that it follows.

Subjective pleasure or self-reported liking is another factor that can obscure the concept of reinforcement. Reinforcement is often experienced as pleasurable (e.g., eating an ice-cream sundae, watching a beautiful sunset, sexual foreplay), but not always. A person might complain about dissatisfaction at wasted hours watching old TV reruns or talking with rude and self-centered friends, but if these activities occupy a large portion of the person's time they are probably functioning as reinforcers. Reinforcing events increase the likelihood of behavior that they follow, but the person consuming the reinforcer may not always describe these events as rewarding or pleasurable.

Reinforcement Through Stimulus Presentation or Removal

The preceding examples represent a certain type of reinforcement in which a stimulus is presented that increases the probability of a behavior. This type is referred to as *positive reinforcement.* Another type of reinforcement operates through the withdrawal or prevention of stimuli, typically aversive or noxious in nature, which increases the probability of a behavior. This second type of reinforcement is referred to as *negative reinforcement.* Asking a family member to turn down the volume on his stereo system is negatively reinforced by the termination or reduction of the loud noise. In a parallel manner, rubbing hydrocortisone ointment on an itchy mosquito bite is negatively reinforced by the cessation of the skin irritation. As with positive reinforcement, negative reinforcement can follow socially inappropriate behavior and sustain it, as when a child fabricates reasons for not doing her chores and then is freed from having to do that work.

In real life the distinction between positive and negative reinforcement is not always clear (Baron & Galizio, 2005; Michael, 1975). For example, when a person in a hot, stuffy room opens the window, his response could be positively reinforced by the addition of the cool, fresh air or negatively reinforced by the removal of the overheated, stale air. In this situation, it may not be possible to separate out the two processes; the significant point is that reinforcing stimulus change has occurred. In clinical work, however, the distinction between positively and negatively reinforced behaviors may be useful because it suggests different intervention strategies (Carr, 1977; Iwata, 1987, 2006). Consider the case of a youth in a residential treatment center who refuses to comply with staff instructions or physically assaults other people. Is the youth's problem behavior being positively reinforced by attention from staff members who try to convince her to do the right thing, or is it being negatively reinforced by her being restricted to the living unit and being held back from school (where classmates tease her or she does poorly on her assignments)? The two suspected causes call for two different treatment approaches. If the youth is acting out to obtain attention from staff, interventions should be used that prompt some appropriate, alternative behavior (e.g., assisting staff with unit chores) and provide ample staff recognition for it. Conversely, if the youth is misbehaving to avoid school, interventions should be aimed at making school less aversive and more gratifying (e.g., separating the youth from peers that tease her, assigning more engaging or academically suited class work). Observing the youth's behavior over time and in other situations can reveal the potent reinforcers for this individual and can suggest underlying motives for her problem behavior.

Factors Affecting the Effectiveness of Reinforcement

Several factors modulate the effectiveness of reinforcers, making them potent or eliminating their potency when these factors reach certain levels. One of these factors is the probabilistic strength of the contingency, or the consistency with which the reinforcement is obtained after the desired response and *only* after the desired response. The stronger the relationship is between a response and reinforcement, the more effective the reinforcer will be, particularly when learning a new behavior. For example, token reinforcement can be an effective consequence for motivating study behavior in an elementary school child, but not if it is administered irregularly or if the child can obtain the same tokens by merely sitting in his chair, by bartering with other children for tokens, or by stealing tokens.

A second factor is the immediacy of reinforcement or the length of time between performance of the behavior and delivery of the reinforcer. Generally speaking, the more closely the reinforcement follows the behavior, the more effective it will be. Given two machines that produce the same result (e.g., two computers, two video games, two microwave ovens), we usually choose the faster one. Quick feedback from teachers on homework assignments and tests promotes learning better than delayed feedback. Delayed consequences can be effective in sustaining behavior, however, if the response has been well established, the delay has been gradually increased, or the delay has been explained to the person who must wait for reinforcement.

A third factor affecting reinforcer effectiveness is the amount of reinforcement. A larger quantity of reinforcement can be more effective than a lesser quantity (Cooper, Heron, & Heward, 2007; Miller, 1997). A teenager might be willing to mow the lawn for $10, but not for $2. A person might be agreeable to driving across town to see a friend for 4 hours, but not for only 40 minutes.

Secondary or Conditioned Reinforcement

Our susceptibility to certain reinforcing or punishing stimuli is part of our genetic endowment and is often crucial for survival. The biological functions of being reinforced by food, water, sleep, and sex, and by avoiding bodily injury and extreme heat and cold, are obvious. However, other reinforcers and punishers are themselves established through learning or are conditioned during the individual's lifetime. Some people's preference for spicy food is due not to spicy food being more nutritious than bland food, but to their history of repeated pairing of those spicy tastes with satisfying meals. Many sorts of garments will protect our bodies from the sun and wind, but our preference for stylish fashions of the day is guided by the reactions of friends and family members to our appearance. Likewise, many young people value good grades and other forms of academic achievement, but some youth groups ridicule high achievers as being "bookworms" or "nerds," turning good grades into a source of shame. It is important to recognize that certain reinforcers are conditioned or secondary reinforcers, because this conditioning varies greatly depending on individual history and cultural background. Some people will go through considerable effort to hear their favorite country music, which puts them in a good mood and relaxes them; yet, that same music might be irritating to someone else. The same could be said for rap or classical music. Recognizing that childhood upbringing and personal history can infuse objects and activities with disparate or even opposite motivational value can heighten appreciation of human diversity.

Generalized reinforcers, such as money, tokens, and praise, are a particularly dependable form of secondary reinforcer that can be used to gain access to a variety of primary and secondary reinforcers. The broad purchasing power and consistent reinforcing capacity of money is well known to all. However, praise—or positive regard and the goodwill of others—has similar worth in that it can be exchanged for favors, special consideration, material objects, and even money. Generalized reinforcers are more reliable reinforcers because they are associated with multiple primary and secondary reinforcers, and their reinforcing capacity is not linked to a specific state of deprivation or motivation. For example, although a cheeseburger and fries may be positively reinforcing when one is hungry, they lose much of that value once one has eaten and is satiated. However, money will have reinforcing value when one is hungry *and* when one is full because it can be used to acquire other desired goods unrelated to one's current state of hunger.

Schedules of Reinforcement

Under most conditions, behavior is reinforced intermittently rather than after each occurrence. Buying and dressing up in a new outfit will sometimes garner a compliment, but not always. If you hold a door open for another person entering a building after you, often the person will say "Thank you," but not every time. In sporting events, basketballs, footballs, and soccer balls are frequently thrown and kicked, but no one expects a goal to be scored with each attempt. The timing and regularity of reinforcement affects the temporal pattern and frequency of the behavior. A *fixed-interval schedule of reinforcement* makes reinforcement available after a certain fixed period of time and affects the temporal distribution of behavior. An example of an ordinary situation involving a fixed-interval schedule would be a person whose mail is delivered every day at around 1 p.m. If we were to observe this person throughout the day we might see that she shows little interest in her mailbox in the early hours of the morning. However, as the time approaches 1:00 p.m. she begins looking out the window at her mailbox, especially whenever she hears a vehicle pass by. After 1 p.m., she begins leaving her house to check her mailbox and continues doing so until she finally picks up her mail. After picking up her mail, she stops looking for mail delivery until the next day, when the whole pattern of checking starts over again. Thus, we would see a gradual increase in response rate as the time for reinforcement approaches and a cessation of responding immediately after reinforcement (which signals a period of time in which reinforcement is unavailable).

Instead of being based on time, reinforcement schedules can be based on the ratio of reinforcements delivered to responses performed. These are referred to as *fixed-ratio schedules of reinforcement*. An example in everyday life is piecework wages, such as one dollar earned for every 50 apples picked or every 50 envelopes stuffed. In such schedules, the amount of reinforcement gained (or money earned) bears a direct relationship to the number of responses performed. If the ratio is not too high, this type of schedule can generate high work rates because the worker earns more by working faster. Piecework wages based on high fixed-ratio schedules of reinforcement may be profitable for owners, but are exhausting for workers. If the ratio is extremely high (e.g., 1:500) "ratio strain" occurs and performance can break down, especially right after delivery of a reinforcer. Disruption usually occurs at this time because delivery of a reinforcer signals a lengthy period in which reinforcement is unavailable, and thus there is a lessened tendency to respond. The subjective experience of working under high-ratio schedules of reinforcement is unpleasant, and people working under these conditions are likely to become irritable or depressed. Conversely, working under low-ratio schedules of reinforcement, where the density of reinforcement is higher, is associated with pleasant sensations and higher levels of satisfaction. So schedules of reinforcement not only influence work rate and other performance measures, but also overall mood and affect.

Reinforcement can be scheduled to occur after varying periods of time, known as a *variable-interval schedule*, or after a varying number of responses, known as a *variable-ratio schedule*. Variable-interval schedules of reinforcement produce a more steady response rate than fixed-interval schedules, without the postreinforcement pause seen in the latter. Variable-ratio schedules of reinforcement produce an even quicker and steadier response rate than fixed-ratio schedules (Miller, 1997). In addition, variable-ratio schedules are notoriously resistant to extinction, as witnessed by some people's addiction to gambling. Despite loss of cash, life savings, possessions, and credit, gamblers are lured back by the variable-ratio schedule in their card game, slot machine, or lottery and the possibility that their next bet will win a big jackpot.

The previous paragraphs discussed simple schedules of reinforcement involving a single schedule and a single response. Operant research has also investigated complex schedules involving more than one reinforcement schedule and one response. A *multiple schedule of reinforcement* is one such complex schedule; it entails the successive presentation of two or more independent simple schedules, each accompanied by its own discriminative stimulus. Multiple schedules of reinforcement are common in everyday life and may take the form of different people or settings. Complaints about one's daily job irritations are likely to be received differently by close friends and family members, strangers on the street, and one's boss. A child throwing a tantrum may get concerned questions from his mother, verbal and physical comforting from his grandparents, ridicule from his siblings, and a spanking from his father. Choosing not to shave and wearing grubby clothes and sandals will generate dissimilar reactions depending on whether one stays at home, visits the corner store, attempts to get a table at fancy restaurant, or goes to a business meeting.

As we know from experience, different consequences for the same behavior in different contexts changes the probability of that behavior; thus employees learn not to complain about their job to their boss and to dress properly for business engagements. In this way, people appear to develop separate facets or multiple personae, but a better way of understanding this complexity is seeing that the different contingencies in these situations control differentiated performances.

Concurrent schedules of reinforcement are another complex schedule; they involve two or more schedules of reinforcement operating on two or more responses at the same time. Concurrent schedules of reinforcement also describe a wide variety of situations that humans experience. Most of the time, a person chooses from an array of responses that are available simultaneously (e.g., work at home, read a newspaper, watch TV, call a friend), with varying types and schedules of reinforcement associated with each response. Matching theory (discussed later under "Advanced

Theoretical Principles'') can help to predict which of these alternatives will draw most of that person's behavior and occupy most of his or her time.

Recent Research on Schedules of Reinforcement With Humans

Schedules of reinforcement held a prominent position in early operant research with infrahuman organisms (Ferster & Skinner, 1957; Zeiler, 1977). The influence of schedules of reinforcement on human behavior in laboratory studies, however, has been shown to be complicated by the presence of instructions and situational demand characteristics that can override schedule effects. The tendency of humans to respond to instructions rather than programmed reinforcement schedules is strong in situations where the instructions produce behavior patterns that cause the person not to come into contact with the actual schedule contingencies. For example, if a person is instructed to respond at a high rate to avoid computerized fines, even though the programmed schedule permits him or her to avoid all fines by responding at a lower rate, the person will usually follow the inaccurate instructions and respond at the higher rate (Galizio, 1979). More significantly, instructions can also modulate or override the effects of reinforcement schedules when people have direct contact with the existing reinforcement contingencies, causing them to lose available reinforcement or to respond unnecessarily (Hayes, Brownstein, Haas, & Greenway, 1986; Hayes, Brownstein, Zettle, Rosenfarb, & Korn, 1986). The beneficial and detrimental impact of humans responding to instructions rather than to actual reinforcement contingencies is discussed later in the section on rule-governed behavior.

Extinction

Effects of reinforcement are not permanent. Extinction is the natural decline in behavior that is no longer reinforced. A person will stop using a computer that will not start or that always crashes. A caller gives up dialing a cell phone number that is never answered. A student who does all of his homework but who nevertheless fails all of his assignments and exams will no longer do his homework. Extinction demonstrates that behavior is functional or ordinarily has some payoff for the person performing the behavior. Organisms do not continue to respond in ways that do not benefit them, and when reinforcers cease, the behavior that fails to produce them eventually disappears, too. The time required for extinction to occur depends partly on the schedule of reinforcement maintaining the behavior, as discussed earlier.

Punishment

Punishment is a stimulus following a response that reduces its future probability. Similar to reinforcement, there are both positive and negative forms of punishment. *Positive punishment* is the *presentation* of a stimulus (unpleasant or painful in nature) following a behavior that reduces its future probability. Examples of positive punishment might include turning up the volume on a stereo so loud that it hurts one's ears, or hurrying through a narrow space and banging one's elbow against a wall, or spanking a child who has misbehaved.

In contrast, *negative punishment* involves the *removal* or *prevention* of a stimulus (pleasant or positively reinforcing in nature) following a behavior that reduces its future probability. Examples of negative punishment might be carelessly unloading a dishwasher and breaking a glass dish, or driving too fast and receiving a speeding ticket (resulting in the loss of time and money).

Punishing stimuli are ubiquitous in real life and people must respond to these stimuli to survive. Ceasing behaviors that bring us into contact with painful stimuli protects us from injury, and terminating behaviors that deprive us of reinforcing stimuli allows us to retain essential resources. However, positive punishment has extremely limited application in human service organizations. For legal and ethical reasons, most state governments prohibit the use of positive punishment, such as corporal punishment or abusive verbal reprimands (e.g., California Code of Regulations, 2011; The 2011 Florida Statutes 400.022 and 402.305). Social workers should fully endorse these prohibitions, since many social service clients have already endured harsh mistreatment and deprivation during their lifetimes. There is some applicability of negative punishment procedures in social services settings (e.g., contingent removal of extra privileges, timeout from reinforcement) if it does not infringe on clients' rights. However, proper use of these procedures is a complicated matter that requires adequate resources, trained staff, technical expertise, and administrative and ethical oversight. Without these safeguards, punishment procedures are very likely to be misused (Wong, 2009). For these reasons, punishment is only briefly covered in this section, and was not mentioned at all in the earlier book chapter upon which this chapter is based (Wong, 2008).

Stimulus Control

The previous sections have focused primarily on stimuli that are consequences of behavior; however, stimuli present prior to the performance of behavior correlated with reinforcing or punishing stimuli also gain control over behavior. *Stimulus control* refers to the effect of these antecedent stimuli on the probability of a response.

Discrimination

Stimuli that are present when a behavior is reinforced gain control over that response, and the behavior becomes more likely when these stimuli are present. A child is likely to approach and talk to a group of children who have accepted him as a playmate. Conversely, this child is less likely to approach and talk with another group of children who have rejected him. A woman is likely to return to a restaurant that has served her delicious and inexpensive food. In contrast, that woman is unlikely to frequent restaurants that have served her unappealing and overpriced dishes. Seeing the front door to one's house brings on a search for one's house keys rather than office or car keys. *Discrimination* is a term that refers to differentiated response patterns that develop in the presence of antecedent stimuli tied to different consequences. Antecedent stimuli, or *discriminative stimuli,* allow us to anticipate consequences before they happen and as such control a large portion of human behavior. The words "Men" and "Women" or the international picture-symbols for male and female painted on a door allow a customer to enter the appropriate restroom of an unfamiliar restaurant and avoid an embarrassing incident. Complex discriminative stimuli obtained from reading maps and street signs, using calendars to keep appointments, and listening to advice from friends about romantic relationships govern more challenging responses in modern life.

Arranging discriminative stimuli to prompt or modify selected behaviors is a simple and often overlooked social intervention. For example, posting signs and making phone calls can be an effective way to increase performance of important tasks, such as attendance at support groups (Martinez & Wong, 2009). Use of paper checklists (Wong, Seroka, & Ogisi, 2000) or cell phone notepads can facilitate completion of complex tasks that exceed one's memory capacity. Verbal instructions also can be beneficial in guiding client behavior or narrowing client responses where there are multiple distractions, such as while conducting searches for community resources on the Internet (Wong & Vakharia, 2011).

Generalization

Whereas stimulus control involves bringing behavior under the control of specific stimuli, *generalization* refers to the opposite process: bringing behavior under the control of a broader range of stimuli. The success of clinical interventions often hinges on producing some form of generalization. Therapy usually is provided in a particular location, such as a clinic or office, and initial therapeutic change may first appear in these circumscribed settings. However, therapy usually aims for the carryover of change to extratherapy settings, such as the client's home, school, workplace, or other settings where therapy was not directly applied. Responding in the presence of stimuli different from those in which the behavior change was previously reinforced is known as *stimulus generalization.* There are empirically validated techniques for promoting stimulus generalization in clinical work (Stokes & Baer, 1977; Stokes & Osnes, 1989), such as bringing elements of the extratherapy setting (e.g., family members) into the therapy setting and varying aspects of the therapy setting so that it more closely resembles extratherapy settings (e.g., training with noise and interruptions like those at home). Using procedures to promote generalization improves the chances that behavioral gains produced by therapy will transfer to relevant situations in the client's living environment.

Building Behavior by Shaping and Chaining

Shaping produces new behavior by reinforcement of successive approximations to the terminal response; or, in simpler terms, by reinforcing small steps in the direction of the desired behavior. In most teaching situations, shaping is combined with verbal instructions, modeling, physical guidance, and other prompts, and so its sole effects are rarely seen. Sports coaches are particularly adroit at this technique. For example, a proper tennis backhand swing can be taught by reinforcing (with verbal feedback and praise) and gradually assembling the combination of movements that constitute the desired response:

1. First, the student is taught to hold the tennis racket properly, emphasizing proper grip, angle, and orientation of the racket.
2. Next, the student is shown how to draw back her arm for the swing, focusing on the direction and arc of the arm.
3. Then, the student taught to step back and turn her torso perpendicular to the incoming ball in preparation for the backhand swing.
4. Next, the student is instructed to initiate the swing, emphasizing the direction and arc of the arm, and orientation of the racket.
5. Simultaneous with the above movement, the student is taught to step forward and turn her torso toward the oncoming ball and execute the swing.
6. Then, the student is instructed to follow through with the swing and hit the ball in the intended direction.
7. Finally, the student is taught to recover from the swing and return to an on-guard position.

A multitude of athletic movements and other skills can be taught through similar procedures involving reinforcement for incremental progress toward the terminal response. Shaping and successive approximation also have numerous clinical applications, such as in the treatment of phobias by reinforcing a client's increasingly closer physical approach toward a feared object (e.g., Thyer, 1981, 1983).

Chaining

A chain is made up of two or more different behaviors, each producing a stimulus change on its completion, which must be performed in a particular sequence. Many complex human activities, such as speaking a language, getting dressed, playing a musical instrument, cooking a meal, and driving a car are behavioral chains. Learning a new behavioral chain (such as when learning to drive a car with a manual transmission) requires the person's close attention and can be difficult to do. However, after the skill is well practiced and mastered, it can be performed automatically with little thought or effort.

Conducting a *task analysis* (Cooper et al., 2007) lays the foundation for teaching a chain by identifying the individual responses composing the chain and the sequence in which they must be performed. Teaching a chain begins by verbally prompting, modeling, or manually guiding the first response in the sequence, and then providing reinforcement for its performance. After several trials in which the first response is performed consistently, the second response is prompted immediately after performance of the first response, and reinforcement is given only after completion of the first *and* second response. After the first and second responses occur together reliably, with reinforcement delivered only after the second response, these two responses may be said to be *linked*. Next, the third response is prompted immediately after the second response, and reinforcement is delivered only after performance of the first, second, *and* third response. This procedure, known as *forward chaining*, is continued until all responses in the chain are linked. Teaching a chain can also be done by starting from the end of the chain and proceeding to the front, known as *backward chaining*.

Modeling and Imitative Behavior

A person visiting a foreign country and trying to get the attention of a waiter at a restaurant is presented with an opportunity to learn by example, one way in which an individual can rapidly acquire behavior from another.

In this situation, the behavior of a model (another customer at the restaurant) serves as discriminative stimuli for the behavior of the observer. The observer watches the model displaying the desired behavior, and then responds to match the behavior of the model. Imitation is more or less likely, depending on what consequences the observer sees the model receiving. If the observer sees the model obtain reinforcement for performing the behavior (e.g., the other customer gets the attention of the waiter by waving his hand or calling out to him), then the observer is prone to imitate that behavior. By contrast, if the observer sees the model fail to obtain reinforcement or get punished for performing a behavior (e.g., the customer who waves his hand is deliberately ignored by the waiter), then the observer is less prone to imitate that behavior. Much imitative behavior is probably *generalized imitation*, in that individuals copy the actions of others due to a history of previous reinforcement for imitative behavior (Baer & Sherman, 1964; Pierce & Cheney, 2004). Observational learning is a quick way to obtain desired outcomes and to avoid aversive stimulation, especially in novel situations wherein one does not know how to act.

Other factors that influence modeling effectiveness and the tendency to imitate are related to characteristics of the model. Models that are similar to the observer based on personal history, appearance, sex, age, and other variables are more likely to be imitated (Bandura, Ross, & Ross, 1963). For example, guidance from a domestic abuse counselor who herself has survived an abusive relationship is more likely to be followed than recommendations of a domestic abuse counselor without such personal experience. Models with high social status and prestige are more likely to be imitated than models of low social standing (Bandura et al., 1963). Hence, high school students are likely to adopt the manner of dress, speech, and even leisure activities of high-status individuals rather than the habits of social outcasts. Social workers should take these factors into account when selecting positive models for public education campaigns, primary prevention programs, and therapy groups.

The common expression "Do as I say, not as I do" refers to the fact that modeling effects occur even when unintended. Performance of socially inappropriate or maladaptive behavior (e.g., aggressive behavior, recreational drug use) can promote that same behavior in others who witness those acts. Perhaps the best example of this is Albert Bandura's (1965) classic Bobo doll experiment, in which modeling prompted physical aggression in children. In Bandura's study, children watched a film in which an adult hit, kicked, or otherwise exhibited physical aggression toward an inflated Bobo doll. In one version of the film, the adult was rewarded with praise, soda, and candy after being aggressive toward the doll; in a second version of the film, the adult was scolded and spanked for hitting or kicking the doll; and in yet a third version, no consequences were given for being aggressive toward the doll. Bandura found that children who observed the adult model being punished were less likely to imitate aggression than children who observed the model being rewarded. However, both the children observing the model being rewarded and those observing the model receiving no consequences were more likely to exhibit aggression than those observing the punished model, with no differences between the former two groups. This study demonstrated how antisocial behavior could be contagious, and it forecast the adverse impact of modeling socially undesirable behavior in television, movies, video games, and other mass media.

Advanced Theoretical Principles

Rule-Governed Behavior

Skinner (1969) posited that a sizable amount of human behavior is controlled by rules rather than by direct reinforcement contingencies. Rules are viewed as "contingency-specifying stimuli" that describe particular responses and the consequences that follow them. Usually the rules are verbal, such as the oral instructions "Go down this street for three blocks, then take a right and go another block, and you will find a gas station," or the written instructions "Push cap down and twist clockwise to open." However, rules also can be conveyed nonverbally (e.g., by demonstrating the proper twisting motions) or can take the form of pictures, diagrams, or even mathematical formulae. Rules can be complex discriminative stimuli (p. 143) generating intricate response patterns, but without a personal history of reinforcement for those responses, such as when a reader uses a map to reach a distant destination he or she has never visited before.

Rule-governed behavior is valuable to groups and societies because it allows people to benefit from the experience of others. The transmission of rules permits people to respond to dire consequences that have a low probability ("Buckle your seatbelt when you drive") or that may occur in the distant future ("Smoking causes lung cancer"). Many preventive programs currently being developed and evaluated by social worker researchers can be seen as forms of public education aimed at providing youth and adults with rules to protect them from dangers for which personal experience provides inadequate preparation.

Although human reliance on rules allows us to more successfully navigate our social and physical environment and avoid harm without the tedious and haphazard process of individual learning, it also has disadvantages. Rules and verbal instructions can overpower the actual reinforcement contingencies currently in place (Hayes, Brownstein, Zettle, et al., 1986; Hayes, Zettle, & Rosenfarb, 1989). Unlike lower organisms that respond to subtle temporal features or response frequency requirements of the prevailing reinforcement schedules, humans will follow explicit or implicit instructions and forgo available reinforcement or make many unreinforced responses (in other words, behave inefficiently). In addition, rules are not merely information entered into a computer; these verbal stimuli possess their own motivational properties (Hayes et al., 1989). The words "We must be on alert for the next terrorist attack" may evoke emotional responses similar to those of being physically injured or having family members killed during guerrilla warfare (e.g., staying indoors, viewing people of certain ethnicities with fear and suspicion, voting for politicians who go to war against "terrorist states"). At a societal level, our susceptibility to verbal stimuli and insensitivity to the discrepancy between faulty rules and actual reinforcement contingencies is reflected in our vulnerability to mass media campaigns, commercial advertising, and political propaganda.

Self-Control

Operant learning is usually associated with external controls, such as those captured in the image of a behavioral psychologist working with a rat in a Skinner Box. However, B. F. Skinner was acutely aware of the self-regulatory capability of humans and wrote about it at length in *Science and Human Behavior* (Skinner, 1953). He observed that people can exert self-control by applying the same behavior control procedures to themselves that they use to alter the behavior of animals and other people. Skinner also listed and described self-control techniques in an account that is still timely and unsurpassed in its abundant, everyday-life examples. Skinner first observed that instances of self-control arise in situations in which people are affected by conflicting consequences, such as those that follow excessive eating. Excessive eating is associated with the reinforcing events of gustatory pleasure and relief from hunger as well as the punishing events of becoming overweight, being unhappy with one's appearance, and suffering from numerous health problems. In such conflictive situations, individuals can perform *controlling responses* to alter the probability of *controlled responses* (e.g., excessive eating), with the controlling responses taking as many forms as there are methods of behavioral control.

People can use physical restraint as a self-controlling response by refraining from purchasing high-caloric foods (e.g., ice cream) or by buying these foods only in small quantities. (One is most likely to do this when one is satiated and capable of "self-control," which fits with contemporary advice not to shop for groceries while one is hungry.) They can also dispose of food items with high fat and high sugar content or lock them in a closet or cabinet and give the key to a strong family member. People can choose to patronize restaurants that have appealing low-calorie entrées on their menu. If one is going to a party where fattening food will be served, one can change the reinforcing properties of the available food by snacking freely on healthier food before the gathering. People trying to manage their food intake can surround themselves with other people with similar intentions, join official weight-loss groups, and read articles and books on the subject (exposing themselves to discriminative stimuli for eating the proper amounts of the right foods). Conversely, people should avoid cooking instruction and cuisine programs on TV, as well as food and restaurant commercials. People can substitute alternative responses to eating fattening foods, such as exercise (e.g., going for a walk), getting involved in a hobby, drinking water, or eating low-calorie snacks and meals. They can also self-monitor (Stuart & Davis, 1972; Watson & Tharp, 2007) their food intake with daily logs to become more aware of their eating and facilitate positive reactivity, as well as to devise better strategies for modifying their eating patterns. The present list only scratches the surface of available self-control strategies and for the sake of space was limited to the problem of excessive eating behavior.

Recent Theoretical Developments

Although operant learning is a mature scientific topic, it is far from settled. Research in the experimental analysis of behavior and applied behavior analysis has both extended the reach of operant learning principles and made discoveries requiring substantial realignment of those principles. In this section I briefly review three of the latter developments that are particularly relevant to social work practice: functional analysis, matching law, and stimulus equivalence and relational frame theory.

Functional Analysis of Problem Behaviors

Functional analysis (Carr, 1977; Iwata, Dorsey, Slifer, Bauman, & Richman, 1982) is an assessment procedure that seeks to identify the reinforcement contingencies that maintain a problem behavior, whether that behavior is self-injury, physical aggression, disruptive behavior, bizarre speech, or some other socially undesirable response. Before functional analyses, behavior therapists and behavior analysts selected interventions without investigating what consequences might have been currently reinforcing the problem behavior. For example, a middle-aged man diagnosed with schizophrenia who exhibited delusional statements might be treated with social skills training, token reinforcement for accurate statements, and response cost (token fines) for delusional statements. The reinforcement and response-cost procedures would be applied to override whatever unknown sources of reinforcement were sustaining the inappropriate behavior (Mace, Lalli, Lalli, & Shea, 1993). Such a traditional behavior modification approach might be effective in reducing delusional speech, but its therapeutic effects would be based solely on the superior potency of extrinsic reinforcers introduced by the therapists. Because preexisting reinforcement contingencies that supported the bizarre speech in this setting were neither identified nor systematically altered, these contingencies could remain to threaten the client's improvements whenever the behavioral program faded or was removed. In contrast, a functional analysis attempts to isolate the specific reinforcers currently maintaining the problem behavior, and this information is then used to design procedures that remove or block those reinforcers for problem behavior and instead make them contingent on appropriate behavior. Theoretically, this approach should produce better outcomes and a higher probability of generalization and long-term maintenance.

The hallmark of a functional analysis is an empirical test utilizing a series of brief (5- to 15-minute) sessions during which various contingencies hypothesized to maintain the problem behavior are simulated and the client's behavior is recorded. These conditions are alternated in random order (forming a multiple schedule of reinforcement), and the amount of problem behavior occurring in each of these conditions is then compared. For example, Wilder, Masuda, O'Connor, and Baham (2001) assessed the contingencies that were maintaining delusional speech in a middle-aged man with schizophrenia by presenting four alternating conditions: (1) *escape from demand* (the therapist asked the client to work on a task, e.g., a simple household chore, until the client made a bizarre statement, after which the therapist allowed the client to take a 30-second break from the task); (2) *attention* (the therapist pretended to be preoccupied and ignored the client until the client made a bizarre statement, after which the therapist made eye contact and told the client that he "shouldn't talk" like that); (3) *alone* (the client was left alone in the room and observed to see if the bizarre statements would occur without any social consequences, and thus were self-stimulatory or self-reinforcing); (4) *control* (the therapist interacted with the client until he made a bizarre statement, after which the therapist broke eye contact and terminated all conversation for 10 seconds). Because these four conditions were presented in random order and the only difference between them was the social contingency, differences in the amount of delusional behavior observed in the four conditions logically should have been due to the type of reinforcement made available for delusional speech in the various conditions.

In the study by Wilder et al. (2001), bizarre speech occurred in a substantially greater percentage of the scored intervals with attention (mean = 26%) as compared to escape from demand (mean = 2%), alone (mean = 0%), and control (mean = 5%) conditions. Utilizing this data, an intervention consisting of differential reinforcement of alternative vocalizations (attention for appropriate speech) plus extinction for bizarre vocalizations was designed. When this invention was applied and evaluated in a reversal design, it was shown to nearly eliminate the client's psychotic speech. Results of this study were later replicated with a second client also diagnosed with schizophrenia who displayed bizarre vocalizations in the form of tangential remarks (Wilder, White, & Yu, 2003).

This clinical assessment methodology has been used successfully with expanding numbers of clients, predominantly children with developmental disabilities residing in hospitals or institutions (Hanley, Iwata, & McCord, 2003; Iwata et al., 1994). However, functional analyses have also been utilized effectively with developmentally disabled youth in an outpatient clinic (Derby et al., 1992) and with clients of normal intelligence (14% of the clients) who underwent brief stays (average = 10 days) in an inpatient setting (Asmus et al., 2004). Thus, functional analysis is a clinical assessment tool whose validity has been repeatedly established with numerous clients in various settings, and that yields interventions that harness motives underlying problem behavior.

Matching Law

Herrnstein (1961, 1970) formulated the matching law based on his research with pigeons in a two-response apparatus where responses were reinforced with food on concurrent variable interval/variable interval (VI VI) schedules. Herrnstein noted that his subjects "matched" or allocated their responses to the two alternative schedules in proportion to the reinforcements obtained from them. For example, if one third of the reinforcements were obtained from the first alternative and two thirds from the second, then approximately one third of the animal's responses would be directed toward the first alternative and two thirds to the second. This discovery was important because it showed that responding is affected by its overall context and the *relative amount of reinforcement* for each response alternative. This also meant that the frequency and duration of one response would change when reinforcement for a concurrent response was varied. For example, if the frequency or density of reinforcement for the second alternative response were increased from two thirds to four fifths of all available reinforcement, then four fifths of all responses would be directed toward that alternative. Consequently, the proportion of responses that would be directed toward the first alternative would drop from one third to one fifth, even though there was no change in the absolute number of reinforcements available for that choice. Thus, responding cannot be predicted solely on the basis of the amount of reinforcement provided for a response, but rather on the *relative payoff* for that response as compared to its alternatives. While this law was first demonstrated with pigeons in the laboratory under specific concurrent VI VI schedules, its generality has since been established with a wide variety of species, including humans, in naturalistic and clinical situations, and with different combinations of reinforcement schedules (McDowell, 1982, 1988; Pierce & Epling, 1983; Plaud, 1992).

McDowell (1982, 1988) elucidated how this law could be applied to ameliorate various clinical disorders. Problem behaviors are usually treated with extinction or mild punishment, but the matching law suggests that they can also be reduced by either increasing the rate of reinforcement for concurrent alternative responses or by increasing the rate of "free" or noncontingent reinforcement. Ayllon and Roberts (1974) implemented the former strategy in a fifth-grade class with students who frequently exhibited disruptive behavior. These investigators erected a token economy that reinforced reading in the classroom, and they recorded large increases in reading behavior and simultaneously large decreases in disruptive behavior. Improvements in both desired and undesired behavior were reversed during a withdrawal phase and then restored during the final treatment phase in an ABAB design. This study demonstrated how problem behavior can be effectively treated in an indirect manner by reinforcing alternative, appropriate behavior occurring in the same context. Although matching law has been applied in only a handful of clinical studies, it provides an empirical and theoretical foundation for positive interventions with a wide array of social problems, such as aggressive behavior, crime, addictive behavior, and psychotic disorders, just to name a few.

Stimulus Equivalence and Relational Frame Theory

These two areas of research examine the development of stimulus-stimulus associations and investigate how symbols and words acquire their meanings. Stimulus equivalence was originally discovered while teaching developmentally disabled students how to read (Sidman, 1971, 1994). In a study demonstrating one form of stimulus equivalence known as *transitivity,* students were first prompted to match spoken words, such as the word "car" (A), with the corresponding picture of a car (B) by reinforcing subjects for pointing to the appropriate picture after hearing the spoken word. Next, students were taught to match spoken words, for example, the word "car" (A) with the corresponding written text, for example, "CAR" printed on a card (C), by reinforcing subjects for pointing to the correct set of letters after hearing the spoken word. After the students were taught to consistently match these two pairs of stimuli (A = B, and A = C), the instructor performed a test presenting B and C together along with a number of other stimuli. Subjects who received the training matched B with C and C with B, even though they had *never received direct training* associating these two stimuli. The emergence of stimulus equivalence B = C and C = B indirectly from training A = B and A = C is an anomaly for operant learning and has required the proposal of new theoretical schema (Sidman, 2000b). Aside from its theoretical significance, being able to match pictures of objects with their corresponding written and spoken names has practical significance because it constitutes a form of reading comprehension and demonstrates partial understanding of the *meaning* of words. Stimulus equivalence is usually connected with a history of verbal learning, and this capacity for abstraction is rarely observed in nonhumans (Hayes, 1989; Schusterman & Kastak, 1993).

Relational frame theory (S. Hayes & Hayes, 1992; Hayes & Wilson, 1993) extends this paradigm by noting that stimulus equivalence is only one of a seemingly endless variety of stimulus relations that can be taught with formats like the one just described. For example, if subjects are taught that "A is greater than B" and "B is greater than C," subjects are likely to respond that "A is greater than C" without any direct training involving A and C. In this case, the *relational frame* controlling behavior is *greater than* rather than the equivalence of paired stimuli. Such relations are arbitrarily defined (the subject could have taught that "X is greater than Y" and "Y is greater than Z," leaving the subject to infer that "X is greater than Z"), and they may or may not accurately reflect relationships between objects and events in the real world. With verbal symbols and their relational frames, humans are able to evoke past, future, distant, and nonexistent events (e.g., childhood memories, anticipation of one's own death, the Tooth Fairy), as well as to manipulate and transform these stimuli by placing them in different relational frames. This enables people to conduct complex analyses and engage in long-term planning, but it can also make them susceptible to faulty rationalizations and debilitating thoughts.

Acceptance and commitment therapy (Hayes & Wilson, 1994) is a new psychotherapy that has sprung from relational frame theory. This approach proposes that certain problematic behaviors and emotional reactions persist due to clients' verbal behavior (overt and covert) that supports patterns of avoidance. For example, a person may rationalize his missing an appointment with the statement, "I was too anxious to go to the job interview." This verbal statement adds to the problem in two ways: (1) The client reifies "anxiety" as an emotional condition that he cannot tolerate or overcome, and (2) the client presents a socially acceptable explanation for his avoidance. Therapists attempt to undermine relational frames that support problematic avoidance patterns through the use of paradoxical parables (showing the futility of attempting to avoid all anxiety-provoking situations), experiential exercises, deconstruction of the meaning of words (e.g., "anxiety"), and other techniques. They also strive to heighten clients' awareness of the *present moment* and help them select the best course of action for that situation. Acceptance and commitment therapy has been described as part of "the third wave of behavioral and cognitive therapy" and has produced positive preliminary outcomes with such diverse clinical problems as anxiety, depression, psychosis, substance disorders, chronic pain, eating disorders, and work-related stress (Hayes, 2004a, 2004b).

Relevance to Social Work Practice

Probably the greatest benefit that operant learning offers to social work practice is that it is a comprehensive framework for understanding and changing human behavior in the social environment (Thyer, 1987). It could be argued that there is no other biological, psychological, or social science theory that can provide such a broad, exacting, and data-based account of human behavior as the principles of operant learning. This approach also can be utilized to analyze and treat a wide spectrum of human problems, ranging from relatively narrow disorders such as phobias and anxieties to pervasive disturbances such as antisocial behavior, psychoses, and mental retardation. It can also be used to study and ameliorate seemingly macro-level problems, such as differences in intellectual and academic ability correlated with socioeconomic status, by changing patterns of daily parent-child interactions in the home (Hart & Risley, 1995). See Pelaez, Gewirtz and Wong (2008) for a more detailed discussion of this application.

The following sections review some of the direct applications of operant learning methodology to social work practice, including assessment, intervention, and prevention.

Uses in Assessment

The data of operant learning are observable behaviors qualified with clear descriptions of the target behaviors and quantified along parameters such as frequency, duration, intensity, and latency. Many forms of socially significant behavior can be precisely measured along these dimensions, such as frequency of initiating conversations or pursuing job leads, duration of engaging in school homework or household chores, force in hammering nails, or latency before making an assertive reply. Socially problematic or clinical behaviors also can be quantified by these dimensions, such as frequency of drinking alcohol or making self-deprecating comments, duration of arguments or obsessive rituals, voice volume while screaming at others, or latency before complying with parental requests. Certain complex performances might exist as behavioral chains, and assessing completion of component responses in the correct order can be facilitated by a task analysis and a task checklist (e.g., Wong et al., 2000). The precision and objectivity of such varied behavioral measures can help to clarify social work concerns and goals, which otherwise might be vague and nebulous.

Quantification and precision of behavioral measures do not, however, guarantee their *social validity*, *clinical validity*, or practical utility. Increases in the frequency of positive comments or in the duration of eye contact during casual conversations are measurable, but they may not have substantial impact on listeners' evaluations of the speaker's social competence or attractiveness. The social validity of behavioral measures should be established by showing their relationship to primary concerns of clients, clients' family members, referral and funding sources, and significant persons in the clients' community (e.g., teachers, prospective employers, police officers; I. S. Schwartz & Baer, 1991; Wolf, 1978). The clinical validity of behavioral measures should be demonstrated through their correlations with ratings of clients' subjective distress, level of functioning, ability to fulfill role demands, capacity to engage in desired activities, and overall quality of life (Kazdin, 1999).

Uses in Intervention

Evidence-based applications of operant learning principles are extensive and have been the subject of enough textbooks to fill a small library. So, this chapter merely offers a sample of empirically validated applications of operant learning approaches with particular relevance to social work practice. This section briefly covers evidence-based foundations in four areas: parent and staff training, social skills training, safety and prevention, and interventions with clinical disorders.

Parent and Staff Training

Because parents and staff members regulate many aspects of clients' environment and they are authority figures, training parents and staff in behavioral techniques has been a prime strategy for structuring contingencies to foster desired behavior. Parents and staff have been taught to set reasonable performance expectations, to prompt adaptive behavior with verbal instructions or modeling, and to reinforce performance of this behavior with attention, praise, and tangible reinforcers. They also have been trained in the sometimes difficult technique of ignoring minor misbehavior as a means of extinguishing it. Using this approach, parents have been taught how to deal with children's problematic behavior, such as noncompliance (Briggs, Leary, Briggs, Cox, & Shibano, 2005; O'Reilly & Dillenburger, 2000; Stein & Gambrill, 1976), temper tantrums (Pinkston, Polster, Friedman, & Lynch, 1982), bizarre verbalizations (Pinkston & Herbert-Jackson, 1975), failure to thrive (Koepke & Thyer, 1985), and sleep disturbances (Brophy, 2000). Court-mandated parents in the child welfare system (Smagner & Sullivan, 2005) and parents with a developmentally disabled child (Gammon & Rose, 1991) have been taught a variety of skills to cope with the special needs of their families. Recent research on parent training in behavioral techniques continues to yield positive outcomes, including work with immigrants (Leung, Tsang, & Dean, 2010, 2011) and novel in-home instructional formats (Lanier et al., 2011).

In a parallel manner, staff members in institutions have been trained to use reinforcement contingencies to manage urinary incontinence in elderly residents (Pinkston, Howe, & Blackman, 1987) and to reduce delusional verbalizations and disruptive behavior (Wong, Woolsey, & Gallegos, 1987), to restore appropriate conversational speech (Wong & Woolsey, 1989), and to improve grooming skills and personal hygiene (Wong, Flanagan, et al., 1988) in persons with severe mental disorders. Behavioral procedures have also been utilized to teach technical skills to professional staff or interns, such as facilitative and supportive utterances during family therapy (Gallant, Thyer, & Bailey, 1991), clinical interviewing skills (Iwata, Wong, Riordan, Dorsey, & Lau, 1982; Schinke, Gilchrist, Smith, & Wong, 1978), management of visits between parents and children in foster care (Kessler & Greene, 1999), behavior management skills to staff in group homes for persons with mental retardation (Schinke & Wong, 1977) and adult day care centers (DeRoos & Pinkston, 1997), and behavior analysis skills to graduate social work students (Dillenburger, Godina, & Burton, 1997).

Social Skills Training

Social skills training (SST) can improve clients' competence in a variety of important interpersonal encounters, such as initiating conversations, dealing with conflict, and conducting successful job interviews. Coming from social learning theory rather than an operant learning perspective, Richard M. McFall (1976) developed a versatile technique for teaching interpersonal skills as well as noninteractive behavior. Although inspired by social learning theory (Bandura, 1969, 1976), this format embodies operant learning principles in its main procedures of (a) giving instructions that describe and explain the skill to be taught; (b) demonstrating or modeling the skill for the student; (c) having the student practice or rehearse the desired response, usually in role-play situations; and (d) giving the student positive or negative feedback on his or her performance. A major difference between SST and other operant learning procedures is that prompts and reinforcement are delivered in *simulated encounters* and not in the actual interactions in which the behavior typically occurs. It was implicitly assumed that skills learned in role-play simulations would generalize to extratherapy settings. However, this assumption was overly optimistic and specific procedures to promote generalization to extratherapy settings are often required (Wong et al., 1993; Wong, Morgan, Crowley, & Baker, 1996).

Utilizing the SST protocol, social workers have taught interpersonal skills for initiating and maintaining positive interactions with peers to fifth-grade students (Hepler, 1994), for maintaining social support to women at risk of child maltreatment (Richey, Lovell, & Reid, 1991), for facilitating vocational and community adjustment to mentally retarded clients (Hall, Schlesinger, & Dineen, 1997; Sundel, 1994), for carrying out appropriate conversations with persons with severe mental disorders (Wong et al., 1993), for increasing assertiveness and drug avoidance to drug users in residential treatment (Hawkins, Catalano, & Wells, 1986), and for problem solving and avoiding future acts of delinquency to youths in detention (Hawkins, Jensen, Catalano, & Wells, 1991). The range of client populations and concerns to which SST procedures have been effectively applied gives some indication of their flexibility and robustness.

Safety and Prevention

Operant learning and SST procedures have been successfully used to instill safe practices that avert accidents or reduce dangers that arise in familiar places, such as the home and family car. Besides preventing possible injury or death, these interventions can also head off the emotional harm that is a frequent aftermath of these traumatic events. Some self-protective skills that have been taught are automobile safety belt usage to youth (Sowers-Hoag, Thyer, & Bailey, 1987; M. Williams, Thyer, Bailey, & Harrison, 1989), safe responses when finding a gun in a house (M. Himle, Miltenberger, Flessner, & Gatheridge, 2004; Miltenberger et al., 2005), skills for young children to avoid abduction (Johnson et al., 2005, 2006; Miltenberger & Thiesse-Duffy, 1988), steps for identifying and treating children's illnesses for parents at risk of child abuse and neglect (Bigelow & Lutzker, 2000), ways to reduce home safety hazards for parents reported for child neglect (Metchikian, Mink, Bigelow, Lutzker, & Doctor, 1999), and self-preservation and emergency responses for battered families (Lund & Greene, 2003).

One of the most promising applications of social and operant learning procedures has been in the area of prevention. Prevention programs seek to reduce high-risk behavior and the development of clinical disorders by building adaptive strengths and coping skills (Gilchrist, Schinke, & Maxwell, 1987; Task Panel on Prevention, 1988). Social work researchers have employed an expanded form of the SST procedure to transmit information and teach skills to prevent unplanned pregnancy in high school students (Schinke, Blythe, & Gilchrist, 1981), cigarette smoking in middle school students (Schinke & Gilchrist, 1985), drinking and driving in adolescents (Wodarski, 1987; Wodarski & Bordnick, 1994), drinking and substance abuse in minority adolescents (Botvin, Schinke, Epstein, Diaz, & Botvin, 1995; Schinke et al., 1988), and to improve self-image and social competence in adolescent girls (Lecroy, 2004, 2005).

Combining strategies of prevention and early intervention, Fraser and his colleagues evaluated multicomponent training programs aimed at preventing the development of aggressive behavior in third-grade children. One component of their program, Making Choices, consisted of teaching children social problem solving, social information processing, and social skills during 25 to 30 45-minute group sessions (Fraser, Day, Galinsky, Hodges, & Smokowski, 2004; Smokowski, Fraser, Day, Galinsky, & Bacallao, 2004). A second component was Strong Families, a parent-training curriculum covering topics of limit setting, problem solving, and rewarding of prosocial behavior, delivered during 15 1- to 2-hour sessions conducted in the parents' home (Fraser et al., 2004). In a series of controlled studies with hundreds of subjects, these interventions were shown to produce statistically significant improvements for trained groups over comparison groups on teacher ratings of social aggression (i.e., verbal aggression, teasing, hostility) and overt aggression (i.e., threats, physical attack), with effect sizes for the different studies ranging from small to large (Fraser et al., 2004, 2005; Smokowski et al., 2004). Finally, children participating in the Making Choices program were rated significantly less aggressive than children in a control group at a 6-month follow-up assessment (Fraser, Lee, Kupper, & Day, 2011).

All of the previous studies reported success in accomplishing at least some of their goals; however, effect sizes associated with these interventions were not always large, measurement of generalization varied considerably across studies, and improvements were often assessed by self-report data. The impact of these preventive interventions might be amplified in future research by taking greater pains to objectively measure generalization of desired behavior to extratherapy settings, considering strategies for promoting generalization across stimuli and responses extrapolated from operant learning principles (Rzepnicki, 1991; Stokes & Baer, 1977; Stokes & Osnes, 1989), and modifying antecedent and consequent environmental stimuli more proximal to the target behaviors.

Another area of prevention research with potentially far-reaching ramifications is the reduction of television viewing and exposure to its words and images encouraging "violence, rampant consumerism, sedentary lifestyles and early sexual activity" and its dulling of "intellectual and social development" (Jason & Fries, 2004, p. 129). Jason and his colleagues have developed devices and techniques (e.g., television locks, televisions operated by token meters, and contingency contracts between parents and their children) for regulating exposure to this ubiquitous mass media that promotes sensationalism, materialism, and immediate gratification. By utilizing such devices and techniques, millions of parents can regain control over the unwanted messages that are broadcast directly into their homes and viewed by their families.

Clinical Disorders

Evidence-based applications of operant learning principles come from the fields of behavior therapy, applied behavior analysis, and behavioral social work in effectively treating mental disorders delineated in the *Diagnostic and Statistical Manual of Mental Disorders*, fourth edition, text revision (American Psychiatric Association, 2000). These myriad disorders are associated with personal suffering, functional impairments, and risks to health and life; therefore, the success of operant and behavioral interventions in ameliorating these problems proves their utility. Because the literature on applying operant learning procedures with clinical disorders is vast, the present section focuses on the research of social workers addressing these problems.

Phobic Disorders   Excessive, crippling fears and avoidance responses have been a major target of behavior therapy, and a few social work researchers have been active in this arena. Treatments based on learning theory often entail *prolonged exposure* to the feared stimuli, thereby habituating clients to conditioned aversive properties of the stimulus and extinguishing their avoidance behavior. In an archetypal study of this approach, Thyer (1981) used graduated and prolonged in vivo exposure to dogs of various sizes and breeds to eliminate extreme fear of dogs in a 70-year-old woman. Thyer (1983) also successfully treated morbid fear of frogs in a 26-year-old woman by having the client gradually approach and eventually touch a live frog. Working with a situation causing distress in a nonclinical population, Thyer and colleagues (1981) reduced test anxiety in a group of 19 college students by teaching a combination of cognitive restructuring and muscle relaxation techniques (responses incompatible with fear). In another clinical application Vonk and Thyer (1995) utilized sex education and graduated exposure therapy to successfully treat fear of vaginal penetration in a 25-year-old heterosexual woman who was unable to have sexual intercourse. Most recently, in an evaluation of a short-term intervention, Hindo and Gonzáles-Prendes (2011) reported significant improvements in the public speaking anxiety of 32 women with social anxiety disorder who participated in one 3-hour session of graduated exposure therapy.

Obsessive-Compulsive Disorder Persistent and distressing thoughts, images, or impulses that are often accompanied by repetitive rituals that clients enact to reduce anxiety have also been the target of behavioral interventions. Behavioral treatment often involves prolonged exposure to the objects or situations that provoke the obsessional fears and *response prevention* or persuading clients not to engage in the rituals that they usually perform to reduce their anxiety (e.g., washing or checking; Steketee, 1987). Thyer (1985a) treated a 36-year-old woman with homicidal obsessions of stabbing family members with sharp objects that were unaccompanied by compulsive rituals with repeated exposure to tape recordings of herself reading detailed accounts of her disturbing thoughts. J. Himle and Thyer (1989) later reported the successful use of exposure in eliminating obsessive thoughts in a 50-year-old man. This client's obsessions were blasphemous thoughts about religious figures and sex ("The Virgin Mary is a whore"), which were treated by having the client listen to tape recordings of himself repeating these repugnant phrases and having him repeatedly write out these phrases on paper. Williams, Chambless, and Steketee (1998) described the treatment of two African American women, one obsessed with fears of contamination and the second obsessed with hoarding beer. Both clients showed dramatic improvements after exposure exercises; the former client was able to touch grimy trash and the latter was able to give away beer or pour perfectly good beer down the drain. Exposure and response prevention have also been applied with larger groups of clients with obsessive-compulsive behavior, showing that outcomes are generally better when these procedures are applied in combination (Foa, Steketee, Grayson, Turner, & Latimer, 1984).

Schizophrenic Disorders Operant learning principles have been applied with some of the most severe behavior disorders in adults involving the emergence of bizarre or grossly disorganized behavior and the associated deterioration in social functioning, vocational performance, and self-care. Wong and his colleagues (Wong, 1996; Wong, Wilder, Schock, & Clay, 2004) have recommended that the treatment of these disorders be multipronged and address the specific behavioral excesses and deficits exhibited by the individual client. In an early study, Patterson and Teigen (1973) used token reinforcement and verbal feedback to reestablish factual statements about personal background in a 60-year-old woman with a long history of delusional speech. Wong, Woolsey, et al. (1987) later applied positive reinforcement to increase accurate verbalizations and response cost (removal of positive reinforcement for inappropriate behavior) to reduce delusional speech in a 24-year-old woman with the diagnosis of paranoid schizophrenia. In a series of studies that examined the relationship between psychotic behavior and appropriate alternative behavior, Wong and his colleagues (Corrigan, Liberman, & Wong, 1993; Wong, Terranova, et al., 1987; Wong, Wright, Terranova, Bowen, & Zarate, 1988) demonstrated that a broad array of bizarre and repetitive responses could be displaced by both sedentary and strenuous recreational activities in 14 persons with severe mental disorders bearing varied diagnoses.

Beginning the lengthy process of restoring functional repertoires in clients with long histories of severe mental disturbances, Wong and Woolsey (1989) used a highly structured, discrete trials format to restore rudimentary conversational skills (e.g., saying "Hi" or "Hello") in four actively psychotic patients with schizophrenia. Working with three higher functioning patients with schizophrenia, Wong et al. (1993) applied traditional social skills training procedures to teach more sophisticated conversational skills (e.g., conversational questions such as "How is the weather outside?"). Addressing the common problem of clients' poor self-care and appearance, Wong, Flanagan and colleagues (1988) utilized verbal prompts, modeling, praise, and consumable reinforcement to improve grooming and personal hygiene skills in a group of 50 regressed mental patients residing in a state hospital. Finally, focusing on clients' fitness and productive use of leisure time, Thyer, Irvine, and Santa (1984) used consumable reinforcement to motivate two former mental patients in a group home to exercise on a stationary bicycle.

More recently, Bradshaw (1997) applied a combination of cognitive and behavioral techniques over an 18-month period to reduce psychotic symptoms and to improve functioning in four outpatients with schizophrenia. After spending a month to establish empathetic and supportive relationships with clients, the investigator taught them stress-reduction techniques (e.g., progressive relaxation, exercise) and social skills. Clients were also instructed in three cognitive techniques: negative thought stopping, empirical testing and invalidation of negative thoughts, and generating positive self-statements. Outcome data analyzed in four AB, single-subject designs showed that treatment was associated with substantial reductions in ratings of symptoms and gains in ratings of role functioning. Using a larger participant sample, Bradshaw and Roseborough (2004) applied a similar combination of cognitive and behavioral treatment procedures during 18 months of treatment with 22 outpatients diagnosed with schizophrenia. Outcome measures consisted of clinical ratings of symptoms and adaptive functioning, and aggregated group data were evaluated within a multiple-baseline design. This study also documented significant improvements in symptoms and adaptive functioning that resulted from treatment.

Aggressive Behavior   Although not linked to any specific diagnosis, aggression is a serious problem behavior and one that is frequently treated with techniques derived from operant learning principles. Persons with developmental disabilities are a population that exhibits a variety of challenging behaviors, including physical aggression. Wong, Slama, and Liberman (1985) outlined skill acquisition and response reduction procedures available for persons with developmental disabilities or mental disorders, and presented case illustrations with positive outcome data. Wong, Floyd, Innocent, and Woolsey (1991) applied brief compliance training and differential reinforcement of other behavior (DRO) schedule to reduce physically aggressive behavior in an autistic man. The DRO schedule required the client not to display aggressive behavior (perform any behavior other than aggressive behavior) for a certain period of time (e.g., 15 minutes) to earn positive reinforcement (e.g., praise and a small piece of candy). As the duration of appropriate behavior increased and the frequency of aggressive behavior lessened, the DRO interval was gradually lengthened (e.g., to 30 minutes, to 45 minutes). Figueroa, Thyer, and Thyer (1992) employed extinction and a DRO schedule to reduce physical aggression in a 7-year-old boy with severe mental retardation. Extinction in this case involved a burly therapist who wore heavy, protective clothing and gloves and who ignored, blocked, or otherwise neutralized the boy's physical attacks until they gradually subsided.

Youth in residential or psychiatric treatment are another population with difficult-to-manage behavior, including verbal and physical aggression. Dangel, Deschner, and Rasp (1989) described a cognitive-behavioral anger control program used to decrease the verbal aggression of adolescents in residential treatment. The training program included cognitive retraining in identifying triggers for anger, considering alternatives to aggressive behavior, and increasing self-awareness of feelings and self-statements associated with anger buildup. Subjects were also taught alternative behaviors to aggression, including thought-stopping, muscle relaxation, and walking away from the situation. Rates of daily verbal aggression were recorded, and results evaluated within a multiple-baseline across-groups design showed modest declines in verbal aggression in the treatment phase and substantial declines in the follow-up phase. Finally, Wong (1999) showed that long-term treatment with a modified Achievement Place program (Phillips, Phillips, Fixsen, & Wolf, 1974) with response-cost procedures was associated with substantial decreases in aggression and other severe antisocial behavior in a group of 29 adolescent inpatients with histories of treatment failure. In addition to being linked to behavioral improvements, program components received generally high consumer satisfaction ratings by the youth in its care.

Critiques of the Operant Learning Approach

The operant learning model is frequently misrepresented and misunderstood (Thyer, 2004). In earlier times, a common criticism of this approach was that the model was too simplistic and mechanistic. Human behavior was characterized as being inherently too complex to be analyzed in terms of mere stimulus-response units. This criticism has fallen silent in the present era of biomedical and pharmacological treatments in which the activity of synaptic-neurotransmitters is boldly claimed to pattern human behavior, while highly profitable psychotropic drugs are advanced as solutions for a spectrum of psychological and interpersonal difficulties (see, e.g., Wong, 2006). Another factor that has tended to quell this criticism is the growing body of research that has produced more advanced and elegant operant theory and techniques, some of which were discussed in this chapter.

It has also been suggested that operant learning overemphasizes the external control of behavior, and its principles may eventually result in mind/behavior control technologies that will be used by authoritarian or punitive agents, such as those artistically portrayed in the film *A Clockwork Orange*. However, with rare exception, behavioral researchers and practitioners are keenly aware of their position as human service professionals and their ethical responsibilities as behavior change agents. Furthermore, because behavioral practitioners' attempts to alter behavior are open and recognizable, they are probably less prone to use this influence in authoritarian and self-serving ways as compared to other groups, such as religious or business organizations, whose behavioral control activities are less obvious and less subject to public censure. Thyer's (2004) comment regarding the misreading or failure to read behavioral literature is also pertinent here. Leading behavioral researchers have written extensively about the shortcomings of punishment and reasons not to apply it as a behavioral control procedure, including its long-term ineffectiveness, its lack of teaching desired behavior, its negative emotional side effects, its tendency to produce escape or countercontrol behavior, and its modeling of aversive control that the student is later predisposed to use against the teacher (Sidman, 2000a; Skinner, 1953).

Another criticism of the operant learning approach is that because it changes behavior by engineering environmental stimuli, it is suited only for tightly controlled environments such as laboratories or closed institutions (e.g., hospitals, prisons, schools). This impression might have arisen due to the many early applications of operant principles in these types of settings. However, recent research reviewed in this chapter should help to correct this misconception, demonstrating that these principles can be utilized as educational techniques in prevention and early intervention programs applied in open organizations and communities.

Contrary to these criticisms, operant learning's focus on the malleability of behavior within the environment speaks for a progressive view of human nature and society. Because this approach sees behavior as largely the product of environmental stimuli and individual experience, it predicts that human potential will be optimized by making the most of these factors. Thus, operant theorists strive to expand people's opportunities and to provide them with nurturant and supportive environments, positive learning experiences, and skills for self-sufficiency and responsible citizenship. These are essentially humanitarian goals mirrored in the primary values of social work.

Key Terms

Behavior chain

Discriminative stimulus

Extinction

Functional analysis

Imitative behavior

Matching Law

Modeling

Negative punishment

Negative reinforcement

Positive punishment

Positive reinforcement

Relational frame theory

Rule-governed behavior

Schedules of reinforcement

Secondary or conditioned reinforcers

Self-control

Shaping

Stimulus generalization

Review Questions for Critical Thinking

1. List five of your own behaviors that would eventually disappear after reinforcement for the behavior ceased. For each of the five behaviors also describe the reinforcing consequence (i.e., reward, avoidance of an aversive stimuli) maintaining the behavior.

2. From your own personal experience or from observation of another person, describe two situations in which a neutral or an insignificant stimulus was transformed into something valuable or repugnant based on its association with another stimulus.

3. Recall a new skill that you learned in the past. Identify component skills or behaviors that you had to learn and put together to perform the full skill. Did the component skills have to be performed in a certain order, and what was that order?

4. Distinguish between how behavior is acquired through direct contact with environmental contingencies (e.g., reinforcement, punishment) and through exposure to verbal rules. What are advantages and disadvantages of each method?

5. Based on the information in this chapter, what are some behavioral prevention or intervention strategies for dealing with a serious behavior problem (e.g., physical aggression, substance abuse)?

Online Resources

Website for the *Journal of Applied Behavior Analysis* (JABA), the leading journal in applied behavior analysis, which contains research in developmental disabilities, special education, public safety, and staff training. From links at this site the reader can obtain free, full-text PDF copies of articles from all issues of JABA except those from the most recent six months.

http://seab.envmed.rochester.edu/jaba/

Website for the Association for Behavior Analysis International (ABAI), the major organization for the field of behavior analysis. Contains general information on experimental and applied behavior analysis, links to state chapters of ABAI, conference announcements, and other resources.

www.abainternational.org/index.asp

Website of Behavior Analysis: Division 25 of the American Psychological Association (APA). This division of the APA advances experimental, applied, and conceptual analyses derived from the science of behavior. The organization conducts its own program within the annual APA convention and issues a newsletter, both of which can be retrieved from the website.

www.auburn.edu/~newlamc/apa_div25/index.htm

Website of the Association of Contextual Behavioral Science, which is "[D]edicated to the advancement of functional contextual cognitive and behavioral science and practice so as to alleviate human suffering and advance human well being." The website contains a large number of resources on Relational Frame Theory and Acceptance and Commitment Therapy. Full access to these materials requires paid membership in the organization; however, at the time of this writing, membership dues are "value based" and can be a minimum contribution of $1 per year.

http://contextualpsychology.org/

Website for the Cambridge Center for Behavioral Studies, a behavior analysis organization whose mission is "to advance the scientific study of behavior and its humane application to the solution of practical problems, including the prevention and relief of human suffering." This site contains links to a large number of related organizations with similar interests and perspectives.

www.behavior.org/index.php

Website for the journal *Behavior and Social Issues* (BSI), a free-access, online journal that advances the scientific analysis of behavior, particularly with regard to important social problems. BSI has published articles on topics such as cultural analysis, social justice, human rights, and environmental sustainability.

www.uic.edu/htbin/cgiwrap/bin/ojs/index.php/bsi/index

References

American Psychiatric Association. (2000). *Diagnostic and statistical manual of mental disorders* (4th ed., text rev.). Washington, DC: Author.

Asmus, J. M., Ringdahl, J. E., Sellers, J. A., Call, N. A., Andelman, M. S., & Wacker, D. P. (2004). Use of a short-term inpatient model to evaluate aberrant behavior: Outcome summaries from 1996 to 2001. *Journal of Applied Behavior Analysis, 37*, 283–304.

Ayllon, T., & Azrin, N. (1965). The measurement and reinforcement of behavior of psychotics. *Journal of the Experimental Analysis of Behavior, 8*(6), 357–383.

Ayllon, T., & Azrin, N. (1968). *The token economy: A motivational system for therapy and rehabilitation.* Englewood Cliffs, NJ: Prentice Hall.

Ayllon, T., & Michael, J. (1959). The psychiatric nurse as a behavioral engineer. *Journal of the Experimental Analysis of Behavior, 2*, 323–334.

Ayllon, T., & Roberts, M. D. (1974). Eliminating discipline problems by strengthening academic performance. *Journal of Applied Behavior Analysis, 7*, 71–76.

Baer, D. M., & Sherman, J. A. (1964). Reinforcement control of generalized imitation in young children. *Journal of Experimental Child Psychology, 1*, 37–49.

Baer, D. M., Wolf, M. M., & Risley, T. R. (1968). Some current dimensions of applied behavior analysis. *Journal of Applied Behavior Analysis, 1*, 91–97.

Bandura, A. (1965). Influence of model's reinforcement contingencies on the acquisition of imitative responses. *Journal of Personality and Social Psychology, 1*, 589–595.

Bandura, A. (1969). *Principles of behavior modification.* New York, NY: Holt, Rinehart, and Winston.

Bandura, A. (1976). *Social learning theory.* Englewood Cliffs, NJ: Prentice Hall.

Bandura, A., Ross, D., & Ross, S. A. (1963). A comparative test of the status envy, social power, and secondary reinforcement theories of identificatory learning. *Journal of Abnormal and Social Psychology, 67*, 527–534.

Baron, A., & Galizio, M. (2005). Positive and negative reinforcement: Should the distinction be preserved? *Behavior Analyst, 28*, 85–98.

Bigelow, K. M., & Lutzker, J. R. (2000). Training parents reported for or at risk for child abuse and neglect to identify and treat their children's illnesses. *Journal of Family Violence, 15*(4), 311–330.

Botvin, G. J., Schinke, S. P., Epstein, J. A., Diaz, T., & Botvin, E. M. (1995). Effectiveness of culturally focused and generic skills training approaches to alcohol and drug abuse prevention among minority adolescents: Two-year follow-up results. *Psychology of Addictive Behaviors, 9*(3), 183–194.

Bradshaw, W. (1997). Evaluating cognitive-behavioral treatment of schizophrenia. *Research in Social Work Practice, 7*(4), 419–445.

Bradshaw, W., & Roseborough, D. (2004). Evaluating the effectiveness of cognitive-behavioral treatment of residual symptoms and impairment in schizophrenia. *Research in Social Work Practice, 14*(2), 112–120.

Briggs, H. E., Leary, J. D., Briggs, A. C., Cox, W. H., & Shibano, M. (2005). Group treatment of separated parent and child interaction. *Research in Social Work Practice, 15*(6), 452–461.

Brophy, G. (2000). Social work treatment of sleep disturbance in a 5-year-old boy: A single-case evaluation. *Research in Social Work Practice, 10*(6), 748–758.

California Code of Regulations (2011). Title 9. Rehabilitative and Developmental Services. § 784.34. Abuse and Corporal Punishment. Retrieved from http://

government.westlaw.com/linkedslice/default.asp?SP=CCR-1000&SPC= Timeout

Carr, E. G. (1977). The motivation of self-injurious behavior: A review of some hypotheses. *Psychological Bulletin, 84*, 800–816.

Cooper, J. O., Heron, T. E., & Heward, W. L. (2007). *Applied behavior analysis* (2nd ed.). Upper Saddle River, NJ: Pearson.

Corrigan, P. W., Liberman, R. P., & Wong, S. E. (1993). Recreational therapy and behavior management on inpatient units: Is recreational therapy therapeutic? *Journal of Nervous and Mental Diseases, 181*, 644–646.

Dangel, R. F., Deschner, J. P., & Rasp, R. R. (1989). Anger control training for adolescents in residential treatment. *Behavior Modification, 13*(4), 447–458.

Derby, K. M., Wacker, D. P., Sasso, G., Steege, M., Northup, J., Cigrand, K., & Asmus, J. (1992). Brief functional assessment techniques to evaluate aberrant behavior in an outpatient setting: A summary of 79 cases. *Journal of Applied Behavior Analysis, 25*, 713–721.

DeRoos, Y. S., & Pinkston, E. M. (1997). Training adult-day-care staff. In D. M. Baer & E. M. Pinkston (Eds.), *Environment and behavior* (pp. 249–257). Boulder, CO: Westview Press.

Dillenburger, K., Godina, L., & Burton, M. (1997). Training in behavioral social work: A pilot study. *Research in Social Work Practice, 7*(1), 70–78.

Ferster, C. B., & Skinner, B. F. (1957). *Schedules of reinforcement.* Englewood Cliffs, NJ: Prentice Hall.

Figueroa, R. G., Thyer, B. A., & Thyer, K. B. (1992). Extinction and DRO in the treatment of aggression in a boy with severe mental retardation. *Journal of Behavior Therapy and Experimental Psychiatry, 23*(2), 133–140.

Fischer, J., & Gochros, H. (1977). *Planned behavior change: Behavior modification in social work.* New York, NY: Free Press.

Foa, E. B., Steketee, G., Grayson, J. B., Turner, R. M., & Latimer, P. R. (1984). Deliberate exposure and blocking of obsessive-compulsive rituals: Immediate and long-term effects. *Behavior Therapy, 15*(5), 450–472.

Fraser, M. W., Day, S. H., Galinsky, M. J., Hodges, V. G., & Smokowski, P. R. (2004). Conduct problems and peer rejection in childhood: A randomized trial of the Making Choices and Strong Families programs. *Research on Social Work Practice, 14*(5), 313–324.

Fraser, M. W., Galinsky, M. J., Smokowski, P. R., Day, S. H., Terzian, M. A., Rose, R. A., & Guo, S. (2005). Social information-processing skills training to promote social competence and prevent aggressive behavior in the third grade. *Journal of Consulting and Clinical Psychology, 73*(6), 1045–1055.

Fraser, M. W., Lee, J.-S., Kupper, L. L., & Day, S. H. (2011). A controlled trial of the Making Choices program: Six-month follow-up. *Research on Social Work Practice, 21*(2), 165–176.

Gallant, J. P., Thyer, B. A., & Bailey, J. S. (1991). Using bug-in-the-ear feedback in clinical supervision: Preliminary evaluations. *Research on Social Work Practice, 1*(2), 175–187.

Galizio, M. (1979). Contingency-shaped and rule-governed behavior: Instructional control of human loss avoidance. *Journal of the Experimental Analysis of Behavior, 31*(1), 53–70.

Gambrill, E. (1977). *Behavior modification: Handbook of assessment, intervention, and evaluation.* San Francisco, CA: Jossey-Bass.

Gammon, E. A., & Rose, S. D. (1991). The coping skills training program for parents of children with developmental disabilities: An experimental evaluation. *Research on Social Work Practice, 1*(3), 244–256.

Gilchrist, L. D., Schinke, S. P., & Maxwell, J. S. (1987). Life skills counseling for preventing problems in adolescence. *Journal of Social Service Research, 10*(2/3/4), 73–84.

Hall, J. A., Schlesinger, D. J., & Dineen, J. P. (1997). Social skills training in groups with developmentally disabled adults. *Research on Social Work Practice, 7*(2), 187–201.

Hanley, G. P., Iwata, B. A., & McCord, B. E. (2003). Functional analysis of problem behavior: A review. *Journal of Applied Behavior Analysis, 36*, 147–185.

Hart, B., & Risley, T. R. (1995). *Meaningful differences in the everyday experiences of young American children.* Baltimore, MD: Brookes.

Hawkins, J. D., Catalano, R. F., & Wells, E. A. (1986). Measuring effects of a skills training intervention for drug abusers. *Journal of Consulting and Clinical Psychology, 54*(5), 661–664.

Hawkins, J. D., Jensen, J. M., Catalano, R. F., & Wells, E. A. (1991). Effects of a skills training intervention with juvenile delinquents. *Research on Social Work Practice, 1*(2), 107–121.

Hayes, S. C. (1989). Nonhumans have not yet shown stimulus equivalence. *Journal of the Experimental Analysis of Behavior, 51*(2), 385–392.

Hayes, S. C. (2004a). Acceptance and commitment therapy and the new behavior therapies. In S. C. Hayes, V. M. Follette, & M. M. Linehan (Eds.), *Mindfulness and acceptance: Expanding the cognitive-behavioral tradition* (pp. 1–29). New York, NY: Guilford Press.

Hayes, S. C. (2004b). Acceptance and commitment therapy, relational frame theory, and the third wave of behavioral and cognitive therapies. *Behavior Therapy, 35*, 639–665.

Hayes, S. C., Brownstein, A. J., Haas, J. R., & Greenway, D. E. (1986). Instructions, multiple schedules, and extinction: Distinguishing rule-governed from schedule-controlled behavior. *Journal of the Experimental Analysis of Behavior, 46*(2), 137–147.

Hayes, S. C., Brownstein, A. J., Zettle, R. D., Rosenfarb, I., & Korn, Z. (1986). Rule-governed behavior and sensitivity to changing consequences of responding. *Journal of the Experimental Analysis of Behavior, 45*(3), 237–256.

Hayes, S. C., & Hayes, L. J. (1992). Verbal relations and the evolution of behavior analysis. *American Psychologist, 47*(11), 1383–1395.

Hayes, S. C., & Wilson, K. G. (1993). Some applied implications of a contemporary behavior-analytic account of verbal events. *Behavior Analyst, 16*(2), 283–301.

Hayes, S. C., & Wilson, K. G. (1994). Acceptance and commitment therapy: Altering the verbal support for experiential avoidance. *Behavior Analyst, 17*(2), 289–303.

Hayes, S. C., Zettle, R. D., & Rosenfarb, I. (1989). Rule-following. In S. C. Hayes (Ed.), *Rule-governed behavior: Cognition, contingencies, and instructional control* (pp. 191–220). Reno, NV: Context Press.

Hepler, J. B. (1994). Evaluating the effectiveness of a social skills program for preadolescents. *Research on Social Work Practice, 4*(4), 411–453.

Herrnstein, R. J. (1961). Relative and absolute strength of response as a function of frequency of reinforcement. *Journal of the Experimental Analysis of Behavior, 4*, 267–272.

Herrnstein, R. J. (1970). On the law of effect. *Journal of the Experimental Analysis of Behavior, 13*, 243–266.

Himle, J., & Thyer, B. A. (1989). Clinical social work and obsessive compulsive disorder. *Behavior Modification, 13*(4), 459–470.

Himle, M. B., Miltenberger, R. G., Flessner, C., & Gatheridge, B. (2004). Teaching safety skills to children to prevent gun play. *Journal of Applied Behavior Analysis, 37*, 1–9.

Hindo, C. S., & Gonzáles-Prendes, A. A. (2011). One-session exposure treatment for social anxiety with specific fear of public speaking. *Research on Social Work Practice, 21*(5), 528–538.

Iwata, B. A. (1987). Negative reinforcement in applied behavior analysis: An emerging technology. *Journal of Applied Behavior Analysis, 20*, 361–378.

Iwata, B. A. (2006). On the distinction between positive and negative reinforcement. *Behavior Analyst, 29*, 121–123.

Iwata, B. A., Dorsey, M. F., Slifer, K. J., Bauman, K. E., & Richman, G. S. (1982). Toward a functional analysis of self-injury. *Analysis and Intervention in Developmental Disabilities, 2*, 3–20.

Iwata, B. A., Pace, G. M., Dorsey, M. F., Zarcone, J. R., Vollmer, T. R., Smith, R. G., ... Willis, K. D. (1994). The functions of self-injurious behavior: An experimental–epidemiological analysis. *Journal of Applied Behavior Analysis, 27*, 215–240.

Iwata, B. A., Wong, S. E., Riordan, M. M., Dorsey, M. F., & Lau, M. M. (1982). Assessment and training of clinical interviewing skills: Analogue analysis and field replication. *Journal of Applied Behavior Analysis, 15*, 191–203.

Jason, L. A., & Fries, M. (2004). Helping parents reduce children's television viewing. *Research in Social Work Practice, 14*(2), 121–131.

Jehu, D. (1967). *Learning theory and social casework.* London, UK: Routledge & Kegan Paul.

Johnson, B. M., Miltenberger, R. G., Egemo-Helm, K., Kelso, P., Jostad, C., Flessner, C., & Gatheridge, B. (2005). Evaluation of behavioral skills training procedures for teaching abduction-prevention skills to young children. *Journal of Applied Behavior Analysis, 38*, 67–78.

Johnson, B. M., Miltenberger, R. G., Knudson, P., Egemo-Helm, K., Kelso, P., Jostad, C., & Langley, L. (2006). A preliminary evaluation of two behavioral skills training procedures for teaching abduction-prevention skills to schoolchildren. *Journal of Applied Behavior Analysis, 39*, 25–34.

Kazdin, A. E. (1999). The meanings and measurements of clinical significance. *Journal of Consulting and Clinical Psychology, 67*(3), 332–339.

Kessler, M. L., & Greene, B. F. (1999). Behavior analysis in child welfare: Competency training caseworkers to manage visits between parents and their children in foster care. *Research in Social Work Practice, 9*(2), 148–170.

Kimble, G. A. (1961). *Hilgard and Marquis' conditioning and learning* (2nd ed.). New York, NY: Appleton-Century-Crofts.

Koepke, J. M., & Thyer, B. A. (1985). Behavioral treatment of failure to thrive. *Child Welfare Journal, 65*(5), 511–516.

Lanier, P., Kohl, P. L., Benz, J., Swinger, D., Moussette, P., & Drake, B. (2011). Parent-child interaction therapy in a community setting: Examining outcomes, attrition, and treatment setting. *Research in Social Work Practice, 21*(6), 689–698.

Lecroy, C. W. (2004). Experimental evaluation of "Go Grrrls" preventive intervention for early adolescent girls. *Journal of Primary Prevention, 25*(4), 457–473.

Lecroy, C. W. (2005). Building an effective primary prevention program for adolescent girls: Empirically based design and evaluation. *Brief Treatment and Crisis Evaluation, 5*(1), 75–84.

Leung, C., Tsang, S., & Dean, S. (2010). Evaluation of a program to educate disadvantaged parents to enhance child learning. *Research in Social Work Practice, 20*(6), 591–599.

Leung, C., Tsang, S., & Dean, S. (2011). Outcome evaluation of the Hands-On Parent Empowerment (HOPE) Program. *Research in Social Work Practice, 21*(5), 549–561.

Lindsley, O. R. (1960). Characteristics of the behavior of chronic psychotics as revealed by free-operant conditioning methods [Monograph supplement]. *Diseases of the Nervous System, 21,* 66–78.

Lindsley, O. R., & Skinner, B. F. (1954). A method for the experimental analysis of the behavior of psychotic patients. *American Psychologist, 9,* 419–420.

Lund, C. J., & Greene, B. F. (2003). Developing a capacity for self-preservation and emergency management among battered families. *Journal of Family Violence, 18*(4), 181–192.

Mace, F. C., Lalli, J. S., Lalli, E. P., & Shea, M. C. (1993). Functional analysis and treatment of aberrant behavior. In R. V. Houten & S. Axelrod (Eds.), *Behavior analysis and treatment* (pp. 75–99). New York, NY: Plenum Press.

Martinez, K. K., & Wong, S. E. (2009). Using prompts to increase attendance at groups for survivors of domestic violence. *Research in Social Work Practice, 19*(4), 460–463.

McDowell, J. J. (1982). The importance of Herrnstein's mathematical statement of the law of effect for behavior therapy. *American Psychologist, 37*(7), 771–779.

McDowell, J. J. (1988). Matching theory in natural human environments. *Behavior Analyst, 11*(2), 95–109.

McFall, R. M. (1976). Behavioral training: A skill-acquisition approach to clinical problems. In J. T. Spence, R. C. Carson, & J. W. Thibaut (Eds.), *Behavioral approaches to therapy* (pp. 227–259). Morristown, NJ: General Learning Press.

Metchikian, K. L., Mink, J. M., Bigelow, K. M., Lutzker, J. R., & Doctor, R. M. (1999). Reducing home safety hazards in the homes of parents reported for neglect. *Child and Family Behavior Therapy, 21*(3), 23–34.

Michael, J. (1975). Positive and negative reinforcement: A distinction that is no longer necessary, or a better way to talk about bad things. *Behaviorism, 3,* 33–44.

Miller, L. K. (1997). *Principles of everyday behavior analysis* (3rd ed.). Pacific Grove, CA: Brooks/Cole.

Miltenberger, R. G., Gatheridge, B., Satterlund, M., Egemo-Helm, K. R., Johnson, B. M., Jostad, C.,... Flessner, C. A. (2005). Teaching safety skills to children to prevent gun play: An evaluation of in situ training. *Journal of Applied Behavior Analysis, 38,* 395–398.

Miltenberger, R. G., & Thiesse-Duffy, E. (1988). Evaluation of home-based programs for teaching personal safety skills to children. *Journal of Applied Behavior Analysis, 21,* 81–87.

O'Reilly, D., & Dillenburger, K. (2000). The development of a high-intensity parent training program for the treatment of moderate to severe child conduct problems. *Research on Social Work Practice, 10*(6), 759–786.

Patterson, R. L., & Teigen, J. R. (1973). Conditioning and post-hospital generalization of nondelusional responses in a chronic psychotic patient. *Journal of Applied Behavior Analysis, 6*, 65–70.

Pelaez, M., Gewirtz, J. L., & Wong, S. E. (2008). A critique of stage theories of human development. In B. A. Thyer (Ed.), *Comprehensive handbook of social work and social welfare: Vol. 2. Human behavior in the social environment* (pp. 503–518). Hoboken, NJ: Wiley.

Phillips, E. L., Phillips, A. E., Fixsen, D. L., & Wolf, M. M. (1974). *The teaching family handbook.* Lawrence, KS: University of Kansas, Bureau of Child Research.

Pierce, W. D., & Cheney, C. D. (2004). *Behavior analysis and learning* (3rd ed.). Mahwah, NJ: Erlbaum.

Pierce, W. D., & Epling, W. F. (1983). Matching and human behavior: A review of the literature. *Behavior Analyst, 6*(1), 57–76.

Pinkston, E. M., & Herbert-Jackson, E. W. (1975). Modification of irrelevant and bizarre verbal behavior using parents as therapists. *Social Service Review, 49,* 46–63.

Pinkston, E. M., Howe, M. W., & Blackman, D. K. (1987). Medical social work management of urinary incontinence in the elderly: A behavioral approach. *Journal of Social Service Research, 10*(2/3/4), 179–194.

Pinkston, E. M., Levitt, J. L., Green, G. R., Linsk, N. L., & Rzepnicki, T. L. (Eds.). (1982). *Effective social work practice: Advanced techniques for behavioral intervention with individuals, families, and institutional staff.* San Francisco, CA: Jossey-Bass.

Pinkston, E. M., Polster, R. A., Friedman, B. S., & Lynch, M. A. (1982). Intervention for coercive family interactions. In E. M. Pinkston, J. L. Levitt, G. R. Green, N. L. Linsk, & T. L. Rzepnicki (Eds.), *Effective social work practice: Advanced techniques for behavioral intervention with individuals, families, and institutional staff* (pp. 247–260). San Francisco, CA: Jossey-Bass.

Plaud, J. J. (1992). The prediction and control of behavior revisited: A review of the matching law. *Journal of Behavior Therapy and Experimental Psychiatry, 23*(1), 25–31.

Reid, W. J. (2004). Contribution of operant theory to social work practice and research. In H. E. Briggs & T. L. Rzepnicki (Eds.), *Using evidence in social work practice: Behavioral perspectives* (pp. 36–54). Chicago, IL: Lyceum Books.

Richey, C. A., Lovell, M. L., & Reid, K. (1991). Interpersonal skill training to enhance social support among women at risk for child maltreatment. *Children and Youth Services Review, 13*(1/2), 41–59.

Rose, S. (1977). *Group therapy: A behavioral approach.* Englewood Cliffs, NJ: Prentice Hall.

Rzepnicki, T. (1991). Enhancing the durability of interventions gains: Challenge for the 1990s. *Social Service Review, 65*(1), 92–111.

Schinke, S. P., Blythe, B. J., & Gilchrist, L. D. (1981). Cognitive-behavioral prevention of adolescent pregnancy. *Journal of Counseling Psychology, 28*(5), 451–454.

Schinke, S. P., & Gilchrist, L. D. (1985). Preventing substance abuse with children and adolescents. *Journal of Consulting and Clinical Psychology, 53*(5), 596–602.

Schinke, S. P., Gilchrist, L. D., Smith, T. E., & Wong, S. E. (1978). Interviewing skills training: An empirical evaluation. *Journal of Social Service Research, 1,* 391–401.

Schinke, S. P., Orlandi, M. A., Botvin, G. J., Gilchrist, L. D., Trimble, J. E., & Locklear, V. S. (1988). Preventing substance abuse among American-Indian adolescents: A bicultural competence approach. *Journal of Counseling Psychology, 35*(1), 87–90.

Schinke, S. P., & Wong, S. E. (1977). Evaluation of staff training in group homes for retarded persons. *American Journal of Mental Deficiency, 82*(3), 130–136.

Schusterman, R. J., & Kastak, D. (1993). A California sea lion (Zalophus californianus) is capable of forming equivalence relations. *Psychological Record, 43,* 823–839.

Schwartz, A., & Goldiamond, I. (1975). *Social casework: A behavioral approach.* New York, NY: Columbia University Press.

Schwartz, I. S., & Baer, D. M. (1991). Social validity assessments: Is current practice state of the art? *Journal of Applied Behavior Analysis, 24,* 189–204.

Sidman, M. (1971). Reading and auditory-visual equivalences. *Journal of Speech and Hearing Research, 14,* 5–13.

Sidman, M. (1994). *Equivalence relations and behavior: A research story.* Boston, MA: Authors Cooperative.

Sidman, M. (2000a). *Coercion and its fallout* (rev. ed.). Boston, MA: Authors Cooperative.

Sidman, M. (2000b). Equivalence relations and the reinforcement contingency. *Journal of the Experimental Analysis of Behavior, 74*(1), 127–146.

Skinner, B. F. (1948). *Walden Two.* Oxford, UK: Macmillan.

Skinner, B. F. (1953). *Science and human behavior.* New York, NY: Free Press.

Skinner, B. F. (1966). Operant behavior. In W. K. Honig (Ed.), *Operant behavior: Areas of research and application* (pp. 12–32). Englewood Cliffs, NJ: Prentice Hall.

Skinner, B. F. (1969). *Contingencies of reinforcement: A theoretical analysis.* Englewood Cliffs, NJ: Prentice Hall.

Skinner, B. F. (1971). *Beyond freedom and dignity.* New York, NY: Knopf.

Smagner, J. P., & Sullivan, M. H. (2005). Investigating the effectiveness of behavioral parent training with involuntary clients in child welfare settings. *Research on Social Work Practice, 15*(6), 431–439.

Smokowski, P. R., Fraser, M. W., Day, S. H., Galinsky, M. J., & Bacallao, M. L. (2004). School-based skills training to prevent aggressive behavior and peer rejection in childhood: Evaluating the Making Choices program. *Journal of Primary Prevention, 25*(2), 233–251.

Sowers-Hoag, K. M., Thyer, B. A., & Bailey, J. S. (1987). Promoting automobile safety belt use by young children. *Journal of Applied Behavior Analysis, 20*(2), 133–138.

Stein, T., & Gambrill, E. D. (1976). Behavioral techniques in foster care. *Social Work, 21*(1), 34–39.

Steketee, G. (1987). Behavioral social work with obsessive-compulsive disorder. *Journal of Social Service Research, 10,* 7–35.

Stokes, T. F., & Baer, D. M. (1977). An implicit technology of generalization. *Journal of Applied Behavior Analysis, 10,* 349–367.

Stokes, T. F., & Osnes, P. G. (1989). An operant pursuit of generalization. *Behavior Therapy, 20,* 337–355.

Stuart, R. B., & Davis, B. (1972). *Slim chance in a fat world: Behavioral control of obesity.* Champaign, IL: Research Press.

Sundel, M., & Sundel, S. (1975). *Behavior modification in the human services.* New York, NY: Wiley.

Sundel, S. S. (1994). Videotape training of job-related social skills using peer modeling: An evaluation of social validity. *Research on Social Work Practice*, *4*(1), 40–52.

Task Panel on Prevention. (1988). Report of the Task Panel on Prevention. In G. W. Albee, J. M. Joffe, & L. A. Dusenbury (Eds.), *Prevention, powerlessness, and politics: Readings on social change* (pp. 25–52). Newbury Park, CA: Sage.

The 2011 Florida Statutes (2011). 400.022 Residents' Rights (o). Retrieved from www.flsenate.gov/laws/statutes/2011/400.022 and 402.305 Licensing standards; child care facilities. (12) Child discipline (a) 3. Retrieved from www.flsenate.gov/laws/statutes/2011/402.305

Thomas, E. J. (Ed.). (1967). *The socio-behavioral approach and applications to social work*. New York, NY: Council on Social Work Education.

Thomas, E. J. (Ed.). (1974). *Behavior modification procedure: A sourcebook*. Chicago, IL: Aldine.

Thyer, B. A. (1981). Prolonged in vivo exposure therapy with a 70-year-old woman. *Journal of Behavior Therapy and Experimental Psychiatry*, *12*, 69–71.

Thyer, B. A. (1983). Treating anxiety disorders with exposure therapy. *Social Casework*, *64*, 77–82.

Thyer, B. A. (1985a). Audio-taped exposure therapy in a case of obsessional neurosis. *Journal of Behavior Therapy and Experimental Psychiatry*, *16*, 271–273.

Thyer, B. A. (1985b). Textbooks in behavioral social work: A bibliography. *Behavior Therapist*, *8*, 161–162.

Thyer, B. A. (1987). Contingency analysis: Toward a unified theory for social work practice. *Social Work*, *32*, 150–157.

Thyer, B. A. (2004). The misfortunes of behavioral social work: Misprized, misread, and misconstrued. In S. A. Kirk (Ed.), *Mental disorders in the social environment: Critical perspectives* (pp. 330–343). New York, NY: Columbia University Press.

Thyer, B. A., Irvine, S., & Santa, C. A. (1984). Contingency management of exercise by chronic schizophrenics. *Perceptual and Motor Skills*, *58*, 419–425.

Thyer, B. A., Papsdorf, J. D., Himle, D. P., McCann, B. S., Caldwell, S., & Wickert, M. (1981). In-vivo distraction-coping in the treatment of test anxiety. *Journal of Clinical Psychology*, *37*, 754–764.

Vonk, M. E., & Thyer, B. A. (1995). Exposure therapy in the treatment of vaginal penetration phobia: A single-case evaluation. *Journal of Behavior Therapy and Experimental Psychiatry*, *26*, 359–363.

Watson, D. L., & Tharp, R. G. (2007). *Self-directed behavior* (9th ed.). Belmont, CA: Thomson Wadsworth.

Wilder, D. A., Masuda, A., O'Conner, C., & Baham, M. (2001). Brief functional analysis and treatment of bizarre vocalizations in an adult with schizophrenia. *Journal of Applied Behavior Analysis*, *34*, 65–68.

Wilder, D. A., White, H., & Yu, M. L. (2003). Functional analysis and treatment of bizarre vocalizations exhibited by an adult with schizophrenia: Replication and extension. *Behavioral Interventions*, *18*, 43–52.

Williams, K. E., Chambless, D. L., & Steketee, G. (1998). Behavioral treatment of obsessive-compulsive disorder in African Americans: Clinical issues. *Journal of Behavior Therapy and Experimental Psychiatry*, *29*, 163–170.

Williams, M., Thyer, B. A., Bailey, J. S., & Harrison, D. F. (1989). Promoting safety belt use with traffic signs and prompters. *Journal of Applied Behavior Analysis*, *22*, 71–76.

Wodarski, J. S. (1987). Evaluating a social learning approach to teaching adolescents about alcohol and driving: A multiple variable evaluation. *Journal of Social Service Research, 10,* 121–144.

Wodarski, J. S., & Bagarozzi, D. (1979). *Behavioral social work.* New York, NY: Human Services Press.

Wodarski, J. S., & Bordnick, P. S. (1994). Teaching adolescents about alcohol and drinking: A 2-year follow-up study. *Research on Social Work Practice, 4*(1), 28–39.

Wolf, M. M. (1978). Social validity: The case for subjective measurement or how applied behavior analysis is finding its heart. *Journal of Applied Behavior Analysis, 11,* 203–214.

Wong, S. E. (1996). Psychosis. In M. Mattaini & B. A. Thyer (Eds.), *Finding solutions to social problems: Behavioral strategies for change* (pp. 319–343). Washington, DC: American Psychological Association.

Wong, S. E. (1999). Treatment of antisocial behavior in adolescent inpatients: Behavioral outcomes and client satisfaction. *Research on Social Work Practice, 9,* 25–44.

Wong, S. E. (2006). Behavior analysis of psychotic disorders: Scientific dead end or casualty of the mental health political economy? *Behavior and Social Issues, 15*(2), 152–177.

Wong, S. E. (2008). Operant learning theory. In B. A. Thyer (Ed.), *Comprehensive handbook of social work and social welfare, Volume 2: Human behavior in the social environment* (pp. 69–99). Hoboken, NJ: Wiley.

Wong, S. E. (2009). Assessment of behavior management and behavioral interventions in state child welfare facilities. In R. Rodenhiser (Ed.), *Assessment in residential care for children and youth* (pp. 105–116). New York, NY: Routledge.

Wong, S. E., Flanagan, S. G., Kuehnel, T. G., Liberman, R. P., Hunnicutt, R., & Adams-Badgett, J. (1988). Training chronic mental patients to independently practice personal grooming skills. *Hospital and Community Psychiatry, 39,* 874–879.

Wong, S. E., Floyd, J., Innocent, A. J., & Woolsey, J. E. (1991). Applying a DRO schedule and compliance training to reduce aggressive and self-injurious behavior in an autistic man: A case study. *Journal of Behavior Therapy and Experimental Psychiatry, 22,* 299–304.

Wong, S. E., Martinez-Diaz, J. A., Massel, H. K., Edelstein, B. A., Wiegand, W., Bowen, L., & Liberman, R. P. (1993). Conversational skills training with schizophrenic inpatients: A study of generalization across settings and conversants. *Behavior Therapy, 24,* 285–304.

Wong, S. E., Morgan, C., Crowley, R., & Baker, J. N. (1996). Using a table game to teach social skills to adolescent psychiatric inpatients: Do the skills generalize? *Child and Family Behavior Therapy, 18,* 1–17.

Wong, S. E., Seroka, P. P., & Ogisi, J. (2000). Effect of a checklist on self-assessment of blood glucose level by a memory-impaired woman with diabetes mellitus. *Journal of Applied Behavior Analysis, 33,* 251–254.

Wong, S. E., Slama, K. M., & Liberman, R. P. (1985). Behavioral analysis and therapy for aggressive psychiatric and developmentally disabled patients. In L. H. Roth (Ed.), *Clinical treatment of the violent person* (DHHS Publication No. ADM 85-1425, pp. 22–56). Washington, DC: U.S. Government Printing Office.

Wong, S. E., Terranova, M. D., Bowen, L., Zarate, R., Massel, H. K., & Liberman, R. P. (1987). Providing independent recreational activities to reduce stereotypic vocalizations in chronic schizophrenics. *Journal of Applied Behavior Analysis, 20,* 77–81.

Wong, S. E., & Vakharia, S. (2011, September). *Improving web browsing for community resources by clients with severe mental disorders.* Paper presented at the 31st Annual Meeting of the Florida Association for Behavior Analysis, Daytona, Florida.

Wong, S. E., Wilder, D. A., Schock, K., & Clay, C. (2004). Behavioral interventions with severe and persistent mental disorders. In H. E. Briggs & T. L. Rzepnicki (Eds.), *Using evidence in social work practice: Behavioral perspectives* (pp. 210–230). Chicago, IL: Lyceum Books.

Wong, S. E., & Woolsey, J. E. (1989). Re-establishing conversational skills in overtly psychotic, chronic schizophrenic patients: Discrete trials training on the psychiatric ward. *Behavior Modification, 13*(4), 415–430.

Wong, S. E., Woolsey, J. E., & Gallegos, E. (1987). Behavioral treatment of chronic psychiatric patients. *Journal of Social Service Research, 10,* 7–35.

Wong, S. E., Wright, J., Terranova, M. D., Bowen, L., & Zarate, R. (1988). Effects of structured ward activities on appropriate and psychotic behavior of chronic psychiatric patients. *Behavioral Residential Treatment, 3,* 41–50.

Zeiler, M. (1977). Schedules of reinforcement: The controlling variables. In W. K. Honig & J. E. R. Staddon (Eds.), *Handbook of operant behavior* (pp. 201–232). Englewood Cliffs, NJ: Prentice Hall.

Chapter 4
Cognitive-Behavioral Theory

Paula S. Nurius and Rebecca J. Macy

> Overarching Question: How can human beings think about their thinking to create therapeutic change in their thoughts, feelings, and behaviors?

Relevance to Contemporary Practitioners

Social workers and practitioners from allied disciplines use interventions based on cognitive-behavioral theory (CBT) to address a wide range of psychosocial problems, including depression, anxiety, chronic pain, substance abuse, violent trauma, and difficult family relationships (J. S. Beck, 2011; Berlin, 2002; Iverson et al., 2011; Nurius, 2008; O'Donohue & Fisher, 2009; Ronen & Freeman, 2007). Cognitive-behavioral therapy (CBT) has been applied and found effective with an array of clients from a range of socioeconomic and sociocultural backgrounds (Hays & Iwamasa, 2006; Koh, Oden, Munoz, Robinson, & Leavitt, 2002; Voss Horrell, 2008), LGBTQ populations (Martell, Safren, & Prince, 2004), and a range of developmental ages including youth (Christner, Stewart, & Freeman, 2007; Lecroy, 2008; Manassis, 2009; Weisz & Kazdin, 2010) and older adults (Laidlaw, Thompson, Dick-Siskin, & Gallagher-Thompson, 2003; Lau & Kinoshita, 2006). In addition, CBT can be used in a variety of settings, from private practice offices to inpatient hospitals to community outreach services (e.g., A. Nezu & Nezu, 2010).

Over the course of its development, the underlying cognitive-behavioral theory has been subjected to extensive research. These research results are a highly favorable body of findings that show the therapeutic effectiveness of CBT and its theoretical foundations (A. T. Beck, 2005). The results of one recent meta-analytic study recommended CBT as a "first-line psychosocial treatment of choice" for clients with anxiety and depressive disorders (Tolin, in press). Another strength of the theory base is its considerable versatility and adaptability. As social work professionals are increasingly asked to use evidence-based practices and to show that their interventions make a difference in the lives of the people with whom they work, many practitioners turn to cognitive-behavioral therapy because of the combination of its utility, adaptability, and strong record of effectiveness (Macy, 2006).

Cognitive-behavioral therapy has at its foundation a set of well-documented and detailed intervention techniques (see, e.g., J. S. Beck, 2011; Leahy, 2002) that are widely available and straightforwardly applied. Such clear-cut application is particularly salient to practitioners. CBT's emphasis on articulating implementation methods provides a basic template for how to translate theory into therapeutic practice. Nonetheless, the effectiveness of any therapeutic method can be diluted by adherence to technique that is insufficiently attentive to the characteristics, complexities, and context of any given case. Grounding in the underlying theory, awareness of emerging developments, and balanced attention to limitations as well as strengths of this model of practice are essential to making decisions about the appropriateness of CBT for a given client as well as adaptation to foster good fit.

As with any intervention, the effectiveness of cognitive-behavioral therapy is dependent on the practitioner's ability to use the theory and related techniques in clearly formulated, deliberate, and thoughtful ways. Practitioners will be most effective in their use of cognitive-behavioral interventions if they have a nuanced understanding of the theoretical premises and are skilled in a range of CBT intervention techniques and tools. This level of mastery requires study, practice, and supervision from others well versed in this intervention theory. In addition, effective application of cognitive-behavioral interventions is incumbent on the social worker's ability to appropriately adapt and modify cognitive-behavioral theory and therapy techniques to clients' sociocultural and socioeconomic backgrounds, as well as clients' development in the life course (Cormier, Nurius, & Osborn, in press; Hays & Iwamasa, 2006). To provide readers with a theoretical foundation for using this therapy effectively in assessment and intervention, we provide an overview of the theory and its developmental history, basic and advanced theoretical principles, and recent developments and critiques.

Overview of Cognitive-Behavioral Theory

The cognitive-behavioral theoretical framework of human functioning is based on the premises that thoughts, emotions, and behaviors are inextricably linked and that each of these aspects of human functioning continuously effects and influences the others. Cognitive-behavioral theory posits that thoughts about the self, relationships, the world, and the future shape emotions and behaviors. Feelings and behaviors shape thoughts and thought processes in a kind of ongoing reciprocal feedback loop. Moreover, cognitive-behavioral theory posits that cognitive-affective-behavioral *processes* are similar and analogous across human beings and human experience. However, the *content* within the cognitive-affective-behavioral processes is specific, unique, and personal to the individual (Alford & Beck, 1997; DeRubis, Tang, & Beck, 2010).

This distinction is critically important. There is a lot yet to learn about processes—*how* exactly thoughts and feelings interact with each other as well as with genetics, physiology, and prior lived experience, and how these systematically relate to and with behavior. Yet to date, it appears that there is a high degree of comparability in how processes operate as with other aspects of the human body and functioning. The defining *content* of memories, beliefs, understandings, expectations, and values can be highly variable, reflecting differences across people. These differences flow into the operating system of cognition–affect–body–behavior processes in a continuous reciprocal interchange to generate an intricate, contextualized set of thoughts, feeling and behaviors.

In other words, how human beings construct the reality of their lives and the meaning human beings give to their lives, their selves, their relationships, their environments, and their futures is distinct. This distinctiveness comes from uniquely individual experience, knowledge, and memory. When this cognitive-affective-behavioral system works well, human beings are able to take in information from their experiences and their environment, process and manage that information, and then use the information to direct emotions and behaviors toward meeting their needs and goals in ways that are adaptive, efficient, and functional.

However, serious difficulties in human thinking, feeling, behaving, and functioning can occur when there are problems in thoughts and thought processes (J. S. Beck, 2011). Central to cognitive-behavioral theory is the notion of cognitive mediation—that the meaning people bring to and take from their experiences shapes how they feel and respond. Accordingly, our cognitive activity is an active and crucial part of both positive and negative functioning. When our emotions and behaviors are guided by thoughts and beliefs that are seriously unhelpful in some manner, it is likely that we will have difficulty meeting our needs, pursuing our goals, and experiencing life in a satisfied, comfortable manner. When our needs are unmet and goals are not achieved, we are then likely to experience distress and anguish. In turn, these negative feelings will reinforce or create new problems in our thoughts and beliefs, our emotional and social experience, as well as our views of ourselves and what the future holds.

As a counterpoint to this, cognitive-behavioral theory also posits that we human beings have the capacities to monitor, examine, and change our thoughts, beliefs, and thought processes. We have the ability to think about thinking, and thus we have the capacity to alter and replace problematic, inaccurate, or in some other way unhelpful thoughts. By directing attention to and modifying thoughts and beliefs, we can also change and direct emotions and behaviors to better meet our needs and goals toward more beneficial outcomes (Leahy, Tirch, & Napolitano, 2011). This premise that people can think about their thinking, referred to as metacognition, is foundational to the change processes in cognitive-behavioral therapy.

However, cognitive-behavioral theory also posits that we do not tend to regularly reflect on our thoughts and thought processes, leaving us largely unaware of problems in our own thinking that may be at least partially contributing to our unease (Mischel, 2007). For brevity's sake, we are using such terms as thoughts and beliefs. However, the notion of cognition and cognitive activity is quite broad. As Dobson and Dozois (2010) note, a wide range of cognitive constructs and processes have been implicated, including but not limited to thoughts, beliefs, attitudes, assumptions, perceptions, interpretations, attributions, self-statements, scripts, rules for living, values, expectancies, narratives, cognitive distortions, schemas, narratives, and private meanings. In sum, cognitive-behavioral theory proposes that practitioners can play an important role in helping clients with understanding the impact that their thoughts have on their emotions and behaviors, the ways that self and social factors can shape their cognitive activity, and ways that clients can learn how to reflect on and make choices about modifying their thoughts and thought processes to better meet their needs and goals.

Historical and Conceptual Origins

> There was a time, not too long ago, when the term cognitive-behavioral therapy was considered an oxymoron.... Only a quarter century ago, it was inconceivable to many that there could be anything legitimately called "mind sciences." Now it is difficult to imagine an adequate approach to psychotherapy that does not appreciate basic contributions from the cognitive sciences. (Mahoney, 2004a, p. 5)

This quotation captures the rapid development and dramatic impact of cognitive-behavioral theory and the therapeutic methods it informs. In many respects, cognitive-behavioral theory reflects an ongoing evolution in theorizing, clinical application, and empirical evidence. Definitional boundaries can also be unclear. Some refer to cognitive theory and therapy and others to cognitive-behavioral theory and therapy. Some therapists see themselves predominantly as behaviorists who incorporate findings related to ways that thought, feeling, and action are interrelated. Others see themselves more rooted in the cognitive realm of understanding key processes through which cognitions—particularly errors, distortions, and maladaptive patterns of cognition—give rise to serious problems in living. Still others see themselves as working at an interface that integrates CBT premises with premises or findings from other arenas, such as cognitive science, constructivism, human biology, ecology, psychopharmacology, and substantive factors anchored in respective arenas of practice (e.g., addictions, child and youth development, stress-related problems, problems associated with medical conditions).

A strict rendering of the historical origins of cognitive-behavioral theory is made difficult by differing perspectives and a general sense of merging between cognitive and behavioral lines of theorizing relative to therapeutic techniques (although not without dissent or controversy). Behavior therapy, for example, can be seen as developing in a context that stood in contrast to a medical model of psychopathology and to psychoanalysis as the prevailing therapeutic approach, instead emphasizing pragmatism, symptom relief, use of well-specified methods, and adherence to empirical evidence of underlying theorized principles and therapeutic outcomes. As behavior theories are addressed elsewhere in this volume, we do not review these here. O'Leary and Wilson (1987) identify the following as characteristics typifying behavior therapy (cited in Prochaska & Norcross, 2003, p. 244):

Most abnormal behavior is acquired and maintained according to the same principles as normal behavior.

- Assessment is ongoing and focuses on currently functioning determinants of behavior.
- People are best described by what they think, feel, and do in specific life situations.
- Treatment is based on theory and empirical findings.
- Practice methods are detailed and replicable.
- Treatment is tailored to different problems and people.
- Intervention goals and methods are mutually developed and agreed upon with the client.
- Specific therapeutic techniques are evaluated as to their effects on specific problems.
- Outcomes are evaluated on the basis of observed behavior change, its generalization to real-life settings, and its maintenance over time.

We list these background dimensions of behavior therapy as they have carried forward to a considerable extent in the development of cognitive-behavioral theory and therapy. Although effective for a wide range of specific problems, particularly those associated with anxiety, both clinical and empirical experience with behavior therapy began to reflect limitations. Behavior theory underwent dramatic change as a function of the cognitive therapy movement that began in the 1960s and blossomed in subsequent decades. Major early contributors to the cognitive therapy movement include Albert Ellis, Aaron Beck, Michael Mahoney, Joseph Cautela, Donald Meichenbaum, Albert Bandura, and others who introduced cognitively oriented therapies such as rational-emotive therapy, cognitive therapy, self-control and self-regulatory methods, covert sensitization, self-instructional and stress inoculation techniques, coping skills training, problem-solving training, and structural and constructivist perspectives (Foreyt & Goodrick, 2001, and Dobson & Dozois, 2010, provide useful overviews of early major contributors).

Models that emphasized conditioning of human behavior by environmental forces began to share space and integrate with models that argued for cognitive *mediational processes*. These models assert that particular thoughts and cognitive styles shape how stimuli (external events as well as one's own thoughts and feelings) are experienced and interpreted, which shapes behavioral responding. The shift from behavioral to cognitive-behavioral theory entailed a shift from environmental determinism (that one's functioning is primarily shaped by the external environment) to reciprocal determinism (that one is an active participant in shaping one's development as well as being affected by the nature of that environment, in a continual transaction between person and environment).

A number of factors have been identified as contributing to the initial theoretical specification of cognitive-behavioral therapy and its rapid ascendance as a preeminent therapeutic approach. Dobson and Dozois (2010) note the following:

- The behavioral perspective was increasingly being seen as insufficient to account for important dimensions of human behavior, yet cognitive extensions were generally not embraced as consistent with behavioral theory.
- The strongest alternative at the time, the psychodynamic model, had not amassed a persuasive body of evidence documenting its effectiveness.
- The mediating processes offered by cognitive-behavioral theory articulated a different understanding of mechanisms and, thus, cognitive and affective targets and guidelines for intervention.
- Basic and applied research on cognitive processes was flourishing, providing empirical support for new and clinically relevant cognitive models.
- Cognitive-behavioral therapy took hold as an organizing construct and body of work, manifested by major contributors and forums such as new journals that served to establish a focus and platform for exchange about provocative ideas and evolving findings.
- The growing body of research findings supporting CBT became particularly significant in a context of cost containment and workplace pressures to document use of empirically supported interventions.

The following three propositions are central to cognitive behavioral theory: (1) cognitive activity affects behavior; (2) cognitive activity can be monitored and altered; and (3) desired behavior change can be affected through cognitive change. These propositions are found throughout CBT in all its manifestations. However, CBT is not static intervention theory. Theorists and practitioners have continued to develop and refine CBT. Mahoney (1995, 2004b) indicates the major conceptual developments in the cognitive psychotherapies over the past three decades:

- The differentiation of rationalist and constructivist approaches to cognition. Although not inherently unrelated, this distinction distinguishes a relative emphasis on cognitive content. The rationalist approach emphasizes logic, errors, distortions, and (ir)rationality. Alternatively, the constructivist approach emphasizes a proactive (constructive) view of the nature of cognition that includes a complex system of interchanges among thought, feeling, and action contextualized within a developmental perspective of the self and social systems.

- The recognition of social, biological, and embodiment issues. Increasingly, factors such as genetics and biological functioning, bodily experiences, physiology, and powerful social forces important to shaping, understanding, and intervening were incorporated into theory.

- The reappraisal of unconscious processes. There was growing recognition that not all cognition is available to consciousness and that some processes, including automatic thoughts, typically operate without awareness. Such contemporary notions of the unconscious are not the same as those deriving from Freudian theory. However, there is an active effort to illuminate tacit experience and learn its function in psychological health.

- An increasing focus on self and social systems. Early cognitive approaches tended to be internally focused and relatively inattentive to historical events or to the social and emotional relationship between client and social worker. More recent approaches emphasize complexity of the self and social embeddedness.

- The reappraisal of emotional and experiential processes. CBT's early emphasis was on conscious reason as the key vehicle for correcting problems of perception. There is now more focus on cognitive change strategies that emphasize emotion and experiential techniques. Recent decades have witnessed a lessening of sibling rivalries among different psychotherapy theoretical adherents and greater dialogue and conceptual integration among behavioral, cognitive, humanistic, and psychodynamic theorists and practitioners. Accordingly, cognitive psychotherapies have likewise contributed to the psychotherapy integration movement.

Research and theorizing have continued with vigor since CBT's early foundations, to the point that CBT now ranks among the most dominant therapies identified by practitioners, supported by empirical findings, and listed as recommended methods (Cormier et al., in press; Dobson & Dozois, 2010; Prochaska & Norcross, 2010). The combination of theoretical evolution (openness to revisiting and revising theoretical propositions based on new findings), relatively precise documentation of intervention strategies, and a sturdy base of positive outcomes evidence has positioned cognitive-behavioral theory and practice to gain wide support. We now turn to an outline of cognitive-behavioral therapy principles as well as recent theoretical development.

Basic Theoretical Principles

As discussed earlier, cognitive-behavioral *therapy* is essentially the application of cognitive-behavioral *theory* to the individual client's situation or problem. The specific therapeutic strategies a practitioner may use with coping skills applications, problem-solving skills development, or cognitive restructuring across different clients will vary to fit the change goals. However, there is a common theoretical base that undergirds these different types of cognitive-behavioral therapy. In this section we briefly review several basic theoretical principles of cognitive-behavioral therapy that are critical to understanding the organizing premises used to develop, apply, and adapt cognitive-behavioral interventions. Specifically, we discuss the theoretical principles of the (a) mediational model—how thoughts and beliefs determine emotions and behaviors; (b) information processing—how we human beings manage all the stimuli from our environments and ourselves to meet our needs and goals and how cognition is fundamental to this process; (c) self-regulation—how human beings are active agents with the capacity to alter their thoughts, feelings, behaviors, and environments, and how self regulation can be used as the basis for change in cognitive-behavioral therapy; and (d) the importance of the environment—how a person's environment, including socioeconomic and sociocultural context, plays a critical role in shaping and activating cognitive content.

Mediational Model

The premise of the mediational model is that stimuli, such as experiences we encounter in life, do not directly determine feelings or lead to behavior but rather go through a filtering process of meaning making, led by the cognitive system that has to attend to and undertake interpretation of the experience and its implications for the person. This interpretative process draws from several levels of thinking, including automatic thoughts, underlying assumptions and rules, and core beliefs. Neenan and Dryden (2004, p. 7) describe negative automatic thoughts as those that involuntarily pop into a person's mind when experiencing emotional distress; these thoughts are often outside immediate awareness and difficult to turn off. Underlying assumptions ("*If* I impress others, *then* I should get ahead in life") and rules ("I *should* not let people down") are typically not explicitly articulated and yet tend to be reflective of and to reinforce core beliefs (e.g., "I am incompetent"). Core beliefs, which we further address later, take form as schemas that are stored in memory and drawn by relevant life events into information processing, shaping meaning making and thus emotional and physiological states and behavioral responding.

The mediational model does not propose a strictly linear process whereby thoughts or beliefs lead to emotions and physiological states, which then dictate behaviors. Rather, there is a dynamic interplay and presumed reciprocal relationships among these elements, such that changing any one should affect change in the other elements, or at least the overall dynamic. Assuming that an individual has developed negative automatic thoughts, assumptions and rules, and core beliefs that have become deeply established in patterned, habitual responding (e.g., depression, anxiety, poor self-esteem), change in the cognitive architecture that is operating in problematic situations is pivotal. In short, acknowledging dynamic interplay, the mediational model generally posits that emotions and behaviors in a situation flow from the cognitive activity that gets engaged in relating to the experience (e.g., the content of thoughts and beliefs salient in the moment and cognitive processes that carry these in anticipating, interpreting, and reacting, inclusive of thoughts and beliefs about the self, relationships, the world, and the future).

To illustrate, two students receive disappointing grades on an assignment in one of their first courses in graduate school. The first student's cognitive content about the disappointing grade reflects the following beliefs: "I'm not good at this school stuff and now it's showing. If I continue to try to get through this, then my incompetence will become more and more apparent. I'm a second-rate student and I'm going to be humiliated in front of my classmates." The second student's cognitive content about the grade reflects these beliefs: "Wow! I was not expecting graduate school to be this tough. If I work a lot harder and study more, then I'm going to do better or at least have a better picture of what help I need. I am disappointed about this grade, but I have to keep my focus on my goals, and I know I can do better next time."

The cognitive content exhibited by the first graduate student will result in emotions such as embarrassment and anxiety and behaviors of ruminatively worrying about future performance and starting to avoid studying, as that prompts episodes of anxiety, negative self-talk, and a sense that the material is over his head. Alternatively, the cognitive content from the second graduate student will likely result in emotions of resolve and determination and behaviors such as going to the library to study after class. With both students in this example, it is evident that their cognitive content shapes and influences their emotions and behaviors, as well as that the cognitive content mediated the relationship between the life experience of getting a disappointing grade and the subsequent emotions and behaviors. These examples also illustrate ways that behavior contributes to a vicious cycle of emotional distress. People typically act as they think (e.g., if I don't think I can be successful with something, I'll likely behave in a manner consistent with this, which serves to sustain my unhappiness with my perceived incompetence). In short, the mediational model posits that problems in one's behaviors and emotions are indicative of problems in one's underlying thoughts and thought processes, most likely negative, unhelpful beliefs, assumptions, and automatic response patterns.

In first thinking about the idea of the mediational model, it may not be initially clear why emotions play an important role. However, theory and findings show complex relationships; thoughts and beliefs trigger and amplify emotions, emotional content associated with cognition stimulates and alters behavior, and powerful emotions can reinforce thoughts and thought processes, as well as make thoughts seem all the more urgent (Leahy, 2007). Although cognitions are targeted as key inroads to lasting change and behaviors are monitored as indicators of cognitive change and improvement, therapeutic change is predicated on eliciting and managing relevant emotional patterns. Emotions need to be activated in therapeutic work to gain access to emotionally charged cognitions. It is this activated state that allows the social worker to go beyond an abstract, cerebral exchange to actively work with the feeling–thinking linkages and to begin to foster different patterns not only of thinking and behaving, but of feelings (Neenan & Dryden, 2004).

Information Processing

At any given moment of our lives, we human beings are receiving large amounts of information. Often this information is complex, and it originates from multiple sources. To manage this constant exposure to massive amounts of information that come from within us as well as from our environment, we have developed elaborate thinking, feeling, and behavioral processes that enable us to screen out and ignore information that may not be useful or important at a given moment or in a particular situation (A. Beck, 2002). These filtering processes enable us not only to avoid being overwhelmed but also to focus—selectively attending to, interpreting and responding to information that is relevant and that makes is possible for us to progress toward meeting our needs and goals. How exactly is it possible that human beings can manage all the complex information we experience day in and day out and across the development of our life course? Cognitive-behavioral theory maintains that human beings have complex cognitive and affective structures (schemas) that allow us to manage the multiplicity and complexity of internal and external information in efficient and consistent ways. Although these structures generally function with impressive sophistication and utility, this information-processing system has its vulnerabilities. It is, for example, highly conservative and what some have characterized as "miserly"—inclined to search in a self-confirmatory manner for what is familiar, self-relevant, and anticipated, to overlook or resist information that is contradictory, to not see information that is beyond one's base of experience or imagination, and to extend minimal processing resources unless compelled to do so.

Here is an example of how information processing works. Think about the last time you went to a party. You probably had a conversation with a good friend while you were at the party. During your conversation, many other things were probably happening at the party, too. Other people were talking, and there may have been music playing. Let us say that your friend was telling you some important information about promotions at the place you both work and that being promoted is a long-standing career goal of yours. Let us also say that you came to the party hungry and had not made it to the buffet table before you ran into your friend. In addition to all the activity in the environment, you are also feeling ravenous. For you to attend to your friend's words (which may give you information to meet a life goal), it was also necessary to screen out all the information and activity going on around you at the party and within you internally. This screening process allowed you to focus on the conversation in such a way that you probably were not even aware that you were filtering out all this other information and activity. In fact, you were probably able to manage all this external and internal information smoothly and fairly easily and were also able to engage in this important conversation. Though shortly after this conversation ended, you probably began searching for the buffet table!

The task of attending to a conversation at a party is a fairly simple example of information processing. In fact, information processing occurs in an intricate, interconnected, and interdependent system of cognitive-affective-behavioral structures (A. Beck, 1996). These structures take in information, assign meaning, and evoke corresponding emotions, which all lead to behavioral responses in reaction to the information. Keep in mind that information processing occurs during every activity and behavior, from driving a car to playing basketball with friends to giving a presentation at work. Consider, too, ongoing activities and behaviors that occur over time, such as planning and taking a vacation, developing and completing a project at work, and parenting a child, just to name a few examples. Information processing is an operative part of every waking moment, sometimes functioning in a fairly automatic way (walking down the street, doing the laundry), sometimes in a more deliberate way that involves more explicit attention (hearing a child scream as one is walking down the street, coming across contraband material in your son's pants pocket as you do the wash).

Human beings have patterned and stable cognitive-affective information processes for all aspects of our lives and our personalities. On the one hand, the stability and consistency of these information-processing structures is adaptive, even essential, and facilitates human functioning in an efficient manner, conserving energy for needed times (Berlin, 2002; Macy, 2006). Consider the example of driving a car. Imagine if every time you drove your car you had to consciously think through *every* step and decision—all the mechanics of driving, from getting into the car to turning the steering wheel, as well as the vast attentional energy required to purposely examine every bit of visual, auditory, and tactile information one encounters along the way. It would take a long time to get to your destination, would be exhausting and stressful (given that one has to sustain a continuous level of high alert and highly active processing trivial environmental information), and might even increase your risk of an accident given that attentional focus is so diffuse and taxing, reaction time to truly significant information is impaired.

However, the stability and consistency of cognitive-affective structures can also cause problems. To the extent that an individual has, for example, schematic structures underlying core beliefs about the self and the world containing information or ideas that are dominantly negative, that person's expectancies, interpretations, feelings, and responses are going to be infused and directed by this dominantly negative content in a system that will resist challenge or change, as do all well-developed cognitive-affective structures (Nurius, 2008). These difficulties in thinking, feeling, and behaving will pose problems for the person in terms of getting needs met and pursuing life goals. Although the person may be fully aware that needs and goals are not being successfully met, the person may not understand why the problems exist because the underlying cognitive-affective-behavioral processes, which contain unhelpful information, are so efficient and automatic that the person is not aware of the problematic information (Mischel, 2007). Erroneous cognitive-affective structures tend to be self-perpetuating, as the act of processing information through a specific structure serves to reinforce the underlying content and the relative ease or accessibility of that structure for future processing. On the one hand, information processing that draws on predominantly healthy and adaptive cognitive-affective structures is key to human beings' capacity to survive and thrive in a complex world. On the other hand, information processing that draws on predominantly unhealthy and maladaptive cognitive-affective structures can cause serious problems that impair a person's capacity to survive and thrive.

Self-Regulation

Fortunately, as discussed earlier, our ability to think about our thinking (metacognition) gives us the capacity to become aware of our cognitive content and processes. With increased awareness of these generally automatic processes, we can then alter and replace problematic, inaccurate, and unhelpful beliefs and thoughts that underlie our problems in feeling and functioning. Although cognitive structures must be resistant to change to provide coherence and stability, they can be altered, modified, and replaced (J. Beck, 2011). By directing attention to and modifying problematic thoughts and underlying schemas that thwart our efforts to meet our needs and pursue our goals, we can also change and direct emotions and behaviors to better meet our needs and goals (Dobson & Dozois, 2010). As Berlin (2002) emphasizes, we humans are active agents in our own lives in the way we seek out, select, and manage information and experiences. Although we are constantly and consistently showered with information, we are not sponges simply soaking up information. We can also use our metacognitive capacity to think about our thinking to better direct our thoughts, feelings, and behaviors in ways that help us meet our needs and goals. This capacity to observe and reflect on our thinking, as well as our ability to direct our thoughts, feelings, and behaviors in ways that help us best meet our needs and goals, is termed self-regulation and is another basic principle of cognitive-behavioral theory.

Cognitive-behavioral theory views the person as an active agent in the construction of perceived reality and the social and psychological interchanges both among and within individuals. Beyond reacting to the world, we also dynamically search for, choose, and use information to construct our realities and make meaning in our lives, including our understandings of our self, our relationships, the world, and our future. Although much of the way that people are exercising their agency or influence in this regard resides beyond common awareness, cognitive-behavioral theory views our cognitive-affective-behavioral patterns as knowable, accessible, and modifiable. This theoretical premise is the cornerstone of cognitive-behavioral interventions, be they cognitive restructuring, coping skills training, emotional regulation, or other specific strategies.

Recall the example of the graduate student who received the unsatisfactory grade and thought to herself, "I am disappointed about this grade, but I can do better next time," and then headed off to the library; this is an illustration of self-regulation. Let's assume that both students had the abstract knowledge that academic performance can generally be improved through study, perseverance, and tutoring. One student had a core belief consistent with herself as being able to accomplish this connection, whereas the other did not. Clearly, the self-regulatory task for the student with a negative core belief is considerably more difficult than for the other student. Self-regulation for the former student would involve observing and reflecting on cognitive patterns (negative automatic thoughts, assumptions and rules, and core beliefs about her academic competence), feeling states (embarrassment, anxiety, disappointment), and behaviors (avoidance strategies) that are contributing to her problems and then undertaking activities to interrupt these patterns and work to invoke and reinforce new patterns. A number of specific strategies could be used to assist with this effort. However, central to the effort will be the incremental progress toward challenging the negative core belief and reinforcing a new positive belief structure and information-processing habits regarding her academic competence, the possibility of achieving success, and the "how-tos" and "what-ifs" for self-regulating through challenges and backslides along the way. Self-regulation often involves not only deliberate, explicit focus on changing beliefs and thought patterns, but also explicitly working to manage one's physiology (e.g., bodily reactions associated with anxiety, embarrassment), coping patterns, and mood.

What is noteworthy about the example of the positive belief student is how she automatically engaged in positive, helpful thinking patterns that supported behaviors that are adaptive for success in her academic goals. Part of what makes self-regulation difficult is this automaticity; both adaptive and problematic patterns are typically implicit and unscrutinized (Dunkley, Blankstein, & Segal, 2010). Experientially, it feels like "what is," a kind of truth or reality ("I'm just not good at this—never have been, never will be"). The theoretical premises underlying self-regulation essentially frame the client as a personal scientist. Embedded within an overarching social learning and psychoeducational framework, self-regulation entails an assumed ability, with assistance, for clients to (a) gain awareness of their heretofore unobserved and automatic patterns, (b) test the validity of their problematic beliefs and thoughts, and (c) collaborate with the counselor to modify these patterns (Neenan & Dryden, 2004). Although the process of self-regulation requires energy and overcoming an inherently conservative cognitive-affective-behavioral system, humans are also inherently motivated to understand, gain meaning, and be agentic in their own functioning—assets to the process of self-regulatory change. How this capacity can be used for therapeutic purposes is discussed in greater detail later in the chapter.

The Importance of Environment

Social work professionals frequently work from a biopsychosocial perspective and often use frameworks that emphasize the importance of the environment, such as person-in-environment perspective, the metatheory of systems, and the ecological framework. The emphasis on the individual client's interactions with various aspects of his or her environment (e.g., family, neighborhood, community, government) is critical for social work professionals because we conceptualize problems in human functioning in terms of disruptions and problems in our clients' environment as much as we conceptualize problems in human functioning as stemming from within the person. Because of this emphasis, social workers may wonder to what extent cognitive-behavioral theory is useful for social work practice. We have noted that cognitive-behavioral theory sees the individual as deeply and continuously embedded within complex social environments, with functioning a product of reciprocal relationships between persons and their environments.

Nonetheless, we have emphasized (as does much of the literature) the cognitive, affective, and behavioral processes that happen within the individual. It would be a mistake, however, to assume that cognitive-behavioral theory conceptualizes problems in human functioning as lying entirely within the individual. In fact, person-in-environment interactions are essential in how cognitive-behavioral theory understands problems in human functioning, as well as in how social workers use cognitive-behavioral interventions to address a client's problems. Neenan and Dryden (2004) emphasize a focus on correcting the *combination* of psychological and situational factors that are contributing to an individual's distress and working collaboratively with the client to understand how objectively unpleasant situations are experienced as well as how these may be exacerbated by how the client appraises or makes meaning of these situations in ways that impair his or her ability to cope with them.

Let us consider two ways in which a client's environmental milieu, which includes the client's socioeconomic and sociocultural context, come into play in a cognitive-behavioral theory perspective (Macy, 2006; Nurius, 2008). First, people's environment will inevitably play a considerable role in forming and presenting the opportunities, experiences, and information to which they have access. As a result, the characteristics of their environment will likely shape the thoughts, beliefs, and ideas that form the basis of people's information processing and capacity to self-regulate their thinking, feeling, and behaving. Patterned ways of responding typically derive from formative experiences with the social environment.

For example, a person who lives on the flat plains may never have the experience of downhill skiing because the geographic environment limits the person's opportunities to have this experience. Without mountains and considerable snow, a person may never learn to ski and thus will never develop cognitive-affective-behavioral processes for the activity of skiing. However, if this person has economic resources and can travel, then he or she may go to a snowy, mountainous geographical area on vacation, take skiing lessons, and subsequently become proficient at this activity. Again, the person's environmental realities—in this case, the fact that the person has economic resources—have provided the opportunity for the development of cognitive-affective-behavioral processes for the activity of skiing.

This is a fairly benign example of how a person's environmental context can shape cognitive-affective-behavioral processes. However, given the social work profession's emphasis on social change and social justice, the reader may wish to consider how deleterious aspects of a person's environment, for example, poverty, racism, and neighborhood crime, also impact a person's cognitive, affective, and behavioral functioning. As Berlin (2002) emphasizes, the opportunities to which human beings have access may limit their capacity to create alternative ways of seeing themselves, relationships, future, and the world.

Second, established cognitive-affective-behavioral patterns are often activated by the environmental context. A person's internal experience (thoughts, feelings, bodily sensations) also activate relevant cognitive-affective-behavioral systems. Think of your own thinking, feeling, and behaving processes when you find yourself hungry or sleepy. In the flow of everyday life, we are constantly experiencing thoughts and beliefs being activated and made momentarily salient and influential by the experiences, events, or situations we are encountering.

As an example, think back to our two graduate students who both received disappointing grades on their assignments. Let's consider the student who began to anxiously ruminate, leading to avoidance coping behaviors. Let's further imagine that this student found out right before class that his partner of 1 year decided to break up with him. As a result, of receiving these two pieces of bad news so close together, which are examples of external events, our student is feeling particularly discouraged, sad, and hopeless. But let's also imagine that on the way to a student bar with the intent to drown his sorrows a bit, the student runs into a good friend. This friend joins him for a beer but also provides a listening ear and a clear-eyed shoulder to cry on. As a result of this friend's help and support, our graduate student feels more hopeful and heartened. The next day, he joins the other graduate student for an all-day study session in the library. This illustration provides multiple examples—the assignment grade, the problem relationship, the supportive friend—of how the current environmental context can activate relevant cognitive content in a way that shapes a person's thinking, feeling, and behaving.

Clearly, the kinds of problems and contexts with which many social work clients are struggling carry many levels of stress, hurt, inequity, and impoverishment. No one change or support approach will be a panacea, and cognitive-behavioral theory lays no claim to being a vehicle to correct environmental oppression and ills. Rather, this theory illuminates the ways that individuals can gain awareness of both the stresses and resources of their environments as well as the ways they are engaging with that environment to exert influence in the best interest of their own needs, goals, and well-being. To accomplish this, practitioners who use cognitive-behavioral therapy, guided by an understanding of their client's environmental context, including developmental and cultural history, family and friend relationships, economic realities, and environmental factors, may well pair CBT with interventions targeted at external resources or problem contributors.

Advanced Theoretical Principles

Although the theoretical principles we selected as basic apply across the range of cognitive-behavioral intervention strategies, other theoretical constructs will be pertinent when more in-depth cognitive challenges and restructuring are involved. These may pertain, for example, to work with individuals who are suffering from serious depression or chronic maladaptive behaviors and deeply patterned interpersonal functioning problems. It is beyond the scope of this chapter to detail applications of CBT methods or to elaborate in depth. We select core beliefs and cognitive errors as two features of cognitive-behavioral theory that build on and go beyond underlying basic principles. Additional resources for recent summaries of advanced cognitive-behavioral theory and therapeutic techniques, with emphasis on schemas, the role of emotions, and complex cases include A. T. Beck (2005), Leahy et al. (2011), Persons (2008); Safran, Eubanks-Carter, and Muran (2010), and Young, Rych, Weinberger, and Beck (2008).

Core Beliefs

Earlier we introduced the construct of core beliefs as the deeper cognitive structures (typically assumed to be stored in memory as schemas and situationally activated) that carry the content—positive or negative—of what individuals believe to be fundamentally true about themselves and their world. In applying cognitive-behavioral therapy to human problems at a foundational level, the distinctions among different types of cognitions are not always critical. However, at an advanced level of understanding, knowing the distinctions among cognitions will help to refine and advance a clinician's assessment and intervention.

Core beliefs, also called *schemas*, are the underpinnings of information processing because they are the memory structures that store descriptive information, beliefs, judgments, and ideas about the self, relationships, the world, and the future (DeRubis et al., 2010; Martin & Young, 2010). Core beliefs take time and repeated use to become well-elaborated and overgeneralized. Once well-developed, they tend to be experienced as tacit truths and are stable, complex, and resistant to change. Core beliefs are storage repositories, but they are by no means static. These cognitive schemas are theorized to be the main drivers directing what we attend to, how we make interpretations, what feeling states are evoked, and what behaviors we are then predisposed to. In relation to information processing, the resilience of core beliefs is often adaptive and helpful because they allow us to process and to make sense of new information in efficient and consistent ways. However, when core beliefs contain unhelpful, inaccurate, or maladaptive information, they can cause considerable problems in thinking, feeling, and behaving.

Core beliefs generally comprise foundational information about the self, relationships, the world, and the future and are theorized to have had their initial formation in childhood and early adolescence. Cognitive-behavioral theory hypothesizes that formative life experiences develop and reinforce these central cognition structures because they were functional and useful during these key developmental periods. With repeated application colored by the conservative, self-confirmatory bias of the cognitive system, these schemas were maintained and strengthened, being used to interpret and assign meaning to new experiences that further elaborate them. To identify a client's fundamental core beliefs, which may hold problematic information for the client's current life, a comprehensive developmental assessment can provide information and insight to the contexts from which a client's core beliefs emerged and what functions they served at the time.

Because core beliefs so powerfully shape a person's thoughts, emotions, and behaviors, they are essential and critical targets for deep-level change from a cognitive-behavioral theory perspective (J. Beck, 1995; DeRubis et al., 2010). In fact, many who do research on and write about cognitive-behavioral theory hypothesize that lasting cognitive, affective, and behavioral change requires an alteration in problematic core beliefs. There are several challenges to altering core beliefs. One is the process of helping clients become aware of these underlying cognitive processes that contain negative, maladaptive information. Because these cognitive structures have become so embedded in a person's sense of identity, life philosophy, understanding of reality, and patterned way of being in the world, the intervention tasks of identifying, challenging, and disrupting habitual thought processes and then developing and reinforcing competing, more adaptive core beliefs require considerable skill and sustained commitment by client and counselor alike. However, core beliefs can be altered in a way that is helps clients to better address their needs and goals (Dowd, 2002; Leahy, 2003a).

Cognitive Errors

In our discussion of the mediational model we described how unhelpful thoughts and beliefs contribute to problems in feeling, behaving, and functioning. Some of this stems from maladaptive cognitive content, such as negative core beliefs. Some stems from maladaptive patterns of thinking or cognitive processes. Cognitive errors are one such set of problematic patterns of thinking stipulated in cognitive-behavioral theory. Cognitive errors can occur at various levels of thought, including core beliefs as well as surface thoughts. Thus, cognitive errors are found both within a person's fundamental beliefs about the self, relationships, the world, and the future, as well as in spontaneous, transitory thoughts. In some respects, the term cognitive error is a misnomer to the extent that it conveys a notion of some absolute reality or truth against which an individual's perceptions are gauged for accuracy. Consistent with the educational, learning approach of cognitive-behavioral therapy, the term "error" conveys a pattern of cognitive responding that can be reflected on as to its helpfulness to the person and modified to bring patterns of responding more in alignment with the individual's comfort and goals.

Within the general concept of cognitive errors there are several types of cognitive errors that have been broadly observed in clinical and empirical work, particularly those associated with emotional states. DeRubis et al. (2010) review common examples of cognitive error. *Magnifying problems* reflects the tendency to make one small event or problem bigger than it actually is or might fair-mindedly be viewed to be. For example, a person who is planning an once-in-a-lifetime, dream vacation and who runs into some problems as she tries to reserve a hotel room may think to herself, "The hotel I really wanted to stay at on my vacation is overbooked. This is awful! I might as well not go on the trip at all then, because it will ruin my whole vacation if I cannot stay at that hotel!" It is unlikely that this is the only suitable hotel in which our vacation planner can stay (although this would need to be explored). She may begin thinking about the entire vacation, not just the overbooked hotel, in a negative way, which in turn may lead to negative feelings, including disappointment, about her vacation plans. The fact that her thinking is focused on this one apparently minor factor is likely magnifying the problem in a way that colors her entire view of what was once her dream vacation. We all magnify (or minimize) at times. It becomes a problem, though, when there are repeated patterns—particularly when the individual is unaware of the polar extremes that are coloring her or his interpretations and feelings, patterns that lead to ongoing unhappiness and imbalance.

Another cognitive error, *jumping to conclusions,* reflects the tendency to come to a conclusion before gathering all the information, particularly conclusions that reinforce a negative existing belief. For example, a recent high school graduate who is looking for a job may think to himself, "It's been a day, and I have not heard back from my job interviewer, so I must not have gotten the job." Likely this thought will lead to other negative thoughts (e.g., "Why do I bother looking? No one will want to hire me") and negative feelings, such as frustration and despondency. These negative thoughts and feelings may in turn lead to unhelpful actions and behaviors (e.g., deciding to watch TV all day instead of sending follow-up e-mails to places where he sent his resume), which may also cause difficulty in his search for a job.

Discounting positives refers to the propensity to concentrate on negative experiences or aspects of a situation rather than the positive experiences or aspects. For example, a college instructor received many positive reviews from students about his teaching, but he can only focus on the few negative comments, possibly dismissing the positives as naive perspectives whereas the negatives show "the real truth" about his teaching.

Overgeneralizations reflect the inclination to view one negative experience as the rule (e.g., "I asked a guy out once, but he said no. So I will never ask another guy out because they all will say no to me"); this is likely accompanied by affective states like embarrassment and a sense of hopelessness about this changing.

Mind reading takes form through believing we know what other people are thinking, believing, and feeling, irrespective of whether we have any information in this regard. A person who is engaging in this cognitive error may think to herself, "My supervisor did not speak to me in the hall when she passed me! That's not like her. I bet she is thinking of including me in the next round of layoffs and does not want to speak me." There could be many reasons why this person's supervisor did not stop to say hello. She may have been busy or distracted. However, a person who is engaged in one cognitive error may also tend to disregard any information that disconfirms the unhelpful thought and instead focus only on thoughts and feelings that support his or her unhelpful belief. Unfortunately, as the mediational model posits, cognitive errors generally lead to difficult, negative emotions, as well as unhelpful and maladaptive actions and behaviors.

Dobson and Dozois (2010) list other forms of cognitive error: *All-or-nothing thinking* segments experiences into two, often extreme or reductionistic, categories (e.g., flawless or defective). In *fortune-telling,* one's beliefs and/or feelings about the future are how things will be, discounting or ignoring other possibilities. *Emotional reasoning* is perceiving things to be true on the basis of one's feelings; if something "feels true" (e.g., is consistent with how one is feeling about oneself or others), this is evidence of its truth. Clients who make *"should"* statements blur duty and desire; they frame events in evaluative "should" terms (should have done; not done) when "would like to have done/not done" is more accurate. *Labeling* is applying a label to describe a behavior, then ascribing other meanings that the label carries (e.g., "I'm a 'bad mother' for losing my patience with my child. Bad mothers are negligent, unkind, and undeserving of their children."). *Inappropriate blaming* is a restrictive view of events that funnels into an overly narrow blaming stance (e.g., using hindsight to judge what should have been done even if that could not have been known at the time; discounting others' contributions to a problem or mitigating factors).

As you are reading about these different types of cognitive errors, it may occur to you that we human beings frequently engage in many of these types of problematic thinking and unhelpful beliefs on a regular basis. In fact, from a cognitive-behavioral theory perspective, all human beings are prone to thinking in ways that do not always help us to meet our needs and to reach our goals and to think in ways that can cause problems for us. Fortunately, as we emphasized in our discussion of the basic theoretical principles of cognitive-behavioral theory, human beings can also think about their thinking and change their thoughts, beliefs, and ways of thinking. As a result of this capacity, we are not necessarily stuck with our unhelpful, problematic, and maladaptive thoughts and beliefs. As human beings use their capacity to reflect on problems in their thinking, they can also change their thoughts and beliefs to be helpful and adaptive. In our discussion of the relevance of cognitive-behavioral theory for social work practice, we discuss how practitioners can use specific cognitive-behavioral therapy techniques to help clients change their thinking to support adaptive ways of thinking, feeling, and behaving.

Recent Theoretical Developments

Over the past decade there have been several substantial developments. Some have characterized these as third-generation or third-order developments, following first-generation traditional behavioral therapy and second-generation behavioral therapies that integrated cognitive science (i.e., cognitive-behavioral therapy). These new directions embrace concepts such as acceptance, dialectics, spirituality, relationship, and mindfulness (Arch & Craske, 2009; Hayes, Follette, & Linehan, 2004). This third generation of therapy has been defined in the following way (Hayes, 2004b, cited in Hayes, 2004a, p. 6):

> Grounded in an empirical, principle-focused approach, the third wave of behavioral and cognitive therapy is particularly sensitive to context and functions of the psychological phenomena, not just their form, and, thus tends to emphasize contextual and experiential change strategies in addition to more direct and didactic ones. These treatments tend to see the construction of broad, flexible, and effective repertoires over an elimination approach to narrowly defined problems, and to emphasize the relevance of the issues they examine for clinicians as well as clients. The third wave reformulates and resynthesizes previous generations of behavioral and cognitive therapy and carries them forward into questions, issues, and domains previously addressed primarily by other traditions, in hopes of improving both understanding and outcomes.

Orsillo, Roemer, Lerner, and Tull (2004) provide an overview of developments in and beyond traditional CBT, particularly related to anxiety disorders. They acknowledge the important evidence base supporting CBT (albeit with limitations) as well as concerns that most individuals receiving community-based psychotherapy do not receive empirically supported forms of intervention. Modern learning theory has pointed to the importance of personal meaning both in how problematic symptoms (such as anxiety) arise as well as methods to interrupt dysfunctional patterns of cognitive and emotional responding, such as panic. Personal meaning points to the variability in how similar events can hold very different connotations and significance for different people. This strain of theorizing points to ways to build on techniques such as exposure therapy—for example, through assessing meaning and context in designing treatment—to better incorporate different emotionally charged meanings and life conditions that may otherwise impede therapeutic efforts. This growing attention to variation in personal meaning may provide important inroads for appreciating cultural diversity in underlying beliefs, values, expectations, and spiritual or existential philosophy as well as variation in how predictable or controllable any given event may be and the perceived implications of disturbing events for one's fundamental identity and worth.

Acceptance-based methods are a new wave of CBT-derived clinical approaches that explicitly address treatment impediments, such as clients' fear and avoidance of internal experiences. These emerging methods address a critical clinical dilemma. Avoidance of deeply distressing thoughts and feelings (such as those associated with trauma) is associated with later increased distress and symptom severity (Gilboa-Schechtman & Foa, 2001) and may incline some clients to avoid or refuse traditional CBT interventions and/or increase their risk of dropping out of treatment. Acceptance and commitment therapy, one such third-wave outgrowth, targets experiential avoidance and increasing acceptance. Experiential acceptance is defined as "willingness to experience internal events, such as thoughts, feelings, memories, and physiological reactions, in order to participate in experiences that are deemed important and meaningful" (Orsillo et al., 2004, p. 76). Similar emphasis on experiential acceptance is also evident in dialectical behavior therapy (Dimeff & Koerner, 2007; Linehan, 1993), integrative behavioral couple therapy (Christensen et al., 2004), and mindfulness-based cognitive therapy (Segal, Williams, & Teasdale, 2002) and mindfulness-based stress reduction (Roth & Calle-Mesa, 2006). Acceptance-based approaches work to assist individuals to be able to tolerate exposure to thoughts and feelings that are highly aversive and uncomfortable to them, moving to the capacity to observe both external and internal stimuli with an openness to acceptance rather than attempts to judge, flee, avoid, or change them (Segal et al., 2002).

Although acceptance-based methods are similar in several ways to CBT methods, the former emphasizes core values and quality of life, commitment to actions likely to help actualize these values and goals, metacognitive awareness that helps one observe distressing internal events more neutrally, a shift from changing thought content to changing one's relationship to one's own internal responding, and concern that attempts to directly control internal responses will more likely foster problem maintenance than resolution (Orsillo et al., 2004). Mindfulness practice is gaining supportive evidence (Baer, 2006; Bowen, Chawla, & Marlatt, 2011; Shapiro & Carlson, 2009) as an acceptance technique for augmenting tolerance of one's negative affect and cognition, fostering changes in attitude about one's internal events, ability to self-monitor and manage thoughts and feelings that are highly aversive, and facilitating relaxation

(Orsillo et al., 2004). However, evidence is as yet preliminary. How these techniques function is not yet clearly established, nor has there been sufficient comparative analysis (e.g., to discern whether acceptance-based approaches significantly extend the effectiveness of CBT theories and interventions). Nonetheless, theoretical and clinical work is under way (e.g., Roemer & Orsillo, 2009) to better specify how this spiritual tradition fits into current theory and clinical methods.

Relevance to Social Work Practice

Consistent with the mediational model, a core emphasis in cognitive-behavioral interventions is on changing cognitions to produce and sustain change in emotional distress and maladaptive behavior patterns. Frequently, these therapies are applied in a fairly specific problem-focused manner within relatively limited time frames (although more in-depth schema-based change involves more extensive therapeutic effort). In addition, these therapies aim for well-delineated goals as outcomes, typically including behavioral evidence. For example, a person is behaviorally functioning in a manner more in line with change goals such as less depressed, more adaptive coping, more effective problem solving. As a result of these emphases, cognitive-behavioral therapies are particularly relevant for today's practice in many areas of human service and across a variety of problems. In addition to being required to use evidence-based practices, many human service providers are also struggling with diminished resources and frequently being asked to serve more people in efficient ways. In this section we illustrate specific ways in which cognitive-behavioral theories and therapies can be used in social work practice.

Uses in Assessment

Because problematic thoughts sustain a client's intrapersonal and interpersonal problems, practitioners are applying CBT work to identify relevant unhelpful and maladaptive cognitions, both surface thoughts and core beliefs (DeRubis et al., 2010). However, as discussed earlier, cognitive content and processes are often not realized or easily recognized by the client. This is particularly the case for thoughts that are part of clients' core beliefs. That is, clients may be more aware of their negative automatic thoughts, but they are less likely aware of the core beliefs that underlie these automatic thoughts and thought processes. For example, few clients will say to a practitioner something like, "I have a view of myself, my relationships, and the world that is fundamentally negative, and it is causing me serious problems." Rather, in a first meeting with a practitioner, clients are more likely to describe a presenting problem in terms of their difficult and negative feelings or in terms of the interpersonal problems they are experiencing (Macy, 2006). As a result, practitioners using cognitive-behavioral therapy need to use strategies to identify the cognitive activity that is most related to the client's presenting problem. We present several of these strategies.

Strategies for Identifying Cognitive Content

Cognitive-behavioral therapy is predicated on the educational premise that the more clients understand the basic logic behind the model, the better positioned they will be to incorporate these strategies into their own repertoire. This will give clients the ability to step outside patterns that are troubling to them to assess the "how come" questions, consider their options, and gain skills that they can apply to this and future problems in functioning. Thus, many cognitive-behavioral assessment strategies can be used both in meetings between practitioner and client as well as outside formal sessions. Most assessment strategies can also be used in a variety of settings: in a practitioner's office, during a home visit, or in a situation or setting that is part of the client's presenting problem (e.g., in a work setting if the client is having difficulty there). These strategies may need to be appropriately adapted to different settings and clients.

One cognitive assessment strategy entails asking a client to *think aloud* during a task, situation, or role-play (Dunkley et al., 2010). In this strategy, the client is encouraged to report and describe any thought, idea, or belief in order to identify cognitive content that is related to the presenting problem or difficulty. To facilitate activation of relevant cognitive structures, the client is coached to enact this exercise in a task, situation, or context that is related to the presenting problem or is causing the client distress. For example, if a client presents with problems in his or her role as a parent, a practitioner can have the client role-play an activity that is related to this problem (e.g., helping the child with homework). During the role-play, the client will report thoughts, beliefs, and ideas that generally happen when engaged in this activity. The practitioner may need to prompt the client to report and describe these ideas and thoughts, and the practitioner may want to record the think-aloud ideas in writing to obtain all the information elicited by the client. This kind of technique generally begins with negative automatic thoughts, progressing to underlying assumptions and rules, and, if needed, identifying negative core beliefs (see Leahy, 2003a; Neenan & Dryden, 2004, for elaboration).

Another broadly applied cognitive assessment strategy is *self-monitoring* (Cormier et al., in press; DeRubis et al., 2010). One type of self-monitoring is the *thought record log*, in which the client is asked to record ideas, thoughts, and beliefs that occur during a specific activity, in a certain situation, or over a certain period of time (J. Beck, 2011). Or the practitioner can have the client record thoughts in relation to a specific activity or time. For example, a client who has a presenting problem of distressing anxiety during public speaking and who also must frequently speak publicly might be asked to record his thoughts while preparing to speak and then immediately after speaking. Information from this client's thought record log will provide helpful information to the practitioner who is conceptualizing the client's case.

Another example of self-monitoring is *thought listing* (Dunkley et al., 2010). In this exercise, the client is asked to list any thoughts he or she may have had during an experience related to the presenting problem or during a distressing situation, either through enactment methods in a formal helping session or in the context of relevant experiences outside of formal sessions. For example, a practitioner may ask a client who is having difficulty at work to take a few minutes to record all her thoughts about work the next time she is feeling particularly anxious or distressed there, bringing these notes in for examination with the social worker.

Information about relevant cognitive content gathered outside of client-worker meetings can be particularly informative, because cognition patterns of responding are typically activated by particular situations, experiences, contexts, activities, and mood states. Visualization, guided imagery, role-play, and other invoking strategies can often be significantly supplemented by monitoring in relevant situations as these emerge. This reflects another dimension of cognitive-behavioral theory highly relevant to social work: careful attention to patterned interchanges between environmental factors and cognitive-affective-behavioral configurations related to the client's presenting problem. As discussed earlier, cognitions do not occur without a context or stimulus; both are formative in a client's history and operative in clients' present-day habits and conditions. Cognitive-behavioral theory is influenced by social psychological findings regarding the ongoing self-social interface (Nurius, 1991, 2008); thus the practitioner will pay attention to clients' life development, including their current stage of life development as well as their life developmental history (Dobson & Dozois, 2010). However, the focus of change efforts is more likely to be anchored in the present, examining and working to reconstruct ways that current cognitive activity embedded in current environmental conditions are serving to sustain problematic patterns.

Working Hypothesis

Cognitive-behavioral theory is generally undertaken within an experimental frame of reasoning. That is, as the practitioner is identifying the cognitive content relating to the client's present problem, the practitioner will also begin to develop and eventually refine a theory of the client's presenting problem. This theory serves as a tentative working hypothesis of the problem and is the basis for the treatment plan and interventions with the client. In a working hypothesis, the practitioner will specify the relevant events, situations, or activities that activate the problematic core beliefs, which give rise to the unhelpful automatic thoughts and assumptions, which are followed by consonant emotional responding and maladaptive behaviors (Persons & Davidson, 2010). In short, this working hypothesis strives to operationalize on a case-by-case basis the mediational model components and how these appear to be functioning in producing outcomes distressing to the client. Thus, identifying the underlying core beliefs that may be causing the presenting problem, as well as what internal or external stimuli appear salient and activate the unhelpful beliefs, is critical and forms the basis of the working hypothesis (DeRubis et al., 2010; Persons, 2008). The working hypothesis is typically developed in an educational, collaborative manner with the client—assessing how the counselor's picture fits with the client's reported experiences and patterns—and is then used to target intervention efforts.

Uses in Intervention

Guided by this working theory, the practitioner, together with the client, use cognitive-behavioral theory to articulate interventions designed to modify a client's unhelpful and problematic cognitions and to develop and reinforce adaptive and beneficial cognitive-affective-behavioral patterns. As discussed throughout this chapter, all human beings have this capacity to reflect on and alter their thinking. However, not all of us realize that we can develop these skills or know how to effectively apply these cognitive change skills. In this section, we review selected specific cognitive-behavioral intervention strategies that practitioners can use to help clients with their presenting problem.

Cognitive-Behavioral Intervention Principles

Cognitive-behavioral therapeutic interventions rely on two important principles. The first principle emphasizes the importance for clients, as well as practitioners, to understand the fundamentals of the mediational model and how thoughts are seen to interact with and influence feelings and behaviors (Dobson & Dozois, 2010). This reflects a transparent, educational orientation intended to assist clients to apply self-monitoring to gain awareness of their unique patterns, to reflectively assess dimensions of (mal)adaptiveness, to articulate and undertake change goals, and to marshal supports to reinforce and sustain desired changes in content and process. Toward these ends, a cognitive-behavioral practitioner will frequently use psychoeducational tools and strategies to teach clients about the fundamentals of the mediational model.

The second fundamental principle of cognitive-behavioral interventions is the importance of collaboration between practitioner and client (J. S. Beck, 2011; Cormier et al., in press; Dobson & Dozois, 2010). Cognitive-behavioral interventions maintain that both the practitioner and the client bring expertise to the working, therapeutic relationship. Practitioners understand cognitive-behavioral theory and know how to create change in the lives of their clients. However, just as important to the success of cognitive therapy, clients bring their expertise about their thought content, ways of thinking, and meaning making. Without clients' information about their internal thought processes, the practitioner cannot successfully apply the cognitive-behavioral theory to the presenting problem. Because of this, the success of cognitive-behavioral therapy replies on both the positive nature of the working relationship and the client's level of participation during the change process (Leahy, 2008). Thus, it is critical that clients are active in the cognitive-behavioral interventions and the change process.

Homework outside of meetings between the client and practitioner is frequently part of cognitive-behavioral interventions as one means to gather contextual information relevant to activating the problematic patterns and to practice the cognitive-behavioral change skills that clients are learning in formal sessions (J. S. Beck, 2011; Cormier et al., in press; DeRubis et al., 2010). One way the practitioner can help foster success with these application activities is to break the homework activities down into small, achievable parts (Kazantzis, Deane, Ronan, & L'Abate, 2005). The practitioner may also want to practice homework activities with clients or to coach clients through the activities during meetings to make certain the clients fully understand and are able to carry out the assignments. Last, it is important for practitioners to help clients think through barriers to carrying out the homework activities, as well as ways to work around these barriers. Although it is critical for clients to be active participants in the cognitive-behavioral change process both inside and outside of therapeutic meetings, it is also critical for the practitioner to fully prepare clients to be successful in their efforts.

These principles combine to support empowerment outcomes. At the end of a successful collaborative working relationship between the client and practitioner, and with the resolution of the presenting problem, the client will have developed a new set of cognitive-behavioral change skills that will enable him or her to adaptively and effectively manage new problems. Once clients learn how to apply cognitive and behavioral change skills to one set of life problems, they are better positioned to generalize these skills to other problems in their life and to future problems.

Strategies for Cognitive Change

Dobson and Dozois (2010) distinguish three primary types of cognitive-behavioral therapies: coping skills therapies, problem-solving therapies, and cognitive restructuring therapies. Briefly, coping skills therapies aim to help clients more effectively manage biopsychosocial stressors and problems through the development and enhancement of coping skills. Problem-solving therapies aim to help clients find and create new strategies, skills, and resources to address their presenting problems. Cognitive restructuring therapies aim to create cognitive change to ameliorate clients' presenting problem (Cormier et al., in press). Although these three cognitive-behavioral therapies entail specific strategies that distinguish them from one another, each involves some degree of cognitive restructuring. As a result, we focus our discussion of intervention strategies on cognitive restructuring.

A key intervention strategy in cognitive restructuring involves asking clients to test the validity of their thoughts and beliefs, including both automatic thoughts and core beliefs. In considering the validity of a thought or belief, the client is asked to carefully assess whether the thought or belief is accurate, a fact, the truth, and meaningful. Frequently, problematic thoughts and beliefs rest on incomplete or distorted perceptions of relevant contributors and situational dynamics, may not be meaningful, or are not wholly accurate. Helping clients see how their unhelpful beliefs reflect biases or inaccuracies (such as confirming negative expectancies and discounting contradictory evidence) or are not meaningful is the beginning to cognitive change and is an important step in cognitive restructuring. One example of a specific intervention strategy is the downward arrow technique (Neenan & Dryden, 2004). In this technique the practitioner uses a series of questions following the client's answers. For example, consider a client who has come to a practitioner because of difficulty with public speaking. The practitioner asks the client, "What is the worst thing possible that could happen to you while you are giving a talk in front of people?" The client tells the practitioner, "I get so anxious up there in front of everyone because I am so afraid that I'll misspeak and make a complete fool out of myself." The practitioner responds to the client with another question, such as, "Well, let's say your worst fears came true. What would that mean to you?" This question may help the client begin to see that the consequences of misspeaking may not be quite as bad as she thinks, with subsequent questions helping to illuminate underlying beliefs about negative outcomes and their implications.

Dobson and Dozois (2010) recommend that practitioners help clients distance themselves from unhelpful and problematic thoughts so they can identify, tolerate, and begin the process of challenging these seeming truths. This process of distancing can help the client examine the thoughts or beliefs in a more objective light. For example, in cognitive restructuring clients can be encouraged to take on the role of scientist or private detective with their thoughts and ways of thinking. In this role, the client will be looking for evidence to support or disconfirm the thought or belief. If in this process the client finds that there is little support for the thought or belief, the client may also begin to see the fallibility of the belief and the possibility of constructing alternatives.

Cognitive restructuring interventions also help create helpful, positive, and adaptive cognitions to replace the unhelpful cognitions (Cormier et al., in press). Cognitive change is more likely to be successful and clients are less likely to slip back into unhelpful ways of thinking when armed with constructive, well-elaborated, and sustainable alternative response patterns. Again, let us consider the client who has difficulty with public speaking and has made progress in challenging her catastrophizing core beliefs and automatic thoughts. Toward developing positive, helpful thoughts about her public speaking, the practitioner may ask the client about a time in her past when she experienced success in a public presentation or, that failing, identify the kinds of thoughts she imagines a comfortable speaker would have in that context. Once the success is identified (e.g., "I was very anxious and nervous, but I kept thinking that if I kept taking a deep breath and focused on how well I really knew this material, I could get through it okay"), the practitioner may build on this to coach and encourage the client to engage in positive self-talk during role-plays, exercises, and her next speaking engagement, guiding development of positive thoughts and core self-messages meaningful to the client.

Likewise, the practitioner might couple this positive self-talk intervention with a behavioral intervention that emphasizes teaching the client relaxation breathing skills, which is an example of a coping skills strategy. In combination, the mitigation of the client's negative beliefs ("I make a complete fool of myself every time I speak in public"), with the development of positive thoughts ("I have given other talks and made it through them just fine. I can make it through this one"), and the use of self-monitored self-talk, the client and practitioner have worked together to create a comprehensive cognitive restructuring intervention to address the client's presenting problem.

Changing Core Beliefs

Although the cognitive change intervention strategies just described apply to automatic core beliefs as well as surface thoughts, practitioners may find it more challenging to restructure clients' core beliefs relative to their automatic thoughts. Dowd (2002) posits that core beliefs are more stable and less alterable because they are long-standing and were once functional and adaptive (and they may continue to be adaptive and functional in other aspects of the client's life). As a result, clients may be unwilling to consider and alter these beliefs. Berlin (2002) gives this apparent unwillingness a slightly different slant. She states that this unwillingness may be "an effort to preserve the integrity of continuous identity and a coherent life story" (p. 15). Thus, practitioners should carefully assess and consider problematic core beliefs in their efforts to change them, because unhelpful and problematic core beliefs may continue to give the client a sense of self and identity.

Still, CBT literature often emphasizes the importance of changing problematic core beliefs if these appear to be causing problems in multiple areas of a client's life or if other forms of skill development (such as coping or problem solving) will be insufficient. The practitioner may work with a client to change automatic thoughts at one time point, only to find a few months later that the client continues to struggle with the same presenting problem. A reoccurrence of a presenting problem suggests that an underlying core belief requires modification and restructuring. In a related vein, when clients and practitioners are successful in changing core beliefs to be more adaptive and helpful, clients will be provided with a kind of inoculation against future problems and difficulties because they have at their disposal a set of helpful, adaptive core beliefs that will aid them in facing future problems and challenges (Cormier et al., in press). Consistent with the cognitive restructuring interventions presented earlier, A. Beck (1996) maintains that there are three ways to change core beliefs: neutralize them, modify them, or create more adaptive core beliefs that inhibit and mitigate the maladaptive core beliefs. Thus, the same cognitive restructuring interventions that work effectively with automatic thoughts will also work on core beliefs. However, practitioners must realize and account for the fact that the foundational nature of core beliefs requires careful thought and active work on the part of both the client and the practitioner.

Adapting Intervention Strategies

Although the fundamental elements of cognitive-behavioral interventions can be successfully used to address a range of biopsychosocial problems across different groups of people, it is critical that these interventions be appropriately adapted to clients' sociocultural, socioeconomic context and gender identity, cognitive development, and physical capacities and abilities. As discussed earlier in this chapter, cognitive-behavioral theory maintains that cognitive-affective-behavioral processes are similar across human beings. However, the content within the cognitive-affective-behavioral processes is specific, unique, and personal to the individual. An individual's cognitive content is, in part, derived from the individual's cultural heritage and background, socioeconomic status, and the political realities of his or her existence, as well as his or her life history and life experiences. As a result, by adapting cognitive-behavioral interventions to the individual client's background, life history, and experiences, the practitioner is helping to ensure the meaningfulness and ultimately the effectiveness of the interventions for that individual client.

Fortunately, research provides some guidance on how to adapt cognitive-behavioral intervention strategies to be appropriate for various people (Voss Horrell, 2008). For example, in their assessment of a client's presenting problem, it is important for practitioners to consider cognitions related to the presenting problem; in their formulation of a working hypothesis, they should consider how social and cultural factors may make a problem worse. As Berlin (2002, p. 149) states, "In the midst of all the other difficulties (i.e., social problems), the overwhelmed individual is less able to think his or her way through problems." Thus practitioners should assess and recognize the client's capacity to think through his or her problem in the face of the social problem with which the client may be struggling. Practitioners should also consider how social and environmental factors may limit a client's ability to participate in the interventions and the change processes (Organista, 1995), as well as ways to assist clients to surmount barriers to their participation. Although for the most part, cognitive-behavioral change interventions emphasize intrapersonal change, some therapists also emphasize the importance of environment change. Practitioners who are able to help clients with changes to their environment, context, and situations as well as cognitive-behavioral changes may be the most effective change agents relative to practitioners who focus solely on cognitive-behavioral change. Changes to an individual's environment, context, or situation will likely provide new experiences and new ways of seeing the self, the world, and the future. Moreover, significant reductions in environmental and social stressors will also likely help clients think their way through and out of a problem.

Practitioners should carefully adapt their language when teaching clients cognitive-behavioral theory and the mediational model. For example, practitioners should use terms that do not discount the client's life experiences or reinforce marginalization, such as using the terms *rational* and *irrational* when describing a client's thoughts and thought processing. (Consider the terms we have used throughout the chapter to describe maladaptive cognitions, such as *problematic* and *unhelpful*.) Practitioners should also avoid jargon in their work with clients. As much as possible, practitioners should adapt the language used in cognitive-behavioral change interventions to the client's primary language, age, educational level, and hearing, seeing, and reading abilities. Practitioners should also strive to adapt cognitive-behavioral intervention strategies to the client's values and to address issues of discrimination and marginalization in the intervention work together, when appropriate (Carter, Sbrocco, Gore, Marin, & Lewis, 2003; Koh et al., 2002). Practitioners may need to consult and collaborate with others informed about a client group to better understand the situational and social problems with which their clients are struggling, as well as the internal meaning making in which their clients are engaged.

Evidence-Based Foundations

One reason for the advancement and expansion of CBT has been the rapidly growing body of empirical findings indicative of effective outcomes (Tolin, in press). The base of original research testing CBT outcomes is far too extensive to report here. However, a number of sources have summarized research outcomes across a range of clinical problems (Cormier et al., in press; Dobson, 2010; Nurius & Green, in press; O'Donohue & Fisher, 2009; Prochaska & Norcross, 2010; Simos, 2009): affective disorders (depression, anger, anxiety, panic, trauma, and phobia), addictions (substance abuse, gambling, smoking), obsessive-compulsive disorders, relationship problems (couples treatment, parenting, social ineffectiveness, assertion), self-esteem issues, problem-solving skill needs, stress management and coping skills, and medical conditions (pain, epilepsy, cancer, asthma).

As previously noted, various forms of CBT have been applied with diverse client populations, across a wide age range, for both sexes, for gender-related issues, and with cultural and racial minorities. Cormier et al. (in press) and Hays and Iwamasa (2006) review some of these findings, indicating a generally positive record among published studies. However, these reviews and others also highlight the importance of explicit attention to cultural factors, at times indicating adaptations of CBT techniques (see Hays, 2008, for recommendations for cultural adaptation of cognitive-behavioral methods). Advances both in clinical research with diverse populations and in theorizing that better articulates cognitive-cultural and transactional models (e.g., DiMaggio, 2002; Whaley & Davis, 2007) are critical sources of input to guide cognitive-behavioral theory and method refinement for effectiveness.

The growing pressures to use interventions established as empirically supported have combined with calls to distill key targets of change for particular problems and pressures to maximize cost and time efficiency to encourage research examining brief CBT. Although there are as yet no formal norms for what constitutes brief CBT, the generally recognized standard is treatment consisting of fewer than 10 sessions (in contrast to the more typical 10- to 20-session range for standard CBT treatment; Key & Craske, 2002). Brief CBT is generally targeted to a specified presenting problem and may be offered in a typical time sequence or in massed delivery, such as condensed over a 7- to 10-day period. Brief CBT may either reduce the amount of materials generally offered in standard CBT or may rely to a greater extent on the client taking a highly active role beyond time with the therapist, using materials such as workbooks, books, audiotapes, or computer programs.

Similar to standard CBT, brief CBT has been effective for depression, anxiety, and phobia-related disorders (Beck & Bieling, 2004). Although the general body of research is favorable with respect to both CBT and brief CBT, as with many other therapies there remain gaps in our evidence base. For example, findings are incomplete as to which individual differences (e.g., attitudes toward treatment, chronicity and/or severity of problem, problem type) affect treatment outcome under what treatment conditions (Hazlett-Stevens & Craske, 2002). Thus far, evidence supporting effectiveness centers primarily on problems that are relatively circumscribed, with well-specified targets for change. However, to date there are few unconfounded comparisons between standard and brief CBT. Thus, further investigation is needed to ascertain the individuals and conditions under which brief CBT appears to be a well-suited choice over standard CBT.

Critiques of This Approach

Given the fuzzy definitional boundaries between behavior therapy, cognitive therapy, and cognitive-behavioral therapy, critiques are similarly indistinct. It is not always clear to what exactly critics are referring. Moreover, critiques of CBT, as with all clinical theories, vary somewhat as a function of the theoretical lens of the analyst. Some are uneasy with the highly systematic and perceived "mechanistic" characteristics inherited from behavior therapy, whereas others see that it is the behavioral techniques more than the focus on what are seen as ill-defined cognitions that carry the load of therapeutic change. Some find the focus on cognitions to be overly rationalistic and/or judgmental (e.g., regarding the irrationality of some cognitive patterns). Others argue that cognitive/behavioral therapy is too simplistic, basically reflects positive thinking, delivers little more than symptom relief, and is inattentive to client history or to dimensions of the therapeutic relationship. Not surprisingly, others rebuke such claims (see Neenan & Dryden, 2004; Prochaska & Norcross, 2010, for discussions).

Some are concerned by what they see as insufficient attention to contextual factors in terms of socializing forces such as gender, sexual identity mores, and culture, as well as the more direct effects of external contingencies (e.g., poverty, oppression) that do not have to "go through the head" to be felt and do damage to people (Kantrowitz & Ballou, 1992). Hays (1995) notes, for example, that some of the underlying tenets of CBT may not be well-suited for all clients, for example, emphasis on self-control, greater focus on an individual's thoughts relative to environmental factors that may be contributors to the root problems, challenging beliefs or thoughts that are seen as underlying client problems yet also reflect cultural or other personal values. On the other hand, strengths of cognitive-behavioral theory relative to use with culturally diverse people include its focus on individual uniqueness, empowerment and collaborative practice, conscious processes and specific events and behaviors, and recognition of variability in individual meaning and histories that are shaping current experience (Muroff, 2007). Recognition of need is incrementally being met with therapeutic adaptations and direct tests. Goodheart (2006) illustrates the attention to diversity factors and context and the blending of concepts from cognitive-behavioral therapy and other approaches.

Other critiques illuminate gaps and weaknesses in testing the theoretical base of CBT. The theorized cognitive process underpinnings have not yet been thoroughly empirically modeled or tested as to their causative functions in producing change. Cognitive units such as schemas, associative networks, belief and expectancy systems, and priming functions are difficult to directly tap and test. In reviewing empirical shortcomings, Orsillo et al. (2004) and Hayes (2004a) review research highlighting the following: (a) insufficient demonstration of how irrational cognitions are acquired, who acquires them, and how they can be measured independent of the associated emotions, such as fear or anger; (b) lack of direct evidence to support the theoretical premise that cognition not only predicts but causes behavior; (c) findings of bidirectionality between cognitions and emotions, which raises questions as to temporal, causal processes; (d) the fact that clinical improvement has been observed with CBT before the key theorized features have been fully implemented; (e) component analysis that has been equivocal as to the additive benefits of cognitive interventions; and (f) changes in cognitive mediators, which are the presumed agents of change, that do not always explain outcomes of CBT. Increasing pressure to develop innovative theory and to secure outcomes evidence across groups or subpopulations is, in some cases, leading to new models that diverge from standard CBT theory and methods.

There are also issues related to the match of CBT with client, problem, and therapist characteristics. This is particularly salient with short-form or abbreviated versions of CBT. Brief CBT is based on assumptions that a target for change is well-defined and circumscribed and that the client is motivated, ready to undertake focused cognitive and behavioral changes, and capable of active engagement in activities in and between intervention sessions (Beck & Bieling, 2004). However, in many cases, neither the problem nor the client is consistent with these assumptions, which raises serious questions about the appropriateness of brief CBT in these instances

(Hazlett-Stevens & Craske, 2002). In a related vein, there needs to be good match with therapist characteristics. For example, therapists need a high level of skill in effecting change in a limited time, positive expectancies, an ability to work in a highly targeted manner, and openness to outcomes being framed more in terms of teaching skills than in full symptom resolution (Key & Craske, 2002).

These issues are by no means unique to CBT. In many respects, they reflect the ongoing nature of advances in social science theory, clinical application, and changing consciousness and value perspectives that characterize society at large as well as clinical and research communities. Examples include assertions of the need for greater contextualism, the impact of postmodern and postcolonial theories, the need for inclusion of cultural diversity factors, and calls for multilevel theorizing that links individual with structural forces toward problem development and effective interventions—which bring challenging forces to bear on all practice-related theories. Part of what has characterized CBT theory is its elasticity. That is, the essential cognitive paradigm has been applied and adapted to a remarkably broad array of clinical problems.

As both Hayes et al. (2004) and Scrimali and Grimaldi (2004) illustrate, there is an ongoing flow to clinical and scientific clinical movements that illuminates limitations in conjunction with new possibilities. Cognitive-behavioral theory reflects the ebb and flow of research findings; theoretical challenges and innovations; and pragmatic, "on the ground" clinical implementation feedback. As more is being learned about the complex systems that contribute to our functioning as humans—both internally and in self-social exchanges—we anticipate that cognitive-behavioral theory and its theoretical successors will evolve as well.

Key Terms

Active agents	Core beliefs	Thought record log
Automatic thought	Information	Working hypothesis
Cognitive errors	processing	
Cognitive	Metacognition	
restructuring	Self-regulation	

Review Questions for Critical Thinking

1. Explain how cognitive behavioral theory conceptualizes the relationships among thoughts, feeling, and behaviors.

2. Compare and contrast the difference between *automatic thoughts* and *core beliefs*. How are they both similar and different? What is their relationship to one another?

3. In your own words, explain *information processing*. Explain how human beings' information processing systems can be both helpful and unhelpful for human beings.

4. In your own words and ideas, explain *the mediational model* from cognitive behavioral theory. Explain the importance of the mediational model for the creation of therapeutic change in cognitive-behavioral therapy.

5. In your own words and ideas, explain the idea of *metacognition*. Explain the importance of metacognition for the creation of therapeutic change in cognitive-behavioral therapy.

6. Explain how a person's context and environment are relevant and important in conducting cognitive-behavioral therapy.

Online Resources

Beck Institute for Cognitive Behavioral Therapy (www.beck institute.org). The Beck Institute is a training and resource center for health and mental health professionals, educators, and students that offers training programs and resources in cognitive-behavioral therapy.

The American Institute for Cognitive Therapy (www.cognitive therapynyc.com), headed by Dr. Robert Leahy, provides evaluations and treatment for psychological problems, state-of-the-art cognitive-behavioral therapy, and training for other professionals.

The Schema Therapy Institute (www.schematherapy.com/id201.htm), headed by Dr. Jeffrey Young, focuses on schema theory and schema-based approaches to cognitive therapy. Similar to other institutes, this one provides training, assessment tools, consultation, and other practice-oriented resources.

The American Psychological Association (http://search.apa.org/search?query=cognitive-behavioral therapy) provides a wide range of resources related to cognitive behavioral therapy, include publications, web page recommendations, media sources, and direction to applications for varied audiences.

Seeking Safety (www.seekingsafety.org). Seeking Safety is a manualized, evidence-based cognitive-behavioral therapy that helps clients with co-occurring trauma (e.g., Posttraumatic Stress Disorder and substance abuse).

TF-CBT Web (http://tfcbt.musc.edu). This is a free web-based learning course for trauma-focused cognitive-behavioral therapy, which is an evidence-based therapy for children and youth who have experienced a traumatic event (e.g., auto accident, child sexual abuse, natural disaster).

References

Alford, B. A., & Beck, A. T. (1997). *The integrative power of cognitive therapy*. New York, NY: Guilford Press.

Arch, J. J., & Craske, M. G. (2009). First-line treatment: A critical appraisal of cognitive behavioral therapy developments and alternatives. *Psychiatric Clinics of North America, 32*(3), 525–547. doi:10.1016/j.psc.2009.05.001.

Baer, R. A. (2002). Mindfulness training as a clinical intervention: A conceptual and empirical review. *Clinical Psychology: Science and Practice, 10*, 125–143.

Beck, A. T. (1996). Beyond belief: A theory of modes, personality and psychopathology. In P. M. Salkovskis (Ed.), *Frontiers of cognitive therapy* (pp. 1–25). New York, NY: Guilford Press.

Beck, A. T. (2002). Cognitive models of depression. In R. L. Leahy & E. T. Dowd (Eds.), *Clinical advances in cognitive psychotherapy theory and application* (pp. 29–61). New York, NY: Springer.

Beck, A. T. (2005). The current state of cognitive therapy: A 40-year retrospective. *Archives of General Psychiatry, 62*, 953–959.

Beck, J. S. (1995). *Cognitive therapy basics and beyond*. New York, NY: Guilford Press.

Beck, J. S. (2011). *Cognitive therapy: Basics and beyond* (2nd ed.). New York, NY: Guilford Press.

Beck, J. S., & Bieling, P. J. (2004). Cognitive therapy: Introduction to theory and practice. In M. J. Dewan, B. N. Steenbarger, & R. P. Greenberg, (Eds.), *The art and science of brief psychotherapies: A practitioner's guide* (pp. 15–49). Washington, DC: American Psychiatric Press.

Berlin, S. B. (2002). *Clinical social work practice: A cognitive-integrative perspective*. New York, NY: Oxford University Press.

Bowen, S., Chawla, N., & Marlatt, G. A. (2011). *Mindfulness-based relapse prevention for addictive behaviors: A clinician's guide*. New York, NY: Guilford Press.

Carter, M. M., Sbrocco, T., Gore, K. L., Marin, N. W., & Lewis, E. I. (2003). Cognitive-behavioral group therapy versus a wait-list control in the treatment of African American women with panic disorder. *Cognitive Therapy and Research, 27*, 508–518.

Christensen, A., Atkins, D. C., Berns, S., Wheeler, J., Baucom, D. H., & Simpson, L. E. (2004). Traditional versus integrative behavioral couple therapy for significantly and chronically distressed married couples. *Journal of Consulting and Clinical Psychology, 72*, 176–191.

Christner, R. W., Stewart, J. L., & Freeman, A. (Eds.). (2007). *Handbook of cognitive-behavior group therapy with children and adolescents: Specific settings and presenting problems*. New York, NY: Routledge.

Cormier, S., Nurius, P. S., & Osborn, C. J. (in press). *Interviewing and change strategies for helpers* (7th ed.). Pacific Grove, CA: Cengage.

DeRubis, R. J., Tang, T. Z., & Beck, A. T. (2010). Cognitive therapy. In K. S. Dobson (Ed.), *Handbook of cognitive-behavioral therapies* (3rd ed., pp. 277–316). New York, NY: Guilford Press.

DiMaggio, P. (2002). Why cognitive (and cultural) sociology needs cognitive psychology. In K. A. Cerulo (Ed.), *Culture in mind: Toward a sociology of culture and cognition* (pp. 272–281). New York, NY: Routledge.

Dimeff, L., & Koerner, K. (Ed.). (2007). *Dialectical behavior therapy in clinical practice: Applications across disorders and settings.* New York, NY: Guilford Press.

Dobson, K. S. (Ed.). (2010). *Handbook of cognitive-behavioral therapies* (3rd ed.). New York, NY: Guilford Press.

Dobson, K. S., & Dozois, D. J. A. (2010). Historical and philosophical bases of the cognitive-behavioral therapies. In K. S. Dobson (Ed.), *Handbook of cognitive-behavioral therapies* (3rd ed., pp. 3–38). New York, NY: Guilford Press.

Dowd, E. T. (2002). History and recent developments in cognitive psychotherapy. In R. L. Leahy & E. T. Dowd (Eds.), *Clinical advances in cognitive psychotherapy theory and application* (pp. 15–28). New York, NY: Springer.

Dunkley, D. M., Blankstein, K. R., & Segal, Z. V. (2010). Cognitive assessment. In K. S. Dobson (Ed.), *Handbook of cognitive-behavioral therapies* (3rd ed., pp. 133–171). New York, NY: Guilford Press.

Foreyt, J. P., & Goodrick, G. K. (2001). Cognitive behavior therapy. In R. Corsini (Ed.), *Handbook of innovative therapy* (2nd ed., pp. 95–108). New York, NY: Wiley.

Gilboa-Schechtman, E., & Foa, E. B. (2001). Patterns of recovery from trauma: The use of intraindividual analysis. *Journal of Abnormal Psychology, 110*, 392–400.

Goodheart, C. D. (2006). Evidence, endeavor, and expertise in psychology practice. In C. D. Goodheart, A. E. Kazdin, & R. J. Sternberg (Eds.), *Evidence-based psychotherapy: Where practice and research meet* (pp. 37–61). Washington, DC: American Psychological Association.

Hayes, S. C. (2004a). Acceptance and commitment therapy and the new behavior therapies: Mindfulness, acceptance, and relationship. In S. C. Hayes, V. M. Folette, & M. M. Linehan (Eds.), *Mindfulness and acceptance: Expanding the cognitive-behavioral tradition* (pp. 1–29). New York, NY: Guilford Press.

Hayes, S. C. (2004b). Acceptance and commitment therapy, relational frame theory, and the third wave of behavioral and cognitive therapies. *Behavior Therapy, 35*, 639–665.

Hayes, S. C., Folette, V. M., & Linehan, M. M. (Eds.). (2004). *Mindfulness and acceptance: Expanding the cognitive-behavioral tradition.* New York, NY: Guilford Press.

Hays, P. A. (1995). Multicultural applications of cognitive behavioral therapy. *Professional Psychology: Research and Practice, 26*, 309–315.

Hays, P. A. (2008). *Addressing cultural complexities in practice: Assessment, diagnosis, and therapy* (2nd ed.). Washington, DC: American Psychological Association.

Hays, P. A., & Iwamasa, G. Y. (2006). *Culturally responsive cognitive-behavioral therapy.* Washington, DC: American Psychological Association.

Hazlett-Stevens, H., & Craske, M. G. (2002). Brief cognitive-behavioral therapy: Definition and scientific foundations. In F. W. Bond & W. Dryden (Eds.), *Handbook of brief cognitive behaviour therapy* (pp. 1–20). Chichester, West Sussex, UK: Wiley.

Iverson, K. M., Gradus, J. L., Resick, P. A., Suvak, M. K., Smith, K. F., & Monson, C. M. (2011). Cognitive–behavioral therapy for PTSD and depression symptoms reduces risk for future intimate partner violence among interpersonal trauma survivors. *Journal of Consulting and Clinical Psychology, 79*(2), 193–202.

Kantrowitz, R., & Ballou, M. (1992). A feminist critique of cognitive-behavioral therapy. In L. S. Brown & M. Ballou (Eds.), *Personality and psychopathology: Feminist reappraisals* (pp. 70–87). New York, NY: Guilford Press.

Kazantzis, N., Deane, F. P., Ronan, K. R., & L'Abate, L. (Eds.). (2005). *Using homework assignments in cognitive behavior therapy*. New York, NY: Routledge.

Key, F. A., & Craske, M. G. (2002). Assessment issues in brief cognitive-behavioral therapy. In F. W. Bond & W. Dryden (Eds.), *Handbook of brief cognitive behaviour therapy* (pp. 21–34). Chichester, West Sussex, UK: Wiley.

Koh, L. P., Oden, T., Munoz, R. F., Robinson, A., & Leavitt, D. (2002). Adapted cognitive behavioral group therapy for depressed low-income African American women. *Community Mental Health Journal, 38*, 497–504.

Laidlaw, K., Thompson, L. W., Dick-Siskin, L., & Gallagher-Thompson, D. (2003). *Cognitive behavioral therapy with older people*. West Sussex, UK: John Wiley & Sons.

Lau, A.W., & Kinoshita, L.M. (2006). Cognitive-behavioral therapy with culturally diverse older adults. In P. A. Hays & G. Y. Iwamasa (Eds.), *Culturally responsive cognitive-behavioral therapy* (pp. 179–197). Washington, DC: American Psychological Association.

Leahy, R. L. (2002). Cognitive therapy: Current problems and future directions. In R. L. Leahy & E. T. Dowd (Eds.), *Clinical advances in cognitive psychotherapy theory and application* (pp. 418–434). New York, NY: Springer.

Leahy, R. L. (2003). *Cognitive therapy techniques: A practitioner's guide*. New York, NY: Guilford Press.

Leahy, R. L. (2007). Emotion and psychotherapy. *Clinical Psychology: Science and Practice, 14*(4), 353–357.

Leahy, R. L. (2008). The therapeutic relationship in cognitive-behavioral therapy. *Behavioural and Cognitive Psychotherapy, 36*, 769–777.

Leahy, R. L., Tirch, D., Napolitano, L. A. (2011). *Emotion regulation in psychotherapy: A practitioner's guide*. New York, NY: Guilford Press.

Lecroy, C.W. (Ed.). (2008). *Handbook of evidence-based treatment manuals for children and adolescents* (2nd ed.). New York, NY: Oxford University Press.

Linehan, M. M. (1993). *Cognitive-behavioral treatment of borderline personality disorder*. New York, NY: Guilford Press.

Macy, R. J. (2006). Cognitive therapy theory. In A. Rochlen (Ed.), *Applying counseling theories: An online, case-based approach* (pp. 157–176). Upper Saddle River, NJ: Pearson.

Mahoney, M. J. (1995). Theoretical developments in the cognitive psychotherapies. In M. J. Mahoney (Ed.), *Cognitive and constructive psychotherapies* (pp. 3–19). New York, NY: Springer.

Mahoney, M. J. (2004a). Human change processes and constructive psychotherapy. In A. Freeman, M. J. Mahoney, P. Devito, & D. Martin (Eds.), *Cognition and psychotherapy* (2nd ed., pp. 5–24). New York, NY: Springer.

Mahoney, M. J. (2004b). Synthesis. In A. Freeman, M. J. Mahoney, P. Devito, & D. Martin (Eds.), *Cognition and psychotherapy* (2nd ed., pp. 349–365). New York, NY: Springer.

Manassis, K. (2009). *Cognitive behavioral therapy with children: A guide for the community practitioner*. New York, NY: Routledge.

Martell, C. R., Safren, S. A., & Prince, S. E. (2004). *Cognitive–behavioral therapies with lesbian, gay, and bisexual clients*. New York, NY: Guilford Press.

Martin, R. & Young, J. (2010). Schema therapy. In K. S. Dobson (Ed), *Handbook of cognitive-behavioral therapies* (3rd ed., pp. 317–346). New York, NY: Guilford Press.

Mischel, W. (2007). Toward a science of the individual: Past, present, future? Persons in context: Building a science of the individual. In Y. Shoda, D. Cervone, & G. Downey (Eds), *Persons in context: Building a science of the individual* (pp. 263–277). New York, NY: Guilford Press.

Muroff, J. (2007). Cultural diversity and cognitive behavior therapy. In T. Ronen & A. Freeman, (Eds.), *Cognitive behavior therapy in clinical social work practice* (pp. 109–146). New York, NY: Springer.

Neenan, M., & Dryden, W. (2004). *Cognitive therapy: 100 key points and techniques.* New York, NY: Brunner-Routledge.

Nezu, A. M., & Nezu, C. M. (2010). Cognitive-behavioral case formulation and treatment design. In R. A. DiTomasso, B. A. Golden, & H. J. Morris (Eds.), *Handbook of cognitive-behavioral approaches in primary care* (pp. 201–222). New York, NY: Springer.

Nurius, P. S. (1991). Possible selves and social support: Social cognitive resources for coping and striving. In J. Howard & P. Callero (Eds.), *The self-society dynamic* (pp. 239–258). Cambridge, UK: Cambridge University Press.

Nurius, P. S. (2008). Cognition and social cognitive theory. In T. Mizrahi & L. Davis (Eds.), *Encyclopedia of social work* (20th ed.). Washington, DC: NASW.

Nurius, P. S. & Green, S. (in press). Cognitive behavior therapy with diverse and stressed populations. In E. J. Mullen (Ed.). *Oxford Bibliographics in Social Work.* New York, NY: Oxford University Press.

O'Donohue, W. T. & Fisher, J. E. (Eds). (2009). *General principles and empirically supported techniques of cognitive behavior therapy.* Hoboken, NJ: Wiley.

O'Leary, K. D., & Wilson, G. T. (1987). *Behavior therapy: Application and outcome* (2nd ed.). Englewood Cliffs, NJ: Prentice-Hall.

Organista, K. C. (1995). Cognitive-behavioral treatment of depression and panic disorder in a Latina client: Culturally sensitive case formulation. *In Session: Psychotherapy in Practice, 1*(2), 53–64.

Orsillo, S. M., Roemer, L., Lerner, J. B., & Tull, M. T. (2004). Acceptance, mindfulness, and cognitive-behavioral therapy. In S. C. Hayes, V. M. Folette, & M. M. Linehan (Eds.), *Mindfulness and acceptance: Expanding the cognitive-behavioral tradition* (pp. 66–95). New York, NY: Guilford Press.

Persons, J. B. (2008). *The case formulation approach to cognitive-behavior therapy.* New York, NY: Guilford Press.

Persons, J. B., & Davidson, J. (2010). Cognitive-behavioral case formulation. In K. S. Dobson (Ed.), *Handbook of cognitive-behavioral therapies* (3rd ed., pp. 172–195). New York. NY: Guilford Press.

Prochaska, J. O., & Norcross, J. C. (2010). *Systems of psychotherapy: A transtheoretical analysis* (75th ed.). Pacific Grove, CA: Thompson/Brooks/Cole.

Roemer, L. & Orsillo, S. M. (2009). *Mindfulness- and acceptance-based behavioral therapies in practice.* New York, NY: Guilford Press.

Ronen, T., & Freeman, A. (Eds.). (2007). *Cognitive behavior therapy in clinical social work.* New York, NY: Springer.

Roth, B., & Calle-Mesa, L. (2006). Mindfulness-based stress reduction (MBSR) with Spanish- and English-speaking inner-city medical patients. In R. A. Baer (Ed.). *Mindfulness-based treatment approaches* (pp. 263–284). New York, NY: Academic Press.

Safran, J. D., Eubanks-Carter, C., & Muran, J. C. (2010). Emotion focused/interpersonal cognitive therapy. In N. Kazantzis, M. A. Reinecke, & A. Freeman (Eds), *Cognitive and behavioral theories in clinical practice* (pp. 332–362). New York, NY: Guilford Press.

Scrimali, T., & Grimaldi, L. (2004). The entropy of mind: A complex systems-oriented approach to psychopathology and cognitive psychotherapy. In A. Freeman, M. J. Mahoney, P. Devito, & D. Martin (Eds.), *Cognition and psychotherapy* (2nd ed., pp. 297–322). New York, NY: Springer.

Segal, Z. V., Williams, J. M., & Teasdale, J. D. (2002). *Mindfulness-based cognitive therapy for depression: A new approach to preventing relapse*. New York, NY: Guilford Press.

Shapiro, S. L. & Carlson, L. E. (2009). *The art and science of mindfulness*. Washington, DC: American Psychological Association.

Simos, G. (Ed). (2009). *Cognitive behavior therapy: A guide for the practicing clinician, vol. 2*. New York, NY: Routledge/Taylor & Francis.

Tolin, D. F. (2010). Is cognitive-behavioral therapy more effective than other therapies? A meta-analytic review. *Clinical Psychology Review, 30*, 710–720. doi:10.1016/j.cpr.2010.05.003.

Voss Horrell, S. C. (2008). Effectiveness of cognitive–behavioral therapy with adult ethnic minority clients: A review. *Professional Psychology: Research and Practice, 39*(2), 160–168. doi:10.1037/0735–7028.39.2.160.

Weisz, J. R., & Kazdin, A. E. (Eds.). (2010). *Evidence-based psychotherapies for children and adolescents*. New York, NY: Guilford Press.

Whaley, A. L., & Davis, K. E. (2007). Cultural competence and evidence-based practice in mental health services: A complementary perspective. *American Psychologist, 62*, 563–574.

Young, J. E., Rych, J. I., Weinberger, A. D., & Beck, A. T. (2008). Cognitive therapy for depression. In D. H. Barlow (Ed.), *Clinical handbook of psychological disorders* (4th ed., pp. 250–305). New York, NY: Guilford Press.

Chapter 5
Attachment Theory

Michelle Mohr Carney and Phen M. Young

> What role does childhood attachment play in adulthood?

Social work is an applied helping profession that has roots in all of the other allied professions (e.g., psychology, sociology). Like these other helping professions, social work uses theory to both seek explanations for patterns in client problems and guide its search for solutions in collaboration with clients. Among the many theories, both explanatory and for intervention, that social work embraces, perhaps none is more important than attachment theory. Given the breadth and depth of attachment-related research (e.g., a literature search on PsycINFO yields more than 10,000 hits), the purpose of the chapter is not to provide an exhaustive review of this substantial body of literature. Rather, because such critical reviews already exist, the purpose of this chapter is to briefly explain attachment theory and link it to professional social work practice. Specifically, this chapter provides an explanation of attachment theory and traces both its historical origins and recent theoretical advancements. Particular attention is given to empirical support for the theory as well as to its application to social work practice and to the profession of social work as a whole.

Attachment theory emerged from the seminal works of John Bowlby and Mary Ainsworth. Drawing on a range of theoretical frameworks from the fields of psychology, ethology, cybergenics, and psychoanalysis, among others (Bretherton, 1992), Bowlby developed a theory that transformed our thinking about the importance of the mother-child bond and the effects its disruption could have on the developing child. In his conceptualization of the attachment model, Bowlby sought to investigate the development of the mother–child relationship, beginning at birth, and explore the relationship between the quality of the mother–child connection and the emergence of different personality traits in children. In his model, he studied infant behavior toward the attachment figure, the adult, during times of separation and reunion. It was Bowlby's belief that the attachment behaviors formed in infancy would transcend childhood and shape the attachment relationships people have as adults (Ainsworth & Bowlby, 1991).

At the time of Bowlby's writing, the field of psychology was preoccupied with psychoanalysis and the inner workings of the mind. With his attachment model, Bowlby challenged the widely accepted beliefs of his era in a lifelong effort to validate the effect of environmental factors on human development. Unlike many of his contemporaries, Bowlby believed existence to be multidimensional and dynamic, with interpersonal relationships playing a pivotal role in determining future patterns of perception and adaptation. His accomplishments were primarily theoretical, but through the groundbreaking studies of Mary Ainsworth, empirical support for his ideas was generated, which led to the acceptance of his model in the professional community. Since its inception, Bowlby's attachment theory has established itself as an invaluable and respected psychological approach, currently considered to be "the leading perspective for understanding continuity and change in personality development" (Thompson & Raikes, 2003, pp. 691–692). In recent years, attempts have been made to extend its scope by applying its fundamental premises to areas outside of its original domain, further exemplifying its far-reaching and powerful influence.

Historical and Conceptual Origins

Edward John Mostyn Bowlby, born in England in 1907, began his studies in 1925 at Cambridge, with a focus in psychology and preclinical sciences. Continuing his education in clinical medicine, he attended University College Hospital, London, before acquiring his first practical experience teaching at a school for maladjusted children. Bowlby's volunteer work at the school proved to be an influential experience. Often noted are his interactions with two young boys who differed markedly in their reaction to Bowlby's presence. One was insular and reluctant to show affection; the other would not leave Bowlby's side. Bowlby was fascinated by their differences and desired to discover the factors contributing to their remarkably different reactions to him. Interestingly, his experiences with these two boys are largely believed to have heavily contributed to his decision to focus on children in his future studies (Ainsworth & Bowlby, 1991; Bretherton, 1992).

Bowlby's career in psychology officially began with his training at the Maudsley Hospital in London in 1933. Over the course of the next several years he would qualify as a psychiatrist, begin working as a child analyst in the London Child Guidance Clinic, and train with the Institute of Psychoanalysis in London. At the London Child Guidance Clinic, Bowlby (1944) performed his first research experiment, the objective of which was to determine whether extended periods of mother–child separation were more common in his group of 44 juvenile delinquents relative to his control group of youth without felony charges. Results of this study suggested that the incident of separation between mother and child was less prevalent among those individuals in the control group (Bretherton, 1992).

Until this time, although his ideas regarding mother–child relationships had begun to emerge, he was still affiliated with the more Freudian and Kleinian schools of thought (Bretherton, 1992). Bowlby worked for many years with colleagues, including Joan Riviere and Melanie Klein, whose perspectives differed from his own. Consequently, because he was in the early stages of his clinical career, the degree to which his own beliefs diverged from theirs went unspoken for some time. A significant event in Bowlby's life was his recognition of just how far he had strayed from the beliefs he once embraced. Apparently, the turning point involved his work with a child whose mother was admitted to a psychiatric hospital in the midst of treatment. Whereas Bowlby, influenced by his postgraduate training with two psychoanalytically trained social workers, was more interested in the family experiences as a whole and the effects of the mother's illness on the child, Klein was concerned with the projections of the child onto the mother (Ainsworth & Bowlby, 1991; Bretherton, 1992). Comparing his own assessments to those of his colleagues helped him to better differentiate his beliefs from the model embraced by them, giving him the confidence to not only acknowledge his newfound beliefs, but to actively explore them. As a result of this discomfort, in 1948 Bowlby developed a research unit to further explore his emerging interests in mother–child separation by engaging the social worker James Robertson to naturalistically observe institutionally hospitalized children who had been separated from their parents. This 2-year study would provide the first attachment-related data, which Ainsworth would later analyze at Tavistock Clinic and which would spark her lifelong interest in naturalistic observation methodology (Bretherton, 1992).

In addition to the development of these programs, a request made by the World Health Organization (WHO) was significant to the progress of Bowlby's life and work. In 1950, Bowlby was asked to provide advice to the WHO on the psychological well-being of homeless children. In preparation for this task, he sought to increase his knowledge of mother–child separation by delving even further into the existing research surrounding this issue. What emerged from this endeavor was Bowlby's report, *Maternal Care and Mental Health* (1952; Bretherton, 1992). Penguin Books published a second edition called *Child Care and the Growth of Love* in 1965 that included chapters written by Mary Ainsworth (Bowlby, 1965). This research laid the preliminary groundwork for Bowlby's attachment theory, elaborating on his beliefs relative to the quality of mother-child relationships and their effect on the child's developing mental health. Bowlby's major conclusion, as quoted in Bretherton (1992, p. 765), was that in order to grow up mentally healthy, "the infant and young child should experience a warm, intimate, and continuous relationship with his mother (or permanent mother substitute) in which both find satisfaction and enjoyment."

In understanding the events that led to Bowlby's formation of attachment theory, it is necessary to include the contributions of Mary Ainsworth. Studying at the University of Toronto under William E. Blatz, Ainsworth became well-versed in Blatz's security theory, an approach to personality development sharing some similarities to attachment theory (Ainsworth &

Bowlby, 1991; Bretherton, 1992). After finishing her dissertation, she applied for a job at the Tavistock Clinic as a developmental researcher. Though her time spent at the clinic was brief, her experiences there marked the beginning of a career dedicated to the principles of attachment theory and led to the development of the now famous research experiment known as the Strange Situation (Ainsworth & Bell, 1970; Ainsworth, Bell, & Stayton, 1971; Ainsworth, Blehar, Waters, & Wall, 1978).

Although Ainsworth's next step involved the study of attachment formation in East Africa, Bowlby continued in his quest to more clearly define and articulate the groundbreaking evidence of their attachment-based studies. Consequently, the development of the theory in its concrete form was a gradual process that stretched across many years and was the result of a variety of influences. In the mid-1950s, Bowlby's interactions with Robert Hinde brought to his awareness the potential importance of animal behavior in furthering his understanding of the origins of human attachment. Bowlby and his colleagues became particularly interested in observing the relationship between animal mothers and their young. For example, Bowlby and Hinde engaged in an extensive study of rhesus monkeys, which underscored the importance of external factors, such as the presence of social groups and family networks, in explaining animal behavior. Bowlby then applied information drawn from his ethological studies of animals to better understand his work with humans, paying careful attention to the interplay between individual and environment (Ainsworth & Bowlby, 1991; Bretherton, 1992).

Basic Theoretical Principles

Prior to the work of Bowlby and Ainsworth, theoretical work on mother–child interactions frequently concentrated on specific, often singular behaviors. For example, according to Sigmund Freud's psychoanalytic view, mother–child attachment occurred during the oral stage and was a function of the mother meeting the baby's basic needs through nursing (Ainsworth & Bowlby, 1991).

In the late 1950s, a classic study conducted by Harlow (1959) with rhesus monkeys began to question Freud's psychoanalytic view of attachment. Specifically, Harlow was interested in studying the relative importance of nourishment and comfort in determining whether attachment was simply a function of the mother providing for the child's basic needs. To investigate this question, he separated rhesus monkeys from their mothers at birth and placed them with surrogate mothers—one a wire cloth-covered "mother" with a face, the other simply made from wire. He found that the monkeys preferred the cloth-covered mother to the wire figure even when the wire mother was the source of nourishment (Harlow, 1959). Further, he found that when he introduced fear, the monkeys went to the mother they were using as a source of warmth and comfort, demonstrating that "physical contact, tactile stimulation, and the clinging response (which they labeled contact comfort) was more critical to the attachment bond between mother and baby monkey than was the feeding relationship" (Liebert & Wicks-Nelson, 1981, p. 374).

Extrapolating from animals to humans, Bowlby (1958, 1969) has argued persuasively that mother–child attachment has an evolutionary basis, encompassing a wide range of mother–child interaction behaviors that together demonstrate attachment. He believed that the predisposition to become attached was inherited and necessary for survival. Specifically, if a mother did not feel attached to her child, that child's ability to survive would subsequently be placed at risk, which would potentially prevent the child from passing on his or her inherited inability to attach (Dworetzky, 1984). Consequently, Bowlby (1958) believed that attachment between infant and adult was immediate, necessary, and a key element of human behavior, equivalent to eating and procreating. He further asserted that children's attachment relationship to their parents will in many ways predict the types of relationships they will enjoy throughout their entire life (Bowlby, 1969, 1982). More specifically, children construct expectations regarding how others will react to them based on the examples set by their experiences with their parents (Bowlby, 1973). Another important tenet of Bowlby's (1944) theory is that physical disconnection from one's parents is directly related to delinquent or even criminal behavior later in life. Protection by one's caregivers, which Bowlby (1969, 1982) states is a crucial element of secure attachments, is another important theme. Parents, government, police, and even friends and partners are expected to protect us from physical or emotional harm. We discuss these macro applications of attachment theory later in the chapter.

Advanced Theoretical Principles

Bowlby identified four essential features related to forming attachment bonds: "(1) proximity maintenance (wanting to be physically close to the attachment figure), (2) separation distress, (3) safe haven (retreating to caregiver when sensing danger or feeling anxious), and (4) secure base (exploration of the world knowing that the attachment figure will protect the infant from danger)" (Sonkin, 2005, p. 2). Additionally, he identified four stages of attachment: (1) preattachment, (2) attachment in the making, (3) clear-cut attachment, and (4) goal-corrected partnership. The preattachment stage, beginning at birth and lasting through the first few weeks of life, is characterized by a desire to maintain close proximity to the mother by engaging in behavior that promotes attachment (crying, smiling, sucking, closely watching mother). During the stage of attachment in the making, the infant's behavior becomes more personal and individualized. Specifically, whereas in the preattachment stage the infant would indiscriminately engage in attachment-promoting behaviors, in the second stage (i.e., attachment in the making), which lasts until the second half of the first year, the child focuses those behaviors on familiar figures (Bowlby, 1969; Dworetzky, 1984). By the third stage of attachment, clear-cut attachment, the infant is able to move around and physically seeks proximity to the identified attachment figure. The fourth stage, goal-corrected partnership, begins during the second year of life and is characterized by a more sophisticated child engaging in behavior designed to manipulate the attachment figure to meet the child's own needs (Dworetzky, 1984).

Mary Ainsworth provided strong empirical support for Bowlby's attachment theory by first, studying the quality of the mother–child attachment and second, investigating differences in attachment patterns. She began studying the strength and quality of the mother–child attachment in Uganda with mother–infant pairs. Her objective was to observe mothers and babies in their natural environment to document the presence and frequency of attachment-based behavior (Ainsworth & Bowlby, 1991; Bretherton, 1992). Ainsworth (1963, 1967) found that mothers varied in their responses to their infants' signals in what she considered to be three important ways. Through her observations, she identified what she called *securely attached infants* (babies who cried little and were not afraid to explore when the mother was present); insecurely attached infants (babies who cried a great deal, even while being held by the mother and who tended to not explore); and not-yet-attached infants (babies who were indifferent to the mother; Bretherton, 1992).

Back in the United States, Ainsworth began a second project — similar to her study in Uganda — in Baltimore, Maryland. Again she observed the mothers in their own homes to identify differences in their responses to infant signals. Over the course of the yearlong study, she gathered more than 72 hours of data on each of the 26 participating families to explore maternal sensitivity to their infants (Bretherton, 1992). She found that those mothers who attended quickly and tenderly to their baby's signals in the first quarter of the study had babies who cried less in the fourth quarter of the study. Similarly, those mothers who held and cuddled their infants often in the first quarter of the study had babies who needed to be held less in the fourth quarter of the study (Bretherton, 1992). Her home visits were followed by a laboratory experiment designed to provide the opportunity for more controlled observation (Ainsworth & Bowlby, 1991; Bretherton, 1992). In what is known as the *Strange Situation*, Ainsworth examined the relationship between the early attachment behaviors she observed in the infants in their home with their desire to explore a new environment in a controlled setting. She was interested in determining the extent to which the helpless infant relies on the mother, who serves as a "secure base" for the young child's exploration of the world (Ainsworth & Bowlby, 1991; Bretherton, 1992).

Ainsworth ultimately identified three classifications of attached children: the securely attached child, who protests or cries when the mother leaves the room but is easily consoled when she returns; the ambivalent child, who tends to be very clingy and unwilling to explore his or her surroundings without the mother present; and the avoidant child, who shows signs of independence but in actuality is rather angry with the mother (Karen, 1990, p. 36).

Further revealing the importance of early attachment, Karen (1990, p. 36) states that "at age two, insecurely attached children tend to lack self-reliance and show little enthusiasm for problem solving," which strongly indicates that the child is conditioned by the level of responsiveness exhibited by his or her mother. Karen further explains that "Ainsworth's central premise was that the responsive mother provides a secure base" (p. 36) for the child, from which he or she can safely develop autonomy, comforted by the knowledge that he or she is supported by the mother. Karen does acknowledge, however, that,

> [B]eing securely attached hardly ensures that babies will grow up free of neuroses or even of insecurities. It means only that they have been given confidence that someone will be there for them and that they are thus at least minimally capable of forming satisfying relationships [emphasis added] and of passing on that ability to their children. (p. 38)

It follows that these past relationships determine patterns for future relationships (Kobak & Hazan, 1991) and that these patterns can be accurately predicted based on an understanding of the quality of the initial attachment relationship (Bowlby, 1988). Given this, anxious attachment during early childhood would be a compelling determinant of the individual's likelihood of experiencing relationship difficulties later in life (Ainsworth, 1985).

Recent Theoretical Developments

The relationship between childhood attachment style and adult relationship patterns is widely studied (Campbell, Simpson, Boldry, & Kashy, 2005; Mikulincer & Shaver, 2005; Moore & Leung, 2002). Adult relationship attachment styles are believed to parallel childhood attachment styles, shaping the type of relationships in which individuals engage (Hazan & Shaver, 1987; Mikulincer & Florian, 1998; Moore & Leung, 2002; Waters, Kondo-Ikemura, Posada, & Richters, 1991; Yarrow, 1972). Paralleling the childhood attachment bonds identified by Ainsworth and colleagues (1978) — secure, anxious/resistant, avoidant, or disorganized/disoriented — similar patterns in adult relationships have been identified: secure, clingy, casual, and uninterested. Bartholomew (1990) created a four-category model of attachment (secure, dismissing, fearful, and preoccupied) to assess the quality of adult attachment relationship along two dimensions: positivity of representations of self and positivity of representations of others. The type of adult relationship formed has further been suggested to be an important determinant of quality of life generally, across the life span, in two distinct domains: "the internal psychological (emotional and affective) domain and the external sociocultural (behavioral) domain" (Moore & Leung, 2002,

p. 245; Searle & Ward, 1990). The internal domain reflects "social and emotional well-being, mental health and/or levels of psychological distress or experienced stress," and the external domain reflects larger life stressors (Moore & Leung, 2002, p. 245). These life stressors, external to the individual, vary by culture and society and change with political and economic shifts. The individual's capacity to cope with these external stressors has been linked to adult relationship style and thereby early attachment bond (Mikulincer & Florian, 1998; Moore & Leung, 2002).

Recent developments in attachment theory have identified a pattern of transmission of attachment styles from one generation to the next (Besser & Priel, 2005; Godbout, Dutton, Lussier, & Sabourin, 2009; Obegi, Morrison, & Shaver, 2004; Rodriguez, 2006). Women who are distrustful of or overly reliant on others are more likely to engage in physical maltreatment of their children (Rodriguez, 2006). Furthermore, there is evidence that insecure attachment styles in a parent adversely impacts their relationship with their child, which would, in turn, amplify the risk for abuse (Howe, Brandon, & Hinings, 1999; Rodriguez, 2006). Survivors of child abuse tend to develop an internal working model that shows an avoidance of intimacy and anxiety with close relationships (Godbout et al., 2009). The intergenerational transmission of attachment style is particularly true for mothers and daughters (Obegi et al., 2004). Besser and Priel (2005) examined a community sample of 300 participants comprising 100 three-generation triads of women and found an intergenerational congruence of trait vulnerabilities. A mother's level of avoidance and discomfort with physical and emotional closeness in romantic relationships is the strongest predictor of her daughter's attachment style (Obegi et al., 2004).

In her manuscript describing the origins of attachment theory, Bretherton (1992, pp. 765–766) remarks that an often neglected aspect of Bowlby's attachment theory is his "emphasis on the role of social networks and on economic as well as health factors in the development of well-functioning mother-child relationships." Interestingly, Sonkin (2009) describes the current economic crisis as a mass social trauma with the potential to cause untold psychological stress, which he ties to implicit memory, a relatively new area of research. Implicit memory is conceptualized through behaviors, feelings, and other patterns in which little or no conscious thought is put into remembering how to do things (e.g. driving a car, working on the computer) so that individuals can multitask efficiently (Sonkin, 2009). For those who grew up in families with financial difficulties, this recession may trigger times of anxiety, fear, abuse, and unhealthy coping strategies. The stronger the emotion, the more extreme the coping mechanism will be. When people understand how the past can intrude on their present emotions, they can reevaluate the current situation with a sense of perspective, which hopefully leads to better problem-solving methods (Sonkin, 2009). A macro case example illustrating a larger system application of attachment theory is discussed later in the chapter.

Relevance to Social Work Practice

In the next section we discuss the use of attachment theory in social work practice, including its applications to the assessment of children, the assessment of adults, and how this approach may be used as intervention. We next illustrate its application in some specific problem areas, including domestic violence and minority disenfranchisement.

Uses in Assessment

Measuring Attachment in Children

Mary Ainsworth's naturalistic observational studies, discussed previously, were initially used to assess and measure attachment in infants and were followed by the Strange Situation laboratory experiments. More recently, researchers designed an alternative to the Strange Situation called the *Attachment Q-set*, also to determine children's use of the attachment figure as a secure base from which to explore their environments (Waters & Deane, 1985). This process uses an observer (sometimes expert, sometimes mother) to monitor a wide range of attachment-related behaviors in children and categorize them relative to their accurate description of the child (i.e., ranging from highly descriptive to not descriptive at all). In research evaluating the relationship between the results of the Q-set assessments and the Strange Situation attachment classification, it was discovered that the Q-set assessments performed by experts corresponded well to the Strange Situation assessments, although those done by mothers were less consistent (Van Dam & Van IJzendoorn, 1988; Vaughn & Waters, 1990).

Measuring Attachment in Adults

Measuring attachment in adults is typically done via interviews or self-report measures. Over the past 20 years, multiple scales and interview formats have been created, all of which are designed to assess attachment (for a review of the most frequently used methods, see Sonkin, 2005; Sperling, Foelsch, & Grace, 1996). Although it is beyond the scope of this chapter to review all of them, we briefly discuss a few of the most often used instruments that have been created to measure attachment in adults.

The Adult Attachment Interview uses open-ended questions to determine the influence of childhood attachment relations on adult attachment development (Main & Goldwyn, 1993). More structured is the attachment scale developed by Hazan and Shaver (1987) that is designed to gather similar broad information about attachment and links responses to attachment-related questions to one of three attachment styles that best describe subjects' feelings about romantic relationships. "Securely attached people indicate that they find it relatively easy to get close to others ... avoidantly attached people indicate that they are uncomfortable being close to others, find it difficult to completely trust ... and anxiously attached people indicate that they find others are reluctant to get as close as they would like, [and] frequently worry that their romantic partners don't really love them'' (Simpson, 1990, p. 971).

The Adult Attachment Style Questionnaire (Bartholomew, 1990; Bartholomew & Horowitz, 1991) is a prototype measure using a Likert scale to determine how individual relationship characteristics approximate one of four identified categories: secure, dismissing, fearful, and preoccupied.

The Experiences in Close Relationships Scale (Brennan, Clark, & Shaver, 1998) is a 36-item self-report measure of adult romantic attachment created from most of the existing self-report measures. Revised by Fraley, Waller, and Brennan in 2000, the Experiences in Close Relationships Scales—Revised is again a 36-item self-report scale that yields the same two subscales: Avoidance (or Discomfort with Closeness and Discomfort with Depending on Others) and Anxiety (or Fear of Rejection and Abandonment).

The Adult Attachment Projective developed by George and West (2001) uses a series of drawings depicting scenes designed to trigger responses relative to the individual's level of attachment (Sonkin, 2005).

Uses in Intervention

Professional social workers rely, in part, on existing evaluation research to make informed clinical decisions regarding choosing an effective intervention model for clients. Determining which interventions may be helpful is made easier when they are viewed in a theoretical framework. Attachment theory suggests that the absence of secure attachment very early in life can have lifelong negative implications. High-stress family settings where there is child abuse and neglect, poverty, incarceration, divorce, or domestic violence, prove to be hazardous environments for children to form the secure attachments necessary for healthy psychological development (Aber & Allen, 1987).

From an attachment perspective, social workers can choose particular methods or services for clients that serve to address the early attachment problems. This is possible because attachment theory has been used as a framework for creating intervention programs that address almost every aspect of human behavior. Specifically, research on attachment theory has been used to influence child welfare (Andersson, 2005; Barth & Miller, 2000; Bennett, 2003; Daniel, Wassell, & Ennis, 1997; Dyer, 2004; Grigsby, 1994; Haight, Kagle, & Black, 2003; Houston, 2001; Howe et al., 1999; McMillen, 1992; Mennen & O'Keefe, 2005; Penzerro & Lein, 1995; Riggs, 2005; R. Solomon, 2002) as well as to identify the negative impact of disrupted attachment patterns across the life span. Researchers have linked attachment theory to various social problems, including child abuse and neglect (Aber & Allen, 1987; Bacon & Richardson, 2001; Bolen, 2002; Crittenden, 1992; Crittenden & Ainsworth, 1989; George, 1996; Howe, Dooley, & Hinings, 2000; Hughes, 2004; Olafson, 2002; Page, 1999; Wasserman & Rosenfeld, 1986), poverty (Bakermans-Kranenburg, van IJzendoorn, & Kroonenberg, 2004; Erickson, Korfmacher, & Egeland, 1992; Gauthier, 2003), delinquency (Bowlby, 1944; Gauthier, 2003), divorce (Birnbaum, Orr, & Mikulincer, 1997; Brennan & Shaver, 1998; Cohen & Finzi, 2005; Cohen, Finzi, & Avi-Yonah, 1999; Corrie, 2002; Fausel, 1986; Rogers, 2004; J. Solomon, 2005; Thewatt, 1980; Todorski, 1995; Waters, Merrick, & Treboux, 2000), incarceration (Eloff & Moen, 2003; Fearn & Parjer, 2004; Mackenzie, 2003; Martin, 1997; Poehlmann, 2005; Pollock, 2002), the ability to form adult relationships (Bartholomew, 1990; Campbell et al., 2005; Feeney & Noller, 1990; Fraley & Davis, 1997; Hazan & Shaver, 1987, 1990; S. Johnson, 2004; S. Johnson, Makinen, & Millikin, 2001; Mikulincer & Shaver, 2005; Moore & Leung, 2002; Waters et al., 1991), and domestic violence (S. Bond & Bond, 2004; Carney & Buttell, 2005, 2006; Dutton, 1995, 2000; Dutton, Saunders, Starzomski, & Bartholomew, 1994; Kesner, Julian, & McKenry, 1997; Kesner & McKenry, 1998; Murphy, Meyer, & O'Leary, 1994; Sonkin & Dutton, 2003), to name a few. Our research has been in the field of forensic social work, primarily concentrated in work with batterers in court-mandated domestic violence intervention programs. Therefore, we will use this research area as an example of attachment theory as it relates to professional social work intervention. Following that discussion is an application of attachment theory at the macro level.

Domestic Violence and Attachment

Bowlby believed that human beings react with anger when their attachment needs go unmet (Kesner & McKenry, 1998). This anger is meant to be a signal for the attachment figure to address the unmet need. A consistent state of unmet needs creates attachment patterns that Bowlby asserted were both lifelong and critical in forming the individual's internal working model of self. Consistent, warm, supportive responses to the proximity-promoting signals given from an infant create secure attachment and an "internal working model of self as valued and self-reliant" (Bretherton, 1992, p. 70). Conversely, rejected bids for closeness and security cause an "internal working model of self as unworthy or incompetent" (p. 70). Fonagy and his colleagues (Fonagy, Gergely, Jurist, & Target, 2002, p. 65) purport that, in adults, "a secure attachment relationship promotes the ability to mentalize, that is, to perceive and interpret behavior as based on intentional mental states."

What does it mean to mentalize? Using physical violence as an example, what causes some individuals to react to their own feelings of aggression with physical attacks rather than handling those feelings in a nonviolent manner? Fonagy (1999) would argue that those who engage in physical violence are unable to think about aggression in relation to attachment, or in other words, have inadequate mentalizing capacities. These individuals are often victims of child abuse who as children sought the comfort of their attachment figure while at the same time experiencing confusion about why they were being abused by that caregiver. This mental anguish causes children to create mental distance between their experienced acts of violence and their physical need for closeness. In doing this, they form inadequate patterns of thoughts relative to behaviors which continue throughout the life span and affect adult relationships as well (Fonagy, 1999). The securely attached adult is not encumbered by this need to create mental distance while seeking physical closeness, suggesting a synergistic relationship between having the capacity to mentalize, which demands secure attachment, and having a securely attached attachment figure. Thus, initial patterns of attachment shape interpersonal experiences and form the template from which future relationships are formed. This level of attachment in the adult, or the security of the attachment bond, is therefore a determining factor in the type of adult relationships individuals form and a factor in whether those relationships involve the use of physical violence (S. Bond & Bond, 2004).

Researchers have found the strength and type of attachment bond to be significantly associated with the use of violence in the home (S. Bond & Bond, 2004; Carney & Buttell, 2005, 2006; Dutton, 1995, 2000; Dutton et al., 1994; Kesner et al., 1997; Kesner & McKenry, 1998; Murphy et al., 1994; Sonkin & Dutton, 2003). Interestingly, the focus on attachment theory was the direct result of observations made in clinical practice that batterers were overly dependent on their intimate partner but incapable of initiating and maintaining an emotionally supportive relationship. As a result, these men desired closeness with their partner but, given their inability to achieve emotional closeness, engaged in violent and controlling behaviors to ensure physical closeness rather than emotional closeness (Murphy et al., 1994).

Dutton and Sonkin (2003) generated a treatment model for male domestic violence offenders grounded in attachment theory that speaks to many issues that occur within relationships with domestic violence. According to Goldenson, Geffner, Foster, and Clipson (2007), this approach may also be germane when treating female offenders. Dutton and Sonkin's framework involves (a) helping offenders better understand the impact that their upbringing has had on their patterns of behavior in romantic relationships, and (b) teaching self-regulation during periods of attachment-related anxiety instead of offenders' typical responses of distancing, clinging, or approach-avoidance (Dutton & Sonkin, 2003).

Conceptually, excessive interpersonal dependency among abusive men is viewed as a consequence of insecure attachment in childhood (Dutton, 1995; Holtzworth-Monroe, Bates, Smultzer, & Sandin, 1997). In brief, attachment theory proposes that the overall quality of the infant–caretaker relationship during infancy and early childhood is both the primary determinant of dependent traits in adulthood (Ainsworth, 1969) and a model for later interpersonal relationships (Bowlby, 1980). Regarding the development of excessive interpersonal dependency among batterers, Dutton has argued that battered mothers cannot adequately attend to the demands of the attachment process while simultaneously attempting to negotiate a hostile and dangerous home environment. Consequently, children in this situation become insecurely attached and, in adulthood, exhibit excessive dependency on their partners (Dutton, 1995; Holtzworth-Monroe et al., 1997; Murphy et al., 1994). Recently, Sonkin and Dutton (2003, p. 109) have reviewed the literature on attachment theory and domestically violent men and suggest that "men whose violence was predominantly or exclusively in intimate relationships probably have an attachment disorder." Therefore, they conclude, "incorporating attachment theory into batterer treatment is well founded" (p. 110). Despite this apparent connection, there are several factors not addressed in the available literature on attachment theory and domestically violent men that could militate against the inclusion of attachment theory into batterer intervention efforts.

First, a close evaluation of some of the studies supporting the connection between attachment theory and batterers reveals that some have serious measurement limitations. For example, in a study investigating the relationship between dominance needs and attachment style among maritally violent men, Mauricio and Gormley (2001) discovered that 58% of the 60 court-mandated batterers in their study reported an insecure attachment style. However, by the authors' own admission, the findings of the study were compromised by a significant association between social desirability and attachment style and the use of a single-item measure of attachment, the reliability of which was established on a college population. This highlights a common problem among studies attempting to investigate attachment issues in adults, namely, attempting to retrospectively assess the quality of the infant–caretaker bond in adult samples. Consequently, researchers often use indirect measures, most commonly interpersonal dependency, to judge the quality of childhood attachment in adults.

Second, among the studies investigating interpersonal dependency among abusive men (an indicator of insecure attachment in adulthood), there have been conflicting results from studies employing court-mandated and voluntary subjects. Specifically, those studies that employed voluntary subjects have suggested that domestically violent men exhibit excessive levels of dependency on their intimate partner relative to nonviolent men (Holtzworth-Munroe et al., 1997; Murphy et al., 1994).

Finally, it has been argued that all batterers have attachment issues (e.g., Dutton, 2000; Murphy et al., 1994; Sonkin & Dutton, 2003). Specifically, Dutton has argued persuasively that insecure attachment, when combined with parental shaming and observing violence in childhood, results in the development of an abusive personality in adult men. In his developmental model for explaining male-initiated physical abuse, Dutton argues that childhood exposure to parental shaming, insecure attachment, and physical abuse form the core of an abusive personality, which, in adulthood, leads these individuals to abuse their partners. However, in a compelling review of Dutton's developmental model, Lawson (2001) notes that, among other things, Dutton fails to acknowledge that his argument pertains to only one type of batterer, namely, the borderline/dependent batterer, which accounts for only 25% of the batterers in Dutton's typology. Further, Lawson correctly indicates that Dutton's model completely ignores feminist theory and systems theory and minimizes social learning theory as workable explanations for the development of abusive behaviors among men. Taken as a whole, these three issues suggest that attachment theory may be an important component of theoretical explanations of battering and intervention efforts with some batterers, but it appears premature to suggest that attachment theory has relevance to all batterers.

In the field of domestic violence, rapid changes are occurring in forensic work with batterers. Importantly, two issues at the heart of batterer intervention programs (BIPs) are diverging and creating programmatic tension for social workers providing intervention services to domestically violent men and women. Specifically, increasingly rigorous evaluations of BIPS are suggesting that they are not as effective as initial research indicated they were, while, simultaneously, states are passing legislation that mandates a "one size fits all" BIP for all treatment providers statewide (currently more than 30 states have legislation governing BIP program standards; Maiuro, Hagar, & Lin, 2002). Consequently, through the enactment of state laws governing the treatment of batterers, treatment providers are becoming married to a BIP model that empirical research is suggesting may be ineffective (Davis & Taylor, 1999; Davis, Taylor, & Maxwell, 1998; Dunford, 2000; Feder & Forde, 2000). Despite the obvious problems associated with this initiative, the push for legislative standards moves forward. Among the many suggestions addressed by these standards is to formalize program structure and length. As a result, most treatment programs nationally, regardless of theoretical perspective, offer a feminist-informed, cognitive-behavioral, group treatment approach for batterers (Gelles, 2001; Holtzworth-Munroe, 2001). Perhaps the greatest problem associated with this legislative trend is that it poses a risk of institutionalizing a treatment approach that may not be working well.

In an interesting parallel, in a recent study investigating childhood attachment patterns via levels of interpersonal dependency among women in treatment for domestic violence offenses, we found the women to also be overly dependent on their partner, an adult indicator of insecure attachment style (Carney & Buttell, 2005). Perhaps more important, we found this excessive level of interpersonal dependency to be significantly associated with the women's use of psychological aggression tactics, physical assault, sexual coercion, and severe injury directed at their intimate partner. In this regard, these women appear to be much like male batterers in that there seems to be a positive linear relationship between interpersonal dependency and a multidimensional definition of violence.

While there is still much to discover about interpersonal dependency, recent research concerning the impact of attachment theory on domestic violence has found that exposure to domestic violence in childhood or later on in life appears to impact the development of insecure attachment in adult women (Godbout et al., 2009). According to Godbout et al. (2009), feelings of psychological victimization are related to women's adult anxious attachments. Additionally, being exposed to domestic violence is associated with avoidant style attachments in adult women (Godbout et al., 2009). The exposure to parental violence was positively related to women who have experienced domestic violence with a male partner who is anxiously attached (Godbout et al., 2009).

Similarly, strength of attachment has been found to be a factor in determining whether an abused woman stays in her abusive situation or leaves (Dutton, 1988; Dutton & Painter, 1993; Henderson, Bartholomew, & Dutton, 1997). Based on the social-psychological theory of traumatic bonding, the abuse can strengthen the attachment bond. A battered woman's loyalty to her abuser is linked to the power imbalance and the intermittent nature of the violence in their relationship (Dutton, 1988; Dutton & Painter, 1993; Henderson et al., 1997). The working model of self, embodied in the battered woman as worthless, intensifies as the abusive partner becomes more abusive. As her negative view of self escalates, she becomes more fearful, less confident, and more dependent on her abuser (Dutton, 1988; Henderson et al., 1997). This power imbalance, coupled with the intermittent nature of the violence, where periods of violence are followed by pleasant, affectionate, seemingly loving behavior on the part of the abuser, creates a cycle (Walker, 1979). This cyclical pattern of behavior serves to strengthen the bond between the battered woman and her abuser, thus interfering with her ability to leave (Dutton & Painter, 1993).

As the preceding discussion illustrates, attachment theory holds considerable potential for explaining the actions of both abusers and victims in domestic violence situations. Unfortunately, in the current climate of increasing state standards and legislative requirements for BIPs (Maiuro et al., 2002), wholesale programmatic change would, at best, be unlikely. Nevertheless, in terms of interpersonal dependency and attachment theory, the literature on male batterers is evolving in the direction of incorporating these constructs into existing treatment protocols (Sonkin & Dutton, 2003). Consequently, if future research confirms that all batterers, regardless of sex, have dependency issues that should be addressed in BIPs, then dependency and attachment issues may become vital in batterer intervention programming.

Case Example

An Application of Attachment Theory at the Macro Level to Explain Minority Disenfranchisement in the United States

As discussed previously, an often neglected aspect of Bowlby's attachment theory is the impact of macro influences on the attachment process. In fact, he argued that "just as children are absolutely dependent on their parents for sustenance, so in all but the most primitive communities, are parents, especially their mothers, dependent on a greater society for economic provision. If a community values its children it must cherish their parents" (Bowlby, 1951, p. 84, as cited in Bretherton, 1992). Consequently, while many studies focus on attachment principles in the context of the family, according to Bowlby, one can also expand the basic tenets of this theory to apply on a societal level. The remainder of this section considers the African American experience through the lens of attachment theory. Although no research is currently available that explores this avenue with a particular focus on African Americans, it seems evident that the disenfranchisement of African Americans in the United States can be at least partially accounted for by attachment theory.

In "The Political Context," Mowlam (1996) proposes that the inconsistent availability of the government to its citizens has led to a sense of insecurity on the part of American society as a whole. Of particular interest here, however, is the specific nature of the African American population's anxious or avoidant attachment to society and the government, within the framework of the typically microlevel dynamics of the mother–infant relationship that Bowlby (1982) and Ainsworth (1985) have explored. In short, although all human beings are affected by the early attachment dynamics of their parents or caregivers, the African American population as an entire culture has also been profoundly affected by the inconsistent responsiveness of the American government as well as dominant society at large, in much the same way as an infant is affected by an insecure or anxious attachment to his or her parents. For example, a recent study on the history of youth delinquency (Cross, 2003) emphasizes that the coexistence of high African American crime rates and high levels of social capital can be explained by looking at the long-term negative emotional effects of slavery (which, more clearly than any other example in history, illustrates the absence of secure bonds with the government and society). The parallel between attachment theory at micro and macro levels is undeniable.

The main principle of Bowlby and Ainsworth's theory of attachment is that the securely attached child possesses the knowledge that his or her mother is dependable and consistently available (Karen, 1990). As attachment theory shows, a client who is currently experiencing relationship and intimacy difficulties may perhaps be better understood when examined in the framework of the relationships with his or her parents. To illustrate this point, consider the example of a young African American female client at a local community mental health facility. This client has expressed concern about a pattern of difficulty finding a romantic partner. She attributes this difficulty to the fact that she has a tendency to terminate her relationships at the first sign of a lack of trustworthiness. Her reluctance to trust (both in herself and others) has also been compounded by several painful and unsuccessful attempts to form friendships with Caucasian women. These relationships in particular have been thwarted by both racist concerns of the Caucasian parents and by an unwillingness on the part of her Caucasian friends to accompany her to African American clubs. As with her romantic partners, this client has a history of abandoning friendships as opposed to making efforts, through open communication, to arrive at some sort of mutual understanding. This client's pattern of avoidant attachments, through no fault of her own, can be traced all the way back to an avoidant attachment to her mother, whose boyfriend systematically and sexually abused the client for years. Her mother, in response, accused the client of seducing the man and therefore threatening her mother's relationship with him. The suspicious and destructive nature of this early relationship with authority figures seems to have set the stage for her current difficulties in achieving intimacy. As Colin (1996, p. 298) points out, "Adult avoidance of intimacy may have its roots in early experiences in which emotional vulnerability was associated with parental rejection." In this case, the client experienced both physical and emotional rejection by her mother, both of which have impacted her current relationship patterns on micro and mezzo levels.

However, related to the application of attachment theory at the macro level, one also could argue that her current relationship and attachment difficulties have also been largely affected by her culture's extensive history of social and political rejection. In this case, both the client's personal history of rejection and the specific history of the African American culture have affected her adult relationships. This connection gains further clarity when viewed in relation to the theme of trust that is evident throughout the principles of attachment theory. Specifically, an exploration of African Americans' attachment patterns as they relate to government and the dominant society uncovers many parallels to the dynamics of parent-child relationships. As discussed earlier, insecure or avoidant attachments result from a lack of protection and responsiveness from the parent. Enlarging this concept to a cultural level, though, reveals a similar pattern. Just as Mowlam (1996, p. 23) asserts that Americans in general are suffering from a "widespread, profound sense of insecurity" as a result of mistrusting the government, it follows that the very same (but greatly intensified) lack of trust would be present among African Americans when one considers that they, as a collective group, have never enjoyed the feeling of availability of and responsiveness from dominant society or the American government. In this respect, the theme of protection operates on micro, mezzo, and macro levels, with many of the same patterns emerging.

In the context of family and friend systems, protection provides comfort, safety, self-confidence, and security. In the sociopolitical (macro) realm, protection enhances the same qualities, but also affects the ability to successfully acculturate oneself into larger society. While African Americans are already faced with the need to assimilate into two cultures ("bicultural socialization"; Norton, 1993), the additional anxiety that arises from an overwhelming sense of being unwelcome or unimportant to their government (metaphorical parents, as it were) makes the effort to belong that much more difficult.

Continuing with our theme of linking attachment theory and domestic violence, another example of a macro application of attachment theory is the case of two clients, one female and one male, who came to a community mental health center seeking help with the female's depression and were referred for conjoint therapy sessions. At the time of the second session, the female showed up late and disheveled, stating that the male had physically attacked her in the parking lot. After talking for a few minutes while she calmed down, it was suggested that she call the police and report the incident. She had serious reservations about reporting the incident because she was afraid that the police would arrest her.

In the context of an avoidant attachment to authority figures, her reaction makes perfect sense. In her experience, she had no reason to trust that the police would protect or help her. It is precisely this awareness of the larger person-in-environment perspective that will enable clinicians to not only respond empathically, but also to begin to understand the effects of a lifelong experience that includes continuous rejection by authority figures on a sociopolitical level.

The reality of her fear is reflective of Bowlby's (1973) elucidation that children construct their expectations of others' reactions to them in terms of the history of their experiences with their parents, but on an enlarged scale. In this case, the police are a metaphorical replacement for the parents, and the concept then applies on a macro level.

In this aspect, the presence of increased social capital among African Americans is also reminiscent of sibling bonding patterns that may occur in the absence of consistent or nurturing parental care. In a study conducted by Van IJzendoorn, Van der Veer, and Van Vliet-Visser (1987), five families were observed to examine the effects of the birth of a sibling. In this study, the anxiously attached firstborn responded very warmly to the newborn, differing from the patterns exhibited by other subjects (Van Vliet-Visser & Van IJzendoorn, 1987). An explanation of this phenomenon, provided by Dunn and Kendrick (1981) is that when the parents have failed to establish a secure bond with the firstborn, the child with anxious attachment will attempt to bond with the sibling in order to minimize the feeling of complete abandonment. This dynamic is also applicable to Hines, Preto, McGoldrick, Almeida, and Weltman's (1999) essay, "Culture and the Family Life Cycle." Hines and colleagues explain that a common practice of African Americans is to refer to each other as brothers and sisters as a reflection of the sense of attachment to each other that they possess. In the framework of sibling bonding patterns, this cultural attachment may be viewed as a direct reaction to members having suffered together through slavery and discrimination (an extreme lack of secure bonds with authority figures or metaphorical parents).

Additionally, Mowlam (1996, p. 26) asserts that this "lack of belonging" is one of the fundamental causes of the recent collapse between all young people today and their government. In an attachment theory framework, the concept of belonging is directly linked to avoidant attachment as well as the themes of trust and rejection.

The principles set forth by attachment theory therefore do not apply exclusively to individuals in the context of their family and upbringing. Attachment dynamics on a macro level also affect one's relationships as well as one's ability to function in society. African Americans and Caucasians still maintain some degree of separation from each other (although, admittedly, the relations have improved). It is also interesting to note that while African Americans as a culture enjoy high levels of social capital, the Caucasian culture by comparison is somewhat lacking in this resource.

In addition to increased awareness, acknowledgment, and validation of the African American culture's avoidant attachment history, the social worker must also help clients to identify and resolve these macro level avoidant attachment patterns—pretending not to care when actually they are probably quite angry—in order for clients to feel less resentful about a more integrated level of socialization into dominant society, which may in turn lead to increased opportunities. The emphasis here is on bicultural socialization, and not complete abandonment of the African American culture. The fact that there is a dominant society does logically, right or wrong, require some level of adjustment in order for other cultures to increase their opportunities for success. While the decision to embrace both cultures lies with each individual, the decision should be made free of any anger that has resulted from cultural rejection and an appalling lack of protection. The resolution of these avoidant attachments may also provide a therapeutic and productive channel in which to direct the intense feelings of anger that are likely to surface by using social capital to focus a collective effort on cultural advocacy.

In this sense, a strengths perspective (Saleebey, 1992) emphasizes the value of existing social capital among African Americans as a creative and effective defense against a consistently hostile environment. Culturally specific social capital may also be utilized as a solid foundation from which one is better equipped to confront adversity. As Hewitt (1996, p. xv) notes, social capital is not only essential in terms of economics, but is also part of "the conditions for a good life." Existing attachment patterns used to establish social capital among African Americans may also provide opportunities to apply these same patterns to other populations. Because social capital is based on relationships and attachments (Putnam, 2000), the clinician's awareness and encouragement of this resource is vital.

As clinicians, we must be aware of and sensitive to the fact that attachment issues among African American clients may exist on several levels. Social workers must therefore make a special effort to explore these avenues when working with any client who has been oppressed. It is also essential to good practice that social workers acknowledge and validate African Americans' history of oppression so as not to add to the feelings of rejection, mistrust, and lack of responsiveness by authority figures. As mentioned earlier, the strengths perspective (Saleebey, 1992) guides us toward both encouraging and utilizing social capital as a resource, especially in light of the unlikelihood that the American sociopolitical system, in which African Americans live and function, is going to change any time soon. Given the progress that has been achieved thus far, however, it would not be surprising for the macro level application of attachment theory with regard to oppressed populations to gain more understanding, recognition, and support in the near future.

Critiques of This Approach

Attachment theory has been widely tested and criticized (Bretherton, 1992). Scholars from virtually every discipline have questioned Bowlby's assertions regarding attachment theory's biological and physiological base, its universality, its intergenerational transmission, and its stability across time (Bolen, 2000). Additionally, research suggests that studies supporting Bowlby's attachment model have been plagued with methodological problems, calling into question the legitimacy of the interpretations and findings (Bolen, 2000; Hazan & Shaver, 1987; Lamb, 1987; Rheingold & Eckerman, 1973). Critics have suggested that the traditional view of the mother as the primary caregiver is sexist (Chodorow, 1978; M. Johnson, 1988), yet attachment theory does not specifically name the mother as the attachment figure, and evidence suggests that most important is a committed caregiver relationship (Marris, 1982). Opponents also advise that more research should be conducted relative to fathers as attachment figures and attachment within the family system (Bronfenbrenner, 1979).

The interrelations of early childhood attachment and later-in-life attachment relationships—across the spectrum—need to be further investigated. The impact of early disrupted attachment on later involvement in violence either as a perpetrator or as a victim needs to be further delineated. Finally, using the information gained about individual attachment patterns to create programming to address social problems such as delinquency and domestic violence is particularly warranted.

Key Terms

Attachment	Intergenerational	Mentalize
Attachment styles	transmission of	Naturalistic
Attachment theory	attachment styles	observation
Domestic violence	Interpersonal	Strange Situation
Implicit memory	dependency	

Review Questions for Critical Thinking

1. This chapter refers to both attachment and bonding. What are the differences between attachment and bonding?

2. Comment on the importance of measuring attachment styles. What are the advantages and disadvantages of labeling a client with an attachment style? What strategies could be utilized to ameliorate these disadvantages?

3. As the chapter states, measuring attachment in adults is typically done via interviews or self-reported measures. What challenges do self-reported surveys, such as the Adult Attachment Style Questionnaire, face regarding measuring a person's accurate attachment style?

4. Many theoretical concepts born from psychoanalysis have been criticized for their inability to be used cross-culturally. Does attachment theory suffer from this same limitation? Why or why not?

Online Resources

The Bowlby Centre is an organization committed to the development, promotion and practice of an attachment-based and relational approach to psychotherapy. It offers training in psychotherapy and produces a journal.

www.thebowlbycentre.org.uk

The International Association for the Study of Attachment is a multidisciplinary association of mental health professionals that focuses on how humans cope with danger, how attachment relationships affect this, and how later adaptation to life circumstances draws on these experiences.

www.iasa-dmm.org

Attachment Across Cultures provides lists of authors, books, journals, and articles in the area of attachment theory.

www.attachmentacrosscultures.org

The Attachment Theory Website contains lists of authors, books, journals, and articles in the area of attachment theory. Many articles have summaries attached and links to full-text where available or assistance with seeking full-text on the web where not.

www.richardatkins.co.uk/atws

Relationship Matters is a psychotherapist's website where mental health professionals and the general public will find information about family violence and how to provide psychotherapy with attachment and the neurosciences in mind.

www.daniel-sonkin.com

Attachment theory information and research from the State University of New York and the New York Attachment Consortium.

www.psychology.sunysb.edu/attachment

References

Aber, J. L., & Allen, J. P. (1987). Effects of maltreatment on young children's socioemotional development: An attachment theory perspective. *Developmental Psychology, 23*, 406–414.

Ainsworth, M. D. S. (1963). The development of infant-mother interaction among the Ganda. In B. M. Foss (Ed.), *Determinants of infant behavior* (pp. 67–104). New York, NY: Wiley.

Ainsworth, M. D. S. (1967). *Infancy in Uganda: Infant care and the growth of love.* Baltimore, MD: Johns Hopkins University Press.

Ainsworth, M. D. S. (1969). Object relations, dependency, and attachment: A theoretical review of the infant-mother relationship. *Child Development, 40*, 969–1025.

Ainsworth, M. D. S. (1985). Patterns of infant-mother attachment: Antecedents and effects on development. *Bulletin of the New York Academy of Medicine, 61*, 771–791.

Ainsworth, M. D. S., & Bell, S. M. (1970). Attachment, exploration, and separation: Illustrated by the behavior of 1-year-olds in a Strange Situation. *Child Development, 41*, 49–67.

Ainsworth, M. D. S., Bell, S. M., & Stayton, D. J. (1971). Individual differences in Strange Situation behavior of 1-year-olds. In H. R. Schaffer (Ed.), *The origins of human social relations* (pp. 17–57). London, UK: Academic Press.

Ainsworth, M. D. S., Blehar, M. C., Waters, E., & Wall, S. (1978). *Patterns of attachment: A psychological study of the strange situation.* Hillsdale, NJ: Erlbaum.

Ainsworth, M. D. S., & Bowlby, J. (1991). An ethological approach to personality development. *American Psychologist, 46*, 333–341.

Andersson, G. (2005). Family relations, adjustment, and well-being in a longitudinal study of children in care. *Child and Family Social Work, 10*, 43–56.

Bacon, H., & Richardson, S. (2001). Attachment theory and child abuse: An overview of the literature for practitioners. *Child Abuse Review, 10*, 377–397.

Bakermans-Kranenburg, M., van IJzendoorn, M., & Kroonenberg, P. (2004). Differences in attachment security between African-American and White children: Ethnicity or socio-economic status? *Infant Behavior and Development, 27*, 417–433.

Barth, R., & Miller, J. (2000). Building effective post-adoption services: What is the empirical foundation? *Family Relations, 49*, 447–455.

Bartholomew, K. (1990). Avoidance of intimacy: An attachment perspective. *Journal of Social and Personal Relationships, 7*, 147–178.

Bartholomew, K., & Horowitz, L. M. (1991). Attachment styles among young adults: A test of a four-category model. *Journal of Personality and Social Psychology, 61*, 226–244.

Bennett, S. (2003). Is there a primary mom? Parental perceptions of attachment bond hierarchies within lesbian adoptive families. *Child and Adolescent Social Work Journal, 20*, 159–173.

Besser, A. & Priel, B. (2005). The apple does not fall far from the tree: Attachment styles and personality vulnerabilities to depression in three generations of women. *Personality and Social Psychology Bulletin, 31*, 1052–1073.

Birnbaum, G. E., Orr, I., & Mikulincer, M. (1997). When marriage breaks up: Does attachment style contribute to coping and mental health? *Journal of Social and Personal Relationships, 14*, 643–654.

Bolen, R. (2000). Validity of attachment theory. *Trauma, Violence, and Abuse, 1*, 128–153.

Bolen, R. (2002). Child sexual abuse and attachment theory: Are we rushing headlong into another controversy? *Journal of Child Sexual Abuse, 11*, 95–124.

Bond, S., & Bond, M. (2004). Attachment styles and violence within couples. *Journal of Nervous and Mental Diseases, 192*, 857–863.

Bowlby, J. (1944). Forty-four juvenile thieves: Their characters and home life. *International Journal of Psychoanalysis, 25*, 19–52.

Bowlby, J. (1952). *Maternal care and mental health.* Geneva, Switzerland: World Health Organization.

Bowlby, J. (1958). The nature of the child's tie to his mother. *International Journal of Psychoanalysis, 39*, 1–23.

Bowlby, J. (1965). *Child care and the growth of love* (2nd ed.). Harmondsworth, UK: Penguin Books.

Bowlby, J. (1969). *Attachment and loss: Vol. 1. Attachment.* New York, NY: Basic Books.

Bowlby, J. (1973). *Attachment and loss: Vol. 2. Separation, anxiety, and anger.* New York, NY: Basic Books.

Bowlby, J. (1980). *Attachment and loss. Vol. 3: Loss.* New York, NY: Basic Books.

Bowlby, J. (1982). Attachment and loss: Retrospect and prospect. *American Journal of Orthopsychiatry, 52,* 664–678.

Bowlby, J. (1988). *A secure base: Clinical applications of attachment theory.* London, UK: Routledge.

Brennan, K., Clark, C. L., & Shaver, P. R. (1998). Self-report measurement of adult romantic attachment: An integrative overview. In J. A. Simpson & W. S. Rholes (Eds.), *Attachment theory and close relationships* (pp. 46–76). New York, NY: Guilford Press.

Brennan, K., & Shaver, P. (1998). Attachment styles and personality disorders: Their connections to each other and to parental divorce, parental death, and perceptions of parental caregiving. *Journal of Personality, 66,* 835–878.

Bretherton, I. (1992). The origins of attachment theory: John Bowlby and Mary Ainsworth. *Developmental Psychology, 28,* 759–775.

Bronfenbrenner, U. (1979). *The ecology of human development.* Cambridge, MA: Harvard University Press.

Campbell, L., Simpson, J., Boldry, J., & Kashy, D. (2005). Perceptions of conflict and support in romantic relationships: The role of attachment anxiety. *Journal of Personality and Social Psychology, 88,* 510–531.

Carney, M., & Buttell, F. (2005). Exploring the relevance of attachment theory as a dependent variable in the treatment of women mandated into treatment for domestic violence offenses. *Journal of Offender Rehabilitation, 41,* 33–61.

Carney, M., & Buttell, F. (2006). Exploring the relevance of interpersonal dependency as a treatment issue in batterer intervention. *Research on Social Work Practice, 16,* 276–286.

Chodorow, N. (1978). *The reproduction of mothering: Psychoanalysis and the sociology of gender.* Berkeley, CA: University of California Press.

Cohen, O., & Finzi, D. (2005). Parent-child relationships during the divorce process: From attachment theory and intergenerational perspective. *Contemporary Family Therapy, 27,* 81–99.

Cohen, O., Finzi, R., & Avi-Yonah, O. K. (1999). An attachment-based typology of divorced couples. *Family Therapy, 26,* 167–190.

Colin, V. (1996). *Human attachment.* Philadelphia, PA: Temple University Press.

Corrie, S. (2002). Working therapeutically with adult stepchildren: Identifying the needs of a neglected client group. *Journal of Divorce and Remarriage, 37,* 135–150.

Crittenden, P. (1992). Children's strategies for coping with adverse home environments: An interpretation using attachment theory. *Child Abuse and Neglect, 16,* 329–343.

Crittenden, P., & Ainsworth, M. D. S. (1989). Child maltreatment and attachment theory. In D. Cicchetti & V. Carlson (Eds.), *Child maltreatment: Theory and research on the causes and consequences of child abuse and neglect* (pp. 432–463). New York, NY: Cambridge University Press.

Cross, W. E. Jr. (2003). Tracing the historical origins of youth delinquency and violence: Myths and realities about Black culture. *Journal of Social Issues, 59*(1), 67–82.

Daniel, B., Wassell, S., & Ennis, J. (1997). Critical understandings of child development: The development of a module for a post-qualifying certificate course in child protection studies. *Child and Family Social Work, 2*, 209–219.

Davis, R., & Taylor, B. (1999). Does batterer treatment reduce violence? A synthesis of the literature. *Women and Criminal Justice, 10*, 69–93.

Davis, R., Taylor, B., & Maxwell, C. (1998). *Does batterer treatment reduce violence? A randomized experiment in Brooklyn.* Washington, DC: National Institute of Justice Final Report.

Dunford, F. (2000). The San Diego Navy experiment: An assessment of interventions for men who assault their wives. *Journal of Consulting and Clinical Psychology, 68*, 468–476.

Dunn, J. & Kendrick, C. (1981). Interaction between young siblings: Association with the interaction between mother and firstborn child. *Developmental Psychology, 17*, 336–343.

Dutton, D. (1988). *The domestic assault of women: Psychological and criminal justice perspectives.* Boston, MA: Allyn & Bacon.

Dutton, D. (1995). *The batterer: A psychological profile.* New York, NY: Basic Books.

Dutton, D. (2000). Witnessing parental violence as a traumatic experience shaping the abusive personality. *Journal of Aggression, Maltreatment and Trauma, 3*, 59–67.

Dutton, D., & Painter, S. (1993). Emotional attachments in abusive relationships: A test of traumatic bonding theory. *Violence and Victims, 8*, 105–120.

Dutton, D., Saunders, K., Starzomski, A., & Bartholomew, K. (1994). Intimacy-anger and insecure attachment as precursors of abuse in intimate relationships. *Journal of Applied Social Psychology, 24*, 1367–1368.

Dutton, D., & Sonkin, D. (2003). *Intimate violence: Contemporary treatment innovations.* New York, NY: Haworth Trauma and Maltreatment Press.

Dworetzky, J. (1984). *Introduction to child development.* St. Paul, MN: West.

Dyer, F. J. (2004). Termination of parental rights in light of attachment theory: The case of Kaylee. *Psychology, Public Policy, and Law, 10*, 5–30.

Eloff, I., & Moen, M. (2003). An analysis of mother-child interaction patterns in prison. *Early Child Development and Care, 176*, 771–720.

Erickson, M. F., Korfmacher, J., & Egeland, B. R. (1992). Attachments past and present: Implications for therapeutic intervention with mother-infant dyads. *Development and Psychopathology, 4*, 495–507.

Fausel, D. (1986). Loss after divorce: Helping children grieve. *Journal of Independent Social Work, 1*, 39–47.

Fearn, N., & Parjer, K. (2004). Washington state's residential parenting program: An integrated public health, education, and social service resource for pregnant inmates and prison mothers. *California Journal of Health Promotion, 2*, 34–48.

Feder, L., & Forde, D. (2000). *A test of the efficacy of court-mandated counseling for domestic violence offenders: The Broward experiment.* Washington, DC: National Institute of Justice Final Report.

Feeney, J., & Noller, P. (1990). Attachment style as a predictor of adult romantic relationships. *Journal of Personality and Social Psychology, 58*, 281–291.

Fonagy, P. (1999, May). *Transgenerational consistencies of attachment: A new theory* [Electronic version]. Paper presented at the Developmental and Psychoanalytic Discussion Group, American Psychoanalytic Association meeting, Washington, DC. Available from http://psychematters.com/papers/fonagy2.htm

Fonagy, P., Gergely, G., Jurist, E. L., & Target, M. (2002). *Affect regulation, mentalization, and the development of the self.* New York, NY: Other Press.

Fraley, R., & Davis, K. (1997). Attachment formation and transfer in young adults' close friendships and romantic relationships. *Personal Relationships, 4,* 131–144.

Fraley, R., Waller, N., & Brennan, K. (2000). An item response theory analysis of self-report measures of adult attachment. *Journal of Personality and Social Psychology, 78,* 350–365.

Gauthier, Y. (2003). Infant mental health as we enter the third millennium: Can we prevent aggression? *Infant Mental Health Journal, 24,* 296–309.

Gelles, R. (2001). Standards for programs for men who batter? Not yet. *Journal of Aggression, Maltreatment and Trauma, 5,* 11–20.

George, C. (1996). A representational perspective of child abuse and prevention: Internal working models of attachment and caregiving. *Child Abuse and Neglect, 20,* 411–424.

George, C., & West, M. (2001). The development and preliminary validation of a new measure of adult attachment: The Adult Attachment Projective. *Attachment and Human Development,* 30–61.

Godbout, N., Dutton, D., Lussier, Y., & Sabourin, S. (2009). Early exposure to violence, domestic violence, attachment representations, and marital adjustment. *Personal Relationships, 16*(1), 365–384.

Goldenson, J., Geffner, R., Foster, S. L., & Clipson, C. R. (2007). Female domestic violence offenders: Their attachment security, trauma symptoms, and personality organization. *Violence and Victims, 22*(5), 532–545.

Grigsby, R. (1994). Maintaining attachment relationships among children in foster care. *Families in Society, 75,* 269–276.

Haight, W., Kagle, J., & Black, J. (2003). Understanding and supporting parent-child relationships during foster care visits: Attachment theory and research. *Social Work, 48,* 195–207.

Harlow, H. (1959). The development of learning in the rhesus monkey. *American Scientist, 7,* 459–479.

Hazan, C., & Shaver, P. (1987). Romantic love conceptualized as an attachment process. *Journal of Personality and Social Psychology, 52,* 511–524.

Hazan, C., & Shaver, P. (1990). Love and work: An attachment-theoretical perspective. *Journal of Personality and Social Psychology, 59,* 270–280.

Henderson, A., Bartholomew, K., & Dutton, D. (1997). He loves me; he loves me not: Attachment and separation resolution of abused women. *Journal of Family Violence, 12,* 169–190.

Hewitt, P. (1996). Preface. In S. Kraemer & J. Roberts (Eds.), *The politics of attachment* (pp. xv–xvi). London, UK: Free Association Books.

Hines, P. M., Preto, N. G., McGoldrick, M., Almeida, R., & Weltman, S. (1999). Culture and the family life cycle. In B. Carter & M. McGoldrick (Eds.), *The expanded family life cycle: Individual, family, and social perspectives* (3rd ed., pp. 215–248). Needham Heights, MA: Allyn & Bacon.

Holtzworth-Munroe, A. (2001). Standards for batterer treatment programs: How can research inform our decisions? *Journal of Aggression, Maltreatment and Trauma, 5*, 165–180.

Holtzworth-Munroe, A., Bates, L., Smultzer, N., & Sandin, E. (1997). A brief review of the research on husband violence. *Aggression and Violent Behavior, 2*, 65–99.

Houston, S. (2001). Transcending the fissure in risk theory: Critical realism and child welfare. *Child and Family Social Work, 6*, 219–228.

Howe, D., Brandon, M., & Hinings, D. (1999). *Attachment theory, child maltreatment and family support: A practice and assessment model.* Mahwah, NJ: Erlbaum.

Howe, D., Dooley, T., & Hinings, D. (2000). Assessment and decision-making in a case of child neglect and abuse using an attachment perspective. *Child and Family Social Work, 5*, 419–437.

Hughes, D. (2004). An attachment-based treatment of maltreated children and young people. *Attachment and Human Development, 6*, 263–278.

Johnson, M. (1988). *Strong mothers, weak wives.* Berkeley, CA: University of California Press.

Johnson, S. (2004). Attachment theory: A guide for healing couple relationships. In W. S. Rholes & J. Simpson (Eds.), *Adult attachment: Theory, research, and clinical implications* (pp. 367–387). New York, NY: Guilford Press.

Johnson, S., Makinen, J., & Millikin, J. (2001). Attachment injuries in couple relationships: A new perspective on impasses in couples therapy. *Journal of Marital and Family Therapy, 27*, 145–156.

Karen, R. (1990). Becoming attached. *Atlantic Monthly, 265*(2), 35–69.

Kesner, J., Julian, T., & McKenry, P. (1997). Application of attachment theory to male violence toward female intimates. *Journal of Family Violence, 12*, 211–228.

Kesner, J., & McKenry, P. (1998). The role of childhood attachment factors in predicting male violence toward female intimates. *Journal of Family Violence, 13*, 417–432.

Kobak, R., & Hazan, C. (1991). Attachment in marriage: Effects of security and accuracy of working models. *Journal of Personality and Social Psychology, 60*, 861–869.

Lamb, M. (1987). Predictive implications of individual differences in attachment. *Journal of Consulting and Clinical Psychology, 55*, 817–824.

Lawson, D. (2001). The development of abusive personality: A trauma response. *Journal of Counseling and Development, 79*, 505–509.

Liebert, R. M., & Wicks-Nelson, R. (1981). *Developmental psychology* (3rd ed.). New York, NY: Prentice-Hall.

Mackenzie, M. (2003). *The relationship between adult attachment and psychopathy in a sample of incarcerated male offenders.* Dissertation Abstracts International: Humanities and Social Sciences, *64*(2), 662A.

Main, M., & Goldwyn, R. (1993). *Adult attachment classification system.* Unpublished manuscript, University of California at Berkeley.

Maiuro, R. D., Hagar, T. S., & Lin, H. (2002). Are current state standards for domestic violence perpetrator treatment adequately informed by research? A question of questions [Special issue]. *Journal of Aggression, Maltreatment and Trauma, 5*, 21–44.

Marris, P. (1982). Attachment and society. In C. M. Parkes & J. Stevenson-Hinde (Eds.), *The place of attachment in human behavior* (pp. 185–201). New York, NY: Basic Books.

Martin, M. (1997). Connected mothers: A follow-up study of incarcerated women and their children. *Women and Criminal Justice, 8,* 1–12.

Mauricio, A., & Gormley, B. (2001). Male perpetration of physical violence against female partners: The interaction of dominance needs and attachment insecurity. *Journal of Interpersonal Violence, 16,* 1066–1082.

McMillen, J. C. (1992). Attachment theory and clinical social work. *Clinical Social Work Journal, 20,* 205–218.

Mennen, F., & O'Keefe, M. (2005). Informed decisions in child welfare: The use of attachment theory. *Children and Youth Services Review, 27,* 577–593.

Mikulincer, M., & Florian, V. (1998). The relationship between adult attachment styles and emotional and cognitive reactions to stressful events. In J. Simpson & W. S. Rholes (Eds.), *Attachment theory and close relationships* (pp. 143–165). New York, NY: Guilford Press.

Mikulincer, M., & Shaver, P. (2005). Attachment theory and emotions in close relationships: Exploring the attachment-related dynamics of emotional reactions to relational events. *Personal Relationships, 12,* 149–168.

Moore, S., & Leung, C. (2002). Young people's romantic attachment styles and their association with well-being. *Journal of Adolescence, 25,* 243–255.

Mowlam, M. (1996). The political context. In S. Kraemer & J. Roberts (Eds.), *The politics of attachment* (pp. 21–26). London, UK: Free Association Books.

Murphy, C., Meyer, S., & O'Leary, D. (1994). Dependency characteristics of partner assaultive men. *Journal of Abnormal Psychology, 103,* 729–735.

Norton, D. (1993). Diversity, early socialization, and temporal development: The dual perspective revisited. *Social Work, 38*(1), 82–90.

Obegi, J. H., Morrison, T. L., & Shaver, P. R. (2004). Exploring intergenerational transmission of attachment style in young female adults and their daughters. *Journal of Social and Personal Relationships, 21*(5), 625–638.

Olafson, E. (2002). Attachment theory and child abuse: Some cautions. *Journal of Child Sexual Abuse, 11,* 125–129.

Page, T. (1999). The attachment partnership as conceptual base for exploring the impact of child maltreatment. *Child and Adolescent Social Work Journal, 16,* 419–437.

Penzerro, R., & Lein, L. (1995). Burning their bridges: Disordered attachment and foster care discharge. *Child Welfare, 74,* 351–366.

Poehlmann, J. (2005). Representations of attachment relationships in children of incarcerated mothers. *Child Development, 76,* 679–696.

Pollock, J. (2002). Parenting programs in women's prisons. *Women and Criminal Justice, 14,* 131–154.

Putnam, R. D. (2000). *Bowling alone: The collapse and revival of American community.* New York, NY: Simon & Schuster.

Rheingold, H. L., & Eckerman, C. O. (1973). Fear of a stranger: A critical examination. In H. W. Reese (Ed.), *Advances in child development and behavior* (Vol. 8, pp. 185–222). New York, NY: Academic Press.

Riggs, S. A. (2005). Is the approximation rule in the child's best interests? A critique from the perspective of attachment theory. *Family Court Review, 43,* 481–493.

Rodriguez, C. M. (2006). Emotional functioning, attachment style, and attributions as predictors of child abuse potential in domestic violence victims. *Violence and Victims, 21*(2), 199–212.

Rogers, K. N. (2004). A theoretical review of risk and protective factors related to post-divorce adjustment in young children. *Journal of Divorce and Remarriage, 40*, 135–147.

Saleebey, D. (Ed.). (1992). *The strengths perspective in social work practice.* New York, NY: Longman.

Searle, W., & Ward, C. (1990). The prediction of psychological and socio-cultural adjustment during cross-cultural transitions. *International Journal of Intercultural Relations, 14*, 449–464.

Simpson, J. (1990). Influence of attachment styles on romantic relationships. *Journal of Personality and Social Psychology, 59*, 971–980.

Solomon, J. (2005). An attachment theory framework for planning infant and toddler visitation arrangements in never-married, separated, and divorced families. In L. Gunsberg & P. Hymowitz (Eds.), *A handbook of divorce and custody: Forensic, developmental, and clinical perspectives* (pp. 259–279). Hillsdale, NJ: Analytic Press.

Solomon, R. (2002). A social constructionist approach to theorizing child welfare: Considering attachment theory and ways to reconstruct practice. *Journal of Teaching in Social Work, 22*, 131–149.

Sonkin, D. (2005). Attachment theory and psychotherapy [Electronic version]. *The Therapist.* Available from www.daniel-sonkin.com/attachment_psychotherapy.htm

Sonkin, D. (2009). Angst in the face of economic meltdown: How neurobiology and attachment theory can inform our response. *The Therapist, 21*(4), 67–69.

Sonkin, D., & Dutton, D. (2003). Treating assaultive men from an attachment perspective. *Journal of Aggression, Maltreatment and Trauma, 7*, 105–133.

Sperling, M. B., Foelsch P., & Grace, C. (1996). Measuring adult attachment: Are self-report instruments congruent? *Journal of Personality Assessment, 67*, 37–51.

Thewatt, R. (1980). Divorce: Crisis intervention guided by attachment theory. *American Journal of Psychotherapy, 34*, 240–245.

Thompson, R., & Raikes, A. (2003). Toward the next quarter-century: Conceptual and methodological challenges for attachment theory. *Development and Psychopathology, 15*, 691–718.

Todorski, J. (1995). Attachment and divorce: A therapeutic view. *Journal of Divorce and Remarriage, 22*, 189–204.

Van Dam, M., & Van IJzendoorn, M. H. (1988). Measuring attachment security: Concurrent and predictive validity of the Parental Attachment Q-set. *Journal of Genetic Psychology, 149*, 447–457.

Van IJzendoorn, M. H., Van der Veer, R., & Van Vliet-Visser, S. (1987). Attachment three years later: Relationships between quality of mother: Infant attachment and emotional/cognitive development in kindergarten. In L. W. C. Tavecchio & M. H. Van IJzendoorn (Eds.), *Attachment in social networks: Contributions to the Bowlby-Ainsworth attachment theory* (pp. 185–223). Amsterdam, The Netherlands: Elsevier.

Vaughn, B. E., & Waters, E. (1990). Attachment behavior at home and in the laboratory: Q-sort observations and Strange Situation classifications of 1-year-olds. *Child Development, 61*, 1965–1973.

Walker, L. E. (1979). *The battered woman.* New York, NY: Harper & Row.

Wasserman, S., & Rosenfeld, A. (1986). Decision-making in child abuse and neglect. *Child Welfare, 65*, 515–529.

Waters, E., & Deane, K. (1985). Defining and assessing individual differences in attachment relationships: Q-methodology and the organization of behavior in infancy and early childhood. *Monographs of the Society for Research in Child Development*, *50*(S1–S2, Serial No. 209).

Waters, E., Kondo-Ikemura, K., Posada, G., & Richters, J. (1991). Learning to love: Mechanisms and milestones. In M. Gunnar & L. A. Sroufe (Eds.), *Self processes and development: The Minnesota Symposia on Child Psychology* (pp. 217–255). Hillsdale, NJ: Erlbaum.

Waters, E., Merrick, S., & Treboux, D. (2000). Attachment security in infancy and early adulthood: A 20-year longitudinal study. *Child Development, 71*, 684–689.

Yarrow, L. (1972). Attachment and dependency: A developmental perspective. In J. Gewirtz (Ed.), *Attachment and dependency*. Oxford, UK: Winston.

Chapter 6
Psychosocial Theory

Roberta R. Greene

> How is the development of behavior and the human personality accomplished through a series of proposed stages across the life span?

The purpose of this chapter is to discuss and critique Erik Erikson's eight-stage psychosocial theory. Erikson's theory, a departure from the classic psychoanalytic tradition of his day, made several contributions to the understanding of human development. First, he viewed development as occurring throughout the life cycle, starting with the infant at birth and ending with old age and death. As a result, the life cycle perspective drew new attention to middle and old age (Hogan, 1976). Second, Erikson contended that each stage of development is a new plateau, at which time the developing self can achieve a greater sense of mastery over the environment. This concept refocused research and treatment on a more positive understanding of personality development (Greene, 2008a). Finally, Erikson proposed that development takes place within a social context in which the individual has an expanding number of significant relationships throughout life. This broader developmental context foreshadowed developmental psychologists' interest in the ecological approach to person-environment.

Developmental Theory

A theory is a logical system of general concepts that provides a framework for organizing and understanding observations. Theories help identify the orderly relationships that exist among many diverse events. They guide us to those factors that will have explanatory power and suggest those that will not (B. Newman & Newman, 2005). Furthermore, theories should account for stability and change; describe the interactions among cognitive, emotional, and social functioning; and predict the impact of the social context on individual development (Greene, 2008b).

Developmental theory offers a means of comprehending the client's behavior within the broader context of the life span and within the composite of biopsychosocial events. The purpose of developmental theory is to account for both the stability and change of human behavior across

Table 6.1   Developmental Theory: Its Applicability

Developmental theory can:

- Provide a framework for ordering the life cycle
- Describe a process that is both continuous and changing from conception to death
- Address stability and change in the unfolding of life transitions
- Account for the factors that may shape development at each specific stage
- Discuss the multiple biopsychosocial factors shaping development
- Explore the tasks to be accomplished at each life stage
- Consider each life stage as emerging from earlier stages
- Explain successes and failures at each stage as shaped by the outcome of earlier stages
- Identify personal differences in development

Note. Adapted from ''Eriksonian Theory'' (pp. 107–136), by R. R. Greene, 2008a, in *Human Behavior Theory and Social Work Practice* (2nd ed.), R. R. Greene, Hawthorne, NY: Aldine de Gruyter.

the life cycle (Table 6.1). Before 1940, most social scientists thought that development did not occur until after an individual became physically mature. Today, it has been generally established that development, particularly in the cognitive and affective areas, takes place across the life cycle (Kastenbaum, 1979). Social workers use various theories to assess clients' situations and develop interventions that resolve their difficulties. Theories also help social workers explain why people behave as they do, understand better how the environment affects behavior, shape interventions, and predict the likely result of a particular social work intervention (Fischer, 1981).

Life span development, as envisaged by Erikson, draws on a number of theories and, due to the complexity of the subject matter, includes many scientific disciplines. In considering human development in an environmental context, this approach addresses an individual's genetic endowment, physiology, psychology, family, home, community, culture, education, religion, ethnicity/race, gender, sexual orientation, and economic status (Rogers, 1982). Developmental theory falls under the rubric of the person-in-situation construct, allowing social workers to view a client's functioning both longitudinally over time and cross-sectionally in the light of stage-specific factors.

Historical and Conceptual Origins

This next section briefly covers the influence of psychodynamic theory on the development of Erikson's Psychosocial Theory, as well as how Erikson's own personal history and background helped shaped his stage theory of human growth.

Freudian Origins

Erikson, who considered himself a Freudian (1968, p. 64) and was trained as an analyst by Freud's daughter Anna Freud, elaborated psychodynamic theory by adding a social dimension. In contrast to Freud, who believed that individuals are impelled by unconscious and antisocial sexual and aggressive urges that are basically biological in their origin, Erikson (1975) proposed that individuals are influenced positively by social forces about which they are highly aware (Greene, 2008a; Table 6.2). Although Erikson agreed with Freud that an individual must deal with unconscious conflicts, he viewed development as the outcome of the interaction of the individual with his or her environment.

Again, unlike Freud and other classical psychoanalysts who emphasized the *id* (the innate and primitive part of the personality) in their study of development, Erikson (1959, 1980) was concerned with the capacity of the *ego* (the executive arm of the personality) to act on the environment. The key to Erikson's formulation was its concentration on the interaction between people's striving ego and their mastery of the environment.

Despite his departures from Freud's psychodynamic point of view, Erikson (1975, p. 23) credited Freud with a "radical change in the concept of the role and the self-perception of the healer as well as the patient." Unlike some theorists (Weick, 1983) who perceive Freud and the medical model as an authoritative approach to treatment, Erikson (1975, p. 24) held that Freud's goals were to "free a person from inner bondage . . . and come to terms with his own unconscious . . . thus becoming collaborators in the job." Erikson's own view was that his training as a psychotherapist was both liberating and indoctrinating.

Table 6.2 Framework for Personality Development According to Freud and Erikson

Theorist	Personality development is:
Freud	Based on a relatively closed energy system
	Impelled by strong sexual and aggressive drives
	Dominated by the id
	Threatened by anxiety and unconscious needs
	Dominated by behaviors that attempt to reduce anxiety and to master the environment
	Conflicted by contradictory urges and societal expectations
	Intended to place impulses under control
	Formed in early childhood stages, culminating in early adulthood
Erikson	Based on a relatively open energy system
	Shaped by weak sexual and social drives
	Governed by the ego
	Based on social interaction
	Bolstered by historical and ethnic group affiliation
	Formed through ego mastery and societal support
	Based on the historical and ethnic intertwining of generations
	Intended to prepare a healthy member of society who can make positive contributions to that society
	Shaped over the life cycle
	Intended to convey principles of social order to the next generation

Note. Adapted from "Eriksonian Theory" (pp. 107–136), by R. R. Greene, 2008a, in *Human Behavior Theory and Social Work Practice* (2nd ed.) R. R. Greene, Hawthorne, NY: Aldine de Gruyter.

Erikson's Historical View

Erikson was born in Frankfurt, Germany, in 1902, and died in the United States in 1994. His perspective that developmental theory must be understood in the context of the historical times in which it is written is mirrored in his own life. The majority of Erikson's written works spanning the years 1936 to 1984 do not reveal much about his personal beliefs and sociohistorical times. However, Carol Hoare's (2002) *Erikson on Development in Adulthood* provides additional information from the Erikson collection at the Houghton Library at Harvard University and a transcript of the Conference on the Adult sponsored by the American Academy of Arts and Sciences. Her review of the unpublished papers used a process of grounded theory to examine Erikson's works and to cluster various ideas into content categories, enabling her to reveal "new images" of his developmental concepts (p. vi). Following the completion of her study, Hoare declared Erikson to be not only creative but "an originator" and a major author of 20th-century thought (p. 9).

According to Hoare (2002), Erikson's interest in identity may have stemmed from the fact his biological father was Danish and his stepfather was Jewish. His sense of alienation was said to have grown because he was taunted as being a gentile by the Jewish community and as being a Jew by other Germans. He lived throughout World War I in Germany, where his hometown was bombed on the day of his bar mitzvah.

In an attempt to clarify his own beliefs as a young adult, he read thinkers such as Kierkegaard, Freud, Lao-Tse, Schopenhauer, and St. Augustine. Trained as a psychoanalytic thinker at Freud's Vienna Psychoanalytic Institute by Anna Freud, he soon rejected the idea that development is primarily based on internal drives. His papers reveal that, although he was an admirer of Freud and incorporated some of Freud's thinking into his later works, he gradually came to find the atmosphere of the Institute too conservative. At that time, he earned a Montessori teacher's diploma, embarking on the path to his own philosophy of adult development "in which people strive beyond themselves to make human connections with others in their social world" (Hoare, 2002, p. 13).

After Erikson immigrated to the United States in 1933, his scholarship and clinical papers propelled him into a prestigious career at such institutions as Harvard, Yale, University of California at Berkeley, and Massachusetts General Hospital. He was the first child psychoanalyst in Boston and continued work as a clinician throughout his life. His views on public matters are sometimes revealed in his Harvard papers. For example, at the end of World War II, he commented on the first use of nuclear weapons, stating that the human race had "overreached itself" and that nuclear bombs were a "historical maladaptation" in species evolution (Erikson, 1984). Erikson's stance of nonviolence deeply informed his participation in the disarmament conference of the American Academy of Arts and Sciences, where he observed that the only antidote to the global arsenals of total destruction was Gandhi's nonviolent alternative to change. Later, in a lecture in 1972, he said that the "American Dream" had turned into a "nightmare" with the Vietnam War. His clinical work was extended to returning veterans. Erikson (1977a) also continued to struggle with the question of what it means to be an adult in a "busy, possession-oriented society" at a time when such a question appeared irrelevant.

Often commenting on and critiquing his own works, Erikson appeared well aware of the historical and conceptual origins of his writings. Erikson (1959, 1980) believed that the society into which one is born strongly influences how one solves the tasks posed by each stage of development. He also thought that people who share an "ethnic area, a historical era, or an economic pursuit were guided by a common image of good and evil" (1959, p. 17). He urged psychoanalysts to study the historical influences of the times in which they work. In his *Identity Youth and Crisis*, first published in 1968, he reflects on the "revolutionary minds of the middle class of the nineteenth century" (p. 25), including Marx, Darwin, and Freud.

Erikson (1958/1993, p. 16) believed he could use "psychoanalysis as a historical tool." At some level, as he writes in *Young Man Luther* in 1958/1993, he saw himself as a clinical worker and a scholar interested in the history of thought. He compares his subject, Martin Luther, to Freud. He attributes to both men the ability to engage in introspective analysis, which led to radical changes in society: "I have applied to Luther, the first Protestant at the end of the age of absolute faith, insights developed by Freud, the first psychoanalyst at the end of the era of absolute reason" (p. 252).

Basic Theoretical Principles

Psychosocial Theory

Erikson considered human development to be a biopsychosocial process, thereby agreeing with Freud that behaviors are propelled by sexual and aggressive drives. But, in contrast to Freud, Erikson suggested that there are three social drives: a need for attention, a need for competence, and a need for order in life's affairs. Erikson also concurred with Freud about the human unconscious having biological origins (Greene, 2008a). Nonetheless, he proposed a psychosocial theory—a theory that examines human behavior as the outcome of the interaction between a person's individual needs and abilities, and societal expectations and responsibilities (B. Newman & Newman, 2005; Table 6.3).

Psychosocial theory is "a theoretical approach that explores issues of growth and development across the life cycle as a product of the personality interacting with the social environment" (Greene, 2008a, p. 109).

Table 6.3   Eriksonian Theory: Basic Assumptions

Development is biopsychosocial and occurs across the life cycle.

Development is propelled by a biological plan; however, personal identity cannot exist independent of social organization.

The ego plays a major role in development as it strives for competence and mastery of the environment. Societal institutions and caretakers provide positive support for the development of personal effectiveness. Individual development enriches society.

Development is marked by eight major stages at which time a psychosocial crisis occurs. Personality is the outcome of the resolution—on a continuum from positive to negative—of each of these crises. Each life stage builds on the success of the former, presents new social demands, and creates new opportunities.

Psychosocial crises accompanying life stages are universal, occurring in all cultures. Each culture offers unique solutions to life stages.

The needs and capacities of the generations are intertwined.

Psychological health is a function of ego strength and social supports.

Confusions in self-identity arise from negative resolution of developmental crises and alienation from societal institutions.

Therapy involves the interpretation of developmental and historical distortions and the curative process of insight.

Note. Adapted from "Eriksonian Theory" (pp. 107–136), by R. R. Greene, 2008a, in *Human Behavior Theory and Social Work Practice* (2nd ed.) R. R. Greene, Hawthorne, NY: Aldine de Gruyter.

According to Erikson, to say that his concept of the identity crisis was both psychological and social meant:

- Identity is a subjective and observable quality related to an individual's sameness and continuity. Thus, a person's identity is a reflection of choices made, values carried out, and mentors met.

- Identity is a state of being and becoming and may be conscious or unconscious. Therefore, developing a sense of identity may produce mental conflicts.

- Identity is most prevalent during the developmental period of adolescence and youth. It results from the interaction of somatic, cognitive, and social factors.

- Identity is dependent on the past and the roles offered an individual during childhood. It also depends on communal models.

In short, psychosocial identity is related to an individual's personal coherence and integration in his or her group, the guiding images and ideologies of his or her day, and the historical moment in which development occurs (Erikson, 1975, pp. 18–20).

Epigenetic Principle

The epigenetic principle, which follows a biological plan, suggests that individual growth occurs systematically, with each developmental stage building on another in an orderly pattern (B. Newman & Newman, 2005). The epigenetic principle suggests that "anything that grows has a ground plan, and that it is out of the ground plan that the *parts* arise, each part having its *time* of special ascendancy, until all parts have arisen to form a *functioning whole*" (Erikson, 1959/1980, p. 53).

Erikson (1950/1963) conceived of the developmental plan as unfolding over a lifetime, and retreating or regressing to an earlier stage was not possible. However, themes of earlier stages can emerge and a new resolution of an earlier conflict occur (Greene, 2008a). According to Erikson's wife, Joan Erikson (1988), who was actively involved in the conceptualization of these theoretical ideas, when a strength does not adequately develop during its scheduled period, support from the environment may bring about a further resolution of the development crisis at a later period in time.

Psychosocial Crisis

According to Erikson (1950/1963), a psychosocial crisis is not really a crisis, but a heightened sense of normal demands. These demands, which arise from the epigenetic principle, represent "a crucial period or turning point in a person's life when there is increased vulnerability and heightened potential. [It is] a time when particular efforts must be made to meet a new set of demands presented by society" (Greene, 2008a, p. 135; Table 6.7).

Erikson contended that an individual's personality is a function of the outcome of the crisis of each life stage. Each of the eight psychosocial crises listed in Table 6.4 may be thought of as a state of tension or stress precipitated by societal expectations for an individual's behavior. The resolution of a psychosocial crisis falls on a continuum from very successful to less successful. The two extremes or poles of the continuum from positive to negative are known as *polarities*. The psychological outcome of a crisis is a blend of ego qualities resting between the two

Table 6.4 The Psychosocial Crisis

Life Stage	Psychosocial Crisis
Infancy	Trust versus mistrust
Early childhood	Autonomy versus shame and doubt
Play age	Initiative versus guilt
School age	Industry versus inferiority
Adolescence	Individual identity versus identity confusion
Young adult	Intimacy versus isolation
Adulthood	Generativity versus stagnation
Old age	Integrity versus despair

Note. Adapted from *Identity and the Life Cycle,* by E. H. Erikson, 1959/1980, New York: Norton; *The Life Cycle Completed,* by E. H. Erikson, 1982, New York, NY: Norton; *Vital Involvement in Old Age,* by E. H. Erikson, J. M. Erikson, and H. Q. Kivnick, 1986, New York, NY: Norton.

contradictory polarities. For example, although an individual may be characterized as trusting, the outcome of the first psychosocial crisis is truly a mixture of trusting and mistrustful personality features. However, in some individuals the qualities associated with one pole will predominate or be more apparent.

Another important distinction made by Erikson was that a crisis may be considered a *normative event*, that is, one that is anticipated. Normative events have been defined as age-graded events, determined by universal biological and social norms, including birth and divorce. Sometimes normative events are historical events, experienced by an entire cohort (people born during the same era), such as the Great Depression. Non-normative events are not expected and are limited to a relatively small number of people, such as violent death (Borden, 1992). Erikson also proposed that psychosocial crises accompanying each developmental stage are universal, occurring in every culture. However, each culture offers unique solutions at each life stage.

Ego Qualities Versus Core Pathologies

Ego qualities are the positive features that become apparent following a psychosocial crisis; *core pathologies* are the negative qualities that emerge as a result of severely negative resolutions of the crisis. Ego qualities are the mental states that orient a person to life events. On the other hand, core pathologies are negative forces that develop following a crisis and also act as a guide to behavior. However, core pathologies usually are seen in resistance and avoidance of change (B. Newman & Newman, 2005; Table 6.5 and Table 6.6). For example, following the crisis of trust versus mistrust, is the person full of hope, or does he or she withdraw from life? Erikson, Erikson, and Kivnick (1986) suggest that those who are hopeful throughout life are better able to cope with adversity and attain their goals.

Radii of Significant Relationships

As an individual faces a psychosocial crisis, he or she has a significant other (or others) who acts as a communicator of and buttress to the societal demands of that period. For example, a mother or father often begins to put a child on a sleeping and eating schedule, but protects the child from hunger and malnutrition. This process begins to sensitize the child to social expectations and to stimulate the resolution of the crisis: trust versus mistrust. As the child develops, siblings, close relatives, teachers, and peers become part of the societal network that provides the social developmental context. In short, the radius of significant relationships refers to "the developing individual's expanding number of social relationships through life" that influence his or her multifaceted social life (Greene, 2008a, p. 109; Table 6.7).

Table 6.5   Prime Adaptive Ego Qualities

Life Stage	Ego Quality	Definition
Infancy	Hope	An enduring belief that one can attain one's deep and essential wishes
Early childhood	Will	A determination to exercise free choice and self-control
Play age	Purpose	The courage to imagine and pursue valued goals
School age	Competence	The free exercise of skill and intelligence in the completion of tasks
Adolescence	Fidelity to others	The ability freely to pledge and sustain loyalty to others
Young adulthood	Love	A capacity for mutuality that transcends childhood dependency
Adulthood	Care	A commitment to concern about what has been generated
Old age	Wisdom	A detached yet active concern with life itself in the face of death

Note. Adapted from "Reflections on Dr. Borg's Life Cycle" (pp. 1–31), by E. H. Erikson, 1978, in *Adulthood*, E. H. Erikson (Ed.), New York, NY: Norton.

Table 6.6   Core Pathologies

Life Stage	Core Pathology	Definition
Infancy	Withdrawal	Social and emotional detachment
Early childhood	Compulsion	Repetitive behaviors motivated by impulse or by restrictions against the expression of impulse
Play age	Inhibition	A psychological restraint that prevents freedom of thought, expression, and activity
School age	Inertia	A paralysis of action and thought that prevents productive work
Adolescence	Repudiation	Rejection of roles and values that are viewed as alien to oneself
Young adult	Exclusivity	An elitist shutting out of others
Adulthood	Rejectivity	Unwillingness to include certain others or groups of others in one's generative concern
Old age	Disdain	A feeling of scorn for the weakness and frailty of oneself and others

Note. Adapted from "Reflections on Dr. Borg's Life Cycle" (pp. 1–31), by E. H. Erikson, 1978, in *Adulthood*, E. H. Erikson (Ed.), New York, NY: Norton.

Table 6.7 Stage and Modalities

Stage	Approximate Age	Radius Relationships	Modalities	Freudian Stage
I	Infancy: Birth to 2 years	Maternal person	To get / To give in return	Oral
II	Early childhood: 2–4 years	Parental person	To hold on / To let go	Anal
III	Play age: 4–6 years	Basic family	To make things (going after something)	Latency
IV	School age: 6–12 years	Neighborhood and school	To make things / To make things together	Puberty
V	Adolescence: 12–22 years	Peer group	To be oneself (or not to be oneself)	Genitality
VI	Young adult: 22–34 years	Partners in friendship	To lose and find oneself in another	
VII	Adulthood: 34–60 years	Divided labor and shared household	To make be / To take care of others	
VIII	Old age: 60 years–death	"Mankind" "my kind"	To be through having been / To face not being	

Note. Adapted from *Identity and the Life Cycle,* by E. H. Erikson, 1980, New York, NY: Norton; *The Life Cycle Completed,* by E. H. Erikson, 1982, New York, NY: Norton; *Vital Involvement in Old Age,* by E. H. Erikson, J. M. Erikson, and H. Q. Kivnick, 1986, New York, NY: Norton.

Psychosocial Stage Theory

Erikson emphasized that one stage of development builds on the successes of previous stages, a time when the individual must reestablish his or her ego functioning or equilibrium. Each stage of development is distinguished by particular characteristics that differentiate it from preceding and succeeding stages (B. Newman & Newman, 2005). The notion that development occurs in unique stages, each building on another and having its own emphasis or underlying structural organization, is called *stage theory.*

Erikson assigned only general ages to his stages. However, he did predict that there would be an age-related movement from one stage to the next at a time of natural ascendancy. Difficulties in resolving earlier psychosocial issues may predict difficulties for later stages. This concept is discussed again under "Assessment."

Stage 1: Trust Versus Mistrust

The first of Erikson's (1959/1980) stages occurs during infancy and centers on the crisis of trust versus mistrust: the "cornerstone of the healthy personality" (p. 56). Erikson believed that "enduring patterns for the balance of basic trust over basic mistrust" were established (pp. 64–65) through positive interaction with a parental caretaking figure. Trust, which is learned from the parental figure, is the perception that people are predictable, dependable, and genuine. This learning takes place, for example, as the child experiences the warmth and joy of being cuddled or fed. "By 'basic trust' [Erikson] meant what is commonly implied in reasonable trustfulness as far as others are concerned and a simple sense of trustworthiness as far as oneself is concerned" (p. 57). On the other hand, *mistrust* may occur as a child senses that he or she is in danger and shies away from the caretaker.

Erikson (1958/1993) expressed his fascination with a child's capacity to form what he termed "object relationships," the ability to love in an individualized sense. Growing cognitive ability and maturing emotional response early converge on the face:

> *An infant of two or three months will smile even at half a face; he will even smile at half a painted dummy face, if that half is the upper half of the face, is fully represented, and has at least two clearly defined points or circles for eyes; more the infant does not need, but will not smile for less. (p. 116)*

The resolution of the first stage is a blend of trust and mistrust. When the resolution results in a more positive pattern, a child will be *hopeful*, exhibiting a sense of confidence. If the resolution is toward the more negative pole, there is a tendency for the child to *withdraw* or become socially detached. These important initial adaptive qualities may filter a person's perceptions over a lifetime unless other critical events affecting this general orientation occur.

Stage 2: Autonomy Versus Shame

Erikson's (1959/1980) second stage, which takes place in toddlerhood, is autonomy versus shame. To develop autonomy, a firmly developed sense of trust is necessary. *Autonomy*, or a sense of self-control without a loss of self-esteem, is the positive aspect of this crisis and involves the psychosocial issues of "holding on" and "letting go" (Greene, 2008a). Autonomy may be seen when a child asserts, "I can do it myself." On the other hand, *shame*, the feeling of being exposed or estranged from parental figures, involves a child feeling that he or she is a failure and is lacking in self-confidence. If a child is overly criticized, he or she may feel less than competent in his or her environment.

Erikson acknowledged Freud's view that this life stage is associated with the child's forcefulness during toilet training and is resolved through interaction with the parents. Erikson (1959/1980, p. 71) asserted that as a result, the matter of mutual regulation between parent and child "faces a severe test." A positive resolution of this crisis allows a child to experience a sense of *will*, seen in his or her resolve in meeting goals. In contrast, children who have a relatively negative outcome at this stage may develop *compulsions* or repetitive ritualized behaviors, contributing to the feeling that they are less able to be in control of their world.

Stage 3: Initiative Versus Guilt

According to Erikson (1959/1980), having come to grips with the crisis of autonomy and become convinced that he or she is a person, a child now must find out what kind of a person he or she is going to be. This crisis takes place in Erikson's third stage of life: initiative versus guilt. Erikson (1950/1963) maintained that, during this stage, the family remains the center of significant relations and that children become more concerned with play and with pursuing activities of their own choosing.

Initiative is expressed through such activities as playful exploration. Erikson (1959/1980, p. 78) stressed that, at this time, three basic developments contribute to the child's ability to engage in an active investigation of his or her environment: (1) The child learns to move around more; (2) the child's sense of language becomes perfected; and (3) both language and locomotion expand the child's imagination.

During the stage of initiative versus guilt, as a result of being "willing to go after things" and "to take on roles through play," the child develops a sense of *purpose* (Erikson (1959/1980, p. 78). A sense of purpose can be observed when a child appears to have a plan or sense of direction, such as building blocks. However, if he or she is overly thwarted or frustrated in carrying out his or her plans, a feeling of *inhibition*, or restraint that prevents freedom of thought and expression, will predominate. Therefore, when parents frequently inhibit planful behaviors, the child can fear parental disapproval. Long after the person has matured, the individual displays, as part of his or her "work ethos as well as in recreation and creativity, behaviors relevant to rebalancing of initiative and guilt" (Erikson et al., 1986, p. 169).

Stage 4: Industry Versus Inferiority

One might say that personality at the first stage crystallizes around the conviction "I am what I am given," and at the second, "I am what I will." The third stage can be characterized by "I am what I can imagine I will be." We must now approach the fourth: "I am what I learn" (Erikson, 1959/1980, p. 87).

Erikson's fourth psychosocial crisis of *industry versus inferiority* occurs between ages 6 and 12. Classical psychoanalysts believed that this was a time when the sexual drive lay dormant and children enjoyed a period of relative rest (Corey, 1986). Erikson (1959/1980) broke with psychoanalytic thinking, suggesting that the central task of this time is to achieve a sense of industry. Industry is showing enthusiasm and self-motivation in relation to work. Developing *industry* is a task involving "an eagerness for building skills and performing meaningful work" (p. 90). On the other hand, *inferiority* is the sense that one is inadequate, or does not compare or compete well with others. It is at this stage that friends and peers present social comparisons.

The crisis of industry versus inferiority can result in the ego quality called *competence*. According to Erikson (1978, p. 30), competence "is the free exercise of dexterity and intelligence in the completion of tasks, unimpaired by infantile inferiority. It is the basis for cooperative participation in technologies, and it relies, in turn, on the logic of tools and skills." The opposite or counterpart of competence is *inertia*, defined as a paralysis of thought and action that prevents productive work. Success at making things and "making things together" with one's neighbors and schoolmates is a critical task in the child's expanding physical and social world at this time (Erikson, 1982).

Erikson (1977b) argued that childhood play is a central factor during this phase of development. He described play as a function of the ego and critical to the synchronization of bodily and social processes. Play may be mere fun or give a child the opportunity to figure out what works as he or she puts together a playful scenario. As the child gains mastery over play-like objects, the environment becomes more manageable. Erikson contended that modern play therapy follows the pattern of a naturally self-healing process in which the child is allowed to "play it out" (i.e., a problem) before a powerful adult (p. 225).

Stage 5: Identity Versus Role Confusion

The fifth psychosocial crisis of adolescence occurs from ages 12 through 22. According to Erikson (1968), *identity* depends on social supports that allow the child to devise consecutive and tentative identifications, culminating in an overt identity crisis in adolescence: "Ego identity, then, develops out of a gradual integration of all identifications, but here, if anywhere, the whole has a different quality than the sum of its parts" (p. 95). Rather, identity is not reducible but can be ascribed to:

- *Soma*: The person's intrinsic nature, that is, his or her biological nature, specifically with reference to inclinations, aptitudes, and talents.
- *Ethos*: The cultural context, in terms of both time and place, by which the person receives greater or lesser exposure to acceptable and unacceptable potential identity elements, and by which particular identity elements may be ascribed.
- *Psyche*: The unique psychological contributions of the individual whereby the person may embrace or resist, in varying ways and to varying degrees, both biological givens and cultural ascriptions.

During adolescence, an individual struggles with the issues of how "to be oneself" and "to share oneself with another" (Erikson, 1959/1980, p. 179). The peer group becomes the critical focus of interaction. Erikson saw the formation of ideological views and choice of future vocations as crucial. The outcome of these challenges may be fidelity or repudiation. *Fidelity* is "an ability to sustain loyalties despite contradictions in value systems"; *repudiation* is a rejection of alien roles and values (Greene, 2008a, p. 98). This is a time when adolescents struggle with their worldviews and may be drawn to others who share their ideas.

Stage 6: Intimacy Versus Isolation

As can be seen in Erikson's (1959/1980, p. 101) words, the process of looking for others who share one's ideas continues into adulthood:

> *Adolescent attachment is often devoted to an attempt at arriving at a definition of one's identity by talking things over endlessly, by confessing what one feels like and what the other seems like, and by discussing plans, wishes, and expectations...a real exchange of fellowship.*

Intimacy versus isolation, Erikson's sixth stage involving a mature person's ability to form intimate, committed relationships, occurs between the ages of 22 and 34. The stage of intimacy versus isolation emphasizes "being able to lose and find oneself in another" (Erikson, 1959/1980, p. 179). The radius of significant relations expands to include partnerships in friendship and love. *Love*, or a mutual exchange and devotion that can overcome "the antagonisms inherent in a divided function," is the positive ego quality that emerges during this stage (Erikson, 1968, p. 289). *Exclusivity*, or shutting out others, is a negative sign that an individual has not been as successful in reaching intimacy.

Although Erikson (1959/1980, p. 101) did not go into detail when describing diverse family forms, he believed that,

> [A]fter a person has formed a "reasonable" identity in adolescence, he or she will establish "real intimacy" with the other sex (or, for that matter, with another person or even with oneself)....Except where mores demand heterosexual behavior, such attachment is often devoted to an attempt at arriving at a definition of one's identity.

Stage 7: Generativity Versus Stagnation

Erikson (1959/1980) did not believe that the terms *creativity* and *productivity* captured his ideas about the crisis of generativity versus stagnation. Referring to people's interest in establishing and guiding the next generation, he focused on parenthood. However, he went on to acknowledge that people may apply their generative gifts "to other forms of altruistic concern and of creativity" (p. 103). In short, Erikson's seventh psychosocial crisis, *generativity versus stagnation*, a stage that occurs in adulthood between ages 34 and 60, emphasizes "establishing and guiding the next generation" (1968, p. 290). The radius of significant relations extends to how people who share each others' lives divide labor and share households. Broadly framed, generativity encompasses creativity through producing a family, mentoring a student, colleague, or friend, and engaging in a career and leisure activity.

The ego quality that evolves from the crisis of generativity versus stagnation involves the ability to take care of others. *Care*, according to Erikson (1982), is an ever-widening commitment to take care of all that one has "stored" over a lifetime, including hope and will, purpose and skill, and fidelity and love, passing on these strengths to the next generation (p. 67). The inability to care for others sufficiently or to include them significantly in one's concerns results in the negative ego quality of *rejectivity*. Erikson extended the idea of rejectivity to people who were overtly discriminatory to or who scapegoat people or ideas different from their own.

Stage 8: Integrity Versus Despair

Integrity versus despair, the eighth psychosocial crisis, takes place during old age, which Erikson indicates begins at age 60 and lasts until death. The issue of this psychosocial crisis is "how to grow old with integrity in the face of death" (1959/1980, p. 104). *Integrity* is realized by individuals who have few regrets, have lived fruitful lives, and cope as well with their failures as with their successes. The person who has successfully achieved a sense of integrity appreciates the continuity of past, present, and future experiences. He or she also comes to have an acceptance of the life cycle, to cooperate with the inevitabilities of life, and to experience a sense of being complete (Greene, 2008a).

Erikson (1959/1980, p. 104) saw integrity as a state of mind—an emotional integration—in which an individual comes to an

> [A]cceptance of one's own and only life cycle and of the people who have become significant to it as something that had to be and that, by necessity, permitted of no substitutions. It thus means a different love of one's parents, free of the wish that they could have been different, and an acceptance of the fact that one's life is one's own responsibility. In contrast, despair is found in those who fear death and wish life would give them another chance. The older adult who has a strong sense of despair believes that life has been too short and finds little meaning in human existence, having lost faith in himself or herself and others. The person in whom a sense of despair dominates has little sense of world order or spiritual wholeness. People who have successfully resolved the crisis of integrity versus despair exhibit wisdom, or the active concern with life in the face of death. Disdain, on the other hand, is an individual's expression of contempt for others and the world. (B. Newman & Newman, 2005)

Advanced Theoretical Principles

In 1970, at 68 years of age, having completed a full career of writing and clinical work, Erikson retired from his professorship at Harvard. As he examined his own work and that of others in the field, he found that adult behaviors were usually stated in the negative and not in terms of what people might yet become. He felt that the linear depiction of development was also limiting and did not capture the complexity of people's lives. Furthermore, he argued that viewing life's milestones, such as marriage and retirement, as the essential elements of development did an injustice to describing the meaning of "adult."

Erikson decided to initiate a conference on adult development to address the difficulties he perceived in the field:

- Freud's idea that adulthood was not a time of growth and further development had been too influential.
- Because of this influence, adults were viewed as physically developed children.

- Theorists appeared to be unable to separate early childhood development from its origins in childhood.
- When adult development was studied, development was addressed as a chronological phenomenon composed of marker events rather than a time of qualitative difference.
- Concepts of adulthood and the views of adult normalcy were limited.
- Developmentalists tended to view behavior from a mainstream perspective limited by class and ethnocentric biases (Hoare, 2002, pp. 28–30).

In short, Erikson critiqued his own work as overly linear and concerned with normative events. He argued for a fresh inquiry into normal adult development, an inquiry that would make known the ideal and images of the generative caring person. His lifelong exploration of what it means to be an adult led him to question why so many adults lead "restricted versions of what they might yet become, whereas others always seem to create resilient, fresh renditions of themselves throughout the adult years" (Hoare, 2002, p. vii).

According to Hoare's (2002) analysis of Erikson's unpublished works, his later writings created six vague categories of overlapping, intriguing images of adults:

1. Prejudiced adult
2. Moral-ethical, spiritual adult
3. Playing, childlike adult
4. Historically and culturally relative adult
5. Insightful adult
6. Wise adult

Perhaps in an attempt to come to terms with the anti-Semitic culture of his youth, Erikson in many of his writings dealt with the nature of prejudice. For example, he wrote with great dismay about injustices to Indians and African Americans in the United States and of Hitler's anti-Semitic methods in Germany. He explained that the prejudiced adult develops as a result of holding membership in one group or another. As a child, a person has a certain degree of cohesiveness with that group and their worldview, often comprised of unconscious biases. Yet Erikson thought that the prejudiced adult who learned personal attitudes and behaviors as a child could overcome such unconscious biases as an adult, transcending prejudice to develop self-awareness and empathy.

Erikson made a distinction between a moral adult, one who is rule-driven and concerned with right versus wrong, and an ethical adult, who is principled. He thought of ethical adults as building on their own strengths and giving to others. The ethical adult assumes intimate, caring, and work roles; when taken together, these attributes are called *maturity* (miscellaneous papers and notes, various dates, Item 95M-2, Erikson Harvard Papers).

Another image of the mature adult is the playing, childlike adult, who is able to adopt a mature form of play in planning, developing models, and appreciating drama. Adult childlikeness, which he considered a rare phenomenon, combines play with wonder and trust.

Erikson's fourth adult image is that of the historically and culturally relative adult, described as a highly abstract, cognitively developed person who lives in history and knows himself or herself. Such an adult is cognizant of cultural differences and rejects ethnic, class, religious, and other types of superiority. Going beyond Freudian concepts, Erikson described insight among insightful adults as both a process and a product. Attributes include the capacity to discern and the ability to understand and take control of oneself. Finally, Erikson decided that it was grandiose to designate wisdom as the strength developed in old age. In *The Life Cycle Completed* (1982), he modified or replaced wisdom with faith, which he defined as the final form of existential hope.

Erikson himself wrote two biographies about men he believed to embody a thoughtful and historically significant adulthood, *Gandhi's Truth* (1969) and *Young Man Luther* (1958/1993). *Gandhi's Truth* traces the historical developments of the militant nonviolence movement that established India's home rule. In his visit to India to outline historical and psychological events of the period, he became fascinated with how the Hindu life stages emerge in a sequence corresponding to his idea of the epigenetic principle. He also saw similarities in the way an adult is perceived to be an aggregate of the strengths developed throughout childhood. His ability to observe and acknowledge differences in the extended Indian family form allowed Erikson to hold a broader view of the Western family upon his return to the United States.

In addition, Erikson's biography of Gandhi contributes to the understanding of the relationship between an individual life cycle and societal movements. Erikson (1969, p. 408) observed that when followers join a leader, they do so because of the complementarity of:

- Their personal lives, that is:
  - The moment when they met the leader, their state of mind, and their stage of life
  - The place of that moment in their life history, especially in lifelong themes transferred to the leader
- Their communities, insofar as these are relevant to their search for an identity by participation, that is:
  - Their generation's search for leadership
  - Traditional and evolving patterns of followership

Throughout his life, Erikson displayed an interest in alleviating people's inner conflicts as well as in human rights. He was attracted to men such as Gandhi and Freud because he believed they both worked to expand a person's self-awareness.

Recent Theoretical Developments

Identity Formation

Several recent studies augment Erikson's concept of identity. For example, Waterman (2004) examines how better identity choices can be distinguished from less promising alternatives. Waterman builds on Erikson's conceptualizations and considers how the role of intrinsic motivation or feelings of personal expressiveness can influence the process of identity formation. Reviewing identity from another perspective, Lachmann (2004, p. 247) proposed that, although Erikson was originally criticized for his sociological or relational view of identity, developmental theory was returning to an "interactional matrix," whereas Ermann (2004) has argued that Erikson's developmental model, in which an individual has gone through the normative identity crisis in adolescence leading to a long-lasting identity, is no longer viable. He contends that because society is in such a state of flux, "today's individual is in a continuous developmental crisis" (p. 209). In an article on the changing nature, if not the end, of the patriarchal family, Sjodin (2004, p. 264) concurs with the dynamic nature of social change, stating that "our entire social contract is being rewritten."

Postmodern theorists have also remarked on the diminishing currency of Erikson's theory (Schachter, 2005). Viewing his psychosocial theory from a postmodern perspective, Schachter made the case that although Erikson's theory was intended to be a universal theory that would transcend time-bound and local contexts, it is increasingly seen as less relevant to current social conditions.

Critical Life Events

Research on an older adult's remembered past is another extension of Erikson's theory. For example, the recall of past experiences has been established as a significant influence on an older adult's quality of life (Rennemark & Hagberg, 1997). In a study of social network patterns, the remembered past, and a sense of coherence, Rennemark and Hagberg found that positive self-evaluations were generally important for well-being, particularly when life events were understood within a context of significant others. Three research questions used to obtain life histories (which may also substitute for social work assessment questions) ask respondents to describe (1) what kind of person they think they are, (2) under what circumstances they have lived, and (3) their relationships with significant others (Table 6.8).

Table 6.8   **Research Questions for Life Histories**

Self-Evaluation (Good, Neutral, or Bad)	Topics	Questions
	Trust/autonomy	To what extent do you think you were well cared for and well guided through your first years?
		How easily do you interact with others without feeling shy or ashamed?
	Initiative	To what extent do you enjoy starting new activities?
		Were you easily kept back by feelings of guilt in your preschool years?
	Industry	Were you a hard-working pupil in the early school years?
		Did your teachers indicate that you were good enough?
	Identity	Did you belong to a group of friends in their teens?
		Did you feel like you knew yourself?
		Did you know how to behave toward other people?
	Intimacy	Do you remember your first love?
		Did you establish a close relationship with anyone?
		How do you remember that person?
	Early generativity	In the first half of your working life, did you do things that were meaningful for other individuals?
		For the next generation?
	Late generativity	In the second half of your working period, did you do things for other people?
		The next generation?

Note. Adapted from "Social Network Patterns Among the Elderly in Relation to Their Perceived Life History in an Eriksonian Perspective," by M. Rennemark and B. Hagberg, 1997, *Aging and Mental Health, 1,* p. 323.

Narrative Gerontology

The idea that it is natural and possibly curative for older adults to talk about the past was first brought to light by Robert Butler, who coined the term *life review* in 1963. He espoused a form of reminiscence therapy based on an Eriksonian psychodynamic perspective in which recall of the past was said to allow for the resolution and integration of past conflicts. Although restructuring of past events has been found to foster adaptation among older adults, the life review approach has been criticized for limitations in terms of its universality (Merriam, 1993; Webster, 1999). Another limitation is that stories revealed during the life review process mainly focus on intrapsychic issues surrounding Erikson's eighth life stage, integrity versus despair.

As is noted in a later section on assessment and intervention, social workers continue to believe in the efficacy of conducting life review. However, as early as 1988, Moody described life review as an "ersatz religion, stubbornly resisting empirical refutation" (p. 12). Critics have called for a fully articulated model or domain-specific model of reminiscence (Fry, 1995; Webster, 1999) and the need for a definition and typology of reminiscence (Haight, 1991).

Postmodern epistemologists have sought to understand reminiscence in a broader context. One such area of study that recognizes people's recall of memories as an important aspect of human development throughout the life course is known as *narrative gerontology*.

Narrative gerontology, a scientific approach to human development, highlights the study of aging by obtaining a story or an account of critical life events as told by an older adult (Kenyon & Randall, 2001). That is, as suggested by Erikson's theory, attention is given to the role of critical life events in their specific sociocultural context (Diehl, 1999). A narrative gerontology approach offers several benefits for studying such critical events. The narrative interview allows researchers and clinicians to understand the multiple dimensions embodied in life stories (Cohen & Greene, 2005). For example, according to Diehl, adverse critical events and the ability to overcome them can be better understood by focusing on the interrelatedness between the developing individual, his or her family, and the changing sociocultural context. An individual's story, told in his or her own words, can "uncover how life reflects cultural themes of the society, personal themes, institutional themes, and social histories" (Creswell, 1998, p. 49). That is, personal stories are recognized as being "nested within a set of larger stories or 'macro' narratives that reflect shared history, values, beliefs, expectations, and myths" (Webster, 2002, p. 140).

The recall of past events can therefore be thought of as a community narrative—a tie to an individual's past and to collective historical events (Andersen, Reznik, & Chen, 1997). As noted by Cole and Knowles (2001, p. 1), narratives or personal stories provide "every in-depth exploration of an individual's life-in-context, [bringing] us that much closer to understanding the complexities of lives in communities."

Relevance to Social Work Practice

Uses in Assessment

Although Erikson did not set out to establish treatment protocols, his theory can be used to guide the practitioner's thinking about a client's relative success in meeting developmental transitions. Assessment is a procedure used to examine and evaluate the client's problem or situation. Through assessment, the social worker identifies and explains the nature of a problem or dysfunction, appraises it within a framework of specific elements, and uses that appraisal as a guide to action (Perlman, 1957). The purpose of an assessment, whether the problem originates with an individual, family, or group, is to bring together the various facets of a client's situation, and the interaction among them, in an orderly, economical manner and to then select salient and effective interventions (Greene, 2000).

Arriving at an assessment plan using Erikson's framework as a theoretical backdrop requires that the social worker explore a client's relative success in reaching the developmental challenges outlined by

Table 6.9 Assessment Questions

Stage	Questions to Explore
Trust versus mistrust	How hopeful is the client?
	How socially attached is the client?
	How well does the client appear to trust the social worker?
Autonomy versus shame	Does the client appear to move ahead with a sense of will or determination?
	Does the client seem to have a strong or relatively weak sense of self-control?
	Does he or she appear lacking in self-confidence?
Initiative versus guilt	To what degree does the client have a sense of purpose?
	Does he or she move into opportunities?
	Does he or she face new events with trepidation?
Industry versus inferiority	How competent does the client seem in handling his or her affairs?
	Does the client seem relatively productive?
Identity versus identity confusion	How comfortable is the client with bonding with others?
	Does the client have a relatively "good" sense of self?
Intimacy versus isolation	How comfortable is the client in loving and sharing with others?
Generativity versus stagnation	How willing is the client to care for others and be cared for himself or herself?
Integrity versus despair	Does the client pass along his or her ideas to the next generation?
	Has the client come to terms with his or her life and with others close to him or her?
	Does he or she have relative comfort with his or her mortality?

Erikson (Table 6.9). For example, the practitioner asks questions that could reveal the extent to which a client has achieved a hopeful and/or trusting personality. This challenge, originally presented in stage 1 and modified by subsequent life events, is evident in people's behavior. Thus, observation of clients' behaviors and how they interact with significant others results in such assessment information.

Uses in Intervention

Erikson's theory suggests that at each stage of development, a person strives to attain the psychosocial orientation associated with that critical time period. For example, the crisis in life orientation associated with the period of old age is integrity versus despair. As assessment discloses the conflicts a client is experiencing resolving this crisis, interventions are then attempted. Interventions are aimed at helping the client gain insight about the challenges and opportunities accompanying the crisis. Adjustments and realignments in roles and relationships may be necessary (Greene, 1982; Table 6.10).

Life Review

Life review is an example of how to use Eriksonian theory to better resolve a psychosocial crisis. In a hallmark 1963 article, Robert Butler,

Table 6.10   Guidelines for the Eriksonian-Style Practitioner

Understand that your client is engaged in a lifelong process of personality development in which you as the practitioner can be instrumental in promoting growth.

Engage the client in a self-analysis that results in a developmental history.

Distinguish with the client his or her relative successes and difficulties in resolving psychosocial crises.

Determine areas of development that have led to a distortion of reality and a diminution in ego functioning.

Interpret the client's developmental and historical distortions. Ask for client confirmation of your interpretations.

Develop the client's insight and understanding about unresolved normative crises and their historical as well as present implications.

Identify ways in which the client can use his or her ego strengths to cope more effectively with his or her environment. Explore how these coping strategies can be put into action.

Clarify how and in what ways various social institutions support or fail to support the client's psychosocial well-being.

Seek means of enhancing the client's societal supports.

Promote the client's developing a new orientation to his or her place in the social environment.

Note. Adapted from "Eriksonian Theory" (pp. 107–136), by R. R. Greene, 2008a, in *Human Behavior Theory and Social Work Practice* (2nd ed.) R. R. Greene, Hawthorne, NY: Aldine de Gruyter.

a major pioneer in the field of geriatric psychiatry, conceptualized the process of life review. As Butler examined his clinical data, he concluded that the "garrulousness" of older adults is not always an indication of psychological dysfunction. Rather, he suggested that the life review process has adaptive value for clients, and that practitioners should actively encourage the recall of the past. He defined life review as the naturally occurring progressive return to consciousness of past experiences in an attempt to resolve and integrate them. It involves a restructuring of past events and is conducive to the individual's adaptation to the aging process. Life review can be enhanced through the use of structured interviews, photographs, music, art, poetry, and dance therapy (Greene, 1977; Weisman & Shusterman, 1977).

Since it was first put forth, life review therapy has become a well-accepted and widely used clinical technique for working with the aged in a number of different treatment approaches and settings. For example, life review is used in social work with individuals and families (Greene, 1977, 1982) and has been effective with groups in nursing homes, senior citizen residences, and community centers (Pratt, 1981; Weisman & Shusterman, 1977).

Evidence-Based Foundations: Erikson on Erikson

Erikson (1968) made a distinction between scientific proof and progress and a field such as psychoanalysis that must account for its methods, practices, and ideology. He commented on his own writings and whether they could be considered "scientific." For example, in relation to the term *identity*, he contrasted his conceptualization to those of social scientists:

> *The dignity of the term seems to vary greatly. The quotation marks [used to set off the term] are as important as the term they bracket: everybody has heard of the "identity crisis" and it arouses a mixture of curiosity, mirth, and discomfort....Social scientists, on the other hand, sometimes attempt to achieve greater specificity by making such terms as "identity crisis," "self-identity," or "sexual identity" fit whatever more measurable item they are investigating at a given time. (p. 16)*

Erikson went on to state that social scientists were motivated by the need to be logical or maintain experimental maneuverability and to keep in academic company. However, he was skeptical about whether the "changing images provided by modern psychology, scientific as they may be in the verification of some details, nevertheless harbor what Freud himself called a 'mythological' trend" (Erikson, 1969, p. 34).

Looking back to his earlier conceptualizations of "normality," Erikson (1959/1980) critiqued his own writings. He acknowledged his reliance on clinical insights in contrast to verifiable knowledge, pointing out that his writings are buttressed by clinical data. This suggested a short treatise on the healthy personality:

> *An expert, it is said, can separate fact from theory, and knowledge from opinion. It is his job to know the available techniques by which statements in the field can be verified. If, in this paper, I were to restrict myself to what is, in this sense, known about the "healthy personality," I would lead the reader and myself into a very honorable but very uninspiring austerity. (p. 50)*

Erikson (1959/1980) stated that psychoanalysis and the social sciences needed to work together to understand the life cycle within the historical period under consideration. He acknowledged the methodological divide between psychoanalytic thought and sociological observations. Putting his psychosocial theory into perspective, Erikson (1975, p. 18) acknowledged the difficulty of conceptualizing "something that is both *psycho* and *social*." He recognized that theory development in the social sciences was not as verifiable as in the natural sciences.

Critiques of This Approach

Gilligan on Erikson

Gilligan (1982), an early and vocal critic of Erikson, disagreed with the traditional approach to stage theory. She argued that human development needed to be reconceived, taking into account the differing socialization and life experiences of women and men. She contended that when women are measured with the same criteria used in the study of men, women come out wanting. In her seminal work, *In a Different Voice* (1987), she addressed the disparity between women's experiences and how these experiences are represented in human development theory. She referred to three studies that discuss the significance of language and how people act. Her interviews are intended to reveal conceptions of self and morality in the early adult years. In contrast to Freud and Erikson, Gilligan is concerned with the depiction of the differences between girls' and boys' development.

For example, her research suggests that there is a problem with Erikson's description of the identity crisis. Of particular concern is his assumption that development is a process leading to more and more autonomy and individuation. She contends that the "celebration of the autonomous, initiating, industrious self through the forging of an identity based on an ideology that can support and justify adult commitments" is a representation of male development (Gilligan, 1987, p. 3). She went on to state that although Erikson does note that for women identity has more to do with intimacy than with separation, he does not carry this theme out in writings. Gilligan (1990, p. 65) wrote, "Listening to girls poised at the edge of adolescence, I hear them speak of their confusion and their fight, their struggle for understanding and a great desire to be heard, to be in authentic relationships, and to know what they know with a sense of personal authority."

Gilligan (1982) and other theorists addressing women's development took issue with Erikson's description of girls' and boys' play as stemming from "biological initiatives" (Erikson, 1959/1980, p. 82).

Paradigm Shifts

As paradigms shift, Erikson's psychosocial theory also has been challenged philosophically. In this case, a critique of theory involves a process of "thinking paradigm" or a process of "continually asking questions about what the information . . . we send and receive reflects about our own and other's views of the world" (Schriver, 2001, p. 7). Similarly, Saleebey (1993) would argue that theories are perspectives, not truths. They are texts, narratives, and interpretive devices.

For example, in a 2005 issue of *Identity: An International Journal of Theory and Research*, Schachter asks how Erikson's classic identity theory meets postmodernism. While defending the concept's humanistic viewpoint, he goes on to say that the influence of Erikson's original concept of identity is slowly diminishing. He acknowledges that Erikson's attempt to write a universalistic theory "intended to transcend time-bounded and local contexts" (p. 139). He equally applauds Erikson's stance that all human development needs to be understood in interaction with context, making the perspective relevant to postmodern thinkers. The postmodern context of development emphasizes two points: (1) identity is formed within the context of continuous and rapid change, and (2) the developing individual is embedded in multiple contexts and affiliations that are sometimes contradictory. Thus, when a person is lacking in self-continuity and self-coherence, this may lead to what Erikson termed "identity confusion."

A Social Work Context on Development

According to Greene (2008b), "A theory has inherent usefulness to the degree that it gives direction to a [sound] social work plan of action" (p. 5). Therefore, Erikson's theory may be critiqued from the vantage point of those values and ideas considered important to social work practice, including whether the approach addresses the person-environment context, human diversity, and social and economic justice. The theory might also be critiqued for its relative consideration of a client's strengths and weaknesses.

Person-in-Environment

Based on the belief that the profession's basic mission requires a dual focus on individual and societal well-being, person-in-environment has been a continuing and unifying theme in the historical development of social work. The person-in-environment perspective has also structured the helping process (Gordon, 1962). By serving as a blueprint or an organizing guide for social work assessment and intervention at a multiple systems level, the person-environment focus has allowed for social workers to intervene effectively "no matter what their different theoretical orientations and specializations and regardless of where or with what client group they practice" (Meyer, 1987, p. 409).

There are two major Eriksonian concepts that might be said to be in the person-environment context: (1) The idea of development taking place in a radius of significant relationships—an ever-widening circle of significant others—mirrors the person-environment point of view; (2) societal institutions must positively reinforce and support the development of a healthy ego.

Life Cycle Versus Life Course

A critique of stage theory itself involves a rejection of the premise that there is a fixed sequence to development. For example, Germain (1997) and others have argued for a life course approach to development that takes account of the personal timing of events, one's personal history in relation to the social structures, and the sociocultural period in which one lives. It thus takes into account the synchronization of individual life transitions with collective family configurations under changing social conditions (Hareven, 1982). In an article on the development of gays and lesbians, Boxer and Cohler (1989), maintain that a life cycle approach does not take into account between-group and intragroup variations. They contend that "it is precisely this social definition of the course of life which transforms the study of the life span or life cycle into the study of the life course" (p. 320).

Diversity and Social and Economic Justice

Stage models that present fixed uniform stages have also been criticized because they do not sufficiently account for culture, historical contexts, sexual orientation, family forms, or the presence of poverty and oppression (Greene, 2008c). For example, Chestang (1972, 1984) pointed out that understanding the dynamics of establishing a sense of identity among African American youth requires awareness of the special factors involved in forming racial identity. He also contended that Erikson's psychosocial theory did not give sufficient attention to the implications of social injustice, inconsistency, and feelings of impotence on personality development in a hostile environment. Chestang went on to say that societal structures that embody institutional racism often impede development through "excessive shaming" and "repeated environmental assault" (pp. 46–48).

Ironically, although Erikson has been criticized for a lock-step approach to development (Boxer & Cohler, 1989), he also needs to be recognized for his cross-cultural studies (Erikson, 1937). For example, in his article "Observations of Sioux Education" (Erikson) written during his stay at the Pine Ridge Reservation in South Dakota, he worked on his report with the Indian commissioner's field representative in applied anthropology. The report reveals sensitivity to the plight of the Sioux as they must adapt to the trauma of historical change and oppression. He related how especially the older Indians can only try to escape as "the three horsemen of their history's apocalypse appear on the horizon: the migration of foreign people, the death of the buffalo, and soil erosion" (p. 103). He went on to say that it is possible to understand why Indian people do not want to adapt to "a conquering and feeding government" (p. 104). He also empathizes with the shock of young children who, in the government's effort to "Americanize" them, are forced from their homes and sent to big boarding schools.

Erikson (1975, p. 25) also expressed concern about inequities in the lives of African Americans:

> Since then [Nazi Germany] there have been national wars, political revolutions, and moral rebellion which have shaken the traditional foundation of human identity. If we wish to find witnesses to a radically different awareness of the relation of positive and negative identity, we only have to change our historical perspective and look to Negro writers in this country today. For what is there is nothing in the hopes of generations past nor in the accessible resources of the contemporary community which could help to overcome the negative image held up to a minority by the "compact majority"?

Strengths and Challenges

Client descriptions and social work helping strategies reflect a theorist's language and belief systems, and thereby may embody a strength or deficit perspective with respective implications for practice (Goldstein, 1990, 1998; Longres, 1997; Saleebey, 1996; Witkin & Nurius, 1997). Theories such as those derived from the psychodynamic school have been criticized for placing too great an emphasis on client weaknesses, such as a client's problems or abnormality. It is said that, in such approaches, practitioners take on the role of expert. However, Erikson's views on the matter are revealed when he credited Freud for his treatment of what was then termed the *hysterical personality*. Erikson states that Freud's approach to psychoanalysis freed his patients from inner repressions. He also said that Freud (contrary to today's popular opinion) "called for a strict equality between patient and doctor, with the dictum that only as long as this nonviolent equality is maintained can the truth emerge" (1969, p. 246). Similarly, in Erikson's biography of Gandhi he applauded Gandhi's introduction of fasting and meditation into the politically charged societal conflicts of his day, saying that this approach to political battles was liberating.

Key Terms

Autonomy	Epigenetic principle	Object relationships
Basic trust	Ethos	Psyche
Core pathologies	Inferiority	Shame
Developmental theory	Life review	Soma
Ego qualities	Narrative gerontology	

Review Questions for Critical Thinking

1. Describe how Erikson's conceptualization of human development significantly differs from that of Freud.

2. Consider the so-called core pathologies depicted in Table 6.6, and discuss whether you judge these to be essential and common reactions that give rise to difficulties.

3. To what extent does the "stage model" advocated by Erikson take into account cultural and temporal differences? Is the emergence and sequence of these patterns affected by the differences across decades, countries, cultures, or racial groups?

4. Seek out a recently published empirical outcome study that involved an intervention derived from Erikson's psychosocial theory (e.g., the therapeutic value of a Life Review). Critically analyze this investigation, in terms of the effectiveness of this intervention.

Online Resources

http://video.google.com/videoplay?docid=-7953598721199398444

A YouTube clip using archival materials and newly shot footage, this film introduces students to the rich wisdom of Erik H. Erikson, best known for his identification of the eight stages of the life cycle. This film combines biographical information about Erikson with his theoretical proposals to give students an understanding of the relationship between the life experience of a theorist and the work that is produced.

www.erikson.edu/default/aboutei/history/erikerikson.aspx

This is a link to the Erikson Institute, an independent institution of higher education founded in 1966 that prepares child development professionals for leadership. Through its academic programs, applied research, and community service and engagement, the institute advances the ability of practitioners, researchers, and decision makers to improve life for children and their families.

http://en.wikipedia.org/wiki/Erik_Erikson

An online biographical entry on the life and work of Erik Erikson.

http://www.youtube.com/watch?v=vYb9_RDrYzQ

A short videoclip of Erik Erikson being interviewed and explaining his views on the intimacy versus isolation stage of human development.

References

Andersen, S. M., Reznik, I., & Chen, S. (1997). The self in relation to others: Cognitive and motivational underpinnings. In J. G. Snodgrass & R. L. Thompson (Eds.), *The self across psychology: Self-recognition, self-awareness, and the self-concept* (pp. 233–275). New York, NY: New York Academy of Science.

Borden, W. (1992). Narrative perspectives in psychosocial intervention following adverse life events. *Social Work, 37*, 125–141.

Boxer, A. M., & Cohler, B. J. (1989). The life course of gay and lesbian youth: An immodest proposal for the study of lives. *Journal of Homosexuality, 17*(3/4), 315–355.

Butler, R. N. (1963). Life review: An interpretation of reminiscence in the aged. *Psychiatry, 26*, 65–76.

Chestang, L. (1972). *Character development in a hostile environment* (Occasional Paper No. 3). Chicago, IL: University of Chicago Press, School of Social Service Administration.

Chestang, L. (1984). Racial and personal identity in the Black experience. In B. W. White (Ed.), *Color in a White society* (pp. 83–94). Silver Spring, MD: National Association of Social Workers Press.

Cohen, H. R., & Greene, R. R. (2005). Older adults who overcame oppression. *Families in Society, 87*(1), 1–8.

Cole, A., & Knowles, J. G. (2001). *Lives in context: The art of life history research.* Walnut Creek, CA: AltaMira.

Corey, G. (1986). *Theory and practice of counseling and psychotherapy.* Monterey, CA: Brooks/Cole.

Creswell, J. W. (1998). *Qualitative inquiry and research design: Choosing among five traditions.* Thousand Oaks, CA: Sage.

Diehl, M. (1999). Self-development in adulthood and aging: The role of critical life events. In C. D. Ryff & V. W. Marshall (Eds.), *The self and society in aging processes* (pp. 150–183). New York, NY: Springer.

Erikson, E. H. (1937). Observations on Sioux education. *Journal of Psychology, 7,* 101–156.

Erikson, E. H. (1959). *Identity and the life cycle.* New York, NY: Norton.

Erikson, E. H. (1963). *Childhood and society.* New York, NY: Norton. (Original work published 1950)

Erikson, E. H. (1968). *Identity youth and crisis.* New York, NY: Norton.

Erikson, E. H. (1969). *Gandhi's truth: On the origin of militant nonviolence.* New York, NY: Norton.

Erikson, E. H. (1975). *Life history and the historical moment.* New York, NY: Norton.

Erikson, E. H. (1977a, February). *Report to Vikram: Further reflections on the life cycle* (Item 1573). Erikson Harvard Papers.

Erikson, E. H. (1977b). *Toys and reason.* New York, NY: Norton.

Erikson, E. H. (1978). Reflections on Dr. Borg's life cycle. In E. H. Erikson (Ed.), *Adulthood* (pp. 1–31). New York, NY: Norton.

Erikson, E. H. (1980). *Identity and the life cycle.* New York, NY: Norton. (Original work published 1959)

Erickson, E. H. (1982). *The life cycle completed.* New York, NY: Norton.

Erikson, E. H. (1984, November 4). *Developmental considerations* (Item 1633). Erikson Harvard Papers.

Erikson, E. H. (1993). *Young man Luther: A study in psychoanalysis and history.* New York, NY: Norton. (Original work published 1958)

Erikson, E. H., Erikson, J. M., & Kivnick, H. Q. (1986). *Vital involvement in old age.* New York, NY: Norton.

Erikson, J. M. (1988). *Wisdom and the senses: The way of creativity.* New York, NY: Norton.

Ermann, M. (2004). Guest editorial. *International Forum of Psychoanalysis, 13,* 209–210.

Fischer, J. (1981). *Effective casework practice: An eclectic approach.* New York, NY: McGraw-Hill.

Fry, P. S. (1995). A conceptual model of socialization and agentic trait factors that mediate the development of reminiscence styles and their health outcomes. In B. K. Haight & J. D. Webster (Eds.), *The art and science of reminiscing: Theory, research, methods, and applications* (pp. 49–60). Washington, DC: Taylor & Francis.

Germain, C. B. (1997). Should HBSE be taught from a stage perspective? In M. Bloom & W. C. Klein (Eds.), *Controversial issues in human behavior in the social environment* (pp. 33–48). Boston, MA: Allyn & Bacon.

Gilligan, C. (1982). *Psychological theory and women's development.* Cambridge, MA: Harvard University Press.

Gilligan, C. (1987). Women's place in a man's life cycle. In S. Harding (Ed.), *Feminism and methodology* (pp. 57–73). Bloomington, IN: Indiana University Press.

Gilligan, C. (1990). Teaching Shakespeare's sister: Notes from the underground of female adolescence. In C. Gilligan, N. Lyons, & T. Hammer (Eds.), *Making connections: The relational worlds of adolescent girls at Emma Willard School* (pp. 65–82). Cambridge, MA: Harvard University Press.

Goldstein, H. (1990). Strength or pathology: Ethical and rhetorical contrasts in approaches to practice with families in society. *Families in Society, 71,* 267–275.

Goldstein, H. (1998). What is social work, really? *Families in Society, 79,* 343–345.

Gordon, W. (1962). A critique of the working definition. *Social Work, 7*(4), 3–13.

Greene, R. R. (1977). *Life review and the use of photographs in family therapy.* Paper presented at the National Association of Social Workers Professional Symposium, San Diego, California.

Greene, R. R. (1982). Life review: A technique for clarifying family roles in adulthood. *Clinical Gerontologist, 2,* 59–67.

Greene, R. R. (2008a). Eriksonian theory. In R. R. Greene (Ed.), *Human behavior theory and social work practice* (3rd ed., pp. 85–112). New York, NY: Aldine de Gruyter.

Greene, R. R. (2008b). Human behavior theory: Person-in-environment and social work practice (3rd ed., pp. 1–27). New Brunswick, NJ: Aldine Transaction.

Greene, R. R. (2008c). Human behavior theory and professional social work practice. In R. R. Greene (Ed.), *Human behavior theory and social work practice* (3rd ed., pp. 27–56). New Brunswick, NJ: Aldine Transaction.

Greene, R. R. (2000). *Social work with the aged and their families.* New York, NY: Aldine de Gruyter.

Haight, B. K. (1991). Reminiscing: The state of the art as a basis for practice. *International Journal of Aging and Human Development, 33,* 1–32.

Hareven, T. L. (1982). The life course and aging in historical perspective. In T. K. Hareven & K. J. Adams (Eds.), *Aging and the life course transitions: An interdisciplinary perspective* (pp. 1–26). New York, NY: Guilford Press.

Hoare, C. H. (2002). *Erikson on development in adulthood: New insights from the unpublished papers.* New York, NY: Oxford University Press.

Hogan, R. (1976). *Personality theory: The personological tradition.* Englewood Cliffs, NJ: Prentice-Hall.

Kastenbaum, R. (1979). *Humans developing: A life-span perspective.* Boston, MA: Allyn & Bacon.

Kenyon, G. M., & Randall, W. (2001). Narrative gerontology: An overview. In G. Kenyon, P. Clark, & B. de Vries (Eds.), *Narrative gerontology* (pp. 3–18). New York, NY: Springer.

Lachmann, F. M. (2004). Identity and self: Historical antecedents and developmental precursors. *International Forum of Psychoanalysis, 13,* 246–253.

Longres, J. (1997). Is it feasible to teach HBSE from a strengths perspective, in contrast to one emphasizing limitations and weaknesses? In M. Bloom (Ed.), *Controversial issues in human behavior in the social environment* (pp. 16–33). Boston, MA: Allyn & Bacon.

Merriam, S. (1993). Butler's life review: How universal is it? *International Journal of Aging and Human Development, 37*(3), 163–175.

Meyer, C. (1987). Direct practice in social work: Overview. In A. Minahan, R. M. Becerra, C. J. Coulton, L. H. Ginsberg, & J. G. Hopps (Eds.), *Encyclopedia of social work* (18th ed., pp. 409–422). Silver Spring, MD: National Association of Social Workers Press.

Moody, H. R. (1988). Twenty-five years of the life review: Where did we come from? Where are we going? *Journal of Gerontological Social Work, 12*(3/4), 7–21.

Newman, B. M., & Newman, P. R. (2005). *Development through life: A psychosocial approach* (8th ed.). Pacific Grove, CA: Brooks/Cole.

Perlman, H. H. (1957). *Social casework: A problem-solving process*. Chicago, IL: University of Chicago Press.

Pratt, H. (1981). *I remember.* Alexandria, VA: Mental Health Association.

Rennemark, M., & Hagberg, B. (1997). Social network patterns among the elderly in relation to their perceived life history in an Eriksonian perspective. *Aging and Mental Health, 1*(4), 321–331.

Rogers, C. R. (1982). *Life-span human development.* Monterey, CA: Brooks/Cole.

Saleebey, D. (1993). Notes on interpreting the human condition: A "constructed" HBSE curriculum. In J. Laird (Ed.), *Revisioning social work education: A social constructionist approach* (pp. 197–217). New York, NY: Haworth Press.

Saleebey, D. (1996). The strengths perspective in social work practice: Extensions and cautions. *Social Work, 4*, 296–305.

Schachter, E. P. (2005). Erikson meets the postmodern: Can classic identity theory rise to the challenge? *Identity: An International Journal of Theory and Research, 5*(2), 137–160.

Schriver, J. M. (2001). *Human behavior and the social environment.* Needham Heights, MA: Allyn & Bacon.

Sjodin, C. (2004). The power of identity and the end of patriarchy: Reflections on Manuel Castells' book on the network society. *International Forum of Psychoanalysis, 13*, 264–274.

Waterman, A. S. (2004). Finding someone to be: Studies on the role of intrinsic motivation in identity formation. *Identity: An International Journal of Theory and Research, 4*(3), 209–228.

Webster, J. (1999). World views and narrative gerontology: Situating reminiscence behavior within a lifespan perspective. *Journal of Aging Studies, 13*(1), 56–78.

Webster, J. (2002). Reminiscence functions in adulthood: Age, race, and family dynamics correlates. In J. D. Webster & B. K. Haight (Eds.), *Critical advances in reminiscence work* (pp. 140–152). New York, NY: Springer.

Weick, A. (1983). Issues in overturning the medical model of social work. *Social Casework, 67*, 551–559.

Weisman, S., & Shusterman, R. (1977). Remembering, reminiscing and life reviewing in an activity program for the elderly. *Concern, 22*–26.

Witkin, S., & Nurius, P. (1997). Should human behavior theories with limited empirical support be included in HBSE classes? In M. Bloom & W. C. Klein, (Eds.), *Controversial issues in human behavior in the social environment* (pp. 49–64). Boston, MA: Allyn & Bacon.

Chapter 7
Person-Centered Theory

Michael J. Holosko, Jeffrey Skinner, and
Catherine A. Patterson

> How have the principles of person-centered theory impacted the broader field
> of social work practice?

Client-centered theory is an ever-evolving approach to human development conceptualized by Carl Rogers in the 1940s, eventually known as person-centered theory (PCT) in the 1970s. The reasoning behind the change of nomenclature was that the words *person-centered* more closely articulated the values of the Rogerian therapeutic approach. For Rogers, what was formerly referred to as the *patient* was indeed a *person* with the same idiosyncrasies of human beings everywhere (i.e., hopes and fears, dreams and aspirations, triumphs and losses, and unrealized potential and struggles).

In Rogers's early years, therapists maintained the accustomed practice of seeing a patient with their back turned to the client. For Rogers, truly *seeing and being with* the client in her or his physical, mental, emotional, spiritual, and experiential space was imperative. For social work professionals, the Rogerian approach to PCT will certainly resonate with core ethics from the social work praxis, particularly the principles of the person-in-environment, the biopsychosocial approach to assessment and intervention, the self-determination of the client, the recognition of the spirituality of the client, and the intrinsic dignity and worth of all human beings, to name a few.

This chapter discusses the historical and conceptual origins, basic theoretical principles, advanced theoretical principles, and recent theoretical developments of PCT and the relevance of PCT to social work practice. Additionally, evidence-based foundations and critiques of this conceptual approach are considered. This chapter presents the conceptual constructs (i.e., of the practice, the human personality, and the therapeutic process) of the person-centered approach to understanding human behavior in our social environment and provides conceptualizations that can assist the practitioner in her or his therapeutic enterprise.

Historical and Conceptual Origins

On January 8, 1902, Carl Ransom Rogers was born in the Chicago suburb of Oak Park, Illinois, to a civil engineer father and a devout Christian mother. Carl was the fourth of six children. Being raised in a strict moral, religious environment, Carl became secluded, autonomous, and a self-regulated person, cultivating knowledge and an appreciation for scientific methodology.

Vocationally, Carl Rogers initially wanted to work in the field of agriculture. Following a trip to an international Christian conference in Beijing in 1922, however, his heart was intent on becoming a clergyman. After 2 years in the seminary, Rogers shifted vocational tracks again and began to focus his energies on helping human beings overcome the obstacles that impeded the realization of their intrinsic worth and value. While completing his PhD he was involved with the Society for the Prevention of Cruelty to Children. In 1930, Rogers became the director of the program.

During this period, several psychotherapeutic elements were brewing in the cauldron of praxis and application. Freud's psychoanalytic understanding of the human being was a dominant theoretical model. The elite Psychoanalytic Society occupied a preeminent place in the mindscape of the praxis milieu. Kurt Goldstein was developing the idea of organismic self-actualization. Edward Thorndike was constructing an educational psychology theorem that tested and measured children's intelligence and their ability to learn. Otto Rank set out to test the previously uncharted territory of American psychoanalysis (deCarvalho, 1999) and introduced the therapeutic process of relationship and will. Abraham Maslow was at the nascent stage of his crusade for humanistic psychology. John Watson's (1913) book, *Psychology as the Behaviorist Views It*, often referred to as the "Behaviorists' Manifesto," thrust him into the spotlight of popular media, and his articles on child development and child rearing became commonplace in advertising and magazines. B. F. Skinner's operant behaviorism, which focused on how behavior can be established, shaped, and maintained through reinforcement processes, loomed large on the horizon of possible practice modalities. And Fredrick Perls was developing Gestalt psychotherapeutic theory and methodology, which sought to synthesize the cognitive, emotional, physical, and spiritual aspects of the human being in her or his pursuit to actualize the full self. Amid the churning of these variegated elements, Carl Rogers was transitioning from the clinician field to the academy.

In 1940, Ohio State University offered Rogers a full professorship. Within 2 years, he wrote his first book, *Counseling and Psychotherapy* (1941), in which he discussed the necessity of the therapist to establish a relationship with the client based on understanding, acceptance, and open communication. These ideas were revolutionary when Rogers first penned them. Three years later (in 1945), the University of Chicago invited Rogers to establish a counseling center on campus applying the elements of his practice modality. While working at the University of Chicago, he authored his œuvre d'une vie, *Client-Centered Therapy* (1951), wherein he outlined the tenets of his theory of psychotherapy.

Carl Rogers is hailed by many as one of the most influential American psychologists in history. As the cofounder of humanistic psychology (along with Abraham Maslow), Rogers wrote 16 books (two of which were published posthumously) and more than 200 articles that influenced the world and changed the whole of therapeutic understanding. He was renowned for nondirective psychotherapy, and the primary goal of his theoretical orientation was to release and empower the individual to achieve her or his full potential.

In Rogers's day, three primary forces informed therapeutic praxis: (1) psychoanalysis, (2) behaviorism, and (3) humanistic psychology. The emergence of PCT was a direct response to the other two modalities of practice. Whereas psychoanalysis sought to find the corollary between clients' past experiences and their present actions, in the Rogerian approach, the therapist is simply present to the client (person) in relationship, offering neither valuation regarding what the client shares, nor interpretation of the meaning of that which is shared. Psychoanalysis sought to offer an answer by imbuing the therapist with the ability to interpret insights, teach, and lead the patient through personal discovery of her or his neurosis. In this theory, the psychoanalyst is the expert teacher and the patient is the recipient of the therapist's expertise. Rogerian therapy sought to transform the therapist from resident expert to transparently honest human sojourning with the client.

The behaviorist approach to therapy sought to modify the patient's behavior through controlling the consequences that follow behavior. By applying learning theory, the behaviorist focused not on the development of personal insights by the patient, but on the understanding and elimination of the presenting problem through an analysis of environmental contingencies possibly involved in maintaining it.

The Rogerian approach countered this therapeutic modality by focusing on the inner experiences of the client and how those inner experiences influenced behavior. The third prevailing force that was influential in therapeutic praxis in Rogers's day was humanistic psychology. Rogerian thought and practice truly resonated with this approach.

Humanistic psychology emphasized the inherent worth and dignity of the human individual and her or his quest and drive toward personal growth. The bedrock of PCT is the Renaissance-inspired esteem for human potentiality. Upon this humanocentric foundation, Rogers constructed a model of practice that was a reaction to the other prevailing therapeutic forces and a celebration of human potential. A comparison of these three modalities is presented in Table 7.1.

For Rogers, the client was not merely a client (customer, patient, or patron) per se, but a person with a face and feelings. Freud never saw the patient's face. It was his general practice to sit with his back to the patient. Freud sought to interpret for clients their neuroses; behaviorists sought to

Table 7.1   Comparing the Main Therapeutic Issues of Psychoanalysis, Behaviorism, and Client-Centered Therapies

Practice Modality	Main Authors	Main Assumptions	Main Treatment Issues	Therapist's Role
Psychoanalysis	Balint, Benjamin, Bion, Bollas, Bowlby, Erikson, Fairbairn, Ferenczi, Fonagy, A. Freud, S. Freud, Gabbard, Grotstein, Horney, Jung, Kernberg, Klein, Kohut, Lacan, Loewald, McDougall, Mitchell, Ogden, Renik, Sandler, Searles, Stoller, Stolorow, Sullivan, Tustin, Winnicott, Wolf	The therapist seeks to liberate the analyst from subconscious obstructions that impede her/his freedom. These obstructions are often unexamined and play out through transference, resistance, and defense mechanisms. Patient is oblivious to the power of self-deception and the influence her/his past has on the present mental health. The nature of the human being is tripartite, consisting of *id* [primitive desires], *superego* [internalized values, norms, and morality] and the *ego* [mediates the other two parts and gives rise to the self].	Pros: Effective treatment modality for issues of intimacy and relationships; good at identifying unconscious sources of problems; recognizes the struggle between values and desires. Cons: Therapist is expert textual interpreter of patient's disclosures and the therapeutic approach intellectualizes feeling process, thus strengthening client's defenses.	Therapist analyzes the free associations of the patients' transference with empathetic neutrality and offers insights. Therapist is the interpreter, teacher, and expert who leads the patient to personal discovery of her/his neurosis. Therapist treats the unconscious [the source of the neurosis] and patient gets well. **Therapist is passive.**
Behaviorism	Beecroft, Binder, Bloom, Boulding, Briggs, Cook, Gagné, Glaser, Kamin, Lindsley, Pavlov, Parrott, Rayner, Reese, Rescorla, Schoenfeld, Skinner, Solomon, Staats, Thorndike, Tolman, Trolfand, Watson, Wyrwicka, Zuriff	Behavior in the client can be investigated scientifically without delving into the unconscious. Human free will is an illusion, and genetics, environment, association, and reinforcement are the primary determinants of action. Observing behavior and treatment of presenting troublesome symptoms can assist the client.	Pros: Recognizes that improving the conditions of the client requires modifying the environment she/he lives in; stresses the objective study of behavior; and establishes the difference between respondent and operant behavior.	Therapist helps client to modify her/his behavior through understanding her/his learning history and adding in modifying current contingencies of reinforcement and punishment.

Table 7.1   (*Continued*)

Practice Modality	Main Authors	Main Assumptions	Main Treatment Issues	Therapist's Role
Behaviorism (cont'd)		Modifying behavior is the goal of this therapeutic approach, not exploring or improving feelings of the client.	Cons: Seen by some as reducing the client to an animalistic nature and minimizes inner knowing and feelings.	Therapist is not concerned with inner knowing of the client but instead with present problematic behavior. **Therapist is directive and active.**
Client-Centered [aka Person-Centered]	Bozarth, Buber, Corsini, Finke, Kirschenbaum, Levant, Maslow, Meador, Mearns, Rank, Shlien, Tomlinson, Zimring	Within the human being are three selves: the self-concept, real self, and ideal self. The real self is the person in actuality. The goal of therapy is to bring greater congruence to the person of these three selves through a person-to-person relationship between client and therapist. Increasing congruence in the client frees her/him to realize full potential [self-actualization]. The more congruence, the greater the whole health of the client.	Pros: This modality prizes the person and respects the inner knowing, feelings, and experiences of the individual; use of reflection and clarification proves clinically useful; stress on clients' self-determination. Cons: Nondirectivity of therapist is often criticized. Person-centered therapy is often considered a theory but not a model.	Therapist establishes with the client a relationship of positive regard, genuineness, and empathetic understanding. The role of therapist is not to be teacher, guru, or problem solver but partner with the client to achieve congruence within her/himself. **Therapist is interactive.**

change the environment and behaviors of their clients; but Rogers endeavored to facilitate a transformation within clients by helping them achieve greater congruence between their real self, self-concept, and ideal self. This fundamental change was contingent upon the relationship between the therapist and the client. Through the conduits of unconditional positive regard, genuineness, and empathetic understanding, the transformation of the client could be engendered. Congruence and the realization of the latent potentiality of the client (her or his self-actualization) was the ultimate goal of Rogers's therapeutic enterprise.

It is relatively easy to discern the influence of Rogers's contemporaries on his psychotherapeutic practice theorem. Rank's theory of will therapy and therapist-client relationship is evident in Rogers's PCT (deCarvalho, 1999). Whereas Freud saw an inexorable link between patients' present neurosis and their past, Rank stressed the importance of the patient's immediate inward experience. Similarly, Rogers's emphasis on *the here and now* of the client and her or his inner knowing is more closely akin to Rank than it is to Freud.

Additionally, Rank (1924) stressed a biopsychosocial proviso of attachment and acceptance in the human being that originates at birth. For Rank, this essential need exists within the therapeutic relationship between the practitioner and the client. Although not entirely asseverating this Rankian presupposition, Rogers did recognize the biopsychosocial importance of nurture and acceptance from the therapist with the client. Rank's inference that "nurturing and intuitive emotional bonding can produce individual growth" is a clearly present tenet in PCT (deCarvalho, 1999, p. 132).

A third juncture of confluence between Rank and Rogers is the significance of and respect for both the individuality of the client and her or his inherent potential and the necessity of noninvasive, nondirective therapy. Although they only met professionally in 1936, Rogers was clearly influenced by the ideas of Rank. Nevertheless, it could not be claimed with any degree of scholarly certainty that Rogers was well informed about Rank's theories.

Although beginning his psychotherapeutic journey with those in the Freudian camp, Rank departed from that discipline and went in a different direction. His encounters with social work clinicians (most of whom were women) in Pennsylvania were certainly of great consequence to the development of his psychotherapeutic understanding. Likewise, Rogers's clinical experiences with children in New York, where he worked as a child psychologist alongside social workers at the Rochester Society, had a developmental influence on his practice modality. For both Rank and Rogers, clinical experiences, encounters with social workers in the field of service, the inadequacy of the preeminent models of psychoanalysis, and the stirring of the cauldron of psychotherapeutic praxis and application helped to formulate new treatment modalities. Even though Rank was the first to articulate a person-centered psychotherapeutic modality, Rogers went on to become one of the "most influential psychologist[s] in American history" (Kirschenbaum & Henderson, 1989, p. xi).

Another significant influence on PCT was Abraham Maslow. A contemporary of Rogers, Maslow studied with the comparative psychologist Harry Harlow at the University of Wisconsin. Following graduation, Maslow returned to New York to study with the behaviorist Edward Thorndike. After a stint teaching at Brooklyn College, Maslow became chairman of the Psychology Department at Brandeis University in Massachusetts, where he began the work for which he is most known (Seeman, 1990).

The early years of Maslow's research revolved around attachment behavior (principally in the nurturing/nonnurturing rhesus monkeys studied by Harlow), the learning process and connectionism, and human sexuality. While at Brandeis, he encountered Kurt Goldstein, a German neurologist, who was steeped in Gestalt theory (a holistic theory of the organism). The psychotherapeutic ramifications of Gestalt theory emphasized the importance of awareness in the patient. Through his relationships with contemporary theorists, Maslow learned about the organismic drive to self-actualize in all human beings and the necessity of clients to become aware of themselves as part of reality. The insights gained from his encounters with these contemporaries gave rise to the model for which Maslow is known, the hierarchy of needs (see Figure 7.1). This model had a contributive influence on the development of Rogers's person-centered paradigm.

The notion of self-actualization, that is, that the person has both the organismic drive as well as the essential resources to reach her or his fullest potential, became a driving force in Rogerian thought. One point of departure for these two psychologists was that Maslow contended that very few people become self-actualized, spending most of their energy on the lower levels of existence (the "D-needs"). Conversely, Rogers maintained that the principle driving force of the human is toward self-actualization. Maslow believed that the development toward actualization was contingent upon the stage-like progression of satisfying lower needs first, whereas Rogers conceived of the inner connectivity of all things and

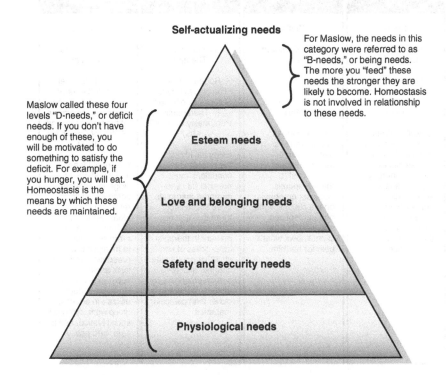

Self-actualizing needs

For Maslow, the needs in this category were referred to as "B-needs," or being needs. The more you "feed" these needs the stronger they are likely to become. Homeostasis is not involved in relationship to these needs.

Maslow called these four levels "D-needs," or deficit needs. If you don't have enough of these, you will be motivated to do something to satisfy the deficit. For example, if you hunger, you will eat. Homeostasis is the means by which these needs are maintained.

Esteem needs

Love and belonging needs

Safety and security needs

Physiological needs

Figure 7.1

Maslow's hierarchy of needs.

needs. Unlike Maslow, Rogers perceived the actualizing tendency in all organisms, not just human beings. Virtually every living thing inherently seeks to reach its latent potential. If certain favorable conditions are present, the minuscule acorn becomes the mighty oak, the egg becomes the elegant swan, the banal granule of sand becomes the lustrous pearl in the oyster, and the human being becomes fully actualized, that is, reaching her or his growth potential and selfhood. Rather typical of Rogers was the tendency to take a basic idea and amplify it to multiapplicable proportions. Rogers applied the concept of self-actualization to micro, mezzo, and macro levels—from seaweed to society, from farm animals to family systems, and from cats to clients.

Earlier, we suggested that PCT is an ever-evolving approach to human development. Among the interesting characteristics of the Rogerian hypothesis is the dynamism of the model. Rogers's therapeutic postulations were not static and were not posited in a vacuum. Some scholars suggest that Rogerian therapy developed over the course of four periods, spanning several decades (Bozarth, Zimring, & Tausch, 2001; Zimring & Rasking, 1992; see Figure 7.2).

In the 1940s, Rogers developed nondirective counseling as a reaction to the predominant psychoanalytical practices of directive therapy, thus challenging the notion that the therapist knows what is best for the patient

Figure 7.2

Periodic development of Rogerian therapeutic approach.

Period One	Period Two	Period Three	Period Four
1940s	1950s	1950s–1970s	1980s–1990s
Non-Directive Counseling	Client-Centered Therapy	Conditions of Therapy	Common Factors Revisited
Rogers' book: *Counseling and Psychotherapy* 1942	Rogers' book: *Client-Centered Therapy* 1951	Rogers' article: "The Necessary and Sufficient Conditions of Therapeutic Personality Change" 1957	Bozarth's paper: *Forty Years of Dialogue with the Rogerian Hypothesis of the Necessary and Sufficient Conditions* 1999
Essential Ideas: Rapport between client and therapist is essential to effective therapy; client needs to accept self; nondirective acceptance of client facilitates the client's self-acceptance.	Essential Ideas: The therapist's attitude, rather than technique, is essential to the therapeutic success; emphasis on the client's world and perceptions; and idea that the client knows what's best for her/him.	Essential Ideas: Six necessary conditions must preexist for client-centered therapists to be successful; three therapeutic attitudes must be present in therapist for process of constructive personality change; and research emphasis on attitude of therapists rather than particular therapies.	Essential Ideas: Investigations of Rogerian thought come full circle, returning to earlier ideas; application of Rogers' basic premises applied to multiplicity of presenting problems from anxiety to substance abuse; Rogerian thought utilized in education, group work, diplomacy, social justice, health care, and policy.

(Rogers, 1942). In the 1950s, he reframed and renamed his theory to reflect the prominence of the client, calling the approach client-centered therapy (Rogers, 1951). During this period, Rogers focused more on the self-actualizing tendency of the client and less on the role of the therapist. Between the 1950s and 1970s, he focused on the conditions essential to the therapeutic process by which the client becomes the self he or she truly is (Rogers, 1961). During this period, Rogers expanded his theory to educational and encounter groups. Finally, in the 1980s and 1990s, the Rogerian approach was expanded "to education, industry, groups, conflict resolution, and the search for world peace" (Corey, 2005, p. 165). Amid the emergent, exponentially increasing application of Rogers's theory, a new name was ascribed to it: person-centered therapy.

According to Corey (2005), the educational, relational, professional, clinical, and theoretical experiences and encounters in Rogers's life all played a role in the formulation of his unique approach to psychotherapy. Ultimately, Rogers defined a psychotherapeutic approach in which the raison d'être was that the client is the essential agent for positive self-change. Rogers embraced salient ideas and theories of his day, rebuffed antiquated postulations, rejected demoralizing practices and principles, and constructed a theorem that has proven its relevance over half a century.

Basic Theoretical Principles

Having considered the historical and conceptual origins of Rogerian therapy, we now turn our attention to the basic principles of the theory itself. In this section we consider (a) human nature, (b) the three values sustaining Rogerian theory and the role of the therapist, and (c) self-actualization. Explicating these principles will provide the clinician with a working knowledge of the essential tenets of person-centered therapy.

Human Nature

The therapist's anthropological perspective and presuppositions regarding human personality will inevitably adjudicate her or his psychotherapeutic practice modality. Ziegler (2002, p. 76) explained that "clients are treated in a particular way consonant with the therapist's theory (explicit or implicit) regarding what client (human) personality is." As practitioners, our estimation of that which constitutes the human being will inform, guide, shape, and delimit our assessment, intervention, advocacy, and relational and interactional dynamics with clients.

Freud saw the human being through the lens of moderate constitutionalism, that is, the perspective that the biological and organismic instincts constitute the essential elements of what it means to be human. Strongly influenced by Darwinism, neuroanatomy, and neurophysiology, Freud nevertheless acquiesced to the causality of environmental factors, particularly in psychosexual development during childhood, although he favored biological determinism. The human being's personality emerged from her or his biological existence, while the environment had some role in development.

Behaviorists such as Watson, Skinner, and Thorndike believed that the human being is a combination of biologically determined behaviors contingent upon genetics as well as reactions to environmental influences, which, through association or reinforcement, shape behavior. The freedom to choose (i.e., free will) is an illusion, according to behaviorists. Additionally, until Skinner began crafting his *radical behaviorism model*, the feelings, emotional states, and contemplative introspection of clients were not generally regarded as real or worthy of treatment.

Rogers apparently concurred with Freud to some extent, often referring to the "nature" of the human being. Central to the hypotheses of PCT is the inherent, intrinsic, and fundamental organismic drive of the human being to live up to her or his fullest potential. Rogers (1961, p. 196) contended that the principal driving force of the human creature was "the inherent tendency of the organism to develop all its capacities in ways which serve to maintain or enhance the person." He believed that positive childhood experience was fundamental to the self-actualization of the human being in adulthood. The environment during the developmental years was, for Rogers, the principal determinant of later positive advancement. For all three of these perspectives, the patient/client's biopsychosocial interconnectedness is of principal import to the therapist.

Regarding the role of rationality, the three main therapeutic modalities differed considerably. Freud did not subscribe to the opinion that the human being was the architect of her or his life or the rational being he or she claimed to be. Rather, from his perspective, the human being was merely a puppet, and the irrational forces of the unconscious neuroses were the puppet master. The id (that part of the human personality that functions outside the realm of conscious, rational awareness) dominated the mindscape of the human being, causing her or him to behave in virtually unpredictable and unreasonable ways. Additionally, the incongruous exigencies of the superego exasperated the neuroses of the subject by placing absolutist claims on the human being that could not be satisfied. Because the human being is essentially a neurotic mess, irrationally controlled by the unconscious, the notion of a reasonable person is a myth (Stachey, 1989).

Behaviorists, being essentially materialists, did not opt for the rationality of human beings either. The intention of the behaviorist is not to deliberate on the person and her or his feelings, but on the person's exposure to past contingencies of reinforcement and punishment. The behavior of the individual, not the reasoning behind it, was of primary interest to the behavioral psychologist. The genetic predisposition of the person, her or his history of respondent and operant learning, and the contravention of punishment, reward, and reinforcement on the person were more significant to the behaviorist than alleged human rationality.

Rogers perceived the human being as strongly rational and exceptionally adept at shaping her or his behavior through reasonableness. According to Rogers (1961, p. 195), the human is "exquisitely rational, moving with subtle and ordered complexity toward the goals the organism is endeavoring to achieve." The inner connectivity of the self-actualizing drive and human reason is strongly emphasized in Rogerian thought and practice. Irrationality occurs as a direct result of the psychosocial conditions of incongruity between the actual self and the ideal self or the actual self and experience. In other words, when people are at odds with their essential (fundamentally reasonable) selves, they behave unreasonably and destructively.

Further along the anthropological lines of personality is the subject of the changeability of the human being. Personality change is often the principal end toward which therapeutic intervention strives. Disagreement among the main theorists exists, however, regarding the possibility of and the extent to which the human subject can change. Freud believed that the adult personality is fashioned during the psychosexual stages of maturation in early childhood (e.g., oral-incorporative stage, anal-retentive stage, and phallic stage, in which the Oedipus complex [for males] or Electra complex [for females] occurs). The developed character structure of the patient is an importunate and impassive configuration that continues through the adult years. The benefit of the therapeutic enterprise is not then change of the neuroses of the patient, but rather, insight as to the source of the neuroses. Freud's contention was that such insight could assuage the annoyance caused by the patient's neuroses. The psychoanalytic approach to therapy did not subscribe to nor try to effect change in the personality of the patient.

Behaviorists asseverated that individual's reactions to stimuli could be modified through positive reinforcement, thus altering maladaptive behavior. Behaviorists did not usually focus on trying to effect personality change in the client based on clients' self-report of their inner feelings. Clients' introspective reports on feelings and inner mental states, though real, are simply descriptions of their private behavior, and are themselves *caused* by biological factors and clients' learning history, but are not *causes* of behavior themselves. The essential goal of the therapeutic enterprise is the modification of aberrant behavior, as defined by the client and/or society.

Rogers was strongly committed to and optimistic about the ability of the human being to change her or his life and personality. The transformative process of human development was, for Rogers, an ever-evolving dynamic fueled by the organismic tendency to achieve one's full potential. Informed by existentialist ideology (i.e., existence precedes essence), Rogers did not believe that the self existed at birth, but rather developed over time as the human being experienced life and challenges. Along the journey to self-actualization, the human is involved in the organismic valuing process whereby she or he determines whether or not experiences develop or depreciate the sense of self. The essential goal of the therapeutic enterprise, for Rogers, is for the therapist to offer the person (client) unconditional positive regard so that she or he can cultivate a pattern of self-acceptance to bring about congruence and facilitate self-actualization.

Hjelle and Ziegler (1992) posited that a therapist's particular anthropological biases adjudicate the praxis modality. As is evident in the brief synopsis of three main therapeutic approaches, not all interventions perceive the patient/client/person in the same way. Similarly, the anticipated outcomes for each methodology are different, as they correspond to the varying presuppositions of the human constitution. The anthropological biases determine the stratagems to effect change in the subject, whether that change is cognitive insight, behavioral modification, or achievement of psychodynamic congruence.

The essential frame of reference for whatever practice modality a clinician chooses to employ rests squarely on her or his anthropology. The essential assumptions regarding human nature, the constitutionality of the human subject, the development of personality, and the ability to change are all factors that inform practice. The differences evident in the three theories reviewed in this subsection highlight the critical issue of the possibility of fundamental transformation within the patient/client/person as a result of therapeutic intervention. A summary of this is presented in Figure 7.3.

The Three Core Conditions Sustaining Person-Centered Theory and the Role of the Therapist

According to Rogers, people are essentially trustworthy. They have the potential for understanding themselves and resolving their own problems without direct intervention from the therapist, and they are capable of self-directed growth if they are involved in a specific kind of therapeutic relationship. Achieving change in therapeutic scenarios can be difficult for both the therapist and the client, even in the most ideal settings (Corey, 2005).

The role of therapists is rooted in their ways of being and their attitudes, not techniques designed to get the client to do something. These attitudes and beliefs affect the change of the personality or inner resources of the client, thus creating the therapeutic climate for growth. Therapists use themselves as instruments of change, and when they encounter a client on a person-to-person level, their role is to be without roles (Corey, 2005). Rogers admitted that his theory was radical, but his three therapeutic core conditions of (1) *congruence*, (2) *unconditional positive regard*, and (3) *accurate empathic understanding*, embraced by many therapeutic schools, are helpful in facilitating therapeutic change. These conditions relate to the shared journey in which therapists and clients reveal their humanness and participate in a growth experience together.

Person-centered therapy reverences the intrinsic value of the living organism and the essential drive to reach its potential. The core conceptual value of PCT is that *life invariably finds a way*. When therapists offer these core values to a client, they are able to offer a social environment that serves to dissolve a client's conditions of worth. The purpose of a PCT therapist's actions is to bring about growth or empower clients. In doing

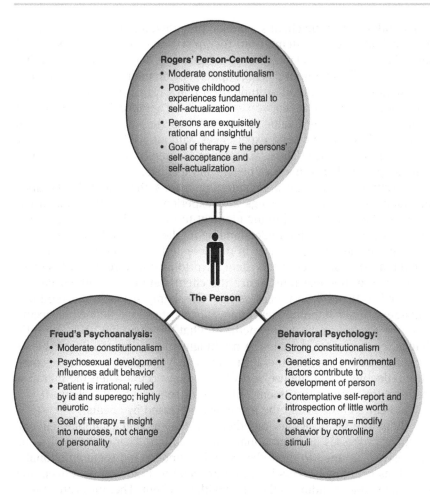

Figure 7.3

Summaries of the theories of human nature.

Rogers' Person-Centered:
- Moderate constitutionalism
- Positive childhood experiences fundamental to self-actualization
- Persons are exquisitely rational and insightful
- Goal of therapy = the persons' self-acceptance and self-actualization

The Person

Freud's Psychoanalysis:
- Moderate constitutionalism
- Psychosexual development influences adult behavior
- Patient is irrational; ruled by id and superego; highly neurotic
- Goal of therapy = insight into neuroses, not change of personality

Behavioral Psychology:
- Strong constitutionalism
- Genetics and environmental factors contribute to development of person
- Contemplative self-report and introspection of little worth
- Goal of therapy = modify behavior by controlling stimuli

so, therapists treat each client with respect and are mindful of individual differences and cultural and ethnic diversity.

Congruence and genuineness implies that therapists are really and truly authentic during therapy sessions. Their inner experiences and outer expressions of those experiences match, and they can openly express feelings, thoughts, reactions, and attitudes that are present in the relationship with the client. Being authentic or congruent also suggests having the capability to relate to the client and disclosing thoughts and events to build an alliance. Through authenticity, the therapist serves as a model of a human being struggling toward greater realness. This does not mean that therapists should impulsively share all their inner feelings and reactions, but self-disclosure should be both appropriate and well-timed (Corey, 2005).

Unconditional positive regard and acceptance entails that therapists needs to communicate ongoing genuineness and openly care for the client as a person. This caring should be unconditional and not contaminated by the judgment of the client's feelings, thoughts, and behaviors as either good or bad. If caring stems from therapists' own need to be liked and appreciated, then the relationship is not genuine. Therapists should value and accept a client without placing stipulations on their acceptance criteria. For example, this is not an attitude of "I'll always accept you when...''; rather, it is one of "I'll accept you as you are." Therapists' behavior should communicate that they value their clients as they are, and that clients are free to have feelings and experiences without risking the loss of their therapist's acceptance. Thus, acceptance is merely the recognition of a client's rights to her or his own beliefs and feelings.

Accurate empathetic understanding means that the PCT therapist understands the client's feelings and experiences sensitively and accurately, as they are revealed in the moment-to-moment interaction during a therapy session. Empathic understanding implies that the therapist strives to sense the client's experiences in the here-and-now. In other words, the PCT therapist should sense the client's world as if it were her or his own. However, the therapist must sense the client's emotions without getting entangled in them. Two processes help the therapist foster and reinforce empathetic understanding: reflection and clarification. Reflection occurs when the therapist repeats fragments of what the client has said with little change, conveying to the client a nonjudgmental understanding of his or her statements. Thus, the therapist consciously enables clients to become more reflective about themselves. Clarification occurs when the therapist abstracts the core or the essence of a set of remarks by the client. It is a way to hear and then echo the meanings expressed by clients.

Empathy is an active ingredient of change that facilitates clients' cognitive processes and emotional self-regulation. Therapists need to be responsively attuned to their clients and to understand them emotionally as well as cognitively. This is not an artificial technique; it is a deep and subjective understanding of the client with the client. Therapists are able to share their own feelings that are like the client's feelings (i.e., disclosure).

Self-Actualization

Self-actualization is a person's lifelong process of realizing his or her potential to become a fully functioning person. The goal of self-actualization is to be that "true self," and the direction is toward the "good life," which is defined by what the client values. Rogers's evolving construct of self-actualization changed significantly in its theoretical meaning and usage over time. In the early period, he presented it as the central motivational construct; in later periods, the tendency toward self-actualization became a part of a larger motivational model. As a master of motivational tendencies, he contended that if a person was self-actualizing, he or she was necessarily optimally healthy and growth-oriented. When actualization explicitly became the master tendency with self-actualization as a subsystem, it no longer meant health and growth were synchronized with one another (Ford, 1991).

Rogers took the approach that every individual has the resources for personal development and growth. It is the role of the counselor to provide the favorable conditions, which for Rogers were congruence, empathy, and unconditional positive regard, for the natural phenomenon of personal development to occur. As such, there is a natural urge within every being to develop in a positive direction. However, before this urge or actualization tendency can operate, it must be liberated by a permissive environment. He often saw personal development as the process of persons becoming more fully themselves (Ford, 1991).

Self-actualization in PCT is not to be confused with self-actualization as presented by Maslow. In PCT, it was illustrated as the central theoretical proposition; the organism has one basic tendency and striving: to actualize, maintain, and enhance the experiencing organism. It is the basic being of motivation. Self-actualization is not a state but a process, and it applies only to the part of the person delineated as the self. The self is a subsystem that becomes differentiated within the whole person (Wilkins, 2003). According to Bradley (1999), when it comes to motivation, even when the primary needs are satisfied and its homeostatic chores are done, an organism is alive, active, and up to something.

The process of self-actualization was associated with enhanced functioning in three areas: (1) openness to experience, (2) living existentially, and (3) placing full trust in organismic institutions. In *being open to experiences*, the client's emotions, thoughts, and perceptions can consciously be considered. The client is aware of all that she or he is experiencing in these areas. When clients *live existentially*, they go with the flow of each moment in life by fully participating. They experience life in the here-and-now, without needing to control how things should be in the future. *Placing full trust in organismic institutions*, the client does what he or she feels is right after weighing all available information. She or he relies loosely on the past or social conventions. The self-actualizing person also appreciates free choice, creativity, and human nature's trustworthiness (Allen, 2003). Boeree (2006) stated that the aspect of being that is founded in the actualizing tendency follows organismic valuing; it needs and receives positive regard. Self-regard is what Rogers calls the real self (see Figure 7.4).

Advanced Theoretical Principles

The following sections review the fundamental conceptual constructs of person-centered theory, including its theory of personality, the presumptive stages of the therapeutic process, and some more recent theoretical advances.

Conceptual Constructs

In PCT, the therapist strives to constantly promote a client's freedom of choice. Rogers maintained that the human organism has an underlying

Figure 7.4

**Real and ideal
self-actualization.**

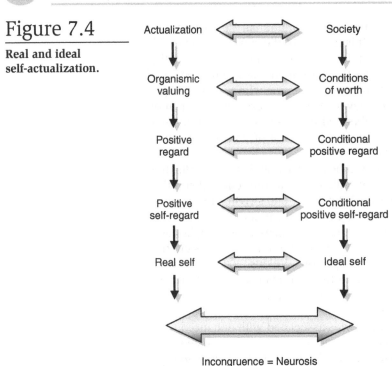

Incongruence = Neurosis

"actualizing tendency" that aims to develop all capacities in ways that maintain or enhance the organism and move it toward autonomy. The concept of the actualizing tendency is the sole motive force in the theory, as it encompasses all motivations, tension, need, or drive reductions, and creative as well as pleasure-seeking tendencies (Rogers, 1977).

Actualization theory viewed people as functioning as well as they can, given their circumstances at a particular time. This theory provided the intellectual grounding for this functional belief. In reciprocation, PCT is an endeavor that constantly tests the actualizing tendency premised with each client (Bradley, 1999).

As PCT developed, Rogers developed an advanced theory as actualizing tendency became more salient to the therapeutic process. The actualizing tendency emerged from a tested hypothesis in human relations that has always remained speculative because it can never truly be conclusively proved or disproved. This hypothesis was to be field-tested with new clients based on assumptions that influence the way that the therapist proceeded as a helper. This theory also elaborated an idea of an inherent motivation, which was a kind of wisdom of the organism, to persist, to maintain its organization, to heal itself if needed, and to develop its capacities (Bradley, 1999).

Rogers observed that clients in psychotherapy who did not benefit or gain skills were soon lost when therapists tried to guide, interpret, or direct them. Favorable circumstances promoted specific survival, integrative, and developmental processes and socially valued outcomes in behavior. The client may be able to function better if certain conditions are changed; if unfavorable internal or external circumstances can be determined and removed; and if favorable circumstances can be created. Understanding the concept of the actualizing tendency clarified the concept of the organism in Rogers's theory. The actualizing tendency is universal and the expression of the tendency is unique to each individual. The functioning of the actualizing tendency and the functioning of the organism as a whole are a changing gestalt, ongoing as its own entity and life force.

Human beings were essentially rational, constructive, positive, independent, realistic, trustworthy, and accepting, and these variables are established through experience, which was the key to Rogerian theory. Rogers stated that experience was the highest authority because each person's perception of his or her own experience is unique, and the client is the only expert on his or her own life. During this experience, a *person's worth* is conditional when his or her self-esteem is based on significant others' evaluation of experiences. Other major constructs, such as *congruence, incongruence, empathetic understanding, genuineness, defense, locus of evaluation, self-experiences,* and *frames of reference,* help each person reach his or her full potential in this regard. To explain how advanced theoretical principles underpin the therapeutic alliance, we will use the examples of genuineness and self-experience.

Genuineness is the state in which there is no difference between the real and the perceived self. Thus, if clients perceive themselves as being outgoing, their actions will mimic this representation. The person's total internal view of self in relation to the experience should match the person's functioning within the environment (self-concept). Similarly, *self-experience* is perceived as any event in the individual's perceptual field that he or she sees as relating to the self, "me," or "I" (Rogers, 1961).

Personality

Personality development is the development of the organized pattern of behaviors and attitudes that makes a person distinctive. Personality is also what makes a person a unique person, and it is recognizable soon after birth. According to Rogers, the main determinant of whether we become self-actualized is childhood experience and the effect these experiences have on personality development. Rogers believed that it is crucial for children to receive positive regard and unconditional positive regard. *Positive regard* is affection and approval from important people in our lives. *Unconditional* positive regard is affection and acceptance with no strings attached (Rogers, 1977).

During therapy, a constructed theory of personality is developed by the client through the dynamics of her or his behavior. According to Rogers, personality theory was not a major concern for PCT; rather, the manner in which change comes about *in the human personality* is the focus (Sperry, 1990). The core characteristics of personality development are (a) *self,* (b) *need for positive regard,* and (c) *need for positive self-regard.* Personality is shaped partly by self-actualization tendencies and partly by others' evaluations. In other words, as the PCT therapist prescribes his or her perception of the individual as he or she appears in therapy, a theory of development of personality and the dynamics of behavior has been constructed. The characteristic of *self* is the person's conscious sense of who and what he or she is. It is available through one's awareness, although it is not always in one's awareness. Once the self is developed, two consequential needs are acquired: *the need for positive regard from others, and the need for positive self-regard.* These are developed through interactions with others and involve awareness of being and functioning. The self-concept is the organized set of characteristics that the individual perceives as peculiar to himself or herself and is based largely on the social evaluations he or she has experienced (Wilkins, 2003).

Central to PCT is the idea that every person has an innate need for positive self-regard. Positive regard was Rogers's umbrella term for emotional or physical pleasures such as love, affection, attention, and nurturance. For example, it is clear that babies need love and attention. In fact, it may well be that they die without them. They certainly fail to thrive, that is, become all they can be, without them. Rogers also stated that humans value positive self-regard, which consists of self-esteem, self-worth, and a positive self-image. Positive self-regard is an intrinsic attitude toward the self that is not dependent on the perceptions of significant others. This is achieved by experiencing the positive regard others show us during our years of growing up. Without this self-regard, we tend to feel small and helpless, and again we fail to become all that we can be (Rogers, 1961).

In the infant beginning stage of therapy, clients perceive their *experience* as reality; as a consequence, they have a greater concept of what reality is than someone else does. The client also has an inherent tendency toward actualizing his or her organism by interacting with his or her reality in terms of his or her basic actualizing tendency. Behaviors then become properly goal-directed in an attempt to satisfy experienced needs for actualization (Rogers, 1961).

Stages of the Therapeutic Process

Person-centered therapy aims for a greater degree of independence and integration of the whole self. Its focus is on the person, not on the person's presenting problem. Rogers contended that the aim of therapy was not to solve problems, but to assist clients in their life growth development. As such, ideally clients should be able to better cope with problems they are currently facing and with their future problems. Therapeutic change depends symbiotically on clients' perceptions of both their own experience in therapy and the counselor's basic attitude (Corey, 2005).

Rogers's ideas about personality development, when applied to PCT, involved the assumption that, if certain conditions exist, then a characteristic process of personality change will occur naturally. The direction of change for clients in Rogerian therapy is from a personality that is fixed, detached from self, and tied to the past, a past that is spontaneous, integrated, and flowing with experiences that occurred in the present. Seven characteristic stages of this process unfold during therapy:

Stage 1: The client's communications are mostly about externals, not about self.

Stage 2: The client describes feelings but does not recognize or own them personally.

Stage 3: The client talks about self as an object, often in terms of past experiences.

Stage 4: The client experiences feelings in the present, but mainly just describes them, with distrust and fear, rather than expressing them directly.

Stage 5: The client experiences and expresses feelings freely in the present; feelings bubble up into awareness with a display of desire to experience them.

Stage 6: The client accepts his or her feelings in all their richness.

Stage 7: The client trusts new experiences and is able to relate to others, openly and freely. (Allen, 2003, p. 215)

When this process occurs, certain cognitive, emotional, and behavioral changes will occur. These changes reflect increases in congruence, openness to experience, adjustment, correspondence between actual and ideal self, positive self-regard, and acceptance of self and others. There is convincing evidence that therapeutic outcome is positively associated with the quality of the therapeutic relationship, particularly when perceived by the client (Cramer & Takens, 1992). The client will be able to express deep and motivating attitudes; will explore his or her own attitudes and reactions more fully than he or she has previously done and will come to be aware of aspects of his or her attitudes that he or she has previously denied; will arrive at a clearer conscious realization of his or her motivating attitudes and will accept himself or herself more completely; and will choose to behave in a different fashion in order to reach these goals.

Recent Theoretical Developments

During the 1940s and 1950s, Rogers and his colleagues developed a theory and a method of therapy that was initially characterized as nondirective, later as client-centered, and then person-centered. Client-centered therapy was practiced in the early days without much of a theoretical base. It was only in the late 1950s that Rogers set out the well-known theoretical schema that asserted that therapeutic movement will occur if and only if six conditions are present: (1) The client and therapist are in psychological contact; (2) the client is in a state of vulnerability and incongruence; (3) the therapist is congruent or integrated in the relationship; (4) the therapist experiences positive regard for the client; (5) the therapist is accepting and empathic toward the client; and (6) the client perceives these attitudes in the therapist (Allen, 2003). Central features of PCT are the motivational constructs of actualization and self-actualization. Later in his life, Rogers (1986) spoke of the importance of the counselor being "present" and "there" for the client, a view that has been reemphasized (Corey, 2005).

According to Zimring and Rasking (1992), a new explanation of PCT is necessary because some of the theories that Rogers used to explain why change occurs do not match his therapy methods. Thus, in line with the old paradigm, his theory refers to experience, not awareness. The framework of a new paradigm may enable practitioners to describe their clients, during supervision, in ways that are respectful of the client, without reference to material they are unaware of.

Relevance to Social Work

Both the social work profession and Rogerian PCT share the intellectual and cultural ideas of humanism and religious humanism. Thus, they promote a strong value-based mission and practice mandate to facilitate opportunities with clients for their human growth and actualization. Embedded within PCT and the social work profession are values and embodied convictions that blend the personal and professional use of self. The relevance of PCT is most lucid when viewing the social work profession as a principle-based approach to practice, as described subsequently by Biestek (1961). Biestek's key principles include the acceptance of clients with their strengths and weaknesses, a nonjudgmental attitude, respect for client self-determination, a duty to assist clients in activating their potential for self-direction, and a respect for the client as an individual human being worthy of full attention. Almost all of these resonate with social work's present Code of Ethics (National Association of Social Workers, 1996).

The social work profession and PCT are mutually congruent in what constitutes a beneficial helping and facilitating relationship with the client. For instance, principle-based approaches require a social worker (or counselor) to manifest grounding and awareness of the attitudes, beliefs, and personal attributes that he or she brings to the client relationship. Similarly, attitudes and manifestations of the Rogerian principles of accurate empathy, unconditional positive regard, genuineness, warmth, and counselor congruence provide the client with the experiences of facilitating, self-congruence, and self-actualization.

Rogerians do not emphasize techniques and psychoeducation, focusing more on the qualities of the helping relationship in a nondirective approach. The overt Rogerian values of client self-direction and determination resonate with the social work profession principle of client self-determination and subsequently the practice principle of meeting the client where the client is. The profound Rogerian genuine respect of client dignity allows for the possibility of empowering the client to become self-congruent and to take the lead in the working relationship through selecting the focus and topics to be discussed. Such a construction of the working relationship and the high regard for self-determination allow for a more equal distribution of power between the client and the counselor. Rogerian PCT promotes, as does the profession of social work, a collaborative model of the helping relationship whereby the social worker stays with the client, minimizes misuse of professional authority, and practices with the client instead of on the client. This avoids dehumanizing and de-personifying the client and provides for a more trusted and authentic experience of self than the client may otherwise feel permitted to experience or have available elsewhere in his or her environment.

Central principles guiding social work practice are empowering the client and building capacities for self-efficacy. Rogerian thought parallels empowering the client, as seen in the goal of promoting client self-actualization and through building developmentally on client strengths. The emphasis in PCT on the facilitative qualities of the helping relationship contribute to the social work understanding of the casework process as foundationally prescribed by the formative social work educator Perlman (1979). The Rogerian mandate of counselor authenticity, empathy, and unconditional positive regard allow for counselor transparency and promote a model for clients that culminates in their regarding the counselor as having their best interest in mind. The effective use and manifestation of the previous three counselor attributes allow clients openly and honestly to explore themselves without having to fear, please, placate, or meet expectations of the social worker.

The humanistic anthropology of regarding people as ends in themselves and self-directed, not as a means to be exploited, can serve as a radically corrective reminder to monitor and repair any potential toxic disruptions during the formation of the treatment relationship. Foundational treatment relationship fractures can occur in managed care social work practices, in which the treatment relationship is driven by the entrepreneurial marketplace. This may result in entrapping the client as consumer and the social worker as provider. Such an institutional helping relationship paradigm in social work practice can corrode the development of a facilitative person-to-person helping relationship. When social workers primarily ground their attitudes toward clients in fiduciary exchanging postures, they can unknowingly characterize clients as means for a monetary or quota end.

The Rogerian principle of unconditional positive regard contributes to the mandate of social work to serve those who are oppressed and marginalized within society, the profession's present preoccupation with social justice (Wakefield, 2001). Oppressed and marginalized clients often feel inner conflicts and diminished self-efficacy. This especially occurs when their sense of self and human potential are derived from pejorative or stigmatic valuations from others in their intimate and larger social environments. Consequently, oppressed and marginalized clients live in a state of conditional positive regard. Person-centered therapy and social casework can promote fuller congruence between the ideal self and the real self through utilizing unconditional positive regard. This provides clients with an opportunity to self-actualize according to their intrinsic beliefs and not according to the restricting dynamics of an oppressive environment. For example, PCT has been utilized in assisting gay adolescent males to achieve greater self-regard and congruence in their process of coming out to their families and communities (Lemoire & Chen, 2005).

Training in PCT focuses on the processes and qualities of the helping relationship, instead of the outcome. Accordingly, Rogers often recorded therapy sessions in an effort to examine the therapist's interviewing skills, authenticity, positive regard, accurate empathy, and attending behaviors toward the client. Social work education and training, among other helping professions, benefit from the contributions that Rogers made in training person-centered therapists. Rogers encouraged what in social work is called "critical self-reflective thinking," whereby a social worker examines in detail the interviewing process with clients and, most important, evaluates his or her benevolent blending of the professional and personal use of self. In social work education, training, and specifically in (baccalaureate- and graduate-level) foundation practice courses, skills labs, and field education, students are evaluated and self-evaluate according to Rogers's three core conditions: empathy, congruence, and unconditional positive regard.

Assessment

Rogers opposed formally diagnosing clients with labels. He promotes the notion that formal and systematic assessments of clients, even history taking, were potentially harmful, unhelpful, and incongruent with the humanistic approach to helping others. Implementing systematic assessments may give clients the idea that the counselor omnisciently has the solution for their presenting issues. This consequently disempowers clients from tapping into their own inner resources and assuming responsibility for their life and the therapy process (Corey, 1996). Such a stance may appear dogmatically dismissive, given the current practice climate of utilizing standardized measures, normed psychometric tests, time-framed structured client interviews, risk-assessment models, and the like, all of which eventually lead to a psychosocial case formulation that may include the classifying of client problems and functioning into the five *DSM-IV* axes.

In PCT, the clients are the experts about themselves, and no other external source of information or data, including the counselor, may serve as a substitute for definitively authentic client self-derived knowledge. Rogers and others in the humanistic and existential traditions in counseling offer helpful arguments and reasons about the harmful effects of assessing and diagnosing clients (Friedman & MacDonald, 2006). Assessments and diagnoses are reductionistic and typify the client as having a problem or, even worse, being the problem. Rogers was more interested in knowing persons and how they experience their lives rather than making judgments and investigating the etiology of the problem. The latter assumes that solving the origin of the problem will lead to a more self-congruent life. Friedman and MacDonald make the point that office-based assessments are artificially contained and take limited pictures of where clients actually live their lives (p. 518).

The phenomenological and existential underpinnings of PCT provide an appreciation of its incompatibility with the assessment and diagnostic protocols used today. The existential influences emphasize experiences and processes in human life more than the content, problems, or rationalizations of human experiences. Subsequently, meaning in life and self-knowledge are derived directly from the client's experiences and not from the essence of an external referent, such as psychometric testing based on general population norms with preconceived standard deviations.

Phenomenological thought posits that nothing has an essence in such a manner for it to stand alone in and of itself, outside of human existence and meaning. This approach to understanding a client's social and personal existence and relating to a client necessitates that counselors acknowledge that they are already in relationship with the client as a human to a human. The client relationship must not be preconceived or biased in any mediated assessment protocol that may discriminately typify a client. Likewise, the phenomenological approaches require the counselor to bracket, put aside, and forsake systematic assessment constructs (personality profiling, etc.). The disciplined and intentional use of the phenomenological approach to knowing the client as a person requires that the counselor create a helping relationship that allows clients to unfold, reveal, and present themselves authentically and uniquely. The basic posture of unconditional positive regard helps clients to reveal themselves willingly without complying with and meeting the performance demands of time-framed systematic assessments, such as psychodiagnostic testing. Therefore, the process of clients knowing themselves more fully is mediated through a direct, immediate experience of the here-and-now moments within the therapy session, which precludes time-framed assessment parameters.

Person-centered therapy does not use the constructs of normalcy and pathology of healthy and unhealthy. Rogers was interested in the process of becoming self-congruent, self-actualized, and authentic within the self and others. For Rogers, symptoms and expressions of such indicate that the client is suffering and seeking relief from inauthentic existence. Schmid (2003) regarded symptoms as unique expressions of the individual person and an invitation from the client to understand himself or herself and to be understood by others. Classifying symptoms and then linking them to uniform standardized treatment protocols is not a part of PCT because Rogers believed that the unique person should not be subsumed and lost in the generic, depersonalized world. As such, each client uniquely discovers his or her own solutions for self-actualization in his or her own time and in his or her own way. For example, a client who is labeled schizophrenic with symptoms of auditory hallucinations can become a more self-congruent and authentic person while manifesting his or her schizophrenic symptoms.

External referents of client data and formal assessments of clients are ideologically incompatible with PCT principles. Post-Rogerian thinkers and humanistic psychologists (Friedman & MacDonald, 2006), however, seek helpful ways to utilize formal assessments in PCT. Thus, they seek to incorporate external referents about the client that contribute to the client's ongoing self-understanding. Assessment measures such as rating scales, diagnostic testing, agency-mandated assessment forms, and personality and vocational testing are conditionally permitted as useful, only insofar as the clients interpret or appropriate the findings in their quest for self-understanding and congruence. In other words, external sources of data may be helpful for the client only when the client is the expert, not the counselor or the authority behind the data, in applying the findings to himself or herself. Few current assessments conducted in social work practice provide for the mutual partnership and empowering of the client in directing this process.

An example of utilizing noninvasive and nonnormed assessments to facilitate client self-awareness was implemented by Rogers early in his career. He adapted the Q-Sort assessment process to PCT. He offered the Q-Sort process as a learning tool for clients to measure their self-congruence between their real self and their ideal self. Rogers's adaptation of the Q-Sort method consisted of a deck of 100 cards, each of which contained an adjective describing various personality traits. Clients then selected each card as applicable or nonapplicable to their immediate, perceived true self. They then placed the cards on a 9-point continuum, ranging from "Not like me at all" to "Very much like me." Clients were instructed to place most of the cards in the middle of the continuum to depict a normal distribution of real self-perceived qualities. To depict the ideal self, clients then placed the cards as to how they would like to see themselves. They then utilized the distribution of personality traits between their real self and ideal self as a depiction of their self-congruence. Repeated Q-Sort assessments could allow clients to empirically gauge their own progress during therapy. Obviously, the more the Q-Sort distribution between the real and the ideal self became similar and correlated, the closer a person came to being self-actualized, congruent, and authentic (Stephenson, 1953).

Intervention

According to *Merriam-Webster's Collegiate Dictionary* (2004), the word "intervention" derives from the Latin word *intervenire*, translated as "to come between." Accordingly, applying the word intervention in a nondirective helping practice of PCT transforms it conceptually into an action-oriented and directive process in which the counselor steps in between the person and his or her problem. A more fitting word, which reflects Rogers's foundational practice principle of the working relationship of two people making direct psychological contact, is "facilitation."

The role of the counselor is to facilitate or to become a catalyst in giving the client a life-changing experience that allows him or her to become self-actualized. The counselor does not employ techniques, apply treatment manuals, ask questions, probe, interpret unconscious materials, or confront defense mechanisms. Instead, the counselor comports himself or herself to embody through intentional speech, attitudes, attending behaviors, reflective listening, and nondirective conversation the three necessary and sufficient dynamics: accurate empathy, congruence, and unconditional positive regard. Additionally, the counselor does not plan comportment as a technique to use with the client. Rather, the comportment is a non-intrusive attended and intentional state of being with himself or herself and the client. This distinctive comportment of counselor posture creates a canopy of care and moral kindness, which in turn openly presents the counselor as another person, whose sole purpose is being alongside the client in such a way that client and counselor can be with one another. The counselor is the agent of change who creates opportunities for the client to change through the unfolding process of the self-actualizing principle. Consequently, the client's experiences of the helping relationship are the treatment. For the student in training, sometimes accomplishing comportment can be frustrating, especially since the student desires foremost to know technically what to do, instead of practicing and experiencing how to be an attentive human being and counselor.

The course of PCT takes the path of clients experiencing discrepancies between the self-perception and the reality experiences within their life and environment. There is uncomfortable incongruence and a lack of authenticity within clients, which are typically expressed as anxiety. As clients gradually experience the empathy, congruence, and unconditional positive regard from the counselor, they become less guarded, feel more understood and accepted, and become more open to their experiences through trusting their own internal dialogues about themselves. Clients are more open to reconciling issues between the real self and the ideal self and thus activate their own healing (self-actualizing) processes. Thus, clients chart their own self-healing paths.

Accurate empathy is one of the three processes that promote a therapeutic relationship, as described earlier. Rogers (1959, pp. 210–211) described it as,

> [P]erceiv[ing] the internal frame of reference of another with accuracy and with the emotional components and meanings which pertain thereto as if one were the person, but without ever losing the "as if" condition. Thus, it means to sense the hurt or the pleasure of another as he senses it and to perceive the causes thereof as he perceives them, but without ever losing the recognition that it is as if I were hurt or pleased and so forth.

Empathy also involves looking into and feeling the client's subjective experiences on behalf of the client. Empathy as experienced by the counselor involves both a cognitive understanding and an affective appreciation for the client's feelings. When clients sense the counselor's empathetic concern, it is almost as if the clients know that the counselor has their mind in his or her mind and can feel their feelings without the counselor losing his or her own selfhood or professional posture. Practicing empathy requires a counselor to attend deeply and in detail to the client's total being.

Empathizing with a client is not the imposing of counselor insights onto the client, but rather reflecting back to the client that the counselor understands and appreciates the client's subjective experiences as framed within the client's worldview. Accurate empathizing does not add any new materials, topics, or dynamics to the client's conversations with the counselor. As counselors offer clients their empathy, clients can reject or modify the counselors' empathy. This back-and-forth dialogue eventually leads to accurate empathizing, as long as the counselor is attentive to the feedback from the client. Accurate empathy also deepens the client's self-disclosure and self-understanding by putting into words what the client cannot yet say and by giving the client the safety within the treatment relationship to say what he or she otherwise could not say in another context. The ongoing process of reflective responding and empathizing gives voice to what otherwise the client might not have words for. Accurate empathy has been shown to be relatively effective with different groups of clients as well as in concert with other forms of therapy (Gallant & Holosko, 2001; Gallant, Holosko, & Gallant, 2005).

The nondirective nature of the practice of PCT requires a counselor "to go at the client's pace" (Joseph, 2004). Staying with the client, as evidenced in a counselor's ongoing reflective listening and the selective use of the response skills of reflection of meaning and reflection of feeling, requires considerable patience and attentiveness. Rogerian reflective responding is commonly misunderstood as parroting verbatim responses from the client. To the contrary, a reflective empathetic response needs to capture the essence of what the client is saying by matching the felt meaning the client expresses without the counselor's taking away or adding content. Effective reflective responding connects more directly the counselor with the client, shows the client the counselor's appreciation for the client's frame of reference, and encourages deeper explication by the client without tempting the counselor to abstract the client's meaning or to exceed or lag behind the client's pace of processing (Sachse, 1990). An example of extracting abstract meaning from a client's conversation is the following dialogue:

Client: I don't know why, but every time my boyfriend says good-bye to me after our date, I feel as though I may never see him again.

Counselor: Sounds to me like you have long-standing issues of abandonment, which must relate to your earlier childhood experiences and lack of object constancy.

An example of the counselor's nondirective, evenly paced empathetic response, without abstracting meaning, is the following:

Counselor: You wonder and are bothered by how it is that you experience your boyfriend's customary good-byes as ultimately signifying the final good-bye.

An example of a counselor response aimed at giving permission and unconditional regard for deepening client explication is as follows:

Client: Yes, I always dread his saying good-bye because I feel desperate about needing him and I try not to show it to him.

Counselor: You have strong and intense feelings for needing your boyfriend, which you keep tightly under wraps.

Client: I am not sure how much longer I can keep my needy feelings hidden from him. I feel ashamed for having them and I can't really tell if I have true love for him.

Rogerian principles of practice are applicable to the foundational structures of a working relationship in treating several kinds of presenting problems or client situations, especially when a supportive relationship is indicated, often in the practice of crisis intervention (Gallant et al., 2005). Utilizing unconditional positive regard, honoring client self-determination through client topic control during interviewing, empathizing, and using nondirective reflective responding to facilitate client exploration are useful in supportive work. For example, Joseph (2004) regarded PCT as helpful in the supportive phases of working with clients who had experienced posttraumatic disorders. Such clients may be fearful or anxious when recapitulating the content of their trauma. When the emphasis is on the process of how clients express themselves during the immediate moments in counseling, and when content focus is minimized, clients can then begin to talk about the difficulties associated with the trauma (Gallant & Holosko, 2001).

Evidence-Based Foundations

Rogers was a proponent of the main tenets of evidence-based psychotherapy before the phrase evidence-based practice (EBP) was embraced by the helping professionals. His vast body of work was modified, adapted, tweaked, and improved by a constant infusion of new theories, facts, ideas and intervention modifications during his life up until today. Rogers himself believed in an ongoing quality assurance model, as he constantly supported and encouraged continuing developments in theory and practice (Cain, 2010, p. 7). Even back in his formative years as a clinical psychologist in Rochester, New York, working with troubled children and parents, his guiding questions were: "Does it work?" and "Is it effective" (p. 8). In an early classic text, he wrote in 1942, *Counseling and Psychology: Newer*

Concepts in Practice, he stated that: "the book endeavors to formulate a definite and understandable series of hypothesis...which may be tested and explored" (pp. 16–17). The evidence-based empirical tradition he established has carried forward to present day and serves to ensure the ongoing development of PCT. Despite his legacy of a commitment to ongoing EBP for PCT, one thing that did not change over time was the core assumptions tabled in 1959 in the cornerstone text that was his life's legacy—"A Theory of Therapy, Personality, and Interpersonal Relationships," which remains today as the definitive work of PCT.

EBP can be simply defined as using empirical evidence to direct and inform practice. It is also anchored in the threads of theory, practice, and research. Rogers himself contended that PCT needed strong threads for these three elements so that they could be braided into a sturdy rope to guide PCT through numerous uncharted waters, such as multiproblem clients/groups/families, complex psychosocial presenting problems, preserving client autonomy at all costs, nondirective versus directive counseling, creating a "definable climate" of facilitative attitudes at all times, and so on. Just how he empirically anchored PCT by braiding these elements together to navigate but a few of PCTs therapeutic challenges will be briefly outlined.

Theory

A simple yet well-worn definition of a theory is "a system of ideas that explains something." Thus, theories seek to understand causes and explain phenomena. EBP has used the term *theory* more in the latter sense, rather than the former, and has linked the importance of theory to practice by insisting that all empirical interventions must be grounded in integrated theory. Rogers fully believed this, as Worsley (2004) stated:

> Responsible integration within the Person-Centered Approach aims at an imaginative use of various theories and philosophies of therapy to stimulate an increased openness to experience within the therapist...[and] to link back the process of integration to the basic philosophy so to demonstrate coherence. (p. 126)

Rogers anchored PCT in nine core theories of: (1) an actualizing tendency, (2) an organismic valuing process, (3) the self, ideal self and self-actualization, (4) experience and openness to experience, (5) locus of evaluation, (6) positive regard and unconditional positive regard, (7) conditions of worth, (8) internal and external frames of reference, and (9) empathy. He used these theories across the life cycle in an "ages and stages" orientation to develop a theory of psychological development and personality. This was derived primarily from his observation of the therapeutic process (Cain, 2010, p. 26). He extended this rudimentary theory of personality and behavior in 1951 with his work *Client-Centered Therapy: Its Current Practice, Implications, and Theory,* which articulated 19 propositions of the subjective world of the client, which assisted the attitudes and roles of therapists in the therapeutic client-centered process.

Practice

Rogers was vigilant about how therapists used PCT. He stated that clients have within themselves the resources for self-understanding and change. Therapists can activate these resources if they can provide a "definable climate of facilitative psychological attitudes (Rogers, 1980, p. 115). Therapists thus serve as role models and teachers for their clients. Over time, clients observed their therapist's manner of [therapeutic] engagement and living, and began to incorporate those qualities and behaviors, for example, optimism, being present, promoting client freedom and autonomy, having congruence, being accepting, being affirming, having unconditional regard, and being empathetic (Cain, 2010). Collectively, these are considered the core conditions of therapy.

Given their radical departure from the rather passive therapist roles expressed by his earlier contemporaries Rank and Freud, Rogers was concerned [for his entire life] about the education and training of PCT psychotherapists. From an EBP approach, training and education promotes overt accountability, as well as intervention fidelity and internal validity of the intervention, which promotes its eventual external validity.

Over his life, Rogers would train psychotherapists and students, and both were deemed as equal partners and collaborators in learning more about how PCT should be used and assessing its efficacy with clients. He was the first to study the counseling process in depth by using live 78-rpm audio recordings, as well as verbatim transcripts for training and research, as early as 1940. The case of "Herbert Bryon" (Rogers, 1942) was the first phonographically verbatim transcript of an entire course of psychotherapy ever recorded for training and education purposes. Although not a smart phone, in its day such use of technology was considered groundbreaking and technologically advanced.

Practice skills of the core conditions, although necessary and essential, served as flexible scaffolding for therapists to have freedom to interpret, as directed by the client's needs. Rogers summarized this by stating:

> It is when the therapist is natural and spontaneous that he seems to be the most effective.... Our experience has deeply reinforced and extended my view that the person who is able openly to be himself in that moment, as he is at the deepest levels he is able to be, is the effective therapist. Perhaps nothing else is of any importance. (Rogers & Stevens, 1967, pp. 188–184)

Research

Consistent with social work's Code of Ethics (National Association of Social Workers, 2008), Rogers firmly believed that it was his ethical responsibility [to clients foremost] to evaluate PCT's efficacy. He did this by careful systematic observation, not trial and error. The research [technically the evaluation of practice] he did anchored PCT to direct and inform practice not only for his life, but spanning a legacy of PCT effectiveness research even until today. Kirschenbaum and Jordan (2005) reported that between 1987 and 2004, a total of 777 PC publications, including 141 books, were published (Cain, 2010, p. 7). In 1984, Patterson conducted a review of reviews of the extensive research on the effectiveness of the core conditions of PCT. He concluded:

> *Considering the obstacles to research on the relationship between the therapist variables and therapy outcomes, the magnitude of the evidence is nothing short of amazing. There are few things in the field of psychology for which evidence is so strong. The evidence for the necessity, if not the sufficiency, of the therapist conditions of accurate empathy, respect or warmth, and therapeutic genuineness is incontrovertible. (p. 435)*

Rogers's systematic observations of what worked compared to what did not work, done on a case-by-case basis, are labeled today as the *case comparison method*. This represents a notable paradigm shift in social work evidence-based research's development from practice wisdom to empirical practice to evidence-based practice (Holosko, 2006). For Rogers, the first domino in this developmental chain was *case wisdom*, not *practice wisdom*, as case wisdom does not just accumulate cases over time and aggregate trends of what works and what doesn't work, but it takes each case separately and poses that very same question. Thus, the client is viewed as a separate individual in their own skin, self, and uniqueness.

In a recent comprehensive review of social work research, Wodarski (2011) criticized its focus as ignoring client complexities, ignoring the uniqueness of clients and their problems, ignoring the context of client problems, and indiscriminately applying homogeneous interventions to heterogeneous clients [in a one-size-fits-all manner]. Also, in a departure from the well-noted social work practice-research gap or schism (Holosko & Leslie, 1998), Rogers epitomized a model in which an ongoing evaluation of practice and effectiveness of *both the process of PCT and its outcomes* were synergistic, with one feeding the other in a symbiotic dynamic fashion. This is referred to as *practice-based evidence* or PBE (Green, 2008; Holosko, 2010). Green (2008) stated that the goal of PBE is for:

> *[C]ontinuous practice-based research and evaluation to adapt the best practice guidelines through the "best processes" of collecting data to diagnose the sociopsychobiological needs of their patients, matching the proposed evidence-based interventions with the use of theory and mutual consultation and the prospective testing of complimentary interventions. (p. 124)*

Rogers not only lived the above quote, he pioneered it! CBT truly was a PBE approach to practice developed by an individual who consciously braided the three threads of theory, practice, and research in a vision that he not only implemented but assessed. He was without question well ahead of his time in this area of practice.

Critiques of This Approach

From the beginning, PCT has had its critics—for the apparent vagueness of its principles, its antipathy to diagnosis, its claim that therapists need less training, and its emphasis on the client's self-evaluation as the primary way to judge the outcome of therapy. Social work practice with individuals, families, and groups is rooted in a vast range of borrowed and indigenous knowledge consisting of concepts, theories, models, practice wisdom, and research findings (Reid, 2002). Indeed, PCT has had a major influence on social work practice overall. Although Rogers's theory of counseling was typically incorporated in social work practice and ideology, his basic assumptions and guidelines for practitioners still permeate current social work practice and education. For instance, social workers developed certain practice values with regard to the people they served. Clients were seen as having inherent worth and dignity as human beings, and their right to self-determination was to be fostered. This remains one of the hallmark and defining characteristics of social work practice today.

Person-centered therapy provided a framework, a purpose, and a field-tested methodology that enabled one-on-one therapy (Neville, 1999). One problem with PCT was that there was no set time frame at which a client would reach self-actualization. Internally, this may affect a client's ability to receive optimal services due to time constraints (i.e., a limited number of therapy sessions). This may also impact the evaluation or outcome of the sessions. Since the requirement of the goals and objectives for clients is to be able to reach a level of self-efficacy, practitioners using the PCT approach would not be able to readily identify these, as PCT is a developmental approach without time constraints. Rogers's classical PCT does not set goals, aside from self-actualization (Reid, 2002). Most therapists conducted therapy behind closed doors. Therefore, little was known about what practitioners did in sessions or if they did what they claimed they did. As a result, little was known about the processes or outcomes of therapy (Hill & Nakayama, 2000).

Conversely, Rogers insisted on testing PCT to show that it worked. To Rogers, that meant objective, quantifiable research. Unfortunately, there were few usable methodological procedures and no real examples of research in psychotherapy to use. Often, such research was considered impossible because therapists had never let anyone listen in, let alone measure, compare, and analyze case materials. Rogers was accused of violating the sanctity of the analytic relationship because he recorded therapy sessions. He sought baseline data and comparative research and he tried hard to get his psychoanalysts in training to record and test their therapy. This, he thought, would show whose sanctity was being protected. Rogers's group was the first to qualitatively analyze every sentence of hundreds of transcripts and to measure outcomes on psychometric (and other newly devised) tests given to clients before and after therapy, and also given to comparison or control groups (Gendlin, 2002).

Practitioners of PCT are required to have the appropriate therapeutic skills in facilitating individuals to identify vast resources that they have within themselves. These skills are (a) self-understanding, (b) self-concept, and (c) self-directed behavior (Coghlan & Mcllduff, 1999). By adhering to strongly ingrained values of nondirectiveness, PCT practitioners sometimes lost sight of the fact that they too needed to feel free and act freely if they were to offer or create optional conditions for growth in their clients

(Cain, 1989). The PCT approach also assumed that all therapists could utilize and implement this approach in any client–worker relationship. However, it required a degree of supervision, continuous education, self-evaluation, and competence in which the practitioner must constantly be in tune with themselves (Hill & Nakayama, 2000).

It was also important not to confuse two related issues: applying principles of therapy and applying the approach on which they have been based. In applying the principles of therapy, one is doing what one knows how to do. In doing so, it may be difficult to avoid therapeutic goals that are important in building a client–worker relationship as well as providing a climate for that client to self-actualize (Wood, 1995).

According to Freire and Tambara (2000), the PCT practitioner's commitment resided in the promotion of the client's growth forces, which is different from the usual helping relationships, which aim to diagnose and resolve. Although PCT itself seems to function effectively, applications of approach to education, small groups for encounter and psychotherapy, and large group workshops to improve transnational understanding, to facilitate conflict exploration, and to learn the nature of culture and its formation have revealed shortcomings in PCT practitioners' psychology. This psychology may have included the belief that people may be counted on to do the right thing and that people are always in charge of their own actions (Wood, 1995).

For example, there is only one technique that Rogerians are classically known for: reflection. Reflection is the mirroring of emotional communication: If the client says "I feel like crap!" the therapist may reflect this back to the client by saying something like "So, life's getting you down, hey?" By doing this, the therapist is communicating to the client that he or she is indeed listening and cares enough to understand. The therapist is also letting the client know what it is the client is communicating. Reflection must be used cautiously, however. Many beginning therapists use it without thinking (or feeling) and just repeat every other phrase that comes out of the client's mouth. Then they think that the client does not notice, when in fact it has become a misattribution of Rogerian therapy, the same way sex and Mom have become misattributions of Freudian therapy. Reflection must come from the heart—it must be genuine, focused, and congruent (Wood, 1995).

Rogers died in 1986, and today only a small number of mental health professionals regard themselves chiefly as taking a client-centered or person-centered approach. But his ideas about personality are still found in numerous textbooks; one survey found 50 journals and 200 organizations all over the world now devoted to some variant of client-centered or person-centered therapy. Beyond that, PCT principles may have influenced the practice of many other therapists. For example, self-disclosure (transparency, congruence) has become more acceptable to psychodynamic and cognitive-behavioral therapists (Gendlin, 2002).

The principles of PCT are also central to anchoring motivational inter-viewing, which has been found to be as effective as cognitive-behavioral therapy in a clinical trial of alcoholism treatment (Wood, 1995). In this method, clients set the agenda, and the therapist acts as a partner in dialogue rather than an authority figure. Motivational interviewers avoid warnings, diagnosis, and direct attempts to argue, persuade, or educate. They try to offer accurate empathy and ongoing reflective listening. Instead of directly confronting resistance to change, they promote self-efficacy, which is related to self-actualization as conceived by Rogers (1995, p. 27).

Today, many practitioners are eclectic in their choice of methods or use several techniques in different situations with the same client. The PCT of motivational interviewing, for example, is designed for early phases of therapeutic change, called the precontemplation and contemplation stages. Rogers wrote in the 1940s that an experienced psychotherapist told him he had made explicit something the therapist had been groping toward for a long time. The legacy of PCT and its facilitating conditions may persist less as a specific technique than as a permanent background influence (Hill & Nakayama, 2000).

Although the PCT approach had its origins purely within the limits of the psychological clinic, it is proving to have implications, often of a startling nature, for very diverse fields of effort. According to Freire and Tambara (2000), there are several present and potential implications. Person-centered therapy may sound simple or limited because there is no particular structure that the therapist is trying to apply, but PCT in action may display a rich and complicated process. People unravel their own identities, they discover new matters, take brave steps, and do not have to cope with a therapist who has used techniques with them. The therapist strives to understand and accept the client's issues. Over time, the client increasingly seeks to understand and accept his or her own self as well (p. 130).

Key Terms

Acceptance	External frame of reference	Process
Accurate empathic understanding	Incongruence	Psychological adjustment
Actualizing tendency	Internal frame of reference	Psychological maladjustment
Conditions of worth	Intervention	Reflection
Congruence and genuineness	Locus of evaluation	Reflective
Critical self-reflective thinking	Nondirective	Self-actualization
	Organismic valuing process	Self, self-concept
Empathizing	Outcomes	Unconditional positive regard and acceptance
	Phenomenological thought	

Review Questions for Critical Thinking

1. How can person-centered therapy (PCT) contribute to macro level social work, as in the alleviation of social injustice and oppression?

2. Describe some key commonalities between core social work values and PCT and describe how these common values promote client self-determination, a core ethic of social work.

3. Describe and analyze the contributions Roger's person-centered theory has made to the understanding and implementing of psychotherapy research.

4. Using a commonly available search database, such as PsycInfo or Web-of-Science, locate a recently published outcome study on PCT. Read and critically analyze this study in terms of its applications to current social work practice. To what extent has evidence-based practice and PCT been developed to successfully direct and inform practice?

5. Identify five core elements of PCT that practitioners would routinely use in administering person-centered therapy. What are two intervention no-no's that proponents of PCT would never use?

Online Resources

www.adpca.org/

Mission Statement: "The Association for the Development of the Person Centered Approach is an international network of individuals who support the development and application of the person-centered approach. ADPCA welcomes the participation of educators, therapists, psychologists, psychiatrists, nurses, social workers, health service providers, counselors, organization development specialists, students and all people who are interested in the field of human relations and personal and interpersonal development."

www.apa.org/about/division/div32.aspx

Website for the Society for Humanistic Psychology, Division 32 of the American Psychological Association. The Society recognizes the full richness of the human experience. Its foundations include philosophical humanism, existentialism, and phenomenology. The Society seeks to contribute to psychotherapy, education, theory/philosophy, research, organization, management, social responsibility, and change. The *Humanistic Psychologist* is the society journal, published quarterly.

www.bapca.org.uk/the-association/bapca/history-of-bapca.html

Formed in 1989, the British Association for the Person-Centered Approach (BAPCA) is a national person-centered organization that has been instrumental in developing the approach in the United Kingdom.

www.carlrogers.info

This website serves as a gateway to the intellectual work of Dr. Carl R. Rogers and the wide variety of disciplines he influenced. Carl Rogers, the creator of client-centered counseling, student-centered education, and person-centered approaches to human relations and community building, is arguably the most influential American psychologist of the 20th century. An array of videos and audiotapes are available for free viewing/listening.

www.centerfortheperson.org

A face-to-face community of scholars, practitioners, and individuals dedicated to the principles of person-centered theory and counseling. It offers programs for personal growth, an extensive library, and training in conflict resolution.

www.tandfonline.com/toc/hthp20/current

Website for the journal called the *Humanistic Psychologist*. This long-established journal, now in its third decade of publication, is devoted to reflective inquiry into humanistic psychologies, broadly defined.

www.youtube.com/watch?v=DjTpEL8acfo

A great 7-minute YouTube video of Carl Rogers explaining the essentials of person-centered counseling.

References

Allen, B. P. (2003). *Personality, theories development, growth, and diversity* (4th ed.). Boston, MA: Pearson.

Biestek, F. (1961). *The casework relationship*. London, UK: Unwin University Books.

Boeree, C. G. (2006). *The ultimate theory of personality*. Unpublished manuscript, available at http://webspace.ship.edu/cgboer/conclusions.html

Bozarth, J. D., Zimring, F. M., & Tausch, R. (2001). Client-centered therapy: The evolution of a revolution. In D. J. Cain & J. Seeman (Eds.), *Humanistic therapies: Handbook of research and practice* (pp. 147–188). Washington, DC: American Psychological Association.

Bradley, B. T. (1999). The actualizing tendency concept in client-centered therapy. *Person-Centered Therapy Journal, 6*(2), 108–120.

Cain, D. J. (1989). The paradox of non-directedness in the person-centered approach. *Person-Centered Review, 5,* 89–99.

Cain, D. J. (2010). *Person-centered psychotherapies*. Washington, DC: American Psychological Association.

Coghlan, D. J., & McIlduff, E. (1999). Facilitating change in organizations: Toward a framework of organization development for person-centered practitioners. *The Person-Centered Journal, 6*(1), 48–58.

Corey, G. (1996). *Theory and practice of counseling and psychotherapy* (5th ed.). Pacific Grove, CA: Brooks/Cole.

Corey, G. (2005). *Theory and practice of counseling and psychotherapy* (7th ed.). Belmont, CA: Brooks/Cole.

Cramer, D., & Takens, R. J. (1992). Therapeutic relationship and progress in the first six sessions of individual psychotherapy: A panel analysis. *Counseling Psychology Quarterly, 5*(1), 25–36.

deCarvalho, R. J. (1999). Otto Rank: The Rankian circle in Philadelphia and the origins of Carl Rogers' person-centered psychotherapy. *History of Psychology, 2*(2), 132–148.

Ford, G. (1991). Rogerian self-actualization: A clarification of meaning. *Journal of Humanistic Psychology, 31*(2), 101–111.

Freire, E., & Tambara, N. (2000). Client-centered therapy: The challenges of clinical practice. *The Person-Centered Journal, 7*(2), 129–138.

Friedman, H. L., & MacDonald, D. A. (2006). Humanistic testing and assessment. *Journal of Humanistic Psychology, 46*(4), 510–529.

Gallant, W., & Holosko, M. (2001). Using music intervention in grief work with clients experiencing loss and bereavement. *Guidance & Counseling, 16*(4), 115–122.

Gallant, W., Holosko, M. J., & Gallant, M. (2005). Using bio-spiritual music focused energetic for social workers to enhance personal identity and transformation: The power of self-reflective-empathy. *Critical Social Work Journal, 6*(2), 60–74.

Gendlin, E. T. (2002). Foreword. In C. R. Rogers and D. E. Russell, *Carl Rogers: The quiet revolutionary, an oral history*. Los Angeles, CA: Penmarium Books.

Green, L. W. (2008). Making research relevant: If it is an evidence-based practice, where's the practice-based evidence? *Family Practice, 25*, i20–i24.

Hill, C. E., & Nakayama, E. Y. (2000). Client-centered therapy: Where has it been and where is it going? A comment on Hathaway (1948). *Journal of Clinical Psychology, 56*(7), 861–875.

Hjelle, L. A., & Ziegler, D. J. (1992). *Personality theories* (3rd ed.). New York, NY: McGraw-Hill.

Holosko, M. (2006). A suggested authors checklist for submitting manuscripts to *Research on Social Work Practice, 16*, 449–454.

Holosko, M. J. (2010). *Challenges of becoming an evidence-based practitioner: The need for a knowledge-based model*. Invited keynote address, International Conference on Social Work and Counseling Practice: Promoting Harmony in a World of Conflict, Hong Kong.

Holosko, M., & Leslie, D. (1998). Obstacles to conducting empirically-based practice. In J. Wodarski & B. Thyer (Eds.), *Handbook of empirical social work. Vol. 2: Social problems and practice issues*. New York, NY: Wiley.

Joseph, S. (2004). Client-centered therapy, post traumatic stress disorder and post traumatic growth: Theoretical perspectives and practical implications. *Psychology and Psychotherapy: Theory, Research and Practice, 77*(1), 101–119.

Kirschenbaum, H., & Henderson, V. L. (Eds.). (1989). *Carl Rogers: Dialogues*. Boston, MA: Houghton Mifflin.

Kirschenbaum, H., & Jordan, A. (2005). The current status of Carl Rogers and the person-centered approach. *Psychotherapy, 42*(1), 37–51.

Lemoire, S. J., & Chen, C. P. (2005). Applying person-centered counseling to sexual minority adolescents. *Journal of Counseling and Development, 83*, 146–154.

Merriam-Webster's Collegiate Dictionary 11th ed., (2004). Springfield, MA: Merriam-Webster.

National Association of Social Workers. (1996). *Code of Ethics.* Washington, DC: Author.

National Association of Social Workers. (2008). *Code of Ethics.* Washington, DC: Author.

Neville, B. (1999). The client-centered ecopsychologist. *The Person-Centered Journal, 6*(1), 59–74.

Perlman, H. H. (1979). *Relationship, the heart of helping people.* Chicago, IL: University of Chicago Press.

Rank, O. (1924). *The trauma of birth.* London, UK: Kegan, Paul, Trench Trubner.

Reid, W. J. (2002). Knowledge for direct social work practice: An analysis of trends. *Social Service Review, 20*(1), 48–58.

Rogers, C. R. (1942). *Counseling and psychotherapy: Newer Concepts in Practice.* Boston, MA: Houghton Mifflin.

Rogers, C. R. (1951). *Client-centered therapy: Its current practice, implications, and theory.* Boston, MA: Houghton Mifflin.

Rogers, C. R. (1959). Theory of therapy, personality and interpersonal relationships, as developed in the client-centered framework. In S. Koch (Ed.), *Psychology: A study of science* (Vol. 3). New York, NY: McGraw-Hill.

Rogers, C. R. (1961). A therapist's view of the good life: The fully functioning person. In C. R. Rogers (Ed.), *Becoming a person.* Boston, MA: Houghton Mifflin.

Rogers, C. R. (1977). *Carl Rogers on personal power: Inner strength and its revolutionary impact.* New York, NY: Delacorte Press.

Rogers, C. R. (1980). *A way of being.* Boston, MA: Houghton Mifflin.

Rogers, C. R. (1986). The interpersonal relationship. *Human Relations, 3*, 151–155.

Rogers, C. R. (1995). What understanding and acceptance mean to me. *Journal of Humanistic Psychology, 35*, 7–22.

Rogers, C. R., & Stevens, B. (1967). *Person to person: The problem of being human.* New York, NY: Pocket Books.

Sachse, R. (1990). Concrete interventions are crucial: The influence of the therapist's processing proposals on the client's intrapersonal exploration in client-centered therapy. In G. Lietaer, J. Rombauts, & R. Van Balen (Eds.), *Client-centered and experiential psychotherapy in the nineties* (pp. 295–308). Leuven, Belgium: Leuven University Press.

Schmid, P. F. (2003). Back to the client: A phenomenological approach to the process of understanding and diagnosis. *Person-Centered and Experiential Psychotherapies, 3*(1), 36–51.

Seeman, J. (1990). Theory as autobiography: The development of Carl Rogers. *Person-Centered Review, 5*(4), 373–386.

Sperry, R. W. (1990). Structure and significance of the consciousness revolution. *Person-Centered Review, 5*(2), 120–129.

Stachey, J. (1989). *Sigmund Freud: The ego and the id.* New York, NY: Norton.

Stephenson, W. (1953). *The study of behavior: Q-technique and its methodology.* Chicago, IL: University of Chicago Press.

Wakefield, J. (2001). *Social work as the pursuit of minimal distributive justice.* Keynote address at the Kentucky Conference on the Working Definition of Social Work. School of Social Work, the University of Kentucky, Lexington, Kentucky.

Watson, J. (1913). Psychology as the behaviorist views it. *Psychological Review, 20,* 158–177.

Wilkins, P. (2003). *Person-centered therapy in focus.* Thousand Oaks, CA: Sage.

Wodarski, J. (2011). The social work practice research conundrum. *Journal of Human Behavior in the Social Environment, 21,* 577–600.

Wood, J. K. (1995). The person-centered approach: Toward an understanding of its implications. *The Person-Centered Journal, 2*(2), 18–35.

Worsley, R. (2004). Integrating with integrity. In P. Sanders (Ed.), *The tribes of the person-centered nation* (pp. 125–147). Ross-on-Wye, UK: PCS Books.

Ziegler, D. J. (2002). Freud, Rogers, and Ellis: A comparative theoretical analysis. *Journal of Rational-Emotive & Cognitive-Behavior Therapy, 20*(2), 75–91.

Zimring, F. M., & Rasking, N. J. (1992). Carl Rogers and client-centered therapy. In D. K. Freeheim (Ed.), *History of psychotherapy* (pp. 629–656). Washington, DC: American Psychological Association.

Chapter 8
Genetic Theory

Laura J. Pankow

> How does knowledge of an individual's genetics contribute to a holistic understanding of the person-in-environment and to social work practice? Is a fundamental understanding of genetic theory crucial to thorough assessment and treatment of clients coping with human social conditions?

Evolution by natural selection is the central theme of biology, and genetic processes are how natural selection shapes the evolutionary development of a species. *Genetics* is the study of inheritance. In human beings this involves the study of characteristics that a child receives from the combined influence of the genetic material possessed by his or her biological mother and father. Genetics contains the basic paradox of similarity and difference between child and parents, for children resemble each parent but are also distinctly different from each parent. Furthermore, children born to the same parents have distinct similarities and differences.

The physical and social environment into which human beings are born does not inscribe its effects on a tabula rasa, a blank slate of a human being. Rather, all people possess a unique genetic history stretching back for generations and ultimately to the origins of humanity itself. Genetics is responsible for a wide array of physical characteristics and aspects of temperament and abilities. Striking advances in the scientific analysis of genetic structure have led to important developments in the treatment and prevention of certain disorders with genetic components. Quite literally, who we are and what we do is to a considerable extent a function of the intersection between genetics (which are largely immutable) and psychosocial environments (which are in a constant state of flux). An understanding of the role of genetics and its influence on human growth and development across the life span, and of pragmatic applications of such an understanding in social work practice, is important knowledge for social workers to be competent practitioners. Knowledge of a client's genetic history can have a role within the processes of social work assessment

(Bernhardt & Rauch, 1993) as well as practice (Bishop, 1993). Many social work clients present with issues related to genetic factors; clients may have health conditions related to inherited characteristics or may be in need of informational or supportive counseling (R. Black & Weiss, 1990; Schild, 1973; Weiss, 1976, 1981, 1993). Prenatal genetic testing revealing the existence of fetal abnormalities can present parents with difficult choices and life-changing decisions (R. Black & Furlong, 1984). Learning that one is affected by an incurable genetic condition, such as Huntington's chorea, presents people with critical issues that must be resolved, such as whether to have children.

In social work's history, members of the profession were collaborators in medical efforts to locate and refer for involuntary sterilization individuals with certain genetic disorders. This occurred in the United States during the early part of the 20th century, in Nazi Germany, and in many other nations that adopted policies related to eugenics, attempts to improve the human race by encouraging the genetically "fit" to reproduce (so-called positive genetics) and discouraging or preventing the genetically "unfit" to have children (so-called negative genetics). This history has recently been reviewed by LaPan and Platt (2005), with E. Black (2003) and Broberg and Roll-Hansen (1996) also being good sources. Papers dealing with eugenics were a frequent topic at national social welfare conferences 100 years ago, and an article titled "Eugenical Social Work" came out in 1930 (Lorimer, 1930). One widely held perspective is summarized as follows:

> If the extension of contraceptive practices is encouraged, perhaps supplemented by a more extensive development of voluntary sterilization procedures, sizes of family among these less privileged groups can quite possibly be reduced to the levels prevailing among the more privileged groups. (Lorimer, 1933, p. 42)

In other words, society was held to have an interest in discouraging the poor from having children.

Many diseases affecting human beings have a genetic basis. All human babies born in hospitals are tested for phenylketonuria (PKU), a condition in which the body lacks an enzyme necessary to metabolize the amino acid phenylalanine. The amino acid builds up in the blood and can cause mental retardation at these abnormally high levels. The condition occurs in approximately 1 in 10,000 births in the United States, and mental retardation can be avoided by feeding the child a diet low in phenylalanine until the age of 7, when higher blood levels of the amino acid no longer affect the brain's rapid development. Genetics has also been used extensively in agriculture to develop desirable characteristics in plants and animals, from sweeter corn to cows producing more milk. Thomas Jefferson performed many experiments with plants before the patterns in plant offspring were reported in the mid-19th century. All of these areas in which genetics is used affect the social environment.

The diversity of genes within a population in a geographical area is an important factor in survival. Laws prohibiting intermarriage between close relatives (e.g., brothers and sisters) were established largely for this reason. Experiments have shown that when closely related individuals have offspring, undesirable traits are more likely to emerge. The genetic disease Huntington's chorea, from which country-western singer Woody Guthrie died, is prevalent in the Ohio River valley in southern Indiana. Due to many generations of intermarriage between cousins in the small communities there, a high prevalence of Huntington's chorea has been reported.

Gregor Mendel, an Austrian monk, published a paper in 1866 that reported his observations of selectively choosing certain characteristics in plants, such as height and color, and recording the percentage of offspring having these same characteristics. The scientific community generally disregarded his work until 1900. Human beings have selectively bred plants and animals for desired characteristics for the past 10,000 years, yet it has only been in the past century that the theoretical explanations for the success of these practices has been available (e.g., genetic transmission via DNA).

Mendel's work provided evidence of hereditary pieces, one of which was received from each parent. These pieces of heredity are now called *genes*. The discipline of genetics studies the composition and operation of genes as well as how genes are conveyed from ancestor to offspring.

In 1953, James Watson, an American, and Francis Crick, of Great Britain, deciphered the chemical structure of DNA (deoxyribonucleic acid) at Cambridge University in England. In the early 1950s, Linus Pauling in California and Maurice Wilkins and Rosalind Franklin in London were also working with gene composition. Watson and Crick, in a one-page paper published in *Nature*, illustrated the double helix composition of DNA, the fundamental structure of the gene (Watson & Crick, 1953).

DNA resembles a twisted ladder. The sides of the ladder are made up of sugars and phosphates. The rungs of the ladder are made up of chemical compounds (amino acids) called *purines* (adenine and guanine) and *pyrimidines* (thymine and cytosine). The rungs of the ladder are paired adenine with thymine and guanine with cytosine. This pairing pattern establishes the code of characteristics that are passed on from one generation to the next. The method by which the passage of hereditary material occurs is discussed later in the chapter.

Watson and Crick's work represents one of the most important discoveries in biology, because it provided the physical structure of the gene, previously only an abstract concept. They, along with Maurice

Wilkins, won the Nobel Prize in medicine or physiology in 1962 for this discovery.

A gene is a section of DNA. Thus, one DNA molecule contains many genes. The information encoded in DNA by each gene controls production of other molecules. The dynamic association between genes, the external environment, and the products of other genes is the mechanism of the function of a living organism.

Watson and Crick's discovery also provided an explanation for how DNA ensures that it can reliably reproduce itself. This process is termed *replication*. Their model also explains the process of *mutation*, by which hereditary material is changed, and *transmission genetics*, the way genetic material is passed from one generation to the next.

The Eukaryotic Cell

Eukaryotic cells have a nucleus enclosed by a membrane. Their functional formed bodies (organelles) are also enclosed by membranes (Campbell, 1996, p. G8). Animals (including humans), plants, and fungi are all composed of this cell type. They contain more structures for capturing and processing energy from the environment than do their evolutionary predecessors, the prokaryotic cells. Eukaryotic cells require oxygen to function. Prokaryotic cells have no nucleus and do not need oxygen. The bacteria Eschericia coli (E. coli) and salmonella are examples of prokaryotic cells.

Cells are the basic structure of all living things, and thus the basic structure of all human body organs and tissues. Muscle cells contract, allowing movement as a result of being stimulated by impulses traveling through nerve cells. Pancreas cells produce insulin to control blood sugar levels. Living things have the ability to reproduce, grow, metabolize (use energy to create chemicals and other substances), and adapt to changes occurring within and outside of the organism. Connective tissue fibers do not meet the definition of being alive, because they do not have these properties.

Under the lower magnification of a light microscope, the eukaryotic cell appears to be a relatively simple entity. However, if viewed under the higher magnification of an electron microscope, it is observed to be more complex. Cells come in a variety of shapes and sizes. Muscle cells are long and spindle-shaped, and red blood cells have a more rounded shape. Sperm cells have tails called flagella, which enable them to move. A general cell's makeup is about 15% protein, 3% fat, 1% carbohydrate, 1% nucleic acids (DNA and RNA) and minerals, and 80% water (Kapit & Elson, 1993, p. 3). Each cell has *organelles*, structures that are responsible for performing the functions necessary for the cell to exist. Human beings have approximately 200 different types of cells.

All cells perform basic processes necessary for life, and thus there are certain functions common to all human cells. The organelles present in cells have been identified largely by examining cells with the combination of the magnification of a microscope and stains.

The *cell membrane* surrounds the cell and provides support for it. Human cells do not have the additional feature of a *cell wall*, which exists in plant, fungal, and prokaryotic cells. The cell membrane is composed of fats, proteins, and a few carbohydrates. It serves as a selective barrier to materials in the external and internal environments of the cell, admitting materials of benefit to the cell and allowing release of detrimental materials inside the cell.

The *nucleus* is the largest organelle in the cell and is surrounded by the *nuclear membrane*. The nuclear membrane serves as a selective barrier to substances inside and outside of the nucleus. The *nucleoplasm* is the major component of the nucleus and contains *chromatin*, thin threads of DNA and protein, which is changed into chromosomes during cell division. Chromatin appears throughout the nucleus and is in the form of filaments, which stain lightly (euchromatin) or darkly (heterochromatin). It is made up of two components, protein and amino acids. The *nucleolus* is composed largely of RNA with some DNA and protein. It produces RNA units, which combine in the cytoplasm to form ribosomes. Under a microscope, the nucleolus and chromatin are prominently observed. *Histone* is the main protein; there are five types, which basically show no diversity in structure in eukaryotic cells. In all, approximately 21 types of proteins are tightly bound to the DNA in the nucleus. Deoxyribonucleic acid is the only type of nucleic acid present in chromatin.

The material outside of the nuclear membrane is the *cytoplasm*. Within the cytoplasm, a protein framework exists called the *cytoskeleton*. Fibers of this framework are seen throughout the cytoplasm, and their microfilaments provide the means through which muscles contract. The cytoplasm is a jelly-like fluid composed of water, sugars, fats (lipids), and proteins (amino acids), which contains the organelles responsible for performing the metabolic functions of the cell.

The cell membrane contains several folds in the cytoplasm. These folds are called the *endoplasmic reticulum*, of which there are two types: *rough* and *smooth*. The folds are flattened in rough endoplasmic reticulum and rounded in smooth endoplasmic reticulum.

Attached to some of these folds are small circular structures called *ribosomes*. Ribosomes are formed by RNA units sent into the cytoplasm by the nucleolus, and are the site where proteins are made from amino acids. Ribosomes are active in cells of the pancreas and muscles, where high levels of protein are produced. Rough endoplasmic reticulum is responsible for carrying protein produced by the ribosomes to other locations in the cell. The *Gorge body* is a group of flat sacs that are lined with membrane. Here proteins and other substances are stored and "packaged" for the cell to use or to be exported from the cell. Smooth endoplasmic reticulum has different functions depending on the cell in which it resides. In liver cells, for example, it is responsible for breaking down substances that are poisonous to the cell; in muscle cells, it stores calcium, which is necessary for muscle movement.

The *centrosome* is situated close to the nucleus. It houses two cylinder-shaped structures called *controls*, which lie perpendicular to each other. They play an integral role in ordering cell division.

Many *mitochondria* are scattered throughout the cytoplasm. They are the cell's source of energy, for they contain many enzymes, which catalyze chemical reactions for the breakdown of carbohydrates to supply simpler chemical compounds that the cell uses to carry out its life processes. Two important features of these organelles are that they contain their own genetic information, exclusive of that contained in the DNA of the nucleus, and they are inherited only from the female parent. Muscle and sperm cells contain many mitochondria as these cells use a great deal of energy: muscles for movement of the various body parts and sperm cells for mobility. The nucleus is the primary site of DNA. Though the mitochondria contain their own DNA, they still require that contained in the nucleus in order to function.

The cell needs a constant supply of enzymes that can break down chemicals that are either poisonous to the cell or cannot be used in their present form. The cell stores enzymes, which break large chemical compounds down into smaller, usable units, in the *lysosome*. Enzymes "digest" substances that are poisonous (toxic) to the cell, which are stored in *peroxisomes*, a large number of which are found in liver cells.

Eukaryotic cells can have two types of extensions: *microvilli* and *cilia*. Microvilli are projections from the cell that resemble fingers and increase the cell's surface area. They exist in the cells of the digestive tract, where one of the major functions of the cells is to absorb nutrients to be shared with the rest of the body. They also appear in the outermost layer of skin tissue, the epidermis. Cilia are longer and thinner than microvilli and resemble hair. They occur in the cells of the lungs and windpipe and capture dust and other particles that may interfere with breathing.

A notable exception to the prototypical eukaryotic cell is the red blood cell (erythrocyte) of mammals. These cells contain no nucleus or mitochondria and thus have no genetic material or means of producing energy through use of oxygen. These cells perform metabolism in a different way than other mammalian body cells. The red blood cells of other vertebrate classes do contain nuclei, so this type of red blood cell is unique to mammals.

Chromosomes

Chromosomes are structures shaped like rods, numbering from 10 to 100, usually paired, in most eukaryotic cells. They are composed of DNA, histones, and other nuclear proteins. Chromosomes are visible in living cells under the microscope, but they are more easily seen in dead cells that have been stained. The stains elicit a banding pattern that is unique to each chromosome pair.

Centromeres are constrictions that occur along the chromosome. *Metacentric* chromosomes have a constriction in the middle. *Submetacentric* chromosomes have a constriction that is somewhat off center. *Achocentric* chromosomes have a constriction almost at one end, and *telocentric* chromosomes have a constriction at the end. Some chromosomes have a second centromere that separates a small fragment from the remainder of the chromosome. This fragment is a *chromosome satellite.*

Karyotype is a term used to refer to a photograph of the chromosomes of a single cell of an individual. This photograph is specially arranged so that the chromosomes appear from largest to smallest. For species with eukaryotic cells, this picture is unique to the species. Individuals within a species usually have the same number of chromosomes, but an exception is found in bees. In this species, males have half the number of chromosomes of females. Each chromosome is identified by such characteristics as the banding pattern, the length, and the location of the centromere. Pairs of chromosomes are then numbered.

In many species, eukaryotic cells have one pair of chromosomes that do not have identical appearances. This pair is the *sex chromosomes.* In these species members of the same sex are identical in chromosome appearance, but those of the opposite sex differ in chromosome appearance. The sex chromosomes, by convention, are given the highest number in the karyotype. All other chromosomes are termed *autosomes.* An important note is that the number of chromosomes has no relationship to the complexity or time in evolutionary history at which the species originated. Human beings have 46 chromosomes; some ferns have more than 1,200.

Diploid species have chromosomes that occur in pairs. One chromosome of each pair came from the female parent and one from the male parent. The members of the pair are termed *homologous*, meaning that each chromosome is similar to the other in appearance and structure and also that the two chromosomes have the same gene sequence.

Each gene has a particular place or *locus* on the chromosome. As stated earlier, a gene is a section of DNA, which can take any one of several forms, called *alleles.* Thus a human being has two alleles for each gene, one on each of the chromosomes in the pair. One of these alleles comes from the mother and one from the father. If the two alleles are identical, the individual is said to be *homozygous* for that allele. If the alleles on the two chromosomes are different, the individual is termed *heterozygous* for that gene. The pair of alleles constitutes the individual's *genotype.* This concept is discussed more fully in a later section of the chapter describing Mendelian genetics.

In species with paired chromosomes, the number of pairs is termed the *haploid* number for that species. The diploid number is the number of chromosomes and the haploid number is the number of pairs. Thus, the haploid number is one half of the diploid number.

Errors may occur when cells are dividing in the process of producing offspring. When a human baby is born with a chromosome number greater or lesser than 46, he or she is termed *aneuploid*. In some cases individuals have extra pairs of chromosomes; these individuals are termed *polyploid*. This condition leads to death in human beings. In grains of wheat and rye, however, this condition results in plants that are more resistant to disease than those in the species with the normal karyotype and thus have a better survival rate.

The number of chromosomes is reflective of the relationship between species from an evolutionary standpoint. Dogs, wolves, foxes, and coyotes all have the same genus (Cani) and all have the same number of chromosomes, 78. Human beings have 46 chromosomes, and chimpanzees and gorillas, which are of the same order (vertebrae), have 48 chromosomes. A new species often originates as the results of a pairing of a set of chromosomes, which is called *fusion*. This reduces the diploid number. In human beings, for example, chromosome 2 is homologous to two chromosomes in chimpanzees and gorillas. Another process that can account for a change in the number of chromosomes, creating a new species, is *fission*. In this case a pair of chromosomes divides into two or more pairs, thus increasing the diploid number. Therefore, while the genes within closely related species may be similar, the way they are organized may be very dissimilar.

When two species are closely related, it is sometimes possible for them to produce offspring. This process is called *hybridization*. A well-known example of this process in the animal kingdom is that of mating a male donkey and a female horse; the result is a mule. It is important to note that mules are sterile, and the only way to produce a mule is to breed a male donkey and a female horse. Hybridization is also common in agriculture, where two species of corn or other crop are cross-pollinated to produce offspring with desirable characteristics, such as enhanced color or taste.

Reproduction

Only the basic processes of cell division and genetics are discussed in addressing reproduction. The more complex elements of reproduction, including differentiation of organs and time periods over which development occurs prior to birth, are not covered here.

In biology there are two types of reproduction, *sexual* and *asexual*. Some species use only one of these methods, and some species use both. In sexual reproduction, the genetic material of two parents come together to form offspring that are different from either parent. In asexual reproduction one parent produces offspring that are identical to itself in terms of genetic material.

In sexual reproduction in the majority of eukaryotic cell species, the uniting of two reproductive cells called gametes forms the offspring. Each gamete has one haploid set of one parent's chromosomes.

Gametes are produced through a process called *meiosis*, which occurs in the reproductive organs of each parent. The gamete formed in the female ovary is called an *ovum*. The gamete formed in the male testis is called *spermatozoa*. Meiosis causes reduction of a cell's chromosomes from the diploid number to the haploid number; the reproductive organs are the only place in the human body where this process occurs. The process of meiosis is discussed later in this chapter.

All cells of the human body, with the exception of gametes (eggs and spermatozoa), are *somatic* cells. These cells reproduce by a process called *mitosis*. In mitosis, unlike meiosis, the cell divides to produce two cells, which each have a diploid number of chromosomes. Mitosis is also the method by which asexual reproduction occurs. Offspring that result from asexual reproduction have genetic material that is identical to that of the parent. The offspring are *clones* of the parent.

Mitosis

During the life of a cell there is a period of a high amount of metabolism and growth, called the *interphase*. There are three parts to the interphase. The first step, called *G1*, is the longest portion of the cell's cycle. Most cells require several hours to complete this step. The "G" notation for this phase stands for "gap" because it was originally thought that nothing was happening during this phase. However, during this period, studies have shown that the cell is preparing, through active metabolism, for the next phase, called *S*.

During the S step, chromosomes are making exact duplicates of themselves (replicating). The "S" notation stands for "sequence." This is a step of synthesis. Mistakes in replication usually lead to the death of offspring, so the accuracy of this synthesis is of the utmost importance. The time necessary for this step varies from one species to another. The *G2* step follows the S step. During this phase the cell is making protein for the active process of cell division.

There are four stages to the visibly dynamic process of mitosis: prophase, metaphase, anaphase, and telophase. In *prophase* the chromosomes become coiled and have two strands. Each strand is called a *chromatid*, and they are attached to a *sister chromosome* at the site of the centromere. As long as only one centromere exists, the composite structure is considered to be a single chromosome. While the chromatids do not have their own centromeres, and thus are not considered chromosomes at this point, they do possess complete genetic material identical to that of the sister chromosome.

During this phase, the nucleus and nuclear membrane disappear and the cytoplasm forms a structure called a *spindle apparatus*. In human and other animal cells, the centrioles separate and form the ends of these spindles. The spindle apparatus facilitates the movement of the chromosomes in later stages of mitosis.

In *metaphase*, the chromosomes are attached to the spindle apparatus by the centromere of each pair of chromatids. The chromosomes then move to the plane midway between the centrioles and perpendicular to the line that connects them. This position is called the *equatorial plate*. All chromosomes then line up at the equatorial plate.

Anaphase begins when each centromere divides. At this point, each chromatid becomes a chromosome in its own right. Thus, for each chromosome in the cell, two new chromosomes now exist. The spindle apparatus then contracts and pulls the chromosomes to opposite ends of the cell. The centromere is the guiding force in this motion, so the chromosomes take on a J, V, or I shape depending on whether they are submetacentric, metacentric, or telocentric. This is the shortest step of mitosis.

Telophase is evidenced by the reappearance of the nuclear membrane. In human and other animal cells a crease appears in the cell membrane, which expands until the cell finally divides in two. The crease also divides the contents of the cytoplasm as it expands, but this division does not occur with the meticulousness of that of the nucleus and chromosomes. It is extremely important that both new cells receive mitochondria. If this does not occur, the new cell has no way to extract energy from the environment, and dies.

When cells increase in number, they are described as *proliferating*. If the body does not control this process, the result is cancer. During the 1980s, understanding of cell division increased greatly. *Cyclin* is a chemical produced continuously by the cell to control mitosis. When a sufficient amount of cyclin is present in the blood, a second chemical, called maturation-promoting factor (*MPF*) is produced. Maturation-promoting factor induces mitosis, degrades cyclin (leading to a decreased amount of MPF in the blood), and thus leads to the production of more cyclin. Thus a check-and-balance system for cell division is present in the cells of the body. Cells divide at different rates, but, as previously mentioned, nerve cells never divide; thus a much more complex set of factors than that outlined here is present in the human body. There is much about the process of mitosis that has yet to be discovered.

All forms of life begin as a single cell, but the majority of life spends most of its existence in a multicellular form. Cells *develop* into structures to perform specifically different functions. The process of this development has two parts: *growth* and *differentiation*. Cells have a limited range of sizes. Mitosis is the method by which an organism grows, and it occurs throughout the life of a multicellular organism. The largest animals known are blue whales, and the largest living organisms known are giant sequoia trees and interconnected underground fungi.

Differentiation describes the method by which cells become specialized to perform a limited range of functions. It is important to remember that, though cells specialize during differentiation, all somatic cells contain all of the genetic material necessary to re-create the entire human being.

Mendelian Genetics

Earlier in the chapter Gregor Mendel was mentioned as a leading figure in the history of genetics. He is the founder of the basic principles of inheritance. Mendel was not able to actually see genes; instead, he studied the *phenotype* of plants, that is, the physical appearance or trait that the gene produces in the organism. Mendel observed whether characteristics such as color and height were the same in a parent and its offspring.

Mendel's experiments are used to teach the model for scientific experimental design and systematic data collection. He focused on seven traits in pea plants (shape of seed, color of pea, color of seed coat, pod form, color of unripe pod, flower position, and stem length), carefully mated plants that differed in these traits, and counted the offspring of the two parents possessing alternative forms of these traits. These seven traits constitute *qualitative* diversity in the pea plants.

Quantitative diversity occurs in a factor such as height or weight, in which the diversity occurs on a continuous scale. It can be argued that stem length is a quantitative variable, but Mendel did not record it as such. The difference in height between plants with long stems and those with short was very distinct so that there was no area of overlap to cause confusion in this categorization.

Mendel began his experiments with *pure breeding* seeds, that is, seeds that had consistently given rise to the same alternative forms as the parent for the seven traits being studied, for several generations. He then mated parent plants that differed in alternative forms of only one trait, long stem and short stem, for example, but the other six traits were identical. These are termed *monohybrid* crosses. All of the monohybrid crosses yielded similar results. The first generation of offspring exhibited the trait being selectively crossed of one parent, and none represented the selected trait of the other. The trait that was not represented in the offspring was termed *recessive*. For example, when white seed coat and gray seed coat parents were crossed, none of the offspring had gray seed coats. Thus, the gray seed coat was a recessive trait. This occurrence is termed *Mendel's law of dominance.*

Mendel also observed that the sex of the parent had no influence on the traits represented in the offspring. This observance is termed *Mendel's law of parental equivalence.*

When monohybrid crosses were made for the seven traits of first-generation offspring, all seven monohybrid crosses resulted in a 3-to-l ratio of dominant trait to recessive trait in the offspring, Thus, in eight offspring plants, six had white seed coats and two had gray seed coats.

Mendel wrote about factors being transmitted from one generation to the next. Today Mendel's factors are called alleles. If an allele results in an observable trait in the individual who possesses it, it is called *dominant*. An allele whose trait is hidden or masked is called *recessive*. Individuals who possess the same allele on homologous chromosomes are called *homozygous* for that trait. Individuals who possess different forms of the same allele on homologous chromosomes are called *heterozygous* for that trait.

The conventional way of denoting the alleles present when attempting to determine expected outcomes for a particular trait in offspring is called a *Punnet square*. Dominant alleles are represented by a capital letter, and recessive alleles are represented with a lowercase letter. The Punnet square has one parent's alleles in the top row of the square and the other parent's alleles in the left hand column of the square. The resulting combinations are then placed in a matrix within the square to determine expected ratios of phenotypes in the offspring.

Mendel also made *test crosses*. A test cross occurs when a heterozygous parent is crossed with a homozygous recessive parent. When Mendel made this test cross for seed color, he found that the ratio of seed coat colors in the offspring were 1:1, white to gray. In this case, no homozygous white offspring exist. Fifty percent of the offspring are heterozygous white and 50% are homozygous gray. Try it with a Punnet square!

When Mendel observed this outcome, he wrote the *law of segregation*. This principle states that each allele of a pair keeps its own integrity, and when sex cells (gametes) are formed, only one allele is transmitted to each gamete.

Mendel crossed parents that were purebred for two of the traits that he was studying. Thus, he was crossing parents that were homozygous for seed color and stem length, for example. The first-generation offspring (conventionally given the notation F1) contained plants that were all white seed color and all had long stems.

Mendel then performed the equivalent of crossing two F1 generation plants by having the plants self-fertilize, as all plants of this generation have the same genotype (WwLl). The resulting ratio of traits in the next generation (denoted F2) is a 9:3:3:1 ratio of nine white seed coat and long stem, three white seed coat and short stem, three gray seed coat and long stem, and one gray seed coat and short stem. The 9:3:3:1 ratio is the standard outcome for a dihybrid cross. This finding demonstrates that seed coat color and stem length do not interact in gametes, which is the basic principle expressed in Mendel's *law of independent assortment*.

As is true of any scientific discovery, when Mendel's laws were read, scientists performed experiments like those of Mendel's but focusing on different phenotypic characteristics. It has been discovered, for example, that some genes have more than two alleles and that in these cases more than one allele may show equal dominance with another. It has also been discovered that sometimes an allele has incomplete dominance. When flower color was studied, for example, flowers that had one allele for red color and one allele for white color (heterozygous for flower color) were pink. It has also been found that some characteristics, such as height, depend on more than one gene. In these cases the characteristic seen in the offspring is dependent on the interaction of these genes. This type of inheritance is termed *polygenic*.

The discovery of *linkage* caused a modification in Mendel's law of independent assortment. In linkage, a group of genes on the same chromosome are transmitted to a sex cell as a group. In cases where genes are linked, the 9:3:3:1 ratio expected in a dihybrid cross does not occur. It has been discovered that the reason all seven traits that Mendel observed in his pea plants demonstrated this expected ratio is the large distance between the genes for these traits on the chromosomes.

Mutation occurs when the DNA of an allele is changed during replication. Any mutations that occurred in Mendel's studies were so infrequent that they did not affect his outcome ratios.

The Process of Meiosis

As in mitosis, *meiosis* has a period of growth and replication of the cell's chromosomes, which is called the interphase. Another similarity to mitosis is that when meiosis begins, each chromosome has a pair of sister chromatids that are bonded by one centromere.

Meiosis I

Meiosis has two sets of divisions, termed *meiosis I* and *meiosis II*. Meiosis I begins with a stage called *prophase I*. This stage is complex and consists of a high degree of chromosome activity. In a process called *synapsis*, the two members of each homologous pair of chromosomes line up in a tight formation side by side. The chromosomes contract to a great degree during this phase, and several attachments between homologous pairs of chromosomes form during this time. The attachments form an X shape and are termed *chiasmata* (*chi* is the Greek letter x). This is the critical event in prophase I as it is the mechanism by which *crossing over* occurs. At the chiasmata, the chromosomes break and reattach to a broken end. If a chromosome repaired itself by reattaching to its own end or that of a sister chromatid, it would keep its original composition of genetic material. However, if it heals by reattaching itself to the broken end of a homologous chromosome or its nonsister chromatid, *genetic recombination* occurs. This is because homologous chromosomes have the same genes but different alleles; thus, when they reattach to each other, an equal exchange of segments occurs. In other words, the same genes will be present, but different alleles may attach to the broken chromosome. This is the process of crossing over. At this point in meiosis, each pair of homologous chromosomes has four chromatids. This entire structure is called a *bivalent*.

At the end of prophase I, the nuclear membrane disappears, a spindle starts to form, and the centromere of each bivalent attaches to the spindle.

In the next stage of meiosis I, *metaphase I*, spindle formation is complete, and the bivalents line up at the center of the spindle in a location called the *metaphase plate*. During this phase, the chiasmata move to the ends of the chromosomes, and the homologous chromosomes are held together only by the chiasmata.

Anaphase I is the next stage. As in mitosis, the centromeres pull each member of the pairs of homologous chromosomes to opposite ends of the spindle. Meiosis differs from mitosis because in anaphase I of meiosis, centromeres do not divide. Remember that centromeres are the defining structures in a chromosome. Thus, because the centromeres do not divide, half the number of original chromosomes exists at the completion of anaphase I. For this reason, meiosis I is termed a *reduction division*. Another difference between meiosis I and mitosis is that after crossing over, the two sister chromatids of each chromosome may no longer have the same genetic material.

Telophase I is similar to telophase in mitosis. The components of the cytoplasm are divided between the two new cells and a new nuclear membrane forms in eukaryotic cells.

Meiosis II

Another period of interphase occurs between meiosis I and meiosis II. This phase is brief. In fact, in some species meiosis II begins immediately following anaphase I, with telophase I and interphase not occurring.

Meiosis II is less complex than meiosis I and resembles mitosis much more closely than meiosis I. In *prophase II*, the nuclear membrane disappears. The chromosomes, widely distributed throughout the cell nucleus at the conclusion of meiosis I, begin to condense again in this phase. In prophase II there is no pairing of chromosomes because now the duplicated chromosomes have nothing with which to pair. Remember that in meiosis I each chromosome made only one duplicate, not two, as in mitosis. At the conclusion of this phase, the formation of a spindle begins.

In *metaphase II*, the chromosomes, which remain duplicated at this point and are each attached to the centromere, move to the middle of the spindle.

In *anaphase II*, the centromere of each chromosome divides, resulting in two single chromosomes. These haploid chromosomes move to opposite ends of the spindle to complete this phase.

Telophase II is constituted by a nuclear membrane forming around each new cell. The chromosomes spread out in the new cell nucleus, and the cytoplasm's contents are divided between the new cells.

Helpful points to remember in clarifying the differences between mitosis and meiosis are that in mitosis one cell division results in two new cells, which are each identical to the cell that divides. In meiosis, the cell goes through two divisions and forms four sex cells, or *spermatozoa* in males, and one functional sex cell, or *oocyte* in females. No two of these sex cells are alike due to the crossover process. The number of possible combinations depends on the species' haploid number. The number of combinations is denoted as 2 to the nth power, where n is the haploid number. Thus, human beings, having 23 chromosome pairs or 46 chromosomes in total, have 2 to the 23rd power (2 multiplied by 2 23 times) for a total number of 8,388,608 different combinations of sex cells possible for each individual human being. Think of the amount of diversity that number has the potential to create when the combination of two individuals with that many different possibilities goes into creating one human baby!

Pedigrees

A *pedigree* is a diagram in which a family's genealogy is depicted. Pedigrees are most commonly developed to demonstrate the path of inheritance of a particular phenotype. An example is the inheritance of sickle cell anemia (a condition in which the red blood cells are sickle-shaped rather than round and have a compromised ability to carry oxygen to the various body organs) that might occur in a family. Those readers familiar with genograms will note the similarity between genograms and pedigrees. Murray Bowen, MD, the psychiatrist who developed the idea of genograms, based them on the pedigree model. Due to the diversity in genetic material that occurs with multiple generations over time, geneticists generally limit pedigrees to 10 generations.

Most inherited conditions that are detrimental to an individual's existence, such as sickle cell anemia and phenylketonuria, are recessive alleles that must occur in the homozygous recessive state to exist in an individual. When close relatives (i.e., cousins) parent children, the chance of the homozygous state of these recessive alleles increases greatly. This is one of the reasons that most states prohibit marriage between siblings and between first cousins.

Individuals with sickle cell anemia and those with sickle cell trait are more resistant to malaria than individuals who do not carry an allele for sickle cell anemia. Therefore, maintenance of the sickle cell anemia allele is important to the survival of the human population.

It is important to dispel a common belief that sickle cell anemia only occurs in human beings of African descent. A genetic mutation was discovered in Portugal that has given rise to cases of sickle cell anemia in Caucasians (Monteiro et al., 1989). Epidemiological studies have demonstrated that Americans of east coast and Caribbean Hispanic descent and Americans of East Asian Indian descent all have shown evidence of sickle cell anemias of various types (Lorey, Arnopp, & Cunningham, 1996).

There are some detrimental traits in human beings that are inherited through dominant alleles. Recall that in this case the individual is either homozygous or heterozygous for the dominant allele because the dominant allele "dominates" the recessive allele. Examples of these conditions are neurofibromatosis (a condition in which noncancerous tumors form all over the individual's body), Huntington's chorea (a disease in which the individual has involuntary muscle spasms and loss of memory and speech), and ptosis (drooping upper eyelids).

Before leaving the topic of pedigrees, a brief discussion of blood groups is in order. Blood groups in human beings are an interesting genetic phenomenon because the gene controlling this trait has three alleles instead of the usual two associated with most human genes. There are several blood groups (A, B, and O are the most common) that have been discovered in human beings, but because the ABO types are the most common, the discussion here is limited to that group.

Classification of blood type is based on chemical substances (antigens) on the red blood cells and chemicals in the blood's liquid portion (serum), which react to the substances on the surface of the red blood cells (antibodies). An individual never has chemicals in the serum that react with the chemicals on his or her red blood cells.

The four human blood types in the ABO group are A, B, AB, and O. A person with blood type A has A antigens and antibodies that react with the B antigen to destroy it. A person with B blood type has antibodies to the A antigen. The person with O blood type has no antigens but A and B antibodies. Finally, the person with AB type blood has no antibodies but has both A and B antigens. If the O allele is present with either an A or B allele, it is masked or dominated by either antigen allele. If a person has A and B alleles, they are codominant; in other words, both antigens exist on the red blood cells.

When blood types are mixed, there can be disastrous effects if the types are not compatible. If a person with type A blood, for example, is given type B blood, the type B blood has antigens to the type A antigen and there is a chemical reaction that destroys the type A red blood cells. This process is called *agglutination*. Because type O blood has no antigens, it can be given to anyone of any blood type and agglutination will not occur. Thus people with type O blood are termed *universal donors*. However, those with type O blood have antibodies to both A and B antigens. Therefore, they can receive only O blood or they will have agglutination problems. People with type AB blood have no antibodies since they have both A and B antigens on their red blood cells. Thus, they can receive blood from any blood type and not experience agglutination. Individuals with this blood type are termed *universal receivers*. It is always preferable to use the same blood type if it is available.

DNA and RNA

The next section covers the important topic of how molecules called nucleic acids store and transmit hereditary material across generations.

The Hereditary Information Molecules

Today, biologists know that the hereditary material for all species is *nucleic acid*. In the vast majority of species, including human beings, the nucleic acid is in the form of DNA (deoxyribonucleic acid). In a few viruses, it is in the form of RNA (ribonucleic acid). The primary functions of these molecules are to store and transmit hereditary material and to translate the hereditary material into protein, a form of information that the body can interpret and use.

Enzymes are a particular class of proteins that speed up (catalyze) chemical reactions necessary for the body to function on a minute-to-minute basis. Other proteins provide a structural brace for cells of the body, and still others (antibodies) help the body defend itself against disease.

Proteins are long chains of amino acids. There are 20 amino acids, which are common to most species, and the human body is able to make 12 of these amino acids. In a protein, two amino acid molecules are held together by a *peptide bond* and a protein, consisting of a chain of many of these bonds, called a *polypeptide*.

The number of possible messages that a protein can carry is a function of the number of amino acids that it contains. The value 20 to the nth power, in which n represents the number of amino acids, determines the number of possible sequences. Therefore, if eight amino acids are present in a protein, 12,800,000 different combinations or hereditary messages are possible.

Because proteins are three-dimensional molecules, they do not exist simply in a straight line. Their structure can be twisted and turned in many different directions to further affect the possible information that they translate.

Until the early 1900s, protein itself was thought to be the material of heredity. However, in 1943, elaborate experiments by the American biologists Avery, MacLeod, and McCarty resulted in a separation of constituents of bacterial cells into DNA, protein, lipids (fatty substances), and carbohydrates.

As mentioned earlier in this chapter, DNA exists in the form of a double helix. The deoxyribose (sugar) and phosphate portions of the DNA, which constitute the sides of the double helix, are identical in all DNA molecules regardless of species or information contained in the DNA. The bases differ from DNA molecule to DNA molecule, which make up the rungs of the twisted ladder. Recall from earlier in the chapter that these bases are adenine (A), guanine (G), cytosine (C), and thymine (T).

On the outside of the double helix, the base is attached to the sugar/phosphate chain. On the inside, the base is connected to another base. This is the gist of the code for hereditary information! Adenine is always paired with thymine, and guanine is always paired with cytosine. The sequence of the bases is the code for genetic information, and the predetermined pairing of the bases ensures that an accurate copy of each strand will be made when replication occurs.

With the four-symbol code of A-T and C-G, the DNA molecule can code an immense amount of hereditary data. Determination of the number of unique messages that a DNA molecule can code is a function of the number of base pairs in the molecule. Thus, with only six base pairs, 4,096 different messages can be contained in the molecule!

RNA resembles DNA but has three important differences in structure. First, the sugar in this molecule is ribose rather than deoxyribose (these two sugars differ only in the fact that deoxyribose has one fewer oxygen atom). Second, RNA typically has one strand rather than two. Third, the base thymine does not exist in RNA. It is replaced by the base *uracil* (U).

Some viruses have only RNA as their mode of coding information concerning heredity. However, all living organisms have three types of RNA. All of these types are copied from DNA in the cell's nucleus, and they are mediators between DNA and protein production. These types of RNA are termed *messenger RNA, ribosomal RNA,* and *transfer RNA.* A more complete discussion of their role in protein synthesis will be imparted following a discussion of the functions of DNA.

Remember from the description of the eukaryotic cell that each cell in an individual human body has an identical set of chromosomes. Each of these chromosomes contains one DNA molecule, which is surrounded by several types of proteins in the cells' nuclei, histones being one of the most important types. The DNA molecule is long and would stretch several inches if uncoiled in a straight line. Histone is believed to serve a role in arranging the coiling of DNA, which enables such an immense amount of hereditary information to be enclosed in the small cell nucleus.

Also recall from the discussion of eukaryotic cell division that both mitosis and meiosis require DNA duplication. At this point, a return to the work of Watson and Crick is required to explain the function of DNA.

Watson and Crick described the double helix model of DNA in 1953. There are several steps in which the hereditary information in DNA is translated into the physical characteristics observed in an individual human body. First, the information in the DNA molecule is copied to messenger RNA. This process is termed *transcription.* In human and all other eukaryotic cells, messenger RNA then moves from the nucleus of the cell to the surrounding cytoplasm, where its hereditary information is read by both ribosomal and transfer RNA. Ribosomal and transfer RNA then produce proteins based on the information they receive from the messenger RNA. Proteins then function as chemicals in the process of development of physical characteristics within the individual. Enzymes are a particularly important type of protein for this job.

Crick also explained that the DNA duplication process ensured that every cell in an individual human body contains the same hereditary material as the original cell that resulted from the combination of a female egg and a male sperm.

Complementary base pairing of adenine and thymine and cytosine and guanine is the method by which DNA is able to duplicate itself precisely, for it enables each DNA strand to synthesize a completely new strand. During replication each DNA strand serves as a *template* for the creation of a new strand of DNA with complementary bases. Enzymes are responsible for this process. One enzyme breaks bonds between the paired bases in the original double helix and "unzips" the DNA. Another enzyme then mediates the linking of the single-strand base with its complementary base. Thus each single strand forms a double strand, and where one DNA molecule existed, now there are two identical molecules.

Crick also proposed that each base pair is the code for a particular amino acid, which is part of a protein. Because he knew there are 20 amino acids, he devised a three-base system for determining amino acids. Each three-base group was termed a *codon*. Messenger RNA (mRNA) production occurs during the G1 and G2 steps of mitosis. This type of RNA is formed from only one DNA strand, called the *sense strand*. Remember that with mRNA uracil pairs with adenine, not thymine, as in DNA replication. Each strand of mRNA has a *leader site* (signified by the base sequence AUG = adenine, uracil, guanine) to which the cell's ribosomes can bind. Recall that the ribosome is the site of protein synthesis for the cell. The ribosomes move down the mRNA strand and *translate* the strand into a series of amino acids dependent on the order of the bases. Each strand of mRNA ends with a codon, which does not code for any amino acid. This tells the ribosome that the protein code is complete. This type of RNA is a long molecule and generally has a life expectancy of only a few minutes.

Ribosomal RNA (rRNA) constitutes approximately 80% of a eukaryotic cell's RNA. This type of RNA, like mRNA, is formed directly from the DNA in the cell's nucleus. It then moves immediately to the cytoplasm, where it connects with proteins to form ribosomes.

Transfer RNA (tRNA) is the smallest of the three types of RNA molecules. Its job is to bring amino acids to the ribosomes for assembly into proteins. Although all RNA is a single strand, tRNA has a twisting form, which causes it to resemble a cloverleaf and appear double-stranded. The tRNA therefore has two free ends. One attaches to the amino acid for which the tRNA is coded at the loop of the cloverleaf, which is located opposite the free ends. This is termed an *anticodon* because it has the exact sequence of bases as the DNA (with the exception of uracil replacing thymine) from which a unique mRNA was formed for the protein of which this amino acid is one component. More than 50 types of tRNA have been identified, each of which is responsible for carrying one amino acid to the cell's ribosome.

A final note to this brief survey of DNA and RNA is the hypothesis of a one-to-one correspondence between genes and polypeptides. Termed the *one gene—one polypeptide hypothesis*, the postulation is that each gene contains the code for one polypeptide, which is most often a protein. The polypeptide then participates in a variety of different chemical reactions, which lead to the production of the physical characteristic of the individual possessing it. Remember the discussion of PKU earlier in this chapter; in this case, an error in coding in a gene causes the absence of an enzyme necessary to metabolize phenylalanine, leading to mental retardation if left untreated.

The Genetics of Gender

The process of reproduction is obviously a crucial part of genetics. In this section, only the genetics of gender are discussed. Remember from earlier in this chapter that male spermatozoa and female oocytes are both produced by a process called meiosis, which reduces the number of chromosomes in the sex cells to the haploid number for the species. The male produces two types of spermatozoa, those containing X chromosomes and those containing Y chromosomes. The female oocytes contain only X chromosomes.

Male offspring possess an X chromosome from the mother and a Y chromosome from the father. Female offspring contain an X chromosome from each parent. Thus, the father determines the gender of the offspring.

There are several genetic gender disorders that result from abnormal numbers of X and Y chromosomes in offspring. *Turner's syndrome* occurs when an individual has only one X chromosome and no Y chromosome. Such a person is a female because she possesses no Y chromosome, but these individuals are usually short in height and have underdeveloped ovaries and breasts. These individuals are incapable of reproduction because both X chromosomes are necessary for a female to produce oocytes. Another type of genetic disorder is labeled *Klinefelter's syndrome*. This occurs when an individual has two X chromosomes and a Y chromosome. This individual is a male because he has a Y chromosome. These individuals have longer arms and legs than those with an XY genotype, and many of the secondary gender characteristics are more feminine than in XY males. These individuals, like those with Turner's syndrome, are unable to reproduce.

Some males are born with one X and two Y chromosomes. These men are taller than XY males but they are able to reproduce. Individuals of this genotype have been a source of study in terms of tendencies toward aggression, as it was discovered that they have a disproportionately high representation in Caucasian males in prisons and mental institutions. Present studies, however, have shown that although men with this genotype may have a higher tendency to be in the penal system, they do not appear to have a higher degree of aggressive tendencies than XY males.

Fragile X syndrome is a condition in which one of the arms of the X chromosome is constricted during mitosis. This condition causes a variety of abnormal characteristics among individuals possessing it, including ears that protrude extensively from the head, large head, long face, a high weight at birth, and flat feet. In males with fragile X syndrome, the testes are larger than in the XY male not having the syndrome.

Taylor and colleagues (2010) conducted a research study that addressed social worker perspectives on use of genetic testing to identify embryonic gender prior to adoption placement. This study sampled recent graduates of social work programs and those who had graduated 25 years earlier, all of whom were members of the National Association of Social Workers (NASW). The study drew two conclusions. First, recent graduates had no better knowledge of human genetics than their colleagues who had graduated 25 years earlier. Second, members who had greater knowledge of human genetics were more likely to support genetic testing for embryonic gender as a consideration in adoption placement than were those who did not have a genetic knowledge base (Taylor, Mapp, Boutte-Queen & Erich, 2010). Problematic are the small sample size (261) and the intervening variable of the NASW policy statement supporting family planning and reproductive choice (National Association of Social Workers, 2009). A social worker's perspective on use of genetic testing to determine gender in adoption is not determined solely by his or her knowledge of genetics. The study's sample may underrepresent social workers with personal objection to abortion, who elect nonaffiliation with the NASW due to this policy statement. Perspectives on genetic testing for embryonic gender to inform social action (i.e., adoption placement) could be interpreted as influencing natural genetic diversity by a social worker who opposes abortion.

Sex-Linked Genetics

Genes that occur on the sex chromosomes X and Y are termed sex-linked. The X chromosome contains many genes. When the term *sex-linked* is used in common language, the speaker is usually referring to the gene causing a physical characteristic being located on the X chromosome. There is only one gene proven to exist on the Y chromosome. This gene codes for the testes to develop in males.

X-linked genes have a unique pattern for expressing their characteristics in offspring because females have two X chromosomes and males have only one. Thus, if a recessive allele is on the one and only X chromosome that a male receives, he will exhibit the trait. In a female, however, if one recessive allele and one dominant allele are received, the female is a *carrier* of the gene for the trait but does not exhibit it. Therefore, males have a 50% chance of inheriting the recessive gene if the mother is a carrier and the father does not have the disease. A female, on the other hand, has no chance of exhibiting the trait of the recessive gene, because even if she receives a recessive allele from her mother, she receives a dominant allele from her father. She has a 50% chance of being a carrier.

One of the best-known cases of this type of inheritance is hemophilia, a blood disorder in which the blood does not have sufficient platelets, and the blood component produces clotting. The person with hemophilia must receive frequent blood transfusions to avoid bleeding to death from injuries that cause bleeding or bruising. When testing for the AIDS virus was not as sophisticated as it is today, many with hemophilia contracted AIDS due to frequent blood transfusions. Queen Victoria of England was a carrier of this disease, and her pedigree is often illustrated as an example of this type of inheritance.

Deuteranopia (red-green color blindness), a condition in which the eye lacks the pigment necessary to differentiate between red, orange, yellow, and green, also has this mode of inheritance. This is the reason that approximately 1 in 30,000 males are born with this defect, but it is rare in females. Approximately 9 million Americans have this form of color blindness, 10% of the population. A particular type of muscular dystrophy called Duchenne is also inherited in this manner. Jerry Lewis has familiarized the public with this type of disease through his extensive work with various forms of muscular dystrophy.

Genetic Counseling

The ability to predict the probability of offspring having inherited diseases has led to the medical service of genetic counseling for potential parents who know that members of their family have experienced these diseases. Potential parents sometimes initiate this process, but more commonly parents who have had a child exhibiting a disease such as sickle cell anemia are referred to genetic counseling to learn about the potential of producing future offspring with the same condition. Sickle cell anemia, in particular, has initiated a great deal of controversy because screening programs for the presence of the disease in infants is mandatory in many states. Because this disease is most prevalent in those of African American origin, these screenings and subsequent mandated genetic counseling have sometimes been perceived to be a method of birth control imposed on the African American minority by the Caucasian majority.

It is obvious that there are many ethical implications in counseling of this type. Social workers and other counselors must be sensitive when discussing options to live birth, such as abortion and adoption, with prospective parents. To date, genetic counseling has not proven to be a deterrent to future childbirth to parents with sickle cell anemia (Neal-Cooper & Scott, 1988; Samuels-Reid, Scott, & Brown, 1984). Other research has shown that the threat of genetic disease is not an important deterrent to parenthood (Frets et al., 1990).

Genetic Engineering

In the past several years, genetic engineering, the ability to change the hereditary information in different living organisms, has become a topic of great discussion and controversy. On one hand, it makes possible the elimination of many inherited diseases; on the other hand, it offers the possibility of creating new individuals from one parent rather than requiring the genetic material of two parents, which can lead to a decrease in diversity with a consequent increased chance of detrimental genetic conditions manifesting themselves. The great debate about the ethics of reproductive cloning human beings after the news of Dolly, the cloned sheep, is an example.

In *DNA cloning*, a bacterial cell is used as a site for combining desired genetic material for reproduction. For example, a desirable trait such as disease resistance might have an identified gene controlling it. The gene is extracted and placed in a virus cell, which then attaches to the host bacterial cell (usually of the species *Escherichia coli*). Enzymes are used to divide the DNA of the gene into segments. The bacterial cell incorporates this DNA fragment into its own DNA. The bacteria are then grown in a culture so that multiple samples of the DNA for the desired trait can be gathered from it.

The DNA is then searched for the desired gene, which may be a lengthy process. When the desired segment of DNA is found, it is analyzed for the method by which this DNA segment was incorporated into the bacterial cell's DNA so that the technique can be reproduced in future cases when it is needed.

Safety is a key issue here, because segments of DNA are often taken from diseased tissues in an effort to determine which gene contains the coding for that disease. Ecologists are concerned about the release of genetically altered organisms into the environment for which no defenses may currently be available. One of the well-known achievements of genetic technology was the creation of human insulin through DNA recombination, which occurred on a widespread basis in the 1980s. Prior to this time human beings with diabetes had to use the insulin of pigs or cows, which is chemically different from that of human beings and has been shown to cause deleterious side effects with use over time. Many individuals developed immunity to these foreign insulins, and over a period of time the insulins became ineffective in lowering blood sugar. Animal insulins were also suspected of contributing to the development of complications of diabetes, such as kidney- and eye disease. There were also cases of allergies to these animal insulins and concerns about what would happen in the case of warfare if a sufficient supply of insulin could not be maintained.

Biologists have identified the genes that contain the hereditary material for many diseases. This enables testing of DNA at any point in life for these detrimental genes. Embryos can be tested in the mother's uterus for such conditions as Huntington's chorea, Down syndrome, sickle cell anemia, as well as many other diseases. This often presents an ethical dilemma. For example, does a person want to be checked at age 15 to determine whether he or she will contract Huntington's chorea at age 35 in an effort to avoid passing the disease on to offspring? There is also a test currently available for alleles that have been shown to present a greater risk for Alzheimer's disease in about 10% of the population. Should insurance companies be allowed to require these tests before life insurance or health insurance will be granted to an individual (Andomo, 2002)?

Finally, the subject of *DNA fingerprinting* became a matter of public knowledge in the O. J. Simpson trial. Because each individual is genetically unique, the banding pattern that DNA exhibits when restricted segments of it are analyzed is unique to each individual, just as his or her fingerprints are. This technique is superior to blood typing in identifying parenthood, in which the tested person could be told with certainty only that he or she was not the parent.

The Human Genome Project

The Human Genome Project began in 1953 when Watson and Crick discovered the structure of DNA. The *genome* of a species is the sequencing of all DNA in the nucleus of each cell of that species. It matches the organism's bases (alanine, thymine, cytosine, and guanine). The human genome is a chain of 3.4 billion bases. The genome of two different human beings varies by one base per thousand on average (www.lexicon-biology.com/biology/definition_56.html). The draft sequence of the human genome was published in *Science* and *Nature* in February 2001. In October 2004, *Nature* published the completed human genome sequence. The sequencing, authored by the International Human Genome Consortium, was the result of work by more than 2,800 scientists in France, Germany, Japan, China, Great Britain, and the United States. The Human Genome Project was completed ahead of schedule and at substantially less expense than originally anticipated, a rare occurrence in funded research.

The completed human genome sequencing covers approximately 99% of the human genome and has precision of approximately 1 event/100,000 bases error, an accuracy rate of 99.999%. This precision level is 10 times the meticulousness of the initial goal. Currently, the human genome has 2.85 billion nucleotides, with only 341 gaps in sequencing. Completing these gaps will require new technological methods (see www.nature.com/nature/journal/v431/n7011/nature03001.html).

Researchers determined that the human genome contains only 20,000 to 25,000 protein-encoding genes, compared to 35,000 predicted in the 2001 draft. The number of protein-encoding genes in the human genome is dramatically lower than estimates of 50,000 to 100,000 genes made in biology texts of the 1990s. The human genome sequencing was deposited into free public databases for research use in April 2003. Continuous sequencing was greatly improved between 2001 and 2003. Genes are "stretches" of DNA that code for particular proteins (www.genome.gov/12513430/). Gene-to-gene high-quality sequencing is currently 475 times longer than the draft sequence published in 2001. These continuous DNA sequences tremendously aid researchers searching for genes and the adjacent DNA sequences that might control the gene's protein-coding activity. The great precision in this sequencing decreases time and cost of locating human genome areas having small and exceptional deviations associated with disease.

The number of gaps decreased from 500,000 in the 2001 draft sequence to 341 in the current human genome sequence. Segment duplication is present in 5.3% of the human genome, compared to 3% in the rat genome. Segment duplications afford observation of how humans and other animals have evolved and continue to evolve. The human Y chromosome has segment duplication over 25% of its length, making it an excellent specimen for study of this phenomenon. Because this duplication often occurs in the middle (centromere) or end (telomere) of the chromosome, scientists have proposed that these two chromosome areas serve as sources of genetic material to create new genes with new roles.

The human genome sequence has also given researchers information about gene birth and death. Since humans diverged from rodents about 75 million years ago, 1,000 new genes have materialized in the human genome. The majority of these new genes have roles in reproductive, immune, and olfactory processes. In contrast, 33 human genes have experienced one or more mutations that have resulted in cessation of role performance, or "death." Ten of these mutant genes appear to have had a role in olfactory reception. The death of these genes provides a partial explanation of the poorer sense of smell in humans compared to rats and mice, in which these genes have full function.

In addition to human beings, plants, other animals, and bacteria have had their genomes completely sequenced. Humans, rats, and mice all have approximately the same gene density of 1 gene/100,000 bases, though these three animal species have different numbers of chromosomes (human 46, rat 42, mouse 40). All of these animals have approximately 30,000 bases as well. Humans have 2.9 billion base pairs, rats have 2.75 billion, and mice have 2.5 billion. In fact, most mammals, including humans, mice, dogs, cats, rabbits, monkeys, and apes, have approximately the same number of nucleotides in their genomes: 3 billion base pairs. This similarity of DNA composition suggests that mammals have about the same number of genes. This proposal is confirmed by the work of the Human Genome Project. The vast majority of mouse genes have a complement in the human genome.

There are social, ethical, and legal implications of the Human Genome Project. The Ethical, Legal, and Social Implications (ELSI) program was initiated in 1990 as a basic component of the Human Genome Project. The ELSI program was charged with recognizing and tackling genome research issues that affect families, individuals, and society. These issues have been addressed by ELSI, resulting in identification of four main areas of possible consequences of genomic research: (1) privacy and justice in use of genetic information, including the potential for genetic bias in employment and insurance; (2) incorporation of new genetic technologies, such as genetic testing, into clinical medical practice; (3) ethical issues surrounding the design and method of genetic research with human subjects, including informed consent; and (4) "education of health care professionals, policy makers, students, and the public" regarding genetics and the sophisticated issues that arise in genomic research (www.ghr.nlm.nih.gov/info=genomic_resesarch/show/elsi/).

The first gene therapy protocol was approved in 1981. Gene therapy has had a mixture of positive and negative outcomes. An interdisciplinary group composed a document in 1984 and 1985 with 110 questions posed to investigators as they pondered a decision regarding use of gene therapy on human patients. The document makes the reader aware of the realm of issues that arise when such a decision is considered. Examples of issues discussed included recipient selection, recipient confidentiality and privacy, other therapy options, and prospective benefits and harms. The document continues to serve as a checklist for contemporary gene therapy.

The early years of gene therapy had a public review process, a crucial component of gene therapy's acceptance. Policy makers knew precisely what was occurring, investigator discussions were open to the public, and the public was privy to questions and had access to a list of approved gene therapy procedures. Since 1981, important information has been gleaned from gene therapy discussion and procedures. First, gene therapy was effectively differentiated from genetic engineering. The goal of *gene therapy* is cure of a genetic disease by placing normal genes in cells containing defective genes so the cell can produce the correct protein (www.lexicon-biology.com/biology/definition_65.html). *Genetic engineering*, also termed *bioengineering*, is a general term referring to any change of an organism's genes for practical purposes (www.library.thinkquest.org/19697/data/OV1Def-b.html).

There are a variety of obstacles to overcome in gene therapy. Delivery tools for the gene have to be investigated. Genes need to be inserted into the body cells via *vectors*. Viruses are the most common vectors currently used, because they have evolved a way to encapsulate their genetic material to place it in the human cell.

Researchers have also experimented with instituting a 47th chromosome into the human body. The chromosome would exist in parallel with the other 46 chromosomes without causing any change in these chromosomes, including mutation.

Another impediment to gene therapy is the lack of knowledge regarding which genes control which body functions. Most genetic diseases are caused by multiple genes. The environment also plays a role in the development of genetic diseases. The fact that two identical twins do not exhibit genetic diseases at the same rate is unquestionable evidence that the environment plays a role in genetic diseases (www.nih.gov/news/panelrep.html).

When a gene is defective, the protein that it codes does not function correctly. Investigators have also suggested that "human gene transfer" may be less biased and emotionally loaded than "human gene therapy," which implies benefit to the recipient. Third, the success of gene therapy was modest in its first 8 years of use. Investigators have expressed regret and disappointment in the researchers and businesses that embellished these early results. Finally, the investigators determined that an optimum location would be required for a national public review body to scrutinize new biomedical technology (www.ornl.gov/sci/techresources/Human_Genome/publicat/hgn/v10n/16walter.shtml).

To date, human gene therapy has involved only somatic cells, not reproductive cells (sperm and egg cells). Somatic cells have already been altered in HIV-AIDS and advanced cancer patients in an attempt to enhance their immune systems. Any changes in the genetic structure of these cells would not be conveyed to offspring. Proposals have been made to perform genetic alteration of sperm and eggs, termed *germ-line gene therapy*. This type of gene therapy would result in an altered future population (www.ornl.gov/sci/techresources/Human_Genome/publicat/v10n/16walter.shtml). There is wide-ranging public consensus that human somatic cell gene therapy must not lead to germ-line transmission of genetic change. However, there are contrasting opinions about the ethics of performing gene therapy on egg and sperm cells. Carter (2002) has expressed the opinion that if germ-line gene therapy can be safely performed and is effective, the principle of beneficence will impose a moral duty on the medical profession to pursue this technology. In 2001, scientists confirmed the birth of 30 genetically changed babies. The mothers had received *ooplasmic transfer,* a procedure in which the mothers who had experienced problems with infertility had their egg cells injected with DNA from a woman who had not experienced infertility problems. The hope was to cause the mitochondria of the embryonic cells to be stronger and thus provide more energy for the developing baby. However, these babies had three parents, a father and two mothers, because they contained DNA from two women. This was an unintentional crossing of the germ-line boundary, but the offspring of these children will all have the mixed mitochondria DNA (http://genome.gsc.riken.go.jp/hgmis/medicine/genetherapy.html).

With the sequencing of the human genome virtually complete, a likely future proposal will be to locate defective genes that cause disease and suffering, remove them, and replace them with genes programmed to properly perform human physiological functions. This type of intervention is the only procedure currently possible to correct diseases that a mother passes on to her baby in the uterus that cause a malfunction in the mitochondria of the embryo's somatic cells. When the embryo consists of four cells, these cells could have their nuclei removed and replaced with the nuclei or a donor who does not have the defective gene. This procedure would consist of germ-line genetic intervention and reproductive cloning.

Gene therapy has the potential to propagate myriad legal questions. Gene therapy may evolve to a stage of being able to prevent, cure, or better treat previously inevitable, permanent, and fatal diseases. If this potential is realized, there will be a huge demand for gene therapy. If the new therapy is more cost-effective than current treatments, major insurers will readily endorse it. However, if the gene therapy proves more expensive, as in the case where treatment was previously unavailable so no treatment costs were incurred, insurers will not be as enthusiastic.

Access to specific medical treatment has a history of being addressed by the court. An individual's decision to challenge an insurer's refusal to pay for a procedure such as gene therapy can take time and delay treatment. Insurers are understandably motivated to save money. Medicare, for example, does not pay for any treatments that are not "medically necessary." Experimental procedures that do not have a proven track record are not considered medically necessary.

Courts will be called on to settle arguments regarding ownership of intellectual property that will undoubtedly arise between scientists and research sponsors. There is also the potential for disputes between researchers and their subjects when scientific findings are used for financial gain. The California Supreme Court has ruled that patients need to be informed and have a right to negotiate a financial gain if they are participating in commercial research.

The courts will also be asked to determine standard of care when gene therapy is available to potentially alleviate or treat a genetic condition that was previously chronic. A patient can learn of gene therapy and demand to receive it when it is yet to be part of standard medical practice. Physicians and other health care providers can be sued for medical malpractice, particularly if they do not inform a patient of a procedure that can offer treatment of genetic disease when nothing is currently available in general medical practice. Genetic counselors are a group at increased risk for legal liability with the advancement of human gene therapy in terms of both apprising patients of potential technological solutions to inherited diseases and poor outcomes if these technological treatments are pursued.

The extent of parental authority to manipulate the genes of their children is an issue that may well come before the court. The judiciary may find itself deciding at what point parental rights to modify a child's genetic material end. Should a parent be able to abort a child if he or she does not have the desired hair color, eye color, or sex? This question involves fundamental philosophical beliefs of our legal system, including equal opportunity and other basic rights.

Court decisions have shown great variance with respect to issues of injustice, making it hard to predict how the judicial system will handle such issues as the inequality of genetic enhancement. In some cases, the court has ignored discrimination; in other cases, the court has ruled that the more powerful party must act in the other party's best interest.

Finally, the courts will be asked to establish the standard of care to which individuals are expected to comply when they cause risk for each other. With the potential for genetic enhancement, should genetically enhanced human beings be held to the standard of an enhanced person in terms of responsibility, as opposed to the standard expected of a nonenhanced person (www.ornl.gov/sci/techresources/Human_Genome/publicat/judicature/article6.html)?

Use of DNA in the courts has been widely reported in the news media. Genetic identification is commonplace in criminal cases. Genetic proof of parenthood is routine in paternity cases. Genetic evidence is now inundating the court, claiming to support both medical and nonmedical assertions. Questions such as "Should long-term care insurance be denied to a person with a family history of Alzheimer's disease?" and "Should a woman with a family history of breast cancer be denied a home mortgage?" are commonplace in this era of genetic testing (www.ornl.gov/sci/techresourcees/Human_Genome/courts/courts.shtml). This type of scientific evidence was responsible for cessation of the death penalty in Illinois when it was determined that a significant number of individuals had been erroneously convicted and punished for murders that they did not commit. In 1999, Attorney General Janet Reno asked the Legal Issues Working Group of the Human Genome Project to ponder several "profound" issues of privacy that had arisen with the use of DNA evidence in the legal system.

One of these issues was preservation of DNA samples after testing is concluded. The attorney general expressed concern that as DNA technology evolved, retained samples would be available for tests to be performed that were not originally intended. Another issue she raised was the right to test arrested individuals versus convicted offenders. While considering this dilemma, the Legal Issues Working Group provisionally advised that the Department of Justice should abstain from advocating a policy supporting DNA sampling of arrestees unless three conditions were met: (1) the convicted offender databases backlog was eradicated; (2) significant resources were provided for examination of nonsuspects; and (3) enough money was allocated for collection and examination of DNA samples from arrested individuals. The major concern was that laboratories were being overworked to provide DNA analysis for convicted offenders, a significantly smaller group than all of those arrested!

The final concern expressed by the attorney general was the issue of the statute of limitation for filing charges as well as appeals. With the ability of DNA testing to investigate crimes that occurred beyond the statutes of limitation in many states, statutes of limitation, which were arbitrarily assigned in many states prior to the advent of DNA technology, may now be limiting factors to victims who could otherwise have had their cases solved (www.ornl.goov/sci/techresources/Human_Genome/publicat/juddicature/article9.html).

In her book *Neuroscience and Social Work Practice: The Missing Link*, Rosemary Farmer (2009) refers to *genetic plasticity* (Andreasen, 2001). She explains that plasticity implies lack of static gene expression. Gene expression can be affected by various factors including age, gender, diet, culture, and environment. She reports that previous studies have postulated genes affect the action of medication, but now studies are investigating how medication affects genes (Kanlow, 2005). The genes directing the enzyme's production have frequent mutations. Dependent upon the genetic programming of the enzyme production (Farmer, 2009), a person may metabolize psychiatric medication well, intermediately, or poorly.

Conclusion

Genetics is a complex topic that has been consolidated into a minimal number of pages in this chapter. Many topics, such as regulation of gene expression, extensive discussion of mutation, and the effect of genes on the immune system, are beyond the scope of this chapter. Further reading in these areas is encouraged for a more complete understanding of this intricate and ethically loaded topic. Technological advances in genetic analysis and possible genetic manipulation have not been matched by corresponding advances in human wisdom regarding how to apply these developments. Knowledge of human genetics has great potential to improve the human condition, as well as great potential to be injurious.

Helping clients make educated decisions requires highly informed social work professionals who are not only armed with technical knowledge but are also well trained in the areas of human ethical conduct.

Key Terms

Allele	Gamete	Mitosis
Chromosome	Gene	Mutation
Deoxyribonucleic acid (DNA)	Genetic engineering	Phenotype
	Genotype	Recessive allele
Dominant allele	Heterozygous	Ribonucleic acid (RNA)
Eugenics	Homozygous	
Eukaryotic cell	Meiosis	Sex-linked gene

Review Questions for Critical Thinking

1. From the standpoint of genetic theory, are there any beneficial aspects of eugenics? If so, what are they? Who or what are the beneficiaries in your example?

2. What steps would you take in counseling a client who recently learned that he or she has a genetic disposition of sickle cell trait?

3. Having read this chapter, how would you answer the question posed at the chapter's outset? ("Is a fundamental understanding of genetic theory crucial to thorough assessment and treatment of clients coping with human social conditions?")

4. Is a person's genetic composition or his or her environment the predominant factor in psychiatric illness? Cite references containing empirical evidence to support your answer.

5. Diversity in a species' gene pool is a primary factor in ensuring survival. What natural and social laws are attributable to this biological principle?

Online Resources

American Eugenics Movement. Retrieved from www.eugenicsarchive.org

This website employs a variety of images with corresponding data to relate the history of the eugenics movement in the United States. Individuals, states, events, and dates are all part of this website's documentation, as well as valuable references.

British Medical Journal Website. (1999). Kevles, D. J. *Eugenics and Human Rights*. Retrieved from www.bmj.com/content/319/7207/435.full.pdf

This website describes the history of selectivity of "desirable human traits" and the expunging of "inferior trains." Although these practices are frequently attributed to Nazi Germany, they have occurred everywhere. Twenty-four of the United States, as well as Canada and Sweden, legalized eugenics at some point in their history.

Centers for Disease Control. (2011). *Facts About Sickle Cell Disease*. Retrieved from www.cdc.gov/nchddd/sicklecell/facts.html

This website is valuable because of the many facts it contains. Different types of sickle cell disease are discussed, as well as the difference between sickle cell disease and sickle cell trait. The causes, diagnosis, treatment, and cure of sickle cell disease are also described.

Nature Education. (2008). *Sex-Linked Diseases: The Case of Duchene [sic] Muscular Dystrophy (DMD)*. Retrieved from www.nature.com/scitable/topicpage/sex-linked-disease-the-case-of-duchene-800

Because it is possible to diagnose Duchenne muscular dystrophy prior to the birth of a baby, scientists question why the frequency of the allele has not decreased in the human population. Duchenne muscular dystrophy is a fatal neuromuscular condition. Scientists have been researching ways to treat the disease since they first became aware of its genetic cause many years ago. However, the disease continues to have a fatal prognosis.

PsychCentral. (2011). *Genetic Regulation of Brain Development Implicated in Mental Illness*. Retrieved from http://psychcentral.com/news/2011/10/27/genetic-regulation-of-brain-development-implicated-in-mental-illness

In this website's study report, researchers at Yale University followed 86% of 17,000 human genes that are thought to be designated as part of the human brain. These genes were identified by their location in the human brain and their expression; 1,300 tissue samples were analyzed from 57 subjects ranging from 40 days to 87 years old. Researchers determined that a large degree of the human brain is functionally determined prior to birth.

U.S. Department of Energy Genomics Website. (2006). *Human Genome Project Information*. Retrieved from www.genomics.energy.gov

The Human Genome Study Information section of this website is devoted to various issues of gene therapy. It describes government policies regulating genetic engineering, current status, and research of this topic as well as ethical and legal considerations on this topic. Other sections of the website deal with microbial genetics and its application in agriculture and energy.

References

Andomo, R. (2002). Biomedicine and international human rights law: In search of a global consensus. *Bulletin of the World Health Organization, 80*, 959–963.

Andreasen, N. C. (2001). *Brave new brain: Conquering mental illness in the era of the genome* (pp. 34–35). New York, NY: Oxford University Press.

Axessens, J. Armstrong, M. Glissen, R. & Cohen, M. (Feb. 2001). The human genome: An introduction. *The Oncologist, 6*(1).

Bernhardt, B., & Rauch, J. B. (1993). Genetic family histories: An aid to social work assessment. *Families in Society, 74*, 195–205.

Bishop, K. K. (1993). Psychosocial aspects of genetic disorders: Implications for practice. *Families in Society, 74*, 207–212.

Black, E. (2003). *War against the weak: Eugenics and America's campaign to create a master race*. New York, NY: Four Walls Eight Windows.

Black, R. B., & Furlong, R. M. (1984). Impact of prenatal diagnosis in families. *Social Work in Health Care, 9*, 37–50.

Black, R. B., & Weiss, J. O. (1990). Genetic support groups and social workers are partners. *Health and Social Work, 15*, 91–99.

Broberg, G., & Roll-Hansen, N. (Eds.). (1996). *Eugenics and the welfare state: Sterilization policy in Denmark, Sweden, Norway, and Finland*. East Lansing, MI: Michigan State University Press.

Campbell, N. A. (1996). *Biology* (4th ed.). Menlo Park, CA: Benjamin/Cummings.

Carter, L. (2002). The ethics of germ line gene manipulation: A five dimensional debate. *Monash Bioethics Review, 21*, S66–S81.

Farmer, R. L. (2009). *Neuroscience and social work practice: The missing link* (pp. 130–131). Los Angeles, CA: Sage.

Frets, P., Duivenvoorden, F., Verhage, F., Niermeijer, M., Van Den Berghe, S., & Galjaard, J. (1990). Factors influencing the reproductive decision after genetic counseling. *American Journal of Medical Genetics, 35*, 496–502.

Furlong, R. M., & Black, R. B. (1984). Pregnancy termination for genetic indications: The impact on families. *Social Work in Health Care, 10*, 17–34.

International Human Genome Sequencing Consortium. (2004). Finishing the euchromatic sequence of the human genome. *Nature, 431*, 931–945.

Kanlow, W. (2005). Pharmacogenomics: Historical perspectives and current status. *Methods of Molecular Biology, 311*, 3–15.

Kapit, W., & Elson, L. M. (1993). *The anatomy coloring book*. New York, NY: HarperCollins.

LaPan, A., & Platt, T. (2005). "To stem the tide of degeneracy": The eugenic impulse in social work. In S. A. Kirk (Ed.), *Mental disorders in the social environment: Foundations of social work knowledge* (pp. 139–164). New York, NY: Columbia University Press.

Lorey, F. W., Arnopp, J., & Cunningham, G. C. (1996). Distribution of hemiglobinopathy variants by ethnicity in a multiethnic state. *Genetic Epidemiology, 13*, 501.

Lorimer, F. (1930). Eugenical social work. *Eugenics, 3*, 93–96.

Lorimer, F. (1933). Discussion of the differential fertility of social classes. *Social Forces, 12*(1), 39–42.

Mendel, J. G. (1866). *Versuche über Pflanzenhybriden* Verhandlungen des naturforschenden Vereines in Brünn, Bd. IV für das Jahr, 1865 Abhandlungen:3–47.

For the English translation, see Druery, C. T., & Bateson, W. (1901). Experiments in plant hybridization. *Journal of the Royal Horticultural Society, 26,* 1–32.

Monteiro, C., Rueff, J., Falcao, A. D., Portugal, S., Weatherall, D. J., & Kulozik, A. E. (1989). The frequency and origin of the sickle cell mutation in the district of Laruche/Portugal. *Human Genetics, 82,* 255–258.

National Association of Social Workers. (2009). Family planning and reproductive choice. In *Social work speaks: 8th edition: 2009–2012 Policy Statements of the National Association of Social Workers* (p. 127). New York, NY: Author.

Neal-Cooper, F., & Scott, R. (1988). Genetic counseling in sickle cell anemia: Experiences with couples at risk. *Public Health Reports, 103,* 174–178.

Samuels-Reid, J., Scott, R., & Brown, W. (1984). Contraceptive practices and reproductive patterns in sickle cell disease. *Journal of the National Medical Association, 76,* 879–883.

Schild, S. (1973). Social workers' contribution to genetic counseling. *Social Casework, 54,* 387–392.

Schmutz, J., Wheeler, J., Dickson, M., Yang, J., Colle., Bajorek, E.... & Myers, R. M. (May, 2004). Quality assessment of the human genome sequence. *Nature, 429*(27) p. 365.

Taylor, P., Mapp, S., Boutte-Queen, N., & Erich, S. (2010). Genetic testing and adoption: Practitioner views and knowledge. *Children and Youth Services Review, 32,* 1473–1478.

Watson, J. D., & Crick, F. (1953). Molecular structure of nucleic acids — A structure for deoxyribose nucleic acid. *Nature, 171,* 737–738.

Weiss, J. O. (1976). Social work and genetic counseling. *Social Work in Health Care, 2,* 5–12.

Weiss, J. O. (1981). Psychosocial stress in genetic disorders: A guide for social workers. *Social Work in Health Care, 6,* 17–31.

Weiss, J. O. (1993). Genetic disorders: Support groups and advocacy. *Families in Society, 74,* 213–220.

Chapter 9
Ecosystems Theory

Mark A. Mattaini and Kristen Huffman-Gottschling

How can a social worker avoid oversimplifying and still integrate the complexities of contemporary practice?

The purpose of social work is to improve the quality of transactions among clients and their physical and social environments in ways that are consistent with social justice (Mattaini & Lowery, 2007). This may seem a simple statement, but the reality is the contrary. Clients (in some cases best framed as members, participants, or consumers) include individual persons, families of many diverse forms, neighborhoods, formed and natural groups, organizations and associations of many kinds, communities of place and interest, even nations. Environments include the built and natural environment; institutions and their policies; personal, collective, and structural oppression; and human, social, ecological, spiritual, and physical assets and needs. Institutions include the education, justice, economic, governmental, and religious systems. The transactions among all of these are an order of magnitude more complex than transactions among individuals alone. Social justice is increasingly recognized as the organizing value of the social work profession (Lowery, 2007; Marsh, 2005; Mullaly, 2007). Social justice can only be actualized, however, in these interlocking patterns of transactions, because justice is active: It can be realized only in action (Young, 1990).

Client experiences may be concurrently affected by many of these variables, and the impacts may be as critical as life or death, or may cause dramatic changes in the potential for a fulfilling, and fully human, life. There is, therefore, no more important profession than social work—and none more complex. Both students and professionals may be drawn to oversimplifications of the work to be done, but the history of the profession convincingly demonstrates that neglecting critical transactional realities leads to poor outcomes for clients. This reality has critical ethical implications.

Social work involves, at its core, work with interconnected transactional networks. The ecosystems perspective has been almost universally accepted in social work, because it provides a framework for exploring and intervening in such networks in their complexity. This strategy for viewing the world can at first seem rather abstract, however, so we begin by exploring why it was developed and has been so widely adopted.

The Ecosystems Perspective in Social Work

In the following section we outline some of the conceptual origins of the ecosystems perspective and how they were introduced into the field of social work. A rationale for this approach, as well as a discussion of the merits of linear and systemic perspectives, is also provided. Concepts from ecological and general systems theories were major contributors to the ecosystems perspective in social work.

Origins of the Perspective

Beginning with Mary Richmond (1917), social work theoreticians have understood that both person and environment are important for understanding people's lives. Although the person-in-environment (psychosocial) concept was defined and redefined throughout the 20th century (e.g., Hamilton, 1951; Hollis, 1972; Richmond, 1917; Sheffield, 1937), its hyphenated structure nonetheless consistently failed to draw balanced attention to each side of the hyphen, and could not seamlessly integrate the two. Practitioners often focus primarily on one side or the other, and as a result fail to note key variables affecting the lives of their clients. Practitioners typically have selected a focus that was compatible with their preferences, largely ignoring either person or environment—usually the environment (Kemp, 2010). Practitioners' preferences commonly lead them to avoid environmental interventions, instead attempting to change individual people amputated from their transactional realities. Research by Rosen and Livne (1992) demonstrated that social workers tend to focus particularly on intrapersonal issues at the expense of transactional problems with significant environmental roots. Nurius, Kemp, and Gibson (1999) similarly found that workers often do not attend to environmental variables unless they are specifically prompted to do so, as did Mattaini (1993a).

No doubt a desire among many to achieve and maintain professional status as psychotherapists equivalent to psychologists and psychiatrists has played a part in the imbalance between person and environment. Social work has also incorporated a more extensive knowledge base to draw from regarding individuals, families, and groups than knowledge related to analyzing and intervening in the networks of transactions that constitute larger systems and their impact on clients. What is commonly known about environments has often seemed like nothing more than organized common sense, providing no practical route into the complexities present (Kemp, 2010). Given the extensive history of the failure of the person-in-environment and psychosocial constructs to provide a guide for intervening in a nonhyphenated way, something new was needed. Drawing on contemporary scientific frameworks, the ecosystems perspective was developed in the 1970s as a response that could facilitate a more integrated understanding of the dynamics of the case (at whatever level).

The Rationale for Ecosystems in Social Work

A fundamental function in all professional practice, including social work, is individualizing the case, for if all cases are to be treated in the same way, there is no need for professional judgment or professional training; simple rules consistently applied by paraprofessionals would do (Meyer, 1993). But not every client with the same goals can be helped in the same way. In social work, this individualizing process is required for practice with client systems of all sizes, including persons, families, groups, and communities. No client system can be understood apart from its defining social context. The ecosystems perspective is designed to ensure that attention is paid to the case in its transactional complexity, reducing the danger of artificially amputating the client system from its environment in assessment and intervention. The perspective can guide the practitioner and client in a partnership of shared power to explore connectedness and recognize the deeply interconnected field of events into which person and environment are seamlessly interwoven.

The purpose of any perspective, including ecosystems, is to provide guidance in determining what to look at, what needs to be examined, what the boundaries of the case are, and how case phenomena are functioning transactionally. The ecosystems perspective should be understood not as a practice model (which tells one what to do), but as a framework that tells one how to look at cases—a process that must happen prior to deciding what to do. Once case realities are clarified, a social worker draws on practice models to suggest what can be done to shift the identified patterns. The data clearly indicate that without such a perspective, social workers are likely to notice dimensions of the case that tend to resonate with their own cognitive biases and to neglect others (Mattaini, 1993a, p. 250). As will become clear subsequently, however, things are not so simple; in important ways, theoretical models of human and other system behavior must be co-present with the ecosystems perspective to achieve coherence (Meyer & Mattaini, 2002).

Systemic Versus Linear Perspectives

Systems thinking, as in the ecosystems perspective, enables the practitioner to notice the transactional realities present in a case and therefore to consider interventions anywhere in the transactional field. Linear thinking, by contrast, oversimplifies, leading to an artificially narrow range of recognized possibilities. As is discussed in detail later, recent advances in systems theories and the emergence of complexity theory have shifted the perspective in many disciplines—including the hard sciences—more and more toward systemic views and away from looking for simple causation (Green & McDermott, 2010; Keenan, 2010, 2011). Interestingly, and importantly, this shift is bringing Western science increasingly in line with indigenous views worldwide (Ross, 2006). The change is epistemological; it involves a change in ways of seeing and knowing.

In systems thinking, unlike linear thinking, causes are recognized as potentially multiple, reciprocal, and often contingent on events and conditions that may be widely dispersed in the transactional field. Many such conditions and events may be involved in maintaining the current situation, and many may offer potential intervention points. Clearly this is a more challenging view and does not have the same air of certainty. If linear thinking tends to lead to conclusions that are comforting but false, it must be discarded. Systems thinking is intended to recognize and accommodate multiplicity, complexity, and uncertainty, and these appear to be characteristic of client realities, both historically and in the 21st century.

The Conceptual Roots of the Ecosystems Perspective

The ecosystems perspective in social work and related fields (Auerswald, 1968; Meyer, 1976) emerged from two conceptual frameworks drawn from the sciences: ecology (e.g., DuBos, 1972) and general systems theory (GST; especially from the work of von Bertalanffy, 1968). In the early and mid-20th century, a variety of thinkers and scientists began to move toward systems thinking and systems theories. Capra (1996) describes a number of examples, including the ecologist Odum (1953), who tried to clarify ecological phenomena by using flow diagrams; Bogdanov's tektology, which sought "to arrive at a systematic formulation of the principles of organization operating in living and nonliving systems" (Capra, 1996, p. 44); and Cannon's (1939) concept of systemic homeostasis.

For social work, and for the field of systems theory in general, Ludwig von Bertalanffy's work was seminal. Von Bertalanffy's (1968, p. 86) aim was breathtakingly ambitious: the "Unity of Science"! He wrote:

> The fact that certain principles apply to systems in general, irrespective of the nature of the systems and of the entities concerned, explains that corresponding conceptions and laws appear independently in different fields of science, causing the remarkable parallelism in their modern development. Thus, concepts such as wholeness and sum, mechanization, centralization, hierarchical order, stationary and steady states, equifinality, etc., are found in different fields of natural science, as well as in psychology and sociology. Reality, in the modern conception, appears as a tremendous hierarchical order of organized entities, leading, in a superposition of many levels, from physical and chemical to biological and sociological systems. Unity of Science is granted, not by a utopian reduction of all sciences to physics and chemistry, but by the structural uniformities of the different levels of reality. (pp. 86–87)

The shift from traditional thinking in this statement, even in the sciences, is profound. A critical point is that von Bertalanffy was not suggesting some sort of metaphysical or metaphoric project in his general system theory (later usually referred to as general systems theory), but rather a deeply scientific perspective for attempting to clarify and model the complexities of dynamic realities.

Similarly, ecology is a science, a division of biology. This science is concerned with the adaptive fit of organisms and their environments and the processes by which they achieve or fail to achieve a dynamic equilibrium that results in survival—and sometimes in flourishing. One of the founders of ecology, Marston Bates (1950/1990, p. 7), described "natural history" (his term for ecology, which only later became the standard terminology) as "the study of life at the level of the individual—of what plants and animals do, how they react to each other and their environment, how they are organized into larger groupings like populations and communities." Ever since, ecological writings (e.g., Wilson, 1992) have emphasized the search for scientific principles to understand such phenomena as diversity and survival at the interfaces of individual, population, and environment.

Before proceeding from here, it is probably important to note that while both ecology and GST have contributed to the ecosystems perspective, a real integration between them has been more a goal than an achievement. In social work each has been developed primarily by separate theorists, and their constructs do not always fit together neatly. Contemporary developments emerging from GST might help explain the dynamics of ecological transactions; as argued later, this is more likely in the more scientifically framed applications.

Ecosystems: Science or Metaphor?

Like GST, ecology is a scientific discipline. The integration of GST and ecology in social work that occurs (if unevenly) in the ecosystems perspective has not always been considered in scientific terms, however. For example, the life model of social work practice uses ecology (and in some cases ecosystems) in an unequivocally and explicitly metaphoric manner (Gitterman & Germain, 2008). Ecological terms such as habitat, niche, adaptation, and pollution, used extensively in the life model, are understood as heuristic constructs rather than in scientific terms. Gitterman and Germain clearly recognize, however, that humans are animals living in transaction with natural, built, and social environments, and ecological concepts even when used heuristically have proven practically helpful in communicating this embeddedness to students and practitioners.

Carol Meyer (1976, 1983, 1988, 1993, 1995), the primary architect of the ecosystems perspective in social work, was concerned that the scientific origins of ecosystems not be lost. She was a strong supporter of the development of research-grounded refinements of the perspective and explicitly rejected ecosystems as primarily metaphoric (Meyer, personal communication, 1987); instead, she emphasized its use as an epistemological framework for understanding reality in its complexity. I argue later in this chapter that the epistemic utility of ecosystems as a way of under-standing phenomena of interest to social work scientifically, however, has been almost universally underemphasized.

Ecological Theory

Ecology, a subdiscipline of biology, is the science of adaptedness. Ecological investigations focus on mutual adaptations between the organism and the environment, with recognition that such adaptation is often (although not always) mutual. In ecological terms, in some cases organisms (includ-ing persons) simply adjust to the environment; the term "adaptation" is generally reserved for those situations where both organism and envi-ronment change in complementary and transactional ways. According to Germain and Bloom (1999, p. 12), "There is a general tendency for each party to this interaction to seek a goodness of fit or positive adaptedness vis-à-vis themselves and the other party." Maladaptation reflects problems in this fit and is commonly regarded as the target of intervention in ecological social work.

An ecological view understands interactions as dynamically trans-actional. Intervention, in the ecological view, usually focuses not on the person, nor the environment, but on the transaction itself (although it may begin at a single point in the field). Note that this understanding is different from that of Meyer (1983, p. 25), who indicated that "in the end, interventions have to be directed to the person or environment." Within the ecological model of social work, best elaborated by Carol Germain and coauthors (e.g., Germain & Bloom, 1999; Gitterman & Germain, 2008) person:environment fit is regarded as the fundamental unit of analysis for an applied social science—not the person, not the group, not the envi-ronment, however understood. This is a bold and intriguing assertion that has been difficult to operationalize (which may be why Meyer resisted it). I suggest later in this chapter, however, that these understandings of fit, particularly when framed transactionally, take us a step closer to a genuinely scientific understanding of ecosystems for social work.

Niche and Habitat

Among ecological concepts that have been emphasized in social work are those of social niche and habitat. The social niche refers to "the status occupied in a community's social structure by its groups and individuals," their "place in a community's web of life" (Gitterman & Germain, 2008, p. 56). Such niches may be growth-supporting—consistent with human needs and rights, or entrapping—failing to provide for basic human needs and leaving few routes to escape (Gitterman & Germain, 2008; Sullivan & Rapp, 2006). Habitat in ecological science refers to the physical and geographic surroundings in which an organism lives; metaphorically, in social work, it is typically used to refer to "physical and social settings within a cultural context" (Gitterman & Germain, 2008, p. 55). Ecological practice may involve targeting dimensions of niche and habitat, often emphasizing considerations of stress and coping, vulnerability and oppression, and social and technological "pollution" that may be transactionally structured into niches or present in the habitat.

Germain and Bloom (1999) and Gitterman and Germain (2008) provide comprehensive discussions of the applications of ecological thinking to social work practice, including rich case examples. Important to note here, however, is that especially more recent statements of their thought (e.g., Gitterman, 2011) clarify that an ecological view does not suggest a sanitizing, Pollyanna-esque view of social and physical realities in which somehow everything and everyone inevitably finds a healthy balance of adaptedness and goodness of fit. These theorists' recent increased emphasis on the ecological dynamics of oppression and social injustice has helped address concerns about an overly optimistic view of human reality.

Ecofeminists in social work take these concerns a step further and concurrently may move ecological thought in social work one step closer to ecological science. (Depending how the approach is interpreted, however, it may also draw the profession further from science.) As the name suggests, ecofeminism emerged from the intersection of ecological science and feminist thought (Besthorn & McMillen, 2002; Mack-Canty, 2004; Spretnak, 1990). Human beings are recognized as simply part of the natural ecosystem, and all oppressive and destructive power structures (e.g., those supporting human trafficking, structural violence, and the devastation of the natural environment) are seen as interrelated. Dominance hierarchies (e.g., man over woman, human over nature, human over other species) are viewed as central to all ecological problems; ecofeminism calls for "wild justice" to challenge those hierarchies. The social justice implications of ecofeminism are important; so is the recognition of human life as genuinely—not just metaphorically—part of the natural world, and therefore amenable to scientific study.

General Systems Theory

According to von Bertalanffy (1968, p. 32):

> There exist models, principles, and laws that apply to generalized systems or their subclasses, irrespective of their particular kind, the nature of their component elements, and the relations or "forces" between them. It seems legitimate to ask for a theory, not of systems of a more or less special kind, but of universal principles applying to systems in general. This is the definition of GST, a theory of universal principles that are understood to apply to all transactional systems, living and nonliving.

All organized systems, as understood by GST and more recent varieties of related systems theories, are characterized by a number of common properties. Following Meyer (1988), these include common structural features, the influences of contextual variables, and hierarchical organization.

Structural Dimensions

Systems have boundaries; as discussed later, living systems often actually create their own boundaries. These boundaries can be reflected in physical space, as in a classroom in which the class is a system. Or they can be drawn conceptually, as the social worker identifies salient transactional patterns that affect the client in systemic ways. (Systems have patterned relationships; students meet regularly in classrooms, for example. In contrast, if an accident happens on the street, the people who gather to watch it are not a system but a random aggregate.) A physical boundary is usually self-evident; a classroom or a school building, for example, has walls. Conceptual boundaries are identified by tracing transactional patterns. A family has a boundary, for example; some people are in the family, and others are not. Who is, and who is not, a member of the family system might be verbally defined by participants differently than if defined by tracing patterns of transactions. Neither is more correct; each is useful for different purposes. In some kinds of practice, the social worker works to become a temporary part of the client system, to take on a role within the boundary. S. Minuchin (1974), for example, emphasizes "joining" the family as a critical step in family treatment, a position from which one can have an impact "from the inside." In highly engaged forms of family treatment like Minuchin's, the therapist may in fact become a central source and nexus of transactions within the family for a period of time.

For living systems to survive, their boundaries must to some extent be open, or permeable. Living systems must at a minimum be able to import energy from the environment and to eliminate waste products; in many cases, there is much more exchange than this, as discussed under the influence of contextual variables. Such exchange enables the system to grow and permits its elements to differentiate and develop. Closed (self-contained) systems cannot survive; they inevitably run down through a process of entropy. All systems move toward disorganization or death without regular importation of energy. Systems that import more energy from the environment than they expend are displaying what is termed negative entropy (which, note, is not a bad thing). As a result of negative entropy, systems can move toward greater complexity through elaboration and differentiation.

Systemic survival requires substantial structural stability. Systems therefore tend to preserve their structure (persistent patterns among elements and transactions). For example, in family therapy, the members of the parental subsystem usually do not change, although the parents may come to behave differently. Within this basic structure, however, living systems are in continuing dynamic process. Stable systems tend to resist extreme change and to maintain a steady state. But because living systems are dissipative structures that cannot survive if transactional processes stop, that steady state must be a dynamic balance, not a static equilibrium.

By definition, systems are characterized by dynamic interconnectedness and reciprocity. An action by one member of the system will often (but not always) have an effect on other members, and actions by other members are likely to have an impact on the first. Active interventions in one or another aspect of the case always resonate through other elements of the case in some way. These reverberating (and in some cases amplifying) effects have great practical implications, because the social worker and client, working together, can sometimes influence relatively distal variables by intervening in more available or accessible areas.

In closed systems, the final state is determined by the initial conditions. If one knows enough about the initial state of a machine, one can predict its state 10 minutes after it has been turned on; the state of the solar system centuries from now can be predicted with great accuracy. This is less true of living systems, however. Because of shifting transactions within the system and exchanges with a complex and dynamic environment, many eventual outcomes are possible given any particular beginning state (multifinality). Similarly, it is possible to reach a particular outcome through many different transactional paths (equifinality). Some level of predictability can often be achieved, but in complex systems outcomes are often uncertain and contingent on changing conditions.

These structural realities can be both advantageous and challenging in practice. A childhood history of trauma may, but need not, lead to lifelong depression (multifinality)—a hopeful perspective compared to traditional linear views that suggest that the effects of childhood trauma cannot be substantially moderated by later events. On the other hand, because of interactions among many conditions and events throughout the transactional field, the same intervention strategy will not lead to the same outcome in every case, emphasizing the need for careful case monitoring even when relying on evidence-informed approaches. For example, there are ways to help with significant depression; if one is blocked, another may lead to just as good a result (equifinality). Multifinality and equifinality are not abstract possibilities; they are characteristic of most complex transactional human realities.

Contextual Factors

As noted earlier, all living systems require regular exchanges with the larger environment. Using the individual as the focal system, Bronfenbrenner (1979) discusses contextual factors in terms of microsystemic factors (family, school, work, peers, etc.), mesosystemic interactions (transactions among microsystemic elements), exosystemic factors (social structures of which the focal individual is not a part but that influence individuals and microsystems), and the macrosystem (larger sociocultural forces). In some of his work, Bronfenbrenner also discussed the chronosystem, which roughly encompassed the place of time and sociohistorical conditions.

The individual or family system, for example, can be powerfully influenced by the very immediate environment (the home, each other, television; Saleebey, 2006, see also Kemp, 2010), as well as by economic forces, social agencies, national social welfare policies, and many contextual variables, and these influences shift over time. Some transactions with environmental forces can nourish, and others can overwhelm the resilience of the system. A functioning system maintains its balance through rich but manageable transactions with the environment.

Hierarchy

General systems theory clarifies that any system may be viewed simultaneously as the focal system (the system considered primary at the moment, say, the family in family therapy), as a subsystem of a larger system (the family as a subsystem of the community), and as a suprasystem constituted of other systems (the family as a suprasystem, with individuals as constituents). Any system is therefore a holon, simultaneously a whole and a part (Anderson & Carter, 1999). It is therefore possible to shift one's frame of reference from one level to another as such shifts are useful. This is precisely what occurred in the history of family therapy. The family had previously been considered primarily as simply background context for work with the individual as focal system. With the coming of family therapy, the family became the primary focus of attention, with individuals as members (and subsets of individuals) seen as subsystems. Salvador Minuchin (1974), for example, talked about the parental subsystem, the couple subsystem (sometimes the same people as those constituting the parental subsystem, but looked at from a different functional perspective), and the sibling subsystem. More recently, the family's essential embeddedness in a powerful environment is increasingly emphasized (Henggeler, Schoenwald, Borduin, Rowland, & Cunningham, 2009; P. Minuchin, Colapinto, & Minuchin, 2006).

Recent Advances in Systems Thought

As in other sciences, knowledge in ecological systems theory continues to advance. Several principles with direct application to social work emerge from recent systemic research and theory, often described as dynamic (or dynamical) systems theory. Important emerging concepts from this work include:

- An understanding (originally emerging from modern physics) that networks of transactional relationships, rather than objects, should be regarded as the basic constituents of reality.
- An appreciation of the central place of self-organization in those networks.
- A recognition that diversity is critical to stability and survival in ecological systems.
- An emerging body of work suggesting that complexity theory may offer unique contributions to our understanding of systems, with potential utility for applied work.

The Primacy of Relationships

Contemporary research and theory in physics and biology suggest that reality is best thought of not as a collection of objects, but as an "inseparable web of relationships" (Capra, 1996, p. 37). The relational components of this web are patterns of transactional events; objects (including organisms) are more like emergent consequences of those transactions, and have reality only within networks of relationships (Esfeld & Lam, 2011). Cells, organisms, and ecosystems are all organized and defined by such network patterns. The hierarchical organization of systems described in GST (subsystems, focal systems, suprasystems) emerges from levels of networks. "Members of an ecological community are interconnected in a vast and intricate network of relationships, the web of life. They derive their essential properties and, in fact, their very existence from their relationships to other things" (Capra, 1996, p. 298). A neighborhood, then, is the relationships among families, residents, businesses, churches, and other elements present within a geographic area, along with their larger context; a family is the relationships among members. This understanding suggests that a tradition "person-in-environment" framework is overly constraining; the person and everything defined as environment exist only as nodes within a single transactional field. The person exists only in those (internal and external) transactions. This is a dramatic epistemological shift, and one with profound implications for practice.

The work of social work is action taken to influence those transactional webs of relationship. The social worker is part of the web as is the client, and the work they do together will be supported, opposed, or both by transactions elsewhere in the web. There is a similarity to indigenous thought here as well; from certain Native perspectives, every action taken can be viewed as strengthening or damaging the web of life (or in some cases some of each; Lowery & Mattaini, 2001). As discussed later, understanding the dynamics of that web may have the potential to resolve certain intractable issues with which contemporary social work is struggling.

Self-Organizing Systems

Recent systems work has also expanded our understanding of the structure and boundaries of living, self-organizing networks. As Hudson notes:

> Self-organizing systems represent a recently identified class of phenomenon. Specifically, they represent a type of emergence that involves the apparently spontaneous development of structure in complex systems in response not so much to external conflicts or the struggle for survival but to the internal logic of the interacting subsystems. (2000, p. 554)

Such systems (networks of transactions) are literally "self-making": At least to some extent, they dynamically organize and construct themselves without guidance from outside. The dynamic patterns of transactions constituting the system are organized by the network itself rather than by outside forces, and construct their own boundaries; the boundary of such a network is a natural result of how it functions. Such natural boundaries (e.g., that of a family or a network of fictive kin) need to be honored in practice, because they are real. They cannot simply be artificially invented by the practitioner; should the practitioner attempt to do so, natural homeostatic processes would likely neutralize the impact of the work being done.

The work of Prigogine (1996) has been particularly important for understanding self-organizing processes in dissipative structures (systems that can exist only in constant dynamic transaction). Families are a social example of such structures. Self-organizing client systems couple with their contextual environments, however loosely, by means of transactions across the boundary, and can be profoundly affected by them. How any particular system responds to an influence from the outside is determined by the state and structure of that system. For example, two economically stressed families may both live in a dangerous, high-crime neighborhood that offers little access to social capital or support. One family may respond by simply dissipating, its diffuse boundaries eventually dissolving and members lost to the street. Another, however, may demonstrate great resilience, taking collective steps to couple with healthier networks (churches and youth organizations, for example) while closing its boundaries to negative influences. Thus the enduring patterns of transactions within each family are key determinants of outcome; that outcome cannot be predicted from knowing only about the impinging environment. (Note also that the resilience literature clarifies that progressively fewer families can survive in healthy ways as environmental stressors increase, and that survival will often involve substantial costs, even for the most resilient; Benard, 2006.)

A key feature of self-organizing systems is the possibility of emergence, of new patterns emerging spontaneously within a system, which then change the experiences of the components of that system. For example, as new family cultures emerge, they may reshape the experiences of family members. Overall, as Hudson notes, emphasis on self-organization is "consistent with traditional social work values, such as mutual support, self-determination, and self-help" (2000, p. 555), and therefore lends support to some forms of practice. At the same time, given the coupling of such systems with the environment, the latter cannot be ignored, so both transactions within the client system and those across the boundaries are relevant. As the science of self-organization advances, it is likely provide more specific guidance for some forms of social work practice.

The Role of Diversity

Ecological science has established that diversity is key to ecosystemic balance: "A diverse ecosystem will also be resilient. The more complex the network is, the more complex its pattern of interconnections, the more resilient it will be" (Capra, 1996, p. 303). Ecological science suggests that variation is critical to survival, and thus that respect and appreciation for those different from oneself and one's group are adaptive and critically important at a sociocultural level. Each enduring cultural group has developed unique ways to survive in the world, each adapted to different environmental and social conditions. As a result, in many cases one cultural group struggling with an apparently intractable social problem can turn to others to find solutions that do not emerge within their own matrix of cultural practices.

For example, the justice systems in the United States and Russia are, from most perspectives, hopelessly broken (see, e.g., Farmer, 2003). Ever-escalating resources are dedicated to those systems, and yet enormous amounts of potentially productive human resources remain locked away—with other enormous amounts of human resources required to keep them that way. There is no obvious route out of this pattern from inside these systems, because they are deeply grounded in existing cultural values and economic arrangements. Other cultures around the world, however, have found entirely distinct approaches to issues of crime and justice, and there is strong evidence that some of those practices can be successfully integrated into cultures that have found no solutions internally (Ross, 2006). Similarly, women in some parts of the world have begun to find ways to challenge sexist oppression. In part as a result of the globalization of communication, increasingly those practices are being adopted and adapted by women in other cultures (Lowery, 2007).

The analogy with biological diversity is evident. Because particular cultural practices have proven adaptive under differing conditions, the diversity of these practices is a source of potentially valuable variations. Maintaining cultural diversity preserves banks of potentially useful possibilities for responding to changing circumstances. In an increasingly globalized world, recognition of the crucial importance of diversity may prove central to the future of the human species.

Complexity Theory

A related advance that may ultimately prove quite important to social work is complexity theory (Green & McDermott, 2010; Warren, Franklin, & Streeter, 1998; Woehle, 2007). As does the related chaos theory, complexity draws on the emerging science of nonlinear dynamics, which moves not only beyond linear causation (as all systems theory does), but also in many cases beyond determinate prediction. This work attempts to model the nonlinear dynamics of such processes as family functioning, in which relationships often do not change along a smooth curve (a bit better, a bit better yet, even a bit better yet); rather at some point a threshold may be reached, and sudden change for better or worse emerges. Self-organization, emergence, and transactional patterns are all central to complexity theory.

Several central concepts from chaos and complexity theory may prove useful for social work. Deterministic chaos, for example, "arises within feedback systems, never precisely repeating itself, but staying within a certain range of possibilities" (Warren et al., 1998, p. 361). Such a pattern may in fact be characteristic of many social systems in which it is astonishingly difficult (or impossible) to know exactly what will happen at any moment due to sensitive dependence on initial conditions and complex feedback networks, but the general limits of what is likely to happen may be predictable. Complexity theory also suggests that the concepts of balance and stability commonly used in traditional systems theory have been overemphasized. In fact, many complex systems operate far from equilibrium (or "at the edge of chaos"), so that they may become more and more complex, often at rapidly accelerating rates; creative variation and change may be most likely under such conditions.

Asserting the emerging importance of complexity theory for social work, Green and McDermott (2010) state that:

> Twenty-first-century social workers will work towards effecting the "climates" that can sustain those conditions (social, ecological, biological, economic, political) essential to enhancing and maintaining human life and well-being. Thus, today's social work must be located at the borders of social, economic, biological and political systems, where, if it is to have any possibility of influencing outcomes, it will be informed by ever emerging explanatory theory. (Green & McDermott, 2010, p. 2428)

Complexity and chaos theories provide a framework that is being applied to help better understand the transaction between the social work professional or agency and those climates. Recent examples of such work include applications to human trafficking, community change, and child protection.

Human Trafficking. Wolf-Branigin (2009) applied complexity theory to the problem of human trafficking, drawing on several key theoretical constructs (agents, heterogeneity, organization or attraction, dynamic, feedback, self-organization and adaption, and emergent behavior). Wolf-Branigin's findings allowed the international NGO that was addressing human trafficking in five countries to identify individual and organizational barriers that prevented clients from seeking services (Wolf-Branigin, 2009).

Community Change. Woehle, Jones, Barker and Piper (2009) used computer models to: "demonstrate community change initiated by interventions that alter social ties and culture, and the systemic and nonlinear social and cultural change that might result" (Woehle et al., 2009, p. 43). The ability to use computer models to understand community-level interactions and the necessary components to effect change could prove exceptionally useful to social workers who are not just involved in individual exchanges but work in systems that are embedded in communities.

Child Protection. Stevens & Cox (2008) applied complexity theory to the field of child protection, stating that: "interventions in the lives of children which are based on a linear understanding can lead to oversimplification of assessment and intervention" (Stevens & Cox, 2008, p. 1332). The framework provided by complexity, they assert, allows workers to better understand their clients and the interactions with the child protection system creating more effective intervention (Stevens & Cox).

Related sciences, particularly behavior analysis, are developing increasingly well-defined and complex models of human and systems behavior on which social work can begin to draw, including some drawing on complexity theory (e.g., McDowell & Popa, 2010). These emerging examples suggest that rigorous understanding of complexity is likely to contribute to social work practice in the future. Still, the level of complexity in most areas of practice is high, and the available research is currently quite limited. Clearly much more work will be required to effectively extend complexity theory into an even more sophisticated, rigorous approach for understanding social reality.

Evaluating the Ecosystems Perspective

The eco-systems perspective is not a model, with prescriptions for addressing cases; it does not draw from a particular theory of personality. It is often misunderstood as being a treatment model, however. When it fails to live up to people's false expectations, it is denigrated as being "too abstract for practitioners to use," "too nonspecific for the case at hand," and "nonclinical in its orientation." Its major claim is that it is a model for assessment, and because it can encompass any treatment model, it has the potential for serving as a unifying perspective in social work practice (Meyer, 1983). Given the proliferation of disparate treatment models, this unifying idea seems vital for the future coherence of practice in social work. (Meyer, 1988, p. 275)

Although the ecosystems perspective has been almost universally accepted in social work over the past three decades, some critiques (e.g., Payne, 2005; Reid, 2002; Wakefield, 1996a, 1996b, 1996c) draw the profession's attention to the perspective's inevitable limitations and have also been helpful in sharpening ecosystemic thought. No single perspective is adequate for work as complex as social work (Mattaini & Lowery, 2007). Other frameworks, such as the strengths and human rights perspectives, clearly are also useful for practice. Perspectives (and practice theories) are valuable to the extent that they contribute to positive outcomes. It is not surprising that no single perspective, theory, or worldview can justifiably be regarded as universally best; this is simply another example of the importance of diversity for survival of any living system, including the social work profession.

The issue of level of abstraction raised in the extract from Meyer (1988) is real; an ecosystemic examination of a social work case does involve substantial complexity, and the perspective probably cannot be meaningfully applied without a grounding in substantive theory(ies). Practitioners are most likely to notice transactions that are consistent with their own personal practice models (Mullen, 1983), for example. And yet, without such a perspective, substantive knowledge and theory may lead one astray, as the multiple studies demonstrating typical lack of attention to environmental factors demonstrate. As discussed further on, graphic models and simulations have proven useful for concretizing the otherwise potentially highly abstract perspective.

Connectedness and the Transactional Focus

Wakefield (1996a, 1996b) raised several important substantive issues related to ecosystems; some of his arguments are clearly correct. (See also

Gitterman, 1996, for further response to Wakefield.) Wakefield (1996a, p. 276) questions, first of all, the ecosystems assertion of connectedness, for example as found in Meyer (1988):

> The underlying philosophical position of the eco-systems perspective is that the person is connected to others, as well as to the social institutions, cultural forces, and the physical space that make up his or her environment. Although there is no explicit assumption about the substantive nature of things or people, there is, in this perspective, heavy reliance upon the person's connectedness.

Wakefield suggests that the connectedness claim is trivial without a "substantive account of the nature of the hypothesized connections" (1996a, p. 10). He is referring here, as I understand it, to domain-specific theory (e.g., various personality theories, social learning theory) as well as empirically grounded knowledge about the phenomenon or issue being examined. With some qualifications, this assertion, I believe, is true. One cannot apply the ecosystems perspective without substantive understandings of how people and the world work (from theory, practice models, and research). And yet as we have seen the evidence suggests that, even with all of this but without a broader perspective, social workers do not in fact examine the transactional field with adequate breadth to notice critical connections. In other words, the perspective can be helpful in drawing attention to connectedness regardless of practice approach, but not without a practice approach.

Wakefield (1996a) also provides several examples where he believes the connectedness construct is potentially distorting and misguided, but his examples, if examined in their full complexity, appear in fact to support the assertion of connectedness. For example, he asserts that child abuse is the result of a one-way linear process, but the child and family literature has clarified that factors such as difficult child temperament and behavior problems, insularity, and poverty, among other child, family, and contextual variables, are associated with increased risk of abuse (Lutzker, 1998; Mattaini, McGowan, & Williams, 1996). This is not to say that there are not times when simple linear interventions can be useful, but that such interventions need to be designed with awareness of the transactional field.

A related issue is Wakefield's (1996a) concern with the "circularity" of causation he believes to be present in ecosystemic thought. His discussion purports to deal specifically with the work of Meyer, but the phrase "circular causality" that he uses throughout his critique does not appear to be present in Meyer's work and is, from my analysis of that work and personal discussions with Meyer, inconsistent with it. Meyer clearly meant to draw attention to the complexity and interactivity present in the social and physical world; there is nothing "circular" in recognizing the reality of interconnectedness and reciprocity. The same is true of Germain and Gitterman's work; feedback processes clearly can be reciprocal and may reverberate and be amplified cyclically (as in many couples and parent-child disputes), but a thorough reading of the ecosystemic literature in social work does not support an assertion of circular causality as a primary theme.

Utility for Assessment

One additional concern raised by critics requires some attention: doubts that the ecosystems perspective has utility for assessment. Wakefield (1996a, p. 14) holds that "assessment is, to a large extent, a matter of defining a client's problem." Only within a narrow, pathology-focused view of social work would this be the case—and only if that view does not recognize the dynamics of living systems. Assessment in social work is a much more complex process of understanding the case in context, contrasting the current state with the desired state, and determining what would be required to get from the former to the latter (Mattaini, 2007; Meyer, 1993). If reality is complex, assessment clearly needs to take that complexity into account in moving toward effective action. Wakefield (1996a, p. 17) is trivially correct in asserting that "no assessment can be infinitely complex"—but a responsible assessment must be complex enough to capture the primary dynamics of the case.

Wakefield (1996a, p. 17) also questions the need to examine contextual factors such as oppression in assessment, asserting that clinicians' role is generally to help clients to cope, "without directly confronting or assessing larger systems." This has, in fact, commonly been true in social work practice, but there is now substantial movement away from this narrow focus. In recent years a number of practice approaches have emerged that involve challenging social justice and human rights issues even in direct practice. Parker (2003) describes practice at the Institute for Family Services in Somerset, New Jersey, for instance, in which clients are assisted through "culture circles" to collectively examine and challenge gender, class, and other systemic forms of oppression. Structural social work as discussed by Mullaly (2007) and others is being taken seriously in the development of most contemporary social work models. Finn and Jacobson (2003) have formulated a "just practice" approach oriented toward supporting social justice in practice in ways that challenge injustice. Vodde and Gallant (2002) have developed an approach designed to bridge micro and macro practice, organized around understanding power and oppression and encouraging collective advocacy. Mattaini and Lowery (2007) discuss how moment-by-moment practice events, even in clinical work, can either support or interfere with justice. These advances would not be occurring if practitioners did not explicitly attend to issues of systemic injustice in practice at all system levels, with recognition of existing power dynamics and willingness to confront them where possible.

At the same time, Wakefield and Reid are clearly correct that the ecosystems perspective cannot stand on its own in assessment. Social workers need ways to understand what the perspective leads them to see, and that understanding comes from practice theory and practice models. Psychodynamic, feminist, and ecobehavioral theories and practice approaches will, and should, understand the patterns of transactions present in a case differently. Wakefield's assertion of the need for substantive knowledge and theory, therefore, is important; it does not, however, invalidate the utility of the ecosystems perspective.

Returning to the Science

"Content-free" ecosystems appears to be indefensible. There clearly is a need for substantive knowledge and theory to apply the perspective. As the ecosystems perspective has played itself out over the past four decades, it appears that there are two approaches that have the potential to use ecosystems in relatively robust ways. One involves practice models that use ecosystems primarily in metaphoric and heuristic ways. The life model (Gitterman & Germain, 2008) and some narrative approaches (e.g., Vodde & Gallant, 2002) are particularly strong examples and are widely used in practice.

A second possibility that I believe has been insufficiently recognized is returning to science. Recall that ecology is a science; general systems theory and its recent expansions are scientific theories, as are dynamic systems and complexity theories. Practice theory and approaches that rely on scientific understandings of human development and behavior, and scientific approaches to sociocultural and environmental processes, should be relatively easy to integrate into a scientific understanding of the ecosystems perspective. In the material that follows, I briefly sketch a scientifically grounded approach to ecosystemic understanding for social work. Readers are urged to explore the references provided for further detail.

Human beings and human systems are part of the natural world, and from a scientific perspective on practice, this fact is not trivial. The ecofeminists are clearly correct in asserting the unity of natural existence, although their strong reservations about the utility of the scientific method are, in my opinion, overdrawn. There is much that science can and has contributed to effective practice, and there is therefore an ethical obligation to avoid premature rejection of approaches to knowledge development that may help vulnerable people. The world, including people, consists ultimately of transactions at a subatomic level; phenomena (molecules, people, stars) emerge from that transactional matrix in organized ways that systems theory attempts to understand. There is therefore every reason to believe that the sciences of human behavior and cultural processes would involve such emergence as suggested in the work on self-organization and complexity, and would find transactional connectedness with the rest of the physical universe. Such a view can contribute to understanding the nature of transactional networks in social work cases.

The basic elements of the science of behavior are not complex: actions, consequences, contextual signals as to when behavior is and is not likely to be effective, simple modeling and social learning processes (R. Malott, Trojan Suarez, & Malott, 2003; Skinner, 1953), coupled with biology and environment. Even cultural practices are constructed of the same simple elements, which, however, are organized in more complex ways than is individual behavior (Mattaini, 1996). Complexity, when it is found, typically emerges from simple elements in transaction; the genetic code is one example. The interface between computer science and natural science suggests the same (Wolfram, 2002). Complexity is real, but is the result of interlocked patterns of simple transactions.

The social worker is part of the client's environment, and transactions between worker and client are transactions between person and environment. The client's environment, however, is much larger than the social worker, and ecosystems thinking, scientifically understood, suggests that many other environmental processes may be not just tangentially but essentially involved in client experience. Recalling that dynamic systems theory views transactions, not objects, as primary, a person can be scientifically understood as "an accumulation of acts grounded in the behavior (i.e., movements and postures) of a single organism" (Lee, 1988, p. 93). Using Lee's terms, acts are not bodily movements, but transdermal events involving the organism and the environment, "things done"—transactions, in ecosystems terms. Further, a scientific understanding of human behavior "resides in the interpenetration of the organism with the contingencies of the culture" (p. 114). In addition, conduct is organic; any particular action "is embedded in a network of overlapping and interlocking actions" (p. 57) and is likely one part of a more complex action (e.g., studying is an act and is part of completing a degree).

Practice that emerges from these principles has been termed ecobehavioral (Lutzker, 1997; Mattaini & Moore, 2004). An ecobehavioral understanding of the sciences of behavior and cultural analysis guides the social worker to notice particular kinds of transactions involving person and environment (Baer & Pinkston, 1997; Goldiamond, 2002). Consistent with understanding behaviors and actions as "things done"—personal activities that have an impact on the environment—consequences are clearly critical to a scientific analysis. Why would a person do what he or she does? For example, why does a child talk back to his or her parent? Patterson's (1976, 1982) model of the escalating coercive cycle that commonly develops in families with aggressive children helps us to understand this. In this pattern, parent and child reciprocally turn to more and more aversive statements or actions until one backs down. The lesson learned from this result is that if one acts aggressively and escalates as necessary, one will ultimately achieve the desired consequences.

At a higher systems level, an analysis of multiple interlocking consequences of common cultural practices leads to deeper understanding than a search for linear causes might. Why, for example, does racial discrimination persist? Briggs and Paulson (1996) and Guerin (2005) provide detailed scientific analyses related to the maintenance of racial discrimination, privilege, and advantage. Extensive interlocks among cultural practices (including in housing, employment, financial, educational, and other institutions) can maintain discriminatory practices even in the absence of intention and overt bias (which, of course, is seldom entirely absent). Such interlocking consequences among multiple classes of actors can be tracked and analyzed scientifically. Antecedent and contextual factors are also powerful environmental determinants of human action and cultural processes that interlock with consequences (see Mattaini, 1997, 1999, for details).

Organizations, communities, nations—in fact, all cultural entities can be viewed ecobehaviorally as organized and constituted of interlocking patterns of "things done": actions in transaction with consequences and environmental context (Mattaini, 1996, 2006). Intervention in those cultural networks often requires the analysis of these patterns. For example, we know that the frequent use of written recognition improves student behavior and achievement in schools (Embry, 2004). It has, however, proven difficult to maintain the practice of providing such recognition on a rich enough schedule over time. An analysis of other practices in the school environment that support or oppose this one can clarify the obstacles, and what might be done about them (Erickson, Mattaini, & McGuire, 2004).

It is always possible to focus narrowly on simple processes, but an ecobehavioral understanding rooted in an ecosystems perspective consistently reminds the social worker that events in the client's world are multiply determined (and often overdetermined), so a single intervention may not result in change that will be maintained. In fact, in many areas of human behavior, achieving change is relatively simple, whereas maintaining change is much more challenging. A single parent may learn effective parenting skills, for example, but is unlikely to maintain them over time without significant environmental support (Dumas & Wahler, 1983; Webster-Stratton, 1997). Similarly, it has proven much more difficult to maintain effective prevention programs in schools and communities over extended periods of time than to establish them (Embry, 2004).

A careful ecobehavioral analysis can clarify the contextual challenges to be addressed (Henggeler et al., 2009) and the kinds of change that are more likely to be naturally maintained through "behavior traps" (Lutzker, 1997; R. Malott et al., 2003). The heart of ecobehavioral practice is the design of interventions that will bring the behavior of actors in the case (whether clients, family members, agency staff members, or anyone anywhere in the ecological matrix) into contact with existing variables that have a realistic chance of maintaining the new repertoires. This can be done only by analysis of the transactional patterns within which the case is embedded. Agent-based models, state-space grids, and other approaches emerging from current work in complexity could easily be integrated into ecobehavioral science, given the emphasis of both on patterns of simple transactions.

Mapping Practice

A broad transactional focus distinguishes much of social work (although not entirely) from other professional disciplines such as psychiatry and psychology. It implies that individuals and their environments are always actually or potentially adaptive to each other, that interventions involve action directed toward the transactions present, and that the results may reverberate through other parts of the network. The ecosystems perspective has enabled social workers to enhance this psychosocial focus through the use of a systemic lens that does not separate the person from the environment but requires that they be seen in their transactional interconnectedness. This, however, is a quite abstract notion as it stands. Graphic visualization and simulations have proven very useful in other scientific and applied areas dealing with the complex (e.g., meteorology, radiology, and theoretical physics). Similarly, the use of the ecomap and related graphic representations to depict the case allows both practitioners and clients to literally see the case in its complexity (Mattaini, 1993a). We established earlier that social workers tend to miss much of this complexity if not specifically prompted to look at it. Preliminary research (Mattaini, 1993a) indicates that social work students are more likely to view a case in its transactional complexity if they prepare a simple ecomap.

Traditional ecomaps as elaborated by Meyer (1976, 1993) and Hartman (1978) were essentially heuristic, using arrows to represent reified "connections," which might be strong, tenuous, or stressful. They are a useful start, and nothing more complex was used in the study with students cited in the previous paragraph. It is possible, however, to quantify the exchanges more specifically, as well as to note that both positive and aversive exchanges may be involved in a relationship (as is relatively typical). This move toward quantification through transactional ecomaps is a valuable support for an emerging scientific understanding of the ecosystems perspective (Mattaini, 1993a). It is also possible to develop computerized approaches to simplify the quantification and presentation of transactional mapping (Mattaini, 1993b).

From the patterns discovered, factors with significant social justice implications are often identified. Young (1990) identified domination (structural or systemic arrangements that exclude people from participating in determining their actions or the conditions of the actions) and oppression (systematic or institutional constraints on self-determination) as the two core dimensions of social injustice. She further identified five "faces of oppression" (p. 39):

1. Exploitation: The transfer of results of labor of one social group to benefit another.

2. Marginalization: Exclusion from system of labor, economic systems, and other important sources of resources.

3. Powerlessness: Lack of voice, authority, status, privilege, and sense of self.

4. Cultural imperialism: Dominant meanings in society that render the perspective of one's own group invisible while simultaneously stereotyping that group and labeling it as *Other*.

5. Violence: Living with the knowledge that one must fear random, unprovoked attacks on persons, property, or self that appear to be motivated to damage, humiliate, or destroy.

Domination and oppression involve the exercise of power, and like all social patterns are grounded in action. Many of those patterns are structural in nature; many different interlocking cultural practices tend to maintain them in systemic and systematic ways (Farmer, 2003; Mullaly, 2007; Young, 1990). What is important here is that social workers who both are able to see the case (whether individual or collective) in its contextual complexity, and are sensitized to recognize regularities of pattern consistent with domination and oppression (both in individual cases and for classes of persons) can see the social justice implications of the case on ecomaps they and their clients construct, drawing on all available sources of information in that process. They will also, based on the scientific underpinnings of the perspective, have a clear view of where change, if it is going to happen, needs to take place.

Drawing an ecomap that clarifies the significant elements of a case and the transactions among them offers the practitioner and client opportunities to explore and assess the dynamic relationships among case variables. Furthermore, although neither systems thinking nor the ecomap prescribes actions, laying out the case as a field of forces enables the practitioner to select intervention approaches likely to influence the primary transactional issues that emerge. An ecomap therefore opens options while ensuring that the most critical factors in the case receive attention.

Conclusion

We have, then, come full circle. The ecosystems perspective emerged in social work in the 1970s from two bodies of scientific theory: general systems theory and ecological theory. There is little doubt, given the research that has been done, that social workers often did and do fail to notice many essential variables in their cases, including patterns of domination and oppression, and there is evidence that the ecosystems perspective or something like it can be of use in minimizing such errors. Even mapping the case in a fairly rough manner appears to be of some use. Since the 1970s, the perspective has been considered primarily a heuristic or metaphoric tool, with little consideration of or reference to science. It appears likely that this lack of attention to rigor has limited the impact of the perspective. Ecosystemic thinking grounded in scientific rigor, however, may have the potential to greatly expand the impact of the perspective.

Contemporary social work research often uses an ecological view for purposes of both design and interpretation, and by leveraging recent advances, the utility of such application could be expanded. Such research may also assist the profession in addressing another intractable challenge. Given larger sociocultural shifts, the costs of continuing to provide services in the way we have are likely to prove increasingly prohibitive. Within this context, in some areas of practice there seems to be no limit to the number of cases requiring services (McKnight, 1996). Ultimately we must attain a sustainable rather than a growth economy (Grant, 2011), and therefore cannot expect resources for services to expand without limit. Adequate ecosystems science, however, may suggest entirely different intervention points that can be both more effective and more efficient, moving away from social toxicity and toward health-enhancing cultures. Even relatively simple analyses can help us move toward such alternatives now (for example, in the use of restorative practices; see also Grant, 2011). The potential for rigorous systems science to contribute to such efforts, while unknown, may be enormous.

In this chapter, we have suggested that an ecological systems understanding of human beings in context is not just a metaphor; transactional connectedness is real. Humans and human societies are essentially woven into the fabric of a larger ecological field, and that ecological field can be understood scientifically. Returning to the science, as in ecobehavioral practice, may be enormously usefully in reconnecting the social work view of cases with the transactional reality in which those cases are embedded. The heuristic use of ecosystems has been and will continue to be useful in social work education and practice; there is also enormous power in science, however, and a transparent, collaborative application of ecosystems science may bring that power to bear for the vulnerable, who often have little access to other sources of power. If this proves to be true, social work has an ethical obligation to enlist that science in everyday practice.

Key Terms

Behavior	Entrapping niche	Maladaptation
Boundary	Equifinality	Mesosystem
Chronosystem	Exosystem	Microsystem
Ecobehavioral social work	General systems theory (GST)	Multifinality
Ecology	Habitat	Social niche
Enabling niche	Macrosystem	

Review Questions for Critical Thinking

1. A fundamental function in all professional practice, including social work, is individualizing the case. What networks of transactions need to be considered to individualize cases in your field of practice, and how would that be done?

2. What are the risks associated with linear thinking in assessing a social work case?

3. How would a social worker identify the transactional boundaries of a case, and why is that important?

4. What roles could diversity play in understanding and intervening in the intractable social problems in which social work clients are often embedded?

5. How could a scientific elaboration of the ecosystems perspective benefit at-risk populations and refine current versions of ecofeminist thought?

Online Resources

www.medicalecology.org/dubos.htm

An essay by Rene Dubos, an important theoretician and scientist in the application of ecological theory to human life.

http://en.wikipedia.org/wiki/Urie_Bronfenbrenner

A brief introduction to Urie Bronfenbrenner, the primary architect of the Social Ecological Model—one of the roots of ecosystemic theory.

http://en.wikipedia.org/wiki/Social_ecological_model

A general introduction to the social ecological model, drawing from Bronfenbrenner's model as well as others, with examples of applications in a number of fields.

http://en.wikipedia.org/wiki/Systems_theory

A basic introduction to several varieties of systems theory originating from Ludwig von Bertanlanffy's General Systems Theory.

www.panarchy.org/vonbertalanffy/systems.1968.html

Selected passages from von Bertalanffy's own work on general systems theory, clarifying its purpose, as well as offering a systemic understanding of the human being as an *active personality system* rather than a mechanical system.

www.istheory.yorku.ca/generalsystemstheory.htm

An excellent beginning bibliography on general systems theory.

http://en.wikipedia.org/wiki/Self-organization

A summary elaboration of the emerging concept of self-organization, one of the key advances in contemporary systems theory that clarifies both the autonomy of living systems and the ways they couple with their environments. Includes applications from physics and cybernetics to human society and collective intelligence.

References

Anderson, R. E., & Carter, I. (with Lowe, G. R.). (1999). *Human behavior in the social environment: A social systems approach* (5th ed.). New Brunswick, NJ: Aldine Transaction.

Auerswald, E. H. (1968). Interdisciplinary versus ecological approach. *Family Process, 7*, 202–215.

Baer, D. M., & Pinkston, E. (1997). *Environment and behavior*. Boulder, CO: Westview Press.

Bates, M. (1990). *The nature of natural history*. Princeton, NJ: Princeton University Press. (Original work published 1950)

Benard, B. (2006). Using strengths-based practice to tap the resilience of families. In D. Saleebey (Ed.), *The strengths perspective in social work practice* (4th ed., pp. 197–220). Boston, MA: Allyn & Bacon.

Besthorn, F. H., & McMillen, D. P. (2002). The oppression of women and nature: Ecofeminism as a framework for an expanded ecological social work. *Families in Society, 83*, 221–232.

Briggs, H. E., & Paulson, R. I. (1996). Racism. In M. A. Mattaini & B. A. Thyer (Eds.), *Finding solutions to social problems: Behavioral strategies for change* (pp. 147–177). Washington, DC: American Psychological Association.

Bronfenbrenner, U. (1979). *The ecology of human development: Experiments by nature and design*. Cambridge, MA: Harvard University Press.

Cannon, W. B. (1939). *The wisdom of the body*. New York, NY: Norton.

Capra, F. (1996). *The web of life*. New York, NY: Anchor Books.

DuBos, R. (1972). *The god within*. New York, NY: Scribner's.

Dumas, J. E., & Wahler, R. G. (1983). Predictors of treatment outcome in parent training: Mother insularity and socioeconomic disadvantage. *Behavioral Assessment, 5*, 301–313.

Embry, D. D. (2004). Community-based prevention using simple, low-cost, evidence-based kernels and behavior vaccines. *Journal of Community Psychology, 32*, 575–591.

Erickson, C., Mattaini, M. A., & McGuire, M. S. (2004). Constructing nonviolent cultures in schools: The state of the science. *Children and Schools, 26*, 102–116.

Esfeld, M. & Lam, V. (2011). Ontic structural realism as a metaphysics of objects. In A. Bokulich & P. Bokulich (Eds.), *Scientific structuralism* (pp. 143–160). Dordrecht, The Netherlands: Springer.

Farmer, P. (2003). *Pathologies of power: Health, human rights, and the new war on the poor*. Berkeley, CA: University of California Press.

Finn, J. L., & Jacobson, M. (2003). Just practice: Steps toward a new social work paradigm. *Journal of Social Work Education, 39*, 57–78.

Germain, C. B., & Bloom, M. (1999). *Human behavior in the social environment: An ecological view*. New York, NY: Columbia University Press.

Gitterman, A. (1996). Ecological perspective: Response to Wakefield. *Social Service Review, 70*, 472–476.

Gitterman, A. (2011). Advances in the life model of social work practice. In F. J. Turner (Ed.), *Social work treatment approaches: Interlocking theoretical approaches*. Oxford, UK: Oxford University Press.

Gitterman, A., & Germain, C. B. (2008). *The life model of social work practice* (3rd ed.). New York, NY: Columbia University Press.

Goldiamond, I. (2002). Toward a constructional approach to social problems: Ethical and constitutional issues raised by applied behavior analysis. *Behavior and Social Issues, 11*, 108–197.

Grant, L. K. (2011). Consumption and climate change. *Behavior Analyst, 34*, 245–266.

Green, D. & McDermott, F. (2010). Social work from inside and between complex systems: Perspectives on person-in-environment for today's social work. *British Journal of Social Work, 40*, 2414–2430.

Guerin, B. (2005). Combating everyday racial discrimination without assuming "racists" or "racism": New intervention ideas from a contextual analysis. *Behavior and Social Issues, 14*, 46–70.

Hamilton, G. (1951). *Theory and practice of social casework.* New York, NY: Columbia University Press.

Hartman, A. (1978). Diagrammatic assessment of family relationships. *Social Casework, 59*, 465–476.

Henggeler, S. W., Schoenwald, S. K., Borduin, C. M., Rowland, M. D., & Cunningham, P. B. (2009). *Multisystemic treatment of antisocial behavior in children and adolescents* (2nd ed.). New York, NY: Guilford Press.

Hollis, F. H. (1972). *Casework: A psychosocial therapy* (2nd ed.). New York, NY: Random House.

Hudson, C. G. (2000). From social Darwinism to self-organization: Implications for social change theory. *Social Service Review, 74*, 533–559.

Keenan, E. K. (2010). Seeing the forest and the trees: Using dynamic systems theory to understand "Stress and Coping" and "Trauma and Resilience." *Journal of Human Behavior in the Social Environment, 20*(8), 1038–1060.

Keenan, E. (2011). From bumps in the road to the edge of chaos: The nature of change in adults. *Journal of Social Work, 11*(3), 306–325.

Kemp, S. P. (2010). Place matters: Toward a rejuvenated theory of environment for direct social work practice. In W. Borden (Ed.), *Reshaping theory in contemporary social work* (pp. 114–145). New York, NY: Columbia University Press.

Lee, V. L. (1988). *Beyond behaviorism.* Hillsdale, NJ: Erlbaum.

Lowery, C. T. (2007). Social justice and international human rights. In M. A. Mattaini & C. T. Lowery (Eds.), *Foundations of social work practice* (4th ed., pp. 63–92). Washington, DC: National Association of Social Workers Press.

Lowery, C. T., & Mattaini, M. A. (2001). Shared power in social work: A Native American perspective of change. In H. Briggs & K. Corcoran (Eds.), *Social work practice: Treating common client problems* (pp. 109–124). Chicago, IL: Lyceum.

Lutzker, J. R. (1997). Ecobehavioral approaches in child abuse and developmental disabilities mirroring life. In D. M. Baer & E. M. Pinkston (Eds.), *Environment and behavior* (pp. 243–248). Boulder, CO: Westview Press.

Lutzker, J. R. (Ed.). (1998). *Handbook of child abuse research and treatment.* New York, NY: Plenum Press.

Mack-Canty, C. (2004). Third-wave feminism and the need to reweave the nature/culture duality. *NWSA Journal, 16*(3), 154–179.

Malott, M. E. (2003). *The paradox of organizational change: Engineering organizations with behavioral systems analysis.* Reno, NV: Context Press.

Malott, R. W., Trojan Suarez, E. A., & Malott, M. E. (2003). *Principles of behavior* (5th ed.). Upper Saddle River, NJ: Prentice Hall.

Marsh, J. C. (2005). Social justice: Social work's organizing value. *Social Work, 50*, 293–294.

Mattaini, M. A. (1993a). *More than a thousand words: Graphics for clinical practice.* Washington, DC: National Association of Social Workers Press.

Mattaini, M. A. (1993b). *The visual ecoscan for clinical practice.* Washington, DC: National Association of Social Workers Press.

Mattaini, M. A. (1996). Public issues, human behavior, and cultural design. In M. A. Mattaini & B. A. Thyer (Eds.), *Finding solutions to social problems: Behavioral strategies for change* (pp. 13–40). Washington, DC: American Psychological Association.

Mattaini, M. A. (1997). *Clinical practice with individuals.* Washington, DC: National Association of Social Workers Press.

Mattaini, M. A. (1999). *Clinical intervention with families.* Washington, DC: National Association of Social Workers Press.

Mattaini, M. A. (2006). Will cultural analysis become a science? *Behavior and Social Issues, 15,* 68–80.

Mattaini, M. A. (2007). Practice with individuals. In M. A. Mattaini & C. T. Lowery (Eds.), *Foundations of social work practice* (4th ed., pp. 217–257). Washington, DC: National Association of Social Workers Press.

Mattaini, M. A., & Lowery, C. T. (Eds.). (2007). *Foundations of social work practice* (4th ed.). Washington, DC: National Association of Social Workers Press.

Mattaini, M. A., McGowan, B. G., & Williams, G. (1996). Child maltreatment. In M. A. Mattaini & B. A. Thyer (Eds.), *Finding solutions to social problems: Behavioral strategies for change* (pp. 223–266). Washington, DC: American Psychological Association.

Mattaini, M. A., & Moore, S. K. (2004). Ecobehavioral social work. In H. E. Briggs & T. L. Rzepnicki (Eds.), *Using evidence in social work practice* (pp. 55–73). Chicago, IL: Lyceum Books.

McDowell, J. J., & Popa, A. (2010). Toward a mechanics of adaptive behavior: Evolutionary dynamics and matching theory statics. *Journal of the Experimental Analysis of Behavior, 94,* 241–260.

McKnight, J. L. (1996). *A twenty-first century map for healthy communities and families.* Chicago, IL: Institute for Policy Studies, Northwestern University.

Meyer, C. H. (1976). *Social work practice: The changing landscape* (2nd ed.). New York, NY: Free Press.

Meyer, C. H. (Ed.). (1983). *Clinical social work practice in an ecosystems perspective.* New York, NY: Columbia University Press.

Meyer, C. H. (1988). The eco-systems perspective. In R. A. Dorfman (Ed.), *Paradigms of clinical social work* (pp. 275–294). New York, NY: Brunner/Mazel.

Meyer, C. H. (1993). *Assessment in social work practice.* New York, NY: Columbia University Press.

Meyer, C. H. (1995). The ecosystems perspective: Implications for practice. In C. H. Meyer & M. A. Mattaini (Eds.), *The foundations of social work practice* (pp. 16–27). Washington, DC: National Association of Social Workers Press.

Meyer, C. H., & Mattaini, M. A. (2002). The ecosystems perspective. In M. A. Mattaini, C. T. Lowery, & C. H. Meyer (Eds.), *Foundations of social work practice* (3rd ed., pp. 3–24). Washington, DC: National Association of Social Workers Press.

Minuchin, S. (1974). *Families and family therapy.* Cambridge, MA: Harvard University Press.

Minuchin, P., Colapinto, J., & Minuchin, S. (2006). *Working with families of the poor* (2nd ed.). New York, NY: Guilford.

Mullaly, B. (2007). *The new structural social work* (3rd ed.). Oxford, UK: Oxford University Press.

Mullen, E. J. (1983). Personal practice models in clinical social work. In A. Rosenblatt & D. Waldfogel (Eds.), *Handbook of clinical social work* (pp. 623–649). San Francisco, CA: Jossey-Bass.

Nurius, P. S., Kemp, S. P., & Gibson, J. W. (1999). Practitioners' perspectives on sound reasoning: Adding a worker-in-context component. *Administration in Social Work, 23*, 1–27.

Odum, E. (1953). *Fundamentals of ecology*. Philadelphia, PA: Saunders.

Parker, L. (2003). A social justice model for clinical social work practice. *Affilia, 18*, 272–288.

Patterson, G. R. (1976). The aggressive child: Victim and architect of a coercive system. In E. J. Mash, L. A. Hamerlynck, & L. C. Handy (Eds.), *Behavior modification and families* (pp. 267–316). New York, NY: Brunner/Mazel.

Patterson, G. R. (1982). *Coercive family processes*. Eugene, OR: Castalia.

Payne, M. (2005). *Modern social work theory* (3rd ed.). Chicago, IL: Lyceum Books.

Prigogine, I. 1996. *The End of certainty: Time, chaos, and the new laws of nature*. New York, NY: Free Press.

Reid, W. (2002). Knowledge of direct social work practice: An analysis of trends, *Social Service Review, 76*(1), 6–33.

Richmond, M. (1917). *Social Diagnosis*. Philadelphia, PA: Sage.

Rosen, A., & Livne, S. (1992). Personal versus environmental emphases in formulation of client problems. *Social Work Research and Abstracts, 29*(4), 12–17.

Ross, R. (2006). *Returning to the teachings: Exploring aboriginal justice* (2nd ed.). Toronto, Canada: Penguin Canada.

Saleebey, D. (2006). *The strengths perspective in social work practice* (4th ed.). Boston, MA: Pearson Allyn & Bacon.

Sheffield, A. E. (1937). *Social insight in case situations*. New York, NY: Appleton-Century-Crofts.

Skinner, B. F. (1953). *Science and human behavior.* New York, NY: Macmillan.

Spretnak, C. (1990). Ecofeminism: Our roots and flowering. In I. Diamond & G. Orenstein (Eds.), *Reweaving the world: The emergence of ecofeminism* (pp. 3–14). San Francisco, CA: Sierra Club Books.

Stevens, I. & Cox, P. (2008). Complexity theory: New understandings of child protection in field settings and in residential care. *British Journal of Social Work, 38*(7), 1320–1336.

Sullivan, W. P., & Rapp, C. A. (2006). Honoring philosophical traditions: The strengths model and the social environment. In S. Saleebey (Ed.), *The strengths perspective in social work practice* (4th ed., pp. 261–278). Boston, MA: Pearson Allyn & Bacon.

Vodde, R., & Gallant, J. P. (2002). Bridging the gap between micro and macro practice: Large scale change and a unified model of narrative-deconstructive practice. *Journal of Social Work Education, 38*, 439–458.

von Bertalanffy, L. (1968). General systems theory. In N. Demerath & R. A. Peterson (Eds.), *Systems change and conflict* (pp. 119–129). New York, NY: Free Press.

Wakefield, J. C. (1996a). Does social work need the eco-systems perspective? Pt. 1. Is the perspective clinically useful? *Social Service Review, 70*, 1–32.

Wakefield, J. C. (1996b). Does social work need the eco-systems perspective? Pt. 2. Does the perspective save social work from incoherence? *Social Service Review, 70*, 183–213.

Wakefield, J. C. (1996c). Does social work need the eco-systems perspective? Reply to Alex Gitterman. *Social Service Review, 70*, 476–481.

Warren, K., Franklin, C., & Streeter, C. L. (1998). New directions in systems theory: Chaos and complexity. *Social Work, 43*, 357–372.

Webster-Stratton, C. (1997). From parent training to community building. *Families in Society, 78*, 156–171.

Wilson, E. O. (1992). *The diversity of life*. Cambridge, MA: Belknap/Harvard University Press.

Woehle, R. (2007). Complexity theory, nonlinear dynamics, and change: Augmenting systems theory. *Advances in Social Work, 8*(1), 141–151.

Woehle, R., Jones, G., Barker, T., & Piper, M. (2009). Theory and modeling of emergent dynamics: The effects of intervention on social and cultural capital. *Social Development Issues, 31*(2), 41–56.

Wolf-Branigin, M (2009). Applying complexity and emergence in social work education. *Social Work Education, 28*(2), 115–127.

Wolfram, S. (2002). *A new kind of science*. Champaign, IL: Wolfram Media.

Young, I. M. (1990). *Justice and the politics of difference*. Princeton, NJ: Princeton University Press.

Chapter 10
Small Group Theory

Lorraine Moya Salas, Dominique Roe-Sepowitz, and Craig Winston LeCroy

> How do the groups to which we belong shape our lives, and how can groups be used to enhance human functioning?

Group work has become an increasingly common form of practice in the social work field and other helping professions. In many settings, social workers provide a broad array of group services, such as educational, supportive, socialization-oriented, therapeutic, community relations, and social activism. In addition to providing direct services to client groups, social workers are often called on to work on multidisciplinary care teams, to be a part of staff work groups, and to serve on community task forces or consumer groups. Involvement in group work is an inevitable component of a social worker's responsibilities, which he or she may partake in either as a member, facilitator, or leader. In the current age of managed care and with an emphasis on cost effectiveness, it is reasonable to expect that group work practice will increase. Thus it is essential for social workers to be knowledgeable about group work and the foundations on which it is built.

There are several advantages to engaging in work with groups. Perhaps the most obvious advantage is that groups are efficient, allowing practitioners to assist many individuals at once. Other benefits include the fact that they help to alleviate isolation and provide members with a sense of hope brought by the other group members (Rose, 2004; Rose & LeCroy, 2005). As individuals in a group share their concerns, members come to recognize that they are not alone in their problems. They are able to receive help in the form of support, validation, and feedback from peers. Group members have the opportunity to observe how peers who may be at different stages in their development have dealt with life issues and troubles and are given the opportunity to learn from the experiences of others. Consequently, peers can become role models for one another. In addition to receiving help, group members have the opportunity to be dispensers of assistance and potentially see themselves in a different light

(Rose & LeCroy, 2005; Toseland & Rivas, 2005). Another benefit is that groups provide the context for individuals to practice new behaviors in a setting that is safe and more similar to real-world situations than individual treatment may be. This increases the likelihood that newly learned skills will transfer to the natural environments of group members (Rose, 2004). As group members share their often different perspectives, this may trigger new thoughts and perspectives in other participants. Thus the synergy of groups creates the potential for new awareness and for consciousness raising. Together the group can achieve what none of the participants could achieve individually. Another and perhaps most significant aspect of group work is that in some settings it has been found to be effective in fostering change within group members. Studies indicate that group treatment is at least as effective as individual treatment and in some instances is more effective (Toseland & Siporin, 1986).

Groups are not without limitations. Groups are not necessarily suitable for everyone, nor are they the intervention of choice for all types of problems. Some of the challenges associated with group work are increased potential for breaches in confidentiality, the chance that members will become dependent on one another, and the possibility that the group may scapegoat particular individuals and/or succumb to group thinking. A few talkative members might monopolize discussion, and the needs of more quiet individuals may not be met. Also, group process often requires a certain level of communication, which may not be appropriate for all individuals, such as children who are nonverbal, adults with a severe mental illness who may be ostracized by other members for their differences, or certain cultural groups for whom it is not acceptable to share personal problems. Ascertaining for whom and when groups are suitable requires some knowledge of group work. Additionally, the ability to modify groups to meet the needs of participants, to create an atmosphere that obviates some of the potential challenges inherent in group work, and to utilize group process to maximize the benefits of group work requires a certain amount of competence (Toseland & Rivas, 2005). Yet, although group work entails many challenges, the power of groups is undeniable and has been repeatedly documented in the literature (Barlow, Burlingame, & Fuhriman, 2005).

Despite the benefits of group work and the likelihood that social workers will engage in group work at some point in their careers, many MSW students graduate without ever receiving training in this modality. A survey conducted by Birnbaum and Auerbach (1994) as cited in Stroizer, 1997) of 89 graduate schools of social work revealed that only 19% of schools require a class in group work, and only 46% of schools surveyed provide group work courses as electives. This indicates that many social workers graduate without ever receiving training in group work and consequently may be ill prepared to engage in small group work. This chapter is designed to enhance social workers' knowledge so that they might be better prepared to engage in effective work with small groups. We focus on the theories that guide small group practice.

Groups are extremely complex, with many factors operating at once. This calls for a theoretical framework that allows the social worker to consider the forces that work simultaneously within a group (Wood, Phillips, & Pedersen, 1996). First, we explore definitions of group work and small groups. This is followed by a review of the history of small group theory and practice so that we might learn from the historic traditions of group workers and more fully understand some of the contemporary issues challenging group workers today. We examine some of the most widely accepted and utilized theories of small groups and their relevance to social work practice. Further, we review the empirical literature to ascertain what works with small groups and what questions remain unanswered.

Definitions

Group work entails bringing together small groups of individuals to serve a need. It is generally agreed that small groups are not a mere aggregate of people in close proximity; they are not distinguished by one ideal or magic number; and they are more than a gathering of people who have similar characteristics (Hutchinson, 2003). Instead, a small group is distinguished by interaction, purpose, a sense of belonging, and the conduct or behavior of group members. It is commonly recommended that small groups range from three to a maximum of 15 participants. Rather than size of the group, however, what is crucial is that members have the opportunity to share thoughts and feelings, respond to other members, and engage in interaction with one another. The size of small groups can vary depending on the purpose of the group (Cathcart, Samovar, & Henman, 1996). For example, socialization and educational groups may be larger than therapeutic groups, where it is crucial for all group members to have the opportunity to address their concerns and to be heard. Small groups are further distinguished by the fact that they are goal-directed and can include an array of purposes. They can be task-oriented, where the purpose is to achieve a goal that may or may not address the needs of the group but rather affects a broader collection of people. They can be treatment-oriented, where the purpose is to meet the socioemotional needs of group members. A unique characteristic of small groups is that the success of the group is connected to the success of its participants. Thus group members develop feelings of mutual interdependence (Cathcart et al., 1996; Toseland & Rivas, 2005). Participants in small groups feel a sense of belonging often based on shared characteristics, values, or purpose, and they self-identify as members of a group. Finally, small groups typically have norms for behavior and roles for group members. These rules may be explicit or implicit, and achievement of goals is partially contingent on members fulfilling these norms (Cathcart et al., 1996).

A definition of small groups provided by D. Johnson and F. Johnson (2006, p. 8) exemplifies many of the qualities of small groups discussed herein:

> Two or more individuals in face to face interaction who are aware of their positive interdependence as they strive to achieve mutual goals, each aware of their membership in the group, and each aware of the others who belong to the group.

Toseland and Rivas (2005, p. 12) provide the following definition of group work:

> Goal directed activity with small treatment and task groups aimed at meeting socioemotional needs and accomplishing tasks. This activity is directed to individual members of a group and to the group as a whole within a system of service delivery.

These definitions reflect the dual foci of group work, that is, on both the individuals and the group as a whole. Practitioners frequently differ in the degree of emphasis they place on the individuals or the group. Most group workers take a group orientation that assumes that when individuals form a group, a new entity is created and the group can no longer be understood solely by looking at individual members. Consequently, the group as a whole must be addressed. In this sense, there are two clients: the group as a whole and the individuals within the group. Toseland and Rivas's definition of group work further notes that groups exist in relation to a larger social context. As such, groups are both influenced by and can influence the larger environment (Toseland & Rivas, 2005).

History and Conceptual Origins

This is not a comprehensive reporting of the history of small group theory and practice, but a summary. We attempt to highlight the evolution of small group practice, with a particular focus on the connection to social work and ultimately professionalization. Further, we look at the philosophy and knowledge base that has informed small group work throughout its development (Andrews, 2001).

Small Group Practice and Professionalization

Early group work is frequently described as a movement, not a method (Papell, 1983, as cited in Middlemann & Wood, 1990; Reid, 1981). This is not surprising given that group work emerged in the context of the progressive movement, the recreation movement, and the adult education movement. In its beginning stages, group workers were not associated with one profession but usually aligned themselves with the agencies with which they worked. Group workers came from recreation, Christian youth organizations, Jewish centers, settlement houses, camps, scouts, and education. Group work was guided by a philosophy rooted in democratic ideals, social reform, and human connection (Andrews, 2001).

During the late 19th century and the beginning of the 20th century, urbanization, industrialization, and massive immigration challenged America. With these changes in the structure of society, numerous social problems emerged, such as "poverty, unemployment, disease, child labor, slum housing, dangerous working conditions and political corruption" (Reid, 1981, p. 77). Group workers attempted to address these social ills by participating in endeavors of social reform and by creating opportunities for human connection. In the recreation movement, there was recognition of the importance of viewing people holistically. It was assumed that an individual's development could be strengthened and the problems of urban living addressed by satisfying people's leisure time. It was also assumed that recreation could assist with the socialization of individuals. There was an emergence of sand gardens, organized sports, clubs, parks, and social centers, and group workers were involved in every aspect of the recreation movement (Reid, 1981).

The adult education movement also surfaced during this time, as adults sought self-advancement. Adult education addressed the needs of immigrants, of those who had not had schooling or had been forced to drop out of school, and of those who had needs related to their new lifestyle. Classes that became available through the adult education movement included reading, writing, English proficiency, citizenship, general health, parenting, child care, homemaking, and occupational training and industrial rehabilitation of people who were without employment due to mechanization. Classes that focused on helping people make good use of their increased leisure time also materialized, and literature, art, drama, and music classes were provided. The adult education movement had a political function as well that was concerned with preparing individuals to participate in and influence the political process. Training was provided on political action, and public forums were sponsored. Mary Parker Follet (1920), a well-known and influential thinker of the time, believed that for democracy to work individuals needed to organize into neighborhood groups and advocate for their needs. Thus neighborhood organizations were born. The adult education movement utilized group process and actively engaged students in their learning. The group worker was tasked with keeping the discussion going in the desired direction, gaining the participation of all members, and pointing out inconsistencies (Reid, 1981).

During this period of social upheaval, social work's focus broadened from the individual to the family and the many socioeconomic factors that could either hinder or promote well-being (Reid, 1981). The settlement movement commenced; social workers lived among the poor in settlement houses that provided playgrounds, kindergartens, and adult education classes, and they engaged in social reform efforts. Small groups were utilized to teach social skills, and efforts were divided between development and environmental reform (Gitterman, 2004). Social workers along with consumers advocated for such things as the regulation of sanitation, prohibition of child labor, and decent, standardized wages (Reid, 1981).

In addition to group work provided in recreation, education, and settlement settings, psychologists also began to experiment with small groups. In 1906, John Pratt established a small group with 15 of his tuberculosis patients, which he referred to as "thought control classes." These groups involved a set of general agreements and consisted primarily of lecture but also allowed time for participants to discuss their problems. Thereafter, other psychologists began to engage in small group work with schizophrenic patients, alcoholics, neurotic patients, and disturbed children in "activity groups." Also in the early 1900s, Freud met with his group of analysts, which came to be known as the Wednesday Evening Society. The group was intended to be educational, with discussion of theoretical concepts, but members regularly engaged in mutual sharing, with Freud in the role of leader. Some of the analysts had experienced Freud as a therapist, and consequently the groups took on the tone of a group therapy session (Rutan & Stone, 2001).

Group workers, however, remained largely concerned with social reform until the 1920s, when there was a shift in focus from environmental factors to the individual and the psyche. This transformation was connected to the many changes occurring in society. Many Americans experienced a higher standard of living, and after World War I the country assumed an isolationist stance. This was the time of the Red Scare. Consequently, there was a desire for conformity and a fear of anything perceived as radical. Furthermore, by this time psychoanalytic theory was pervasive and informed much of social casework, and the settlement movement declined somewhat. Group workers began to work in different settings: as psychiatric social workers with veterans and in child guidance clinics. Group workers continued with this individualistic focus until the stock market crashed and the Depression challenged this country. After this, once again environmental factors could not be denied, and social reform efforts increased. Group workers assembled groups of consumers to study the Depression and to advocate for improved living conditions, for work relief through public works, and for cash benefits for older adults (Reid, 1981).

Despite the renewed interest in social reform, by the 1930s psychoanalytic principles were taught in schools of social work. The first course on group work was provided in 1923 at the School of Social Work at Western Reserve University. Grace Coyle, who drew from the work of John Dewey, taught this initial course. Many social workers thought it was premature to offer group work courses at the university, indicating that group work did not have a comprehensive knowledge base (Reid, 1981). A student at the University of Chicago during the 1930s recounts being told by a teacher that "she was wasting herself by being a person who worked with groups" (Andrews, 2001, p. 49). Many social caseworkers believed that work not informed by psychological dynamics did not belong in social work. In spite of this, there was a steady growth in group work courses, and by 1936, 33 schools of social work offered group work courses. Group workers were cognizant of the need for a reformulation of group work and began to search for other sources of knowledge to inform practice (Reid, 1981).

Coyle (1947, as cited in Reid, 1981, p. 122) wrote the following regarding the need for trained group workers:

> It is not enough merely to open our clubrooms and classrooms, recreation centers and playgrounds. The doors of our agencies have stood open for 50 to 60 years. As we have worked within those clubrooms we have been forced to recognize that, when certain people acted as leaders, the groups were not only more fun for the participants but that more people got more out of them. When others led them, the groups were arid, mechanical, sometimes sentimental, occasionally, actually demoralizing.

Toward the end of World War II, once again there was a change in focus from social reform and preparing group members for social responsibility to a concern with mental health, as 1.5 million men were not accepted in the armed forces or were discharged for emotional problems. When the war ended, social workers were tasked with addressing the needs of millions of soldiers and their families. Services were desired that could meet the needs of large groups of people (Reid, 1981). Alexander Wolf, a psychiatrist, had already begun to apply psychoanalytic concepts and techniques to groups in 1938. His focus was on individuals within a group setting (G. Corey, 1990). Social workers, along with psychologists and psychiatrists, began to work together in therapeutic settings. Group techniques were used in hospitals, correctional institutions, schools, and family agencies (Garvin, 1997). Casework was informed predominantly by Freud's theory of personality, and group work students in social work were also being trained in this knowledge base. Further, the social action component of group work, with its tolerance for diversity and understanding of others, was not appreciated by the anti-Communist and McCarthyist climate of the day (Andrews, 2001). Hence, group work concerned itself with treatment and rehabilitation.

Confusion about the purpose of group work mounted as group workers reflected on whether group work was a medium for individual development or a means of furthering social change and strengthening democracy. Group workers struggled with the nature of group work, their professional identity, and the limited knowledge base that guided group work. As they grappled with some of these issues, in 1936 they formed the National Association for the Study of Group Work (NASGW), dedicated to enhancing the knowledge and skills of group workers and to addressing many of the issues that challenged group work. The NASGW produced several publications that reflected the diversity of group work. It was acknowledged that group work was a "therapeutic tool, a reform movement, an educational method, a small part of the recreation movement and closely akin to the methods and values of social welfare agencies" (Reid, 1981, p. 141).

After much debate about their professional status, in 1946 at the National Conference on Social Work, Grace Coyle, along with other group workers, proclaimed that group work fell under the scope of social work because group workers shared many common concerns with caseworkers.

Ultimately, this led to the formation of the American Association of Group Workers (AAGW), a professional organization (Garvin, 1997). By 1952, the AAGW voted to merge with existing social work professional organizations, and in 1955 this became the National Association of Social Workers (NASW). With this move, group work solidified its identification with social work. Although there were benefits to this union, group workers cited many costs. Group work's connection with recreation and education was weakened, and there was a renewed interest in talk therapy. Group work assumed a more clinical focus, and social action took a back seat to individual development. By the 1960s and early 1970s, the boundaries between caseworkers and group workers were more flexible as an increased number of caseworkers began to engage in small group work, and groups were being provided in numerous settings (Andrews, 2001; Reid, 1981).

As a profession, social work sought unification and to firmly establish the essence of social work. The profession was in search of a common knowledge base that could prepare all social workers to address the needs of clients without trying to fit them into the worker's mode or special-ization. In the 1950s and early 1960s, social work students were required to select a method and field of practice that they would then specialize in (Reid, 1981). In 1962, the NASW Delegate Assembly decided to eliminate practice sections and attempted to integrate the three methods: group work, casework, and community organizing. This generic approach to education resulted in few schools maintaining separate group work programs. Many group workers felt that group work was being washed out of social work and that the generic thrust was biased toward preparing social workers to work with individuals and families. Many often refer to this period as *generocide*. However, work with small groups continued in many settings, often without workers receiving specialized training (Garvin, 1997).

Despite this apparent setback, group workers continued to make advances in group work and continued to explore the diverse purposes of groups. In 1962, Papell and Rothman, building on the work of others, delineated three models of group work: the social goals, remedial, and reciprocal models. All three of these models continue to guide practice theory. The social goals model is primarily concerned with social change. Through participation in groups, members' social consciousness is stim-ulated, citizens are informed, and members are engaged in social action. The role of the group worker is to model desired behavior and to enable participants to engage in responsible citizenship. This model stems from group work's early history and commitment to social reform and is still practiced by citizen, neighborhood, and community groups. The second model outlined by Papell and Rothman is the remedial model and is more closely aligned with the clinical interests of group work. In this model, group leaders are concerned with restoring or rehabilitating individuals who are deviant or behaving dysfunctionally. The individual is the focus of change. The group leader's responsibility is diagnosis and treatment so that individuals can attain a more desirable level of functioning. The goal of the reciprocal model is to create a group that assists members in achieving optimal adaptation. This is achieved by fostering a system of mutual aid among group members. The role of the group worker in this model is that of mediator between the group and society, and the focus is on group processes (Douglas, 1979; Toseland & Rivas, 2005). The three models reflect group workers' commitment to the multiple purposes of group work despite strong pressure to assume an individualistic focus that would narrow the potential of groups.

The second half of the 1970s was characterized by a revitalization in group work that was largely precipitated by practitioners who remained committed to quality group work and to the development of a theoretical knowledge base. Papell and Rothman, in collaboration with Haworth Press, initiated a group work journal entitled *Social Work with Groups: A Journal of Community and Clinical Practice.* This journal filled a void by covering content that other journals had failed to address and provided an outlet for group workers to share their knowledge and expertise. It was devoted entirely to group research and developments in direct practice and community work. In 1978, group workers attending the annual meeting of the Council on Social Work Education gathered to form a committee for the advancement of social work with groups. This later became the Association for the Advancement of Social Work with Groups, International. One of the first tasks of the committee was to plan a group work conference, since other conferences rarely if ever covered group work content. In 1979, the first Group Work Symposium was held, with more than 350 group workers in attendance. Since then, this conference has become an annual event. These series of events laid the groundwork for the rebirth and strengthening of group work that continued into the 1980s (Andrews, 2001; Garvin, 1997).

Theoretical Underpinnings of Small Group Work

Early group work practice reveals that no one theory of human behavior guided all group workers. Rather, group work was influenced by the climate of the day and the many movements that were under way. Through the mid-1930s, group work predominantly utilized methods from progressive education. As small group practice matured, it was increasingly influenced by the practice wisdom of group workers and the research occurring in sociology and psychology. As the 20th century progressed, however, psychology began to overshadow other disciplines in its influence on small group theory (Reid, 1981).

In the early 1900s, sociologists were intrigued by the power of groups. Sociologists such as Cooley, Durkheim, and Simmel were investigating and writing about groups. The concept of "primary groups" originated with Cooley (1943), who described families and playgroups as the primary place where individuals learned standards of behavior, values, mutual identification, and solidarity. He hypothesized that into adulthood, socialization takes place through small primary group associations. The characteristics of groups and how groups formed fascinated Durkheim (1997). He felt that to understand the group, one must look at the structure of the whole group and not just at the characteristics of individual members. Simmel (1950) studied group size and was interested in how this impacted group interactions and power alliances within groups (Reid, 1981).

Psychology also made significant contributions to group work (Reid, 1981). The French psychologist Lebon (1896) began to explore the effect of large groups on individuals. He noted that when individuals become part of a group, their behavior changes and they develop a "group mind." He observed the strength of groups and the contagion and suggestibility that occurs. In 1920, William McDougall published the text *The Group Mind.* He, too, observed the power of groups to change individual behavior and viewed the group process as a potential tool to assist individuals in changing their behavior in positive ways. For this to occur, he felt groups must be organized and have a clear purpose. Freud, too, observed large groups and began to ponder what constitutes a group. He posited that groups require a purpose and a leader. Freud indicated that groups form when individuals develop libidinal connections with the leader and each other. With this sense of identification among group members comes regression and de-differentiation. Consequently, group members lose some individuality and strive to meet group goals. Freud further described the dynamic of the group member relinquishing his or her ego ideal and embracing the group leader's purposes. These suppositions were the first attempts to explain the phenomenon of groupthink (Ashford, LeCroy, & Lortie, 2006). Groupthink occurs when a cohesive group emphasizes consensus at the expense of critical thinking when attempting to solve a problem.

Group workers themselves attempted to add to the knowledge of small groups as they wrote of their experiences and observations. Group workers concerned with continuity of services developed a form for recording what occurs in group sessions. By the 1930s, records from social work students from University Neighborhood Centers were published. These records were used to describe important facets of group organization and development. In 1938, research was published regarding a study of a group of boys on a camping excursion. This study suggested that individuals could grow through group work and focused on the bonding, interaction, and status among group members. In 1930, Grace Coyle published *Social Process in Organized Groups*, in which she addressed the structure and evolution of small groups. In 1938, Liberman published *New Trends in Group Work*; this was a compilation of writings by group workers of the day. A theme in this collection was that group work was educational and contributed to personality development (Reid, 1981).

Contributions to group work came from both researchers and theorists. In the 1940s, the work of Kurt Lewin significantly added to group theory. Field theory is considered the precursor of systems theory in the social sciences. Lewin (1939) was one of the first psychologists to acknowledge that human behavior could best be understood by studying individuals in their environmental context. He presumed that the person and the environment were an interdependent whole, which he referred to as the *life space* or *field*. Specifically, *field* refers to the environment where social units such as individuals or groups are located, where they relate and are impacted by a field of forces (Dale, Smith, Norlin, & Chess, 2006). Individual personality development is influenced by both positive forces that push individuals toward goals and by negative forces that resist movement. The group as a social unit also experiences forces that account for behavior in small groups. Lewin coined the term "group dynamics" to describe these forces occurring in a group. Per Lewin's theory, group workers are tasked with becoming aware of the forces or group dynamics that function within a group so that these forces can be increased or decreased to assist the group and members in achieving change (Douglas, 1979). Whereas practitioners described their work with groups, Lewin experimented with groups by operationalizing some of the forces inherent in the group process. His research provided information about group dynamics and leadership styles and how these factors influence group outcomes. For Lewin, the focus was on the here and now and on personal growth. Although Lewin died in 1947, his work led to the first National Training Laboratory in *group development* and to what is now referred to as t-groups, encounter groups, or sensitivity groups (Rutan & Stone, 2001).

By the 1930s, psychoanalytic principles were widely accepted in the United States as a way of understanding human behavior (Reid, 1981). While Lewin was conducting his research on group dynamics, other theorists were expanding on Freud's theory of personality. Ego psychology, object-relations theory, and other psychoanalytic perspectives emerged, each of which emphasized different aspects of human behavior and development and provided different outlooks on motivation. Eventually group workers began to apply psychoanalytic concepts to small groups (Geller, 2005). Alexander Wolf (Wolf & Schwartz, 1962) and Slavson (1964) were among the first to engage in small group work utilizing psychoanalytic principles. They took an intrapsychic approach and focused on treating the individual within a group milieu and not on treating the group. Wolf used psychoanalytic techniques to bring unconscious conflicts into awareness and to assist the client in reformulating his or her personality system (G. Corey, 1990; Rutan & Stone, 2001).

Interpersonal theories of small group work also emerged. Interpersonal theories assume that the group is a microcosm of the individual's social universe. Through experiences in group, feedback received from other group members, and self-observation, individuals learn about their maladaptive style of interacting with others and of their perceptual distortions. It is assumed that with insight group members are able to change their dysfunctional patterns of interaction (Rutan & Stone, 2001).

Another form of small group theory emerged with the work of Wilfred R. Bion, a psychoanalyst who had been trained in the object-relations tradition (Geller, 2005). Bion conducted his research with small groups at London's Tavistock Institute of Human Relations in the 1940s, but his work did not have influence in the United States until the 1960s. Bion viewed the group as a collective entity and was concerned with both overt and covert aspects of group work. Overt aspects are the task or purpose of the group and group norms; covert aspects of group functioning include hidden agendas and unconscious emotions and the basic assumptions of group functioning. The group leader must attend to both levels of group functioning but is primarily concerned with the basic assumptions: group projections and beliefs about what the group needs to survive. The work group is disturbed by the basic assumptions. Bion (1959) postulated that there are three basic assumptions. The first is the dependency group, which assumes that security and protection can be obtained from a group member, usually the leader. Consequently, group members may act helpless and incompetent in the hopes that the group leader will rescue them. When this does not occur, group members may become angry or express their disappointment in other ways. The second basic assumption is the fight-flight group. Examples of flight include tardiness, absences, and, in extreme cases, dropping out of the group; fight is demonstrated by resisting reflection and self-examination or by engaging in insignificant talk to avoid real issues. The final basic assumption identified by Bion is the pairing group. Here two group members form a bond and invest in planning for the future with the belief that this plan will produce something akin to a Messiah who will save the group. The rest of the group may become inactive as the pair rely on each other and exclude other group members (Rutan & Stone, 2001). Bion did not rule out the possibility that there could be other basic assumptions operating in groups. In fact, Turquet (1974) later identified another basic assumption, oneness, that can interfere with the work group function. Bion assumed that people enter a group with valence, which is an individual's natural tendency for one of the basic assumptions. Per Bion's theory, the function of the group leader is to help the group members become aware of their basic assumptions and their valence. The role of the group leader is at times characterized by noninvolvement, followed by moments of pointing out group behavior. It is assumed that through this process individuals will learn about their problems with authority and peers, which will free them from their historic bonds. In addition to Bion's view of groups as a collective, he brought attention to the unconscious processes that occur in groups and that must be attended to. Later, other theorists built on Bion's work and additional group-as-a-whole theories emerged (Rutan & Stone, 2001).

By the 1960s and 1970s there was a proliferation of theories in the social sciences that influenced social work and, more specifically, group work, including role theory, humanistic and existential theories, and behavioral and systems theories, to name a few (Reid, 1981). These theories emerged partly due to the incompleteness in psychodynamic theories in providing an understanding of human behavior. It is important to note that none of these theories has attained universal acceptance in group work (Rutan & Stone, 2001). Theories have continued to evolve as theorists build on the work of previous researchers, and theories have been adapted for work with small groups; new theories will undoubtedly emerge as we move into the 21st century.

Group work historically has responded to the needs of society by providing recreational and leisure activities, education, rehabilitation, and treatment and has influenced society through social action and reform efforts. Group work is committed to changing both people and society. Group work matured along with the evolution of social theories. Small group work stemmed from a philosophy of people working together for mutual gain and grew from the practice wisdom of individuals and researchers who began to observe and document the power of groups. Gradually, theory emerged to provide clarity regarding the dynamics of groups, to inform the change process, and to provide an understanding of human behavior. There are now numerous theories that inform small group work, some of which focus on the individual within a group milieu and others that focus on the group as a whole. Recently, practitioners have begun to recognize the importance of a dual emphasis. In any event, group work can no longer be criticized for not having a clear theoretical knowledge base. It is rare, however, for practitioners to utilize one theory exclusively. Rather, the group worker is tasked with integrating theory (Rutan & Stone, 2001). It is with this in mind that we move into addressing current theoretical principles of small group work.

Basic Theoretical Principles

Given the diverse beginnings of small group work, it is not surprising that there is no one theoretical orientation that unifies group work. Social workers often equate practice without an explicit theoretical rationale to navigating a plane without a map. Theory is the map that informs one's assumptions about human behavior and guides how we explain behavior and group interactions and decide on group goals and our role in the group process (G. Corey, 1990). It is important to be mindful that not all theories lead to the same destination; nor does one theory reflect the ultimate "truth." Regardless of whether social workers are aware of their theoretical orientation, their behavior is, in all likelihood, informed by their assumptions, and it would serve group practitioners well to reflect on their values and beliefs.

The Association for Specialists in Group Work's "Best Practice Guidelines" indicates the necessity of developing a theoretical framework to guide group practice and support one's techniques and interventions. Practitioners are responsible for formulating their own theoretical framework that is derived from the synthesis of the best of many theories and that is aligned with their natural views and inclinations. To achieve this it is imperative that practitioners be self-aware and grounded in theories of small group work, including the strengths and limitations of numerous theories (M. Corey & Corey, 2002). Only then can the group practitioner select theories and interventions that are advantageous and an appropriate fit for the consumer. Here we consider systems theory, as it provides a means for understanding and working with small groups that goes beyond a focus on the individual or interpersonal exchanges. It provides a lens through which we can look at the whole group and its multiple levels (Connors & Caple, 2005). Additionally, it can be used in combination with other theoretical approaches. Psychoanalytic theory is also addressed, as more than any other theory it has influenced subsequent theories (G. Corey, 1990). Learning theory is reviewed because it has gained momentum in group work practice. Many approaches to group work rely on learning principles, particularly psychoeducational groups and prevention groups (Toseland & Rivas, 2005).

Systems Theory

General systems theory was developed by Ludwig von Bertalanffy in 1968, a biologist who believed that the best way to understand living phenomena was to view them in context, where they could be examined as part of a larger system. Bertalanffy's theory parallels many of Lewin's (1939) ideas, which emphasized the importance of understanding an individual's life space. Like Lewin's field theory, systems theory emphasizes a holistic and interdependent view of organisms and their functioning. Just as there are numerous variants of psychoanalytic theory, there are many forms of systems theory. Here we highlight some of the central tenets of systems theories.

No system or individual acts in isolation but is interconnected with other systems. Every system is part of another system, and every part of a system is also a system itself; therefore, change at any level impacts all systems. A group system is influenced by the interactions of its members, by how the group leader interacts with group members, and by the external environment that impacts individuals and what they bring to the group process. Both nonparticipating group members and group members who dominate discussion influence group dynamics (Connors & Caple, 2005). The method used by the group leader to respond to a particular group member who violates the norms of the group affects that member, the group as a whole, and the group leader. The agency sponsoring a group as a system impacts groups with its mission statement, the employees it hires, and the resources it allocates for group work. With these examples, we see that "all parts of a system interact dynamically and constantly" (p. 14). Further, this interaction is bidirectional: The environment impacts a group, and the group can impact the larger social environment. It is the transaction within and between systems that is central. Linear, cause-and-effect thinking does not sufficiently capture what occurs in groups. The commonly heard phrase "A system is more than the sum of its parts" recognizes the new features that are produced through interaction (Donigian & Malnati, 1997).

In addition to grasping the importance of interaction and connectedness among systems, understanding the group as a whole is primary (Wood et al., 1996). The difference between an individual perspective and a group-as-a-whole perspective is best illustrated with a story shared by Agazarian (1997) in her text *Systems-Centered Therapy for Groups*. She describes sitting near a pond when her companion threw a portion of his hamburger into the water. One of the faster fish got to the food first and swam away with it. It was too big for the fish to gulp down, so the other fish swam along and also nibbled away at it. Her companion reported:

> *From the perspective of the fish in general, we see an efficient distribution and feeding system; one fish is playing a role for the whole shoal of fish by catching the hamburger and holding it in his mouth while the whole group of fish feed. We see something different when we take the perspective of the individual fish, who is having his dinner stolen from him before he can eat it. (p. 8)*

Group workers with a systems orientation are concerned with the big picture or the group as a whole and not just individual needs and perspectives. Consequently, group workers attend to group dynamics and development. (Connors & Caple, 2005)

Systems theory purports that all organisms have a similarity of function and structure, or are isomorphic. Structure includes boundaries and power structures that make decisions regarding the input and output of energy. Boundaries define an entity, contain the energy of a system, and are potentially permeable. When boundaries are open, energy exchange occurs across systems. A change in any part of a system creates change in that system and in the other systems in which it is embedded. Fortunately, systems are naturally self-organizing and goal-directed. They organize themselves to survive and adjust to their ever-changing environment. Systems self-stabilize or attempt to maintain equilibrium by adopting new information into their current structure or by changing their structure, whereby evolution occurs (Connors & Caple, 2005). Systems inevitably transform and move from simple to more complex; closed systems with rigid or impermeable boundaries are a threat to the survival of a system (Agazarian, 1997).

Within groups, systems exchange energy or interact dynamically through communication among group members. Individuals consistently make decisions regarding the rigidness of their boundaries, that is, whether they should be open or closed and whether to share and accept feedback. Some groups can be flexible and accept new members; others are more rigid, resist change of any sort, and have strict group membership requirements. The group leader can assist the group in considering their closedness and their feelings about change. Additionally, group members can challenge each other. Newly formed groups may struggle initially as they seek stability, which is facilitated when group norms, goals, and roles are established (Connors & Caple, 2005).

Generally, systems theorists who work with groups are particularly aware of the power of groups to influence individuals. They recognize the properties that surface from the interaction of individuals in a group. Group workers operating with a systems orientation are attuned to subsystems and external environmental systems that impact the groups' functioning. They recognize that the group, like other systems, is continually in transformation; therefore, the group as a whole moves through its own developmental stages. Group systems, like other systems, struggle to survive when threatened with conflicts and will dissipate when no longer needed (Connors & Caple, 2005; Toseland & Rivas, 2005).

Psychoanalytic Theory

There are multiple psychoanalytic perspectives that have led to intrapsychic, interpersonal, and group-as-a-whole approaches to small group practice. Additionally, many psychoanalytic concepts have found their way into other theories of human behavior. Rather than focusing on the differences among each of these approaches, we highlight the commonalties or the core principles that set psychoanalytic theories apart from other theories (Geller, 2005).

At the crux of psychoanalytic theory is its focus on unconscious processes. It is assumed that people at times are irrational and have unconscious conflicts, thoughts, and feelings. The possibility of the unconscious surfacing leads to anxiety and fear. To protect themselves from this fear and anxiety, individuals employ resistance and defense mechanisms, such as repression, denial, regression, projection, displacement, reaction formation, and rationalism. The therapeutic process is designed to illuminate the unconscious and to make individuals aware of their defense mechanisms. It is presumed that much of human behavior is motivated by the unconscious. Hence, by making the unconscious conscious the individual is freed and can become autonomous (G. Corey, 1990).

The primary mechanism for bringing the unconscious into awareness is transference. Transference occurs when the group member puts feelings, attitudes, or fantasies about significant others onto the therapist or other group members. Countertransference occurs when the group leader puts his or her own feelings onto a group member and the leader's view of that member becomes distorted. It is important to note that transferences can consist of either positive or negative content. Group members are assisted in using transference to relive their past in a setting that will not be harsh and punishing. In this way, group members gain insight and work through unresolved, unconscious conflicts that make it difficult for them to move forward. Small groups potentially provide a reflection of how members relate socially outside of the group, and they allow for the possibility of multiple transferences to occur. To a large degree, the leader's role is to assist group members in exploring the extent to which they relate to group members as they do family members and to aid in re-creating the family of origin in the group setting (G. Corey, 1990).

In psychoanalytic theory the focus is on understanding how present behavior is connected to early development. Therefore, there is a continual weaving back and forth from the here and now to the past. At the core of psychoanalytic theory is identifying and interpreting transference and defense mechanisms. The group leader attempts to explain the underlying meaning of an individual's behavior and/or points out the behavior of the group as a whole (G. Corey, 1990). The basic assumption, as described by Bion (1959), is that the group's collective defense mechanism must be brought to the group's attention. The extent to which various psychoanalytic perspectives focus on the individual or the group as a whole varies. However, there is growing appreciation for the combined boundaries between the self and the group. This relationship is excellently described by Malcolm Pines (1992, as cited in Geller, 2005) in his article "The Self as a Group: The Group as a Self." Pines states, "If we grasp the complexity of the individual both constituted from and functioning as a group, it becomes less problematic to look at the contrasting notion of the group as a self" (p. 94). Consistent with this perspective is the notion that the individual expresses feelings that stem from the whole group. Feelings and thoughts that the group may be unaware of are projected onto a group member, often a scapegoat. If the scapegoat leaves the group, a new scapegoat will likely emerge. It is necessary for the group leader to make members aware of their unconscious feelings and thoughts that are being projected. In this way, the scapegoat is released from the feelings he or she carries for the group, and the group members are able to work through their issues. To some extent, the collective dynamics of the group must be dealt with for growth to occur. Ultimately, psychoanalytic theorists operate under the assumption that problems in behavior are virtually always driven by the unconscious, which remains the domain of all psychoanalytic theories (Geller, 2005).

Social Learning Theory

Many social workers are familiar with social learning concepts. Bandura's (1971) theory is perhaps the most well-known; it attempts to understand people as conscious, thinking beings who can have an influence on their environment. Social learning theorists assume that the behavior of group members is learned based on their interaction with the environment. Further, social learning theorists acknowledge the reciprocal relationship between the individual and the environment. Individuals are not just a product of their environment but can process information to actively influence how the environment controls them.

Perhaps most critical to group work is social learning's emphasis on how observation can lead to learning. It is assumed that learning can occur by observing others, without direct involvement in the learning experience. Thus, social learning theory is an approach that combines learning principles with cognitive processes, plus the effects of observational learning, to explain behavior.

Group workers can make use of social learning theory's emphasis on observational learning. Exposing group members to models can influence behavior. Research on modeling suggests that imitation is enhanced with models of people who are liked and respected. In addition, imitation is more likely when people see similarity between themselves and the model. People are more likely to imitate a model if they see the model's behavior leading to positive outcomes.

An important aspect of social learning theory is the notion of self-efficacy. Self-efficacy refers to a person's belief about his or her ability to perform behaviors that lead to expected outcomes. When people have a strong belief in their ability to perform certain behaviors, their confidence is high. This means they are likely to persist in their endeavors. When people have low self-efficacy, they are not confident and are likely to give up easily. As a result, the decision to engage in a situation, as well as the intensity of the effort expended in the situation, is determined by a person's self-efficacy.

Advanced Theoretical Principles

Systems theory, psychoanalytic theories, and social learning theory are fully developed theories of human behavior that inform practice. Here we look specifically at how these theories have been expanded to apply to small groups. Helen Durkin (1972), for example, first utilized systems theory in group therapy in the early 1970s. Subsequently, others have applied systems theory to work with groups. Agazarian's (Agazarian & Gantt, 2005) formulation of systems theory and its application to small groups is arguably the most comprehensive and will be discussed here. Irving D. Yalom's (1995) interpersonal learning theory is one of the better-known approaches to small group work. A study by Stroizer (1997) that looked at the content of MSW group work courses in the United States revealed that Yalom's text was most often listed in syllabi as the required text in the 51 group work courses in the sample. Hence, this theory will also be addressed. Learning theory gave rise to cognitive-behavioral group work, which has a strong empirical base and is widely utilized. This model is reviewed in the section on recent theoretical developments (Toseland & Rivas, 2005).

Systems-Centered Therapy for Groups

Yvonne M. Agazarian (1997) draws from the work of many theorists and expands on systems concepts with her theory of small group work. As is true of all systems, the primary goal of the systems-centered therapy (SCT) group is survival and transformation. In an SCT group, this entails developing a problem-solving system whereby members learn to resolve their own problems within and outside of the group. This requires mobilizing the energy of the systems toward the group's goals and structuring a group climate conducive to this aim. This climate is referred to as a system-centered culture and "exists when group members are both aware of themselves and of themselves in a hierarchy of contexts" (p. 21).

Agazarian and Gantt (2005) reframe Lewin's (1939) formulation of a field of forces in terms of decreasing restraining forces and increasing driving forces within the field to get to the goal. Problems are conceived of in terms of the permeability of boundaries. Boundaries are permeable if driving forces are stronger than restraining forces. In SCT the task is to minimize restraining forces. Achieving goals necessitates opening boundaries to energy and information and closing boundaries to noise. Noise includes cognitive distortions, contradictions, redundancy, and vague communication. Moreover, Agazarian (1997) elaborates on the tendency of human systems to integrate similarities and close boundaries to differences. Integrating similarity keeps systems stable in the short run, but in the long term this leads to rigidity and is dangerous for the survival of the system. When systems close their boundaries to differences, energy is expelled to deal with the differences. For systems to change and transform themselves, differences must be integrated. When systems reorganize and integrate differences, energy previously used to manage difference is available for working on goals.

To create a system-centered culture and to direct energy toward goals, SCT uses four methods or techniques: functional subgrouping, fork in the road, filtering techniques, and contextualizing. Just as systems theory acknowledges a hierarchy of systems, SCT identifies the core systems of a group as group members, subgroups, and the group as a whole. Subgroups exist within the environment of the group as a whole and are the environment for members. Unlike in other group therapy approaches, the subgroup and not the individual is the basic unit of the group and the target of intervention. Because the subgroup shares boundaries with both individual members and the group as a whole, it is considered most efficient to influence subgroups. Change in any of the core systems leads to change in the other two systems as well (Agazarian & Gantt, 2005).

Systems-centered therapy observes that people naturally gravitate toward that which is similar and separate around differences. This results in splitting in a stereotypical fashion. The status quo is maintained, and groups remain stable for the short term. An alternative to stereotyping that increases the likelihood that differences will be integrated is functional subgrouping. This is when subgroups are deliberately formed around differences or conflicts, and exploration of the unknown is allowed. Typically, groups deny differences by splitting and projecting, and resources for doing the work of the group are lost. Functional subgroups, on the other hand, contain conflicts and differences so that they can later be integrated. It is by integrating differences that systems develop and transform into more complex systems. Additionally, members can avoid ambivalence by working on one side of a personal conflict while allowing another subgroup to work on the other side of the dilemma. The incongruity is contained within the group as a whole, and the member no longer has to bear the conflict alone. Subgrouping around conflicts allows members to experience each half of a conflict rather than projecting, splitting, denying, or acting out while attempting to deal with both sides of an issue. Group leaders look for conflicts and differences that emerge and invite exploration. For example, "yes, but" communication is identified and members are invited to explore. Group leaders may ask whether anyone else agrees with the "yes" portion of the statement, or whether the "yes" resonates for anyone else. The subgroup actively works and members build on each other's experiences until there is a pause in discussion. At this point, the group leader invites other group members to explore the other side of the issue by asking who agrees with the "but" portion of the statement; thus another subgroup is formed and permitted to explore this part of the conflict. As subgroups explore their side of a conflict, small differences within the subgroup surface and are integrated. Differentiation occurs with subgroup members, and similarities between subgroups are also recognized. In this way, differences are integrated in the group as a whole and information is exchanged across systems (Agazarian, 1997).

The fork in the road technique is also used in SCT and puts into practice discriminating and integrating, which is required for transformation. The fork in the road is when members choose one side of a dilemma to explore within a subgroup and energy is vectored or directed toward the system's goals. The first fork in the road requires recognizing the difference between explaining/thinking and exploring/feeling. Rather than explaining and intellectualizing a conflict, members are required to explore it. Explanation leads to what one already knows, whereas exploration allows new experiences to surface (Agazarian & Gantt, 2005). Members describe what they are feeling instead of interpreting, which can lead to cognitive distortions. The boundaries between the two subsystems of the self, the cognitive portion of the self that leads to comprehension and the apprehensive part that stems from intuition, become permeable so that energy and information can cross between the two subsystems. Ultimately, systemic change comes through insight derived from both experience and understanding (Agazarian, 1997).

Another method used in SCT is boundarying, or filtering out noise. By filtering out noise, boundaries become permeable, and clear information comes into the group and is available for group tasks (Agazarian & Gantt, 2005). Systems move from simple to complex when noise is stopped at the boundaries and when clear information and communication cross boundaries. One of the primary tasks of SCT groups is to assist members in recognizing when boundaries are crossed. This includes crossing physical and psychological space and time boundaries and reality and role boundaries. Just as there are geographic boundaries that members cross as they enter the circle of the group at the designated time, there are psychological space and time boundaries as well. Members are made aware of psychological boundaries that include bringing all of their attention to the group process and the ability to focus on the present. In SCT groups, of concern is whether time functions as a restraining or a driving force. Often, when the present becomes too challenging, group members flee into the safety of the past or future. This results in members reliving the past in the present. Instead, members are encouraged to address the past in the here and now and assisted in recognizing the differences between the present and the past. Members may also take flight into the future by making predictions and living in the "as if" world they have created. This too keeps attention away from the present and sets up barriers along the boundaries, and all information that does not fit one's expectations is kept out. Another boundary members are made conscious of is the boundary between reality and irreality. In SCT the group's attention is refocused away from mind reading and prediction to the reality of the group. Members are encouraged to check out their assumptions, fears, and fantasies with other group members. Again, members are required to experience present reality rather than explain it, and misconstructions caused by faulty explanations are compared to reality-tested information obtained through exploration. Group members begin to develop an awareness of different contexts that lead to different interpretations, such as the past, the future, and the irreality of the mind. It is recognized that only in the context of real and current group life can problems be solved (Agazarian, 1997).

Groups using SCT also address role boundaries. Roles are systems in and of themselves, characterized by behavior, function, and goals. They change with context and are not simply a person. This is exemplified by the parental role, for which the goal is rearing children. Parental behavior changes with context; for instance, bedtime behavior differs from playtime behavior. Further, one can assume many roles and can cross boundaries from, say, the marital role back to the parental role. In an SCT group, members become cognizant of their many roles and how behavior and perspective change with roles. Group participants can operate in their person role; the group member role, in which they abide by group norms; a functional subgroup role, in which they operate according to one side of a conflict; or as a member of the group as a whole. Each role embodies a different context, and as roles shift, perspectives change. Members gradually begin to see how behavior, perspective, role, and context are connected and gain the capacity to see problems or situations from more than one perspective. In the end, SCT members are challenged to vector energy across boundaries from outside to inside the group, from the past and future to the present, from irreality to reality, and across group roles (Agazarian, 1997).

The fourth method of SCT, contextualizing, refers to the ability to see multiple contexts. This entails moving from a self-centered system that sees only oneself and consequently personalizes problems to a system-centered system, in which the individual sees himself or herself within a hierarchy of contexts. Here the impact of context is appreciated, and it is recognized that as perspectives change, experience also changes.

Through functional subgrouping, fork in the road, filtering techniques, and contextualizing, a system-centered culture is established and energy is directed toward achieving the goals of the system. For more specific information on how to apply SCT to small groups, readers should consult Agazarian's (1997) text, *Systems-Centered Therapy for Groups*, where a detailed blueprint is provided.

Interpersonal Learning

Yalom's (1995) interpersonal learning theory holds that all problems are in fact the result of interpersonal pathology. Yalom studied with Sullivan;

thus his work emerged from a psychoanalytic tradition and his theory has much in common with this perspective. Interpersonal learning focuses on irrational behavior that is largely unconscious and that causes problems for individuals as they relate with others. The group is the vehicle by which individuals learn of their maladaptive behavior patterns and of their parataxic distortions. Parataxic distortions are similar to transference, as they include distortions of others and refer to all interpersonal relationships. One of the group leader's primary tasks is to set up group conditions that allow members to behave in an unguarded, spontaneous manner. It is assumed that by doing so and with time, group members eventually behave in the group as they do in their social sphere. The group then becomes a microcosm of the group members' social universe. Group members display their interpersonal pathology and receive feedback from other members regarding their behavior. Yalom described the process of consensual validation, whereby individuals compare their interpersonal evaluations with those of the other group members. Through consensual validation group members become aware of their own behavior, how others view them, the feelings their behavior elicits in others, and ultimately how this impacts how they see themselves (Yalom, 1995).

Unlike many psychoanalytic perspectives, interpersonal learning focuses on the here and now and assumes that the power and effectiveness of the group increases as members are able to focus on what happens in the group during the session. Members observe behavior as it unfolds. Consequently, a historical assessment of the lives of group members is not required. Yalom's theory holds that the past is present, or manifests itself in the here and now. When members talk about past situations and their personal history, the group leader moves the group back to a focus on their relationship with one another. For example, if a group member reports that she is consistently angry with her partner, the group leader might ask if she were to be angry like that with someone from the group, who it would be. Yalom (1995) provides numerous examples in his text *The Theory and Practice of Group Psychotherapy* regarding how group leaders can move group members into the here and now.

In addition to moving group members into the here and now, the group leader's role is to illuminate process. Process refers to "the nature of the relationship between interacting individuals" (Yalom, 1995, p. 130). The process, not the content, of group discussion is of primary importance. Group leaders are concerned with the why and how of behavior and of statements made throughout the group process. The difference between focusing on process and focusing on content is made clear in an example provided by Yalom. He describes an incident in which a group member spoke negatively about parenthood to another group member, knowing full well that the majority of group members were parents. The group proceeded to discuss the content of the statements and debated the merits of parenthood. Instead, a concern with process might include exploring why this group member chose to share his sentiments about parenthood with this particular group member and what that indicates about their relationship. Another possibility is to explore why the individual set himself up to be attacked by the group and what that revealed about his way of interacting with others. There are often multiple processes that can be explored, and the leader decides which processes to delve into based on what is deemed most helpful to the individual and the group. Whereas Bion (1959) stressed attention to whole-group processes, Yalom's focus is on interpersonal processes. This is not to say that whole-group processes are unimportant. When the group is presenting obstacles to the working of the entire group, this takes precedence. For example, in the previous scenario, perhaps the individual was filling a role for the group and creating a diversion whereby the group could spend an entire session discussing parenting and thus avoid more honest discussion and self-disclosure. In any event, a central role of the group leader is to help group members examine and understand processes (Yalom, 1995).

Fundamental to assisting group members in addressing their interpersonal pathology is the corrective emotional experience. This entails experiencing an emotional situation within the group in a restorative fashion. In a sense, the group member experiences a past trauma or relives a script that he or she plays out in social interactions, but the group facilitates the elimination of distortions and the experience becomes healing. Within the safety of the group, raw emotions surface, and via honest feedback and consensual validation the group provides the basis for reality testing. Both the emotional experience and intellectual insight are essential to the corrective emotional experience. Catharsis alone is insufficient for change. A cognitive component is needed for individuals to make sense of their feelings and to understand the inappropriateness of their interpersonal behavior. For Yalom, intellectual insight can occur on four levels. The first level is awareness of how one is seen by others. The second level is recognition of patterns of behavior and interaction. The third level entails individuals' understanding why they do what they do. The fourth level is referred to as genetic insight; it is at this level that individuals see how they got to be the way they are. Contrary to psychoanalytic perspectives, it is not necessary to achieve genetic insight or an understanding of the past for change to occur. Insight at any of the first three levels followed by personal responsibility will suffice (Yalom, 1995).

Yalom (1995) conceived of the group both as an agent of change and as providing the conditions that help patients. He specifically explored what it is about group therapy that benefits patients. He recognized that there are many factors that can help group members. Interpersonal learning is key for the achievement of change. Yet this curative factor does not exist in isolation. There are many factors that are interdependent and function together. For example, for interpersonal learning to take place, group cohesion is pivotal. Without a sense of safety and trust that occurs in a cohesive group, it is unlikely that group members will take the risks involved in interpersonal learning. It is also possible that being part of a cohesive group where one belongs and is accepted is in itself sufficient to trigger change. Other therapeutic factors include catharsis, which is a component of the corrective emotional experience, and the corrective recapitulation of the primary family group, in which group members interact with one another as they would with parents and siblings. Although there is no consensus regarding why group members change, Yalom drew from the accounts of group members and leaders and from systematic research to identify 11 therapeutic factors that form the foundation for effective group therapy: instillation of hope, universality, imparting information, altruism, the corrective recapitulation of the primary family group, development of socializing techniques, imitative behavior, interpersonal learning, group cohesiveness, catharsis, and existential factors where individuals ultimately accept responsibility for their life. It is the group leader's task to cultivate these therapeutic factors, thus creating a climate for effective group therapy (Yalom, 1995).

Recent Theoretical Developments

In response to the needs of society, group work has acquired many different modalities that range in focus from social change and social justice goals to the promotion of individual functioning and growth-oriented goals. In this section we discuss two models that currently drive practice, each of which provides a substantially different approach to group work: the cognitive-behavioral model and the mutual aid model (Garvin, Gutiérrez, & Galinsky, 2004).

Cognitive-Behavioral Model

The cognitive-behavioral model is closely aligned with the remedial model. It stems from existing research on what has proven effective, just as the remedial model was derived from its commitment to scientific strategies. It is focused on individual change at either the behavioral, emotional, or cognitive level and utilizes group conditions to achieve these aims. Cognitive-behavioral group work (CBGW) is a highly structured program that draws on behavioral and cognitive theory and small group strategies (Rose, 2004; Rose & LeCroy, 2005).

The structure of group consists of five phases: beginning the group, motivational enhancement, assessment, intervention, and generalization. In beginning the group, the leader is tasked with developing group cohesion, with explaining what the group process entails, and with delineating what is expected of group members. The motivational enhancement phase begins from the moment the group is initiated and continues through subsequent phases. This is where the group leader attempts to increase participants' motivation to work on the problems that brought them to group. Often participants are reluctant to engage in treatment; they may be in denial of their problems or unwilling to self-disclose. This is especially true for involuntary clients. In the assessment phase, the group leader gathers specific information regarding the problem, including the what, where, who, and when of the situation. Particulars are gathered either through formal assessment instruments or through sharing in the group, with the group leader modeling how to describe the issue. Group members are assisted in examining the short- and long-term consequences of the situation, and their level of satisfaction with their current response to the dilemma is noted. Setting measurable goals is essential to the assessment phase, along with specific timelines. Both individual and common treatment goals are formulated. When group members share common goals, the working of the group can be more efficient, with information and activities structured to facilitate goal attainment. Group goals can be formulated that pertain to the interaction of the whole group; for example, attraction of members to the group will increase from the end of one session to the next, as measured by a standardized questionnaire on group cohesion. Both the group leader and members can assist in identifying goals for themselves and other group members. The intervention phase includes a variety of strategies primarily based on social learning principles. A few such interventions are cognitive change strategies, modeling, role-playing, problem solving, guided group exposure, relaxation techniques, and operant procedures. Group members are an active part of many of the interventions. For example, the group leader and multiple group members provide modeling, feedback, and positive reinforcement for desired behaviors and/or withhold reinforcement in an attempt to extinguish behaviors. Group members assist with all of the specified steps in the problem-solving process, that is, in suggesting alternatives and evaluating outcomes. Additionally, group members are available to provide support to each other as they implement identified tasks. The final phase of the group process is generalization. In this phase, group members are prepared to maintain key learning and to take what they have learned during the group process into their natural environment. This occurs, in part, throughout the course of treatment as members are assigned homework activities at the end of each session that are to be completed in real-world settings (Rose, 2004).

Throughout the group process and at the end of each session, members may be asked to rate various aspects of the group process, such as how close they felt to other group members or how much they self-disclosed during the session. Members may also set short-term, measurable goals that are to be met in a few sessions that will lead to fulfillment of long-term goals. Measurement, outcomes, and evaluation are crucial components of CBGW. The role of the group leader is that of change agent and expert in implementing the treatment process, and the group is both the context and the means (Rose, 2004).

Mutual Aid Model

The mutual aid model presented here is an evolution of the reciprocal model, or the interactional model as it has also been referred to. The mutual aid model reflects the reciprocal relationship or interaction among group members and between the group and the larger social environment.

It stems mainly from the work of Schwartz (1962), who utilized systems thinking in his formulation of group work. His systemic approach conceived of the group worker as a mediator within a dynamic system that is mutually influencing. In his view, individuals and society are in a symbiotic relationship, each needing the other for survival and growth; the unique task of the social worker is to act as an intermediary. In the context of group work, this takes the form of assisting group members in establishing a system of mutual aid among themselves and in developing favorable interactions with the environment (Gitterman, 2004).

The role of the group worker is that of external and internal mediator. The group worker acts on behalf of both the group and the agency that employs him or her. He or she is a resource and attempts to improve the fit between group members' needs and the services provided by the agency and/or the larger society. Internally the group worker is focused on minimizing interpersonal tension within the group and strives to establish mutual bonds among group members (Gitterman, 2004). Although all groups to varying degrees recognize the importance of establishing mutual aid among group members, for this model mutual aid is central. Schwartz (1962, as cited in Gitterman, 2004, p. 98) defined the group as:

> [A]n enterprise in mutual aid, an alliance of individuals who need each other, in varying degrees, to work on certain common problems. The important fact is that this is a helping system in which the clients need each other as well as the worker. This need to use each other, to create not one but many helping relationships, is a vital ingredient of the group process and constituted a common need over and above the specific task for which the group was formed.

Engaging members in sharing experiences and developing a common purpose facilitates bonding. Through sharing and listening to the concerns of others, members begin to see that their troubles are not as unique as they originally thought. They gradually begin to feel less isolated and pathologized and begin to see the universality of their situation. Members reach out and help one another and engage in collective problem solving. They discuss issues, disagree, give each other feedback, provide different perspectives, and build on each other's ideas. In the context of a "multiplicity of helping relationships" (Gitterman, 2004, p. 99), group members can change maladaptive perceptions and behaviors. New behaviors can be rehearsed within the safe context of the group. Additionally, members begin to make connections between private issues and societal conditions, and the consciousness of group members is raised. The collectivity of the group often increases the courage of group members who may opt to engage in social change efforts (Gitterman, 2004).

Like CBGW, the mutual aid model has phases that characterize the group process. In the first phase, preparation, the group leader gets ready by considering logistics such as time, location, child care, food, recruitment, and the purpose of the group. The second phase is characterized by the development of mutual agreements. Here group members are assisted in deciding what they will do in the group or the purpose of the group and how they will go about the work and agree on group responsibilities. In the work phase, the group leader assists members to find common-alities between group members and the systems that impact their lives. Group members, with the assistance of the group leader, identify and deal with obstacles to the workings of the group. The group leader facilitates the mutual aid process through modeling and teaching and by reinforc-ing cooperative norms, directing member's comments to one another, and linking the comments of different group members. Engaging group members in collective activities also encourages the mutual aid process (Gitterman, 2004). In the early phases of the group, the leader is active in facilitating the mutual aid process, yet both influences and is influenced by the group. Mutual aid groups are characterized by shared responsibility and partnership (Toseland & Rivas, 2005).

Relevance to Social Work Practice

Group workers make numerous decisions prior to engaging in group work and throughout the group process. Decisions include types of groups to provide, that is, task groups or treatment groups; if a treatment group is selected, whether its focus will be on skill attainment, rehabilitation, growth, socialization, or support, and who gets to decide; how goals will be achieved; how groups will be structured; what the group worker's role will be; and what the responsibilities of the members will be. The theoretical orientation of the worker, the agency, and the climate of the larger social environment influences many of these decisions (G. Corey, 1990). Although not exhaustive, we have reviewed a number of theoretical orientations for small group work. In this section, we demonstrate some of the ways these theories impact assessment and intervention.

Uses in Assessment

Assessment consists of gathering information and making judgments about the data collected to guide interventions. It often begins prior to group formulation with an appraisal of the needs of the community and continues throughout the course of services. There is not one theoretical framework for assessment; rather, assessments differ depending on the theoretical orientation of the worker or agency, the type of group being provided, and the goals of the group. For example, treatment groups often focus on the problems of individual members, whereas the focal point of task groups is the resources and barriers in the community that will help or hinder goal attainment (Toseland & Rivas, 2005). Another example is an agency with a clinical or psychoanalytic orientation where the intake process includes a thorough assessment of early development and family-of-origin issues versus a community center where assessment focuses primarily on current needs and resources. Each agency has a different purpose and in all likelihood a different philosophical orientation about the root cause of human suffering, which in turn influences the assessment process.

Typically, assessment consists of individual assessment, group-as-a-whole assessment, and assessment of the external environment. It is the emphasis on each that varies. Individual assessment entails assessing the functioning of individual members and gathering information about the causes and consequences of behavior. Part of an individual assessment includes looking at the interpersonal functioning of group members, that is, their social skills and the support network of the individual. It also includes looking at the environmental context in which members function (Toseland & Rivas, 2005). Assessment with multicultural group members considers issues of acculturation, discrimination, institutional oppression, and the possibility that dysfunction may stem in part from sociocultural dissonance (Chau, 1992). Further, the group worker must be mindful that social functioning is characterized differently within various social groups and resist the tendency to apply his or her own cultural lens to others as if it were universal truth (Garvin & Reed, 1994). Remedial, CBGW, and some psychoanalytic groups tend to be more individualistically oriented, and consequently assessment is mainly focused on the presenting problems and functioning of individual group members. This is not to say that these types of groups do not assess group conditions as well, but research indicates that among group workers more attention is devoted to individual assessment than to group interaction and broader environmental factors (Toseland & Rivas, 2005).

Group-as-a-whole assessment centers on the functioning of the group and on group processes. The group worker is especially attuned to communication and interaction patterns. Group workers assess such factors as who dominates discussion, who doesn't speak at all, and whether interactions are predominantly member to leader or member to member. Other group dynamics that are monitored include group cohesion, norms, status hierarchies, and roles taken on by group members. The group worker assesses what roles are being played. For example, is there a gatekeeper who is keeping the group from discussing sensitive issues, or a scapegoat who is blamed for all of the troubles of the group, and what does this mean for the group as a whole (Toseland & Rivas, 2005)? The group leader assesses the extent to which members feel attracted to the group and whether it provides sociocultural safety for diverse members. That is, are differences respected and inequities addressed? Questions to consider include how racial and gender composition impact group interaction, whether subgroups are forming around social identities, whether minority group members speak up and are heard, and whether status positions outside of the group are being re-created within the group. The multicultural group worker must continually assess how the social microcosm of the group might be re-creating the micro inequities that exist in society (Garvin & Reed, 1994). Of primary interest is the functioning of the group as a whole and whether group dynamics are conducive to the achievement of group goals.

Mutual aid and systems-oriented groups are particularly interested in group processes. These orientations recognize that groups cannot be understood simply by assessing individual group members. Like the scientist who understands that to know water is to not only recognize its properties but to understand the combination of hydrogen and oxygen, systems theorists and followers of the mutual aid model recognize that it is the interaction produced in groups that must be assessed (D. Johnson & Johnson, 2006). Interpersonal learning theorists too are concerned with group conditions and the presence of curative factors, but assessment is more narrowly focused on interpersonal transactions (Yalom, 1995).

Environmental assessment consists of assessing factors that impact the group as a whole and not simply environmental factors that affect individual functioning. Such environmental factors include the sponsoring agency, its mission statement, and the resources it allocates for the group, and potentially other service providers. Of consideration is whether other organizations will refer participants to the group or will perceive the group as competition and an unnecessary duplication of services. Another factor worthy of assessment is the broader community and its prevailing attitude about groups, the issue being addressed, and the providing agency. Does the agency have a positive reputation for working with diverse clients and staff who look like community members and speak their language (Toseland & Rivas, 2005)? All of these variables can affect the success of the group and are worthy of attention. Groups that are task-oriented or based on the social goals model are apt to be more concerned with environmental assessment. Also, social workers with a strong systems orientation who place more weight on a holistic view of human systems might be more inclined to undertake a thorough environmental assessment. Systems theorists are concerned with all systems in which the group and its members are embedded, and especially with assessing boundary permeability between systems (Toseland & Rivas, 2005). Theoretical orientation influences the assessment process, but in varying degrees group workers engage in assessment at all three levels (Garvin, 1997).

Uses in Intervention

Just as assessment is influenced by theory, so too are interventions. Goals, group structure, role of the group leader, and intervention strategies vary with theoretical orientation. The goal of psychoanalytic groups is mainly to bring the unconscious into the awareness of group members. This is achieved primarily by creating a climate in the group that allows members to delve into the past and explore family-of-origin issues or traumas that continue to impact behavior (Geller, 2005). The group leader is relatively detached and allows members to raise issues through free association. Free association is when group members communicate whatever thoughts or feelings come to mind without censoring them. An adaptation of free association is the go-around technique, in which each member in turn is engaged in free association and is actively involved in group work and making interpretations. The leader assists members in moving unconscious issues into consciousness by interpreting free associations, transference, defense mechanisms, dreams, resistance, slips of the tongue, and group projections. Interpretations are hypotheses that can be accurate or off-base, and it is essential that they be presented as such. Gradually, members engage in making their own interpretations and in sharing insights about other group members. Group members often provide perceptive observations and direct feedback to each other. Having observed interpretations made by the therapist, group members become adept at explaining the underlying meaning of behavior, thus uncovering the unconscious in themselves and other group members. Interpretation of dreams is yet another significant intervention strategy used in psychoanalytically oriented groups. Dream analysis allows unconscious fears, wishes, and repressed experiences to move into consciousness. Members are encouraged to share their dreams and the meaning they derive from them. Group members then give their impressions of the dream, which often consist of interpretation and their own projections. Through free association, dream analysis, and interpretation, members become aware of the causes of their present troubles. However, insight alone is not sufficient; members must be assisted in working through their troubles. This is achieved by reexperiencing the unresolved issue within the context of the group and arriving at a more favorable resolution (G. Corey, 1990).

Group workers with a theoretical orientation based on learning principles often assume a more directive position in group than those from a psychoanalytic tradition. Group workers frequently take on the role of teacher, coach, or trainer, and groups are often highly structured, with activities designed to facilitate new learning. Generally, goals are aimed at behavioral, emotional, or cognitive change that will result in the eradication of maladaptive behaviors. More specifically, measurable goals are formulated in the early phases of the group with group members (G. Corey, 1990). Interventions include modeling techniques, problem-solving techniques, cognitive change procedures, guided group exposure, relaxation training, and operant procedures. Modeling is one of the most effectual strategies used in group work because there are numerous potential models and sources for feedback. Group members are taught early on how to give feedback, which entails giving praise and encouragement for desired behavior and giving specific direction for changing unwanted behavior (Rose & LeCroy, 2005). The group leader can direct role-playing through coaching, thus ensuring that desired behaviors are reinforced and undesirable behaviors modified (LeCroy, 2002). Systematic problem solving is not unlike what occurs in individual services, but in the group, members participate in the process. Group members bring problems to the group, and other group members assist in clearly defining the problem, generating solutions, examining possible consequences, identifying potential resources or obstacles, and evaluating outcomes (Rose & LeCroy, 2005). Group members may role-play the problem situation and the selected solution and then be assigned the homework of carrying out the task in the real world. At the next group session, the member would then report on the outcome. Cognitive change methods are used in group to minimize self-defeating thoughts and irrational self-talk. This entails teaching clients to identify and control cognitive distortions. Group members are engaged in making positive affirmations and in group exercises designed to alter distortions. Group members challenge the distorted thinking of others and receive corrective information through feedback (G. Corey, 1990; Rose & LeCroy, 2005). Another intervention based on learning theory is guided group exposure. This is when members are exposed to a feared situation within the group and later alone in the real world. This is done in stages, while members use cognitive restructuring techniques, relaxation techniques, and the modeling sequence to cope with the situation. Other interventions already alluded to are relaxation and operant methods (see Rose & LeCroy, 2005).

Systems theory has often been criticized for being too broad and not providing specific direction or intervention strategies that can be followed by systems-oriented group workers. With SCT numerous interventions are provided, such as functional subgrouping, the fork in the road technique, and boundarying, which have already been discussed. Also, systems-oriented practitioners frequently combine their orientation with other theoretical approaches. Donigian and Malnati (1997) in their book *Systemic Group Therapy* discuss group interventions that integrate systems theory with concepts from interpersonal learning theory. The group leader observes the interaction between the different systems in the group—member to member, leader to member, leader to subgroup, and leader to the group as a whole—and describes patterns of behavior. The group worker promotes member-to-member interaction and encourages members to provide each other consensual validation. Interventions consist mainly of interpretation, process illumination, and moving members into the here and now. In this way, the goal of "releasing the power of the group" (p. 82) is achieved and members become conscious of their interpersonal interactions.

Multicultural Group Work

We have demonstrated some of the ways that theory at least minimally influences the assessment process and guides interventions. When working with multicultural populations, it is imperative to examine the goodness of fit between different theoretical approaches and various cultural groups. This requires some knowledge of the cultural background, values, and traditions of clients. When little is known about the social identity groups of members, the group worker can provide opportunities for members to share about their cultural background. This simple intervention can be included in virtually all types of groups, regardless of theoretical framework. For example, if the group is addressing assertive communication, the group worker could ask members how cultural background affects one's ability to be assertive. If the group is engaged in problem solving, the leader might ask group members to think about how others from their cultural background might address this issue (Toseland & Rivas, 2005).

Additionally, the group worker must model acceptance, being non-judgmental of differences, and intervene as necessary to prevent discrimination from occurring in the group (Toseland & Rivas, 2005). It is often easier for group workers to identify individual prejudice and more difficult to recognize institutional oppression. For group workers who have difficulty acknowledging societal conditions that lead to personal troubles it may prove extremely challenging to work effectively with diverse populations (Garvin & Reed, 1994). This may be especially true with certain types of groups, such as mutual aid groups and groups based on the social goals model. Further, the group worker would be limited in his or her ability to create an anti-oppressive group structure in any type of group. Hence, it is essential for group workers to engage in considerable self-reflection about their own culture and personal biases about different social identity groups (Toseland & Rivas, 2005).

The group worker must continually assess whether the group process is appropriate for certain cultural groups and how processes can be modified. For example, one must consider how group members from diverse cultures will respond to a psychoanalytically oriented group where the group worker assumes a detached role. This could be problematic for those from a Mexican background, where *personalismo*, maintaining warm interpersonal relationships, is highly valued (Cauce & Domenech-Rodríguez, 2000). Also for consideration is how members of certain cultural groups will respond in groups where members are expected to consistently share personal troubles. For some cultural groups, it may not be acceptable to share family issues in public (Toseland & Rivas, 2005). In this case, groups that are more activity-oriented and structured might be more beneficial, or simply acknowledging difficulties about sharing private issues and respecting cultural values might suffice. Another potential challenge is the expectation in interpersonal learning groups that members provide consensual validation to one another. This could present an obstacle for some group members who are not direct communicators and for those whose values seemingly conflict with this expectation. For instance, in the Mexican culture *simpatía* is highly valued; this is when individuals choose to maintain interpersonal harmony by avoiding conflict (G. Marín & Marín, 1991). Hence, providing others with direct feedback might seem foreign and unacceptable to Mexican group members. If using a systems-oriented approach to group work, one must consider how boundary permeability might differ for different cultural groups and how family systems rather than individual systems can be involved in groups.

In addition to considering which approaches to groups may prove challenging, it is essential to consider which theoretical frameworks and interventions might be particularly suited for diverse groups. For example, for years Mexican women have engaged in conversations as a way of dealing with adversity, perhaps in the form of *platica* around the kitchen table with their sisters, neighbors, or mother (Madriz, 2003). Group workers can build on this cultural strength by forming mutual aid groups in which group members continue to support one another and perhaps engage in social action to alter some of the causes of their personal suffering.

This is not meant to be an exhaustive discussion of potential problems that may surface in groups with multicultural populations, nor is it meant to specifically address how to engage in culturally competent group work. Rather, our aim is to encourage practitioners to continually reflect on their theoretical orientation, assessment process, and group interventions to determine how best to meet the needs of diverse cultural groups.

Evidence-Based Foundations

Just as practitioners engaged in individual practice are increasingly being called on to demonstrate the efficacy of their services, group workers too are being challenged to illustrate the effectiveness of group work. It is expected that group workers be familiar with factors associated with successful groups and that practice be informed by research on group process and outcomes. Some also suggest that group workers should partake in research to bridge the gap between research and practice and to add to the knowledge base of group work (M. Corey & Corey, 2002).

Group research has evolved, as has practice and theory. The complexity of group work, in which multiple interacting variables occur simultaneously, has made group research challenging. Despite numerous methodological challenges, there is now substantial evidence that group work is effective. Barlow et al. (2005), expanding on the seminal work of Furhiman and Burlingame (1994), examined 30 reviews of group work from the 1960s through 2002. They highlighted the growth in knowledge by decade and the ever-increasing rigor in research. By the 1960s, research that included comparison groups was well under way. However, nonequivalent comparison groups were utilized, primarily with patients who were institutionalized. Researchers noted tremendous group variability in therapists, patients, and treatment models. These early studies provided only tentative support for the efficacy of groups. Generally, findings were that groups are complementary when delivered in conjunction with other services. By the 1970s, outcomes were more promising. Studies regularly demonstrated that group work was at least as effective as individual treatment. By this time, studies were utilizing appropriate comparison groups and more representative samples. The past four decades of research reveals that groups are effective for a number of problems using various treatment models. Many have begun to question why groups are not used more regularly given their cost-effectiveness (Barlow et al., 2005).

In 1977, with the introduction of the statistical method of meta-analysis, researchers were able to compare different types of treatment. Meta-analysis yields an effect size, or an estimate of the average amount of change. Hence, studies began to compare the relative effectiveness of groups and individual treatment. Restricting the data to a single index resulted in contradictory findings. In numerous studies, individual treatment had a larger effect size than group treatment. Horne and Rosenthal

(1997, cited in Barlow et al., 2005) noted that individual treatment exceeded the outcomes of group treatment in studies where groups were used as an expedient service, and leaders did not focus on curative factors, nor were these examined in the research process. Studies that focused on therapeutic factors yielded larger effect sizes. Other meta-analyses have compared long-term and short-term formats and different kinds of group formats. These studies indicate that groups are effective regardless of length and specific group format (Barlow et al., 2005). The recent finding that no one type of treatment is superior to another is consistent with earlier research conducted by Lieberman, Yalom, and Miles (1973, as cited in D. Johnson & Johnson, 2006), in which 206 college students were randomly put into one of 18 different types of growth or therapy groups. None of the different groups was found to be superior to the others (as cited in D. Johnson & Johnson, 2006).

There is a great deal of empirical research that looks at the effectiveness of groups with target populations and at the differential effectiveness of various group protocols that are guided by different theoretical orientations. G. M. Burlingame, Kapetanovic, and Ross (2005) looked at several reviews and meta-analyses and found groups to be effective with depressed patients and with those suffering from eating disorders, anxiety disorders, mood disorders, substance abuse, and personality disorders. They did not find any specific theory of change to be more effective than another. Studies of depressed patients found groups to be as effective as individual treatment, and some studies found the rate of effectiveness similar regardless of whether cognitive-behavioral, interpersonal learning, or support group models were used. Four studies also found self-help groups free of professional leadership to be commensurate in member gains to groups guided by formal change theories. This has led researchers to speculate about the factors inherent in groups that make them effective independent of theoretical orientation and group protocols. Similarly, several studies support the efficacy of cognitive-behavioral group therapy in treating bulimia nervosa. In general, outcomes were greater when groups were used in conjunction with other treatment modalities, such as individual treatment or pharmacotherapy. In other research, two studies found interpersonal learning groups are just as effective as cognitive-behavioral therapy groups on indicators of bingeing and emotional eating. Research also demonstrates the effectiveness of CBGT in treating agoraphobia and social phobia. Yet these positive results are clouded by other studies that indicate that unstructured discussion groups or self-help bibliotherapy, a 3-day CBT workshop, and process-oriented groups result in similar patient improvements. Again, this leads to speculation about the unspecified elements of group work that play a part in patient change (G. M. Burlingame et al., 2005).

Given that research indicates that groups are effective across different theoretical frameworks, many have begun to speculate about what it is about groups that makes them effective. By the 1980s, researchers were exploring how process variables connect with outcomes. Researchers began to look at leader characteristics and behavior and how this relates to group outcomes. Additionally, researchers have consistently looked at therapeutic factors and curative factors. A challenge has been that a majority of studies consider only client reports of factors that helped them and do not consider other measurement strategies (Barlow, Fuhriman, & Burlingame, 2004). Numerous studies support the importance of the 11 therapeutic factors Yalom proposed as essential to the group therapy process, yet there is no agreement on the relative importance of each factor in relation to client outcomes (DeLucia-Waack & Kalodner, 2004). Yalom's (1995) research indicates that therapists and clients are rarely in agreement about which therapeutic factors are essential to the change process. Further, different populations, including individual factors and level of functioning, stage in the group process, and type of group all seem to influence which therapeutic factors are most influential. Generally, group members emphasize the importance of relationship factors. This is consistent with research that points to the importance of leader behaviors that convey warmth, acceptance, support, and genuine interest. Regardless of theoretical orientation, effective group leaders demonstrate these characteristics (DeLucia-Waack & Kalodner, 2004; Yalom, 1995).

Future directions in group research include looking at the effectiveness of long-term interventions, examining how process and content interact to produce positive outcomes (G. M. Burlingame et al., 2005), and, as G. Burlingame, MacKenzie, and Strauss (2004) suggest, discovering underlying group principles across group protocols that are essential for successful groups regardless of theoretical orientation (as cited in Barlow et al., 2005).

Critiques of This Approach

Historically group work was denounced for having an insufficient knowledge base and was not considered by many to be a legitimate form of service. Currently, many theories exist to guide group work, and theories based on individual development have been adapted to be more applicable to group work. Systems theories, psychoanalytic theories, interpersonal learning theory, and social learning theories have all been applied to group work. Research consistently indicates that group work is effective, yet there are still many gaps in knowledge. Researchers are now concerned with uncovering which variables lead to effective group outcomes with which populations and under what circumstances. Aspirations for the future include the possibility of matching clients with the appropriate combination of therapeutic factors to maximize positive group outcomes (DeLucia-Waack & Kalodner, 2004).

All theories have their strengths and limitations. Groups based on learning principles have been criticized for being overly concerned with the individual and not focusing sufficiently on group dynamics. Yet learning theorists have made significant contributions to group work, such as stressing the importance of setting measurable goals, evaluating outcomes, and contracting with individual group members (Toseland & Rivas, 2005).

Psychoanalytic theory as a whole is under tremendous scrutiny (Geller, 2005). Like learning theorists, psychoanalytic group workers have been chastised for focusing extensively on the individual in spite of the contributions of numerous group-as-a-whole theorists. Other limitations of psychoanalytic group work include the length of the treatment process, which is at odds with the managed care system, and its heavy focus on the past. Adaptations to psychoanalytic frameworks and interpersonal learning theory now emphasize the here and now and only minimally focus on the past. Despite the limitations of psychoanalytic theory, it has contributed to small group theory and practice. Psychoanalytic concepts such as insight, defense mechanisms, transference, and ego strength have been incorporated into other frameworks of small group practice (Toseland & Rivas, 2005).

Systems theory provides a broad conceptual lens that is used by a plethora of group workers, often in conjunction with other theories of human behavior. This framework allows group workers to look at groups on multiple levels. Systemic group workers bring a holistic view to group work that looks beyond the individual and linear thinking. Systems theory, more than the other theories addressed herein, highlights societal systems, whole group processes, and the energy that is produced when groups of people interact in a group context (Connors & Caple, 2005). However, systemic group work is not beyond reproach. It is often criticized for being too broad and providing inadequate direction for group workers attempting to put theory into practice. Systems theory provides little guidance on how to change oppressive structures and is accused of maintaining the status quo (Schriver, 2004). This is perhaps the greatest criticism of many of the current theories that guide small group work: They are focused on individual change and have lost their interest in social change and reform. Many feel it is imperative for group workers to address not only individual problems but also the societal conditions that produce them. In fact, for many this is the unique mission of social work, and group work is particularly suited for this endeavor as there is strength in numbers and because of the potential of groups to raise consciousness (Garvin & Reed, 1994).

Key Terms

American Association of Group Workers

Association for the Advancement of Social Work with Groups

Catharsis

Free association

Group work

National Association for the Study of Group Work

Primary groups

Process

Self-efficacy

Social Work With Groups

Transference

Review Questions for Critical Thinking

1. It has been suggested that a "best practice" for group work is to have some clearly defined theoretical model for the group leader to follow. Compare and contrast this notion with that of a more empirical and eclectic model of simply employing methods of group work, which have been shown, via prior credible research, to result in favorable outcomes for group members.

2. Using an electronic database such as *PsycInfo* or *Web-of-Science*, locate a recently published empirical outcome study of group work. Describe the model of group work under investigation, the design used to evaluate the outcomes, the outcome measures, and the results. What applications to social work practice may be derived from this study?

3. How has general systems theory been considered a precursor to social work's "person-in-environment" perspective?

4. Describe a group to which you belonged in the past, or belong to now, and how it has influenced your life.

5. Group work has been criticized as providing too little attention to changing oppressive societal conditions, and of having too much of a focus on helping individuals adapt to conditions of social injustice and unfairness. How legitimate do you believe these criticisms to be?

Online Resources

www.aaswg.org/

The website for the *Association for the Advancement of Social Work with Groups*, a not-for-profit organization of group workers, group work educators, and friends of group work who support its program of advocacy and action for professional practice, education, research, training and writing about social work with groups.

www.tandf.co.uk/journals/WSWG

The website for *Social Work With Groups*, a unique quarterly journal of community and clinical practice, and an important reference publication for those in the social work profession who value and seek to understand the small group. The journal addresses the issues of group work in psychiatric, rehabilitative, and multipurpose social work and social service agencies; crisis theory and group work; the use of group programs in clinical and community practice; and basic group competencies for all social work professionals.

www.groupsinc.org/

The website for the American *Group Psychotherapy Association*, an interdisciplinary organization for group workers.

www.groupsinc.org/pubs/IJGPsubmit.html

The website for the *International Journal of Group Psychotherapy*, an interdisciplinary periodical for group workers.

www.apa.org/pubs/journals/gdn/index.aspx

The website for the journal *Group Dynamics: Theory, Research, and Practice*, which publishes original empirical articles, theoretical analyses, literature reviews, and brief reports dealing with basic and applied topics in the field of group research and application. The editors construe the phrase *group dynamics* in the broadest sense—the scientific study of all aspects of groups—and publish work by investigators in such fields as psychology, psychiatry, sociology, education, communication, and business.

www.youtube.com/watch?v=05Elmr65RDg

A 6-minute clip of a group therapy session among inpatients, conducted by Dr. Irving Yalom.

www.youtube.com/watch?v=H6F0nMrMMd8

A 5-minute video describing a randomized controlled trial of group therapy aimed at treating anxiety among children with autism.

References

Agazarian, Y. M. (1997). *Systems-centered therapy for groups*. New York, NY: Guilford Press.

Agazarian, Y. M., & Gantt, S. (2005). The systems perspective. In S. A. Wheelan (Ed.), *The handbook of group research and practice* (pp. 187–200). Thousand Oaks, CA: Sage.

Andrews, J. (2001). Group work's place in social work: A historical analysis. *Journal of Sociology and Social Welfare, 28*(4), 45–65.

Ashford, J. B., LeCroy, C. W., & Lortie, K. (2006). *Human behavior in the social environment: A multidimensional perspective*. Pacific Grove, CA: Brooks/Cole.

Bandura, A. (1971). *Social learning theory*. Englewood Cliffs, NJ: Prentice Hall.

Barlow, S. H., Burlingame, G. M., & Fuhriman, A. J. (2005). The history of group practice: A century of knowledge. In S. A. Wheelan (Ed.), *The handbook of group research and practice* (pp. 39–64). Thousand Oaks, CA: Sage.

Barlow, S. H., Fuhriman, A. J., & Burlingame, G. M. (2004). The history of group counseling and psychotherapy. In J. L. DeLucia-Waack, D. A. Gerrity, C. R. Kalodner, & M. T. Riva (Eds.), *Handbook of group counseling and psychotherapy* (pp. 3–22). Thousand Oaks, CA: Sage.

Bion, W. R. (1959). *Experiences in group and other papers*. New York, NY: Basic Books.

Burlingame, G., MacKenzie, K. R., & Strauss, B. (2004). Small group treatment: Evidence for effectiveness and mechanisms of change. In M. Lambert (Ed.),

Handbook of psychotherapy and behavior change (pp. 213–249). Hoboken, NJ: Wiley.

Burlingame, G. M., Kapetanovic, S., & Ross, S. (2005). Group psychotherapy. In S. A. Wheelan (Ed.), *The handbook of group research and practice* (pp. 387–405). Thousand Oaks, CA: Sage.

Cathcart, R. S., Samovar, L. A., & Henman, L. D. (1996). *Small group communication: Theory and practice.* Madison, WI: Brown & Benchmark.

Cauce, A. M., & Domenech-Rodríguez, M. (2000). Latin families: Myths and realities. In J. M. Contreras, K. A. Kerns, & A. M. Neal-Barret (Eds.), *Latino children and families in the United States: Current research and future directions* (pp. 3–25). Westport, CT: Praeger.

Chau, K. L. (1992). Needs assessment for group work with people of color: A conceptual formulation. *Social Work with Groups, 15*(2/3), 53–65.

Connors, J. V., & Caple, R. B. (2005). A review of group systems theory. *Journal for Specialists in Group Work, 30*(2), 93–110.

Cooley, C. H. (1943). *Social organization.* New York, NY: Schocken Books.

Corey, G. (1990). *Theory and practice of group counseling* (3rd ed.). Pacific Grove, CA: Brooks/Cole.

Corey, M. S., & Corey, G. (2002). *Groups process and practice* (6th ed.). Pacific Grove, CA: Brooks/Cole.

Coyle, G. L. (1930). *Social process in organized groups.* New York, NY: Richard R. Smith.

Coyle, G. L. (1947). *Group experience and democratic values.* New York, NY: Women's Press.

Dale, O., Smith, R., Norlin, J. M., & Chess, W. A. (2006). *Human behavior and the social environment: Social systems theory* (5th ed.). Boston, MA: Pearson Allyn & Bacon.

DeLucia-Waack, J. L., & Kalodner, C. R. (2004). Contemporary issues in group practice. In L. DeLucia-Waack, D. A. Gerrity, C. R. Kalodner, & M. T. Riva (Eds.), *Handbook of group counseling and psychotherapy* (pp. 65–84). Thousand Oaks, CA: Sage.

Donigian, J., & Malnati, R. (1997). *Systemic group therapy: A triadic model.* Pacific Groves, CA: Brooks/Cole.

Douglas, T. (1979). *Group processes in social work: A theoretical synthesis.* New York, NY: Wiley.

Durkheim, E. (1997). *The division of labor.* New York, NY: Free Press.

Durkin, H. E. (1972). Analytic group therapy and general systems theory. In C. J. Sager & H. S. Kaplan (Eds.), *Progress in group and family therapy* (pp. 9–17). New York, NY: Brunner/Mazel.

Follet, M. P. (1920). *The new state.* New York, NY: Longmans, Green.

Freud, S. (1922). *Group psychology and the analysis of the ego.* London, UK: Psychoanalytic Press.

Furhiman, A., & Burlingame, G. (1994). Group psychotherapy: Research and practice. In A. Fuhriman & G. M. Burlingame (Eds.), *Handbook of group psychotherapy: An empirical and clinical synthesis* (pp. 3–40). New York, NY: Wiley.

Garvin, C. D. (1997). *Contemporary group work* (3rd ed.). Boston, MA: Allyn & Bacon.

Garvin, C. D., Gutiérrez, L. M., & Galinsky, M. J. (2004). Introduction. In C. D. Garvin, L. M. Gutiérrez, & M. J. Galinsky (Eds.), *Handbook of social work with groups* (pp. 1–9). New York, NY: Guilford Press.

Garvin, C. D., & Reed, B. G. (1994). Small group theory and social work practice: Promoting diversity and social justice or recreating inequities? In R. R. Greene (Ed.), *Human behavior theory: A diversity framework* (pp. 173–201). Hawthorne, NY: Aldine de Gruter.

Geller, M. H. (2005). The psychoanalytic perspective. In S. A. Wheelan (Ed.), *The handbook of group research and practice* (pp. 87–105). Thousand Oaks, CA: Sage.

Gitterman, A. (2004). The mutual aid model. In C. D. Garvin, L. M. Guitiérrez, & M. J. Galinsky (Eds.), *Handbook of social work with groups* (pp. 93–110). New York, NY: Guilford Press.

Hutchinson, E. D. (2003). *Dimensions of human behavior: Person and environment* (2nd ed.). Thousand Oaks, CA: Sage.

Johnson, D. W., & Johnson, F. P. (2006). *Joining together: Group theory and group skills* (9th ed.). Boston, MA: Pearson Allyn & Bacon.

Lebon, G. (1896). *The crowd*. London, UK: T. Fisher Unwin.

LeCroy, C. W. (2002). Child therapy and social skills. In A. R. Roberts & G. J. Greene (Eds.). *Social work desk reference* (pp. 406–412). New York, NY: Oxford University Press.

Lewin, K. (1939) Experiments in social space. *Harvard Educational Review, 9*, 21–22.

Liberman, J. (Ed.), (1938). *New trends in group work*. New York, NY: Association Press.

Madriz, E. (2003). Focus groups in feminist research. In N. K. Denzin & Y. S. Lincoln (Eds.), *Collecting and interpreting qualitative materials* (2nd ed., pp. 363–387). Thousand Oaks, CA: Sage.

Marín, G., & Marín, B. V. (1991). *Research with Hispanic populations*. Newbury Park, CA: Sage.

McDougall, W. (1920). *The group mind*. New York, NY: Putnam.

Middlemann, R. R., & Wood, G. G. (1990). Reviewing the past and present of group work and the challenge of the future. *Social Work With Groups, 13*(3), 3–19.

Reid, K. E. (1981). *From character building to social treatment: The history of the use of groups in social work*. Westport, CT: Greenwood Press.

Rose, S. D. (2004). Cognitive-behavioral group work. In C. D. Garvin, L. M. Gutiérrez, & M. J. Galinsky (Eds.), *Handbook of social work with groups* (pp. 111–135). New York, NY: Guilford Press.

Rose, S. D., & LeCroy, C. W. (2005). Behavioral group therapy with adults. In M. Hersen (Ed.), *Encyclopedia of behavior modification and therapy* (Vol. 2). Thousand Oaks, CA: Sage.

Rutan, J. S., & Stone, W. N. (2001). *Psychodynamic group psychotherapy*. New York, NY: Guilford Press.

Schriver, J. M. (2004). *Human behavior and the social environment: Shifting paradigms in essential knowledge for social work practice* (4th ed.). Boston, MA: Pearson Allyn & Bacon.

Schwartz, W. (1962). Toward a strategy of group work practice. *Social Service Review, 36*(3), 268–279.

Simmel, G. (1950). *The sociology of Georg Simmel* (Kurt Wolff, Ed. & Trans.). New York, NY: Free Press.

Slavson, S. R. (1964). *A textbook in analytic group psychotherapy*. New York, NY: International Universities Press.

Stroizer, A. L. (1997). Group work in social work education: What is being taught? *Social Work With Groups, 20*(1), 65–77.

Toseland, R. W., & Rivas, R. F. (2005). *An introduction to group work practice* (5th ed.). Boston, MA: Pearson.

Toseland, R., & Siporin, M. (1986). When to recommend group treatment: A review of the clinical and research literature. *International Journal of Group Psychotherapy*, *36*(2), 171–201.

Turquet, P. M. (1974). Leadership: The individual and the group. In G. S. Gibbard, J. J. Hartman, and R. D. Mann (Eds.), *Analysis of groups*. San Francisco, CA: Jossey-Bass.

von Bertalanffy, L. (1968). *General systems theory*. New York, NY: Braziller.

Wolf, A, & Schwartz, E. K. (1962). *Psychoanalysis in groups*. New York, NY: Grune & Stratton.

Wood, J. T., Phillips, G. M., & Pedersen, D. J. (1996). Understanding the group as a system. In R. S. Cathcart, L. A. Samovar, & L. D. Henmen (Eds.), *Small group communication: Theory and practice* (7th ed., pp. 12–23). Madison, WI: Brown & Benchmark.

Yalom, I. D. (1995). *The theory and practice of group psychotherapy* (4th ed.). New York, NY: Basic Books.

Chapter 11
Family Systems Theory

Martha Morrison Dore

> As you read this chapter, think about the family system with which you are most familiar, your own or some other, and ask yourself, "What are the repetitive patterns of interaction (Who talks with whom? Who is allied with whom? Whose voice is strongest and whose is weakest?) in that family system and how do they affect various family members?"

The 20th century was marked by efforts of scholars from a variety of disciplines to conceptualize the role of the family in society and in the life of the individual. As a result, there is no single entity that can be termed *family theory*, but a multiplicity of theories that have informed our understanding of the function of family as shaped by culture, class, and historical context. This chapter briefly examines the historical and conceptual origins of family theory in Western society, culminating in the identification of the contemporary family theory that has the most salience for social work practice: family systems theory. I identify basic and advanced principles of this theory as well as recent theoretical developments that contribute to our 21st-century interpretation and application of this theory in practice. Finally, the evidence base for this theory is examined, as are historical and contemporary critiques of family systems theory and its application to social and individual functioning.

Historical and Conceptual Origins

To understand the origins and development of theories of the family it is necessary to view these theories in the historical context of their times. Prior to the mid-19th century in Western cultures, the primary role of family in society was an economic one. Before the advent of widespread industrialization, families were largely independent economic units, expected to produce sufficient goods to be self-sustaining, whether by their own labor or through the labor of those they maintained. Activities that we now consider functions of the community or state, such as education, care for the ill and disabled, and marketing the results of production, were then managed largely by the family unit. Families supported the larger society, rather than the other way around.

Life during this period was precarious. Pre–Civil War era graveyards are dotted with the graves of young wives dead in childbirth and of infants who failed to survive past toddlerhood. It is not unusual to see a grave marker for a husband and father of the period surrounded by the graves of several wives and the many young children who predeceased him. The exigencies of family life during these times suggest to some historians of the family that the value placed on individual family members, including children, was different than in present times.

Childhood was not a protected and protracted period, as it is today. Children as young as 3 years were expected to contribute their labor to the family's economic well-being. On the farm, even very young children could feed the chickens and gather eggs or help sow seeds at planting time. In urban areas, selling pencils, apples, or newspapers on city streets occupied the waking hours of children who would nowadays be learning their ABCs in kindergarten. With the advent of manufacturing, first in the Northeast and then, after the Civil War, in other parts of the country, children as young as 5 or 6 spent 10 hours a day working the looms of textile plants or sewing buttons on shirts in back alley sweatshops.

Economic survival dominated family life prior to the 20th century and, for some, well into that century. However, after the Civil War, as federal, state, and local governments began gradually to expand their functions, taking on more and more of the responsibilities that formerly belonged to the family, the shape of family life in the United States began to change. As a substantial middle class emerged from the aftermath of the Industrial Revolution and the shift in this country from an agrarian to a manufacturing economy increased in tempo, fewer and fewer families needed to depend on the economic contributions of their youngest members. As a result, domesticity and family life took on heightened meaning. The late 19th and early 20th centuries saw the emergence of women's magazines devoted to the art of homemaking. Except for poor and single women who had no other choice but to work at low-wage jobs, the roles of women became increasingly restricted to those of wife and mother.

At the same time, childhood was increasingly recognized as a special period of psychological and social development in which essential learning and socialization take place. This recognition was codified at the turn of the 20th century in the U.S. public school movement, which sought to prepare youth for participation in the larger society, as well as through federal legislation that limited the working hours of children and banned them altogether from working in certain high-risk occupations. Like the rise in magazines and manuals instructing women in the finer points of caring for a home, there was a similar effort on the part of "experts" to educate parents, more particularly mothers, regarding modern approaches to child rearing.

It was around this time that the first theories of the family were promulgated to explain the changing role of the family in 20th-century society. The first coherent family theory was based on the functionalism of Auguste Comte and Emil Durkheim, social philosophers who held that society is like the human body; it is made up of various parts or structures, such as government and the family, that must function together in a way that ensures equilibrium for the society as a whole. Each of these structures has a specific role to play; however, these roles are interdependent and must function smoothly if the society is to sustain itself. These structural functionalists argued that there is consensus within a society as to roles and functions of the various social structures. Norms and values are expressed through sanctions, punishment, and social approval and disapproval and are transmitted at the most basic level by the family.

During the first half of the 20th century, the developing profession of sociology in the United States was in the forefront of advocating structural-functional theory. Talcott Parsons was perhaps the best-known proponent of this theory. He further refined structural-functional theory and its application to the family, introducing the concepts of expressive and instrumental roles. Parsons recognized that many of the functions that were formerly carried out by the family, such as education and economic production, had been assigned to other social structures in contemporary society. The family in the 20th century, as he saw it, had two primary functions: (1) procreation and the socialization of children and (2) meeting the expressive needs of its adult members.

The intact nuclear family was viewed as the ideal structure to carry out these functions. In this theoretical model, the instrumental functions of the family, that is, the provision of economic resources, were carried out by the male head of household, while the expressive functions were the responsibility of the adult female in the family, in this theory, the wife. She was responsible not only for the care and socialization of the children, but for providing emotional support for her spouse. This division of labor, according to Parsons, was functional not only for the family as a unit, but also for the marital relationship. It was also functional for the larger society in which the family was expected to maintain itself as an autonomous and isolated unit, linked to the larger social system only through the male household head's instrumental role.

In the 1960s, structural-functional theory came under increasing attack for its failure to explain the existence of poverty, social change, and social injustice. The argument that inequity served a functional purpose for society did not satisfy those seeking a more equitable distribution of society's goods and services. The theory appeared to justify the status quo, particularly the dominance and privilege of a patriarchal social system and, by extension, a patriarchal view of the family. The fixed nature of family roles, the family's static position in society, the rigid division between instrumental and expressive functions, and the inherently conservative and consensus nature of this theoretical model were all subjected to severe criticism during this era. Today, structural-functional family theory is largely discredited by sociologists as a reflection of an earlier time, although many recognize Parsons for his pioneering efforts to define the role of the family in society and his description of the internal structure of family life.

An alternative to structural-functional theory, developed primarily by economists and social psychologists beginning in the late 1950s and early

1960s, is social exchange theory (Blau, 1964). This theory is based on the premise that all human interaction is based on exchange of rewards and costs. It assumes that individuals establish and continue social relations based on the expectation of mutual advantage (Nye, 1979). This mutual advantage is framed in concepts such as reward and punishment, pleasure and pain, cost and benefit.

Applying this theory to the family, social psychologists have frequently used it in analyzing mate selection, the underlying rationale for choosing one partner over another (Rosenfeld, 2005). The notion of social exchange as a basis for creating a family is clearly illustrated in the customs of cultures with arranged marriages, where the social and economic value of a potential spouse is carefully weighed by each of the participating families. But even in the United States, where marriages ostensibly occur because of love, not barter, according to exchange theorists there is an underlying expectation of mutual advantage that shapes decisions about who is an appropriate marriage candidate. At its most obvious, this is why elderly rich men can marry beautiful young women. Or why statistics show that highly educated African American women are more likely to remain single than similarly educated White women: The opportunities for equal exchange are fewer because, due to the historical effects of racism, there are fewer highly educated African American males relative to females than White males. Exchange theory suggests that individuals select relationships, particularly long-term relationships, that maximize social and economic advantage.

Social exchange theory also holds that the elements of exchange in a relationship strengthen social bonds of obligation, trust, and solidarity. Exchange does not have to take place at the same point in time; parents may invest emotionally and economically in their children with the expectation that the children will reciprocate by performing well in school, staying out of trouble with the authorities, excelling in sports, or engaging in other behaviors that reflect well on their parents. They may also help support their parents in old age.

Indeed, another frequent application of social exchange theory in family life is in the area of intergenerational assistance as scholars seek to understand the obligations of succeeding generations to those that preceded them (Hogan, Eggebeen, & Clogg, 1993). Why, for example, do many adult children feel obligated to assist elderly parents or grandparents, sometimes to their own detriment? Social exchange theorists view this as a type of exchange in which the younger generation reciprocates for earlier care and support.

Like structural-functional theory before it, social exchange theory has come under fire for its reduction of human relationships to matters of rational choice and for its neglect of the impact of institutional power as opposed to personal power, authority relations, coercion, and other aspects of the larger society on individual capacity for social exchange (Molm, Quist, & Wiseley, 1994). It would also seem to exclude nonrational aspects of human functioning such as intuition and altruism as a basis for social interaction and family relations (Macy & Flache, 1995). Like structural-functionalism, social exchange theory has also been criticized for embracing a patriarchal understanding of family formation. In a society where men hold a disproportionate amount of power and resources, women are left with little bargaining power in exchange relationships except for physical attractiveness and their willingness to accede to the needs of men (Markovsky, Willer, Simpson, & Lovardia, 1997).

A third theoretical perspective that has been widely applied to the family is symbolic interactionism, arguably the most enduring and, some would say, important theoretical framework in contemporary sociology in the United States. Like social exchange theory, symbolic interactionism focuses on understanding and interpreting the interactions between individuals in society (Blumer, 1969). The theory holds that individuals respond not directly to the actions of others, but to their subjective interpretations of these actions. In this theory, human interaction is mediated by the use of symbols, which are used to communicate commonly understood meanings within a society (Berger & Luckmann, 1967).

However, unlike the theories examined previously, in symbolic interactionism the individual interprets and responds to the symbol in his or her own way (Charon, 1979). This may or may not be the interpretation and response determined by the larger society. For example, the flag of the United States is a commonly understood symbol, denoting to many the ideals of participatory democracy, equality, and justice for all. The usual response to the flag as a symbol of these qualities is to treat it as a representational object in a particular, prescribed way. However, for some individuals in society, this symbol may have a different meaning that determines different responses to the flag and results in actions that reflect contempt, anger, frustration, or rejection. The periodic debates in Congress over flag burning are illustrative of how symbols are used to communicate deeper issues that divide a populace.

It is not difficult to see that, when applied to families, symbolic interactionism is a much more nuanced, flexible, and contextual understanding of family interaction and functioning than either structural-functional or social exchange theory. In symbolic interactionism, the individual occupying a familial role, such as mother or father, has considerable flexibility and innovation in determining how that role is carried out overall and in any particular situation. At the same time, there is a common, shared definition of the roles of mother and father in every culture that acts as a symbolic referent of how a mother and father act in a given situation (Blumer, 1969). Contrast this with structural-functional theory in which family roles are rigidly defined by the structure of the family and its function in the larger society, and any failure to conform is viewed as deviant. Research that has focused on the single-parent family as an inherently inadequate family structure reflects a structural-functional interpretation of the family.

The critique of symbolic interactionism as a theory of family has focused on its viewpoint that all participants in social interaction have equal power in relationships. Feminists have questioned, for example, whether women are truly free to create the roles of wife and mother as they wish, or whether these roles are so prescribed by the larger society and the local community that deviation from expected behavior is sanctioned. Consider, for example, that, although 80% of mothers of children over the age of 1 year are in the workforce, there is little or no collective dialogue about public policies that support parents in the workplace, such as the paid parental leave so common in other postindustrialized nations. Publicly funded child care, except for the neediest families and then only for a specified period of time, is a topic that is hardly discussed. Could it be that, despite the overwhelming majority of mothers with small children who are working outside the home, our collective definition of the role of mother is still shaped by the symbol of mother as the primary, or only, source of care and nurture for children?

Although each of these theories of the family has something to offer in broadening our understanding of the role and function of this institution in society, their individual contributions to our understanding of individual psychosocial development and functioning in context are limited. It wasn't until the emergence of family systems theory in the 1960s and 1970s that a theory of the family that could inform both policy and practice with regard to families and individuals came to the fore. Many see family systems theory as the dominant contemporary paradigm for informing understanding and interpretation of the cognitive, social, and emotional functioning of individuals in society.

Family systems theory grew out of general systems theory, promulgated, beginning in the late 1920s, by Ludwig von Bertalanffy (1968), a biologist, who was concerned with understanding the totality of an organism as more than the sum of its individual parts and processes. Borrowing from emerging ideas in mathematics and engineering, von Bertalanffy applied concepts such as wholeness and differentiation, hierarchy, and finality and equifinality to analysis of life forms as well as to symbolic systems such as the family, which he viewed as occupying the highest level of system types. D'Andrade (1986) further developed this hierarchical model of system complexity, with the first level occupied by inanimate systems whose interrelationships can be quantified in mathematical forms. The second level of complexity is reflected in biological systems, the domain of the natural sciences. As in von Bertalanffy's conceptualization, the third and highest level of abstraction is composed of symbol systems constructed from and dependent on the meanings bestowed on them by their participants. Thus, a family is not a family until it is imbued with the symbols that denote the concept of "family" in a culture and among its immediate members.

For example, in the United States, individuals in a long-term same-sex relationship, particularly one that includes children, may identify themselves as a family, as would many others in the larger society. However, there are some who would reject the term *family* for describing this relationship, arguing that a family has historically been composed of a heterosexual couple and their offspring. One symbol of family, the legally sanctioned marriage license, has become increasingly available to same-sex couples, reflecting growing social acceptance of this family form in the United States.

In 1954, the Society for the Advancement of General Systems Theory was established to foment cross-disciplinary discussion and research on von Bertalanffy's theory. Simultaneously there was a growing science called *cybernetics* that focused on feedback systems and communication technology. The principles and concepts of cybernetics were believed to apply to human functioning as much as to the functioning of machines. Cybernetics was a multidisciplinary science, and its developers included social scientists such as Kurt Lewin, a social psychologist, and Gregory Bateson and Margaret Mead, anthropologists. Bateson and Lewin communicated with one another and with von Bertalanffy so that general systems thinking became infused with ideas from cybernetics and vice versa, and the theory was increasingly used to advance understanding of human functioning.

During the mid-1950s, Bateson was part of a research team at the Veterans Administration Hospital in Palo Alto, California, focused on applying principles of cybernetics and communications theory to the study of schizophrenia. Of particular interest to this team were the effects of paradoxical communication on the development of schizophrenia. In addition to Bateson, the research team also included Don Jackson, a psychiatrist who had trained with Henry Stack Sullivan; Jay Haley, who was to become a nationally recognized figure in the family therapy movement in the United States; and John Weakland, a cultural anthropologist who used his training to inform his observations of families and their interactions. These four authored a famous paper on their work entitled "Toward a Theory of Schizophrenia" (Bateson, Jackson, Haley, & Weakland, 1956), which drew on case examples to support their theory that schizophrenia results from a mother's use of paradoxical communication, which places her offspring in a "double bind." In a double bind, the recipient of paradoxical communication cannot respond to one message in the communication without failing to respond to another, literally driving the recipient crazy. Treatment, therefore, must focus on the nature of the communication between mother and child, rather than on the intrapsychic functioning of the individual diagnosed with schizophrenia, as was dictated by Freudian psychodynamic theory widely in use at the time.

Although this theory regarding the genesis of schizophrenia has since been discredited, it marked the first time that interpersonal processes within a family system were examined for their effects on individual family members' functioning. Interestingly, there is a current body of research on "expressed emotion" in families of persons with schizophrenia that supports the belief of the Palo Alto researchers that communication within families has an effect on the course of the illness, just not in the way that they understood (Hooley, 2007).

During the time that the psychiatrist Don Jackson worked with the Palo Alto VA group, he founded the Mental Research Institute, which provided clinical services based on an integration of general systems theory, cybernetics, and communications theory. He was joined in this activity by Paul Watzlawick, a Jungian psychologist, and Virginia Satir, a social worker trained at the University of Chicago School of Social Service Administration. Watzlawick and especially Satir went on to distinguished careers integrating family systems theory into strategies for treating family dysfunction.

Interestingly, once the notion was introduced that the principles of general systems theory were applicable to human systems, small pockets of family researchers and clinicians began to spring up around the country to apply the theory and refine it in practice. In addition to the Palo Alto group, the mid-1950s saw the arrival at the National Institute of Mental Health in Bethesda, Maryland of the psychiatrist Murray Bowen, who was to become seminal in the development and application of family systems theory in clinical practice. He was at NIMH to embark on a study of Schizophrenia in young adults that involved hospitalizing the entire family along with the mentally ill member. He came from the Menninger Foundation in Topeka, Kansas, where he had received his psychiatric training and stayed on to become a staff member in the Menninger Clinic.

It is likely that while at Menninger's, Bowen had become aware of the new approaches to child guidance promulgated by the Menninger Child Guidance Clinic's chief psychiatrist, Nathan Ackerman. Ackerman discarded the traditional child guidance model of having a psychiatrist treat the problematic child, while the parents, or most often, the mother, were seen by a social worker. Instead, Ackerman, though still interpreting family functioning through a psychodynamic lens, advocated seeing all family members together in treating a child with emotional or behavioral problems (Ackerman, 1954, 1958).

A few years before Bowen arrived at Menninger's, Ackerman (1938, as cited in Broderick, 1993) published his first two papers advocating for a whole-family approach to treating psychological problems in individual members, "The Unity of the Family" and "Family Diagnosis: An Approach to the Preschool Child." In his conceptualization of the family, Ackerman drew on elements of social exchange theory, defining the interactions among family members in terms of the exchange of love and material goods. He saw families not as a composite of individual members operating in isolation from one another, but as an interactive whole, in constant interaction, influencing one another, a basic tenet of family systems theory.

Ackerman was also influenced by symbolic interactionism in his emphasis on the influence of social roles, particularly in the ways these roles are defined and carried out within the family. Unlike the communications theorists in Palo Alto, Ackerman believed that communicated understandings about roles within the family are insufficient, that the actual performance of the role is key to understanding family dynamics and functioning. Families got into trouble, according to Ackerman, when role performance was either too rigid and unable to adapt to changing environmental circumstances, or too loose and undefined, thereby failing to carry out significant aspects of role performance.

At the same time that Ackerman and Bowen were beginning to develop their interpretations of family systems theory and apply them in practice, the psychiatrist Carl Whitaker assumed the chairmanship of the Emory University Department of Psychiatry in Atlanta, where he, too, was involved in treating individuals with schizophrenia and their families. Though he left Emory in the mid-1950s, Whitaker continued to develop his approach to working with families with colleagues Thomas Malone and John Warkentin at the Atlanta Psychiatric Clinic. Like Nathan Ackerman, he had been trained in classical psychodynamic theory, and like Ackerman he began to move away from the individual focus of this framework and toward a more systemic understanding of human functioning. Over a period of many years, during which he served as a professor of psychiatry at the University of Wisconsin, Whitaker developed an approach to the clinical treatment of families that he called symbolic-experiential, based on the principles of family systems theory (Whitaker & Bumberry, 1988).

In his seminal work *The Structure of Scientific Revolutions* (1964/1970), Thomas S. Kuhn notes that radical shifts in disciplinary matrices, which are sets of concepts, values, techniques, and methodologies, come when an increasing body of evidence undermines the basic tenets of current practice. Because of contextual changes in the social or cultural environment, traditional matrices no longer seem to fit the existing traditions of scientific practice. Nontraditional thinkers begin to explore alternative theoretical paradigms. The simultaneous exploration and adoption by researchers and theoreticians in widely dispersed locations in the United States of general systems theory as the preferred explanatory model for understanding and interpreting the development of individuals in the context of the family illustrate events described by Kuhn's model.

Basic Theoretical Principles

Although general systems theory has evolved over the years since it was first promulgated by von Bertalanffy and enlarged on according to the discipline to which it is being applied, there are common theoretical principles that span applications. First is the concept of system itself. A *system* is an entity composed of elements in interaction to achieve a specified purpose or goal. The function of a system is to process resources or materials into a product or outcome that achieves that purpose or goal. This resource processing requires energy, whether man-made or naturally occurring, that is sustained in various ways. A system is said to be more than the sum of its various parts. Although each part may be distinguishable within the system, how the parts fit together and produce a unique entity is also distinguishable from other, similar systems. The term *synergy* is used in systems theory to describe the process by which a system's elements or properties work together to generate a whole that is greater than the sum of its parts.

This definition of system can be applied as easily to a single-cell organism as to a built machine or a bureaucratic organization. What differentiates these entities is, first of all, their level of *complexity*.

As noted previously, general systems theory organizes systems according to their level of complexity, which describes their responsiveness to external stimulation or change and their ability to self-regulate. A clock is an example of a system at a low level of complexity. Although its components are organized to achieve a specific goal, that of telling time, it is relatively limited in its ability to respond to events in its environment (being dropped, for example) and its capacity to self-regulate in response (it either breaks or it does not). A clock represents what we would call a *closed system*. There are fixed, automatic relationships among its parts, and it can neither initiate nor respond to events taking place outside its own boundaries. Indeed, the *boundaries* that define what is part of the clock and what is not are easily observed and clearly defined.

In an *open system*, on the other hand, boundaries are more permeable, such that the system itself is influenced by, and in turn influences, its environment. A university is a perfect example of an open system. Its primary function is the creation, generation, and dissemination of knowledge, and, to carry out this function, it must receive *inputs* from the larger environment in which it exists, in the form of students, faculty, financial resources, and information. These inputs are transformed by the university into new materials or *outputs*, which include graduates who are able to contribute to the functioning of the larger social system of which the university is a part, as well as new knowledge of particular aspects of that environment.

The concepts of boundaries and their permeability are key in general systems theory and, as we shall see, in their application to the family as one type of system. Boundaries differentiate a specific system from its larger environmental context. A boundary is the line or point at which something is either outside or inside a particular system. Boundaries also differentiate *subsystems* within a single system. In a bureaucratic organization, for example, boundaries are clearly defined between various organizational levels, such that those individuals on the lowest organizational level must relate only to their immediate superiors in the hierarchy or risk violating rigidly constructed boundaries that define who can discuss various aspects of the organization's day-to-day work with whom. Taking problems or complaints directly to a unit director, bypassing one's immediate supervisor, is usually considered a clear violation of bureaucratic subsystem boundaries and is open to sanction by the organization.

Hierarchy is also a central concept in systems theory, not only denoting a descending level of complexity of various systems, but also describing the levels of organization within more complex systems. Bureaucratic organizations represent an obvious example of systems with clearly defined hierarchies, as suggested by the example just given. An ecological food chain may represent another kind of hierarchy, in which larger animals depend for survival on eating less powerful or agile animals, which in turn depend on even smaller animals, who in turn depend on insects or plants for survival. Although not a system in the same sense as an organizational bureaucracy, an ecological food chain is a system in that its boundaries are clearly defined (lions prey on antelope and wildebeests, not other lions or elephants) and its elements interact to serve a specific purpose or function: survival of the species.

Equifinality is another term associated with general systems theory that has been applied in family systems theory as well. Equifinality refers to the notion that there is more than one way to achieve a particular outcome in a given system. In the education system, for instance, young children can be taught to read using phonetics and sounding out various words, or by memorization and sight reading, or by tactile methods such as cutting letters out of various materials and arranging them in various ways. Each method requires different resources and skills on the part of the teacher and engages different aspects of a child's cognitive and sensory systems. One or another method may be a better fit for an individual child. However, all can eventuate in the same outcome, that of reading.

Finally, von Bertalanffy and his followers recognized that all systems require energy to support system functioning over time. *Homeostasis* represents a system's ideal state, when the energy expended by the system is perfectly balanced by the energy coming into the system from the environment. All systems seek homeostasis and will do whatever it takes to reach and maintain that steady state. *Entropy* is the processes a system uses to balance its inputs, especially its energy inputs, and outputs over time. A university that cannot attract able students or faculty or lacks funding for knowledge development in the form of research begins to lose energy and cannot maintain its output of high-achieving graduates and new knowledge over time. Such an organization is said to be in a state of *negative entropy*, in which it lacks the energy to fulfill its function in the larger environment.

Readers who are familiar with the concepts of family systems theory recognize how the terms used in general systems theory have been applied to describe elements of family functioning and interaction. This application is explicated in the following section.

Advanced Theoretical Principles

As the concepts and principles of general systems theory were increasingly incorporated into the rubric of family systems theory, they were expanded to explain the unique elements in family system functioning. The early pioneers in family systems thinking contributed their own understanding and interpretations to the lexicon of family systems theory. One of the earliest and most remarkable of these contributors was Murray Bowen, whose early research on mothers and their schizophrenic children at the Menninger Clinic and, later, at the National Institute of Mental Health, where he studied whole families, resulted in his concept of *differentiation*.

Differentiation refers to the capacity of the individual for individuation from others and for employing thinking over feeling as a basis for action. In his NIMH study, in which he observed fathers as well as mothers of young adults with schizophrenia, Bowen identified the process of *triangulation* in families, whereby conflict between two family members is diverted by involving a third party, whether this is another family member or an outsider, such as a therapist.

Perhaps Bowen's (1978) most famous contribution to the advancement of family systems theory was his concept of the *multigenerational transmission of nuclear family processes*. This important concept is reflected in the reliance in family treatment on the use of genograms to identify dysfunctional patterns and emotional processes that occur across generations of the same family (Klever, 2004). Bowen held that an individual's level of differentiation was always reflective of that of his or her parents; however, how that level of differentiation manifests in subsequent generations varies and increases or decreases depending on the specific social and political environments in which succeeding generations live and function. Bowen believed, for example, that wartime always brought about a reduction in differentiation among the general populace, resulting in reliance on emotion over thought and opening society to the influence of propaganda. He would not be surprised, for example, at the vulnerability of the American people to manipulation by those in power in the aftermath of the September 11 attack on the World Trade Center in New York, when collective emotions of shock and fear were running high.

Don Jackson, a member of the Palo Alto group discussed earlier, was also at the forefront of advancing systems theory application to families. His conceptualization of the *homeostatic process* in families, in which families organize to resist change, was a defining principle in family systems theory for decades. A clinical example of homeostasis in families is one in which a child becomes symptomatic in order to divert her parents' attention from their increasingly rancorous marital relationship and to provide an opportunity for the parents to work together to address her difficulties.

Jackson (1959) noted what he called the *redundancy* in families' interaction patterns. He observed that each family develops a set of unspoken rules that govern these redundant interaction patterns, which he called his *rules hypothesis*. These rules may limit the options for change available to families when their customary interaction patterns are no longer functional. For instance, a family's rules may require the father to carry full responsibility for the family's instrumental functions, while the mother attends to the affective or emotional needs of family members. If there is no flexibility in these rules and the mother becomes seriously ill and unable to meet the family's affective needs, the system will be unable to adapt, and this need for affective responsiveness will go unfilled or will be filled in dysfunctional ways (e.g., adolescent daughter begins sexual relationship with older man; 10-year-old boy steals beer and liquor from home and begins drinking and hanging out with antisocial peers).

According to Jackson (1965), all husbands and wives establish what he called the *marital quid pro quo*, which determines the rights and responsibilities of each in the relationship. Some of these arrangements are *complementary*, which means that each partner brings something different to the relationship. One might be more social and the other more retiring, for example, or one might be dominant and the other submissive in the relationship. Other marital relationships are more *symmetrical*, with both partners contributing equally in all aspects of the relationship, including in the instrumental and affective realms. As the economic system changed in the United States in the late 20th century, requiring labor force participation by most mothers as well as fathers, the demand for more symmetrical marriages increased, placing a great deal of stress on couples whose marital quid pro quo called for complementarity.

Jackson and other members of the Palo Alto group focused much of their attention on the marital subsystem in families. Salvador Minuchin (1974), on the other hand, focused on the family system in its entirety, particularly on its *structure*, which he defined as those family transactions that, through repetition, develop a patterned regularity. Like Jackson's rules hypothesis, Minuchin saw each couple as negotiating a pattern of behaviors that lend structure to the family system. Each new family experience, such as the birth of a child, generates a process of negotiation, spoken and unspoken, regarding roles and responsibilities that continually shape and reshape the family's structure.

The maintenance of the family structure, according to Minuchin (1974), is accomplished by emotional *boundaries*, which regulate emotional closeness and distance in a family. This emotional closeness/distance ranges from *enmeshment*, in which there are no clear boundaries delineating where one family member's emotional life ends and another's begins, to *disengagement*, in which emotional boundaries between family members are so rigid as to wall off the emotional life of one from another, making them emotionally inaccessible to one another. Most families are somewhere along a continuum between these two extremes, with cultural origins contributing a great deal to the pattern of emotional boundaries in individual families.

Another important principle introduced into family systems theory is the *family life cycle*, which conceptualizes the family as a system moving through time, encountering specific stage-related tasks that must be integrated into the family process. For example, two individuals come together to form a marital or partner system. This coming together is a process that requires the individuals to rework their relationships with their families of origin as well as their friendship networks. The couple must negotiate a new family structure, including the rules that govern the roles and responsibilities of each partner that will characterize the new family system. The family life cycle concept was first developed by sociologists Reuben Hill and Evelyn Duvall. Duvall (1977) proposed an eight-stage model of the family life cycle that formed the basis for later adaptation by family systems theorists.

Perhaps the most thorough and well-known explication of the family life cycle came with the publication in 1980 of the first edition of *The Family Life Cycle* by social workers and family therapists Betty Carter and Monica McGoldrick, who incorporated family systems concepts into Duvall's life cycle stages, including a multigenerational perspective on family processes. In subsequent editions of their book (1989, 2005), Carter and McGoldrick further integrated elements of systems thinking, particularly with regard to family context, including culture, class, and community, as well as the impact of changes in the family system brought about by divorce, single parenthood, and remarriage.

Lee Combrinck-Graham (1985) further elaborated the life cycle concept, which she called the *family life spiral*, incorporating a systemic notion of process into the framework. The effects of changes in the family system were determined to be either centripetal, or drawing family members together, or centrifugal, pushing them apart. A centripetal event would be the birth of a child, and a centrifugal event would be when the last child leaves home. According to Combrinck-Graham's conceptualization, all families move in an oscillating fashion through the family life cycle, experiencing natural periods of emotional closeness and distance. Problems may occur when a family's capacity to manage the demand for closeness or distance is unequal to the task or when the timing or rhythm of the oscillating spiral is out of sync. For example, an adult child returns to live at home after a divorce, or an infant is stillborn; in the first example, the demand for closeness or distance is unclear, and in the second, the demand for closeness occasioned by the birth of a new family member is disrupted by the shock and grief of mourning the child's loss.

Finally, it is important to acknowledge the emphasis of family systems theorists on the concept of *normal family processes* (Walsh, 2011). This concept focuses on the functioning of the family over time within the larger environment in relation to the nurture and psychosocial development of its individual members. It accepts that certain stressors on the family are normative and to be expected, such as the birth of a new baby or the entrance into college of a teenage son or daughter. Most families are able to handle these normative stressors within their customary structures. However, there are stressors that are of such traumatic import as to challenge even the most well-functioning families. How a family system responds as a functional unit to such traumatic events indicates its flexibility and resilience and is critical to restoration of homeostasis. According to the principles of family systems theory, there are multiple paths to mastery over stressful life events (equifinality); the important question is whether these processes are functional for individual family members as well as for the system as a whole.

Recent Theoretical Developments

*Over the past two decades, the family as a relational environment with systems
qualities has received more and more attention from developmental psychologists
and ethnologists. The recognition that individuals and families are embedded
in a larger network of social systems can also be seen in life span theories,
ecological theories and Lewin's psychological field theory.*

(Cox & Paley, 1997, p. 245)

Systems theory has provided the explanatory underpinnings for current explorations of normative and pathological child development in the context of the family and its subsystems. In developmental psychology, the emphasis has traditionally been on the mother-infant dyad, or parent-child subsystem in family systems parlance.

The concept of attachment is thoroughly embedded in our understanding of family relationships, their formation and maintenance (Marvin & Stewart, 1990). Indeed, research on mother–infant attachment has expanded its purview to examine the role that the father plays, directly as well as indirectly through facilitating or hindering the mother-infant bond. For example, conflict in the marital relationship (marital subsystem) has been determined to heighten tension and difficulty in the mother-infant attachment process (Cummings & Davies, 2002; Erel & Burman, 1995). Further, attachment theorists are paying increased attention to the larger environment in which the family resides to enhance understanding of impediments to parent-child attachment (Belsky, 1999).

The concept of attachment in a family systems perspective supports Bowen's theory of the intergenerational transmission of family processes. It appears that attachment styles are often handed down from one generation to the next. Research has found that adults with attachment styles that have been termed "preoccupied" (the individual is anxious and ambivalent in his or her intimate relationships) tend to seek out partners who have more dismissive or avoidant attachment styles (Kirkpatrick & Davis, 1994). Couples with this combination of attachment styles (sometimes called *pursuer–distancer relationships*) are frequently in conflict, manifesting high levels of distress, hostility, and anxiety in their relationship. As noted above, high conflict in the marital subsystem has been shown to interfere with the development of secure attachment between the mother and infant. This, in turn, suggests development of an insecure form of relating to others, which the child will take into adulthood, resulting in a next generation of preoccupied or avoidant relationships.

In addition to its impact on the formation of attachment, conflict in the marital subsystem has direct effects on child functioning (Cummings & Davies, 2002). Multiple studies have found that children who come from families where there is a high degree of stress in the marital relationship demonstrate a range of emotional and behavior problems as early as the preschool years.

Another area that has been further developed in family systems theory in recent years is the relationship of the family to larger systems in the community and how these affect and are affected by the family system. Garbarino's 1980 study of two Chicago neighborhoods, both economically deprived, one with high rates of reported child maltreatment and the other with low rates, was a beginning demonstration of how the social environment in a community can affect families' functioning. Garbarino found that the neighborhood with high child maltreatment also had high rates of housing instability, limiting neighbor-to-neighbor contact, and increasing social isolation of families (Garbarino & Sherman, 1980). Social isolation is a frequent characteristic of abusive and neglectful families.

Similarly, in a study of Cleveland neighborhoods at low, moderate, and high risk of child maltreatment, Coulton (1996) found that a rise in the use of crack cocaine was associated with a significant decrease in community cohesion, such that residents felt they could no longer count on one another during difficult times. Furstenberg (1993) had similar findings in his study of families in low-income Philadelphia neighborhoods. Families living in a violence-prone public housing project isolated themselves and their children, even from organized activities in a local community center that might have provided both children and parents the kind of interpersonal relationships that could help support them in their daily lives. Furstenburg contrasted his findings regarding the social isolation of families in the housing project with another low-income neighborhood that had a high rate of home ownership and strong kinship networks.

Cross-cultural studies of the relationship between community involvement and child maltreatment show similar findings. In a study comparing communities in Spain and Colombia, Garcia and Musito (2003) found that maltreating families in both countries were less integrated into their communities, demonstrated lower participation in community social activities, and made less use of formal and informal support services than nonmaltreating families.

Families who must raise their children in environments that are unsupportive, even hostile, and that lack even the most rudimentary resources for advancing child development, such as community centers, adequate day care, libraries, and safe and accessible parks and play-grounds, are at greatly increased risk for difficulties in functioning in ways that prevent providing nurture and care to individual family members (Bishop & Leadbeater, 1999; Cicchetti & Lynch, 1993).

In addition to looking outward at the ecology of family life, recent work in refining family systems theory has examined the cultural dimensions of this theoretical framework (Rothbaum, Rosen, Ujiie, & Uchida, 2002; Weinstein, 2004). McAdoo was one of the first to raise questions about the cross-cultural applicability of family systems theory in her 1977 article "Family Therapy in the Black Community." Other analyses of the Black family and how its dynamics differed from those of White families also influenced family systems discourse (Allen, 1978; Axelson, 1970; Billingsley, 1968; Hill, 1972; Hines & Boyd-Franklin, 1982; McAdoo, 1980).

Questions raised by these pioneers soon inspired others to examine family systems theory through the lenses of ethnicity, race, class, and gender (Falicov, 1983; Hare-Mustin, 1978; Luepnitz, 1988; McGoldrick, Pearce, & Giordano, 1982). As we shall see, these analyses challenged some of the basic tenets of family systems theory and its application in practice.

Relevance to Social Work Practice

The profession of social work has long embraced the family as its primary focus of attention. The earliest social workers, whether Charity Organization Society field workers or residents of a settlement house, viewed the family as a crucible in which individuals were socialized to fill acceptable social roles. In Mary E. Richmond's landmark 1917 book, *Social Diagnosis*, she clearly viewed the family as the unit of analysis in formulating a diagnostic assessment for case planning. Although the language of general systems theory was not available to Richmond (1917/1944, p. 137), she acknowledges the importance of seeing family members together, "in their own home environment, *acting and reacting upon one another* [italics added], each taking a share in the development of the client's story, each revealing in ways other than words, social facts of real significance." She also anticipates the family systems theory concepts of family cohesion and disengagement when she differentiates between the "united" and the "unstable" family, describing the united family as showing solidarity with one another, as "hanging together through thick or thin," whereas in the unstable family "there is no bond to hold them together at all" (p. 139).

Mary Richmond recognizes the importance of the functioning of the marital subsystem and advocates that the caseworker explore with the couple those factors, individual and environmental, that place particular stresses on the marital relationship, including differences in background and life histories. She seems to anticipate the work of Bowen and his intergenerational transmission of family processes in her case presentation of three generations of women in the Doyle family, in which the theme of alcoholism abounded. She also foreshadows the contextual understanding of family systems theory when she admonishes the caseworker in the Doyle case, who had closed the case once she had obtained support for the family from the missing husband/father, that the focus of work should be on "the synthetic relation of the industrial, physical, moral and social facts which affect [the Doyle family's] welfare" (p. 142). In modern terms, the totality of the system's functioning should be attended to in order to ensure the optimal nurturance and development of each family member.

It is no accident that one of the first journals for the rapidly professionalizing field of social work was entitled *The Family* (later changed to *Social Casework*, and still later to *Families and Society*). Early issues of *The Family*, which began publication in the early 1920s under the aegis of the Charity Organization Society, which later became the Family Service Association of America, are replete with practitioners' descriptions of their casework with multiple members of a single family, recognizing the importance of family interactions to individual functioning. It is clear from these case accounts that social workers were well aware that when a child was in trouble, there was often trouble at home, and that trouble at home frequently stemmed from problems in parenting and/or from stresses originating in the family's social environment.

Despite the strong influence of individual psychodynamic theory in social work beginning in the 1920s, as evidenced by the diagnostic and functional schools of thought based on the respective works of Sigmund Freud and Otto Rank (Dore, 1990, 1999), family-centered practice has been a consistent theme in professional social work practice (Hartman & Laird, 1983). However, it wasn't until the introduction of family systems theory to the field in the 1950s and 1960s that social workers had a theoretical framework to support their practice with families.

In the first edition of her widely used social work textbook, *Casework: A Psychosocial Therapy*, Florence Hollis (1964), a professor at the Columbia University School of Social Work, made brief reference to the new procedure of interviewing whole families together, but it is clear that she sees this as simply informing the diagnostic assessment of the individual and not as a form of treatment of the family as a whole. In her third edition of this text, coauthored with Mary E. Woods and published in 1981, Hollis devotes an entire chapter to the integration of family systems theory into casework practice. Her citations indicate that she is familiar with the seminal literature in family systems theory, although, as the case discussion in her next chapter indicates, aspects of family systems theory, particularly with regard to the influence of environment, are more difficult to integrate for a scholar so immersed in psychodynamic theory and practice.

Interestingly, unlike other theories for social work practice that were developed in the academy and inculcated in students who then practiced them in the field, family systems theory and the family therapy practice that it spawned seemed to influence social work practice in the field first, and then filter inward to the academy. This was despite the introduction of general systems theory to social workers through a series of social work journal articles and books beginning in the late 1960s (Hearn, 1969; Janchill, 1969; Stein, 1971). It may have been that the level of abstraction at which general systems theory was integrated into social work practice in these introductory missives made it difficult for practitioners to see the implications for their work with clients. It was not until Germain and Gitterman published their formulation of the life model for social work practice in 1980 that a practice approach incorporating systems thinking was readily accessible to social work practitioners.

One of the most positive effects of the incorporation of family systems theory into social work practice over the past two decades has been the decline in "family blaming" and the corresponding emphasis on engaging families as partners in the process of change. Although several of the early family systems theorists promulgated theories of mental illness that held families, particularly mothers, responsible for the problems of their offspring, as these same theorists increasingly interacted with families of young people with major mental illnesses they came to appreciate the very difficult struggles that such families encounter in managing the day-to-day effects of their child's illness. The rubric "parents as partners" has come to define provision of mental health services to children and their families in recognition of the primacy of parents in identifying and advocating for appropriate care (Alexander & Dore, 1999). Social workers have been at the forefront of efforts to include families in treatment planning and service delivery across systems of care (Friesen & Poertner, 1995).

Social workers have long been involved with families known to the child welfare system and have sought ways to intervene effectively with these very vulnerable families to prevent child maltreatment and poor psychosocial outcomes for their children. Removing children thought to be at high risk for abuse or neglect from their families and placing them in foster homes, often for years at a time, was once considered standard child welfare practice (Dore & Feldman, 2005). Little effort was made to maintain family ties and to help families overcome the problems that had contributed to the removal of their children. However, influenced by family systems theory and the growing understanding of the importance of attachment and consistent caregiving in a child's life, efforts were increasingly made to stabilize families in crisis and prevent out-of-home placement of children where possible.

Family preservation to prevent child placement and reunify families became the focus of child welfare practice in the 1980s and early 1990s. Over time, however, it became clear that there were some families whose problems were so great, often due to substance abuse, and their ability to adequately parent their children so limited, that preserving the child's biological family was not feasible. Recognizing a child's need for emotional attachment to extended family, placement with relatives, or "kinship care," became the placement of choice. When there was no extended family to care for a child, adoption was seen as providing an opportunity for attachment and stability outside the biological family.

Under the Adoption and Safe Families Act, passed by Congress in 1997, state child welfare agencies were mandated to terminate the rights of parents within a specified period of time and place children of all ages and with a range of psychosocial needs in adoptive homes. There were financial incentives for states to make adoptive placements. However, as researchers studying postadoption family functioning have found, removing children from a dysfunctional family system and placing them in a loving, nurturing family environment is not a panacea (Dore, 2006). Children who have failed to form even tenuous attachments in their family of origin may present significant emotional and behavioral challenges to kin and adoptive families as they struggle to integrate into the family system (Combrinck-Graham & McKenna, 2006). Family systems theory provides a lens though which the problems and processes of absorbing a new member into an established family system through adoption can be viewed and understood.

Uses in Assessment

Assessment from a family systems perspective is an ongoing process that is informed by observation and integration of information about the family as a whole, about its interlocking subsystems, and about the context in which the family is located. It is not a linear, cause-and-effect process, but one that employs the concept of *circular causality*. We don't simply observe 4-year-old Tommy hitting and biting other children in his preschool classroom, interview his mother to determine his developmental and family histories, then conclude in our assessment that Tommy is displacing the anger and aggression on his classmates that he feels toward his mom, who has recently gone back to work full time.

It may well be that Tommy is in fact angry about this change in his life, but a family systems approach would go further and observe Tommy at home with his mom and dad and whoever else is in the home. If we did so, we might see that his mom and dad are engaged in a struggle over the affections of their son and that Tommy is being triangulated into this conflict in the marital subsystem. When a child is triangulated into a marital conflict, this places a great deal of stress on the child, who usually loves and wants to please both parents. In a triangulation, the child is unable to please one parent without displeasing the other, clearly an impossible situation for a young child to manage.

In practice informed by family systems theory, attention is always paid to assessing the functioning not just of the family system as a whole, but of the interlocking subsystems as well. We look at the adult partners in the home, usually but not always the marital subsystem, to determine the dynamics of that relationship apart from their roles as parents in the parenting subsystem. Is there affection and respect between these two individuals, or does one demean or belittle the other? How do they communicate their feelings to one another? Is one a distancer, that is, does he or she withdraw from emotional connection with others, while the other partner pursues and attempts to gain the attention of the distancer through nagging, criticism, helplessness, or other strategies to regain emotional connection? Is there psychological, physical or other forms of violence in the relationship? Does one partner seem to fear the other, while at the same time goading him or her in subtle ways that generate rage?

Assessment from a family systems perspective is about identifying the rules that structure family interactions in predictable patterns. This identification can come only through repeated observations of family dynamics, which is why interviews with all family members present are essential. When we interview a family over time, we frequently observe sequences of behavior that indicate the presence of a particular pattern of interaction between family members. Mom never talks directly to Dad but, instead, delivers her messages through her adolescent daughter. When Billy, age 9, feels demeaned by his father, he strikes out at his younger sister, who, in turn, complains to her mother, with whom she is allied against the father, who takes out on Billy his frustration at his wife's emotional inaccessibility. These are the kinds of patterned behaviors that become apparent in family sessions and can help the clinician assess family system dynamics.

The concept of *boundaries* is an important one in family system assessment. Not only is there a boundary that defines who is in and who is outside the family, but there are boundaries internal to the family that separate subsystems from one another. In a well-functioning family, these boundaries are clear, allowing each subsystem to perform its appropriate function within the family system. For example, when there are clear boundaries that define the marital or partner subsystem; children in the family know that their parents have a relationship that is special to adults and apart from them. In families where incest occurs, the boundaries around the marital or partner subsystem are permeable, and a child becomes a participant in that relationship, with emotionally traumatic results.

In the parental subsystem, boundaries define who can act as a parent to the children in the family. When an older child is given parental authority and responsibilities over younger siblings, this inducts that child into the parental subsystem, which not only changes the dynamics of that subsystem and may result in the adults in the family treating the co-parenting child as an adult before he or she is developmentally prepared, but it also changes the dynamics of the sibling subsystem, which plays an important role in socializing children in their peer relationships outside the family. This is a family pattern that is often seen in single-parent households, where the parent relies on the oldest child, or more often, the oldest girl, as co-parent of younger siblings.

From a family systems perspective, it is important to remember that nontraditional family dynamics are not automatically pathological. Awareness of cultural and ethnic differences in family dynamics has certainly taught us as much. The important determination in a family systems assessment is how the family's unique patterns and structure are facilitating the optimal functioning and development of individual family members. In a family where an older child is part of the parental subsystem, it is essential to assess how this role is impacting the child's psychosocial functioning. Is the child overburdened with responsibilities that he or she cannot handle, or that are interfering with his or her own social and emotional development?

Single parents and parents in an unhappy marriage may also be tempted to induct an older child into the marital or partner subsystem such that the child receives confidences about the parent's adult activities and emotions and is expected to provide comfort and nurture to the parent much as a partner or spouse would. Again, an assessment would examine the subsystem boundaries and functioning to determine whether the child is being exploited in ways that inhibit or distort his or her own development. Children in such situations are often protective of the parent with whom they are allied and feel wanted and needed in their companion role, making systemic changes difficult for all concerned.

Another important dimension of family system interaction that is open to assessment is that of *emotional proximity and distance*, which ranges from emotionally enmeshed to disengaged. An enmeshed family is one in which the affective boundaries among individual family members are highly permeable; it's difficult to know where one person's emotional life ends and the other begins. In interviews, family members feel free to interrupt and/or speak for one another, to express one another's feelings and ideas. If one family member feels stress, they all feel it; if one member is affected by an event outside the family system, whether positively or negatively, they are all affected. Interestingly, families who are highly enmeshed and have poor subsystem boundaries sometimes have rigid boundaries around the family system itself, such that members are highly dependent on one another and have few outside alliances or resources. There are strong rules regarding family loyalty such that members' individuality and autonomy may suffer.

A family on the affectively disengaged end of the proximity-distance continuum has unusually rigid internal boundaries such that communication within and across subsystems is inhibited and infrequent. There is little affective responsiveness or affective involvement within the family system. On the other hand, in disengaged families the boundaries that separate family members from the outside environment can be diffuse. External systems feel free to enter into and impinge on this family system at will. These are the families who are known to and involved with multiple agencies and organizations in the community, yet are unresponsive to these external ministrations because of their internal disarray. Family members, even very young ones, are expected to be autonomous and independent, essentially to care for themselves. Emotional nurturance and dependence are discouraged, and these families often fail in their responsibility to socialize their members to function according to accepted norms.

Again, it is important to emphasize that any assessment of enmeshment and disengagement in families must take into account the cultural context of the family system. Some cultures value a high level of emotional involvement among family members; other cultures reward emotional distance and self-containment. A wonderful illustration of this is a scene from the Woody Allen film *Annie Hall*. In the film Allen, who is Jewish and a New Yorker, is meeting his girlfriend Annie Hall's Midwestern WASP family for the first time. They are all at the dinner table on Easter, and Allen is struck by their distancing communication, which is all about "swap meets and boat basins." He imagines his own family dinners in the Bronx, where family members all talk over one another, reach for food on one another's plates, and introduce highly emotionally charged and personal subject matter such as physical illnesses and complaints. Clearly a highly enmeshed family system! This scene also reminds us that it is essential for clinicians who are assessing the dynamics of other family systems to be acutely aware of the expectations of their own.

Another element of assessment from a family systems orientation is that of the family *hierarchy*. This concept refers to how the family is organized in terms of status and power. Who is in control? In well-functioning families there are clear lines of authority and responsibility. Someone must be in charge, and it shouldn't be the 5-year-old, although in a surprising number of families seen in child guidance clinics this is so. Well-meaning parents who have been brainwashed by the psychodynamic literature on parenting into believing that young children should not be stifled in any way and who have an unusually strongly willed child sometimes abdicate all power and control in the family to the child. And what child wouldn't love to have the adults in their life at their beck and call? Unfortunately for these children, in the real world outside the family system, most adults are not willing to be bossed around by a 5-year-old and they soon run into difficulties in preschool or kindergarten.

Although it is clear to most of us that a 5-year-old should not be at the top of the status and power hierarchy in a family, the question remains as to who should be. In the early years of family systems work, most of the key theoreticians were men, and most of them had a traditional patriarchal view of family hierarchy. This was also the height of the *Leave It to Beaver* era, when the ideal family was thought to be structured around an instrumental male head of household and an affective female as second in command, much like the structural-functional model Talcott Parsons proposed. The feminist critique of this family structure and its incorporation into family theory called attention to alternative ways of organizing the family hierarchy that allowed for power and authority to be shared in partnership or distributed according to family members' capacity or the specific task rather than assigned by gender (Dolan-Del Vecchio, 2008).

However the family hierarchy is organized, it is important to assess how power and authority are distributed and exercised and how family decisions are made and communicated to family members. A well-functioning family has clear lines of authority with open communication regarding family rules and expectations of family members.

Finally, *homeostasis* is an important concept from general systems theory that has been adopted in family systems thinking. Like all systems, families are constantly adapting to change, both externally and internally driven. As the family moves through the life cycle, the system must adjust and readjust to the developmental needs and circumstances of its individual members. Similarly, there are environmental changes that impact the family system: a job loss, a move, a shift in the political climate or cultural expectations. All place stresses and strains on the adaptive capacity of the family. These stresses put pressure on the family system's customary structures and ways of doing things, its homeostasis.

The greater the stressful life event or the more events that occur at the same time, the more likely it is that the homeostatic state will become unbalanced and the family will be challenged to find new ways of adapting to threats to its customary ways of functioning. Families often present themselves in clinical settings when life events have left the system unbalanced and unable to successfully return to a homeostatic state. Loss, whether acute as in death or divorce, or chronic as in underemployment or the birth of a child whose functioning is severely impaired, often precipitates a crisis in the homeostatic functioning of the family system as various family members struggle to adapt to the traumatic event together and alone. Assessing a family's history of stressful life events can provide important information about the family's ability to respond to challenges to its adaptive capacity.

Clinicians working from a family systems perspective have developed some tools that have proven useful in assessing family dynamics. One of these, particularly useful for social workers who are especially attuned to the family's interactions with the environmental context in which it is embedded, is the ecomap (Hartman, 1995). The ecomap is a visual mapping of the family in relation to the variety of individuals, organizations, and institutions to which it relates or fails to relate in the larger environment. Family members who live together in a household are depicted in a circle in the middle of the ecomap. Relevant individuals and organizations in the community to which the family relates or that are potential resources for the family are depicted in a series of circles arranged around the central family circle. These are usually identified in collaboration with the family itself, although information regarding some institutional relationships may come from referral sources or from collateral contacts made as part of the assessment. Lines are then drawn connecting various family members to those individuals, organizations, and institutions to which they are connected or could potentially be connected as resources.

The structure of the line itself—solid, broken, or crosshatched—indicates the nature of the current relationship with the specific community entity. For example, if the household consists of a divorced mother and her two children, a crosshatched line, representing a conflicted or stressful relationship, may extend from the mother to her former husband, who is represented by a circle with his name inside located outside the family's circle. If the children have little or infrequent contacts with their father, the line from each child to him would be a broken one; however, if their relationship with him is a positive source of support for them, the line would be solid.

An ecomap not only illustrates the presence or absence of resources in the community and family members' relationships to these resources, but can also indicate the permeability of a family's external boundaries. A family with rigid boundaries that is socially isolated from the community with few or no relationships with outside individuals or institutions would be quickly identified using this instrument.

Another important assessment tool in the armamentarium of the family systems practitioner is the genogram (McGoldrick, Gerson, & Petry, 2008). The genogram is a graphic representation of complex intergenerational family patterns. It maps relationships, life events, and patterns of functioning across three or more generations. Family systems theorists generally believe that families repeat similar patterns in functioning from one generation to the next. Research has offered support for this belief. Klever (2004, p. 346) conducted a longitudinal study of 49 Midwestern couples and found statistically significant evidence that "nuclear family emotional processes and areas of symptomology were transferred across generations."

Using the genogram in the family assessment process can help the clinician quickly summarize a great deal of information in a way that informs understanding of current family dynamics in the context of the intergenerational family system (McGoldrick et al., 2008). Genograms also help locate critical life events in the intergenerational life cycle. Repetitive family patterns become clear. Intergenerational family themes such as mental illness, substance abuse, loss and abandonment, high achievement, and creativity and artistic talent are highlighted through the use of this tool.

Although the structure of the genogram is too complex to describe fully here, McGoldrick and colleagues (2008) have succinctly presented a standardized format that was agreed on by a committee of family clinicians and is currently in general use in family assessment. The reader is referred to that resource or to the website www.genograms.org for a full description of this tool.

A number of family theorists and researchers have developed standardized instruments to assess various dimensions of family functioning as part of the assessment process. David Olson and his colleagues at the University of Minnesota (Olson, Sprenkle, & Russell, 1979) developed the Family Adaptability and Cohesion Evaluation Scales (FACES), which, as the name suggests, is designed to capture the family's functioning on two dimensions: flexibility and cohesion. Olson's cohesion dimension reflects concepts in family systems theory regarding emotional proximity and distance; that is, it measures enmeshment and disengagement. He defines cohesion as emotional bonding.

His flexibility dimension is related to family system theory's notions of family structure, hierarchy, power, and control. Olson defines flexibility as the family system's potential for change in its organization (rules, roles, authority structure, etc.) in response to internal or external demands. He notes that families need both stability (homeostasis) and the ability to change their ways of doing things when appropriate.

The FACES instrument, which is currently in its fourth version (FACES IV) (Olson, 2011), has been used in hundreds of studies and has been generally found to have good psychometric properties (but see cautionary studies by Daley, Sowers-Hoag, & Thyer, 1990, 1991). Perhaps more important for the discussion here, its properties of flexibility and cohesion have clear clinical applications (Place, Hulsmeier, Brownrigg, & Soulsby, 2005).

Another family assessment instrument that has been widely used in clinical settings is the Family Assessment Device (FAD), developed by family researchers and clinicians who were originally located at McMaster University in Canada and are now affiliated with Brown University Hospital in Rhode Island (Epstein, Baldwin, & Bishop, 1983). The FAD is based on a model of healthy family functioning called the McMaster model, which focuses on those dimensions of family functioning such as communication, problem solving, and affective responsiveness that appear to have the greatest impact on the functioning of individual family members.

The authors of this assessment instrument subscribe to a family systems perspective, noting the importance of family structure and organization (Epstein, Bishop, Ryan, Miller, & Keitner, 1999). Their instrument attempts to capture the transactional nature of family interactions by integrating family members' perspectives on six critical dimensions into a measure of overall family functioning. This instrument has been widely used in the family treatment field, and its scores repeatedly predict family outcomes such as child behavior problems (Kabacoff, Miller, Bishop, Epstein, & Keitner, 1990). The FAD is easily administered and scored and gives clinicians useful information about clinically relevant aspects of family functioning and dynamics.

Other standardized instruments are available to assess the dynamics of family subsystems such as the marital relationship and parent-child interaction. These can be a useful addition to a clinical assessment, particularly if there are problems presented in a family subsystem when the request for treatment is made. However, when using a family systems framework, it is important to focus primarily on assessing the functioning of the family system as a whole, including its interactions with larger social systems, to gain the most understanding of complex family dynamics and their association with the presenting problem or issue.

Uses in Intervention

The family systems practice literature repeatedly emphasizes that the focus of intervention in family treatment is to help the family discover ways of interacting that allow for the optimal development of individual family members and of the family as a whole. The focus in treatment is on the family process: who speaks to whom, what members are aligned with one another, who is valued and who is scapegoated, whose voice is heard and whose is not, and so on. Observation and analysis of this process as well as use of the various assessment tools described earlier allow the clinician to gain a clearer understanding of what is problematic in the family process and where to focus efforts at change.

There are nearly as many approaches to bringing about change in family dynamics as there are family therapists. Some, such as Carl Whitaker (Napier & Whitaker, 1978; Whitaker & Keith, 1981), immerse themselves in the family system, using their ability to join with the family and their own intuitive skills to bring about systems change. This approach is referred to as *experiential*, because it relies on actually experiencing the family interaction to understand the dynamics that require change. *The*

Family Crucible (1978), written by Whitaker with his co-therapist Gus Napier, provides a compelling account of the treatment of a family using an experiential approach.

Other family clinicians focus on communication style and content within the family system. They notice who talks with whom, who has the "big" voice and who has a "small" voice, and whose communications are routinely ignored. They also attend to the content of communication and note whether it is clear and direct or muddled and containing many mixed messages. The family systems theorists who began with the Palo Alto group discussed earlier in this chapter and who made substantial contributions to the development of a treatment approach with families, such as Jay Haley and Virginia Satir, focused on family communication to inform their treatment, although Haley was later aligned with both the structural and strategic schools of family treatment.

The structural approach to family therapy is perhaps the most straightforward of all family systems-informed intervention models. It was developed purposefully by Salvador Minuchin and his colleagues at the Philadelphia Child Guidance Center so that it could easily be learned by therapists without extensive formal education or training. It is primarily based on family system principles of hierarchy and power and authority. Structural family therapists believe that parents should be in charge of children and that, in many families where children are experiencing emotional and behavioral difficulties, parents are not exercising appropriate authority. Either parent-child alliances are undermining the authority of the parental subsystem or the parental subsystem is failing to function because of problems in the marital dyad. At the risk of oversimplifying, the key in the structural approach to family treatment is to empower the adults in the family to assert their authority and control and to work as a team in doing so. If there is only one adult, he or she is encouraged to look outside the family system for support and gratification from other adults, rather than relying on a child to fill that function, which empowers the child and disempowers the parent.

The Bowenian approach to family therapy, based on Murray Bowen's ideas about intergenerational family process and differentiation of self, focuses on increasing the ability of the family to base decision making and problem solving on a rational rather than an emotional process. Many family therapy approaches purposely heighten family anxiety to open up the family system to change. Bowen (1978), on the other hand, believed that change required a rational approach and sought to lower family anxiety rather than increase it. If a family came into treatment in crisis, the first order of business for Bowen and his adherents was to decrease the emotional tone by allowing family members to ventilate their feelings.

Differentiation of self in the Bowenian approach requires that clients actively rework their individual relationships with members of their extended family system. Bowen believed strongly that, until members of a family were freed from participating in the intergenerational family process, which could be accomplished only by reworking disconnected or distorted family relationships, they would be unable to create a functional family system in the present. There is also a great deal of emphasis in Bowen's approach on managing triangulation therapeutically. Conflict between two members of a family, usually husband and wife, is dealt with by bringing someone else into the relationship to deflect the emotional tension between the pair. The triangulated individual is often a child. The therapist's task in such family triangles is to actively work to remove the child from the triangle and help the pair communicate directly with one another, with the therapist as coach.

Another major approach to treating the family system is that of the strategic and systemic family therapists. These clinicians focus primarily on bringing about behavior change to resolve the family's presenting problem. They do this by trying to identify the sequence of actions that support and reinforce problem behavior, much like a behaviorist would do. Except that unlike the behaviorist who looks at an individual behavior sequence, strategic and systemic clinicians study the interactions in the entire family system to understand the complex sequence of events that combine to result in a particular behavior. Rather than directly working to change some family system dynamic, such as the family structure, to bring about change in the presenting problem, strategic and systemic clinicians focus on the problem itself, directing the family's efforts to change the problem behavior as an impetus for systemic change.

Strategic therapists, in particular, rely on such strategies as *enactments*, having the family act out alternatives to the problem situation in a treatment session, and *directives*, assigning homework such as a family outing with particular meaning to the family to help the family experience themselves in a different way. The use of these strategies is very creative, is based on a thoroughgoing understanding of the dynamics of the family system that support the problem situation, and is designed to subtly challenge a family's way of seeing things that keeps them mired in a dysfunctional process. Strategies like these to evoke family change have been widely adopted in the family therapy field.

Evidence-Based Foundations

The research that supports various elements of family systems theory as well as its application in practice is voluminous and growing. What is presented here is a brief overview of the current evidence base.

Much of the research related to family systems theory has focused on patterns of interaction within and across family subsystems and their impact on individual psychosocial development, particularly of children. One major focus of study has been the relationship between parent-child interaction and child functioning. Although this research has traditionally investigated mother–child interaction and its effects on child development, recent work has explored the role of the father both in direct interaction with the child and indirectly as a facilitator of or hindrance to the mother–child relationship (Johnson, 2001). There is increasing evidence that fathers have unique effects on children's psychosocial development, apart from mothers' effects (Marsiglio, Amato, Day, & Lamb, 2000).

Studies of the marital subsystem and how its functioning impacts the family system lend additional support to family systems theory (Erel & Burman, 1995). A substantial body of research has established the relationship between conflict in the marital subsystem and emotional and behavioral problems in children (Buehler & Welsh, 2009; Davies & Cummings, 2006; Gerard, Krishnakumar, & Buehler, 2006; Katz & Woodin, 2002; Rice, Harold, Shelton, & Thapar, 2006). Recently, the focus of study has shifted from establishing a direct relationship between marital conflict and child adjustment problems to observing the process of influence. As predicted by family systems theory, research shows that marital conflict not only directly impacts child functioning, but also influences how the adults involved carry out their other family roles, including parenting and maintaining the family structure (Bradford et al., 2004). When a husband and wife are in conflict, studies indicate that they may be less able to maintain appropriate subsystem boundaries, such that one parent may emotionally ally with a child against the other parent (Grych, Raynor, & Fosco, 2004), or family cohesion may suffer so that there is little affective involvement between family members (Lindahl & Malik, 1999). These indirect impacts on the family system are associated with problematic child adjustment and functioning (Sturge-Apple, Davies, & Cummings, 2010).

In addition to research on subsystem interaction in the family system, researchers have also studied various dimensions of family functioning as a whole (Johnson, 2003). For example, a recent study on the association between family cohesion and the externalizing behavior of adolescent siblings found an inverse relationship between cohesion in the family system and adolescent behavior problems (M. K. Richmond & Stocker, 2006). Other researchers examined four categories of family functioning—cohesion, enmeshment, disengagement, and adequate (high control, low discord, and high warmth)—and found that children in both enmeshed and disengaged families demonstrated more insecurity in their family relationships and more internalizing and externalizing behaviors, both at the time of the study and 12 months later (Davies, Cummings, & Winter, 2004). A third study of family emotional climate found that high conflict and low emotional engagement in families predicted bulimic activity in a sample of adolescent girls diagnosed with bulimia nervosa (Okon, Greene, & Smith, 2003).

Researchers have also examined the concept of family hierarchy, a central concept in family systems theory. One study looked at the development of family hierarchy over time as well as the relationship between strong family hierarchy and children's conduct problems (Shaw, Criss, Schonberg, & Beck, 2004). These researchers found that adolescent parenting and parent–child conflict were directly associated with low levels of family hierarchy. There was an indirect association between low hierarchy and poor marital functioning, negative child behavior, and living in disadvantaged circumstances. The relationship between level of family hierarchy and antisocial behavior in children was mediated by ethnicity and neighborhood context.

In addition to testing various concepts of family systems theory, researchers have also examined specific frameworks informed by this theory, such as that of Murray Bowen. A study by Miller, Anderson, and Keala (2004) provided empirical support for Bowen's concept of differentiation and its association with marital satisfaction. Another study examined Bowen's concept of the intergenerational transmission of family process by examining role reversal, a relationship disturbance in which the parent looks to a child to meet his or her unmet emotional needs rather than to another adult (Macfie, McElwain, Houts, & Cox, 2005). Role reversal is associated with problems in attention, behavior, and social interaction in children. Macfie and colleagues found that women who reported experiencing role reversal with their own mother on the Adult Attachment Interview were significantly more likely to engage in role reversal with their preschool daughters.

Other studies that appear to support Bowen's concept of the intergenerational transmission of family process have looked at patterns of attachment across generations (Kretchmar & Jacobvitz, 2002; van IJzendoorn, 1992) or at intergenerational pathology in parenting (Egeland, Jacobvitz, & Sroufe, 1988; Oliver, 1993; Simons, Whitbeck, Conger, & Wu, 1991). Other elements in Bowen's framework have not received the same empirical support, including the assumption that couples who marry share the same level of differentiation from their families of origin.

There is also a growing body of research that looks at the application of family systems theory in practice. Carr (2009a, 2009b) extensively reviewed research findings regarding the effectiveness of interventions based on this theory for a wide range of problems that affect adults and children. He determined that there is strong empirical support for using family systems-based interventions either alone or as part of a multifaceted approach in treating problems such as anxiety disorders, mood disorders, alcohol abuse, relationship difficulties, schizophrenia, and adjustment to physical illness in adults, as well as a wide range of social, emotional and conduct problems in children from infancy to young adulthood.

Critiques of This Theory

Various critiques of family systems theory have been referenced throughout this chapter. The major criticisms of the framework are based on its origins in the work of White male scholars and clinicians who are perceived as viewing the family through a patriarchal lens. Women scholars, in particular, saw many of the formulations of the early pioneers of family systems theory in practice as reflecting a dominant male point of view

(Goldner, 1985). For example, Bowen's emphasis on differentiation and autonomy and his belief in the primacy of intellect over emotion were interpreted by women scholars as overvaluing a male perspective. The early focus on mothers as singularly responsible for the problems encountered by their children was particularly anathema to women in the field (Caplan & Hall-McCorquodale, 1985).

In addition, some of the efforts in family systems theory to define the structure of a well-functioning family system appeared to privilege male power and control within the family system and contained limited recognition of the impact of social forces such as sexism and wage discrimination in the workplace on the functioning of women within the family system (Bograd, 1984; James & McIntyre, 1983; Taggart, 1985). Women scholars believed that some interpretations of family systems theory reinforced traditional gender roles, blaming wives and mothers for failing to sufficiently attend to the affective needs of husbands and children (Hare-Mustin, 1978).

That family systems theory and its clinical applications were informed by a limited White male perspective was also the criticism of minority scholars, as noted earlier. The emphasis of the theory on a particular model of family structure based on a heterosexual, two-parent couple and their biological or adopted children did not resonate with scholars from racial and ethnic groups where other family forms were widely accepted. The three-generation household, headed by a grandmother, with her adult children, their offspring, and often containing children or other adults who were unrelated by blood, was not addressed in the discourse on well-functioning family systems. Nor were the struggles of these households caused by historical discrimination and poverty entered into the family systems equation. African American and other nonmajority family researchers and clinicians gradually began to find their voices and influence the discourse on family systems theory. The publication in 1982 of the first edition of *Ethnicity and Family Therapy* (McGoldrick et al., 1982) marked a turning point in the recognition of the importance of cultural awareness in applying principles of family systems theory to practice.

Another major challenge to family systems theory and practice came late in the 20th century in the form of postmodernist philosophy and its application in social constructionism and, more recently, poststructuralism (Dickerson, 2010). The latter eschews preconceived notions of family processes such as *differentiation* and the *marital quid pro quo* as based on a positivist paradigm. The primary underlying belief in post-modernist thought is that all meaning is socially constructed and its interpretation depends on the relative power of the individual constructing the narrative (White, 2007). The postmodern expectation of the clinician in any therapeutic endeavor is to let go of the expert role, to free herself of a position of power and of her beliefs about dysfunction, and to allow clients to tell the story of their unique experience with a focus on finding their own solution to the expressed problem or dilemma (Levy, 2006). An example of the influence of these new understandings is seen in the development of solution-focused therapy with families (Macdonald, 2011).

As the review of family systems research above illustrates, aspects of family systems theory are now a widely accepted part of our understanding of how the individual develops in the context of the family and the larger society. There is no longer any question that the child both influences and is influenced by the family system into which he or she is born. Interestingly, however, as the principles and concepts of family systems theory have become increasingly imbued in our therapeutic approaches to working with individuals, emphasis on treating the family as a whole has diminished. Current funding for mental health treatment often calls for a *DSM* diagnosis and psychopharmacological treatment, even for preschool-aged children. In addition, well-established evidence-based interventions such as cognitive-behavioral and dialectical behavioral therapies are primarily focused on treating the individual, whether alone or in groups. Despite these factors, family systems theorists and clinicians have continued to develop and test new family-based models to treat a variety of specific problems and disorders.

One example is multisystemic therapy (MST), a well-supported model for treating conduct-disordered youth (but see Littell, 2005, 2006, for some cautions). MST involves the family in the treatment process, helping the family change the adolescent's behavior by giving them the knowledge and skills to do so. Recently, MST has been applied to other problems with positive results, including serious emotional and behavior disorders in children and adolescents and child abuse and neglect (Swenson, Schaeffer, Henggeler, Faldowski, & Mayhew, 2010). Other family systems–based therapeutic approaches are focused on treating adolescent drug use (Brief Strategic Family Therapy (BSFT); Robbins et al., 2010; Santisteban, Suarez-Morales, Robbins, & Szapocznik, 2006); anorexia nervosa (Family-Based Treatment for Anorexia Nervosa; Courturier, Isserlin, & Lock, 2010; Lock et al., 2010); adolescent substance abuse and conduct disorders (Multidimensional Family Therapy [MDFT]; Rowe, 2010); at-risk and delinquent youth (Functional Family Therapy [FFT]; Waldron & Turner, 2008). BSFT was developed for, and has been found to be especially effective with, Hispanic youth and their families. BSFT, MDFT, and MST-Psychiatric are listed on the SAMHSA National Registry of Evidence-based Programs and Practices, while MST and FFT are found on the Blueprints for Violence Prevention list of model programs for treating delinquent and at-risk youth (www.colorado.edu/cspv/blueprints/modelprograms.html).

The fact that earlier practice applications of family systems theory seemed to blame families for the difficulties of their children may account for current reluctance to focus treatment on the family system as a whole. Yet, given our present knowledge of the dynamics of families and their systemic impact on the development and functioning of all family members, it is important that we do not lose sight of the family system as a focus for change.

Key Terms

Boundary	Ecomap	Hierarchy
Closed system	Enmeshed	Homeostasis
Complementarity	Equifinality	Multigenerational transmission process
Cross-generational coalition	Family structure	
	Family system	Open system
Double bind	Genogram	Triangulation

Review Questions for Critical Thinking

1. Why did family systems theory and therapeutic frameworks built on this theory rise to prominence in the latter half of the 20th century?
2. How is family systems theory useful/not useful as an approach to informing social work practice?
3. Early proponents of family systems theory and practice were faulted for blaming parents, especially mothers, for their children's difficulties. Has that changed in contemporary practice and, if so, how and why?
4. What elements of family systems theory currently inform our approach to assessment and treatment of individuals? Of families?
5. How universal is family systems theory? Can it be applied to families from other cultures or ethnic groups?

Online Resources

www.afta.org

The website of the American Family Therapy Academy, which is an organization of the leading family therapy educators, researchers, clinicians, and others with an interest in family systems interventions. Most of the pioneers in family therapy have been members at one time or another. The organization sponsors an annual conference that brings together innovators and scholars in the field.

www.aamft.org

The website of the American Association for Marriage and Family Therapy, the primary accrediting body in the field of family therapy. This organization sets the standards for specialized training in marriage and family therapy and individuals who graduate from its accredited postgraduate training programs are eligible in most states for licensure as a marriage and family therapist.

www.youtube.com/watch?v=91wTCgPa_xw

This is a 7-minute YouTube video of Salvador Minuchin and structural family therapy. There are other YouTube videos of Carl Whitaker and Virginia Satir, illustrating their approaches to family intervention as well.

www.genograms.org

This is a fact-filled website developed by family therapy educators as an introduction to using the genogram in family treatment. It gives examples of how it is used, and helps the viewer learn how to create his/her own genogram.

www.strongbonds.jss.org.au/workers/cultures/ecomaps.html

This website, created by Jesuit Social Services in Victoria, Canada, is designed to help practitioners understand and use the ecomap. The material is well organized and easily understood and can be printed off as a handout on the topic.

www.facesiv.com

This website contains everything you want to know about the Family Adaptability and Cohesion model and its measurement. It also has information for those who would like to use the instrument based on this model, the FACES IV, in practice, including how to obtain copyright fair use.

www.nrepp.samhsa.gov

This is the website for the National Registry of Evidence-based Practices and Programs. As mentioned in this chapter, Brief Strategic Family Therapy, Multidimensional Family Therapy, and Multisystemic Family Therapy with Psychiatric Supports are all listed on this registry. A visitor to the NREPP website can read about each therapeutic approach, its evidence base, and obtain information about whom to contact to implement it.

www.colorado.edu/cspv/blueprints/modelprograms

Another list of evidence-based intervention models a few of which are based on family systems theory and this time sponsored by the U.S. Department of Justice. Both multisystemic therapy and functional family therapy for delinquents are listed here, along with descriptive information and links to the developers of the models.

References

Ackerman, N. (1954). Interpersonal disturbances in the family: Some unresolved problems in psychotherapy. *Psychiatry, 17,* 367–371.

Ackerman, N. (1958). *The psychodynamics of family life.* New York, NY: Basic Books.

Alexander, L. B., & Dore, M. M. (1999). "Parents as partners" in children's mental health services: The role of the helping alliance. *Journal of Child and Family Studies, 8*, 255–270.

Allen, W. R. (1978). The search for applicable theories of Black family life. *Journal of Marriage and the Family, 40*, 117–129.

Axelson, L. J. (1970). The working wife: Differences in perception among Negro and White males. *Journal of Marriage and the Family, 32*, 457–464.

Bateson, G., Jackson, D. D., Haley, J., & Weakland, J. H. (1956). Toward a theory of schizophrenia. *Behavioral Science, 1*, 251–264.

Belsky, J. (1999). Interactional and contextual determinants of attachment security. In J. Cassidy & P. R. Shaver (Eds.), *Handbook of attachment: Theory, research, and clinical applications* (pp. 249–264). New York, NY: Guilford Press.

Berger, P. L., & Luckmann, T. (1967). *The social construction of reality: A treatise in the sociology of knowledge.* New York, NY: Anchor Books/Doubleday.

Billingsley, A. (1968). *Black families in white America.* Englewood Cliffs, NJ: Prentice Hall.

Bishop, S. J., & Leadbeater, B. J. (1999). Maternal social support patterns and child maltreatment: Comparison of maltreating and nonmaltreating mothers. *American Journal of Orthopsychiatry, 69*, 172–181.

Blau, P. M. (1964). *Exchange and power in social life.* New York, NY: Wiley.

Blumer, H. (1969). *Symbolic interactionism: Perspective and method.* Englewood Cliffs, NJ: Prentice-Hall.

Bograd, M. (1984). Family systems approaches to wife battering: A feminist critique. *American Journal of Orthopsychiatry, 54*, 558–563.

Bowen, M. (1978). *Family therapy in clinical practice.* New York, NY: Aronson.

Bradford, K., Barber, B. K., Olsen, J. A., Maughan, S. L., Erickson, L. D., Ward, D., & Stolz, H. E. (2004). A multi-national study of interparental conflict, parenting, and adolescent functioning: South Africa, Bangladesh, China, India, Bosnia, Germany, Palestine, Columbia, and the United States. *Marriage and Family Review, 35*(3–4), 107–137.

Broderick, C. B. (1993). *Understanding family process.* Newbury Park, CA: Sage.

Buehler, C., & Welsh, D. P. (2009). A process model of adolescents' triangulation into parents' marital conflict: The role of emotional reactivity. *Journal of Family Psychology, 23*(2), 167–180.

Caplan, P. J., & Hall-McCorquodale, I. (1985). Mother-blaming in major clinical journals. *American Journal of Orthopsychiatry, 55*, 345–353.

Carr, A. (2009a). The effectiveness of family therapy and systemic interventions for child-focused problems. *Journal of Family Therapy, 31*, 3–45.

Carr, A. (2009b). The effectiveness of family therapy and systemic interventions for adult-focused problems. *Journal of Family Therapy, 31*, 46–74.

Carter, B., & McGoldrick, M. (Eds.). (1989). *Changing family life cycle: A framework for family therapy* (2nd ed.). Englewood Cliffs, NJ: Prentice Hall.

Carter, B., & McGoldrick, M. (Eds.) (2005). *The expanded family life cycle: Individual, family and social perspectives* (3rd ed.). Boston, MA: Allyn & Bacon.

Charon, J. M. (1979). *Symbolic interactionism: An introduction, an integration.* Englewood Cliffs, NJ: Prentice Hall.

Cicchetti, D., & Lynch, M. (1993). Toward an ecological/transactional model of community violence and child maltreatment: Consequences for children's development. *Psychiatry, 56*, 96–118.

Combrinck-Graham, L. (1985). A developmental model for family systems. *Family Process, 24*, 139–150.

Combrinck-Graham, L., & McKenna, S. (2006). Families with children with disrupted attachments. In L. Combrinck-Graham (Ed.), *Children in family contexts* (pp. 242–264). New York, NY: Guilford Press.

Coulton, C. C. (1996). Effects of neighborhoods on families and children: Implications for services. In A. J. Kahn & S. B. Kamerman (Eds.), *Children and their families in big cities* (pp. 87–120). New York, NY: Columbia University School of Social Work.

Courturier, J., Isserlin, L., & Lock, J. (2010). Family-based treatment for adolescents with anorexia nervosa: A dissemination study. *Eating Disorders, 18*(3), 199–209.

Cox, M. J., & Paley, B. (1997). Families as systems. *Annual Review of Psychology, 48*, 243–267.

Cummings, E. M., & Davies, P. T. (2002). Effects of marital discord on children: Recent advances and emerging themes in process-oriented research. *Journal of Child Psychology and Psychiatry, and Allied Disciplines, 43*, 31–63.

D'Andrade, R. (1986). Three scientific world views and the covering law model. In D. W. Fiske & R. S. Shweder (Eds.), *Metatheory in social science* (pp. 19–41). Chicago, IL: University of Chicago Press.

Daley, J., Sowers-Hoag, K. M., & Thyer, B. A. (1990). Are FACES-II "Family Satisfaction" scores valid? *Journal of Family Therapy, 12*, 77–81.

Daley, J., Sowers-Hoag, K. M., & Thyer, B. A. (1991). Construct validity of the circumplex model of family functioning. *Journal of Social Service Research, 15*(1/2), 131–147.

Davies, P. T., & Cummings, E. M. (2006). Interparental discord, family process, and developmental psychopathology. In D. Cicchetti & D. J. Cohen (Eds.), *Developmental psychopathology. Vol. 3: Risk, disorder, and adaptation* (2nd ed., pp. 86–128). Hoboken, NJ: Wiley.

Davies, P. T., Cummings, E. M., & Winter, M. A. (2004). Pathways between profiles of family functioning, child security in the interparental subsystem, and child psychological problems. *Development and Psychopathology, 16*, 525–550.

Dickerson, V. C. (2010). Positioning oneself within an epistemology: Refining our thinking about integrative approaches. *Family Process, 49*(3), 349–368.

Dolan-Del Vecchio, K. (2008). Dismantling white male privilege within family therapy. In M. McGoldrick & Hardy, K. V. (Eds.), *Re-visioning family therapy: Race, culture and gender in clinical practice* (2nd ed., pp. 250–260). New York, NY: Guilford Press.

Dore, M. M. (1990). The historical development of functional theory and its influence on contemporary social work practice. *Social Service Review, 64*, 358–374.

Dore, M. M. (1999). The retail method of social work: The role of the New York School in the development of clinical practice. *Social Service Review, 73*, 168–190.

Dore, M. M. (Ed.). (2006). *The postadoption experience.* Washington, DC: Child Welfare League of America.

Dore, M. M., & Feldman, N. (2005). Generalist practice with abused and neglected children and their families. In J. Poulin (Ed.), *Strengths-based generalist practice: A collaborative approach* (pp. 431–462). Belmont, CA: Brooks/Cole.

Duvall, E. M. (1977). *Marriage and family development* (5th ed.). Philadelphia, PA: Lippincott.

Egeland, B., Jacobvitz, D., & Sroufe, L. A. (1988). Breaking the cycle of abuse. *Child Development, 59*(4), 1080–1088.

Epstein, N. B., Baldwin, L. M., & Bishop, D. S. (1983). The McMaster family assessment device. *Journal of Marital and Family Therapy, 9*, 171–180.

Epstein, N. B., Bishop, D., Ryan, C., Miller, I., & Keitner, G. (1999). The McMaster model view of healthy family functioning. In F. Walsh (Ed.), *Normal family processes* (2nd ed., pp. 138–160). New York, NY: Guilford Press.

Erel, O., & Burman, B. (1995). Interrelatedness of marital relations and parent-child relations: A meta-analytic review. *Psychological Bulletin, 118*, 108–132.

Falicov, C. J. (Ed.). (1983). *Cultural perspectives in family therapy.* Rockville, MD: Aspen.

Friesen, B. J., & Poertner, J. (1995). *From case management to service coordination for children with emotional, behavioral, or mental disorders: Building on family strengths.* Baltimore, MD: Brookes.

Furstenberg, F. F. (1993). How families manage risk and opportunity in dangerous neighborhoods. In W. J. Wilson (Ed.), *Sociology and the public agenda* (pp. 231–258). Newbury Park, CA: Sage.

Garbarino, J., & Sherman, D. (1980). High-risk neighborhoods and high-risk families: The human ecology of child maltreatment. *Child Development, 51*, 188–198.

Garcia, E., & Musito, G. (2003). Social isolation from communities and child maltreatment: A cross-cultural comparison. *Child Abuse and Neglect, 27*, 153–168.

Gerard, J. M., Krishnakumar, A., & Buehler, C. (2006). Marital conflict, parent-child relations, and youth maladjustment: A longitudinal investigation of spillover effects. *Journal of Family Issues, 27*, 951–975.

Germain, C. B., & Gitterman, A. (1980). *The life model for social work practice.* New York, NY: Columbia University Press.

Goldner, V. (1985). Feminism and family therapy. *Family Process, 24*, 31–47.

Grych, J. H., Raynor, S. R., & Fosco, G. M. (2004). Family processes that shape the impact of interparental conflict on adolescents. *Development & Psychopathology, 16*, 649–665.

Hare-Mustin, R. C. (1978). A feminist approach to family therapy. *Family Process, 17*, 181–194.

Hartman, A. (1995). Diagrammatic assessment of family relationships. *Families in Society, 76*, 111–122.

Hartman, A., & Laird, J. (1983). *Family-centered social work practice.* New York, NY: Free Press.

Hearn, G. (Ed.). (1969). *The general systems approach: Contributions toward a holistic conception of social work.* New York, NY: Council on Social Work Education.

Hill, R. (1972). *The strengths of Black families.* New York, NY: Emerson-Hall.

Hines, P., & Boyd-Franklin, N. (1982). African-American families. In M. McGoldrick, J. K. Pearce, & J. Giordano (Eds.), *Ethnicity and family therapy.* New York, NY: Guilford Press.

Hogan, D. P., Eggebeen, D. J., & Clogg, C. C. (1993). The structure of intergenerational exchanges in American families. *American Journal of Sociology, 98*, 1428–1458.

Hollis, F. (1964). *Casework: A psychosocial therapy.* New York, NY: Random House.

Hollis, F., & Woods, M. E. (1981). *Casework: A psychosocial therapy* (3rd ed.). New York, NY: Random House.

Hooley, J. M. (2007). Expressed emotion and relapse of psychopathology. *Annual Review of Clinical Psychology, 3,* 329–353.

Jackson, D. (1959). Family interactions, family homeostasis and some implications for conjoint family therapy. In J. Wasserman (Ed.), *Individual and family dynamics* (pp. 77–111). New York, NY: Grune & Stratton.

Jackson, D. (1965). Family rules: Marital quid pro quo. *Archives of General Psychiatry, 12,* 589–594.

James, K., & McIntyre, D. (1983). The reproduction of families: The social role of family therapy? *Journal of Marital and Family Therapy, 9,* 119–129.

Janchill, M. P. Sr. (1969). Systems concepts in casework theory and practice. *Social Casework, 15*(2), 74–82.

Johnson, V. K. (2001). Marital interaction, family organization, and differences in parenting behavior: Explaining variations across family interaction contexts. *Family Process, 40,* 333–342.

Johnson, V. K. (2003). Linking changes in whole family functioning and children's externalizing behavior across the elementary school years. *Journal of Family Psychology, 17,* 499–509.

Kabacoff, R. I., Miller, I. W., Bishop, D. S., Epstein, N. B., & Keitner, G. I. (1990). A psychometric study of the McMaster Family Assessment Device in psychiatric, medical, and nonclinical samples. *Journal of Family Psychology, 3,* 431–439.

Katz, L. F., & Woodin, E. M. (2002). Hostility, hostile detachment, and conflict engagement in marriages: Effects on child and family functioning. *Child Development, 73,* 636–651.

Kirkpatrick, L. A., & Davis, K. E. (1994). Attachment style, gender, and relationship stability: A longitudinal analysis. *Journal of Personality and Social Psychology, 66,* 502–512.

Klever, P. (2004). The multigenerational transmission of nuclear family processes and symptoms. *American Journal of Family Therapy, 32,* 337–351.

Kretchmar, M. D., & Jacobvitz, D. B. (2002). Observing mother-child relationships across generations: Boundary patterns, attachment, and the transmission of caregiving. *Family Process, 41,* 351–374.

Kuhn, T. S. (1970). *The structure of scientific revolutions* (2nd ed.). Chicago, IL: University of Chicago Press. (Original work published 1964)

Levy, J. (2006). Using a metaperspective to clarify the structural-narrative debate in family therapy. *Family Process, 45*(1), 55–73.

Lindahl, K. M., & Malik, N. M. (1999). Marital conflict, family processes, and boys' externalizing behavior in Hispanic American and European American families. *Journal of Clinical Child Psychology, 28,* 12–24.

Littell, J. (2005). Lessons from a systematic review of multisystemic therapy. *Children and Youth Services Review, 27,* 445–463.

Littell, J. (2006). The case for multisystemic therapy: Evidence or orthodoxy? *Children and Youth Services Review, 28,* 458–472.

Lock, J., Le Grange, D., Agras, W. S., Moye, A., Bryson, S. W., & Jo, B. (2010). Randomized clinical trial comparing family-based treatment to adolescent focused individual therapy for adolescents with anorexia nervosa. *Archives of General Psychiatry, 67*(10), 1025–1032.

Luepnitz, D. A. (1988). *The family interpreted: Feminist theory in clinical practice.* New York, NY: Basic Books.

Macdonald, A. (2011). *Solution-focused therapy: Theory, research and practice* (2nd ed.). Thousand Oaks, CA: Sage.

Macfie, J., McElwain, N. L., Houts, R. M., & Cox, M. J. (2005). Intergenerational transmission of role reversal between parent and child: Dyadic and family systems internal working models. *Attachment and Human Development, 7,* 51–65.

Macy, M., & Flache, A. (1995). Beyond rationality in matters of choice. *Annual Review of Sociology, 21,* 73–92.

Markovsky, B., Willer, D., Simpson, B., & Lovardia, M. (1997). Power in exchange networks: Critique of a new theory. *American Sociological Review, 62,* 833–837.

Marsiglio, W., Amato, P., Day, R. D., & Lamb, M. E. (2000). Scholarship on fatherhood in the 1990s and beyond. *Journal of Marriage and the Family, 62,* 1173–1191.

Marvin, R. S., & Stewart, R. B. (1990). A family systems framework for the study of attachment. In M. T. Greenberg, D. Cicchetti, & E. M. Cummings (Eds.), *Attachment in the preschool years* (pp. 98–125). Chicago, IL: University of Chicago Press.

McAdoo, H. P. (1977). Family therapy in the Black community. *American Journal of Orthopsychiatry, 47,* 75–79.

McAdoo, H. P. (1980). Black mothers and the extended family support network. In L. F. Rogers-Rose (Ed.), *The Black woman* (pp. 125–144). Newbury Park, CA: Sage.

McGoldrick, M., Gerson, R., & Petry, S. (2008). *Genograms: Assessment and intervention* (3rd ed.). New York, NY: Norton.

McGoldrick, M., Pearce, J. K., & Giordano, J. (1982). *Ethnicity and family therapy.* New York, NY: Guilford Press.

Miller, R. B., Anderson, S., & Keala, D. K. (2004). Is Bowen theory valid? A review of basic research. *Journal of Marital and Family Therapy, 30,* 453–466.

Minuchin, S. (1974). *Families and family therapy.* Cambridge, MA: Harvard University Press.

Molm, L., Quist, T., & Wiseley, P. (1994). Imbalanced structures, unfair strategies: Power and justice in social exchange. *American Sociological Review, 59,* 98–121.

Napier, A. Y., & Whitaker, C. (1978). *The family crucible.* New York, NY: Harper & Row.

Nye, F. I. (1979). Choice, exchange and the family. In W. R. Burr, R. Hill, F. I. Nye, & L. L. Reiss (Eds.), *Contemporary theories about the family* (pp. 1–41). New York, NY: Free Press.

Okon, D. M., Greene, A. L., & Smith, J. E. (2003). Family interactions predict individual symptom variation for adolescents with bulimia. *International Journal of Eating Disorders, 34,* 450–457.

Oliver, J. E. (1993). Intergenerational transmission of child abuse: Rates, research, and clinical implications. *American Journal of Psychiatry, 150,* 1315–1324.

Olson, D. H. (2011). FACES IV and the Circumplex Model: Validation study. *Journal of Marital & Family Therapy, 3*(1), 64–80.

Olson, D. H., Sprenkle, D. H., & Russell, C. (1979). Circumplex model of marital and family systems: Pt. I. Cohesion and adaptability dimensions, family types and clinical application. *Family Process, 18,* 3–27.

Place, M., Hulsmeier, J., Brownrigg, A., & Soulsby, A. (2005). The Family Adaptability and Cohesion Evaluation Scale (FACES): An instrument worthy of rehabilitation? *Psychiatrist, 29,* 215–218.

Rice, F., Harold, G. T., Shelton, K. H., & Thapar, A. (2006). Family conflict inter-acts with genetic liability in predicting childhood and adolescent depression. *Journal of the American Academy of Child and Adolescent Psychiatry, 45,* 841–848.

Richmond, M. E. (1944). *Social diagnosis.* New York, NY: Free Press. (Original work published 1917)

Richmond, M. K., & Stocker, C. M. (2006). Associations between family cohesion and adolescent siblings' externalizing behavior. *Journal of Family Psychology, 20,* 663–669.

Robbins, M. S., Alonso, E., Horigian, V. E., Bachrach, K., Burlew, K., Carrion, I. S.,...Szapocnik, J. (2010). Transporting clinical research to community settings: Designing and conducting a multisite trial of Brief Strategic Family Therapy. *Addiction Science & Clinical Practice,* 54–61.

Rosenfeld, M. J. (2005). A critique of exchange theory in mate selection. *American Journal of Sociology, 110,* 1284–1325.

Rothbaum, F., Rosen, K., Ujiie, T., & Uchida, N. (2002). Family systems theory, attachment theory, and culture. *Family Process, 41,* 328–350.

Rowe, C. L. (2010). Multidimensional Family Therapy: Addressing co-occurring substance abuse and other problems among adolescents with comprehensive family-based treatment. *Child & Adolescent Psychiatric Clinics of North America, 19*(3), 563–576.

Santisteban, D. A., Suarez-Morales, L., Robbins, M. S., & Szapocznik, J. (2006). Brief Strategic Family Therapy: Lessons learned in efficacy research and challenges to blending research and practice. *Family Process, 45*(2), 259–271.

Santisteban, D. A., Szapocznik, J., Perez-Vidal, A., Kurtines, W. M., Murray, E. J., & LaPierre, A. (1996). Efficacy of intervention for engaging youth and families into treatment and some variables that may contribute to differential effectiveness. *Journal of Family Psychology, 10,* 35–44.

Shaw, D. S., Criss, M. M., Schonberg, M. A., & Beck, J. E. (2004). The development of family hierarchies and their relation to children's conduct problems. *Development and Psychopathology, 16,* 483–500.

Simons, R. L., Whitbeck, L. B., Conger, R. D., & Wu, C. (1991). Intergenerational transmission of harsh parenting. *Developmental Psychopathology, 27,* 159–171.

Stein, I. L. (1971). The systems model and social systems theory: Their application to social work. In H. Strean (Ed.), *Social casework: Theories in action* (pp. 35–59). Metuchen, NJ: Scarecrow Press.

Sturge-Apple, M. L., Davies, P. T., & Cummings, E. M. (2010). Typologies of family functioning and children's adjustment during the early school years. *Child Development, 81,* 1320–1335.

Swenson, C. C., Schaeffer, C. M., Henggeler, S. W., Faldowski, R., & Mayhew, A. M. (2010). Multisystemic therapy for child abuse and neglect: A randomized effectiveness trial. *Journal of Family Psychology, 24*(4), 497–507.

Taggart, M. (1985). The feminist critique in epistemological perspective: Questions of context in family therapy. *Journal of Marital and Family Therapy, 11,* 113–126.

van IJzendoorn, M. H. (1992). Intergenerational transmission of parenting: A review of studies in nonclinical populations. *Developmental Review, 12,* 76–99.

von Bertalanffy, L. (1968). *General systems theory: Foundations, development, applications.* New York, NY: Braziller.

Waldron, H. B., & Turner, C. W. (2008). Evidence-based psychosocial treatments for adolescent abusers: A review and meta-analysis. *Journal of Clinical Child and Adolescent Psychology, 37*, 1–24.

Walsh, F. (2011). *Normal family processes: Growing diversity and complexity* (4th ed.). New York, NY: Guilford Press.

Weinstein, D. F. (2004). Culture at work: Family therapy and the culture concept in post–World War II America. *Journal of the History of the Behavioral Sciences, 40*, 23–46.

Whitaker, C. A., & Bumberry, W. A. (1988). *Dancing with the family: A symbolic-experiential approach.* New York, NY: Brunner-Mazel.

Whitaker, C. A., & Keith, D. V. (1981). Symbolic-experiential family therapy. In A. S. Gurman & D. P. Kniskern (Eds.), *Handbook of family therapy* (pp. 56–89). New York, NY: Brunner/Mazel.

White, M. (2007). *Maps of narrative practice.* New York, NY: Norton.

Chapter 12
Organizational Theory

John E. Tropman and Emily J. Nicklett

> How does an understanding of empirically supported principles of organizational behavior contribute to the delivery of social work services?

The 21st century can be called the century of organizations. Organizations not only provide the framework for the way things work, but formal organizations—governmental, commercial, and nonprofit (e.g., nongovernmental organizations)—are a vital element of world society. Organizations are familiar to us as agencies, companies, corporations, and governmental bodies of all kinds. In social work, we are especially interested in organizations called social agencies, human service organizations, people-processing organizations, and people-changing organizations. But social helping does not occur only in social agencies. It occurs in corporations (day care and employee assistance programs, for example), as well as in governmental bodies (departments of social services). Indeed, social work is interested in any organized process that is established and run to assist individuals and families to achieve their potential or that help communities, organizations, and states function more efficiently, effectively, and humanely.

Organizational Behavior

When one thinks about organizations, two types of behavior come readily to mind. One is behavior *of* the organization, on activities in which the organization engages as an organizational entity. Organizational policy is one example of formal organizational action: the agency's office hours, sickness and absenteeism policy, and how many clients should be seen in a day. There is also informal organizational activity, called practice, which may vary from formal policy and yet have the apparent force of policy. For example, it may be practice that, although the agency formally opens at 8:00 a.m., clients are not scheduled until 9:00 a.m.

This material draws on *Supervision and Management in Nonprofit Organizations* (Tropman, 2006). We would like to thank Gerald Davis and Jane Dutton of the Ross School of Business, University of Michigan for their thoughtful commentary on this chapter.

The other type of organizational behavior is behavior *in* the organization, or how people in the organization relate to each other. Here again, there are formal ways in which one interacts with one's supervisor and colleagues; there are also informal ways in which workers interact with each other and with clients.

The word *organization* has multiple referents that it is helpful to clarify. In one meaning, an organization is some entity or process that has parts and elements with understandable and regular interaction. Interaction may occur at a moment in time or over time. Processes are organizations that, typically, exist over time.

Social Organization

The concept of *social organization*, for sociologists at least, refers to the minded interaction that characterizes social structures and the process of developing a structure and culture for that minded interaction over time. It is the movement from unorganized random interactions to patterned ones, guided by rules and norms. The process of social organization produces social organizations.

Social Organizations

Social organizations are groups, communities, organizations, societies, world regions, and the world itself. Social organizations have both structure and culture. Some social organizations have formal properties as well as informal ones.

Levels of Social Organization

Formal organizations exist within a context of levels from small simple ones to larger ones. The dyad, or two-person group, is perhaps the lowest level of social organization. Groups, communities, formal organizations, regions, nation-states, and societies exist as well. Each level is composed of lower levels but has, as well, a reality in and of itself (Tropman & Richards-Schuester, 2000).

Formal organizations are one kind of social organization. Formal organizations are, as just noted, typically what we think of when we use the term *organization*: a formal entity developed to accomplish some specific product or service or to achieve some goal.

Formal Organization

What is a *formal organization*? An early definition of formal organizations comes from Peter Blau (1968, pp. 297–298):

> *[A formal] organization comes into existence when explicit procedures are established to coordinate the activities of a group in the interest of achieving specified objectives. [The formal part involves activities, or directed] procedures for mobilizing and coordinating the efforts of various, usually specialized, subgroups in the pursuit of joint objectives.*

To expand this definition somewhat, formal organizations are rationalized, described relations among individuals and groups that specify organizational positions, roles, processes, and their interconnections over time and space. They are often officially registered and many times have legal status in national and international systems. Common examples are governments and governmental bureaus, corporations, and nongovernmental organizations (NGOs, nonprofits in the United States). The rationalization is comprised of written statements of purposes and goals (ends), the achievement of which is the basis for other documentation concerning the appropriate interactions and procedures for their accomplishment (means). Formal organizations have a structure, often described in an organization chart. They have a culture, which embodies the organization's ideas, values, beliefs, norms, and attitudes. They have a history (short or long), and the conditions and issues crucial and pressing at their founding often have a special and long-term influence on their structure and culture. They typically go through a life cycle, involving stages of founding, growth, maturity, and decline/renewal. Formal organizations usually specify who *belongs* to/with/in them, using categories like citizen, member, employee, and student. This specification also has the property of making it clear who is *outside* of the organization. There are usually rights and responsibilities associated with such membership.

Alternatively, *informal organizations* do not usually possess legal status and are largely voluntaristic and fluid in interactions and membership.

The Importance of Formal Organizations

Formal organizations are vital because they produce results that individuals could not accomplish on their own. They collate diversity (of materials, people, locations, and time periods) into a unity (or series of units) we call products and services. The outcomes we seek from an organization, whether adoption, the development of a personal career path, or the establishment of a recreational and community center that locals would actually use, are all the result of interconnected skills being applied in a disciplined and sequential manner. Although we recognize the product, we often do not recognize or appreciate the upstream set of activities that make our use and/or enjoyment of the product possible. All too frequently we make attribution errors and give credit either to the last element of the organization with which we deal (tipping the server, for example, or making a substantial donation to a hospice) while failing to realize that the server just delivers the organization's product, and that the value of hospice care (and it is valuable) needs to be seen in connection with the large amount of previous medical care that the patient has received. The server example is instructive as one at the bottom of organizational hierarchy; similar attributions are made for executives, who often (in both the nonprofit and the for-profit worlds) receive substantial compensation, as if they are fully responsible for the outcomes produced by the organization. The quality guru W. Edwards Deming (1982) makes a similar point. He argues that a substantial portion of an organization's product is generated by the system, and a small fraction by individuals, although many of us think exactly the reverse is true. His views were well understood and accepted in Japan (where the highest award for quality is the Deming Award) but are still not accepted in the United States in any profound way. A fact that speaks to the overwhelming emphasis on individualism in the United States (the mountain man) in spite of many powerful counter examples (the wagon train).

Historical and Conceptual Origins

There have been several important leaders and theorists in the organizational field; some you have heard about or will want to know about to better understand organizational theory.

Early 20th Century

The scientific study of organizational behavior can be roughly organized chronologically. In this first section, we touch on the work of Max Weber and the American Frederick W. Taylor, and conclude with a review of the famous Hawthorne Studies conducted at the Western Electric factory outside of Chicago.

Max Weber

The German sociologist Max Weber was perhaps the earliest *contemporary* thinker on organizations, in this case, bureaucratic organizations. During his time, Weber explored the topic of authority. His research resulted in the development of three different ideas of authority: traditional authority, charismatic authority, and legal authority. His work with legal authority further inspired him to think about bureaucratic organizations. From his perspective, a bureaucracy is made up of a division of labor and attendant functional interdependence, an administrative apparatus, a hierarchy of authority, and impersonal rules; it is characterized by full-time paying jobs and careers. Bureaucratic work also is based on written documents, and there is a clear separation of home and office (Gearth & Mills, 1947/1958, Chapter 8).

The Principles of Scientific Management

Frederick W. Taylor wrote the first book on *industrial human resources* in 1911. Taylor looked at workers as interchangeable parts that made the assembly lines work. The scientific component of his work was the way he investigated the optimal output efficiency of a line worker. Specifically, Taylor set out to determine the most efficient set of tasks that a worker could accomplish in so many minutes. Ideas such as specialization and differentiation, span of control authoritative coordination, and authoritative delegation came out of this work (Bolman & Deal, 2003, p. 45). Taylor is remembered as the "Father of Scientific Management" (the inscription on his tombstone further supports this designation), but it should be noted that Taylor's scientific merit has been criticized (Stewart, 2009). The extent to which Taylor fudged his data, lied about his successes, and manipulated clients has even been noted in popular newsmagazines (e.g., Lepore, 1999; Stewart, 2009). Such magazines describe Taylor's strategies as "schemes" and the management consulting strategies that emerged from them as less of science and more of "a party trick." The Taylorization of the workforce was a strategy that extended beyond industrial work settings and into the home. This is epitomized by the work and home of Lillian Gilbreth (a close colleague of scientific management enthusiast Justice Louis Brandeis), who raised 12 children in a home setting that would challenge the efficiency of any assembly plant. Two of Gilbreth's children, Frank Bunker Gilbreth, Jr., and Ernestine Gilbreth Carey, authored the book *Cheaper by the Dozen*; it later became the basis for several movies. She had a joint academic appointment at Purdue's School of Home Economics and the School of Management. Although Gilbreth intended for improved efficiency, this was not the result of the Taylorization movement. In the past several decades, Americans are working many more hours per year and juggling concurrent roles (e.g., cook, parent, spouse, employee).

Hawthorne Studies

Elton Mayo and his colleagues conducted the Hawthorne studies in the early 1930s. They studied a group of women working on specific tasks at the Western Electric Plant in Illinois. He and his colleagues manipulated a variety of variables and discovered that no matter what they changed, the women's production seemed to improve. Don Clark (1999) draws four conclusions from the study that generally ring true:

1. *The aptitudes of individuals are imperfect predictors of job performance.* Although they give some indication of the physical and mental potential of the individual, the amount produced is strongly influenced by social factors.

2. *Informal organization affects productivity.* The Hawthorne researchers discovered a group life among the workers. The studies also showed that the relations that supervisors develop with workers tend to influence the manner in which the workers carry out directives.

3. *Work group norms affect productivity.* The Hawthorne researchers were not the first to recognize that work groups tend to arrive at norms of what is "a fair day's work," but they provided the best systematic description and interpretation of this phenomenon.

4. *The workplace is a social system.* The Hawthorne researchers came to view the workplace as a social system made up of interdependent parts.

As other experts have pointed out, though, variables such as the work group itself and the fact that the Depression may have made people hesitant to do anything that would risk their job. However, it was not until 1978 that these factors were carefully examined (Frank & Kaul, 1978).

From a methodological perspective, the Hawthorne studies have flaws that render their conclusions suspect. That said, those results have proven largely correct, and the points D. Clark made have reliability and validity.

The 1930s also saw the beginnings of interest in administration. Leonard D. White (1931) wrote about the city manager as an administrative functionary, and Chester I. Barnard (1938/1962) wrote about the functions of the executive.

1940s and 1950s

Administrative Behavior

In the late 1940s and the 1950s, there was a burgeoning development of studies on *administrative behavior*, the science and art of actually running organizations. This might have been a result of World War II, or just a developing consciousness of the people-organization interface, or even a combination of these and other factors. World War II produced a greater emphasis on and interest in teams and their relationship to organizations. The military is hierarchically organized, yet much of the actual work of the armed forces goes on in teams—patrols, aircraft carriers, bomber squads—and how they function is of vital importance.[1] The war also created interest in *management and managers*, the function of integration, and the behavior of those who do (or do not do) the integrating. Three works are of special importance in exploring this phenomenon: *Administrative Behavior* (Simon, 1947/1957), *TVA and the Grass Roots* (Selznick, 1949), and *Public Administration* (Smithburg & Thompson, 1950).

Nobel Laureate Herbert Simon's (1947/1957) *Administrative Behavior* addressed his interest in rational behavior in organizations and its limits. His book is also focused on decision making within organizations. Simon covers topics such as "Fact and Value in Decision Making" (Chapter 3), "The Psychology of Administrative Decisions" (Chapter 5), and "The Anatomy of an Organization" (Chapter 11). The conclusion of this book offers an appendix considering "What Is Administrative Science?"

In 1949, Phillip Selznick wrote *TVA and the Grass Roots*. It is a study of the development and operation of the Tennessee Valley Authority, specifically the relationship between a developing mega bureaucracy and the locals who lived in the Tennessee Valley. This was a huge administrative undertaking and was intermixed with much ideology (as evidenced by David Lilienthal's 1934/1974 book *The TVA: Democracy on the March*).

The historian Leonard D. White (1954, 1958a, 1958b) got into the act again with three volumes on an administrative history of the United States. Building on his work on municipal management (previously mentioned),

---

[1]Another example of the team effort was the Manhattan Project, the effort that made the atomic bomb. See *The Manhattan Project: Making the Atomic Bomb* by U.S. Department of Energy, National Nuclear Security Administration, Office of the Executive Secretariat and Office of History and Heritage Resources (December 31, 2010).

he turned to national administration in *The Jeffersonians: An Administrative History from 1801–1829*, *The Jacksonians: An Administrative History from 1829–1861*, and *The Republican Era: An Administrative History from 1861–1901*. After reading any of White's work, one has an enhanced appreciation of the role of management in developing the U.S. government.

Herbert Simon and two colleagues, Donald Smithburg and James Thompson, wrote *Public Administration* (1950). This classic book addressed how public (federal) administrators get managerial work accomplished. It deals with issues of formal and informal structures in organizations and the issues of power and change. Chapter 22 of their book addresses the five impediments to change, which the authors refer to as the costs of change and which continue to have amazing relevance for those interested in organizational change today. The five impediments to change are (1) inertia costs, (2) moral costs (we would call them cultural costs today), (3) self-interest costs, (4) rationality costs, and (5) subordination costs.

The large organization of the armed forces in some sense reflected the industrial organization of the first part of the 20th century and became its midcentury model. Civilian organizations tended to look much like the armed forces, with common dress and the "hurry up and wait" ambience of the military. Sloan Wilson's 1955 novel *The Man in the Grey Flannel Suit* addressed these issues in fictional form (Wilson, 1955/2002). William H. Whyte's (1956) book *The Organization Man* picks up this theme in a more analytical way. Whyte begins:

> *This book is about the organization man. If the term is vague, it is because I can think of no other way to describe the people I am talking about. They are not the workers, nor are they the white-collar people in the usual, clerk sense of the word. These people only work for The Organization. The ones I am talking about belong to it as well. They are the ones of our middle class who have left home, spiritually as well as physically, to take the vows of organization life, and it is they who are the mind and soul of our great self-perpetuating institutions. Only a few are top managers or ever will be. In a system that makes such hazy terminology as "junior executive" psychologically necessary, they are of the staff as much as the line, and most are destined to live poised in a middle area that still awaits a satisfactory euphemism. But they are the dominant members of our society nonetheless. They have not joined together into a recognizable elite—our country does not stand still long enough for that—but it is from their ranks that are coming most of the first and second echelons of our leadership, and it is their values which will set the American temper.*
>
> *The corporation man is the most conspicuous example, but he is only one, for the Blood brother to the business trainee off to join Du Pont is the seminary student who will end up in the church hierarchy, the doctor headed for the corporate clinic, the physics PhD in a government laboratory, the intellectual on the foundation-sponsored team project, the engineering graduate in the huge drafting room at Lockheed, the young apprentice in a Wall Street law factory. (p. 3)*

Whyte sees a new conformity arising from the cultural emphasis on organizational compliance. He even includes an appendix titled "How to Cheat on Personality Tests."

Sociologists were also probing the extent and impact of the *organizational culture* that seemed to be pervading America during the middle of the 20th century. C. Wright Mills (1956) explored the new middle class as it existed within organizations in his book *White Collar*. David Reisman (with Reuel Denny and Nathan Glazer) contributed *The Lonely Crowd*. Originally published in 1950, the better known version was issued in 1955 and reissued in 2002 with a foreword by Todd Gitlin. *The Lonely Crowd*'s subtitle is *A Study of the Changing American Character*. That change is really about the American society's increasing organization. They introduce a stimulating theoretical construct about three dominant forces in societies and their nature and succession. First is *tradition direction*, in which a society is guided by the past. The second is *inner direction*, in which society is guided by inner personal reflection and decision. The third is *other direction*, in which societal members are constantly sensing and acting upon what others think. Reisman, Glazer, and Denny argue that America in 1950 was in the third phase. Common phrases of the day, such as "Let's run this idea up the flagpole and see which way the wind is blowing" capture their idea.

The general ideas in these works from the mid-1950s were somewhat akin to that of Taylor and his principles of scientific management. For Taylor, the individual in the organization was reduced to a machine part, and all individuality was lost. For writers in the mid-1950s, the same thing happened except that individuals had been reduced to commonness through an overweening culture. Indeed, one of the editions of *The Lonely Crowd* has a picture of a herd of sheep as its cover. In 1960, Douglass McGregor reminded everyone that organizations were made up of people who needed attention and concern. *The Human Side of Enterprise* called for a humanistic approach to management. The thinkers noted earlier talked a lot about the impact of organizations; they did not actually analyze or explain much about organizations themselves. As March and Simon (1958, p. 1) note, "It is easier ... to give examples of formal organizations than to define the term."

March and Simon's (1958) book *Organizations* really energized the process of organizational analysis. Indeed, their first chapter is "Organizational Behavior," and it is followed by chapters on intra-organizational decisions, considerations of why individuals participate in organizations, and conflict within organizations, among other topics. As they say in the beginning of the first chapter, "This book is about the theory of formal organizations" (p. 1).

The Harvard sociologist Talcott Parsons (1960) offered a theory of organizations in "A Sociological Approach to the Theory of Organizations" and "Some Ingredients of a General Theory of Organizations" in *Structure and Process in Modern Society*. Parsons argued that what we think of as *an* organization—a single entity with a name and address—is actually three intersecting entities, though still with a single name and address. He still kept the triangular form, however. The techno-structure, one of the units in the bottom of the pyramid model, is where the actual work of the organization gets done. The middle of the organization is the managerial level, which organizes the work of the techno-structure but is better viewed as its own organization linked to the bottom portion. The apex of the pyramid is the intuitional level, which connects the organization to the outside resource world. A recent work (Tropman, 2006, pp. 26–27) breaks the institutional structure into two parts: the top team (CEO, COO, CFO, etc.) and the governance structure (the board of directors).

In 1962, Peter Blau and Richard Scott wrote *Formal Organizations*. It continued and expanded the work of McGregor in that it looked at structural effects, or the impact that organizations have on individuals. Jeffery Pfeffer (1991, p. 1) puts it this way:

> *Structural effects represent the influence of an individual's position in social space on that person because of the constraints and opportunities for interaction and social comparison that derive from the structural realities. The effects of structural positions (including network location, physical location, and one's demographic relationship to others) on job attitudes, turnover, performance, and wages illustrate the application of a structural perspective and how that perspective can enrich our understanding of phenomena typically studied from the perspective of individual attributes and dispositions. A structural perspective seeks to put the fact of social relations and organizations back into the study of organizational behavior.*

1980s and 1990s

In 1982 a statistician, W. Edwards Deming, sort of backed into organizational studies, and he was never really embraced by or supported by organizational thinkers, although his conclusions were similar to theirs. Perhaps because Deming was an applied thinker, or so it seemed, aimed at improving organizational outcomes, he was not seen as a scholar. Actually, the U.S. business community did not embrace him either. Scholars ignored him because he was not a scholar as they defined it; business leaders ignored him because his theories require a revamping of the American ideology of success and personal responsibility (although thinkers in the 1950s, such as Wilson, Whyte, and Reisman, had already established the validity of his general premises).

Deming's (1982) book *Out of the Crisis* deals with improving the quality of organizational products. Poor results are due to variation in the production process, and it was eliminating variation that stirred Deming's passions. Variation is due to two fundamental causal sets: common (structural and cultural) causes of variation and special (unique) causes of variation (things individuals do). His startling conclusion struck at the core of American values and the failure of management, two elements that assured his dismissal from the halls of American industry until it was too late. Here is what he said: "I should estimate that, in my experience, most of the possibilities for improvement add up to something like this: 94% belong to the system [common causes of variation]; 6% [belong to] special causes of variation" (p. 315). These proportions were later adjusted slightly to 85% and 15% and can be found at www.well.com/user/vamead/demingdist.html

Deming's conclusion was too much for U.S. business leaders, never a really thoughtful lot anyway, to accept. It was bad enough that problems were not caused by individual workers. One could no longer "fire Harry" as a solution. Even worse was the point that successes were also a product of the system. This was disheartening to the executives, apparently, because it implicated the validity of their own successes and prominence. In any event, Deming's theories were adopted by the Japanese, in part because the greater degree of group orientation of Japanese culture made them more palatable. They were a huge success in Japan, and the quality of Japanese products we see today is largely a result of the combination of Deming's theory and Japanese application.

Organizations have a sort of personality or style of doing their business. We all know this to be true and use that knowledge in our daily selection of organizations and agencies with which we interact. Organizations have a set of ideas, values, beliefs, attitudes, and norms that persist in them over time. This persistence came to be called *organizational culture*. Robert Quinn (1988) was a relatively early writer on the idea of organizational culture in his book *Beyond Rational Management*. Quinn identifies four archetypical cultures: the clan (the fraternity-type organization, which privileges results), the hierarchy (the traditional machine model bureaucracy, which privileges following orders), the market (the outcome-based firm, which privileges results), and the adhocracy (the "pickup game"–type firm, which privileges the entrepreneurial and new type of activities). Quinn looks at the kinds of decision making that are characteristic of each, the kinds of skills needed for each, and the kinds of tensions that exist within and between each. This perspective, which has emerged as the competing values perspective, has been popular among organizations and especially in business schools, where Professor Quinn mainly works. (Quinn is a faculty member of the Ross School of Business at the University of Michigan.)

Cultures are more permanent and long-standing elements of organizations. They take time to emerge and are hard to change. Culture is more like a *climate zone*. Organizations appear to have a climate as well, which is a more temporary, here-and-now set of smaller cultures, more like subcultures in the overall organizational culture. Both cultures and climates vary locally and globally (Cooper, Cartwright, & Earley, 2001).

Henry Mintzberg (1989) returned to and adapted Parson's typology and created a five-part organization archetype. Imagine yourself looking at the end of a railroad track. There is a broad base, curving into a narrower center, which expands out again at the top. Or consider a tree with a large root system, narrow trunk, and large leafy top, almost as large as the root system. These are the essential three Parsonian parts; Mintzberg calls them technical structure (the bottom), middle line (the managerial structure), and strategic apex (the institutional structure). Then Mintzberg adds two eggs, which rest on either side of the middle line. One is the technical structure and the other is the support staff. This basic shape shifts depending on the actual function of the organization. He describes four basic types: machine bureaucracy, professional organization, entrepreneurial startup, and adhocracy (for more detail, see http://istsocrates.berkeley.edu/~fmb/articles/mintzberg/).

In the 1990s, it became clear that one perspective on organizations would not suffice. A couple of frameworks were developed that provided a lens on organizations. Like a kaleidoscope, the organizational stones remained the same, but the prismatics differed as you used different lenses. First issued in 1997, *Reframing Organizations* by Lee Bolman and Terrance Deal offered a range of horizontal perspectives on organizations (Bolman & Deal, 2003). Organizational structure, human resources, politics, culture, and leadership were the frames that they suggested. Tropman and Morningstar (1988), on the other hand, introduced the idea of a vertical taxonomy in *Entrepreneurial Systems for the 1990s* (and later in Tropman's (1998b) *Managing Ideas in the Creating Organization*). This taxonomy involved originally constructed as a five variable model (the five Cs), has been expanded by Tropman and Wooten (2010) to a 7-variable model (the seven Cs): characteristics, competencies, collaborations, crucibles, conditions, contexts, and change.

Characteristics are the personal features of the individuals within the agency, from race and gender to age and temperament. A *collaboration* refers to the personal network of 12 to 18 people on whom the executive (or any of us) relies consistently. A *crucible* considers those life changing/transforming events (occasionally good ones, often negative ones) that remain with us and consciously and unconsciously influence our perspectives. *Competencies* address the issues of what is needed to be known skill-wise to do the job, as well as thinking about how good the worker is at that skill. *Conditions* refer to elements of the organization itself, such as structure, culture and climate, strategy, systems, and staff. *Contexts* refer to those things going on outside the agency that might affect it. *Change* is the turbulence of the internal and external environment of the agency and the velocity with which the turbulence is moving. As an example, think about a child welfare agency. From the perspective of temperament, some people can handle child protection and some cannot (characteristics). Then there are those on whom the worker calls for advice and counsel. Child welfare workers have significant events (crucibles) that form their approach to the work. It might be a successful reunification of child and family, or a child death when the worker did not move quickly enough. Workers need a special set of skills (competencies). Child protection agencies have a certain structure and climate, and that needs to be understood (conditions). There is a lot of turbulence in the child welfare context around issues of child safety, race matching, and so on. Finally, that turbulence is very active and swift, with changes buffeting the agency at a fast pace (change). The seven-C taxonomy provides a structured series of lenses that allow a look at the agency from the bottom (individual workers, employees) to the top (the external environment).

There are hundreds of books and scholarly articles on organizations available at this time. This brief overview simply sets the stage for understanding how organizations and agencies have been conceptualized.

Basic Theoretical Principles

In thinking about basic theoretical principles, we move from the flow of historical development to an enumeration of fundamental agreements that scholars hold to be true about organizations. Although others would surely have variations of this list, these principles reflect our judgment about what most organizational thinkers would find commonly true and important.

Principle 1: Organizations Are Social Institutions

Organizations are one of the forms through which society organizes itself. Formal organizations have some common features. As we look at the disciplines of social science, each has its contribution to make in understanding organizations and its view of them.

Principle 2: Organizations Have a Structure

Organizations have systematic ways to portray themselves to themselves and to the world. The typical Western way to portray the structure of an organization is in an organization chart, based loosely on the medieval pyramid (Pascale & Athos, 1982). However, there are other conceptions of organizational structure, such as the solar system (Tropman, 1998a, p. 194). One might even think about an atom, with the different departments revolving elliptically around the executive nucleus. Mintzberg (1989) also talks about different structural constellations depending on the type of organization. (We return to this point in the discussion about new conceptualizations of organizations.)

Principle 3: Organizations Have Formal and Informal Systems

The organization chart and its list of policies and procedures is the official and formal face of the organization. But agencies have another face as well, their informal system. While the formal organization depicts *reporting relationships*, the informal organization addresses issues of *who knows whom*. Policies have an informal side as well, called practices, and the difference between what the organization says it does and what it actually does is the called the *policy-practice gap*. More informally, the question becomes: Does the agency *walk the talk*?

Principle 4: Organizations Have a Culture

Organizations are characterized by a set of ideas to which emotions and feelings are attached; these are called *values*. Nonprofit human service agencies are especially noted for their values, which are often written into their organizational mission. It is important that organizations be mission-driven, that is, that the structure and culture align with the mission and express it on a daily basis.

Agencies also have subcultures within them. For example, a finance department in a human service organization may have a subculture more like finance departments at for-profit and governmental agencies. It is a challenge to keep all subcultures aligned with the overall mission of the agency. Although *culture* is a more long-standing organizational property, there is also an organizational *climate*, or a shorter term, more *seasonal* or more *local* version of culture (Glisson & James, 2002).

Principle 5: Organizations Have a Life Cycle

Like all systems, organizations go through phases. These conventionally are the startup phase, a new or emerging phase, a growth stage, a stable stage, and a declining or rebirth stage. They tend to follow a sigmoid curve, as one can see in Figure 12.1.

As organizations reach their peak, they begin to die. This process can take a long time. The American steel industry is one famous example;

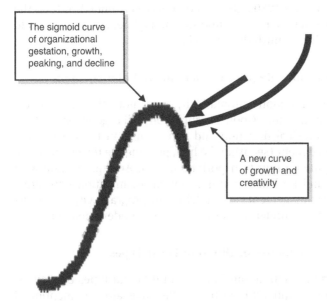

The sigmoid curve of organizational gestation, growth, peaking, and decline

A new curve of growth and creativity

Figure 12.1

The sigmoid curve of organizational growth and decline.

From "Where Are You on the Sigmoid Curve?" by Charles Handy, Fall 1994, *Directors and Boards*, p. 22. Adapted with permission.

General Motors is another. However, in each case, in somewhat different forms, they have risen again, though a fraction of their former selves. Sometimes organizational death should occur; this is one of the differences between profits and nonprofits. Profit-making organizations rely on a market; if no one comes into your restaurant, you are out of business. However, for nonprofits, it is often the case that their consumers and their customers are different. Their consumers are the ones who use the services but often do not pay full price; their customers are those who provide support for the organization. It is possible that the customers remain happy while the consumers are not. Hence the agency continues to offer a service that only a few consumers want but continues to satisfy the customers. A related problem occurs when an agency goes to a local community foundation or other financial angel in search of help and secures a "dysfunctional rescue." Such a rescue occurs when the agency really should die, but it is resurrected for a short time, using from $10,000 to $20,000 to $100,000 (or more) of community resources to sustain a dated service that meets the values of a few but not the needs of the many.

On the other hand, it is possible, and happens with some regularity, that organizations, like people, reinvent themselves at the point when the sigmoid curve begins to turn downward. That is illustrated by the arrow at the downward slope of the curve displayed in Figure 12.1. Perhaps the most well-known example of organizational reinvention in the nonprofit world was the National Foundation for Infantile Paralysis, started in 1938 by President Roosevelt. It provided support for victims of polio and supported research to find a polio vaccine. When a vaccine was discovered in the mid-1950s, its mission effectively ended. It took the March of Dimes as a new name, its fund-raising tagline, and continues to work on the prevention of birth defects today.

Principle 6: Organizations Require Leadership and Management

Organizations do not function automatically, any more than an orchestra performance is automatic. Good organizations, like good orchestras, require leadership (musical direction and conducting, in the case of the orchestra) and management (securing the hall, printing the tickets, printing the program, arranging for tour transportation, etc.). An organization with great management and no leadership is stale; an organization with great leadership and poor management cannot deliver its program. Organizations can be overmanaged and under-led, or over-led and undermanaged.

Principle 7: Organizations Are of Different Focal Types

Organizations can be thought about in terms of different types of entities. Each type may have a different purpose. We have already mentioned Robert Quinn's fourfold typology: clan, hierarchy, market, and adhocracy.

In social work, the human service organization is a common, if not the most common, type. It is a people-changing organization into which individuals enter (clients, customers, consumers), within which they are processed, and from which they are to emerge in an improved state—for example, substance-free, better able to manage anger, having a higher quality of life.

Principle 8: Organizations Sometimes Produce the Opposite of Their Intended Goal

Some human service organizations, such as schools and prisons, are supposed to change people for the better, but actually only process people or change them for the worse. This latter result, in which prisoners are taught how to be better criminals, students actually lose knowledge in school, patients in mental hospitals become sicker, or *organizational iatrogenesis*. It comes from the concept of iatrogenic illness, in which the patient is actually made ill by the physician or catches cold in the doctor's office. This goal subversion can characterize the entire organization or affect a subgroup within the organization.

Principle 9: Organizations Are Central to Meaning Making for Citizens in Industrial Societies

In industrial societies, most citizens spend significant amounts of time in organizations. Typically, from a structural perspective, this connection begins when school attendance for children and continues until the retirement of workers. Preschool children and nonworking mothers are about the only groups in modern society who do not spend much of their day in an organization. Hence, what happens within the organization during the time that most of us are there becomes important, for good or for bad; organizational influence becomes magnified. Organizational influences are magnified by the time we spend within those organizations. And there is a lot of bad, as Scott Adams (1996a, 1996b) points out in *The Dilbert Principle* and *Dogbert's Top Secret Management Handbook*. Especially problematic are workplaces that impair the dignity of the people who work there. Randy Hodson (2001) identifies four *dignity dingers* in his book *Dignity at Work* that he finds common: (1) abusive management, (2) overwork, (3) autonomy constraint, and (4) rascally coworkers. Each of these is found in the nonprofit sector, but overwork is especially common and at times played out as financially pressured executives try to get workers to work for free or for cheap. This is when the organization becomes a thief of self-esteem and positive personal meaning. The reverse is also apparently true: When organizations (and social interactions generally) are positive, we can draw great strength from them. It was this insight that led Dr. Martin Seligman to found the positive psychology movement, which aims to enhance the quality of life in various settings, including the workplace.

Advanced Theoretical Principles

We selected for discussion here eight principles that fit the advanced category.

Interorganizational Theory of Organizational Differentiation

As organizations grow they pass through stages, as described earlier. What the proposition about growth did not describe is the structural properties that emerge as the organization moves from emergent to mature. As an open system, organizations need to fit into their environment (Scott, 2005). As they differentiate structurally, they tend to become as complex as their environments. Organizations that have complex environments need to be internally complex to address all the facets of the environment important to them. That is the first proposition. The second proposition is that the *kinds* of departments organizations tend to produce in their differentiated state tend to be ones that link substantively to vital inputs and outputs. So, for example, a child welfare agency that depends a lot on decisions made at the state capital will most likely have a lobbyist there. A people-processing organization that needs to move clients or patients out to make room for more coming in will probably have a discharge department. This idea of substantive isomorphism as a primary form of structural isomorphism is the second proposition.

Organizational Environments

Organizations are social actors. Early structural theories tended to look at the organization structure as a result of what it *did* in terms of products produced. *Optimal* was defined in relationship to those products. As cultural perspectives developed (which might include informal systems of interaction within the organization), one could think of organizations as being organized by the relationships among the internal and external stakeholders and their values and dispositions. Scott (1992, pp. 132–133) talks about technical (product-related) environments and institutional (structural- and cultural-related) environments.

Scott (1992) does not view these environments as alternatives, but as dimensions to which organizations might have stronger or weaker connections. His useful table gives some examples (p. 427; Table 12.1).

However, the interorganizational theory of differentiation looks at the environment of the organization as critical to the forms it assumes. Organizations are *shape shifters*, and should adapt to what the environment demands or rewards. This approach to institutional linkage, however, portrays the organization as a thoughtless respondent to the external (beyond the organization's skin) elements, as the structural approach did in terms of internal variables (within the organization's skin). New institutional theory posits an important advance—that the organization is a minded actor—which has two important implications. One is that

Table 12.1 **Technical and Institutional Environments with Illustrative Organizations**

		Institutional Environments	
		Stronger	**Weaker**
Technical environments		Utilities	General
	Stronger	Banks	manufacturing
		General hospitals	
Pharmaceuticals			
		Mental health clinics	Restaurants
		Schools	Health clubs
		Legal agencies	Child care
	Weaker	Churches	

Source: *Organizations: Rational, Natural, and Open Systems,* 3rd edition (p. 133), by W. R. Scott, Englewood Cliffs, NJ: Prentice Hall. Reprinted with permission.

the organization selects which elements of the environment to which it responds: There is choice. The organization may make bad choices, but the *environment* is a mélange of stimuli, competing and contradictory ones, but response requires the painful necessity of choice. Second, the organization may seek to influence the environment, or at least the relevant environment. Social advocacy and lobbying is a quick example. Public universities—like the University of Michigan—seek to influence state legislatures on the one hand, and federal research agencies on the other. The environment is multicentric, and provides many opportunities for influence (Elbach & Sutton, 1992). Scott (2001, p. 179) recognizes that "organizations are affected, even penetrated, by their environments, but are also capable of responding to these influence attempts creatively and strategically." (See also Scott's discussion of technical and institutional environments.)

Issues of Organizational Effectiveness

Organizations strive to be efficient (doing things right) and effective (doing the right thing). Those organizations that do both are usually well known as exemplars of their genre (see the list on page 430 from Peter Vaill) and are considered exceptional organizations. The word *exceptional* is important here because it speaks to the point that most organizations do not achieve this status. Some may do things right, but not be doing them on the right things; others are doing the right thing (common among nonprofits) but have managerial issues that mean they are not doing things right. Nonprofit organizations often overly rely on doing good, while failing to understand that they need to do things right (efficiency) and be doing the right things (effectiveness). This distinction between efficiency and effectiveness is very helpful in organizational analysis, yet most organizational analysts do not use it, tending to lump together efficiency, effectiveness, and success (to be mentioned later). Scott (1992, Chapter 13) devotes a chapter to the issue of effectiveness (while managing to avoid actually defining effectiveness). He explores three important concepts: the criteria offered to measure effectiveness, the measurement approaches used to examine the effectiveness question, and the variety of explanations that have been given for "differential effectiveness." The criteria issue is especially difficult for operating organizations. In a famous article titled "On the Folly of Rewarding A While Hoping for B," Steve Kerr (1995) points to many of the faulty measurements that organizations use to measure effectiveness. Three are central to this discussion (these are adaptations of Kerr's):

1. *Face time* is the time on the job when others see you, especially bosses. It bears no relationship to what you actually accomplish; rather, it presents the *face* or illusion of accomplishment. Employees who spend a lot of time at work are often thought to be productive, when in fact they are often not productive. How to actually measure accomplishment is one of the issues in presenteeism and outputs.

2. *Presenteeism* is the on-the-job version of absenteeism. When one is absent, one is not contributing to the agency. Presenteeism is being at your desk but still not working. Sometimes ill workers come to work and cannot function; at other times people give themselves a raise by working less. Presenteeism in effect measures work by being there.

3. *Outputs versus outcomes* is also related to the concepts just mentioned. In the human service field, outputs might be assessed by number of interviews, number of sessions attended, number of meetings attended, and things of that sort. The questions not asked are: Did the clients get better? Did the sessions and meetings have or add value, or were they just putting in the time (presenteeism)? Increasingly agencies are being asked for outcomes—actual results for clients—rather than measures of activity.

Kerr (1995) talks about causes as well. He lists four reasons that organizations become "fouled up":

1. (Over)Fascination with an "objective criterion"
2. Overemphasis on highly visible behaviors
3. Hypocrisy
4. Overemphasis on morality or equity rather than efficiency (this would be Scott's "institutional environment")

It is worth noting that Kerr's original article was published in 1975. In 1995, the Academy of Management asked for an update, and at the same time polled its readership to assess the article's current relevance. Readers overwhelmingly argued that all the things Kerr pointed to still exist. That would have to mean that the bad practices were taught to an *entirely new generation of managers*. Looking at it more than 15 years after the reprint, the piece still has relevance and bite.

Linear (More) Versus Multivariate Concepts of Success and Excellence

One might want to ratchet up the discussion of organizational effectiveness to one of "organizational success." Success in the United States is often thought of in terms of **more** and **bigger** than the counterpart. Individuals in organizations—as well as organizations themselves—struggle with ways to define success, and becoming larger—a "Bigger Mac"—seems to be a frequent choice.

But there are other approaches that do not involve more and bigger. Others think of success in more multifaceted ways. In their article in the *Harvard Business Review*, Laura Nash and Howard Stevenson (2004) provide a multifaceted approach involving four variables: happiness, legacy, significance, and achievement. They were looking at individuals, but if individuals were to alter their first variable—happiness—slightly to *a great place to work*, then an organization might be satisfied as well with possessing these four elements, especially if it is a small agency. But at least two of these areas remain problematic: *great place to work* and *achievement*. Two organizational arenas provide an approach to understanding them.

The first variable, what is a *great place to work*, has been analyzed in some detail by the Gallup organization. Using results from 2 million interviews, Buckingham and Coffman (1999, p. 28) list 12 variables in their book *First Break All the Rules* that, if present, create an organization for which employees enjoy working; or, using human resources jargon, "a workplace of choice":

Base Camp [What do I get?]

1. *Do I know what is expected of me at work?*
2. *Do I have the materials and equipment I need to do my work right?*
3. *At work, do I have the opportunity to do what I do best every day?*

Mid-Camp [What do I give? Do I belong here?]

4. *In the last seven days, have I received recognition or praise for doing good work?*
5. *Does my supervisor, or someone at work, seem to care about me as a person?*
6. *Is there someone at work who encourages my development?*
7. *At work, do my opinions seem to count?*

The Summit [Can we all grow?]

8. *Does the mission/purpose of my company make me feel my job is important?*
9. *Are my coworkers committed to doing quality work?*
10. *Do I have a best friend at work?*
11. *In the last six months, has someone at work talked to me about my progress?*
12. *This last year, have I had the opportunity to grow?*

There are multiple measures of achievement, yet it is still an elusive concept for organizations. In his article, "The Purposing of High Performing Systems," Peter Vaill (1982) suggests eight measures of achievement. He continues exploring the concept in his book *Management as a Performing*

Art (1989). Again, the multifaceted, rather than the linear, approach seems to make more sense:

1. *They are performing excellently against known external standards.*
2. *They are performing excellently against what is assumed to be their potential level of performance.*
3. *They are performing excellently against where they were at some previous point in time.*
4. *They have been judged by informed observers to be doing substantially better qualitatively than other comparable systems.*
5. *They are doing what they do with significantly less [sic] resources than it is assumed they needed to do what they do.*
6. *They are perceived as exemplars of the way they do whatever they do and thus become a source of inspiration to others.*
7. *They are perceived to fulfill at a high level the ideals for the culture within which they exist.*
8. *They are the only organizations that have been able to do what they do at all, even though it might not seem that what they do is a difficult or mysterious thing. (p. 25)*

To these we would add:

9. *They provide values in products and services, and add value to the system.*
10. *They accomplish these tasks without exploiting workers or the environment.*

The Problems of Organization Superperformance and Malperformance

When one talks about organizational outcomes, a couple of assumptions seem to be present. One is that the outcomes are generally positive ones, and another one is that they fall in the normal or average range. But what if the organizational outcomes are awful, such as patients getting sick in hospitals, explosions, and chemical spills? How can we understand these activities? And what about organizations that really have no room for mistakes, such as air traffic control towers, nuclear power plant operators, nuclear submarines, or scientists handling biohazardous material? The first problem was addressed by Charles Perrow (1984) in his book *Normal Accidents*. The second problem was addressed by Karl Weick (1995); Marais, Dulac, and Leveson (2004) provide an excellent overview. Bierly and Spender (1995, p. 1) have a very good summary of the issues here:

> *Perrow defined as "high risk" those organizations that combine complexity and tight coupling with the potential for catastrophic failure. He concluded that accidents are "normal" for such organizations because their managers face irreconcilable structural paradoxes. Centralization, the method of dealing with the tight coupling, must be combined with delegation, the method of dealing with the complexity. Weick, researching the complex and tightly coupled systems found in air traffic control and carrier flight-deck operations, saw these problems differently. He argued that strong organizational cultures provide a centralized and focused cognitive system within which delegated and loosely coupled systems can function effectively. High risk organizations thereby become transformed into high reliability organizations (HROs).*

Organizations Can Enhance or Exhaust the Human System

Organizations do work through staff. Overworking staff can cause burnout and human exhaustion. Sometimes it is a hard-driving boss. Sometimes it is overcommitment to work on the part of the employee. A good work–life balance is essential to sustained employee productivity, and organizations are slow to recognize this. Some do, as Sue Shellenbarger (2006, p. D1) points out in her *Wall Street Journal* article "Companies Retool Time-Off Policies to Prevent Burnout, Reward Performance." Those who are concerned for this group are checking on employees who never take vacations to help prevent the buildup of stress to the point it becomes strain. A study by Landrigan and colleagues (2004, p. 1838) in the *New England Journal of Medicine* concluded that "Eliminating interns' extended work shifts in an intensive care unit significantly increased sleep and decreased attentional failures during night work hours."

Social support for employees is one of the most important elements in preventing burnout. Some of that support comes from other employees, but the agency needs to do its part in showing concern as well.

Burnout has another source, though, which is also important to mention. Agencies are full of ambitious people who want to give service and get ahead. Sometimes that ambition translates into social undermining, in which colleagues (if that is the appropriate term for these people) advance their career by undermining yours. Being undermined by those with whom you work is a strange experience because one simply does not expect it and therefore it takes longer to recognize.

Sometimes agencies themselves participate in this undermining. They engage in a process of social exploitation, or getting employees to work for below-market wages. This typically means that wages are low to begin with ("We simply do not have the resources ... "), and then employees are encouraged, or guilt-tripped, into working extra hours for the same low pay. No wonder they feel used and soon burn out (see Maslach, 2003; Maslach, Jackson, & Leiter, 1996).

Positive Organizational Scholarship

As mentioned in Principle 9, organizations are major locales where meaning is made for people in the modern world. In many ways, the organization replaced the village as a central place where one interacts with others. As Buckingham and Coffman (1999) have pointed out, organizations can be great places to work and locations where the human spirit can be uplifted and the agency members flourish. This perspective is also one developed by the positive organizational scholarship (POS) movement started at the University of Michigan (www.bus.umich.edu/Positive). The mission of POS is as follows: "The Center for Positive Organizational Scholarship is a community of scholars devoted to energizing and transforming organizations through research on the theory and practice of positive organizing and leadership."

What does "positive" mean in this context? The center does work in areas such as compassion, organizational virtuousness, positive emotions, positive identity and experiencing a reflected best self, positive leadership, positive social capital, resilience, and thriving. This approach builds out from and focuses the positive psychology insights in an organizational venue. It is hopeful and inspiring. That said, its existence in some sense recognizes that organizations (a) are a long way from expressing these positive values, (b) need help in getting there, and (c) can, on their own, do serious damage. It is this last point that deserves special mention.

Sick Organizations

If positive organizational scholarship is the sunny side of organizational studies, then looking at *sick organizations* is the dark side. Sick organizations are those that actively harm the physical and mental health of employees and others with whom they come in contact (spouses and partners of employees, for example). If the POS folks are right and organizations can be structured to be uplifting and enhancing, the reverse must also be true. Manfred Kets Devries and Danny Miller (1984) talk about how organizations can have a deleterious impact in their book *The Neurotic Organization*. Kets Devries is an organizational specialist and a psychoanalyst; therefore, his characterizations of organizations take a clinical approach. They define five dysfunctional types of organizational styles. The first is the paranoid style, characterized by suspicion about everything. The second is the rigid and dogmatic agency, which shows a compulsive style. The third is an organization that has a dramatic style; it needs constant reassurance and seeks to wow the external world with its efforts and actions. The fourth is the schizoid style, which is emotionally detached and socially isolated. Finally, there is the depressive style, characterized by a low sense of pride, a preoccupation with the past, lots of talk about organizational death, indecision and risk aversion, and apathetic and inadequate leadership. (From personal observations, far too many social work organizations presented as depressive in Kets Devries and Miller's terms. There is constant weeping and wailing about the lack of resources, the lack of appreciation, the fact that they are always in peril.)

Recent Theoretical Developments

The distinction between *advanced* and *recent* is crisp in organizational studies and not as crisp as it might be in other fields. Some of the advanced items just discussed are recent, and the items in this section might be described as advanced. However, each is important regardless of their classification here.

Emotion Work in the Workplace

In the 1980s the University of California at Berkeley sociologist Arlie Russell Hochschild (1983) became interested in an aspect of organizations that had never been studied: the flow of feelings and emotions within the workplace. As a way to look into this issue she attended flight attendant school, an investigation that produced a book called *The Managed Heart*. She looked at the flight attendants' job as essentially the management of feelings, though nothing like this was mentioned in the job description. She was one of the first people to develop the analytical field called *emotion work*; it has since become a very important area of organization study, extending worldwide (see www.psychologie.uni-frankfurt.de/Abteil/ABO/forschung/emoarbeit_e.htm).

Previous work had looked at the results of poor emotional management at work, certainly one of the causes of burnout. But Hochschild was a true pioneer in articulating the ongoing issue of emotion work in the workplace and the gendered assignment of emotion management work. (To no one's surprise, it has mostly been assigned to or accepted by women.) Emotion work is a large part of social work, and it is a surprise, and a disappointment, that social work has not connected more to the field of emotion work, where it could contribute as well as learn. Research has connected "emotion work" to the labor process in the field of nursing and midwifery.

The development of emotion work led to the idea of the emotion quotient, a concept that has become part of the public discourse. Nancy Gibbs (1995) of *Time* puts it this way:

> The phrase "emotional intelligence" was coined by Yale psychologist Peter Salovey and the University of New Hampshire's John Mayer 5 years ago to describe qualities like understanding one's own feelings, empathy for the feelings of others and "the regulation of emotion in a way that enhances living." Their notion is about to bound into the national conversation, handily shortened to EQ, thanks to a new book, Emotional Intelligence (Bantam, 1995) by Daniel Goleman. Goleman, a Harvard psychology PhD and a New York Times science writer with a gift for making even the chewiest scientific theories digestible to lay readers, has brought together a decade's worth of behavioral research into how the mind processes feelings. His goal, he announces on the cover, is to redefine what it means to be smart. His thesis: When it comes to predicting people's success, brainpower as measured by IQ and standardized achievement tests may actually matter less than the qualities of mind once thought of as "character" before the word began to sound quaint.

New Approaches to Imagining Organizations

For most of the 20th century, the historical powers of the pyramid form of organization, and its connection to and reflection of the hierarchical structure, were a pervasive intellectual point of departure for thinking about organizations. In the past 25 years, additional and exciting ways to think about the organization have emerged. Tom Peters (1988) contrasts the "inflexible mass producer of the past" with the "flexible, porous, fleet-of-foot organization of the future." The second rendering is especially interesting, but even in portraying the older organization he uses a circle instead of a pyramid. See Figures 12.2 and 12.3.

Around this same time Tropman (1989) introduced the concept of *the organizational circle*. It offers a conceptualization of an organization like a solar system or an atom. Levels are gone, replaced by orbits. This approach has some significant differences from the pyramid model. For one thing, the idea of orbits suggests dynamism rather than stasis of organizational position of the subunits. For another, the core, or the executive top team, becomes central to, rather than above, the parts and elements of the organization. Third, organizational subunits are both close and far from the core, especially given an increased ellipsis of their orbit.

Figure 12.2

What have things been like? Tom Peters tells us.

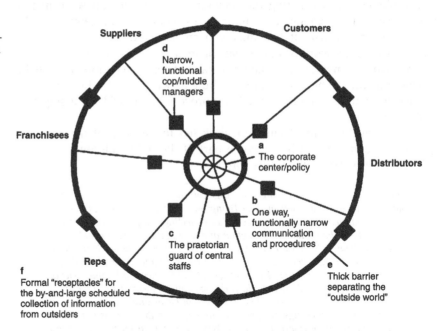

The Inflexible, Rule-determined, Mass Producer of the Past: All Persons Know Their Place

Start with (a), the corporate center/policy. This is the traditional, invisible, impersonal, generally out-of-touch corporate hub. The tininess of the circle representing the corporate center suggests both tightness and narrowness of scope; communication to the outside world (in or beyond the firm's official boundary) is usually via formal declaration—the policy manual or the multivolume plan, by and large determined on high—and communicated via the chain of command (i.e., downward). Within this tiny circle lie the "brains of the organization." It is here, almost exclusively, that the long-term thinking, planning, and peering into the future take place.

Source: "Restoring American Competitiveness: Looking for New Models of Organizations," by Tom Peters, 1988, *Academy of Management Executives*, 2(2), pp. 103–107. Reprinted with permission.

Figure 12.3

So what's new? Tom Peters again.

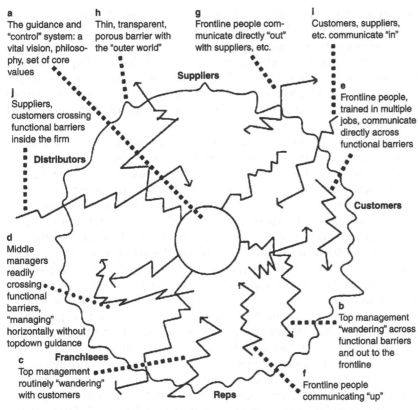

a The guidance and "control" system: a vital vision, philosophy, set of core values

h Thin, transparent, porous barrier with the "outer world"

g Frontline people communicate directly "out" with suppliers, etc.

i Customers, suppliers, etc. communicate "in"

Suppliers

j Suppliers, customers crossing functional barriers inside the firm

Distributors

e Frontline people, trained in multiple jobs, communicate directly across functional barriers

Customers

d Middle managers readily crossing functional barriers, "managing" horizontally without topdown guidance

Franchisees

c Top management routinely "wandering" with customers

Reps

b Top management "wandering" across functional barriers and out to the frontline

f Frontline people communicating "up"

The Flexible, Porous, Adaptive, Fleet-of-Foot Organization of the Future: Every person is "paid" to be obstreperous, a disrespecter of formal boundaries, to hustle and to be fully engaged with engendering swift action and constantly improving everything.

Source: "Restoring American Competitiveness: Looking for New Models of Organizations," by Tom Peters, 1988, *Academy of Management Executives, 2*(2), pp. 103–107. Reprinted with permission.

Organizational Kaleidoscopes: Disciplinary Perspectives

One way to think about organizations is as a set of stones that we look at through a kaleidoscope. Each turn of the kaleidoscope gives a different view of the same set of stones. Gareth Morgan (1998) gives an exciting array of ways to look at the organization in his book *Images of Organization*. Among those he discusses are the organization as an organism, a brain, and a hologram. Each view privileges different elements and aspects of the agency, and the full range gives a rich tapestry of understanding.

Disciplinary perspectives have also been important. Each discipline focuses on different organizational aspects.

Anthropology

For anthropology, culture is a central lens. During the 1980s the phrase *organizational culture* was coined in two separate books: Deal and

Kennedy's (1982) *Corporate Cultures* and Peters and Waterman's (1982) *In Search of Excellence*. Anthropologists were not heavily involved in early organizational culture research, which comes as a surprise because culture and human behavior is what anthropologists thrive on. Organizational theorists were investigating the different layers of organizations during this time. Anthropologists used different measures, such as ethnographic research and case illustrations, to investigate subcultures and other nested sets of networks.

As time progressed into the 1990s, anthropologists were involved in continued organizational research, applying their study of "culture" to "organizational culture." Organizational culture looks at an organization as if it were a culture in order to contextualize and understand organizational behavior. (It is useful to note here that, for anthropologists, "culture" includes *both* ideas, values, beliefs, norms, and attitudes *and* artifacts or structure. For sociologists, culture usually includes only the former set and not artifacts and structure.) At this point, it was thought that organizational culture was being researched to investigate the differences between American and Japanese businesses. Today, anthropologists use other techniques to help improve on organizational theory. Using anthropological techniques, Dennis Weidman (2001) has helped to explain how Florida International University doubled in size despite Hurricane Andrew and continued state budget cuts. He looked at the university as an organization and created a strategic plan to "organize information, symbols, and people that influence the allocations of resources and facilitate change in direction consistent with the goals of the university." A critical component of this investigation was to look at how external forces influenced the organization.

Economics

The economic view of organizations as *the firm* was as a rational economic actor seeking to maximize profits. The following theories help explain the economic relation to organizations, according to Zey (2001, p. 12751):

- *Rational choice theory* (RCT) is used when it is necessary to link the change in actions of individuals with change in characteristics of the organization.

- *Organizational theory* (OT) explains how individual actions articulate with structure.

Agency and transactional theories of the firm fall under the RCT frame of thought, and Weber's capitalist frame of thinking falls under the OT.

There are two approaches to organizational economics: (1) transactional cost economics and (2) agency theory. The first looks at the different transactions both internal and external to the organization. These transactions include those "between owners and managers, managers and subordinates, suppliers and producers, sellers and buyers" (Hodge,

---

Case Example

Organizational Economists Versus Organizational Theorists in Incentives

The organizational economist investigates the details about the organization's incentive systems. The organizational theorist investigates the social context of organizational incentives, which include "critical problems in culture, network structure, framing," and so on (Kaplan & Henderson, 2005, p. 509). The two work separately from one another; however, if they coordinated their efforts, more could be accomplished.

Anthony, & Gales, 1996, p. 23). Agency theory investigates the different interests between the owners and the workers. The owners want to maximize their profits, while the workers want to minimize their efforts.

Transactional cost economics was coined by Oliver Williamson (1975) in *Markets and Hierarchies*. It was established to help answer the question "Why are some exchanges done within an organization's boundaries, while others take place across boundaries?" (Davis, 2006, p. 485). This is important because complications in transactions might be less costly for an organization than complications between partners directly involved with the organization's investments and profits.

Political Science

This discipline looks at the organization as an arena in which and through which power is exercised. One of its important insights is that power in organizations, over time, tends to be concentrated in the hands of a few. This is called *The Iron Law of Oligarchy*. It was developed by Robert Michels in the early part of the century. (A recent translation of his book *Political Parties* is Michels, 1962.) Voss and Sherman (2000) make a similar point. They argue that organizations have a tendency to fall into oligarchy leadership patterns and tend to have conservative goals. In oligarchic leadership, the distance between staff and leaders increases, which allows leaders' interests to prevail. And goals become more conservative as leaders view the survival of the organization and increased (short-term) profit as most important.

Another important concept is the circulation of elites, developed by Vilfredo Pareto (1848–1923, as cited in Coser, 1977, pp. 395–396). This idea suggests that change in power is often the replacement of one elite for another, with the masses playing a distant role, if any. The concept is captured in the parable of the lions and the fox, which illustrates the different methodologies that are required for gaining and maintaining power. Some discontented lions are looking at a regime of wily and corrupt foxes. The lions are brutal and direct, and they attack the foxes, destroy them with their greater strength, and assume power. Their skills of brutality and strength begin to wear down, and they employ some wily foxes to help them. Over time the foxes replace the lions as the core of power, and other, dissident lions begin to flourish outside the inner circle. You know what happens next!

Psychology

Psychological perspectives come from industrial and organizational psychology, as well as from the discipline as a whole. Organizational psychology is used to investigate the relationship between the person and the organization, including attachments and commitment to the organization. It is also used to look at the program evaluation of nonprofits' strategic planning (McDavid & Hawthorn, 2006).

Psychologists tend to view the organization from the perspective of workers' "personality." What is their temperament, their *emotion quotient*, their communication style? Organizations tend to be viewed as packages of individual characteristics. Issues often involve using those individual characteristics to build big performing groups. During the 1990s, the top 10 topics in organizational psychology were the following, according to Katzell and Austin (1992):

1. Future of organizations (culture, climate, productivity, workforce, etc.)
2. Training
3. Organizational culture
4. Work teams and their effectiveness
5. Motivation: theory and practice
6. Competitive organizations
7. Conflict resolution
8. Changing technology, challenges
9. Power and leadership
10. Development of managerial talents

Sociology

"Organizational theory is the branch of sociology that studies organizations as distinct units in society" (Davis, 2006, p. 484). One could also call it the *organizational system*. The sociological perspective on organizational theory looks at the structures of organizations, the linkages between organizations, and how they intertwine over time. Early research on organizations examined how hierarchies work, and the organization's structure; however, as time progressed and research matured, more information was gathered on how the organization works in its environment and as a part of society.

Sociologists, like anthropologists, consider organizational culture. The ideas, values, norms, and beliefs that characterize an organization are part of the "double helix" of organizational structure and culture, interacting together, sometimes supporting and sometimes opposing each other.

Cultural lag occurs when the organizational structure changes faster than or ahead of the values of the organization. *Structural lag* occurs when the values change and the structure is still aligned with the older value system.

Organizational sociology also has some more particular interests. One is on the kind of organization—public, governmental, nonprofit. Although there is much that is similar among all classes of organizations, each type has issues of their own. Another is on organizational developmental and decline processes. Again, each phase has opportunities and challenges to be understood. And at the end of the organizational cycle, there can be reinvention or death and rebirth (and sometimes both—like the General Motors corporation). Going along with the stage of organizational development is organizational size. Small, medium-size, and large organizations have their own subsets of issues. A third is on the formal and informal systems within organizations and how they interact (for better or worse). Fourth, organizational sociologists are interested in how larger social dynamics play out within the organization. Rosabeth Kanter's *Men and Women of the Corporation* (1993, 1977) is a perfect example of this emphasis.

A fourth area is organizational change. More on change is mentioned later in the chapter.

Executive Derailment and Calamity

One of the elements that has characterized organizations recently is the problem of executive acting-out. The names Enron, Qualcom, Health South, and Bernard Madoff bring to mind organizations and executive teams who lie, cheat, and steal the organization's resources for personal enrichment. The case of Jack Abramoff (www.slate.com/id/2116389), the lobbyist who was convicted of bilking Indian tribes and peddling influence in Washington, DC, illustrates that government hanky-panky goes on as well. And the nonprofit sector appears to have its proportional share of over-the-top executives. The United Way scandal in the early 1990s is one example (Glasser, 1994), but there are others (Tropman & Shaefer, 2004; Tropman, Zhu, & Shaefer, 2004). Tropman and colleagues developed a calamity staircase to look at the ramifications of executive malfeasance (see Table 12.2).

The precipitating causes of these problems seem to lie in the nexus between the internal controls of the executive and the external controls of other parts of the organizational structure and (in the case of nonprofits and public companies) the board of directors.

Many organizations, such as the Catholic hierarchy, Andersen Accounting, and the U.S. military (Abu Ghraib prison) seem to have calamities that extend over time and place. Although organizations often characterize these problems as "a few bad apples," we would do well to recall Deming's injunction (and the sociologists' perspective) that the organizational system as a whole produces results both good and bad.

Table 12.2 The Calamity Staircase: Showing the Ramifications of Executive Malfeasance

Steps	Precipitating Event	Predisposing Events and Signature/Symptomatic Elements
1. Periderailment	Negative publicity and ancillary job loss (a board seat, for example)	Public problems, investigations, "smoldering" issues that bring unwanted attention, conflicts of interest that invite attention, behavior that invites public negative comment
2. Derailment	Publicly losing your job	"Resignation," "retirement," "to pursue other interests," "to spend more time with family," let go, reorganized out, "time for a change"
3. Flameout	Losing your job, bringing others with you, causing significant collateral damage, legal issues (indictments, lawbreaking)	Specific problems that go well beyond you that are commented on in the press, mention of others' involvements, mention of actual or potential negative sequelae
4. Calamity	Publicly losing your job, bringing others with you, causing significant organizational collapse	Bankruptcy, layoffs, pension fund collapse
5. Supercalamity	Publicly losing your job, bringing others with you, causing significant organizational collapse, negatively impacting industry/sector/nation	Huge publicity, multisector consequences

Source: The Crow and the Cheese: From Derailment to Calamity in the Executive Suite, by Tropman, Zhu, and Shaefer (2004, March), paper presented at the International Applied Business Research Conference, San Juan, Puerto Rico. Reprinted with permission.

Organizational Decision Making

Organizations run on three fuels: money, people, and ideas. Some organizations and thinkers emphasize one over the other (the economists, for example, tend to emphasize money in the form of costs and profits), but most thinkers agree that each is necessary if an organization is to be successful. If we look at that statement more closely, though, we see that it is not just the presence of money, people, and ideas that is important: It is their application, orchestration, and integration that make all the difference. That means that underlying each of those variables—a building block, as it were—is the process of organizational decision making. Good decisions make organizations successful; great decisions make organizations exceptional; rotten decisions cause organizations to fail. A close look at decision making and the quality of those decisions is vital to understanding organizational operations. One new view is that decisions can be looked at as if they were a business product (which they are). One can ask not only how decisions are made, but also about their quality (Tropman, 2002).

Although the field of analyzing how to *make good decisions* is new, the field of *looking at bad decisions* is much better developed. Bad decisions, it seems, result from bad decision processes (no surprise to Mr. Deming). Four well-known bad decision processes are examples of what can go wrong. Perhaps the most well known is the idea of groupthink, developed by Irving Janis (1983). In groupthink one of two problems can occur: Either the group is so cohesive that no one wants to bring bad news, or the group succumbs to an intimidating boss. Something similar to that occurs in the Abilene Paradox, developed by Jerry Harvey (1974). There, because of a lack of decision clarification, everyone winds up doing something that no one wanted to do.

The concept of defensive routines, what we would call *organizational denial*, develops in organizations. Certain topics are not discussed, and their nondiscussability is not discussed either. Chris Argyris (1985) developed this idea in connection with his exploration of organizational learning. He wondered how organizations learn. While that question is still under investigation, Argyris did introduce the idea of single- and double-loop learning. Single-loop learning is like a thermostat; it gets set and operates at that setting regardless. It is a bit like Robert Merton's (1958) concept of means ritualism. It does not question whether the setting is right. Double-loop learning, on the other hand, questions the setting as well as operating the furnace. Double-loop learning is necessary if organizations are to improve and develop.

Another way to think about decision avoidance is to set a high threshold of trouble before one makes a decision. This almost always leads to reactivity, because one is deciding too late in the process to be effective. Tichy and Devanna (1986) discuss this as the concept of the boiled frog syndrome. They explain that if you place a frog in cold water and then slowly heat the water, the frog will not notice and will boil to death. In organizational decision making, this is called the "just noticeable difference syndrome": Small differences do not hit the threshold, so nothing is done. And the organization dies.

Diversity and Organizations

Issues of diversity are of vital importance to organizational demographics. As globalization increases, organizations are becoming more and more diverse in all possible ways—in ethnicity, nationality, age, color, and gender, to name a few of the more popular dimensions. This diversity does not always (or even frequently) extend throughout the organization; however, in North American as well as European organizations, the leadership is likely to come from the White male group. Indeed, with respect to minorities, "the higher, the fewer" might be a sensible proposition. Increasing diversity is generally thought to be a good thing, not only because it is the right thing to do (which many social work agencies think) but also because it increases connectivity with the organization's customers, clients, and consumers.

Organizations tend to reproduce the top team through cloning (Kanter, 1993, in *Men and Women of the Corporation*, calls this process "homosocial reproduction"). This process means that leaders of organizations prefer to select leaders like themselves, which accounts in part for the great persistence of White male leadership. And women, even executive women, still earn about 75% to 80% of their male counterparts.

Relevance to Social Work Practice

Organizations—we call them agencies—are obviously important to social work because it is through them that much of social work practice goes on. If they are run well, workers are satisfied and can do good work. If they are run poorly, good work is not done, and accomplishment of the mission of the organization becomes impaired. Thomas Holland's (1995, p. 1787) writing in the *Encyclopedia of Social Work* provides an excellent overview of "organizations [as a] context for service delivery" and provides a brief history of perspectives on social service organizations.

Agencies are human service organizations. They are generally organized to help others, though they are not the only organizations with that goal. Churches, law firms, and hospitals are among the others who also have helping aims. Generally, though far from always, human service organizations provide help to those who have difficulty helping themselves at some point—often people marginalized by society in one or many ways. It is important to keep in mind that American society is ambivalent about the process of helping in general, and helping the poor in particular. This ambivalence places social work agencies in a subdominant position, one of suspected appreciation, as it were. In the book *Do Americans Hate the Poor?* the issue of poorhate and speculation on some of its implications are raised (Tropman, 1998a).

Either contributing to this situation or reflecting it, or both, is the fact that most of the helpers are women. Helping is thus a gendered process, which no doubt further complicates the issue. Within the helping system, there are always more needs than resources, and that means that the organizations need to have some kind of internal allocating system: Some get more of their needs met than others do. This process, however, is not unique to social agencies. All organizations have an excess of needs over resources and need to find ways to make the books balance (Tropman & Shaefer, 2006).

To be run well and to be effective and efficient, agencies must be managed and led well (see Principle 6). Although probably no one would disagree with this assertion, it does raise two issues for the field. One is whether management is generic or specific. That is, do social work managers need to *be* social workers (and what kind of social workers?) to carry out a social work mission? This question actually applies in the form of "Does one have to be one to run one?" across all forms of organization. The consensus seems to be that there are indeed common elements of management and leadership that run across all settings and organizations, but that *product knowledge* is also required.

In social work we have approached this question with something of a split personality. On the one hand, we like to think that social work agencies should be led and managed by social workers; they have the in-depth product knowledge to actualize the mission. That said, we have not, on the other hand, done much to train those who become executive leaders in the generic parts of the executive leadership task. The problem with this approach is that someone who is a good player might not make a good coach; someone who is a good cook may not make a good chef. There has been some attention to the process of managerial education. In 1947, Elwood Street, the executive director of the Greater Bridgeport and Stratford (Connecticut) Community Chest and Council, wrote a book called *A Handbook for Social Agency Administration*. In the same year Margaret Clark and Briseis Teall (1947) wrote *The Executive Director on the Job*. Peter Drucker (1990) wrote *Managing the Non-Profit*, emphasizing the importance of mission-driven management and leadership.

In 1991, Edwards and Yankey produced a compilation titled *Skills for Effective Human Services Management.* Then, David Austin (1995) wrote an excellent "Management Overview" in the *Encyclopedia of Social Work*. And in 1998, Edwards, Yankey, and Altpeter edited *Skills for Effective Management of Nonprofit Organizations.* Currently Edwards and Yankey (2006) have an updated version titled *Effectively Managing Nonprofit Organizations.* However, management programs in schools of social work are generally small. (The University of Michigan is one exception.) A plethora of "centers for nonprofit management" are springing up all over the country, including some national centers, like Compass Point (www.compasspoint.org), the Tides Center (www.tidescenter.org/index_tc.cfm), and the Fieldstone Alliance (formerly part of the Amherst H. Wilder Foundation; www.fieldstonealliance.org), which is a testimony to the fact that the profession of social work has dropped the training ball when it comes to management education, both within MSW curricula and afterward.

There is even an organization of assistance organizations (and others interested in issues of nonprofit management), the Nonprofit Alliance (www.allianceonline.org).

Overall Social Work Demographics

How many social workers are there, and where do they work? That number is hard to come by because there are different ways of determining a "social worker." There are, of course, the degrees—master's of social work and bachelor's of social work. In 2009, in terms of this training, there were 468 accredited bachelor's of social work programs (BSW) and 196 master's of social work (MSW) programs (Bureau of Labor Statistics, 2010). But there are also state licensing requirements, which use the term "social worker," that are job related rather than education related.

From the perspective of recent history, June Hopps and Pauline Collins (1995, p. 2275) reported that in 1991 there were 630,000 workers who were called social workers, and 75% of them were employed. Of these, 24% reported working in private for-profit enterprises (though it is not clear whether this means private practice or corporate employment). They also report that the profession was 77% female. That figure rose to 81% in 2004, as compared to a 51% female proportion in the U.S. labor force (Center for Health Workforce Studies & NASW Center for Workforce Studies, 2006). It is clear that the social work profession is highly organizationalized, so what happens in organizations is of vital concern not only to the clients but also to the employees. Further, with such a big proportion of women in the profession, the possibility of gender-based exploitation of those women is a constant threat.

Government workforce figures show fewer numbers, but they are looking at employed persons (Bureau of Labor Statistics, 2010):

Social workers held about 642,000 jobs in 2008. About 54 percent of jobs were in health care and social assistance industries, and 31 percent were employed by government agencies. Although most social workers are employed in cities or suburbs, some work in rural areas. Employment by by type of social worker, in 2008, follows:

Child, family, and school social workers	292,600
Mental health and substance abuse social workers	138,700
Medical and public health social workers	137,300
Social workers, all other	73,400

That same report looks at earnings of social workers in different settings. The following figures provide the most recent data:

Median annual earnings of child, family, and school social workers were $39,530 in May 2008. The middle 50 percent earned between $31,040 and $52,080. The lowest 10 percent earned less than $25,870, and the top 10 percent earned more than $66,430. Median annual earnings in the industries employing the largest numbers of child, family, and school social workers in May 2008 were:

Elementary and secondary schools	$53,860
Local government	46,650
State government	39,600
Individual and family services	34,450
Other residential care facilities	34,270

Median annual earnings of medical and public health social workers were $46,650 in May 2008. The middle 50 percent earned between $35,550 and $57,690. The lowest 10 percent earned less than $28,100, and the top 10 percent earned more than $69,090. Median annual earnings in the industries employing *the largest numbers of medical and public health social workers in May 2008 were:*

General medical and surgical hospitals	$51,470
Home health care services	46,930
Local government	44,140
Nursing care facilities	41,080
Individual and family services	38,370

Median annual earnings of mental health and substance abuse social workers were $37,210 in May 2004. The middle 50 percent earned between $28,910 and $48,560. The lowest 10 percent earned less than $21,770, and the top 10 percent earned more than $61,430. Median annual earnings in the industries employing the largest numbers of mental health and substance abuse social workers in May 2008 were:

Outpatient care centers	$36,660
Individual and family services	35,900
Residential mental retardation, mental health and	33,950
substance abuse facilities	29,110

Median annual earnings of social workers, all other were $46,220 in May 2008. The middle 50 percent earned between $34,420 and $60,850. The lowest 10 percent earned less than $27,400, and the top 10 percent earned more than $74,040. Median annual earnings in the industries employing the largest numbers of social workers, all other in May 2008 were:

General medical and surgical hospitals	$55,940
Local government	51,700
Individual and family services	36,660
Residential mental retardation, mental health and substance abuse facilities	36,460
Community food and housing, and emergency and other relief services	31,890

The median incomes of social workers ($39,530, $46,650, $37,210, and $46,220) yields a group median of $41,930 (dividing the two middle numbers by 2). That is extraordinarily close to the 2008 U.S. per capita income of $40,947 (Bureau of Economic Analysis, 2011). It is 2.3% above the per capita income, in fact. Without question, gender plays a role here. In 2008, male median income was $46,367; the female median was $35,745 (DeNavas-Walt, Proctor, & Smith, 2008). For professional people (women), with a high proportion of advanced degrees, this is a problem.

Nonprofit Sector

Another way to look at the social work organizational field is to look at nonprofit organizations as a sector. One needs to understand that there are many nonprofits that do not perform social services.

What is going on in the nonprofit social service sector? Some facts and figures may help us orient ourselves. Nonprofits are not the only place that social workers work, as we shall see in a moment. There is the public sector and the corporate sector. But at least let's start here.

According to National Center for Charitable Statistics (http://nccs dataweb.urban.org/PubApps/profile1.php), there were 1,581,111 nonprofit organizations in the United States in 2009.[2] Their total 2004 revenue was about $1 trillion, not counting an additional $266.3 billion in charitable contributions (2005 data). Nonprofit organizations employ 9.4 million persons, not counting an additional 5 million or so volunteers.

Independent Sector (2007) also points out that the majority of nonprofit organizations utilize volunteerism along with paid employment to keep their organizations afloat. If someone is asked to volunteer, more than half the time he or she will agree to volunteer. Women are more likely than men to volunteer. In 2002, 44% of adults in the United States reported that they volunteer their time. Almost 60% of teenagers volunteer 3.5 hours a week. In 2000, a total of 15.5 billion hours were clocked in the United States by volunteers, which, when calculated with the 2000 average hourly volunteer value of $15.68, totals $239 billion worth of work. In 2006, that number was up to $18.77.

Finally, the nonprofit sector is notorious for being primarily a female-populated sector. However, when it comes to leadership positions, women as previously noted, continue to earn significantly less than their male counterparts. In addition, females are more likely to lead the smaller organizations (GuideStar, 2004).

There is a growing trend in the sector in how to address the recipients of agency services. Whether a person is referred to as a client, a customer, or a consumer, every sector of the nonprofit sector serves some form of individuals, groups, families, or parts of families. Another component to consider is whether the client is receiving agency services voluntarily or involuntarily.

Trends in the Nonprofit Social Service Sector

There are a number of trends within the nonprofit social service sector, and indeed within the nonprofit sector at large, that are currently under way and will have an impact on the delivery of services.

Confounding of Services Among the Three Sectors

In times past, there was a clearer distinction (though not completely crisp) among public services, private social services, and corporate services. Now, in most areas, services are provided by each of the three sectors. Consider child care, for example. There are public, private, and corporate offerings. The same is true in the aging field and in substance abuse and corrections. It is therefore less clear what organizational location does what.

---

[2]There may actually be close to 1.9 million but the 1.5 figure represents those registered with the IRS. Religious organizations are not required to register.

Nonprofit organizations and social services generally have two sets of customers. One set includes those who use and pay for the service. The other set includes customers who have supplementary entities that pay their bill. Thus the agency needs to respond both to the user of the service and also to the payer of the service. A possible problem is that agencies become overly responsive to the payers, much like your body shop becomes overly responsive to your auto insurer rather than to you. Medical care is another example, when covered by insurance.

Lack of Taxonomy

The nonprofit sector does not have an accepted taxonomy for services. This lacuna is long-standing and harmful for the sector as a whole, because we really do not know, without a study each time, how much of what kinds of services are currently being offered. For example, if one asks how much child care is going on at any point in time, the large number of definitions of child care range from basic care to educationally enriched. This means that the question cannot readily be answered. Further, communication among child care providers and customers or consumers often becomes garbled as the differences in definitions and expectations become apparent. The Urban Institute's *National Taxonomy of Exempt Entities Care Codes*, published in September of 1998, is a very positive step in this direction. Even mental health services are a hodgepodge of this service package and that service package. In the clinical area, the *Diagnostic and Statistical Manual of Mental Disorders* serves this function. We are now at *DSM-IV-TR* (with the *DSM-5* coming out shortly) and while there are conflicts over the categories, it is a useful system for organizing and communicating.

User Nomenclature

Historically, those who used social work services were called *clients*, a term also used by other professions, such as the law. But in recent years some have felt that the term is disempowering, and other terms, such as consumer and customer, are coming into vogue. Different terms have different implications, and the move away from *client* is thought to be an empowering one for any person.

The Name of the Top Job Is Changing

Similar changes are occurring at the executive level. The historical name for the top job was *executive director*, improved from *executive secretary*, which was more popular in the early years of the 20th century. Now, however, there is a terminological escalation of that title, with phrases like *chief professional officer*, *chief executive officer*, and *president* becoming common. The title of *chairperson* is still used for the head of the board of directors, but change is also occurring at this level. There is a movement away from the more phlegmatic term *member* to the more corporate term *director*.

Big Change Coming in the Executiveship Cadre as Boomers Retire

The largest number of executives of nonprofit human services agencies are in the baby boomer generation, and many will be retiring within the next several years. This generational shift creates issues of sustainability for the sector. As the Annie E. Casey Foundation (n.d.) puts it:

> Transitions are becoming increasingly frequent. A Foundation study conducted in 2000 with 130 of its community-based grantees found that 85% of executives will likely leave their positions by 2007. Similar surveys, including a recent arts leadership study, suggest that this is representative of a larger generational shift in the sector's leadership predicted in the coming decade. (www.aecf.org/initiatives/leadership/programs/capacity.htm)

The Staying Problem

If leaving is a problem in many instances, staying is as well. Many executives stay too long, and in each case the problems tend to be heartbreaking. One category of these overstayers is the founders. These are the individuals who founded the organization and often ran it before the first executive was hired. Their time has passed, but the gratification they get out of their legacy encourages them to destroy it. Another problematic category is the ill or sick executive, who, because of medical problems, cannot do his or her work yet cannot seem to work out with the board a suitable exit strategy. A third category is long stayers who have retired in place. Each of these, and others, threatens the sector as well.

The Development of the Idea of Core Competencies

In the midst of all these issues of management and structure, with organizations coming on the scene at a rapid rate, are questions about what the core elements of an organization actually are. Tropman and Lucas (2006) adapted some of that work in Alderfer's (1969) existence, relatedness, and growth model. A design is presented in Figure 12.4. This work incorporates the work of Blumenthal (2003) and organizes it in a sensible way. This taxonomic approach begins to bring together the elements of organizational capacity in ways that clarify and sequence the elements of capacity.

At the bottom of the figure are elements that Tropman and Lucas (2006) culled from the capacity literature that form the base of the elements organizations need to have if they are to achieve functionality. These nine elements fall into two categories, leadership and management, which can be considered a package of one, executive leadership, though there are obviously components and levels within each. On the organizational side, agencies need a functioning governance system, the ability to deliver programs and support that program delivery, a supportive culture that recognizes and reflects the diversity of its clientele, and the ability to change and to connect to the community. Accomplishing satisfactory levels of these elements allows for the *existence* of the organization. Deficiencies threaten its sustainability.

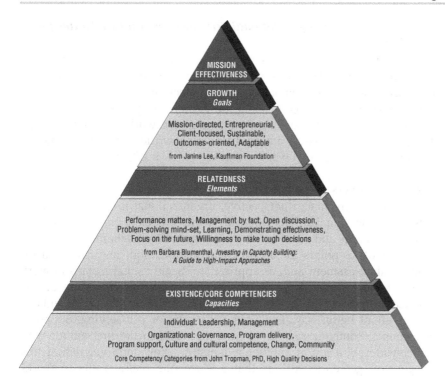

Figure 12.4

The competency pyramid: Existence/ relatedness/growth.

According to Barbara Blumenthal (2003), most of the capacity-building suggestions are anecdotal and have no empirical basis. In her own work involving interviewing 100 grantees and grantmakers in capacity-building programs, she concluded that organizational cultures that support the following practices will be most effective: (a) a belief that performance matters; (b) management by fact (goals and measures); (c) open discussion as the norm (no defensive routines, no groupthink); (d) data-based problem solving; (e) organizational learning that produces proactive change; (f) a requirement to prove effectiveness; (g) a focus on the future, especially financially; and (h) willingness to make tough decisions. If an organization has a culture that supports and reflects these practices, it will likely go beyond *existence* to *relatedness*.

For an organization to grow, however, it needs to go even further. It needs to be constantly infused with a sense of mission (mission-directed); it needs to be outcomes-oriented (as opposed to outputs-oriented, a reflection of Blumenthal's "performance matters" piece); it needs to be nimble (entrepreneurial, adaptable), yet it needs to be sustainable enough that it is not wobbly.

Uses in Assessment and Intervention

How might organization theory (or organizational theories) be useful in assessment? There are several ways.

Understanding That Organizational Structure and Culture Matter for Individual Clients

While it may seem obvious, organizational theory establishes the importance of organizations—good ones and bad ones—in our lives. A supportive and fun work environment can affect the home sphere. Perhaps more important for a counseling profession, negative organizational environments can also do that. Problems in the workplace such as lack of dignity, abusive bosses, and problematic coworkers are not always (if ever!) parts of the job one can leave at the plant or office.

Assessing Workers' Personal Fit

Looking to a more macro perspective, organizational theory can help us understand the organizations where we work to decide, ourselves, if there is a fit between us and our workplace. Using the Buckingham and Coffman (1999) list of 12 points for an excellent organization, one can do a bit of personal assessment and, as appropriate, begin to make plans to work elsewhere. Frequently, because of the *organizationalized* nature of our socialization, we are inclined to think that the organization is right and our feelings about being, say, exploited are wrong or self-serving. Suppose, for example, someone says to you, as they said to the first author who was considering a job at another university, "You don't get rich at this college; you get enriched!" Is that a place one really wants to work? I think not.

Assessing Human Service Organizations

Apart from the personal fit to one's own employment, organizational social workers (consultants, staff of management assistance organizations) can use elements of organizational theory to diagnose or assess the areas of weakness in their organization and assist the organization in fixing them. These assessments will be informed not only by the core competency triangle mentioned before, but also by the stages of organizational development. The competency package will look different for an emerging organization as opposed to one that is more mature. Such an assessment can include staff assays, executive assays, and governance assays, as well as touching base with stakeholders (payers, users, and others).

Working With the Executive and Executive Team

Executive coaching is a new area for social work (Caspi, 2005). Elements involve working with the executive to see the degree of fit between his or her skills and desires and the level of organizational development. Some executives are best at startup, others at mature organizations; still others like to catch the wave at the apex of the sigmoid curve and assist in agency reinvention; others change as the organization needs them to change. Coaching may also involve developing a career path for the executive and assisting that executive in organizing, attending to, and achieving personal and professional growth.

Developing Education and Training for Project Managers, Managerial Supervisors, Middle Managers, and Executives

As noted, there is a great need for more education and training for the executive leaders currently in place and those in the pipeline. More training is needed, and social workers can organize, market, and deliver such training to their peers.

Assisting in Efforts at Organizational Change

Agencies, as social institutions, often need to change but fail to recognize that need. The "boiled frog syndrome" lurks over each of us. Organizational change agents—consultants often, but sometimes those already employed by the agency—can assist the organization in facing its issues and becoming better. The middle of the competency pyramid—establishing a culture and a structure of performance, outcomes, candor, and accountability—is as hard for organizations as for individual clients. This is another area where social work can be of service. Sometimes the changes are evolutionary, sometimes revolutionary; sometimes they are transformational, sometimes transactional; sometimes invention is required, sometimes innovation, sometimes it is change of the system, sometimes it is change in the system. Regardless, social workers, guided by organizational theory, can help facilitate the change.

Evidence-Based Foundations

The concept of evidence-based practice is an excellent one for organizational theory to address. At the theoretical level, there is much agreement among scholars on the general principles outlined here. At the application level, however, Blumenthal's (2003) caution—that much of the best practice material is anecdotal—stands as a cautionary note. There is not much that organizational theory and its derived propositions and suggestions can say for sure is right to do. The most comprehensive work, and work that we consider strongly evidence-based, is the 2 million interviews done over a 2-year period in *First Break All the Rules* by Buckingham and Coffman (1999); that seems about as well-founded as one is going to get. Its format—a popular book—has probably led it to be viewed with less than acceptance by some in the academic community. But the evidence is there, and is presented in a methodological discussion at the end of the book. One can take those principles as reliable and valid and begin to look at one's own organization in light of them.

Still, there is less hard evidence than any of us would like. There are questions the work to date suggests we keep considering. The following are particularly important:

- Mountain Man versus Wagon Train: How can we weight the role of the individual versus the role of the system?
- How can organizations become more self-reflective?

- How can human service organizations care for clients and care for staff? Does use of money for staff care take money away from clients?
- How do human service organizations know whether they are accomplishing anything?
- Why are human service organizations so far behind in technology and human resources practices?

Critiques of This Approach

Organizational theory is not an approach, like a therapeutic or psychological technique. Rather, it is a hawser: a bundle of strands of ideas, perspectives, suggestions, and proposals that come from interviews, focus groups, systematic thought, and experiential mining viewed from a number of different perspectives (anthropology, political science, sociology, psychology, economics, decision science, etc.). Organizational theory needs to be used, but with judgment and prudence. One does not reject organization theory and propositions (or parts of it) because it does not meet an arbitrary standard (recall that there are type 1 *and* type 2 errors), nor does one accept something in a book by a famous CEO without reflection and contemplation.

Conclusion

Organizations are a triumph of somewhat intelligent design. They serve noble and ignoble social purposes. They do things individuals cannot because of their longevity, their reach, and their multifaceted membership. But they are also deeply flawed. There are no standards today for being on a board of directors. One has to go through more training to get a lifeguard patch on one's swimsuit than to be on a profit or nonprofit board. There are no professional standards for managers and CEOs, including ethical ones. Each board works on its own, making and remaking its own errors and those of other organizations. There is little accountability for middle and senior managers. Imagine if those women and men were subjected to the same numerical scrutiny as, for example, a quarterback on a football team. The background announcer in sports broadcasting is chock full of every conceivable nanobit of information about the sports figures in the game he or she is announcing. Managers and executives enjoy freedom from such numerical scrutiny. This means that errors in executive appointments can contain many more error terms than picking your draft choice; and errors are made even so. Although organizations have a greater social impact than sports, in aggregate, they escape the scrutiny that sports require. The next big task of organizational theory is to take a deep dive into the societal impact of organizational actions to help us understand who is a star player and who is a social loafer.

Key Terms

Effectiveness

Efficiency

Emotion work

Formal
organizations

Hawthorne studies

Organizational
behavior

Organizational
culture

Organizational
iatrogenesis

Organizational
policy

Organizational
practice

Positive organiza-
tions approach

Sick organizations

Review Questions for Critical Thinking

1. Do "organizations" exist, apart from the aggregated behavior of the individuals who comprise them?
2. Why is an understanding of empirically supported organizational principles of importance to social work practice?
3. Think of an organization with which you are familiar. Describe and distinguish between its formal and informal systems.
4. What does it mean for an organization to be "effective"?

Online Resources

Catalyst works with businesses and the professions to build inclusive environments and expand opportunities for women at work.

www.catalyst.org

Chronicle of Philanthropy is a news source for charity leaders, fund raisers, grant makers, and others involved in *philanthropic* enterprises.

http://philanthropy.com/section/Home/172

Deming Institute—The W. Edwards Deming Institute® is a nonprofit organization that was founded in 1993 by noted consultant Dr. W. Edwards Deming.

http://deming.org/

Harvard Business Review is a journal that publishes business management case studies, articles, books, and more addressing today's topics and challenges in business

http://hbr.org/

National Society of Female Executives is one of the country's largest associations for women professionals and business owners. It provides resources—through education, networking, and public advocacy—to empower its members to achieve both career and personal success.

www.nafe.com

References

Adams, S. (1996a). *The Dilbert principle.* New York, NY: Harper & Row.

Adams, S. (1996b). *Dogbert's top secret management handbook.* New York, NY: Harper & Row.

Alderfer, C. (1969). An empirical test of a new theory of human needs. *Organizational Behavior and Human Performance, 4,* 142–175.

Argyris, C. (1985). *Strategy, change, and defensive routines.* Upper Saddle River, NJ: Longman.

Austin, D. (1995). Management overview. In R. Edwards (Ed.), *Encyclopedia of social work* (19th ed., pp. 1642–1658). Washington, DC: National Association of Social Workers Press.

Barnard, C. I. (1962). *The functions of the executive.* Cambridge, MA: Harvard University Press. (Original work published 1938)

Bierly, P. E., & Spender, J. C. (1995). Culture and high reliability organizations: The case of the nuclear submarine. *Journal of Management, 24*(4), 639–656.

Blau, P. (1968). Organizations: Theories of organizations. In D. L. Sills (Ed.), *International encyclopedia of the social sciences* (Vol. 2, pp. 297–305). New York, NY: Macmillan and Free Press.

Blau, P., & Scott, R. (1962). *Formal organizations.* San Francisco, CA: Chandler.

Blumenthal, B. (2003, November). *Investing in capacity building: A guide to high-impact approaches.* New York, NY: Foundation Center.

Bolman, L., & Deal, T. E. (2003). *Reframing organizations* (3rd ed.). San Francisco, CA: Jossey-Bass.

Buckingham, M., & Coffman, C. (1999). *First break all the rules: What the world's greatest managers do differently.* New York, NY: Simon & Schuster.

Bureau of Economic Analysis, U.S. Department of Commerce. (2011). Per capita personal income by state, 1990 to 2010. Retrieved from http://bber.unm.edu/econ/us-pci.htm

Bureau of Labor Statistics. (2010). Social workers. *Occupational Outlook Handbook, 2010–11.* Retrieved from www.bls.gov/oco/ocos060.htm#outlook/

Caspi, J. (2005). Coaching and social work: Challenges and concerns. *Social Work, 50*(4), 359–362.

Center for Health Workforce Studies & NASW Center for Workforce Studies. (2006). Licensed social workers in the United States, 2004. Retrieved from http://workforce.socialworkers.org/studies/chapter2_0806.pdf

Clark, D. (1999). Hawthorne effect. Retrieved from www.nwlink.com/~donclark/hrd/history/hawthorne.html

Clark, M., & Teall, B. (1947). *The executive director on the job.* New York, NY: Women's Press.

Cooper, C. A., Cartwright, S., & Earley, P. C. (Eds.). (2001). *Handbook of organizational culture.* London, UK: Blackwell.

Coser, L. (1977). *Masters of sociological thought.* New York, NY: Harcourt Brace.

Davis, G. F. (2006). Organization theory. In J. Beckert & M. Zafirovski (Eds.), *International encyclopedia of economic sociology* (pp. 484–488). London, UK: Routledge.

Deal, T. E., & Kennedy, A. A. (1982). *Corporate cultures: The rites and rituals of corporate life.* Reading, MA: Addison-Wesley.

Deming, W. E. (1982). *Out of the crisis.* Cambridge, MA: MIT Press.

DeNavas-Walt, C., Proctor, B. D., & Smith, J. C. (2008, September). Income, poverty, and health insurance coverage in the United States: 2008 (Current population reports: Consumer income). Washington, DC: U.S. Census Bureau. Retrieved from www.census.gov/prod/2009pubs/p60–236.pdf

Drucker, P. (1990). *Managing the nonprofit organization: Practices and principles.* New York, NY: HarperCollins.

Edwards, R., & Yankey, J. (Eds.). (1991). *Skills for effective management of nonprofit organizations.* Washington, DC: National Association of Social Workers Press.

Edwards, R., & Yankey, J. (Eds.). (2006). *Effectively managing nonprofit organizations.* Washington, DC: National Association of Social Workers Press.

Edwards, R., Yankey, J., & Altpeter, M. (Eds.). (1998). *Skills for effective management of nonprofit organizations.* Washington, DC: National Association of Social Workers Press.

Elbach, K. D., & Sutton, R. I. (1992). Acquiring organizational legitimacy through illegitimate actions: A marriage of institutional and impression management theories. *Academy of Management Journal, 35*(4), 699–738.

Frank, R. H., & Kaul, J. D. (1978). The Hawthorne experiments: First statistical interpretation. *American Sociological Review, 43,* 623–643.

Gearth, H., & Mills, C. W. (1958). *From Max Weber.* New York, NY: Galaxy. (Original work published 1947)

Gibbs, N. (1995). The EQ factor. *Time, 46*(14). Available from www.seorf.ohiou.edu/~af313/Brain/EmotionalQ/eq.htm

Glasser, J. S. (1994). *An insider's account of the United Way scandal: What went wrong and why.* New York, NY: Wiley.

Glisson, C., & James, L. R. (2002). The cross-level effects of culture and climate in human service teams. *Journal of Organizational Behavior, 23,* 767–794.

GuideStar. (2004). Gender, geography, and nonprofit compensation. Retrieved from www.guidestar.org/news/features/2004_comp_findings.jsp

Handy, C. (1994, Fall). Where are you on the sigmoid curve? *Directors and Boards.*

Harvey, J. B. (1974, Summer). The Abilene paradox. *Organizational Dynamics,* 63–80.

Hochschild, A. R. (1983). *The managed heart.* Berkeley, CA: University of California Press.

Hodge, B. J., Anthony, W. P., & Gales, L. M. (1996). *Organizational theory: A strategic approach* (5th ed.). Upper Saddle River, NJ: Prentice-Hall.

Hodson, R. (2001). *Dignity at work.* New York, NY: Cambridge University Press.

Holland, T. (1995). Organizations: Context for social service delivery. In H. L. Lurie (Ed.), *Encyclopedia of social work* (19th ed., pp. 1787–1793). Washington, DC: National Association of Social Workers Press.

Hopps, J. G., & Collins, P. M. (1995). Social work profession overview. In H. L. Lurie (Ed.), *Encyclopedia of social work* (19th ed., pp. 2266–2282). Washington, DC: National Association of Social Workers Press.

Independent Sector. (2007). Facts and figures about charitable organizations. Retrieved from www.independentsector.org/programs/research/Charitable_Fact_Sheet.pdf

Janis, I. (1983). *Groupthink: Psychological studies of policy decisions and fiascoes.* Boston, MA: Houghton Mifflin.

Kanter, R. M. (1993)[1977]. *Men and women of the corporation.* New York, NY: Basic Books.

Kaplan, S., & Henderson, R. (2005). Inertia and incentives: Bridging organizational economics and organizational theory. *Organizational Science, 16*(5), 509–521.

Katzell, R. A., & Austin, J. T. (1992). From then to now: The development of industrial-organizational psychology in the United States. *Journal of Applied Psychology, 77*(6), 803–835.

Kerr, S. (1995). On the folly of rewarding A while hoping for B. *Academy of Management Executive, 9*(1), 7–14. (Original work published 1975)

Kets Devries, M., & Miller, D. (1984). *The neurotic organization.* San Francisco, CA: Jossey-Bass.

Landrigan, C. P., Rothschild, J. M., Cronin, J. W., Kaushal, R., Burdick, E., Katz, J. T., … Czeisler, C. A. (2004). Effect of reducing interns' work hours on serious medical errors in intensive care units. *New England Journal of Medicine, 351,* 1838–1848.

Lepore, J. (1999, October 12). Not so fast: Scientific management started as a way to work. How did it become a way of life? *New Yorker,* 114–127.

Lilienthal, D. (1974). *The TVA: Democracy on the march.* Westport, CT: Greenwood Press. (Original work published 1934)

Marais, K., Dulac, N., & Leveson, N. (2004, March). Beyond normal accidents and high reliability organizations: The need for an alternative approach to safety in complex organizations. MIT. Available from http://esd.mit.edu/symposium/pdfs/papers/marais-b.pdf

March, J. G., & Simon, H. (1958). *Organizations.* New York, NY: Wiley.

Maslach, C. (2003). Job burnout: New directions in research and intervention. *Current Directions in Psychological Science, 12*(5), 189–192.

Maslach, C., Jackson, S. E., & Leiter, M. P. (1996). *The Maslach burnout inventory* (3rd ed.). Palo Alto, CA: Consulting Psychologists Press.

McDavid, J. C., & Hawthorn, L. R. L. (2006). *Program evaluation and performance measurement: An introduction to practice.* Thousand Oaks, CA: Sage.

McGregor, D. (1960). *The human side of enterprise.* New York, NY: McGraw-Hill.

Merton, R. (1958). *Social theory and social structure.* Glencoe, IL: Free Press.

Michels, R. (1962). *Political parties.* New York, NY: Free Press.

Mills, C. W. (1956). *White collar: The American middle class.* New York, NY: Oxford University Press.

Mintzberg, H. (1989). *Mintzberg on management.* New York, NY: Free Press/Macmillan.

Morgan, G. (1998). *Images of organizations.* San Francisco, CA: Berrett-Koehler.

Nash, L., & Stevenson, H. (2004). Success that lasts. *Harvard Business, 82*(2), 102–109.

Parsons, T. (1960). *Structure and process in modern societies.* Glencoe, IL: Free Press.

Pascale, R., & Athos, T. (1982). *The art of Japanese management.* New York, NY: Warner.

Perrow, C. (1984). *Normal accidents.* New York, NY: Basic Books.

Peters, T. (1988). Restoring American competitiveness: Looking for new models of organizations. *Academy of Management Executives, 2*(2), 103–107.

Peters, T., & Waterman, R. (1982). *In search of excellence.* New York, NY: Harper & Row.

Pfeffer, J. (1991). Organization theory and structural perspectives on management: Special forum–Integrative perspectives on organizations. *Journal of Management.* Available at www.findarticles.com/p/articles/mi_m4256/is_n4_v17/ai _11817397

Quinn, R. (1988). *Beyond rational management.* San Francisco, CA: Jossey-Bass.

Reisman, D., Glazer, N., & Denny, R. (1950). *The lonely crowd.* New Haven, CT: Yale University Press.

Scott, W. R. (1992). *Organizations: Rational, natural and open systems* (3rd ed.). Englewood Cliffs, NJ: Prentice-Hall.

Scott, W. R. (2005). Institutional theory: Contributing to a theoretical research program. In K. G. Smith & M. Hitt (Eds.), *Great minds in management: The process of theory development* (pp. 450–484). New York, NY: Oxford University Press.

Selznick, P. (1949). *TVA and the grass roots.* Berkeley, CA: University of California Press.

Shellenbarger, S. (2006, January 5). Companies retool time-off policies to prevent burnout, reward performance. *Wall Street Journal,* D1.

Simon, H. (1957). *Administrative behavior.* New York, NY: Macmillan. (Original work published 1947)

Smithburg, D. W., & Thompson, V. A. (1950). *Public administration.* New York, NY: Knopf.

Stewart, M. (2009). *The management myth: Why the experts keep getting it wrong.* New York, NY: Norton.

Street, E. (1947). *A handbook for social agency administration.* New York, NY: Harper & Row.

Taylor, F. W. (1911). *The principle of scientific management.* New York, NY: Harper & Row.

Tichy, N., & Devanna, M. (1986). *The transformational leader.* New York, NY: Wiley.

Tropman, J. (1989). The organizational circle. *Administration in Social Work, 13,* 1.

Tropman, J. (1998a). *Do Americans hate the poor? The other American dilemma.* Westport, CT: Praeger.

Tropman, J. (1998b). *Managing ideas in the creating organization.* Westport, CT: Quorum Books.

Tropman, J. (2002). *Making meetings work* (2nd ed.). Thousand Oaks, CA: Sage.

Tropman, J. (2006). *Supervision and management in the human services.* Pecosta, IA: Eddie Bowers.

Tropman, J., & Lucas, C. (2006, March). The *five-C theory of leadership.* Paper presented at the Benchmark 3 Conference on Nonprofits, Phoenix, Arizona.

Tropman, J., & Morningstar, G. (1988). *Entrepreneurial systems for the 1990s.* Westport, CT: Quorum Books.

Tropman, J., & Richards-Schuester, K. (2000). A tale of the bored board. *Children's Voice, 9,* 1.

Tropman, J., & Shaefer, L. (2004). Flameout at the top: Executive calamity in the nonprofit sector. In Schmid (Ed.), *Organizational and structural dilemmas in nonprofit human service organizations.* New York, NY: Haworth.

Tropman, J., & Shaefer, L. (2006). *Social exploitation.* Unpublished manuscript.

Tropman, J. E., & Wooten, L. (2010). Executive leadership: a 7C approach. *Problems and Perspectives in Management, 8*(4), 47–57.

Tropman, J., Zhu, L., & Shaefer, L. (2004, March). *The crow and the cheese: From derailment to calamity in the executive suite.* Paper presented at the International Applied Business Research Conference, San Juan, Puerto Rico.

Vaill, P. (1982, Autumn). The purposing of high performing systems. *Organizational Dynamics, 11*(2), 23–39.

Vaill, P. (1989). *Management as a performance.* San Francisco, CA: Jossey-Bass.

Voss, K., & Sherman, R. (2000). Breaking the iron law of oligarchy: Union revitalization in the American labor movement. *American Journal of Sociology, 106,* 303–349.

Weick, K. (1995). *Sensemaking in organizations.* Thousand Oaks, CA: Sage.

Weidman, D. (2001). Directing organization culture change through strategic planning and leadership. *National Association for the Practice of Anthropology Bulletin, 18*(1), 164–175.

White, L. D. (1931). *The city manager.* Chicago, IL: University of Chicago Press.

White, L. D. (1954). *The Jeffersonians: An administrative history from 1801–1829.* New York, NY: Macmillan.

White, L. D. (1958a). *The Jacksonians: An administrative history from 1829–1861.* New York, NY: Macmillan.

White, L. D. (1958b). *The Republican era: An administrative history from 1861–1901.* New York, NY: Macmillan.

Whyte, W. H. (1956). *The organization man.* New York, NY: Doubleday.

Williamson, O. (1975). *Markets and hierarchies, analysis and antitrust implications: A study in the economics of internal organizations.* New York, NY: Free Press.

Wilson, S. (2002). *The man in the grey flannel suit.* New York, NY: Four Walls Eight Windows Press. (Original work published 1955)

Zey, M. (2001). Rational choice and organization theory. In N. J. Smelser & P. B. Baltes (Eds.), *International encyclopedia of the social and behavioral sciences* (pp. 12751–12755). New York, NY: Elsevier Science and Technology Books.

Chapter 13
The Potentially Harmful Effects of Theory in Social Work

Bruce A. Thyer

Under what circumstances can a psychosocial theory result in harm to the social work profession?

From my earliest training in the human services, beginning in community college and continuing through my doctoral studies, I was taught the value of theory. Specifically, I was inculcated with the belief that the major purpose of scientific research is the development of what can be called theory, more specifically "deductive" theory, which is "an attempt to increase human understanding by providing explanations of why certain things occur" (Burr, 1973, p. 3). In earlier publications, I reviewed a number of similar definitions of deductive theory found in various social work texts (Thyer, 2001a, 2001b), and I distinguished deductive theory from related constructs, such as models for practice (e.g., task-centered), perspectives on practice (e.g., an ecosystems perspective), one's philosophical assumptions (realism versus constructivism), and one's statistical assumptions or choice of research methodologies. I am aware that other people hold more expanded, or perhaps weaker, views of what constitutes a theory (e.g., it is simply a guess or prediction), so to make it clear from the onset, I am referring only to conceptual attempts to explain the causes (e.g., etiologies) of psychosocial problems and the mechanisms of actions of psychosocial treatments.

The field of social work purports to highly prize the development of theory that provides both logically supported and empirically based explanations of the causes of social problems and of the presumptive mechanisms of action of psychosocial interventions. A theory's initial propositions supposedly lead to testable hypotheses capable of being

This chapter was originally presented at a doctoral colloquium on social work theory at the University of Chicago School of Social Service Administration on October 21, 2004, and later given as a plenary address at the Evaluation for Practice conference held at the University of Huddersfield, England, on July 14, 2005. I am grateful to Professor Michael Holosko with the University of Georgia, who provided a very helpful review of this chapter.

459

supported or rejected via empirical analysis of various types: descriptive analyses, correlational studies, quasi-experiments, true experiments, meta-analyses, and systematic reviews. Social work research was to take these leads from theory, to develop some means of testing these derived hypotheses, and through a series of corroborating or disconfirming investigations derive general conclusions regarding that theory's level of empirical support and, ideally, its congruence with nature's realities. This view of the role of theory is similar to the stance advocated by Ernest Greenwood in his seminal article appearing in a 1955 issue of the *Social Service Review:* "Research, to be scientific, must proceed from a body of theory and feed back into that theory; its goal always is to test and to expand scientific theory" (p. 22). This view is also supported by the policies and practices of our major professional organizations, such as the Council on Social Work Education, the Group for the Advancement of Doctoral Education in Social Work, the National Association of Social Workers, as well as in major social work textbooks (cf. Thyer, 2001a).

Ironically, there is little discussion in our disciplinary literature of the potentially harmful effects of theory in social work research and practice, and this concluding chapter attempts to correct this conspicuous omission. One of the few comments dealing with this topic is by Gambrill (1983, p. 235):

> *Problems in causal analysis arise when social workers do not use theories when they would be helpful and* and when they do use theories in areas in which they are inappropriate. *Both actions result in erroneous conclusions and failure to attain outcomes desired by clients. (emphasis added)*

Plionis (2004) authored "Teaching Students How to Avoid Errors in Theory Application," in which she outlined and discussed some common problems encountered in applying theory to social work practice. Similarly, Shaw and Compton (2003, p. 192), in "Theory, Like Mist on Spectacles, Obscures Vision," noted, "While theory is helpful in focusing evaluator's attention and facilitating investigation, it also excludes evidence that does not fit within its framework." Much earlier, Meyer (1973, p. 86) critiqued the proliferation of practice models (which she linked to theory development) in social work and similarly observed:

> *The selling of those models has tended to lead each of us to the brink of premature closure. As long as we "do" our special model we will have no need of the other fellow's. Moreover, the more we work at our models and the more refinement we achieve in honing techniques and educating adherents, the greater our investment becomes in our invention. (emphasis in original).*

However, such critical analyses are rare and only scratch the surface of this important matter.

In an earlier article (Thyer, 2001a), I commented that I have seen doctoral students forced to insert inappropriate or tangential theories in their dissertations because their faculty advisors judged that dissertations simply needed to have some sort of theoretical discussion, no matter how seemingly gratuitous. This is a fairly benign example of how theory can have deleterious consequences. In the remainder of this chapter, I would like to review some more serious consequences of using bad theory in social work in an effort to help us become more discriminating in our incorporation of theory into social work education about human behavior and its development across the life span and our use of theory in practice, as well as to guide and inform our research efforts.

Some Harmful Effects of Bad Theory

The next few sections of this chapter describe the various ways in which theory can have a destructive influence in diverse areas of social work. Included among these harms are the wasting of time in social work education and in social work research, and the development of ineffective or harmful practices. Bad theory can also bias one's perspective in viewing research or practice, and may lead researchers into attempting to prove that their preferred theory is "true," rather than engaging in an objective search for truth. Theory, with its corresponding need for "theoreticians," can lead to the elevation of persons over principles, and to the development of cult-like phenomena. Bad theory also promotes pernicious divisions between practitioners and researchers.

Teaching Bad Theory Wastes Time in Education and Training

The prior accreditation standards of the Council on Social Work Education (CSWE; 2003, p. 33) stated that one foundation program objective is to have students "use theoretical frameworks *supported by empirical evidence* to understand individual development and behavior across the life span and the interactions among individuals and between individuals and families, groups, organizations and communities" (emphasis added).

On the face of it, this seems like a reasonable standard, and one consistent with a discipline trying to ground itself in the hallmarks of the traditional professions. The *Educational Policy and Accreditation Standards* further stated, "The master's program has a concentration curriculum that includes (a) concentration objectives, (b) a conceptual framework built around relevant theories," and some other features (CSWE, 2003, p. 37). This standard is reiterated several places further on in the benchmarks section. Clearly, it is required by CSWE that accredited BSW and MSW programs educate students in the use of theoretical frameworks. Unfortunately, the stipulation that such frameworks be those "supported by empirical evidence" was often honored more in the breach than in reality, in our textbooks and course syllabi. A review of such books reveals sometimes extensive content on stage theories such as those of Sigmund Freud, Erik Erikson, Jean Piaget, Lawrence Kohlberg, and Carol Gilligan, approaches to understanding human development that, to put it kindly, have not been well supported by empirical evidence and in some cases seem to have been largely refuted. Apart from general theories of human development, there is a plethora of highly specialized theories, sometimes originating in a broader framework but sometimes of novel origin, addressing social work practice in circumscribed problem areas, for example, alcohol abuse, depression, trauma, family violence, or with particular populations, for example, juvenile delinquents, the very young, the very old, and people of color. These too can be given undue attention in our curriculum, often with a disregard for the empirical research (or lack thereof) addressing them.

In time, this cascades into our professional journals, our conferences, and our continuing education offerings. Students and practitioners are faced with a sometimes indigestible mass of theories, models, perspectives, frameworks, and lenses, many of which contradict each other, unified often only by their lack of supportive research. For example, the *Journal of Social Work Education* contained an article extolling the value of the Myers-Briggs Type Indicator (MBTI) as an assessment tool for use with social work students (Moore, Dettlaff, & Dietz, 2004). The MBTI is based on the theory of personality of Carl Jung, and there are a number of references to its use with social work students over the years.

Unfortunately, the theory underlying the MBTI is either weakly supported or reasonably refuted, and the validity of the instrument itself is seriously open to question (cf. Hunsley, Lee, & Wood, 2003). And this has been known for years (Druckman & Bjork, 1991; Pittenger, 1993). How many thousands of students complete this invalid assessment instrument each year? How many erroneous decisions regarding students based on MBTI results are made by faculty and supervisors annually?

Moore et al. (2004) recommended that field instructors and other faculty get training in using and interpreting the MBTI. In my opinion, this is a squandering of precious in-service and continuing education resources. In recent years, I have similarly seen continuing education offerings approved for social workers to learn about past-life regression psychotherapy, how to heal clients using invisible energy forces unknown and undetectable to science, to use yoga, to prescribe herbal therapies, to help clients by structuring their eye movements, and creating mandalas. How far we have come from our historic role of working with clients at all levels to effect change in their life circumstances and focusing on the interactions within and among families, groups, communities, and organizations.

And if the empirical support of various approaches to social work practice with individuals remains fairly thin in many areas, how much more attenuated are the solid research findings that can be taught to students relating to practice with families, groups, organizations, and communities? It would be a very interesting exercise indeed to analyze to what extent the theories we teach about families, groups, and larger systems are supported by empirical research.

Teaching Bad Theory Detracts From Time Spent Teaching Evidence-Based Content

The social work curriculum and the amount of time devoted to an individual course are finite elements. One can provide only so much content in the context of any given course, or throughout an entire MSW program. To the extent that time and energy are devoted to reviewing unsupported social work theory, or theory that is known to be incorrect, there is that much less time and energy available to providing coverage on what the CSWE really mandated — that is, teaching frameworks supported by empirical research. Replacement of speculative or erroneous theoretical content with theories reasonably well supported by empirical research seems unlikely until the CSWE begins to take seriously its own standard regarding the evidentiary foundations of theoretical frameworks, which is mentioned only in the education policy portion of the accreditation standards, not in the later actual accreditation benchmarks. For example, Accreditation Standard M2.0.1 mandated only the provision of "a conceptual framework built on relevant theories" (CSWE, 2003, p. 47) used in evaluating candidacy or the accreditation review itself, not providing coverage on empirically supported theories. Any general education policy that lacks the teeth of operationally defined accreditation benchmarks is one that will be slow to be adopted, if at all. The result has been described by Rehr, Showers, Rosenberg, and Blumenfield (1998, p. 89): "So many theories exist that little guidance is given to practice." Carol Meyer (1973, p. 88) had a similar observation: "In our field, we are theoretical hoarders; we do not seem ever to clear out the attic, but instead we keep adding new items, hoping that they will somehow fit in with the old."

Let us be honest here. We cannot possibly do a good job at teaching all relevant theories to our social work students, be they in our bachelor's, master's, or doctoral programs. Therefore, each program, indeed, every instructor, is faced with making an important choice: What theoretical frameworks shall I cover in my classes? Sometimes we take the path of least resistance and teach those theories that happen to be covered in our assigned textbooks and consider that we have done a satisfactory job if we get good course evaluations. We are content if our students do well on the standardized multiple-choice tests the publishers provide us with in the instructor's manual accompanying the assigned textbook.

I am advocating here, and have elsewhere, that the scientific foundations supporting a given theory should be an important consideration in such choices about what we teach, and this is congruent with past and current CSWE education policy, although not apparently enforced with any degree of regularity. To the extent that we persist in teaching the outdated, the unfounded, and (the worst case) the false, we have less room to provide instruction for the contemporary, the empirically investigated, and the reasonably well validated. And for all of us, this is not a good thing.

In a number of social work programs with which I am familiar, advanced practice classes are often little more than something akin to the sociological study of a problem or client group. For instance, a class titled Social Work Practice with Substance Abusers is often laden with content, readings, and discussion about the descriptive features of various drugs and of the people most prone to abuse them, the correlates and antecedents of substance abuse, its costs, theoretical causes, and consequences. Almost dismissed on the agenda is attention to evidence-based approaches to actually help individuals stop abusing drugs, of which much is considerably known now. Similarly, a course titled Social Work Practice with the Elderly is likely to be overburdened with theories of aging and descriptive features of senior citizens and their most pressing problems and to present little on empirically supported ways of helping the elderly maintain or regain health and independence or to cope effectively with specific physical or behavioral problems.

In part, our preoccupation with theoretical importance at the expense of evidence-based interventions may be the result of the heavy emphasis laid on theory in our profession. It may also be due to the unfamiliarity among some of the professoriate with the latest advances being made in effective practices in so many areas in the human services.

Investigating Bad Theory Wastes Researchers' Time and Resources

Like the classroom instructor, the social work researcher has a finite amount of time to devote to investigating psychosocial phenomena. The time spent thinking about, reading, and designing studies on spurious or invalid theory, much less conducting them, could be considered a waste of the investigator's time. Factor in analyzing the data, writing it up for publication, and sending it in for peer review, and one is faced with the fact that any given investigation is a tremendous investment in the career of a researcher. Now, I am not advocating for anything like a ban on investigating certain topics or theories. Far from it. I too support the freedom within the academy that permits us to pursue a range of topics without oversight from on high (except perhaps with the exception of our university human subjects review committee) for the purposes of expanding knowledge. I am urging a little bit of critical thinking and discrimination in choosing topics to research, because the consequences of choosing something trivial or investigating a fallacious theory can be great. One cannot always be sure, in advance, which theoretical frameworks will ultimately prove to be the most valid or congruent with nature or useful in practice. But to give an example, based on related existing theory, logic, internal inconsistencies, and related factors, I was reasonably sure that the theory underlying the novel technique of eye movement desensitization and reprocessing (EMDR) was incorrect when it initially erupted on the scene. Nevertheless, I had a colleague who had been trained in the approach, and she wanted to conduct an outcome study of EMDR using a novel client population. Despite my personal reservations, we worked together on this empirical adventure and found EMDR to be essentially equivalent to a placebo treatment, not at all capable of producing any of the miracle cures touted by its advocates. I thought this project was well designed, and it was eventually published, but the experience was far less satisfying to me as a practitioner, academic, and social scientist than one grounded on a more solid theory and more likely to lead to some advance in our knowledge about helping clients. It is both tempting and perhaps easier to gravitate toward the novel, unusual, or (apparently) dramatically successful approaches to practice, rather than to investigate the outcomes and processes of widely used social work interventions whose mechanisms and effectiveness remain murky (which is all too often the case).

Currently we find professional books and journals providing coverage on numerous discredited theoretical frameworks and practices, such as transactional analysis, neurolinguistic programming, sensory integration, recovering repressed memories, facilitated communication, and thought field therapy. This last bogus treatment was taught during the summer of 2006 as a clinical MSW elective in one of the more highly respected social work programs in the United States. We flirt with the faddish, being quick to embrace and write about, for example, vague notions of quantum and chaos theories as having applications to social work practice. The reality is that quantum (e.g., the behavior of subatomic particles) phenomena have no applications or extensions to the macro world in which we all live, and the apparent similarities (e.g., we can inadvertently change someone's behavior by observing them) are metaphorical at best (Stenger, 1997) and actually have nothing to do with quantum theory. I suspect that few of my social work colleagues can follow the complex mathematics that undergird quantum or chaos theory. I certainly cannot.

Are these the theoretical roads we wish students and practitioners to travel? Our disastrous embrace of watered-down and vague principles of general systems theory and its derivatives, such as the ecosystems perspective, has sidetracked the profession for years. It provides a Potemkin patina of theoretical rationale for just about anything one chooses to do in practice. In my judgment, Wakefield's (1996a, 1996b) incisive critiques dealt a devastating blow to the scientific credibility of these approaches, but systems theory remains a revered orientation in social work education, although one of precious little heuristic value in terms of generating empirical research or specific interventions (Gallant & Thyer, 1999).

Basing Practice on Bad Theory Can Result in Ineffective or Harmful Practices

On April 18, 2000, a 10-year-old girl by the name of Candace Newmaker, accompanied by her adoptive mother, walked into the home of a woman named Connell Watkins, a social worker with an MSW from a CSWE-accredited program. With three other adult therapy assistants, Candace was tightly wrapped head to toe in a blue flannel blanket, curled into a fetal position, and placed under four large pillows. The four adults then pushed against her to simulate birth contractions, and Candace was urged, via yelling and being hit by the therapists, to emerge from this cloth cocoon and be reborn. Altogether, the four adults weighed over 670 pounds. Candace began to complain that she could not breathe. She cried. She finally said, in a pitiful voice, "Okay, I am dying. I am sorry." The therapists shouted back, "You want to die, okay then, die. Go ahead and die right now" When, after about an hour, Candace was unwrapped, she had been silent and unresponsive for some minutes. She was unconscious and not breathing. She had soiled herself with vomit and feces. This entire procedure was captured on videotape. Candace died the next day from this suffocation. The adoptive mother had been present and urged her daughter to be reborn during this therapy session, having paid about $7,000 for Candace to be treated in a 2-week intensive session of therapy. The social worker was charged with child abuse leading to death, served a prison sentence (Crowder & Lowe, 2000), and is now released.

What happened here? Well, it is called "rebirthing therapy" and is based on a theory of human behavior that asserts that one's current emotional problems are caused in part by the trauma one experienced during birth. Resolution of one's current problems can therefore be attained by experiencing a more successful rebirthing experience via this simulated exercise. There is little empirical support for this theory, and no sound research to suggest that rebirthing techniques are genuinely helpful in resolving emotional problems. This case tragically illustrates how a bad theory can promote injurious social work treatments. Sometimes bad theory can lead to decidedly harmful interventions, and sometimes to more benign treatments that, at the least, waste the time and money of social work clients and perhaps detour them from obtaining legitimately effective care.

There are many such tragic illustrations of how bad theory can promote bad practice. For example, Bruno Bettelheim's theory that autism was caused in part by emotionally distant caregivers, the so-called "refrigerator mother," led to the intervention of removing children from their biological homes and placing them in institutional care, sometimes for many years. Psychoanalytic theories of the etiology of homosexuality led to the decades-long stigmatization of gay and lesbian individuals as mentally ill and to their being referred for therapy to change their sexual orientation. More recently, practitioners using religiously derived theories continue efforts to "convert" gays and lesbians into heterosexuals using faith and psychotherapy (Spitzer, 2003), despite numerous position statements by major professional associations against such "reparative therapies." Relatedly, religiously derived theories about the role of parents led a few states to pass laws prohibiting gay or lesbian couples from adopting children, to the detriment of children thus deprived of a possibly advantageous permanent home. My point is that all theory is not good theory, and sometimes it is very bad indeed.

Some voices in our profession claim that the accuracy or truthfulness of the theories used in social work is either unimportant or simply impossible to determine. For example, Morris (1997, p. 76) asserted, "Our role as students of theory is not to decide which theories are correct or which are obsolete." The radical skeptics claim that no certain knowledge is obtainable via scientific inquiry, whereas others assert that all potential scientific methodologies are of equal value in uncovering truth. These views are, in my opinion, intellectual dead ends, and ultimately of great harm to the profession.

Theory Can Place Intellectual Blinders on Practitioners and Researchers

Just as adoption of a good theory can help a practitioner or researcher make sense of a given psychosocial phenomenon, sometimes adherence to a bad theory places intellectual blinders on a professional, so that everything is viewed as consistent with a particular perspective. Contravening evidence can be ignored or discounted and the congruent instances seen as an ever-mounting accumulation of solid evidence in support of one's favored perspective. This can in turn compromise our ability to see or hear what clients really bring to us, or lead researchers astray. Martin Bloom (1965, p. 12) mentioned this many years ago, noting:

> Usually, worker's preferences are expressed at the very onset of the case, and clients begin to show just those symptoms that preferred theory requires. In other words, this preferential approach leads to theory selection that may be a long, false lead.

Nisbett and Ross (1980) wrote extensively about this confirmation bias, or availability heuristic, in everyday judgments under uncertainty, and the results have application to the decisions made by researchers as well as practitioners. They specifically noted, "People have little appreciation for strategies of disconfirmation of theories and often persist in adhering to a theory when the number of exceptions to the theory exceeds the number of confirmations" (p. 16).

The difficulties of objectively surveying large numbers of research studies and drawing legitimate conclusions from these aggregated studies are well known. Even efforts to minimize subjective judgments in this process, replacing narrative reviews of complex literature with sophisticated strategies such as meta-analyses, have been criticized as remaining subject to bias on the part of the researchers (Wilson, 1985). Theory, especially bad theory, can lead researchers astray.

Legitimate Research Aimed at Testing Theory May Degenerate Into Attempting to Prove That a Given Theory Is True

According to the idealized standards of scientific inquiry, the researcher strives to be an objective investigator whose goal is to determine whether his or her data corroborate or refute the specific hypotheses derived from a given theory. Over time, presumably, an accumulation of well-designed refutations of a theory's propositions (e.g., a failure to reject the null hypothesis) leads to an eventual determination that a particular theory, or at least significant aspects of a particular theory, are unsupported and may be considered false. Having reasonably excluded certain explanations from the domain of plausible theories, a field then moves on to test others. Slowly, by excluding likely explanations or theories, one begins to narrow in on an increasingly circumscribed set of theories that have not yet been falsified and presumably contain more truthful accounts. This approach has been called *falsificationism*, or strong inference (see Platt, 1964, for a lucid account of this process), and has been widely written about by Karl Popper, among others.

Although complete objectivity is unlikely to occur among human beings, by subscribing to the tenets of mainstream science one has some level of control over bias and subjectivity, which is indeed the whole point of employing scientific methodology. This is not a perfect system for uncovering knowledge, but it seems to be the best approach developed so far. However, it is often the case that researchers embark on a given study, not in an effort to dispassionately examine the merits of their hypotheses, but to garner evidence that will serve to support the hypotheses or, more broadly, to try to show that a given theory or part thereof is true. This is particularly prone to happen among doctoral students, who in many instances have been taught, perhaps implicitly, that a failure to find predicted results represents a failure of their dissertation project or reflects poorly on their research skills. It also seems likely to occur in situations in which program evaluations are undertaken by individuals with a vested interest in promoting the social service program under investigation or among researchers who have received significant external funding.

One current example I have heard about occurred recently when child welfare researchers gathered together to discuss evaluating the practice effectiveness of BSWs versus child welfare workers holding non-social work degrees. Rather than framing the role of the research as being to see which educational background yields better child welfare workers, some stakeholders asserted that the function of the research is to "prove that BSWs make better child welfare workers"—in other words, to support an *a priori* conclusion, rather than find the true facts. This is a terrible distortion of the scientific method. Frankly, it can be difficult to get as excited over a failure to reject the null hypothesis (e.g., finding out that a novel treatment is no better than an existing one), as when your results come out as bravely predicted by the given theory. It is much more fun to reject the null hypothesis in favor of some proposition or in support of a novel program of social care, compared to, say, no intervention or treatment as usual.

For a variety of reasons, philosophical and practical, it is difficult in social work research to prove that a given theory is true (justificationism), but perhaps somewhat more possible to demonstrate that it is false (falsificationism). Both approaches have inherent problems. It may well be that a given result was predicted by Theory X and the outcomes are seen as supportive of Theory X. But it is often true that many other theories would have predicted a similar result from one's study, so that the results can be seen as corroborative not only of Theory X but of Theories Y, Z, and others. It is difficult to design a study capable of yielding results that corroborate Theory X and not other rival explanations. It is also true that most studies, even those designed with the utmost rigor, possess significant methodological flaws of such magnitude as to cause critics to claim that no meaningful conclusions may be drawn. Examples include the Fort Bragg Study on child mental health services and the Collaborative Depression Treatment Study, both funded by the NIMH, among others.

However, the approach of falsificationism also has its philosophical and methodological uncertainties. Such studies are also likely to possess methodological limitations that will cause the advocates of Theory X to claim that the null result apparently falsifying Theory X was due to other factors. Such factors may involve the use of poorly chosen dependent variables or the inappropriate application of the independent variable. Many psychotherapy outcome studies with null results have been attributed, after the fact, to inadequately trained therapists, demand characteristics, poor or absent supervision, or a failure to provide sufficiently prolonged or intense treatment. Another response to negative outcome studies is to develop *post hoc* revisions of the original theory being tested so that the study results are seen as strengthening, rather than falsifying, the theory.

Greenwald, Pratkanis, Leippe, and Baumgardner (1986), in their paper "Under What Conditions Does Theory Obstruct Research Progress?" address this by noting the tendency of investigators to engage in *theory-confirming* research as opposed to the more legitimate approach they call *theory-centered* inquiry. These authors review how adherence to a particular theory leads researchers in the field of social psychology to undertake a series of theory-confirming studies about a particular phenomenon, the end result of which was to delay legitimate (and presumably more accurate) advances in theoretical knowledge about this phenomenon. As they see it:

> Both Popper and Kuhn maintain that theory testing is the central pole around which scientific activity revolves. In contrast, our analysis suggests that theory should not play so pivotal a role. The researcher who sets out to test a theory is likely to become ego-involved with a theoretical prediction, to select procedures that will lead eventually to prediction-confirming data, and thereby, to produce avoidably overgeneralized conclusions. (p. 223)

These authors bluntly concluded:

> Under what conditions does theory obstruct research progress? Theory obstructs research progress when testing theory is taken as the central goal of research, if (as often happens) the researcher has more faith in the correctness of the theory than in the suitability of the procedures that were used to test it....Theory obstructs research progress when the researcher is an ego-involved advocate of the theory and may be willing to persevere indefinitely in the face of prediction-disconfirming results. (p. 226)

Attempts to confirm that a theory is true, what Gambrill (1999) and others have labeled justificationism, contorts scientific methods. It does science no service to undertake, say, an evaluation of a multimillion-dollar social work program with the aim of showing that it "works." Evaluators, like researchers in general, should be expected to adhere to a commitment to finding out the actual outcomes and to reporting them honestly. This is not simply pie-in-the-sky idealism. The *Guiding Principles for Evaluators* published by the American Evaluation Association (AEA; 2007, D.3) asserts, "Because justified negative or critical conclusions from an evaluation must be explicitly stated, evaluations sometimes produce results that harm client or stakeholder interests." This can be a difficult standard to cling to in the face of powerful stakeholders who have vested interests in promoting a particular program of social service or in fostering the credibility of a given theory. Although I am not aware of anyone who openly advocates the converse, hiding undesirable findings, I am sure that it does sometimes happen in the social services, tantamount to what has happened in the pharmaceutical and tobacco industries.

Theory Can Promote the Rise of Authority Figures and of Cult-Like Phenomena

Henry Adams (1984; the late psychologist, not the novelist) wrote about this in his little gem of an article titled "The Pernicious Effects of Theoretical Orientations in Clinical Psychology." Adams (please forgive the dated male-centered language) observed:

> *Theoretical orientations are instigated by a great man or men who have developed a comprehensive theory of the nature of man ... whose controversial ideas elicit criticism and frequently emotional behavior on the part of persons representing the "establishment." This opposition is associated with the recruitment of disciples to spread the "message." If the ideas are controversial, unusual, or threatening, then they often become the object of public attention. Like fashions, these movements often become "fads." (p. 90)*

Adams mentions Sigmund Freud, B. F. Skinner, and Carl Rogers as examples of individuals who were seen as authority figures in their respective fields. We often see new journals, training institutes, clinics, websites and blogs, specialized societies, and foundations established to promote these authorities and their ideas. Although such practices are not necessarily antithetical to good science, the interests of self-promotion and financial gain are very real influences that can distort the objective pursuit of truth. Adams likened professional psychology to a collection of cults centered on revered authority figures, as opposed to being a system of applied clinical science.

For me, warning signs that one is dealing with cult-like interventions include:

- Claims that cures are complete or surefire
- Words or phrases such as "amazing," "never dreamed of," "unique," and "special"
- Belittlement of other approaches

- The complaint that the advocates of the new approach are being excluded or ignored by the "establishment" or the "mainstream"
- Portrayal of the establishment as too set in its ways to accept anything new, or as protecting its interests against new ideas
- Invoking mysterious forces unknown to science as responsible for change
- Vagueness or secrecy about methods or training
- Charging exorbitant fees for training or supervision in the new approach
- A reliance on anecdotal claims as evidence of effectiveness
- A reluctance to subject the new intervention to independent, rigorous evaluation
- Lack of a clear linkage to credible theory

Discretion prevents me from giving illustrations of contemporary human service professionals whose practices contain some of these elements, but it is possible that a reader can come up with his or her own examples of such.

Theory Can Promote Division Between Researchers and Practitioners

There have been a number of studies evaluating the content of research published in social work and other disciplinary journals, and it seems clear that a majority of social work articles are not reports of empirical research, and the minority of studies that are empirical do not usually address those issues of highest concern to practitioners, namely, evaluations of methods of social work assessment and outcome studies on social work practice. In fact, only about 3% of our field's journal articles report the results of well-designed outcome studies (Rosen, Proctor, & Staudt, 1999), while a far greater proportion are designed to test some aspect of a theory, which may have only ambiguous or spurious applications to practice. This schism between the interests of researchers and those of practitioners has long been with us. For example, Greenwood (1955) noted:

The history of the relations between social science and social work practice, by and large, has been one of estrangement. (p. 20)

In his efforts to develop theory, the social scientist need not be, and very often is not, concerned with its applicability. He subordinates the requirements of utility to that of theoretical significance. (p. 22)

The social scientist's prime aim is the accurate description of the social world, control is a secondary end. The practitioner's chief end is the effective control of that world, and to this all knowledge is subjugated. (p. 25, emphasis in original)

Even if social work practitioners were thoroughly conversant with the very best in social science theory, the knowledge would not be directly usable by them.

The theoretical formulations of the social sciences are too abstract in form to be directly applicable to problems of practice. (p. 29)

Similar comments have been made by others in our field:

Small wonder that practitioners have such little use for formal theory.

(Bloom, 1965, p. 19)

To try and build a social work house on the shifting sands of social science theory is asking for trouble.

(Stevenson, 1971, p. 226)

In our midst we have our abstract theorists who intimidate those very social workers who should be actively involved in research.

(Meyer, 1973, p. 96)

Practitioners in turn criticize the disconnect between our disciplinary research output and social work practice (Cheers, 1978), and social work researchers lament the relative ignorance of practitioners in terms of research knowledge and of their use of empirical evidence in making practice decisions. In a survey of more than 1,700 professionally trained British social workers, Sheldon and Chilvers (2004) found that fewer than 5% could recall having read a randomized controlled trial and fewer than 4% could explain what is meant by statistical significance. This is apparently not a new problem. As Greenwood (1955, p. 29) noted 50 years ago, "The plain truth is that social work practitioners are unable to understand the language of social science."

One proposed solution to this problem has been for practitioners to become "more scientific," more literate in the methods of social science, more scientifically discriminating in their adoption of theories, and to undertake systematic evaluations of their own practice, using small-scale nomothetic and single-system research designs. This approach has been called *empirical clinical practice* and has been widely written about in the social work literature for several decades. The ultimate success of this approach remains to be seen, although it has had some clear merits, and, in my opinion, has had a positive impact on the profession. However, the obvious parallel effort is to encourage social work researchers to become more "applied" in their work, to write more simply, and to focus on issues more relevant to social work; these suggestions have received much less attention. The work of Robert Schilling (1997) in establishing the Social Intervention Group at the Columbia University School of Social Work is a fine example of another problem-focused approach to undertaking intervention research in agency settings, with modest budgets and without a complex research infrastructure. Another step in this process is to encourage doctoral students to undertake outcome studies as their dissertation topic (see Harrison & Thyer, 1988).

All too often, it seems that doctoral students opt for dissertation research that consists of asking one or more groups of individuals (sometimes college students, sometimes social work clients, usually some form of convenience sample of unknown representativeness) to complete one or more survey instruments in an effort to test some hypothesis derived from some theory. Also increasingly common is the practice of having doctoral students obtain access to some source of secondary data, perhaps a national survey study, perhaps data collected in one's state, or perhaps data from a faculty member, and conduct a secondary analysis of these data originally gathered by someone else. I am not disputing the usefulness of conducting such secondary analyses, but I very much regret that doctoral students miss the opportunity to design a study from the ground up, involving the evaluation of their own practice or of an existing social work program, selecting outcome measures, prospectively testing novel hypotheses, getting involved in the nitty-gritty of field research with real live clients wrestling with serious problems. To undertake such a study under the careful mentorship of a major professor, guided by a supervisory committee, in the context of earning the research PhD, is literally a once-in-a-lifetime opportunity that, once lost, cannot be re-created.

The psychologist Ron Blount (Blount, Bunke, & Zaff, 2000, p. 81) has written about the analogous situation in clinical psychology training:

> In many graduate programs, a lack of theory building or theory testing for a thesis or dissertation often brings negative comments by some of the voting faculty members on committees. The threat of failure is enough to assure that most clinical students will attempt to design their study around theory development or testing. An additional reason for the preponderance of explicative research in graduate programs is the need for the student to finish the study in a short period of time. The existence of large data banks, which may have already been collected, promotes the student's design of time-efficient studies using those data.

Blount and colleagues argue for the value of what they call "treatment research" (basically, outcome studies) as opposed to the far more prevalent "explicative" or theory-testing research found in clinical psychology. Similar calls can now be widely found within the social work literature.

The point here is to suggest that social workers refocus our research endeavors into more applied investigations since, as suggested by Holosko and Leslie (1998), client-centered empirical research is one of the characteristics that define a given study as *social work* (and not social science) research. Across the nation, in every state and in virtually every community, there are social service programs that are attempting to serve numerous clients with complex problems, even as we speak. Many millions of dollars of taxpayers' money, as well as substantial support from the private sector, go into the provision of welfare programs, various prevention efforts, substance abuse treatment services, mental health care, child abuse and neglect prevention, foster care and adoption services, the alleviation of homelessness, the promotion of health care, and more. Each and every one of these programs, from Big Brothers and Big Sisters, Habitat for Humanity, and Alcoholics Anonymous, to wraparound services for emotionally disturbed youth and hospice care, is crying out for talented social work researchers to undertake well-designed studies of the long-term outcomes of such interventions. Undertaking such program evaluations would be a far more practical and useful undertaking for both doctoral students and established faculty researchers than most of what passes for serious scientific research in our field.

In some cases, but not all, these existing social service programs are genuinely grounded in some form of social science theory, and a well-designed outcome study may have potential implications for the validity or falsity of the theories on which these programs may be based. In some cases, a genuine social science theory is conspicuously absent from the conceptual foundations of a particular program and the daily awareness of the practitioners implementing these programs. The true litmus test for this is to review a given program's mission statement and founding documents to see if reference to social science theory is present. After this, simply ask the practitioners who are daily providing services something like "Can you tell me what theory your program is based on?" or "Can you give me a theoretical explanation as to why you do things this way here?" In many cases, you will fail to find any conceptual foundation in a formal theory, and practitioners will respond with a blank stare, a quizzical look, or a rueful smile, as they acknowledge the absence of formal theory guiding their actions. Researchers have actually gone to agencies and asked practitioners these types of questions, and found that a substantial proportion of them seem to be working relatively free from the benefits or disadvantages of formal theory. This is not something to be lamented—it is reality, and although grounding a program in formal theory may have its advantages, these have yet to be well established. In the meantime, we should acknowledge that often our social work services are not based on theory (and most certainly not empirical research), but are sometimes derived from religious convictions, tradition, history, authority, supervisory preferences, educational backgrounds, the whims of funding agencies, or the influence of persuasive politicians. It is no service to deductive theory to claim that a given theory is actually in operation, hidden, so to speak, only that the program's founders and current service providers are unaware of it. Theory, for it to be worthy of the name, must be something held in conscious awareness, explicit, and providing guidance for many of one's daily actions undertaken in the name of intervention.

Christie (2003, p. 26) surveyed 138 program evaluators active with Healthy Start programs throughout California and found that "a very small percentage of Healthy Start evaluators reported using an explicit theoretical approach to guide their work," only about 1 in 10. In a survey of the usefulness of various reading topics potentially consulted by practitioners and clinical researchers from the discipline of psychology, it was found that both groups rated "theoretical orientations" as the least valuable (Beutler, Williams, Wakefield, & Entwistle, 1995), relative to reading about psychological interventions or topics such as the therapeutic alliance. This suggests that, as a practical matter, grounding evaluation in formal theory is not an essential requirement. It may well be useful to do this, but it appears that program outcome studies can be and are being undertaken lacking such foundation. The distinguished psychotherapy researcher Alan Kazdin (2001, p. 59) provides some related observations on the current state of affairs in the context of an article arguing for *more* theoretically based research:

> There is little in the way of theory that underlies current therapies for children and adolescents. We are in an odd position of having no clear understanding of therapeutic change, no clear set of studies that advance our understanding of why treatment works, and scores of outcome studies that are at the same time wonderfully but also crassly empirical.

The seminal evaluation methodologist Michael Scriven (1998) has also addressed this topic, by describing what he deemed "black box," "grey box," and "clear box" evaluation studies. In the first type, virtually nothing can be determined about how change occurs, although outcomes can be ascertained. In the gray box evaluation, there is some knowledge available about change mechanisms, and in clear box studies, both outcomes and change processes are well established. In Scriven's words:

> One may have no Theory of X but be able to see how it produces its effects . . . as in the classic case of aspirin, one may have no theory of how it works to produce its effects, but nevertheless be able to predict its effects and even its side effects—because we found out what they were from direct experimentation. That does not require a theory. (p. 60)

Although arriving at clear box evaluations is a desirable goal for both social scientists and practitioners, this does not reduce the value of black box appraisals, simply determining outcomes, in the absence of a theory of the mechanisms of change. Such studies may be an important preliminary to gray box and clear box evaluations, or as valuable one-time studies in their own right.

There are many examples of interventions that are based on theory and that translate propositions from that theory into practice. Psychoanalysis, Azrin's Job-Finding Club, the Community Reinforcement Approach to Alcohol and Drug Abuse, systematic desensitization, Alcoholics Anonymous, cognitive therapy for depression, Lovaas's early intensive behavior therapy for autistic youth, exposure therapy and response prevention for certain of the anxiety disorders, and feminist psychoeducational work for the victims of domestic violence are all examples of theory-based interventions. This is not to say that the theories undergirding these interventions are correct—it is obvious that in many cases they are not.

Alcoholics Anonymous is based on the medical theory that alcoholics suffer from a biologically based allergic-like reaction to alcohol and that ingesting alcohol triggers an almost irresistible lifelong craving for more alcohol. This theory, at least, has several virtues. It is eminently testable. In fact, double-blind studies involving giving alcoholics ethanol surreptitiously have rejected this theory rather convincingly. The etiological theory of AA has also led to clear applications to treatment, namely, the recommendation of complete abstinence. The effectiveness of AA as a treatment for alcoholism remains unclear (MacKillop, Lisman, Weinstein, & Rosenbaum, 2003; Ferri, Amato, & Davoli, 2006), but the AA 12-Step program has the virtues of transparency and replicability. It is possible that in time AA will demonstrate that it is indeed a highly effective treatment for those who drink too much. This would not be the first time that an effective treatment emerged from an incorrect etiological theory. Programs like AA and others mentioned earlier do illustrate how theory can inform practice. However, the extensive focus we give to testing explicit theory in our research does a disservice to practitioners who do not need to know if a theory is true or false, but who need to know, with objective data, if the clients they are serving are getting better. We in the academy need to lend our talents more to answering the questions of greatest concern to practitioners, not those derived from theories we are curious about.

Where Can We Go From Here?

The following sections describe some possible alternatives to our traditionally strong reliance on theory in social work. One is to take a more problem-oriented approach, teaching empirically based assessment and interventive approaches centered around particular practice issues, irrespective of the theory (if any) these approaches are based on. Social work research can embrace a more practice focus on the design and testing of new (and the many existing) social work programs, policies, and practices, examining them to see if they are helping clients to accomplished stated goals.

What Are Alternatives to Basing Education, Practice, and Research Primarily on Theory?

Among a large segment of the community of professional social workers, our educational curricula, practice interventions, and choice of research projects are primarily guided by formal theory. As reviewed in this chapter, this can sometimes pose problems, especially if the theory is a bad theory. What are some alternatives to a theory-based profession?

I am very much in favor of one model that had its origins at the University of Chicago School of Social Service Administration through the pioneering work of Professor William Reid, Ann Shyne, and Laura Epstein, which came to be known as task-centered practice (TCP). As originally conceived, TCP was not wedded to any particular psychosocial theory. As described by the authors, "We have drawn upon a range of theories and practices. We have been guided by the findings of research, when such were available or obtainable, and by our clinical experience, when empirical evidence was lacking" (Reid & Epstein, 1972, p. 1). This is remarkably congruent with the tenets of contemporary evidence-based practice. Reid also wrote, "A different mode of developing social work technology is needed. *Instead of an esoteric theory*, the starting point in the process would be the specific types of problems and theories relevant to them" (Reid, 1977, p. 377, emphasis added).

A precursor to this view can be found in the work of Loeb (1959, p. 15): "Although therapeutics should be derivable from theory, it may be appropriate at this point to work at effecting change and to capture as much evidence as possible of what occurs, without primary preoccupation with theory." Echoes of these views can be readily found in related fields, such as psychology:

> *The continued prominence of theoretical-orientation classification belies a breakdown in its applicability to contemporary psychology. Psychotherapy remains a stronghold. However, with internal and external forces endorsing particular approaches, theoretically based practices will be forced to yield to evidence-based ones.*

> *(Smith, 1999, p. 269)*

Task-centered practice was not explicitly based by its founders on any particular social science theory, either of general human functioning or specific problems, and it was not wedded to any particular approach to intervention (e.g., individual practice, group work, family therapy). Over time, Reid and his colleagues undertook and published a marvelous series of randomized controlled studies of TCP, in the context of a widening array of clients and problems, and the development of a model more specific to TCP was undertaken. However, many of the central practices of TCP can be parsimoniously explained by their overlap with social learning theory and behavioral interventions, something that Gambrill (1994) contended was seriously underplayed or unrecognized by Reid. Nevertheless, regardless of the true theoretical frameworks undergirding TCP, the model is an apparently useful one, as defined by its ability to be applied by professional social workers to effectively alleviate pressing human problems. In time, Reid (2000) developed *The Task Planner*, a textbook designed to provide human service professionals with what are, in effect, modest practice guidelines to help apply TCP to a wide array of common psychosocial problems. In general, I support a problem-focused approach to social work education, practice, and research whereby professionals choose selected issues of societal or interpersonal importance and relate their training, practice, or investigations to those issues, drawing on relevant scientific research studies as well as sound theory, professional values, ethical standards, and client preferences (Thyer, 1994).

Alternatives in Social Work Education

Consistent with CSWE educational policy, I do believe that the theoretical content provided in our professional programs should be primarily those reasonably well supported by empirical research, and we should leave to a well-deserved rest and as historical footnotes those that fail to meet this standard. This would not be an easy task. It would be akin to the rigorous purging of the medical school curriculum engendered by the Flexner (1910) report more than 100 years ago (his influential study documenting the lack of an empirical foundation in medical education, and his suggested replacement of quack theories and practices with those more firmly supported in science). We are notoriously reluctant to critique the validity of one another's theories, as this sort of behavior violates a "gentlemen's agreement" within the academy to leave each other alone to pursue our own interests. As an example, David Howe (1980, p. 319) wrote a nice article titled "Inflated States and Empty Theories in Social Work," in which he noted:

> Social work has rarely discarded any of its "theories," leaving them to accumulate in books and courses, swelling of what is taken to be the occupation's knowledge base, giving an impression of development whereas all that may be happening is the steady accumulation of unrelated relics.

In general, Howe contended that our preoccupation with theory was in part an effort to acquire one of the features of supposedly professional and scientific professions—in other words, our "theoretical knowledge," which

> furnished social work with its credentials and provided observers with a yardstick by which to judge the occupation's activities. The integration of the profession's theories into expert practice has become one of the main criteria by which we are told we might recognise the competent social worker. (p. 321)

This might be good for the professionalization and prestige of the field of social work, but such opportunistic reasons hardly make for the genuine integration of social science theory into our education, practice, and research.

Closer to home than Howe's article written 35 years ago, during a CSWE conference in Atlanta, I had occasion during a public question-and-answer session to ask the distinguished social work educator Werner Boehm, "Dr. Boehm, are there any theories of social work practice which you do *not* recommend should be taught to students?" With a rueful smile, he acknowledged his reluctance to cite any specific ones, implying that this would be too conflictual to "get into." Perhaps he was right to take this approach.

In any event, I hope to see the day when social work classes titled, say, Social Work Practice: Psychodynamic Approaches or Behavioral Social Work are gradually expunged from the curriculum and replaced with problem-oriented courses, titled, say, Social Work Practice in the Field of Substance Abuse or Social Work Practice in the Field of Child Abuse and Neglect, wherein the faculty would provide some empirically supported theoretical content, but where the majority of instruction would involve learning to provide evidence-based interventions related to that class's topic. Evidence-based practice guidelines, of which there are a growing number, could also play an important role in social work education. And field placements, in part, could be selected on their basis to reinforce this didactic training. Some small steps are being taken in this direction, such as at Washington University, which has adopted evidence-based practice as its program's conceptual framework (Edmond, Rochman, Megivern, Howard, & Williams, 2006; Howard, McMillan, & Pollio, 2003).

History teaches that practice methods can be effectively taught without a foundation of valid theory. For example, one of the earliest known psychosocial treatments subjected to experimental outcomes research, systematic desensitization (SD), was based on the theory called reciprocal inhibition, and students of SD spent a fair amount of time learning this. However, it gradually emerged in the 1960s and early 1970s that the mechanism of action for the success of SD was *not* reciprocal inhibition. Therefore, of what value was this theoretical training? Perhaps it made some sort of heuristic sense and provided the therapist with a line of plausible patter he or she could deliver to the client, maximizing, perhaps, the placebo power of this treatment. But few of us would be comfortable recommending that contemporary students be knowingly taught a theory now known to be false as a component of training in practice skills. It is interesting to note that SD seemed then (and still seems) to work pretty well, even though it was based on a theory that ultimately proved to be invalid. This illustrates the less than intimate connection that may exist between interventions and theories.

More recently, in the early 1990s, teaching the techniques of EMDR was prefaced by fairly extensive exegesis into the presumptive theoretical mechanisms of actions of how saccadic eye movements affected the brain's neurophysiology, and the proper sequencing and timing of such back-and-forth eye movements was held to be absolutely crucial to obtaining a cure. We now know that the purported benefits of EMDR have absolutely no bearing on one's eye movements, and that all the time and writing devoted to this theory was also meaningless patter.

Similarly, many evidence-based practice guidelines can be adhered to by individuals lacking a genuine theoretical (much less factual) understanding on the part of the practitioner of the treatment's purported mechanisms of action. Please note that I am *not* suggesting that this is a desirable state of affairs. I am merely asserting that this can sometimes happen. If the end results are social workers who can genuinely help clients, my concern that they be able to provide a theoretical rationale for their actions is far less pressing. Remember also that the converse position has been dominant for many years in social work—we have spent more energy ensuring competence in "theory" than we did in empirically based practice skills. And for the most part this has not been wise.

Alternatives in Social Work Practice and Research

Recommendations similar to those outlined earlier have been around for many years in social work. For example:

> Although therapeutics should be derivable from theory, it may be appropriate at this point to work at effecting change and to capture as much evidence as possible of what occurs, without primary preoccupation with theory.

(Loeb, 1959, p. 15)

The idea that casework needs a superordinate theory or theories is no longer tenable. The knowledge base of future practice will likely consist of a variety of empirically demonstrated propositions from different perspectives, tied together by at least one major thread, that is, their utilization leads to success in helping clients.

(Fischer, 1972, p. 108)

The rise of empirically based treatment manuals and practice guidelines has shown that very specific and highly detailed psychosocial interventions can be taught to human service professionals, who can then apply them in practice and obtain positive results with clients (cf. LeCroy, 2008). These manuals more often than not focus on what to do in certain circumstances and can be thin in terms of communicating theory related to a problem's etiology or the proposed mechanisms of change upon which the intervention is based. To the extent that such evidence-based treatment manuals and practice guidelines can be used to train practitioners who can effectively help clients, this is a good thing for the profession. I also freely admit that developing valid etiological theories for the psychosocial problems of concern to social workers is an important undertaking and should be a focus of our attention. However, we need not wait on the emergence of such theories to develop and test specific social work interventions. Indeed, for every conceivable problem, interventions already exist, and investigating these is also a good thing for social workers to undertake.

Sometimes a given field of practice is so undeveloped that exploring theoretical formulations and proposing tests of these is seen as premature. For example, in the September 2004 issue of *Social Service Review*, Krisberg critiqued a recent book on juvenile delinquency as follows:

The editors of this book asked the invited authors to put forward theoretical formulations on the causes of juvenile delinquency and to propose bold hypotheses that could be tested empirically. In this, the editors assumed that much is known about patterns of juvenile delinquency behavior and that the most pressing scientific task is theory construction. I am not certain where the editors got these assumptions. The world of juvenile misconduct is so varied and nuanced that it is difficult to imagine that "we know enough." (p. 521)

In critiquing a typology of juvenile delinquency, the author claims, "Such a distinction is not sufficient for theory building or for planning intervention strategies" (p. 521).

Thus, despite the tenets of science, whereby ideally research is guided by theory, I believe that there are occasions when legitimate research can and should be undertaken without being guided by theory. I believe that this happens far more often than we recognize, in part because we sometimes apply a gratuitous veneer of theory, sometimes before, but sometimes after, we write up our work. Practice, too, is more often than we recognize not guided by formal deductive social science theory. As noted by Gottesfeld and Pharis (1977, p. 13):

> *Early social workers—those bold or foolish men and women who chose to wrestle with these problems—*had no convenient theories to help them plan their activities.... *Americans who would help their fellow man had no legislation and* little helping theory *to rely on. (emphasis in original)*

Jay Haley (1963, p. 214), a pioneer in the field of marital therapy, said, "Marital therapy has not developed because of theory; it appears that people were struggling to find a theory to fit practice." What was true in the early days of formal social work still holds today. A review of 252 empirical studies on psychotherapy published in the *Journal of Consulting and Clinical Psychology* found a two-decades-long decline in theory-guided research and a rise in pragmatic, clinically oriented studies. By the 1980s, only about 31% of the psychotherapy studies had a theoretical rationale (Omer & Dar, 1992). It may well be that to have an explicit theoretical rationale is more the exception than the rule in psychotherapy research.

As in practice, so, too, do we find analogous situations in research:

> *Modern theorists of science—Popper, Hanson, Polanyi, Kuhn, and Feyerabend included—have exaggerated the role of comprehensive theory in scientific advance and made experimental evidence seem almost irrelevant. Instead, exploratory experimentation* unguided by formal theory, *and unexpected experimental discoveries tangential to whatever theory motivated the research, have repeatedly been the source of great scientific advances, providing the stubborn, dependable, replicable puzzles that have justified theoretical advances at solution.*
>
> (Cook & Campbell, 1979, p. 24, emphasis added)

Social work education and research, as you might begin to suspect, is something that I hope to see become more applied and outcome-oriented, with a greater proportion of program evaluation and other forms of outcome studies being represented in our professional literature. When training BSW and MSW students to be consumers of research, we could use more examples of services research for them to read, to critique, and to learn how to use contemporary sources of information, such as the websites of the Campbell Collaboration and the Cochrane Collaboration, sources of current information on evidence-based practices. Learning to read and critique a randomized controlled trial or even a systematic review is a professional skill that will have lifelong value (Holosko, 2006).

Conclusion

I began this chapter by stating my respect for good theory that is used to guide well-crafted research, in a recursive process that yields closer approximations to nature's truths about the reality of social problems, and of the mechanisms of action of psychosocial interventions. This is how I was trained as a professional social worker, and this is how, to a large extent, I have guided my own research agenda over the past 25 years. Personally, I believe that the tenets of contemporary social learning theory, involving an amalgam of respondent, operant, and observational learning, have much to contribute to both social work research and practice. A substantial proportion of my empirical research has indeed been guided by social learning theory, as have many of the interventions I have investigated. I have also written extensively on the theoretical contributions of social learning theory to social work across the spectrum of practice, from one-to-one therapy to group work, community practice, and the design and analysis of social policy on a national level. By no means should I be considered to be anti-theory.

At the same time, I have described how our discipline's preoccupation with theory, much of it bad theory, has exerted a deleterious effect on social work education, practice, and research. In regard to false conceptual frameworks, I believe that social workers need theory like birds need ornithology, and I have gone so far as to state, "There is nothing as harmful as a bad theory" (Thyer, 2004, p. 141). Although there is much in our social work literature extolling the virtues of theory, there is little commentary on how the incorporation of bad theory, or the giving of superficial attention to theory, instead of genuinely integrating theoretical concepts into research projects from their conception, can have harmful consequences. I hope that my attention to these latter consequences of the use of bad theory in social work education, practice, and research are taken in the constructive manner in which they are intended: not as a call for the abolishment of theory, or its repudiation, but for a more informed and critical appraisal and selection of theories constituting the edifice of professional social work. At the same time, I believe that the education of professional social workers and the choice of interventions used by practitioners can and should be more evidence-based and less theoretically driven.

Key Terms

Black box evaluation	EPAS	Task-centered practice
CSWE	Falsificationism	
Deductive theory	Grey box evaluation	White box evaluation
	Justificationism	

Review Questions for Critical Thinking

1. Why do you suppose that the potentially harmful effects of theory in social work have been so little recognized?

2. Does the premise of this chapter seem to be "anti-theory"? Why or why not?

3. When might social work research, and social work practice, *not* be based on an explicit theory? Does this seem legitimate to you? Why or why not?

4. Explain how it could be that an invalid theory might yield an effective treatment, and a valid theory lead to ineffective treatments.

5. Try to come up with an example of a research project that is clearly *not* explicitly based on a particular theory (e.g., the U.S. census). Provide a rationale for your choice.

6. Try to come up with an example of a social work service or program which is clearly *not* explicitly based on some etiological theory for the problem being addressed, or mechanism of action for the intervention (e.g., child protective service investigations). Provide a rationale for your choice.

Online Resources

http://socialworkpodcast.blogspot.com/2009/08/theories-for-clinical-social-work.html

A podcast of an interview with social work faculty member Joseph Walsh, conducted by Jonathan Singer, on the topic of theories for clinical social work. This website also provides a number of podcasts devoted to individual theoretical orientations used in social work.

www.psych.ucalgary.ca/thpsyc/default.html

The website for the journal *Theory & Psychology*, a fully peer-reviewed forum for theoretical and metatheoretical analysis in psychology. It focuses on the emergent themes at the center of contemporary psychological debate. Its principal aim is to foster theoretical dialogue and innovation within the discipline, serving an integrative role for a wide psychological audience.

www.wiley.com/bw/journal.asp?ref=0735–2751

The website for the journal *Sociological Theory*, published for the American Sociological Association. This important journal covers the full range of sociological theory—from ethnomethodology to world systems analysis, from commentaries on the classics to the latest cutting-edge ideas, and from reexaminations of neglected theorists to metatheoretical inquiries.

www.blackwellpublishing.com/journal.asp?ref=0021–8308

Website for the *Journal for the Theory of Social Behavior*, which aims at advancing understandings of social behavior, that is, people acting in relation to, or being constituted through, the social world of other people, institutions, and material and symbolic culture. Any discipline or approach that contributes to the journal's aim is welcome.

www.umaine.edu/jmb/

The website for the *Journal of Mind and Behavior* (JMB), a periodical dedicated to the interdisciplinary approach within psychology and related fields—building on the assumption of a unified science. Mind and behavior position, interact, and causally relate to each other in multidirectional ways; JMB urges the exploration of these interrelationships.

References

Adams, H. E. (1984). The pernicious effects of theoretical orientations in clinical psychology. *Clinical Psychologist, 37*(3), 90–94.

American Evaluation Association. (2007). *Guiding principles for evaluators.* Retrieved from www.eval.org/Publications/GuidingPrinciplesPrintable.asp

Beutler, L. E., Williams, P. E., Wakefield, P. J., & Entwistle, S. R. (1995). Bridging scientist and practitioner perspectives in clinical psychology. *American Psychologist, 50*, 984–994.

Bloom, M. (1965). Connecting formal behavioral science theory to individual social work practice. *Social Service Review, 39*(1), 11–22.

Blount, R. L., Bunke, V. L., & Zaff, J. F. (2000). Bridging the gap between explicative and treatment research: A model and practical implications. *Journal of Clinical Psychology in Medical Settings, 7*, 79–90.

Burr, W. (1973). *Theory construction and the sociology of the family.* New York, NY: Wiley.

Cheers, B. (1978). Things and theories: Me, people I help, and theories. *Clinical Social Work Education, 2*(2), 99–107.

Christie, C. A. (2003). What guides evaluation: A study of how evaluation practice maps onto evaluation theory. *New Directions for Evaluation, 97*, 7–35.

Cook, T. D., & Campbell, T. D. (1979). *Quasi-experimentation: Design and data analysis for field settings.* Chicago, IL: Rand McNally.

Council on Social Work Education, Commission on Accreditation. (2003). *Handbook of accreditation standards and procedures* (5th ed.). Washington, DC: Author.

Crowder, C., & Lowe, P. (2000, May 19). Four accused in rebirthing death: Affidavit states girl, 10, smothered while adults pushed and therapist yelled "Die right now." *Rocky Mountain News*, 5A.

Druckman, D., & Bjork, R. A. (Eds.). (1991). *In the mind's eye: Enhancing human performance.* Washington, DC: National Academy Press.

Edmond, T., Rochman, E., Megivern, D., Howard, M., & Williams, C. (2006). Integrating evidence-based practice and social work field education. *Journal of Social Work Education, 42*, 377–396.

Ferri, M. Amato, L. & Davoli, M. (2006). Alchoholics Anonymous and other 12-step programmes for alcohol dependence. *Cochrane Database of Systematic Reviews*, 2006, Issue 3. Art. No.: CD005032. DOI: 10.1002/14651858.CD005032.pub2

Fischer, J. (1972). A review of theories for social casework. *Social Work, 17*, 105–108.

Flexner, A. (1910). *Medical education in the United States and Canada: A report to the Carnegie Foundation for the Advancement of Teaching, Bulletin no. 4*. New York, NY: Carnegie Foundation for the Advancement of Teaching.

Gallant, J. P., & Thyer, B. A. (1999). Usefulness of general systems theory in social work practice. In R. R. Greene (Ed.), *Human behavior theory and social work practice* (2nd ed., pp. 250–257). New York, NY: Aldine de Gruyter.

Gambrill, E. (1983). *Casework: A competency approach*. Englewood Cliffs, NJ: Prentice Hall.

Gambrill, E. (1994). What's in a name? Task-centered, empirical, and behavioral practice. *Social Service Review, 68*, 578–599.

Gambrill, E. (1999). Evidence-based practice: An alternative to authority-based practice. *Families in Society, 80*, 341–350.

Gottesfeld, M. L., & Pharis, M. E. (1977). *Profiles in social work*. New York, NY: Human Sciences Press.

Greenwald, A. G., Pratkanis, A. R., Leippe, M. R., & Baumgardner, M. H. (1986). Under what conditions does theory obstruct research progress? *Psychological Review, 93*, 216–229.

Greenwood, E. (1955). Social science and social work: A theory of their relationship. *Social Service Review, 29*, 20–33.

Haley, J. (1963). Marriage therapy. *Archives of General Psychiatry, 8*, 214–234.

Harrison, D. F., & Thyer, B. A. (1988). Doctoral research on social work practice. *Journal of Social Work Education, 24*, 107–114.

Holosko, M. J. (2006). *A primer for critiquing social science research: A student guide*. Belmont, CA: Thomson.

Holosko, M. J., & Leslie, D. (1998). Obstacles for conducting empirically-based research. In J. S. Wodarski & B. A. Thyer (Eds.), *Handbook of empirical social work practice: Vol. II. Social problems and practice issues* (pp. 433–451). New York, NY: Wiley.

Howard, M. O., McMillan, C. J., & Pollio, D. (2003). Teaching evidence-based practice: Toward a new paradigm for social work education. *Research on Social Work Practice, 13*, 234–259.

Howe, D. (1980). Inflated states and empty theories in social work. *British Journal of Social Work, 10*, 316–340.

Hunsley, J., Lee, C. M., & Wood, J. M. (2003). Controversial and questionable assessment techniques. In S. O. Lilenfeld, S. J. Lynn, & J. M. Lohr (Eds.), *Science and pseudoscience in clinical psychology* (pp. 39–76). New York, NY: Guilford Press.

Kazdin, A. E. (2001). Bridging the enormous gaps of theory with therapy research and practice. *Journal of Clinical Child Psychology, 30*, 59–66.

Krisberg, B. (2004). A book review of Causes of Conduct Disorder and Juvenile Delinquency. *Social Service Review, 78*, 520–522.

LeCroy, C. W. (Ed.). (2008). *Handbook of evidence-based treatment manuals for children and adolescents*. New York, NY: Oxford University Press.

Loeb, M. (1959). The backdrop for social work research: Theory-making and model-building. In L. S. Kogan (Ed.), *Social science theory and social work research* (pp. 3–15). New York, NY: National Association of Social Workers Press.

MacKillop, J., Lisman, S. A., Weinstein, A., & Rosenbaum, D. (2003). Controversial treatments for alcoholism. In S. O. Lilienfeld, S. J. Lynn, & J. M. Lohr (Eds.), *Science and pseudoscience in clinical psychology* (pp. 273–305). New York, NY: Guilford Press.

Meyer, C. H. (1973). Practice models—The new ideology. *Smith College Studies in Social Work, 43,* 85–98.

Moore, L. S., Dettlaff, A. J., & Dietz, T. J. (2004). Using the Myers-Briggs type indicator in field education. *Journal of Social Work Education, 40,* 337–349.

Morris, T. (1997). Is it possible to know when theories are obsolete? In M. Bloom & W. C. Klein (Eds.), *Controversial issues in human behavior in the social environment* (pp. 71–78). Boston, MA: Allyn & Bacon.

Nisbett, R., & Ross, L. (1980). *Human inference: Strategies and shortcomings of social judgement.* Englewood Cliffs, NJ: Prentice-Hall.

Omer, H., & Dar, R. (1992). Changing trends in three decades of psychotherapy research: The flight from theory into pragmatics. *Journal of Consulting and Clinical Psychology, 60,* 88–93.

Pittenger, D. J. (1993). The utility of the Myers-Briggs Type Indicator. *Review of Educational Research, 63,* 467–488.

Platt, J. R. (1964). Strong inference. *Science, 146,* 347–352.

Plionis, E. M. (2004). Teaching students how to avoid errors in theory application. *Brief Treatment and Crisis Intervention, 4,* 49–56.

Rehr, H., Showers, N., Rosenberg, G., & Blumenfield, S. (1998). Profiles of published social work practitioners: Who wrote and why. *Social Work in Health Care, 28*(2), 83–94.

Reid, W. J. (1977). Social work for social problems. *Social Work, 22,* 374–381.

Reid, W. J. (2000). *The task planner.* New York, NY: Columbia University Press.

Reid, W. J., & Epstein, L. (1972). *Task-centered casework.* New York, NY: Columbia University Press.

Rosen, A., Proctor, E., & Staudt, M. (1999). Social work research and the quest for effective practice. *Social Work Research, 23,* 4–14.

Schilling, R. F. (1997). Developing intervention research programs in social work. *Social Work Research, 21,* 173–180.

Scriven, M. (1998). Minimalist theory: The least theory that practice requires. *American Journal of Evaluation, 19,* 57–70.

Shaw, I., & Compton, A. (2003). Theory, like mist on spectacles, obscures vision. *Evaluation, 9,* 192–204.

Sheldon, B., & Chilvers, R. (2004). Evidence-based practice in England. In B. A. Thyer & M. A. F. Kazi (Eds.), *International perspectives on evidence-based practice in social work* (pp. 45–80). Birmingham, UK: Venture Press.

Smith, D. A. (1999). The end of theoretical orientations? *Applied and Preventive Psychology, 8,* 269–280.

Spitzer, R. L. (2003). Can some gay men and lesbians change their sexual orientation? 200 participants reporting a change from homosexual to heterosexual orientation. *Archives of Sexual Behavior, 32,* 403–417.

Stenger, V. J. (1997, January/February). Quantum quackery. *Skeptical Inquirer, 21,* 37–40.

Stevenson, O. (1971). Knowledge for social work. *British Journal of Social Work, 1*(2), 226.

Thyer, B. A. (1994). Are theories for practice necessary? No! *Journal of Social Work Education, 30,* 147–151.

Thyer, B. A. (2001a). Research on social work practice does not benefit from blurry theory. *Journal of Social Work Education, 37,* 51–66.

Thyer, B. A. (2001b). The role of theory in research on social work practice. *Journal of Social Work Education, 37,* 9–25.

Thyer, B. A. (2004). Thyer response [Letter]. *Social Work, 49,* 141.

Wakefield, J. C. (1996a). Does social work need the eco-systems perspective? Pt. I. Is the perspective clinically useful? *Social Service Review, 70,* 1–32.

Wakefield, J. C. (1996b). Does social work need the ecosystems perspective? Pt. II. Does the perspective save social work from incoherence? *Social Service Review, 70,* 183–213.

Wilson, G. T. (1985). Limitations of meta-analysis in the evaluation of the effects of psychological therapy. *Clinical Psychology Review, 5,* 35–47.

Author Index

Aber, J. L., 174
Ackerman, N., 376
Adams, H. E., 470
Adams, S., 425
Agazarian, Y. M., 340, 341, 344, 345, 346, 347
Ainsworth, M. D. S., 165, 166, 167–168, 170, 171, 174, 176, 180
Alderfer, C., 448
Aldwin, C. M., 37
Alexander, L. B., 387
Alford, B. A., 127
Alford, R. R., 25, 26, 27
Allen, B. P., 239, 244
Allen, J. P., 174
Allen, W. R., 384
Almeida, R., 181
Altpeter, M., 443
Amato, P., 397
Andersen, S. M., 212
Anderson, R. E., 306
Anderson, S., 398
Andersson, G., 174
Andomo, R., 285
Andreasen, N. C., 291
Andrews, J., 330, 332, 333, 334, 335
Anthony, W. P., 436–437
Anyon, Y., xxxiii, 1
Arch, J. J., 144
Argyris, C., 441
Arhin, A., 65
Arnett, J. J., 21
Arnopp, J., 277
Ashford, J. B., 336
Aslin, R. N., 51
Asmus, J. M., 100
Athos, T., 422
Auerswald, E. H., 300
Austin, D., 443
Austin, J. T., 438
Austin, M., 5, 10, 11, 28, 31
Austin, M. J., xxxiii, 1
Avi-Yonah, O. K., 175
Axelson, L. J., 384

Ayllon, T., 84, 101
Aylwin, A. S., 65
Azrin, N., 84

Babbie, E., xvii
Bacallao, M. L., 106
Bacon, H., 174
Baer, D. M., 93, 95, 104, 107, 315
Baer, R. A., 145
Baeyens, F., 66
Bagarozzi, D., 85
Baham, M., 99
Bailey, J. S., 105, 106
Baker, J. N., 105
Bakermans-Kranenburg, M., 174–175
Baldwin, L. M., 394
Ballou, M., 156
Bandura, A., 95, 96, 105, 343
Barker, R., xv, xix
Barker, T., 310
Barlow, S. H., 328, 359–360, 361
Barnard, C. I., 416
Baron, A., 86
Bar-Tal, D., 66
Barth, R., 174
Bartholomew, K., 171, 174, 175, 179
Bass, M. J., 55
Bates, L., 176
Bates, M., 301
Bateson, G., 375
Baum, M., 67
Bauman, K. E., 98
Baumgardner, M. H., 469
Beck, A. T., 125, 127, 134, 135, 140, 152
Beck, J. E., 397
Beck, J. S., 125, 126, 127, 136, 140, 141, 147, 149, 150, 155, 156
Bell, S. M., 168
Belsky, J., 383

Benard, B., 308
Bennett, S., 174
Berger, P. L., 373
Berlin, S. B., 125, 135, 136, 139, 152, 153
Bernard, J., 51
Bernhardt, B., 264
Berzin, S., xxxiii, 1
Besharov, D. J., 21
Besser, A., 172
Besthorn, F. H., 303
Beutler, L. E., 475
Bieling, P. J., 155, 156
Bierly, P. E., 430
Biestek, F., 244
Bigelow, K. M., 106
Billingsley, A., 384
Bion, W. R., 342, 349
Birnbaum, G. E., 175
Birsinger, P., 67
Bishop, D., 394
Bishop, D. S., 394
Bishop, K. K., 264
Bishop, S. J., 384
Bjork, R. A., 462
Black, E., 264
Black, J., 174
Black, R. B., 264
Blackman, D. K., 104
Blandford, D. H., 66
Blanken, P., 68
Blankstein, K. R., 137
Blau, P., 412
Blau, P. M., 372
Blehar, M. C., 168
Bloom, M., 2, 12, 13, 302, 303, 467, 472
Blount, R., 473
Blumenfeld, S., 463
Blumenthal, B., 448, 449, 451
Blumer, H., 373
Blythe, B. J., 106
Boeree, C. G., 239, 243
Bograd, M., 399
Boldry, J., 171
Bolen, R., 174, 182

Bolman, L., 414, 421
Bond, M., 175, 176
Bond, S., 175, 176
Borden, W., 200
Bordnick, P. S., 68, 70, 106
Borduin, C. M., 306
Botvin, E. M., 106
Botvin, G. J., 106
Bourdieu, 27
Bourdieu, P., 23, 26, 27
Boutte-Queen, N., 283
Bowen, L., 109
Bowen, M., 380, 395
Bowen, S., 145
Bowlby, J., 165, 166, 167–168,
    169, 170, 171, 175, 176,
    179, 180, 181
Boxer, A. M., 217, 218
Boyd-Franklin, N., 384
Boyle, S., 10
Boynton, K. E., 63
Bozarth, J. D., 232
Bradford, K., 397
Bradley, B. T., 239, 240
Bradshaw, W., 109
Brandon, M., 172
Brennan, K., 174, 175
Bretherton, I., 165, 166, 167,
    168, 170, 172, 175, 179,
    182
Briggs, A. C., 104
Briggs, H. E., 104, 315
Broberg, G., 264
Bronfenbrenner, U., 22, 305
Brooks, W., 10
Brooks-Gunn, J., 21
Brophy, G., 104
Brown, L., 29
Brown, W., 284
Brownrigg, A., 393
Brownstein, A. J., 91, 97
Bruno, F., xiii, xxi, 48
Buckingham, M., 429, 431, 450,
    451
Buehler, C., 397
Bumberry, W. A., 377
Bunke, V. L., 473
Burch, P., 27
Burke, A., 65
Burlingame, G., 359, 361
Burlingame, G. M., 328, 360,
    361
Burman, B., 383, 397
Burr, W., 459
Burrish, T. G., 63
Burton, M., 105

Busnel, M.-C., 51
Butler, R. N., 213–214
Buttell, F., 175, 176, 178
Butterfield, W. H., 71

Cain, D. J., 251–252, 254, 256
Calle-Mesa, L., 145
Cameron, O. G., 61
Campbell, C. B., 73
Campbell, L., 171, 175
Campbell, N. A., 266
Campbell, T. D., 481
Canda, E. R., 2
Cannon, W. B., 300
Caplan, P. J., 399
Caple, R. B., 340, 341, 342, 362
Capra, F., 300, 306, 307, 308
Carey, E. G., 57
Carey, M. P., 63
Carlisle, J. M., 65
Carlson, L. E., 145
Carney, M., 175, 176, 178
Carney, M. M., xxxiii, 165
Caronna, C. A., 26
Carr, A., 398
Carr, E. G., 87, 98
Carter, B., 382
Carter, I., 306
Carter, L., 289
Carter, M. M., 154
Cartwright, S., 420
Caspi, J., 450
Catalano, R. F., 105
Cathcart, R. S., 329
Cauce, A. M., 358
Chambless, D. L., 108
Charon, J. M., 373
Chatterjee, P., 2
Chau, K. L., 354
Chawla, N., 145
Cheers, B., 472
Chen, C. P., 246
Chen, S., 212
Cheney, C. D., 95
Chess, W. A., 337
Chestang, L., 218
Childress, A. R., 62
Chilvers, R., 472
Christensen, A., 145
Christie, C. A., 475
Christner, R. W., 125
Cicchetti, D., 5, 384
Clark, C. L., 174
Clark, D., 415
Clark, M., 443
Clay, C., 108

Clipson, C. R., 176
Clogg, C. C., 372
Cloward, R., 22, 23
Coan, J. A., 62
Cobbs, P. M., xxiii
Coffman, C., 429, 431, 450, 451
Coghlan, D. J., 255
Cohen, H. R., 212
Cohen, O., 175
Cohler, B., 20
Cohler, B. J., 217, 218
Colapinto, J., 306
Cole, A., 212
Coleman, J. S., 23
Colin, V., 180
Collins, P. M., 444
Colyvas, J., 26
Combrinck-Graham, L., 382,
    387
Compton, A., 460
Conger, R. D., 398
Conklin, C., 68
Connors, J. V., 340, 341, 342,
    362
Cook, T. D., 481
Cooley, C. H., 335
Cooper, C. A., 420
Cooper, J. O., 88, 95
Cooper, P. J., 63
Cooper, R. P., 51
Corey, G., 204, 233, 236, 237,
    242, 244, 246, 333, 337,
    339, 340, 342, 353, 356,
    357, 359
Corey, M. S., 339, 359
Cormier, S., 126, 131, 147, 149,
    150, 152, 154
Cornell, K. L., 2
Corrie, S., 175
Corrigan, P. W., 109
Corsini, R., xvii, xxiv
Coser, L., 34
Coulton, C. C., 384
Courturier, J., 400
Cowan, P. A., 5
Cox, M. J., 383, 398
Cox, P., 310
Cox, W. H., 104
Cramer, D., 243
Craske, M. G., 144, 155, 157
Creswell, J. W., 212
Crick, F., 265
Criss, M. M., 397
Crittenden, P., 174
Crolley, J., 68
Cross, W. E., Jr., 180

Crowder, C., 466
Crowley, R., 105
Cummings, E. M., 383, 397
Cunningham, G. C., 277
Cunningham, P. B., 306
Curnoe, S., 69
Curtis, G. C., 61

Dale, O., 337
Daley, J., 393
Dalton, K. M., 62
D'Andrade, R., 374
Dangel, R. F., 110
Daniel, B., 174
Dar, R., 481
Davidson, J., 148
Davidson, R. J., 62
Davies, P. T., 383, 397
Davis, B., 98
Davis, G. F., 25, 26, 437, 438
Davis, K., 175
Davis, K. E., 154, 383
Davis, R., 178
Dawe, S., 68
Dawson, G., 5
Day, R. D., 397
Day, S. H., 106
Deal, T., 414
Deal, T. E., 421, 435–436
Dean, S., 104
Deane, F. P., 64, 150, 173
de Arce, F., 68
Deater-Decker, K., 22
de Carvalho, R. J., 225, 230
DeCasper, A. J., 51
DeLucia-Waack, J. L., 361
Deming, W. E., 413
DeNavas-Walt, C., 445
Denny, R., 418
de Quiros Aragon, M.-B., 68
Derby, K. M., 100
DeRoos, Y. S., 105
de Rosnay, M., 63
DeRubis, R. J., 127, 140, 141,
        142, 146, 147, 149, 150
Deschner, J. P., 110
Dettlaff, A. J., 462
Devanna, M ., 441
Diaz, T., 106
Dickerson, V. C., 399
Dick-Siskin, L., 125
Diehl, M., 212
Dietz, T. J., 462
Dillenburger, K., 104, 105
DiMaggio, P., 25, 26, 27, 154
Dimberg, U., 54

Dimeff, L., 145
Dineen, J. P., 105
Dobson, K. S., 128, 129, 130,
        131, 136, 143, 148, 149,
        150, 151, 154
Doctor, R. M., 106
Dolan-Del Vecchio, K., 391
Domenech-Rodríguez, M., 358
Donigian, J., 340, 357
Dooley, T., 174
Dore, M. M., xxxiii, 369, 386,
        387
Dorsey, M. F., 98, 105
Douglas, T., 335, 337
Dowd, E. T., 141, 152
Downs, T. M., 30, 35
Doyo, M. C., 66
Dozois, D. J. A., 128, 129, 130,
        131, 136, 143, 148, 149,
        150, 151
Drucker, P., 443
Druckman, D., 462
Dryden, W., 132, 134, 138, 147,
        151, 155
DuBos, R., 300
Dulac, N., 430
Dulmus, C. N., xxxi
Dumas, J. E., 316
Duncan, G. J., 21
Dunford, F., 178
Dunkley, D. M., 137, 147, 148
Dunn, J., 181
Durkheim, E., 23, 335
Durkin, H. E., 344
Dutton, D., 172, 175, 176, 177,
        179
Duvall, E. M., 382
Dworetzky, J., 169, 170
Dyer, F. J., 174

Earley, P. C., 420
Eccles, J., 21
Edmond, T., 479
Edward, G. C., 5
Edwards, B., 24
Edwards, R., 443
Eelen, P., 66
Egeland, B., 398
Egeland, B. R., 175
Eggebeen, D. J., 372
Ehrman, R., 62
Elbach, K. D., 427
Elder, G. H., Jr., 15, 16, 17, 20
Eleonora, G., 64
Elkins, R. L., 70
Eloff, I., 175

Elson, L. M., 266
Embry, D. D., 316
Ennis, J., 174
Entwistle, S. R., 467
Epling, W. F., 101
Epstein, J. A., 106
Epstein, L., 476
Epstein, N. B., 394
Erel, O., 383, 397
Erich, S., 283
Erickson, C., 316
Erickson, M. F., 175
Erikson, E. H., 194, 195, 196,
        197, 198, 199, 200, 201,
        202, 203, 204, 205, 206,
        207, 209, 214, 215, 218,
        219
Erikson, J. M., 199, 200, 202
Erk, S., 61
Ermann, M., 210
Esfeld, M., 307
Eubanks-Carter, C., 140

Faldowski, R., 400
Falicov, C. J., 385
Farley, O., 10
Farmer, P., 309, 318
Farmer, R. L., 291
Fausel, D., 175
Fearn, N., 175
Feder, L., 178
Feeney, J., 175
Fehm-Wolfsdorf, G., 62
Feldman, N., 387
Fellin, P., xvi, 30, 33
Ferster, C. B., 91
Feuer, M. J., 26
Feynman, R. P., xv
Fiedler, F. E., 34
Field, A. P., 64
Fifer, W. P., 51
Figueroa, R. G., 110
Finn, J. L., 313
Finzi, D., 175
Fischer, J., 47, 85, 194, 480
Fisher, J. E., 125, 154
Fixsen, D. L., 110
Flache, E., 373
Flanagan, S. G., 104, 109
Flessner, C., 106
Flexner, A., xv, xviii, 477
Florian, V., 171, 172
Floyd, J., 110
Foa, E. B., 108, 145
Foelsch, P., 173

Foley, M. W., 24
Folkman, S., 37
Follet, M. P., 331
Follette, V. M., 144
Fonagy, P., 175, 176
Ford, G., 238, 239
Forde, D., 178
Foreyt, J. P., 129
Fosco, G. M., 397
Foster, S. L., 176
Fraley, R., 174, 175
Frank, R. H., 416
Franken, I. H. A., 68
Franklin, C., 309
Fraser, M., 36
Fraser, M. W., 3, 106
Frawley, P. J., 70
Freeman, A., 125
Freire, E., 256, 257
French, J. R. P., 34
Frets, P., 284
Friedland, R., 25, 26, 27
Friedman, B. S., 104
Friedman, H. L., 246, 247, 248
Fries, M., 107
Friesen, B. J., 387
Fry, P. S., 211
Fuhriman, A., 359
Fuhriman, A. J., 328, 361
Furlong, R. M., 264
Furstenberg, F. F., 384

Gabrieli, J. D. E., 74
Galatzer-Levy, R., 20
Gale, E. N., 61, 66
Gales, L. M., 436–437
Galinsky, M., 3, 36
Galinsky, M. J., 106, 350
Galizio, M., 86, 91
Gallagher-Thompson, D., 125
Gallant, J. P., 105, 313, 314, 465
Gallant, M., 250, 251
Gallant, W., 250, 251
Gallegos, E., 104
Galley, L., 61
Gambrill, E., 85, 460, 469, 477
Gambrill, E. D., 104
Gammon, E. A., 104
Gannon-Rowley, T., 24
Gantt, S., 344, 345, 346
Garbarino, J., 384
Garcia, E., 384
Garvin, C., xvi
Garvin, C. D., 333, 334, 335,
    350, 354, 355, 358, 362
Gatheridge, B., 106

Gauthier, Y., 175
Gearth, H., 414
Geffner, R., 176
Geller, M. H., 337, 342, 343,
    355, 362
Gelles, R., 178
Gendlin, E. T., 255, 256
George, C., 174
Gerard, J. M., 397
Gergely, G., 175
Germain, C. B., 217, 301, 302,
    303, 314, 386
Gerson, R., 392
Gewirtz, J. L., 103
Gibbs, L. E., 13
Gibbs, N., 433
Gibbs, P., 8
Gibson, J. W., 298
Gilboa-Schechtman, E., 145
Gilbreth, F. B., 57
Gilchrist, L. D., 105, 106
Gilligan, C., 215, 216
Giordano, J., 385
Gitlin, T., 418
Gitterman, A., 6, 301, 302, 303,
    312, 314, 331, 352, 353,
    386
Glasser, J. S., 439
Glazer, N., 418
Glisson, C., 423
Gnadler, M., 62
Gochros, H., 85
Gochros, H. L., 47
Godbout, N., 172, 178, 179
Godina, L., 105
Goldenson, J., 176
Goldhaber, D. E., 5
Goldiamond, I., 47, 85, 315
Goldner, V., 399
Goldstein, H., 3, 4, 219
Goldwyn, R., 173
Goleman, D., 433
Gonzales-Prendes, A. A., 108
Goodheart, C. D., 156
Goodrick, G. K., 129
Gordon, W., 217
Gore, K. L., 154
Gorman, J., 67
Gormenzano, I., 47
Gormley, B., 177
Gottesfeld, M. L., 481
Grace, C., 173
Graham, J. R., xviii
Granier-Deferre, C., 51
Grant, L. K ., 318, 319
Grayson, J. B., 108

Green, 154
Green, D., 2, 300, 309, 310
Green, G. R., 85
Green, L. W., 254
Greene, A. L., 397
Greene, B. F., 105, 106
Greene, R. R., xxxiii, 193, 194,
    195, 197, 198, 199, 200,
    203, 205, 207, 212, 213,
    214, 217, 218
Greenfield, E., 14, 39
Greenwald, A. G., 469
Greenway, D. E., 91
Greenwood, E., 460, 471, 472
Grier, W. H., xxiii
Griffin, J. H., xxiii
Grigsby, R., 174
Grimaldi, L., 157
Grist, T. M., 62
Grych, J. H., 397
Guerin, B., 315
Gutiérrez, L. M., 350

Haas, J. R., 91
Hagar, T. S., 178
Hagberg, B., 210, 211
Haight, B. K., 211
Haight, W., 174
Haley, J., 375, 481
Hall, J. A., 105
Hall-McCorquodale, I., 399
Hamilton, G., 298
Han, C. S., 5
Handy, C., 423
Hanley, G. P., 100
Hardiker, P., 47
Hare-Mustin, R. C., 385, 399
Hareven, T. L., 217
Harlow, H., 168
Harold, G. T., 397
Harrison, D. F., 106, 472
Hart, B., 103
Hartman, A., 317, 386, 392
Harvey, J ., 441
Hasenfeld, Y., 30, 34
Haskell, T. L., xix
Hawkins, J. D., 105
Hawthorne, L. R. L., 438
Hayes, L. J., 102
Hayes, S. C., 91, 97, 102, 144,
    156, 157
Hays, P. A., 125, 126, 154, 156
Hazan, C., 171, 173, 175
Hazlett-Stevens, H., 155, 157
Hearn, G., 386
Heather, N., 68

Henderson, A., 179
Henderson, R., 437
Henderson, V. L., 230
Hendriks, V. M., 68
Henggeler, S. W., 306, 316, 400
Henman, L. D., 329
Hennessey, T. M., 50
Hepler, J. B., 105
Herbert-Jackson, E. W., 104
Heron, T. E., 88
Herrnstein, R. J., 100
Heward, W. L., 88
Hewitt, P., 182
Hill, C. E., 255, 256, 257
Hill, R., 384
Himle, J., 108
Himle, M. B., 106
Hindo, C. S., 108
Hines, P., 384
Hines, P. M., 181
Hinings, D., 172, 174
Hjelle, L. A., 236
Hoare, C. H., 196, 208
Hochschild, A. R., 433
Hodge, B. J., 436–437
Hodges, V. G., 106
Hodgson, R. J., 65
Hodos, W., 73
Hodson, R., 425
Hogan, D. P., 372
Hogan, R., 193
Holland, T., 442
Hollis, F., 386
Hollis, F. H., 298
Holmes, D., 26
Holosko, M. J., xxxiii, 225, 250,
    251, 254, 473, 481
Holtzworth-Munroe, A., 176,
    177, 178
Hooley, J. M., 375
Hopps, L. G, 444
Horowitz, L. M., 174
Houston, S., 174
Houts, R. M., 398
Howard, M., 479
Howard, M. O., 71, 479
Howe, D., 172, 174, 478
Howe, M. W., 104
Hudgins, C. V., 59
Hudson, C. G., 307, 308
Huffman-Gottschling, K., xxxiii,
    297
Hughes, D., 174
Hull, C. L., 55
Hulsmeier, J., 393
Hunsley, J., 462

Hunt, S., 15, 16, 17
Hutchinson, E. D., 15, 17, 329
Hygge, S., 54

Innocent, A. J., 110
Irvine, S., 109
Isserlin, L., 400
Iverson, K. M., 125
Iwamasa, G. Y., 125, 126, 154
Iwata, B. A., 87, 98, 100, 105

Jackson, D., 380, 381
Jackson, D. D., 375
Jackson, S. E., 431
Jacobson, M., 313
Jacobson, M. B., 61, 66
Jacobvitz, D., 398
Jacobvitz, D. B., 398
James, K., 399
James, L. R., 423
Janchill, M. P., Sr., 386
Janis, I., 441
Jason, L. A., 107
Jehu, D., 47, 85
Jencks, C., 24
Jensen, J. M., 71, 105
Jensen, M. A., 32
Jewelewicz, R., 65
Johnson, B. M., 106
Johnson, D. W., 330, 355, 360
Johnson, F. P., 330, 355, 360
Johnson, P. E., 3, 4
Johnson, S., 175
Johnson, V. K., 397
Jones, G., 310
Jordan, A., 253
Joseph, S., 250, 251
Julian, T., 175
Jurist, E. L., 175

Kabacoff, R. I., 394
Kagle, J., 174
Kalin, N. H., 62
Kalodner, C. R., 361
Kang, H., 8
Kanlow, W., 291
Kanter, R. M., 439, 442
Kantrowitz, R., 156
Kapetanovic, S., 360
Kapit, W., 266
Kaplan, S., 437
Karen, R., 171, 180
Kasatkin, N. I., 51
Kashy, D., 171
Kastak, D., 102
Kastenbaum, R., 194

Katz, L. F., 397
Katzell, R. A., 438
Kaul, J. D., 416
Kaye, H., 60
Kazantzis, N., 150
Kazdin, A. E., 104, 125, 476
Keala, D. K., 398
Keith, D. V., 394
Keitner, G., 394
Keitner, G. I., 394
Kemp, S. P., 298, 305
Kendrick, C., 181
Kennedy, A. A., 435–436
Kenyon, G. M., 212
Kern, W., 62
Kerner, W., 62
Kerr, S., 428
Kesner, J., 175, 176
Kessler, M. L., 105
Kets Devries, M., 432
Key, F. A., 155, 157
Kimble, G. A., 83
King, N. J., 64
Kinoshita, L. M., 125
Kirkpatrick, L. A., 383
Kirschenbaum, H., 230, 253
Kirst-Ashman, K., 49
Kisilevsky, B. S., 51
Kivnick, H. Q., 199, 200, 202
Klein, W. C., 2, 12, 13
Klever, P., 380, 393
Klosterhalfen, W., 62
Knowles, J. G., 212
Kobak, R., 171
Koepke, J. M., 104
Koerner, K., 145
Koh, L. P., 125, 154
Kondo-Ikemura, K., 171
Kondrat, M. E., 1, 5
Korfmacher, J., 175
Korn, Z., 91
Kravetz, D. F., 54
Kretchmar, M. D., 398
Krisberg, B., 480
Krishnakumar, A., 397
Kroonenberg, P., 174–175
Kuhn, T. S., 377
Kupper, L. L., 106

L'Abate, L., 150
Labrador, F. J., 68
Lachmann, F. M., 210
Laidlaw, K., 125
Laird, J., 386
Lalli, E. P., 99
Lalli, J. S., 99

Lam, V., 307
Lamb, M. E., 397
Landrigan, C. P., 431
Lang, R., 69
Langevin, R., 69
Lanier, P., 104
LaPan, A., 264
Latimer, P. R., 108
Lau, A. W., 125
Lau, M. M., 105
Lawson, D., 177
Lazarus, R., 37
Leadbeater, B. J., 384
Leahy, R. L., 126, 127, 134, 140, 141, 147, 149
Leary, J. D., 104
Leavitt, D., 125
Lebon, G., 336
Lecanuet, J.-P., 51
LeCroy, C. W., xxxiii, 106, 125, 327, 328, 336, 350, 356, 357, 480
Lee, C. M., 462
Lee, J., 68
Lee, J.-S., 106
Lee, V. L., 315
Leighninger, L., 6
Lein, L., 174
Leippe, M. R., 469
Leiter, M. P., 431
Lemoire, S. J., 246
Lepore, J., 415
Lerner, J. B., 144
Leslie, D., 254, 473
Leukefeld, C. G., 71
Leung, C., 104, 171, 172, 175
Levande, D., 8, 10
Leveson, N., 430
Levikova, A. M., 51
Levitt, J. L., 85
Levy, J., 400
Lewin, K., 336, 340, 344
Lewis, E. I., 154
Lewis, M., 7
Liberman, R. P., 109, 110
Liebert, R. M., 169
Liehr, P., 3
Liepman, M., 61
Lilienthal, D., 416
Lin, H., 178
Lindahl, K. M., 397
Lindsley, O. R., 84
Linehan, M. M., 144, 145
Linsk, N. L., 85
Lipsett, L., 60
Lisman, S. A., 475–476

Littell, J., 400
Livne, S., 298
Lock, J., 400
Loeb, M., 477
Loeb, M. B., xvi
Longres, J., 219
Lorey, F. W., 277
Lorimer, F., 264
Lortie, K., 336
Loury, G. C., 23
Lovardia, M., 373
Lovegreen, L. D., 20
Lovell, M. L., 105
Low, J. A., 51
Lowe, P., 466
Lowery, C. T., 297, 307, 309, 311, 313
Lucas, C., 448
Luckmann, T., 373
Luepnitz, D. A., 385
Lund, C. J., 106
Lussier, Y., 172
Lutzker, J. R., 106, 312, 315, 316
Lynch, M., 384
Lynch, M. A., 104

Macdonald, A., 400
MacDonald, D. A., 246, 247, 248
Mace, F. C., 99
Macfie, J., 398
Mack-Canty, C., 303
MacKenzie, K. R., 361
Mackenzie, M., 175
MacKillop, J., 475–476
Macy, M., 373
Macy, R. J., xxxiii, 125, 126, 135, 138, 146
Madriz, E., 358
Mahoney, M. J., 128, 130
Mailick, M., 10, 12
Main, M., 173
Maiuro, R. D., 178, 179
Makinen, J., 175
Maletzky, B. M., 69
Malik, N. M., 397
Malnati, R., 340, 357
Malott, M. E., 314
Malott, R. W., 314, 316
Manassis, K., 125
Mapp, S., 283
Marais, K., 430
March, J. G., 418
Marín, B. V., 358
Marín, G., 358
Marin, N. W., 154

Marissen, M. A., 68
Markovsky, B., 373
Marlatt, G. A., 145
Marsh, J. C., 297
Marsiglio, W., 397
Martell, C. R., 125
Martin, M., 175
Martin, R., 140
Martinez, K. K., 93
Marvin, R. S., 383
Maslach, C., 431
Mason, J., 37
Masuda, A., 99
Mateer, F., xiii
Mattaini, M. A., xxxiii, 297, 298, 299, 307, 311, 312, 313, 315, 316, 317
Mattick, P., 68
Maugeais, R., 51
Mauricio, A., 177
Maxwell, C., 178
Maxwell, J. S., 106
Mayer, S. E., 24
Mayhew, A. M., 400
McAdoo, P. H., 384
McCord, B. E., 100
McDavid, J. C., 438
McDermott, F., 2, 300, 309, 310
McDiarmid, C. G., 50
McDowell, J. J., 101, 310
McElwain, N. L., 398
McFall, R. M., 105
McGoldrick, M., 181, 382, 385, 392, 393, 399
McGowan, B. G., 312
McGuire, M. S., 316
McGuire, R. J., 65
McIlduff, E., 255
McIntyre, D., 399
McKenna, H. P., 3, 4
McKenna, S., 387
McKenry, P., 175, 176
McKnight, J. L., 318
McMillan, C. J., 479
McMillen, D. P., 303
McMillen, J. C., 174
Megivern, D., 479
Mendel, P. J., 26
Mennen, F., 174
Merriam, S., 211
Merrick, S., 175
Merton, R., 441
Merton, R. K., 3, 5, 14, 23
Messick, S., 6, 38
Metchikian, K. L., 106
Meyer, C., xvi, 217

Meyer, C. H., 299, 300, 301, 302, 303, 311, 312, 313, 317, 460, 463, 473
Meyer, H. J., xvi
Meyer, J. W., 25, 26
Meyer, S., 175
Michael, J., 84, 85
Michels, R., 437
Middlemann, R. R., 330
Mikulincer, M., 171, 172, 175
Miller, A. W., 66
Miller, D., 432
Miller, I., 394
Miller, I. W., 394
Miller, J., 174
Miller, L. K., 88, 90
Miller, N. E., 60, 66
Miller, R. B., 398
Millikin, J., 175
Mills, C. W., 414, 418
Miltonberger, R. G., 106
Mineka, S., 64
Mink, J. M., 106
Mintzberg, H., 420, 422
Minuchin, P., 306
Minuchin, S., 304, 306, 381
Mischel, W., 128, 136
Moen, M., 175
Mohan, B., 8, 10
Molm, L., 372
Monteiro, C., 277
Moody, H. R., 211
Moore, J. W., 47
Moore, L. S., 462
Moore, S., 171, 172, 175
Moore, S. K., 315
Moos, R. H., 37, 38
Morenoff, J. D., 24
Morgan, C., 105
Morgan, C. L., xxiv
Morgan, G., 435
Morgan, L., 73
Morgan, R., 70
Morningstar, G., 421
Morris, T., 466
Morrison, T. L., 172
Mower, O. H., 69
Mower, W. M., 69
Mowlam, M., 180, 181
Muir, D. W., 51
Mullaly, B., 297, 313, 318
Mullen, E. J., 311
Mulroy, E., 1, 5, 10, 11, 28, 31
Munoz, R. F., 125
Muran, J. C., 140
Muroff, J., 156

Murphy, C., 175, 176, 177
Murray, L., 63
Murray, S. J., 26
Musito, G., 384
Myers, L. L., 49

Nakayama, E. Y., 255, 256, 257
Napier, A. Y., 394
Napolitano, L. A., 127
Nash, L., 429
Nathan, P., 67
Neal-Cooper, F., 284
Neenan, M., 132, 134, 138, 147, 151, 155
Nesse, R. M., 61
Neville, B., 255
Newman, B. M., 193, 197, 199, 200, 202, 207
Newman, K., 18
Newman, P. R., 193, 197, 199, 200, 202, 207
Nezu, A. M., 125
Nezu, C. M., 125
Nichols, S., xvii
Nicklett, E. J., xxxiv, 411
Nicotera, N., 8
Nisbett, R., 467
Noller, P., 175
Norcross, J. C., 129, 131, 154
Norlin, J. M., 337
Norton, D., 181
Novak, 74
Nurius, 154
Nurius, P., 219
Nurius, P. S., xxxiv, 125, 126, 136, 138, 148, 298
Nye, F. I., 372

Obegi, J. H., 172
O'Brien, C. P., 62
Ocasio, W., 25, 26, 27
O'Conner, C., 99
Oden, T., 125
O'Donohue, W. T., 125, 154
Odum, E., 300
Ogisi, J., 93
Ohlin, L., 22, 23
Ohman, A., 54
O'Keefe, M., 174
Okon, D. M., 397
Olafson, E., 174
O'Leary, D., 175
O'Leary, K. D., 129
Oliver, J. E., 398
Ollendick, T. H., 64
Olson, D. H., 393

Omer, H., 481
O'Reilly, D., 104
Organista, K. C., 153
Orr, I., 175
Orr, T. E., 70
Orsillo, S. M., 144, 145, 146, 156
Osborn, C. J., 126
Osnes, P. G., 93, 107

Page, T., 174
Painter, S., 179
Paley, B., 383
Pankow, L. J., xxxiv, 263
Pareto, V., 437
Parjer, K., 175
Parker, L., 313
Parsons, T., 418
Pascale, R., 422
Passeron, 27
Patterson, C. A., xxxiv, 225
Patterson, G. R., 315
Patterson, R. L., 108
Patton, B. R., 30, 35
Paulson, R. I., 315
Pavlov, I. P., 47
Payne, M., 311
Pearce, J. K., 385
Pedersen, D. J., 329
Pedhazur, E. J., 3
Pelaez, M., 103
Perlman, H. H., 245
Perron, A., 26
Perrow, C., 430
Persons, J. B., 140, 148, 149
Peters, T., 434, 435, 436
Petry, S., 392
Pfeffer, J., 419
Pharis, M. E., 481
Phillips, A. E., 110
Phillips, E. L., 110
Phillips, G. M., 329
Pierce, W. D., 95, 101
Pinkston, E., 315
Pinkston, E. M., 85, 104, 105
Piper, M., 310
Pittenger, D. J., 462
Place, M., 393
Platt, J. R., 468
Platt, T., 264
Plaud, J. J., 101
Plionis, E. M., 460
Poehlmann, J., 175
Poertner, J., 387
Polansky, N., xxiv, xxv
Polissar, N. L., 70

Pollio, D., 479
Pollock, J., 175
Polster, R. A., 104
Popa, A., 310
Popple, P. R., 6
Posada, G., 171
Powell, W., 25, 26, 27
Pratkanis, A. R., 469
Pratt, H., 214
Preto, N. G., 181
Priel, B., 172
Prigogine, I., 308
Prince, S. E., 125
Prochaska, J. O., 129, 131, 154
Proctor, B. D., 445
Proctor, E., 471
Putnam, R., 23

Quinn, R., 420
Quist, T., 372

Rachman, S., 65
Raikes, A., 166
Rail, G., 26
Randall, W., 212
Rank, O., 230
Rapp, C. A., 302
Rasking, N. J., 232, 244
Rasp, R. R., 110
Rauch, J. B., 264
Raven, B., 34
Ray, W. S., 51
Raynor, S. R., 397
Reddon, J. R., 65
Reed, B. G., 354, 358, 362
Rees, V. W., 68
Rehr, H., 463
Reid, K., 105
Reid, K. E., 330, 331, 332, 333,
    334, 335, 336, 337, 338
Reid, L. D., 67
Reid, W., 311
Reid, W. J., xvi, 85, 255, 476
Reisman, D., 418
Rennemark, M., 210, 211
Reznik, I., 212
Rice, F., 397
Richardson, S., 174
Richards-Schuester, K., 412
Richey, C. A., 105
Richman, G. S., 98
Richman, J., 36
Richmond, M., 298
Richmond, M. K., 385, 397
Richters, J., 171
Riggs, S. A., 174

Riordan, M. M., 105
Risley, T. R., 103
Rivas, R. F., 328, 329, 330, 335,
    340, 342, 344, 353, 354,
    355, 357, 358, 361, 362
Robbins, M. S., 400
Robbins, S. J., 62
Robbins, S. P., 2
Roberts, M. D., 101
Robinson, A., 125
Rochman, E., 479
Rodriguez, C. M., 172
Roemer, L., 144, 146
Roe-Sepowitz, D., xxxiv, 327
Roeser, R., 21
Rogers, C. R., 194, 226, 227,
    232, 233, 234, 235, 240,
    241, 242, 244, 249,
    251–252, 253, 257
Rogers, K. N., 175
Rogoff, B., 22
Rohsenow, D. J., 62
Roll-Hansen, N., 264
Ronan, K. R., 150
Ronen, T., 125
Ronnau, J ., 10
Rose, S., 85
Rose, S. D., 104, 327, 328, 350,
    351, 356, 357
Roseborough, D., 109
Rosen, A., 298, 471
Rosen, K., 384
Rosenbaum, D., 475–476
Rosenberg, G., 463
Rosenfarb, I., 91, 97
Rosenfeld, A., 174
Rosenfeld, M. J., 372
Ross, D., 95
Ross, L., 467
Ross, R., 300, 309
Ross, S., 360
Ross, S. A., 95
Roth, B., 145
Rothbaum, F., 384
Rovee-Collier, C., xiii
Rowan, B., 25, 26
Rowe, C. L., 400
Rowland, M. D., 306
Roys, D., 68
Rubin, A., xvii
Rucker, W. B., 50
Ruef, M., 26
Runyan, W. M., 6
Russell, C., 393
Rutan, J. S., 332, 337, 338, 339
Ryan, C., 394

Rych, J. I., 140
Rzepnicki, T., 107
Rzepnicki, T. L., 85

Sabourin, S., 172
Sachse, R., 250
Safran, J. D., 140
Safren, S. A., 125
Salas, L. M., xxxiv, 327
Saleebey, D., 182, 216, 219, 305
Salter, A., 48
Samovar, L. A., 329
Sampson, G. L., 66
Sampson, R. J., 24
Samuels-Reid, J., 284
Sandin, E., 176
Santa, C. A., 109
Santisteban, D. A., 400
Saunders, K., 175
Sbrocco, T., 154
Schachter, E. P., 210, 216
Schaefer, H. S., 62
Schaefer, J. A., 37, 38
Schaeffer, C. M., 400
Schild, S., 264
Schilling, R. F., 472
Schinke, S. P., 105, 106
Schlesinger, D. J., 105
Schmelkin, L. P., 3
Schmid, P. F., 247
Schock, K., 108
Schoenwald, S. K., 306
Schon, D. A., 35
Schonberg, M. A., 397
Schriver, J. M., 216, 362
Schuchts, R. A., 69
Schusterman, R. J., 102
Schwartz, A., 47, 85
Schwartz, E. K., 337
Schwartz, I. S., 104
Schwartz, W., 352
Scott, R., 284
Scott, W. R., 25, 26, 27, 426, 427
Scrimali, T., 157
Scriven, M., 476
Searle, W., 171
Seeman, J., 230
Segal, Z. V., 137, 145
Seinfeld, J., 60
Selznick, P., 416
Seroka, P. P., 93
Settersten, R. A., Jr., 20
Shaefer, L., 439, 440, 442
Shapiro, S. L., 145
Shavelson, R. J., 26
Shaver, P., 171, 173, 175

Shaver, P. R., 172, 174
Shaw, D. S., 397
Shaw, I., 460
Shaw, M., 47
Shea, M. C., 99
Sheffield, A. E., 298
Sheldon, B., 472
Shellenbarger, S., 431
Shelton, K. H., 397
Sherman, D., 384
Sherman, J. A., 95
Sherman, R., 437
Shibano, M., 104
Shortle, B., 65
Showers, N., 463
Shusterman, R., 214
Sidman, M., 101, 102, 111
Simmel, G., 336
Simon, H., 416, 418
Simons, R. L., 398
Simonton, D. K., xv, xvii
Simos, G., 154
Simpson, B., 373
Simpson, J., 171, 174
Singer, J. E., 69
Siporin, M., 328
Sitharthan, T., 68
Sjodin, C., 210
Skinner, B. F., 84, 91, 96, 97, 111, 314
Skinner, J., xxxiv, 225
Slama, K. M., 110
Slavson, S. R., 337
Slifer, K. J., 98
Smagner, J. P., 104
Smith, D. A., 477
Smith, J. C., 445
Smith, J. E., 397
Smith, J. W., 70, 71
Smith, L., 10
Smith, M., 3
Smith, R., 337
Smith, T. A., 71
Smith, T. E., 105
Smithburg, D. W., 416, 417
Smokowski, P. R., 106
Smultzer, N., 176
Solomon, J., 175
Solomon, R., 174
Sonkin, D., 169, 172, 173, 174, 175, 176, 177, 179
Sontag, L. W., 51
Soulsby, A., 393
Sowers, K. M., xxxi
Sowers-Hoag, K. M., 106, 393

Spence, M. J., 51
Spender, J. C., 430
Sperling, M. B., 173
Sperry, R. W., 242
Spitzer, M., 61
Spitzer, R. L., 466
Sprenkle, D. H., 393
Spretnak, C., 303
Sroufe, L. A., 398
Staats, A. W., 66
Staats, C. K., 66
Stachey, J., 234
Starzomski, A., 175
Staudt, M., 471
Stayton, D. J., 168
Stein, I. L., 386
Stein, T., 104
Steketee, G., 108
Steketee, G. S., 67
Stenger, V. J., 465
Stephenson, W., 248
Stevens, B., 253
Stevens, I., 310
Stevenson, H., 429
Stevenson, O., 473
Stewart, J. L., 125
Stewart, M., 415
Stewart, R. B., 383
Stocker, C. M., 397
Stockhorst, U., 62
Stokes, T. F., 93, 107
Stone, S., 7, 15
Stone, S. I., xxxiv, 1
Stone, W. N., 332, 337, 338, 339
Strauss, B., 361
Streeter, C. L., 309
Stroizer, A. L., 328, 344
Stuart, R. B., 98
Sturge-Apple, M. L., 397
Suarez-Morales, L., 400
Sullivan, M. H., 104
Sullivan, W. P., 302
Sundel, M., 47, 85
Sundel, S., 85
Sundel, S. S., 47, 105
Sutton, J., 64
Sutton, R. I., 427
Swenson, C. C., 400
Szapocznik, J., 400

Taggart, M., 399
Takens, R. J., 243
Tambara, N., 256, 257
Tang, T. Z., 127
Target, M., 175
Tausch, R., 232

Taylor, B., 178
Taylor, J. E., 64
Taylor, P., 70, 283
Taylor, S., xxxiv, 1, 10, 11
Teall, B., 443
Teasdale, J. D., 145
Teigen, J. R., 108
Terranova, M. D., 109
Thapar, A., 397
Tharp, R. G., 98
Thewatt, R., 175
Thiesse-Duffy, E., 106
Thomas, E. J., 85
Thompson, J., 417
Thompson, L. W., 125
Thompson, R., 166
Thompson, V. A., 416
Thornton, P. H., 25, 26, 27
Thyer, B. A., xxxiv, 4, 47, 49, 61, 63, 64, 65, 67, 68, 70, 74, 85, 94, 103, 104, 105, 106, 107, 108, 109, 110, 111, 393, 459, 460, 465, 472, 477, 482
Thyer, K. B., 110
Tichy, N., 441
Tiffany, S. T., 68
Timms, F. M., 71
Tirch, D., 127
Todorski, J., 175
Tolin, D. F., 125
Tolson, E., xvi, xvii
Toro, J., 68
Toseland, R., 328
Toseland, R. W., 328, 329, 330, 335, 340, 342, 344, 353, 354, 355, 357, 358, 361, 362
Towne, L., 26
Treboux, D., 175
Tripodi, T., xvi
Troester, J . D., 67
Trojan Suarez, E. A., 314
Tropman, J., 412, 419, 421, 422, 439, 440, 442, 448
Tropman, J. E., xxxiv, 411, 421
Tsang, S., 104
Tsigaras, N., 63
Tuchman, B. W., 32
Tull, M. T., 144
Turkkan, J. S., 71
Turner, C. W., 400
Turner, F. J., xiv, 4, 38
Turner, R., 70
Turner, R. M., 108
Turquet, P. M., 338

Uchida, N., 384
Ujiie, T., 384

Vaill, P., 429
Vakharia, S., 93
Van Dam, M., 173
Van den Bergh, O., 66
Van Den Brink, W., 68
Van der Veer, R., 181
Van De Ven, A. H., 3, 4
Van IJzendoorn, M. H., 173,
    174–175, 181, 398
Van Vliet-Visser, S., 181
Vaughn, B. E., 173
Vigilante, F., 10, 12
Vodde, R., 313, 314
von Bertalanffy, L., 300, 303,
    374
Vonk, M. E., 64, 67, 108
Voss, K., 437
Voss Horrell, S. C., 125, 153
Vygotsky, L., 22

Wahler, R. G., 316
Wakefield, J., 245
Wakefield, J. C., 6, 311, 312,
    313, 465
Wakefield, P. J., 467
Waldron, H. B., 400
Walker, L. E., 179
Wall, S., 168
Waller, N., 174
Walsh, F., 382
Walter, H., 61
Walters, P., 70
Ward, C., 171
Warren, K., 309
Warren, R., 29, 34
Wassell, S., 174
Wasserman, S., 174
Waterman, A. S., 210
Waterman, R., 436
Waters, E., 168, 171, 173, 175
Watson, D. L., 98
Watson, J., 47, 226
Watson, J. D., 265
Wayland, H. L., xviii

Weakland, J. H., 375
Webster, J., 211, 212
Webster-Stratton, C., 316
Weick, A., 2, 3, 195
Weick, K., 430
Weidman, D., 436
Weil, M., 32
Weinberger, A. D., 140
Weinstein, A., 475–476
Weinstein, D. F., 384
Weisman, S., 214
Weiss, J. O., 264
Weisz, J. R., 125
Wells, E. A., 105
Welsh, D. P., 397
Weltman, S., 181
West, M., 174
Whaley, A. L., 154
Whitaker, C., 394
Whitaker, C. A., 377, 394–395
Whitbeck, L. B., 398
White, H., 100
White, L. D., 416
White, M., 399
Whyte, W. H., 417
Wickens, C., 51
Wickens, D. D., 51, 73
Wicks-Nelson, R., 169
Wideman, M. V., 69
Wilder, D. A., 99, 100, 108
Wilkins, P., 239, 242
Willer, D., 373
Williams, C., 479
Williams, G., 312
Williams, J. M., 145
Williams, K. E., 108
Williams, M., 106
Williams, P. E., 467
Williamson, O., 437
Wilson, E. O., 301
Wilson, G. T., 129, 467
Wilson, K. G., 102
Wilson, S., 417
Winter, M. A., 397
Wiseley, P., 372
Witkin, S., 219
Witkin, S. L., 69

Wodarski, J., 254
Wodarski, J. S., 1, 85, 106
Woehle, R., 309, 310
Wolf, A., 337
Wolf, M. M., 104, 110
Wolf-Branigin, M., 310
Wolfe, R. W., 71
Wolfram, S., 315
Wong, S. E., xxxiv, 83, 92, 93,
    103, 104, 105, 108, 109,
    110, 111
Wood, G. G., 330
Wood, J. K., 256, 257
Wood, J. M., 462
Wood, J. T., 329, 340
Woodin, E. M., 397
Woods, M. E., 386
Woolsey, J. E., 104, 109, 110
Wooten, L., 421
Worsley, R., 252
Wright, J., 109
Wu, C., 398
Wunderlich, A. P., 61

Yalom, I. D., 344, 347, 348, 349,
    350, 355, 361
Yankey, J., 443
Yarrow, L., 171
Yelloly, M., 47
Young, B. G., 65
Young, G., 70
Young, I. M., 297, 318
Young, J., 140
Young, J. E., 140
Young, P. M., xxxiv, 165
Yu, M. L., 100

Zaff, J. F., 473
Zaparanick, T. L., 1
Zarate, R., 109
Zastrow, C., 49
Zeiler, M., 91
Zettle, R. D., 91, 97
Zey, M., 436
Zhu, L., 439, 440
Ziegler, D. J., 233, 236
Zimring, F. M., 232, 244

Subject Index

Abuse and domestic violence:
attachment theory on, 172,
174, 175–179, 180, 181
community interaction
impacting, 384
ecosystems theory on, 312
family systems approach to,
384, 387, 400
Acceptance and commitment
therapy, 102, 145
Ackerman, Nathan, 376–377
Administrative Behavior
(Simon), 416
Adolescents. *See* Children and
adolescents
Adoption, 387
Adult education movement,
330, 331
Agazarian, Yvonne M.,
340–341, 344–345, 347
Age, life course perspective on.
See Life course or life
cycle approach
Agency, life course perspective
on, 15, 19, 27
Aggressive behavior, 110. *See
also* Abuse and domestic
violence
Ainsworth, Mary, 165, 166,
167–168, 170, 173
Alcoholics Anonymous,
475–476
Alcohol use. *See* Substance
abuse
All-or-nothing thinking, 143
American Association of Group
Workers (AAGW), 334
American Social Science
Association, xviii
Anxiety and anxiety disorders.
See also Phobic disorders
attachment theory on, 172,
178–179, 180, 181
cognitive-behavioral theory
applied to, 125, 129, 133,
144, 155

operant learning theory
applied to, 102, 103, 108
respondent learning of,
60–61, 62–63, 65, 67
Aristotle, 47
Association for Specialists in
Group Work "Best
Practice Guidelines," 339
Association for the
Advancement of Social
Work with Groups,
International, 335, 363
Associative learning, 73. *See
also* Respondent learning
theory
Attachment theory:
advanced theoretical
principles of, 169–171
assessment protocols based
on, 173–174
basic theoretical principles of,
168–169
classification of attachment,
170–172
critiques of, 182–183
domestic violence and
attachment, 172, 174,
175–179, 180, 181
family systems theory
influenced by, 383
historical and conceptual
origins of, 166–168
intergenerational
transmission of
attachment styles, 172
intervention strategies based
on, 174–182
juvenile delinquency under,
166, 169, 180
measuring attachment,
173–174
minority disenfranchisement
under, 179–182
online resources on, 184
overview of, 165–166

recent theoretical
developments in,
171–172
relevance to social work,
173–182
stages of, 169–170
Aversion therapies, 70–71

Babinski reflex, 50
Baer, Donald, 85
Barnard, Chester I., 416
Bates, Marston, 301
Bateson, Gregory, 375
Behavioral approaches. *See also*
Human behavioral
theories
behaviorism as, 47–49,
71–74, 129–130, 227,
228–229, 234, 237
cognitive-behavioral theory
as, 125–158, 350–351,
356–357
ecobehavioral practice as,
315–316
operant learning theory as,
83–113
respondent learning theory
as, 47–75
Bekhterev, Vladimir, 47
Beliefs, cognitive-behavioral
theory on, 132, 137,
140–141, 146, 152–153.
See also Thoughts and
thinking
Bettelheim, Bruno, 466
Beyond Rational Management
(Quinn), 420
Bias, theoretical, 467–471
Bion, Wilfred R., 337–338,
349
Blaming, 143, 386–387
Blau, Peter, 419
Blood groups/blood types,
277–278
Boehm, Werner, 478

Bowen, Murray, 277, 376, 377, 379–380, 383, 385, 395–396, 398, 399
Bowlby, John, 165–168, 169, 170, 175, 182
Brief Strategic Family Therapy (BSFT), 400
Butler, Robert, 211, 213–214
Butterfield, William, 85

Carter, Betty, 382
Casework: A Psychosocial Therapy (Hollis), 386
Chaining, 94–95
Chaos theory, 309–310
Charity Organization Society, 385
Child Care and the Growth of Love (Bowlby), 167
Children and adolescents:
    abuse of (see Abuse and domestic violence)
    adoption of, 387
    attachment theory applied to, 165–184, 383
    babies' sucking reflex, 47, 50, 58, 59–60
    child labor, 370
    complexity theory applied to child protection, 310
    diseases in, 264–265
    enuresis or bedwetting by, 69–70
    family systems theory involving, 369–402
    genetic inheritances of, 263–293
    juvenile delinquency of, 22–23, 166, 169, 180, 400
    life course perspective on development of (see Life course or life cycle approach)
    operant learning theory applied to, 86, 87, 90, 96, 101, 105, 106, 110
    prenatal situations, 50, 51, 69, 264, 282–283, 285
    respondent learning theory applied to, 47, 49–51, 58, 59–60, 66, 69–70
    small group participation of, 328, 332

Chromosomes, 267, 268–270, 271–272, 275–276, 280, 282, 288
Classical conditioning theory. See Respondent learning theory
Client-Centered Therapy (Rogers), 227, 232, 252. See also Person-centered theory
Cognitive-behavioral theory:
    advanced theoretical principles of, 140–144
    assessment protocols based on, 146–149
    basic theoretical principles of, 132–140
    cognitive errors in, 141–144
    cognitive restructuring in, 150–153, 356–357
    core beliefs in, 132, 137, 140–141, 146, 152–153
    critiques of, 155–157
    environmental importance in, 138–140, 148, 153, 155–156
    evidence-based foundations of, 154–155
    historical and conceptual origins of, 128–131
    homework used in, 150
    information processing in, 134–136, 140–141
    intervention strategies based on, 149–154
    mediational model of, 132–134
    online resources on, 158
    overview of, 126–128
    recent theoretical developments in, 125, 130–131, 144–146, 154–155
    relevance to social work, 125–126, 146–154
    self-regulation in, 136–138
    small group theory influenced by, 350–351, 356–357
    strategies for identifying cognitive content under, 147–148
Combrinck-Graham, Lee, 382
Communities:
    community-based organizations, 30

    complexity theory applied to, 310
    conflict and change in, 34, 36
    diversity of, 33, 36
    family systems theory on role of, 384
    groups in, 30–32
    integrating mechanisms in, 34–35, 36
    life course perspective on, 24–25
    neighborhood-based (see Neighborhoods)
    power and leadership in, 33–34, 36
    practitioner-environment interaction in, 35, 36
    stages of development of, 32, 36
    structure and process of, 29–35, 36
    systems of exchange in, 32–33, 36
Complexity theory, 309–311, 315, 378
Comte, Auguste, xix, 370–371
Conclusions, jumping to, 142–143
Conditioned Reflex Therapy (Salter), 48
Conditioned stimuli, 50–51
Conference of Charities, xviii
Conflict and change, environmental process of, 34, 36
Context. See Environment
Coping strategies. See Stress and coping
Council on Social Work Education (CSWE):
    group work advancement through, 335
    human behavior and the social environment curriculum standards, xiii, 1, 7, 8–9, 10
    theoretical frameworks supported by, xiv–xv, 460, 461, 463
Counseling and Psychotherapy (Rogers), 226, 232, 251–252
Coyle, Grace, 332, 333, 336
Crick, Francis, 265–266, 280–281, 285
Cue exposure therapy, 67–68

Cult-like interventions, 471–472
Cultural issues. *See also* Racial and ethnic issues
  attachment theory on minority disenfranchisement, 179–182
  cognitive processes influenced by, 145, 156
  cross-cultural theories, xxii–xxiii
  diversity as, 33, 36, 308–309, 442
  ecosystems theory on, 308–309, 313, 314–315, 315–316, 317–318
  families reflecting, 373–374, 374–375, 384–385, 389, 390, 399
  globalization of, 17
  institutional theory on, 26
  life course perspective on, 17, 22, 26
  multicultural group work, 354, 357–359
  operant learning theory on, 88
  organizational culture, 418, 420, 423, 435–436, 438–439, 449, 450
  psychosocial theory on, 205, 208, 218
  small group theory on, 354, 357–359
Cybernetics, 375

Decision making, organizational, 440–441
Delinquency. *See* Juvenile delinquency
Deming, W. Edwards, 413–414, 419–420
Depression and depressive disorders:
  cognitive-behavioral theory applied to, 125, 133, 140, 155
  ecosystems perspective on, 305
  respondent learning foundations in, 72
Descartes, René, 47
Deuteranopia, 283
Dewey, John, 332
Dialetical behavior therapy, 145

Differentiation:
  family systems theory on, 379–380, 395–396, 398, 399
  genetic theory on, 270, 272
  operant learning theory on, 110
  organizational, 426
  small group theory on, 336, 346
Discrimination, 54–55, 92–93
Diseases and disorders, inheritance of, 264–265, 277, 281, 282, 283–285, 287–290. *See also* Mental health issues
Diversity:
  ecosystems theory on, 308–309
  environmental structure of, 33, 36
  organizational, 33, 36, 442
DNA (deoxyribonucleic acid), 265–266, 267, 268, 278–281, 284–285, 290–291
Domestic violence. *See* Abuse and domestic violence
Down syndrome, 265, 285
Dream analysis, 356
Drug use. *See* Substance abuse
Durkheim, Emil, 370–371
Durkin, Helen, 344
Duvall, Evelyn, 382

Eating disorders, 67, 68, 360, 397, 400
Ecosystems theory:
  assessment protocols based on, 311, 313–314
  complexity theory in, 309–311, 315
  conceptual roots of, xvi–xvii, 300–311
  connectedness and transactional focus in, 311–312, 316–317, 319
  contextual factors in, 305, 313, 316
  cultural issues in, 308–309, 313, 314–315, 315–316, 317–318
  diversity role in, 308–309
  ecology as basis of, 301–303, 314
  evaluation of, 311–314

hierarchy in, 306
linear perspectives in, 299–300
mapping, 316–318, 392–393
online resources on, 320
origins of, 298–299
primacy of relationships in, 306–307
rationale for, 299
relevance to social work, 297–320
returning to science of, 314–316
self-organizing systems in, 307–308
structural dimensions in, 303–305
systems theory as basis of, 299–301, 303–311, 314–315
Education. *See also* Training
  adult education movement, 330, 331
  alternatives to reliance on theory in, 476–479
  Council on Social Work Education standards of, xiii, xiv–xv, 1, 7, 8–9, 10, 335, 460, 461, 463
  debates and controversial issues in, 12–14
  empirical perspectives on, 10–12
  evidence-based content lack in, 463–464
  group-focused, 332–333, 334, 335
  harmful effects of bad theory in, 461–464
  history of, 7–8
  human behavior and the social environment (HB&SE) curriculum in, xiii, 1, 7–14
  life course or life cycle approach in, 10–11, 12, 14–28, 37
  linking knowledge to practice, 36–38
  managerial, 443, 450–451
  online resources on, 40–41
  psychoanalytic principles taught in, 332
  Rogers' focus on, 253, 255–256

Education. *See also* Training
    (*continued*)
  social environment
    conceptualization in,
    28–36
  systems approach to, 11, 12
    (*see also* Systems theory)
  theory approach to, xiv–xv,
    11, 12, 460, 461–462,
    463 (*see also* Human
    behavioral theories)
Emotions and feelings:
  aggression as, 110 (*see also*
    Abuse and domestic
    violence)
  all-or-nothing thinking
    impacting, 143
  anxious (*see* Anxiety and
    anxiety disorders)
  cognitive impacts on,
    125–158, 350–351,
    356–357
  core beliefs influencing, 132,
    137, 140–141, 146,
    152–153
  corrective emotional
    experiences, 349–350
  depressive (*see* Depression
    and depressive disorders)
  discounting positives
    impacting, 143
  emotional reasoning, 143
  emotion work in workplace,
    433
  empathetic understanding of,
    238, 249–250
  environmental influences on,
    138–140, 148, 153,
    155–156
  familial emotional proximity
    and distance, 390, 397
  fortune-telling of, 143
  inappropriate blaming
    impacting, 143
  internal stressors related to,
    37
  jumping to conclusions
    impacting, 142–143
  labeling impacting, 143
  magnification of problems
    impacting, 142
  mind reading impacting, 143
  operant learning theory on,
    97, 102, 106, 110, 111
  overgeneralizations
    impacting, 143

psychosocial theory on crises
    of, 199–200, 202–207,
    211, 213
  reflecting or mirroring, 229,
    238, 250–251, 256
  respondent learning theory
    on, 48, 49, 61, 66, 71, 72,
    74
  self-regulation of (*see*
    Self-control or
    self-regulation)
  systems-centered therapy
    exploration of, 346–347
Enuresis or bedwetting,
    treatment of, 69–70
Environment:
  abuse and violence in (*see*
    Abuse and domestic
    violence)
  attachment theory on
    importance of, 165–184,
    383
  characterization of
    person-environment
    relationship, 6–7
  cognitive-behavioral theory
    on, 138–140, 148, 153,
    155–156
  communities as (*see*
    Communities)
  conditioned stimuli in, 50–51
  conflict and change in, 34, 36
  connectedness in, 311–312,
    316–317, 319
  cultural issues in (*see* Cultural
    issues; Racial and ethnic
    issues)
  diversity of, 33, 36, 308–309,
    442
  ecological perspective on,
    301–303, 314
  ecosystems theory on,
    297–320, 392–393
  educational HB&SE
    curriculum, 1, 7–14
  family-based, 369–402
  genetic intersection with, 263,
    288
  globalization of, 17
  groups in (*see* Groups)
  institutional theory on, 25–28
  integrating mechanisms in,
    34–35, 36
  key concepts related to,
    28–36
  mapping, 316–318, 392–393

neighborhood as (*see*
    Neighborhoods)
  niche and habitat in,
    302–303
  online resources on, 40–41
  operant learning changes to,
    83–113
  organizational, 426–427 (*see
    also* Organizations)
  power and leadership in (*see*
    Power and leadership)
  practitioner-environment
    interaction, 35, 36
  process in, 29–32, 33–35, 36
  psychosocial theory
    consideration of,
    193–220
  respondent learning response
    to, 47–74
  risk and resilience in, 36–37
  small group theory on
    influence of, 330–332,
    336–337, 340–341,
    344–345, 351–353, 354,
    355, 362
  social learning theory on, 343
  stages of development of, 32,
    36
  stress and coping with,
    37–38, 150, 172
  structure of, 29–33, 36
  systems of exchange in,
    32–33, 36
  systems theory on, 340–341,
    344–345, 352, 362
  theories on contextual human
    behavior in (*see* Human
    behavioral theories)
  in therapeutic relationships
    (*see* Therapeutic
    relationships)
  timing of events in (*see*
    Timing)
  unconditioned stimuli in,
    49–50
Epigenetic principle, 198–199
Epstein, Laura, 476
Equifinality, 379
Erikson, Erik, 193, 194–200,
    202–209, 212–219. *See
    also* Psychosocial theory
*Erikson on Development in
    Adulthood* (Hoare), 196
Ethical issues:
  Codes of Ethics, 7, 244, 253

genetic practices creating, 264, 282–283, 284–285, 287–292
punishment usage as, 92, 111
Rogers' focus on, 253
Ethnic issues. *See* Racial and ethnic issues
Ethnicity and Family Therapy (McGoldrick et al.), 399
Eugenics, 264
Eukaryotic cells, 266–268, 269, 280
Evidence-based research. *See* Research
Executive coaching, 450
Exposure therapy and response prevention (ETRP), 67–68, 107–108
Extinction:
   operant learning theory on, 91
   respondent learning theory on, 53, 57, 67–68
Eye movement desensitization and reprocessing (EMDR), 464–465, 479

Family Adaptability and Cohesion Evaluation Scales (FACES), 393
Family Assessment Device (FAD), 393–394
The Family Crucible (Whitaker and Napier), 395
The Family journal, 385–386
The Family Life Cycle (Carter and McGoldrick), 382
Family systems theory:
   advanced theoretical principles of, 379–382
   assessment protocols based on, 388–394
   attachment theory influencing, 383
   basic theoretical principles of, 377–379
   boundaries in, 378, 381, 389–390
   critiques of, 398–400
   cultural issues considered in, 373–374, 374–375, 384–385, 389, 390, 399
   differentiation in, 379–380, 395–396, 398, 399
   ecomaps in, 392
   emotional proximity and distance in, 390, 397

equifinality in, 379
evidence-based foundations of, 396–398
family blaming decline under, 386–387
family life cycles in, 381–382
family life spirals in, 382
gender roles in, 371, 373–374, 380–381, 391, 398–399
genograms in, 392–393
hierarchy in, 378–379, 391, 395, 397–398
historical and conceptual origins of, 369–377
homeostatis in, 379, 380, 391–392
intergenerational transmission in, 380, 383, 385, 392–393, 395–396, 398
intervention strategies based on, 394–396, 400
multisystemic therapy applying, 400
normal family processes in, 382
online resources on, 401–402
recent theoretical developments in, 383–385
relevance to social work, 385–396
same-sex families in, 374–375
Feelings. *See* Emotions and feelings
Fight or flight response, 50, 338
First Break All the Rules (Buckingham and Coffman), 429, 451
Flexner, Abraham, xv, xviii
Follet, Mary Parker, 331
Formal Organizations (Blau and Scott), 419
Fortune-telling, 143
Forty Years of Dialogue with the Rogerian Hypothesis of the Necessary and Sufficient Conditions (Bozarth), 232
Fragile X syndrome, 282
Franklin, Rosalind, 265
Freud, Sigmund/Freudian theory:
   attachment theory *vs.*, 166, 168

cognitive-behavioral theory *vs.*, 131
cult-like interventions based on, 470
Erikson's psychosocial theory influenced by, 194–195, 196, 197, 202, 207, 215, 219
family systems theory despite, 386
Rogers' person-centered theory *vs.*, 226, 227, 228, 230, 233–234, 237, 253
small group theory influenced by, 332, 333, 336, 337, 340, 342–343, 355–356, 362
Wednesday Evening Society including, 332
Functional analysis, 98–100

Gambrill, Eileen, 85
Gandhi's Truth (Erikson), 209, 219
Gay/lesbian relationships, 374–375, 466
Gender issues:
   ecofeminism addressing, 303, 314
   family systems impacting, 371, 373–374, 380–381, 391, 398–399
   genetic theory on, 269, 281–285
   organizational diversity and, 442
   psychosocial theory critiques addressing, 215–216
   sex chromosomes impacting, 269, 282
   social work demographics highlighting, 444, 445, 446
General systems theory:
   boundaries in, 341, 343, 344–345, 346–347, 378, 381, 389–390
   complexity theory in, 309–311, 315, 378
   contextual factors in, 305
   differentiation in, 346, 379–380, 395–396, 398, 399
   diversity role in, 308–309

General systems theory
    (*continued*)
  ecosystems theory based on,
      299–301, 303–311,
      314–315
  equifinality in, 379
  family-based, 369–402
  hierarchy in, 306, 378–379,
      391, 395, 397–398
  homeostatis in, 379, 380,
      391–392
  multisystemic therapy
      applying, 400
  primacy of relationships in,
      306–307
  self-organizing systems in,
      307–308, 341
  small group theory influenced
      by, 339–342, 344–347,
      352, 354–355, 357, 362
  structural dimensions in,
      303–305
  Systems-Centered Therapy for
      Groups based on,
      340–341, 344–347, 357
Genetic theory:
  blood groups in, 277–278
  chromosomes in, 267,
      268–270, 271–272,
      275–276, 280, 282, 288
  DNA and RNA in, 265–266,
      267, 268, 278–281,
      284–285, 290–291
  dominant *vs.* recessive traits
      in, 273–274, 277, 283
  ethical issues in, 264,
      282–283, 284–285,
      287–292
  eugenics and sterilization
      based on, 264
  eukaryotic cell in, 266–268,
      269, 280
  gender in, 269, 281–285
  gene therapy in, 287–290
  genetic counseling and, 284,
      290
  genetic engineering and,
      284–285, 288, 290
  genetic evidence and
      identification in,
      290–291
  genetic plasticity in, 291
  Human Genome project in,
      285–291
  meiosis process in, 271,
      275–277

Mendelian, 265, 273–275
mitosis in, 271–272, 276
online resources on, 292–293
pedigrees in, 277–278
relevance of social work to,
    263–266
reproduction in, 264,
    270–271, 282, 284–285,
    288–289
research on, 265–266, 273,
    279, 280–281, 282–283,
    285–291
Genograms, 277, 392–393, 402
Gilbreth, Lillian, 415
Gilligan, C., 215–216
Globalization, life course
    perspective on, 17
Goldstein, Kurt, 226, 231
Group for the Advancement of
    Doctoral Education in
    Social Work, 460
The Group Mind (McDougall),
    336
Groups:
  boundaries in, 341, 343,
      344–345, 346–347
  community- and
      organization-based,
      30–32 (*see also*
      Communities;
      Organizations)
  conflict and change in, 34, 36
  diversity of, 33, 36
  dynamics in, 337, 338,
      340–341, 342, 345–346,
      348–350, 350–353,
      355–359
  family-based, 369–402
  groupthink in, 328, 336, 441
  integrating mechanisms in,
      34–35, 36
  leadership of, 33–34, 36, 337,
      338, 340–341, 342,
      345–346, 348–350,
      350–353, 355–359
  multicultural, 354, 357–359
  practitioner-environment
      interaction in, 35, 36
  scapegoats in, 328, 343, 354
  small group theory on,
      327–364
  stages of development of, 32,
      36
  structure and process of,
      29–35, 36
  subgrouping in, 345–346, 357

systems of exchange in,
    32–33, 36
transference and
    countertransference in,
    342–343
Group Work Symposium, 335

Haley, Jay, 375, 395, 481
Harlow, Harry, 230, 231
Harmful effects of theory:
  alternatives to reliance on
      theory, 476–481
  authority figure rise and
      cult-like phenomena as,
      471–472
  bias as, 467–471
  educational time wasting as,
      461–462
  evidence-based educational
      content lack as, 463–464
  ineffective or harmful
      practices based on bad
      theory as, 465–467
  intellectual blinders as,
      467–468
  online resources on, 483–484
  overview of, 459–461,
      481–482
  research degeneration to
      prove theory true as,
      468–471
  researcher-practitioner
      divisions as, 472–476
  research time and resource
      wasting as, 464–465
Hawthorne studies, 415–416
Hemophilia, 283
Hierarchy:
  ecosystems theory on, 306
  family systems theory on,
      378–379, 391, 395,
      397–398
Hill, Reuben, 382
Hinde, Robert, 168
Hochschild, Arlie Russell, 433
Hollis, Florence, 386
Homeostatis, 379, 380, 391–392
Homosexual relationships,
    374–375, 466
Human behavioral theories:
  alternatives to reliance on,
      476–481
  attachment theory as,
      165–184, 383
  characteristics of good
      theories, xxii–xxvi

characterization of person-environment relationship in, 6–7

cognitive-behavioral theory as, 125–158, 350–351, 356–357

cultural issues addressed by (*see* Cultural issues; Racial and ethnic issues)

ecosystems theory as, 297–320, 392–393

educational curriculum including (*see* Education)

empirical perspectives on, 10–12 (*see also* Research)

family systems theory as, 369–402

genetic theory as, 263–293

harmful effects in social work, 459–484

levels or units of analysis in, 5–6

life course perspective in (*see* Life course or life cycle approach)

middle range theories, utility of, 3–4, 4–5

operant learning theory as, 83–113

organizational theory as, 411–454

overview of, xiii–xiv, 1–2

person-centered theory as, 225–259

philosophical assumptions of, xvii–xxii

psychosocial theory as, 193–220

research on (*see* Research)

respondent learning theory as, 47–75

scholarly and professional dilemmas related to, 2–7

small group theory as, 327–364

social environment conceptualization and, 28–36 (*see also* Environment)

theory, defined, xv–xvii

theory-practice linkages, 3–4

theory-research linkages, 3, 459–460

Human Genome project, 285–291

Humanistic psychology, 227

Human nature, person-centered theory on, 233–236

The Human Side of Enterprise (McGregor), 418

Human trafficking, 310

Huntington's chorea, 264, 265, 277, 285

Hybridization, 270, 273–275

Identity formation, 196–197, 198–199, 205–206, 209, 210, 211, 213, 215, 216–218. *See also* Personality

Identity Youth and Crisis (Erikson), 197

Imitative behavior. *See* Modeling and imitative behavior

In a Different Voice (Gilligan), 216

Information processing, 134–136, 140–141

Institutions:
life course perspective on, 25–28

organizations as social institutions, 422

staff training in, 104–105

Integrating mechanisms, environmental process of, 34–35, 36

Integrative behavioral therapy, 145

Internet-based resources. *See* Online resources

Interpersonal learning theory, 337, 347–350, 355, 356–357, 361–362

Jackson, Don, 375–376, 380–381

Jefferson, Thomas, 264

Journal of Applied Behavior Analysis, 85, 113

Juvenile delinquency:
attachment theory on, 166, 169, 180

family systems approach to, 400

opportunity framework on, 22–23

Kerr, Steve, 428

Kets Devries, Manfred, 432

Klinefelter's syndrome, 282

Knowledge base, 3–4, 36–38. *See also* Education

Labeling, 143, 246

Lamaze training, 69

Language, 73, 154, 204, 216

Laws and regulations, 25, 178

Leadership. *See* Power and leadership

Learning theories. *See* Associative learning; Interpersonal learning theory; Operant learning theory; Respondent learning theory; Social learning theory

Legitimacy, institutional theory on, 26

Lewin, Kurt, 336–337, 340, 344, 375

Life course or life cycle approach:
adolescence and early adulthood, 19, 20–21, 199, 201, 205–206

application of, 17–28

comprehensiveness of theory using, xxii

cultural understanding in, 17, 22, 26

early childhood and school age, 19, 21–22, 199, 201, 202–205

educational curriculum based on, 10–11, 12, 14–28, 37

epigenetic principle in, 198–199

extension of, 16–17

family life cycles, 381–382

human agency and self-regulation in, 15, 19, 27

institutional theory in, 25–28

life cycle *vs.* life course, 217–218

life review or reminiscence therapy, 211–212, 213–214

linked lives in, 15–16, 19

lives in time and place in, 15, 18, 19, 20–21

mid- and late adulthood, 18, 19, 20, 199, 201, 206–207, 207–209

Life course or life cycle
    approach (*continued*)
neighborhood effects in,
    24–25
opportunity framework in,
    22–23
organizational life cycles,
    423–424, 439
psychosocial theory on,
    193–194, 197–219
social capital theory in, 23–24
stress and coping framework
    in, 37
timing of lives in, 15, 19
The Lonely Crowd (Reisman
    et al.), 418

Making Choices program, 106
Malone, Thomas, 377
Management as Performing Art
    (Vaill), 429–430
Mapping, ecosystem, 316–318,
    392–393
Maslow, Abraham, 226, 227,
    230–232, 239
Masturbatory reconditioning,
    68–69
Matching law, 100–101
*Maternal Care and Mental
    Health* (Bowlby), 167
Mayo, Elton, 415
McGoldrick, Monica, 382, 399
McGregor, Douglass, 418
Mead, Margaret, 375
Meiosis, 271, 275–277
Mendel, Gregor/Mendelian
    genetics, 265, 273–275
Mental health issues:
    aggressive behavior as, 110
        (*see also* Abuse and
        domestic violence)
    anxiety as (*see* Anxiety and
        anxiety disorders; Phobic
        disorders)
    attachment theory on,
        171–172, 174, 175–179,
        180, 181
    cognitive-behavioral theory
        applied to, 125, 129, 133,
        140, 144, 154, 155
    depression and depressive
        disorders as, 72, 125,
        133, 140, 155, 305
    eating disorders as, 67, 68,
        360, 397, 400
    functional analysis of, 98–100

obsessive-compulsive
    disorders as, 108
operant learning theory
    applied to, 84–85,
    98–100, 102, 103, 106,
    107–110
phobic disorders as, 61,
    63–64, 67, 107–108
posttraumatic stress disorder
    as, 56
respondent learning theory
    applied to, 60–61,
    62–65, 67–72
schizophrenia as, 99–100,
    108–110, 332, 375, 376,
    377, 379–380
sexual paraphilias as, 64–65,
    68–69, 70
social anxiety as, 62–63, 108
substance abuse as (*see*
    Substance abuse)
Methodological behaviorism,
    71–72
Meyer, Carol, 301, 302, 312, 317
Middle range theories, utility of,
    3–4, 4–5. *See also
    specific theories*
Miller, Danny, 432
Mills, C. Wright, 418
Mindfulness-based therapy, 145
Mind reading, 143
Minorities. *See* Cultural issues;
    Racial and ethnic issues
Mintzberg, Henry, 420–421
Minuchin, Salvador, 381, 395
Mitosis, 271–272, 276
Modeling and imitative
    behavior:
    behaviorism including, 48
    mental health issues impacted
        by, 63, 64, 96
    operant learning theory on,
        94, 95–96
    small group theory on, 356,
        358
Morgan, Lloyd/Morgan's canon
    of parsimony, xxiv–xxv
Moro reflex, 49–50
Motivational interviewing,
    256–257
Multisystemic therapy, 400
Muscular dystrophy, 283–284
Mutual aid model of group
    work, 351–353, 354–355
Myers-Briggs Type Indicator
    (MBTI), 462

Narrative gerontology, 211–212
National Association for the
    Study of Group Work,
    333
National Association of Social
    Workers (NASW):
    Code of Ethics, 7, 244, 253
    establishment of, xix, 334
    research including members
        of, 282–283
    research on theory supported
        by, xix, 460
National Conference of Charities
    and Corrections, xviii
National Conference on Social
    Work/Welfare, xviii
*The Necessary and Sufficient
    Conditions of Therapeutic
    Personality Change*
    (Rogers), 232
Neighborhoods:
    conflict and change in, 34, 36
    diversity of, 33, 36
    family systems theory on role
        of, 384
    groups in, 30–32
    integrating mechanisms in,
        34–35, 36
    life course perspective on,
        24–25
    power and leadership in,
        33–34, 36
    practitioner-environment
        interaction in, 35, 36
    stages of development of, 32,
        36
    structure and process of,
        29–35, 36
    systems of exchange in,
        32–33, 36
The Neurotic Organization
    (Kets Devries and
    Miller),
    432
Newmaker, Candace, 465–466
New Trends in Group Work
    (Liberman), 336
Norms, institutional theory on,
    25–26
Observations of Sioux
    Education'' (Erikson),D
    218

Obsessive-compulsive disorders,
    108
Olson, David, 393

Online resources:
    on attachment theory, 184
    on cognitive-behavioral
        theory, 158
    on ecosystems theory, 320
    on family systems theory,
        401–402
    on genetic theory, 292–293
    on harmful effects of theory,
        483–484
    on human behavior and the
        social environment,
        40–41
    on operant learning theory,
        113
    on organizational theory,
        453–454
    on person-centered theory,
        258–259
    on psychosocial theory, 220
    on respondent learning
        theory, 75
    on small group theory,
        363–364
    On the Folly of Rewarding A
        While Hoping for B''
        (Kerr),D
        428
Operant learning theory:
    advanced theoretical
        principles of, 96–98
    assessment protocols based
        on, 103–104
    basic theoretical principles of,
        85–96
    critiques of, 111–112
    extinction in, 91
    functional analysis in, 98–100
    historical and conceptual
        origins of, 83–85
    intervention strategies based
        on, 104–110
    matching law in, 100–101
    mental health issues/clinical
        disorders under, 84–85,
        98–100, 102, 103, 106,
        107–110
    modeling and imitative
        behavior in, 94, 95–96
    online resources on, 113
    parent and staff training
        under, 104–105
    punishment in, 91–92, 111
    recent theoretical
        developments in, 98–102

    reinforcement in, 85–91, 94,
        95, 97, 98–101, 109–110
    relational frame theory in, 102
    relevance to social work,
        103–110
    respondent learning vs., 84
    rule-governed behavior in,
        96–97
    safety and prevention under,
        105–107
    self-control in, 97–98
    shaping and chaining in,
        94–95
    social skills training under,
        105
    stimulus control in, 92–93
    stimulus equivalence in,
        101–102
Opportunity framework, 22–23
Organizational theory:
    administrative behavior in,
        416–419
    advanced theoretical
        principles of, 426–432
    assessment protocols based
        on, 449–450
    basic theoretical principles of,
        422–425
    core competencies in,
        448–449
    critiques of, 452
    decision making in, 440–441
    demographics of social
        workers in, 443–451
    disciplinary perspectives on,
        435–439
    diversity in, 442
    emotion work in, 433
    evidence-based foundations
        of, 451–452
    executive derailment and
        calamity in, 439–440
    groupthink in, 441
    Hawthorne studies on,
        415–416
    historical and conceptual
        origins of, 414–422
    human enhancement or
        exhaustion in, 431
    intervention strategies based
        on, 450–451
    leadership and management
        in, 424, 437–438,
        439–440, 442–443,
        447–448, 450–451, 452
    online resources on, 453–454

    organizational behavior in,
        411–414
    organizational change in, 451
    organizational culture in, 418,
        420, 423, 435–436,
        438–439, 449, 450
    organizational differentiation
        in, 426
    organizational efficiency and
        effectiveness in, 427–428
    organizational environment
        in, 426–427
    organizational life cycles in,
        423–424, 439
    organizational structure in,
        422, 433–435, 438–439,
        450
    positive organizational
        scholarship in, 431–432
    recent theoretical
        developments in,
        432–442
    relevance to social work, 411,
        442–451
    scientific management in,
        414–415, 418
    sick organizations in, 432
    success and excellence
        concepts in, 429–430
    super- and malperformance
        in, 430
The Organization Man (Whyte),
    417
Organizations:
    administrative behavior in,
        416–419
    change in, 451
    community-based, 30
    conflict and change in, 34, 36
    core competencies of,
        448–449
    culture of, 418, 420, 423,
        435–436, 438–439, 449,
        450
    decision making in, 440–441
    differentiation in, 426
    disciplinary perspectives on,
        435–439
    diversity of, 33, 36, 442
    efficiency and effectiveness
        of, 427–428
    emotion work in, 433
    environment of, 426–427
    executive derailment and
        calamity in, 439–440
    formal, 412–414, 422

Organizations (*continued*)
groups in, 30–32
groupthink in, 441
human enhancement or
exhaustion in, 431
integrating mechanisms in,
34–35, 36
leadership of, 33–34, 36, 424,
437–438, 439–440,
442–443, 447–448,
450–451, 452
life cycles of, 423–424, 439
organizational theory on,
411–454
organization behavior in/of,
411–414
positive organizational
scholarship on, 431–432
practitioner-environment
interaction in, 35, 36
sick, 432
social, 412
stages of development of, 32,
36
structure and process of,
29–35, 36, 422,
433–435, 438–439, 450
success and excellence
concepts in, 429–430
super- and malperformance
of, 430
systems of exchange in,
32–33, 36
Organizations (March and
Simon), 418
Out of the Crisis (Deming), 419
Overgeneralizations, 143

Parsons, Talcott, 371, 391,
418–419, 420
Pauling, Linus, 265
Pavlov, Ivan, 47, 75, 84
Pedigrees, 277–278
Perls, Fredrick, 226
Perrow, Charles, 430
Personality. *See also* Identity
formation
Freudian theory on (*see*
Freud,
Sigmund/Freudian
theory)
person-centered theory on,
233–236, 241–242, 243
psychosocial theory on, 193,
195, 197–198, 199–200,
202–207

Person-centered theory (PCT):
advanced theoretical
principles of, 239–243
assessment protocols in,
246–248
basic theoretical principles of,
233–239
behaviorism *vs.*, 227,
228–229, 234, 237
conceptual constructs of,
239–241
critiques of, 254–257
evidence-based foundations
of, 251–254
Freudian theory *vs.*, 226, 227,
228, 230, 233–234, 237,
253
historical and conceptual
origins of, 226–233
human nature in, 233–236
intervention strategies based
on, 248–251
online resources on, 258–259
overview of, 225
personality in, 233–236,
241–242, 243
positive regard focus in, 229,
233, 236, 237–238, 239,
240, 241–242, 244,
245–246, 247, 249, 251
recent theoretical
developments in,
243–244
reflection in, 229, 238,
250–251, 256
relevance to social work,
244–251
self-actualization in, 229,
231–232, 234, 235–236,
238–239, 240–242, 244,
255
stages of therapeutic process
in, 242–243
therapeutic relationships in,
225–233, 236–238, 239,
240–241, 243, 244–246,
249–251, 253
training in, 253, 255–256
Phenylketonuria (PKU),
264–265, 277, 281
*The Philosophical Legacy of
Behaviorism* (Thyer), 74
Phobic disorders, 61, 63–64, 67,
107–108. *See also*
Anxiety and anxiety
disorders

Positive organizational
scholarship, 431–432
Positive regard, person-centered
theory on, 229, 233, 236,
237–238, 239, 240,
241–242, 244, 245–246,
247, 249, 251
Positivism, xix
Posttraumatic stress disorder
(PTSD), 56
Power and leadership:
domestic violence power
imbalances, 179
environmental process of,
33–34, 36
executive derailment and
calamity in, 439–440
group dynamics influenced
by, 337, 338, 340–341,
342, 345–346, 348–350,
350–353, 355–359
hierarchy based on, 306,
378–379, 391, 395,
397–398
job titles for, 447
managerial education in, 443,
450–451
organizational, 33–34, 36,
424, 437–438, 439–440,
442–443, 447–448,
450–451, 452
Pratt, John, 332
Prenatal situations:
genetic testing in, 264,
282–283, 285
Lamaze training in, 69
respondent learning theory
applied in, 50, 51
Problems, magnifying, 142
Problem-solving therapies, 150
Professional organizations,
xviii–xix. *See also*
specific organizations
Psychoanalytic theory. *See also*
Freud,
Sigmund/Freudian
theory
family systems theory
despite, 386
Rogers' person-centered
theory *vs.*, 227, 228, 237
small group theory influenced
by, 332, 333, 336, 337,
340, 342–343, 355–356,
362

Psychological issues. *See* Mental health issues
Psychosocial theory:
    adult development in, 207–209
    advanced theoretical principles of, 207–210
    assessment protocols based on, 212–213
    autonomy *vs.* shame in, 199, 203, 211, 213
    basic theoretical principles of, 197–207
    critical life events and life review in, 210–212, 213–214
    critiques of, 215–219
    developmental theory of, 193–194, 210
    ego qualities *vs.* core pathologies in, 200, 201
    epigenetic principle in, 198–199
    evidence-based foundations of, 214–215
    Freudian theory influencing, 194–195, 196, 197, 202, 207, 215, 219
    generativity *vs.* stagnation in, 199, 206–207, 211, 213
    historical and conceptual origins of, 194–197
    identity formation in, 196–197, 198–199, 205–206, 209, 210, 211, 213, 215, 216–218
    identity *vs.* role confusion in, 199, 205, 211, 213
    industry *vs.* inferiority in, 199, 204–205, 211, 213
    initiative *vs.* guilt in, 199, 204, 211, 213
    integrity *vs.* despair in, 199, 207, 213
    intervention strategies based on, 213–214
    intimacy *vs.* isolation in, 199, 206, 211, 213
    life course perspective in, 193–194, 197–219
    online resources on, 220
    psychosocial crisis in, 199–200, 202–207, 211, 213

    radii of significant relationships in, 200, 206, 217
    recent theoretical developments in, 210–212
    relevance to social work, 212–214
    stage theory in, 202–207
    trust *vs.* mistrust in, 199, 202–203, 211, 213
Public Administration (Smithburg and Thompson), 416, 417
Punishment, operant learning theory on, 91–92, 111
Punnet square, 274

Q-Set/Q-Sort assessments, 173, 248
Quinn, Robert, 420, 424

Racial and ethnic issues. *See also* Cultural issues
    attachment theory on minority disenfranchisement, 179–182
    cross-cultural theories, xxii–xxiii
    diversity as, 33, 36, 308–309, 442
    ecosystems theory on, 308–309, 315–316
    family systems theory on, 384–385, 389, 390, 399
    psychosocial theory on, 218
    respondent learning of racism, 65–67
Radical behaviorism, 71
Rank, Otto, 226, 229–230, 253, 386
Rebirthing therapy, 465–466
Recreation movement, 330, 331
Reflection, 229, 238, 250–251, 256
Regulations and laws, 25, 178
Reid, William, 476–477
Reinforcement:
    chaining via, 95
    differential reinforcement of other behavior, 110
    factors affecting effectiveness of, 87–88
    functional analysis of, 98–100
    generalized, 88–89

    matching law on, 100–101
    negative, 86–87
    operant learning theory on, 85–91, 94, 95, 97, 98–101, 109–110
    positive, 85–87, 109
    research on, 91, 98–101
    rules overpowering, 97
    schedules of, 89–91, 100–101
    secondary or conditioned, 88–89
    shaping via, 94
Reisman, David, 418
Relational frame theory, 102
Relationships:
    abuse in (*see* Abuse and domestic violence)
    attachment theory on, 165–184, 383
    community-based (*see* Communities)
    conflict and change in, 34, 36
    ecosystems theory on primacy of, 306–307
    family-based, 369–402 (*see also* Children and adolescents)
    group-based (*see* Groups)
    integrating mechanisms in, 34–35, 36
    intimacy *vs.* isolation in, 199, 206, 211, 213
    life course perspective on, 15–16, 19, 20, 21–22, 24–25
    organizational (*see* Organizations)
    power and leadership in (*see* Power and leadership)
    psychosocial theory on radii of significant, 200, 206, 217
    same-sex, 374–375, 466
    social capital from/in, 23–24, 181–182
    stages of development of, 32, 36
    systems of exchange in, 32–33, 36
    therapeutic (*see* Therapeutic relationships)
Reminiscence therapy, 211–212, 213–214
Reno, Janet, 290–291

Reproduction, genetic theory on, 264, 270–271, 282, 284–285, 288–289

Research:
alternatives to reliance on theory in, 476–477, 477–481
on attachment theory, 165–169, 170, 171–172
on cognitive-behavioral theory, 125, 130–131, 144–146, 154–155
definition of, xix
degeneration of, to prove theory true, 468–471
on ecosystems theory, 306–311
falsificationism and justificationism in, 468–471
on family systems theory, 383–385, 396–398
on genetic theory, 265–266, 273, 279, 280–281, 282–283, 285–291
harmful effects of theory in, 459–460, 464–465, 467–476
intellectual blinders in, 467–468
on operant learning theory, 91, 98–104
on organizational theory, 432–442, 451–452
on person-centered theory, 243–244, 251–254, 255
philosophy of science supporting, xvii–xxii
on psychosocial theory, 210–212, 214–215
on reinforcement, 91, 98–101
researcher-practitioner divisions, 472–476
on small group theory, 335, 337–338, 350–353, 359–361
on systems theory, 375
theory-research linkages, 3, 459–460
time and resource wasting by investigating bad theory in, 464–465
Resources. See Online resources
Respondent learning theory:
anticipatory nausea under, 51–53, 63

aversion therapies based on, 70–71
babies' sucking reflex under, 47, 50, 58, 59–60
conditioned stimuli in, 50–51
conditioned taste aversion in, 52–53
creating conditioned reactions in, 69–71
cue exposure based on, 67–68
enuresis/bedwetting treatment based on, 69–70
experimental examples of, 59–62
exposure therapy and response prevention based on, 67–68
Lamaze training based on, 69
learned social anxiety under, 62–63
masturbatory reconditioning based on, 68–69
naturally occurring examples of, 56–59
one-trial learning in, 52
online resources on, 75
operant learning vs., 84
overview of, 47–49
philosophical foundations of, 71–74
phobic disorders under, 61, 63–64, 67
private event respondent conditioning under, 60–62, 71–72
pupillary constriction under, 47, 49, 50, 59
racism under, 65–67
relevance to social work, 67–69
respondent discrimination in, 54–55
respondent extinction in, 53, 57, 67–68
respondent learning of psychosocial problems, 62–67
respondent processes, 49–56
second- or higher-order conditioning in, 56
sensitization in, 55–56
sexual conditioned responses and sexual paraphilias

under, 50, 56, 64–65, 68–69, 70
spontaneous recovery in, 54
substance abuse issues under, 62, 67–68, 70–71
timing of stimuli in, 51–53
unconditioned stimuli in, 49–50
vicarious conditioning in, 53–54
Rewards and recognition, 86
Richmond, Mary, 298, 385
Risk and resilience, 36–37
Risley, Todd, 85
RNA (ribonucleic acid), 267, 278–281
Rogers, Carl, 225–256, 470. See also Person-centered theory
Rule-governed behavior, 96–97

Safety and prevention, 105–107
Same-sex relationships, 374–375, 466
Satir, Virginia, 376, 395
Scapegoats in groups, 328, 343, 354
Schizophrenia:
family system involvement with, 375, 376, 377, 379–380
functional analysis of, 99–100
operant learning theory applied to, 99–100, 108–110
small group treatment of, 332
Schwartz, W., 352
Science and Human Behavior (Skinner), 97
Scientific management, 414–415, 418
Scott, Richard, 419
Sechenov, I. M., 47
Second- or higher-order conditioning, 56
Self-actualization, 229, 231–232, 234, 235–236, 238–239, 240–242, 244, 255
Self-control or self-regulation:
behaviorism addressing, 74
cognitive-behavioral theory on, 136–138
life course perspective on, 15, 19, 27

operant learning theory on, 97–98

psychosocial theory on, 199, 203, 211, 213

Self-monitoring, 147–148

Seligman, Martin, 425

Selznick, Phillip, 416

Sensitization:
eye movement desensitization and reprocessing, 464–465, 479
respondent learning theory on, 55–56
systematic desensitization, 479

Settlement movement, 331, 332

Sexual issues. *See also* Gender issues
aversion therapies for, 70
masturbatory reconditioning for, 68–69
operant learning theory applied to, 108
reproduction as, 264, 270–271, 282, 284–285, 288–289
sexual conditioned responses, 50, 56, 64–65, 68–69, 70
sexual paraphilias, 64–65, 68–69, 70

Shaping, 94

Shorkey, Clayton, 85

Shyne, Ann, 476

Sickle cell anemia, 277, 284, 285

Simon, Herbert, 416, 417

Situational factors. *See* Environment

Skinner, B. F., 71, 72, 83–84, 96, 97, 226, 234, 470

Small group theory:
adult education movement influencing, 330, 331
advanced theoretical principles of, 344–350
assessment protocols based on, 351, 353–355
basic theoretical principles of, 339–344
boundaries in, 341, 343, 344–345, 346–347
cognitive-behavioral model of, 350–351, 356–357
critiques of, 361–362
definitions related to, 329–330

education in, 332–333, 334, 335
evidence-based foundations of, 359–361
group dynamics in, 337, 338, 340–341, 342, 345–346, 348–350, 350–353, 355–359
groupthink in, 328, 336
historical and conceptual origins of, 330–339
interpersonal theories in, 337, 347–350, 355, 356–357, 361–362
intervention strategies based on, 351, 355–357
leadership role in, 337, 338, 340–341, 342, 345–346, 348–350, 350–353, 355–359
models of, 334–335, 350–355
multicultural group work based on, 354, 357–359
mutual aid model of, 351–353, 354–355
online resources on, 363–364
overt and covert aspects of, 337–338
overview of, 327–329
psychoanalysis influencing, 332, 333, 336, 337, 340, 342–343, 355–356, 362
recent theoretical developments in, 350–353
recreation movement influencing, 330, 331
relevance to social work, 327–329, 330–335, 351, 353–359
scapegoats in, 328, 343, 354
settlement movement influencing, 331, 332
social learning theory influencing, 340, 343–344, 356–357, 361
subgrouping in, 345–346, 357
Systems-Centered Therapy for Groups in, 340–341, 344–347, 357
systems theory influencing, 339–342, 344–347, 352, 354–355, 357, 362
transference and countertransference in, 342–343

Smithburg, Donald, 417

Smoking. *See* Substance abuse

Social anxiety, 62–63, 108. *See also* Anxiety and anxiety disorders

Social capital, 23–24, 181–182

Social Diagnosis (Richmond), 385

Social exchange theory, 371–373, 376

Social learning theory, 340, 343–344, 356–357, 361, 482. *See also* Operant learning theory; Respondent learning theory

Social Process in Organized Groups (Coyle), 336

Social skills training, 105

Social work:
alternatives to reliance on theory in, 476–481
attachment theory relevance to, 173–182
cognitive-behavioral theory relevance to, 125–126, 146–154
demographics of, 443–451
ecosystems theory relevance to, 297–320
education in (*see* Education)
ethical issues in (*see* Ethical issues)
family systems theory relevance to, 385–396
genetic theory relevance to, 263–266
harmful effects of theory in (*see* Harmful effects of theory)
human behavior in (*see* Human behavioral theories)
income earned in, 444–445
knowledge base development in, 3–4, 36–38 (*see also* Education)
operant learning theory relevance to, 103–110
organizational theory relevance to, 411, 442–451
person-centered theory relevance to, 244–251
practitioner-environment interaction in, 35, 36

Social work (*continued*)
  professional organizations in,
    xviii–xix (*see also*
    specific organizations)
  psychosocial theory relevance
    to, 212–214
  research in (*see* Research)
  respondent learning theory
    relevance to, 67–69
  small group theory relevance
    to, 327–329, 330–335,
    351, 353–359
  theory-practice linkages in,
    3–4
  therapeutic relationships in
    (*see* Therapeutic
    relationships)
Social Work Research Group,
  xix
Social Work Theory: Interlocking
  Theoretical Approaches
  (Turner), xiv
Social Work with Groups: A
  Journal of Community
  and Clinical Practice,
  335, 363
Society for Social Work and
  Research, xix
Society for the Advancement of
  General Systems Theory,
  375
Spontaneous recovery, 54
Status. *See* Power and
  leadership
Strange Situation experiment,
  168, 170, 173
Stress and coping:
  attachment theory on, 172
  conceptualization of, 37–38
  coping skills therapies, 150
Strong Families program, 106
Structural-functional theory,
  371, 391
Structure and Process in Modern
  Society (Parsons),
  418–419
Substance abuse:
  Alcoholics Anonymous
    treatment for, 475–476
  aversion therapy for, 70–71
  cue exposure therapy for,
    67–68
  family systems approach to,
    400

motivational interviewing
  interventions for,
  256–257
operant learning theory
  applied to, 106
respondent learning theory
  on, 62, 67–68, 70–71
small group treatment of, 332
Sundel, Martin, 85
Symbolic interactionism,
  373–374, 376
Systematic desensitization, 479
Systemic Group Therapy
  (Donigian and Malnati),
  357
Systems-Centered Therapy for
  Groups (Agazarian),
  340–341, 347
Systems-Centered Therapy for
  Groups (SCT), 340–341,
  344–347, 357
Systems of exchange,
  environmental structure
  of, 32–33, 36
Systems theory:
  boundaries in, 341, 343,
    344–345, 346–347, 378,
    381, 389–390
  complexity theory in,
    309–311, 315, 378
  contextual factors in, 305
  differentiation in, 346,
    379–380, 395–396, 398,
    399
  diversity role in, 308–309
  ecosystems theory based on,
    299–301, 303–311,
    314–315
  equifinality in, 379
  family-based, 369–402
  hierarchy in, 306, 378–379,
    391, 395, 397–398
  homeostatis in, 379, 380,
    391–392
  multisystemic therapy
    applying, 400
  primacy of relationships in,
    306–307
  self-organizing systems in,
    307–308, 341
  small group theory influenced
    by, 339–342, 344–347,
    352, 354–355, 357, 362
  structural dimensions in,
    303–305

Systems-Centered Therapy for
  Groups based on,
  340–341, 344–347, 357

Task-centered practice, 476–477
The Task Planner (Reid), 477
Taylor, Frederick W., 414–415,
  418
Theories of human behavior.
  See Human behavioral
  theories
The Theory and Practice of
  Group Psychotherapy
  (Yalom), 348
The Theory of Social Work
  (Bruno), 48
A Theory of Therapy,
  Personality, and
  Interpersonal
  Relationships (Rogers),
  252
Therapeutic relationships:
  cognitive-behavioral theory
    on, 149, 155
  Freudian or psychoanalytic,
    226, 227, 228, 230,
    233–234, 237, 253, 355
  person-centered theory on,
    225–233, 236–238, 239,
    240–241, 243, 244–246,
    249–251, 253
  small group theory on, 337,
    338, 340–341, 342,
    345–346, 348–350,
    350–353, 355–359
Thomas, Edwin J., 85
Thompson, James, 417
Thorndike, Edward L., 83, 85,
  226, 230, 234
Thoughts and thinking:
  all-or-nothing thinking, 143
  cognitive-behavioral theory
    on, 125–158, 350–351,
    356–357
  cognitive restructuring of,
    150–153, 356–357
  core beliefs influencing, 132,
    137, 140–141, 146,
    152–153
  critical thinking skills, 11, 13
  discounting positives in, 143
  emotions influencing (*see*
    Emotions and feelings)
  environmental influences on,
    138–140, 148, 153,
    155–156

fortune-telling of, 143
groupthink, 328, 336, 441
inappropriate blaming
    impacting, 143
information processing of,
    134–136, 140–141
jumping to conclusions
    impacting, 142–143
labeling impacting, 143
magnification of problems
    impacting, 142
mentalizing, 73, 175–176
mind reading, 143
overgeneralizations in, 143
respondent learning
    influencing, 60–62, 65,
    71–73
self-monitoring of, 147–148
self-regulation of, 136–138
    (see also Self-control or
    self-regulation)
strategies for identifying
    cognitive content of,
    147–148
thinking aloud, 147
thought record logs/thought
    listing, 147–148
unconscious, 26, 131, 195,
    197–198, 208, 228, 234,
    337–338, 342–343,
    355–356 (see also
    Psychoanalytic theory)
Timing:
    life course perspective on, 15,
    18, 19, 20–21
    operant learning theory on,
    87–88, 89–91, 100–101

person-centered theory lack
    of time constraints,
    255
respondent learning theory
    on, 51–53
Tobacco use. See Substance
    abuse
Training. See also Education
    executive, 443, 450–451
    parent and staff, 104–105
    person-centered theory, 253,
    255–256
    safety and prevention,
    105–107
    social skills, 105
Transference and
    countertransference,
    342–343
Treating Anxiety Disorders
    (Thyer), 67
Trust, psychosocial theory on,
    199, 202–203, 211,
    213
Turner's syndrome, 282
TVA and the Grass Roots
    (Selznick), 416

Unconditioned stimuli, 49–50
Unconscious thoughts, 26, 131,
    195, 197–198, 208, 228,
    234, 337–338, 342–343,
    355–356. See also
    Psychoanalytic theory

Vaill, Peter, 429–430
Vicarious conditioning, 53–54

Violence. See Abuse and
    domestic violence;
    Aggressive behavior
von Bertalanffy, Ludwig,
    300–301, 303, 340,
    374–375, 379

Warkentin, John, 377
Watson, James, 265–266, 280,
    285
Watson, John, 47, 71–72, 226,
    234
Watzlawick, Paul, 376
Weakland, John, 375
Weber, Max, 414
Weick, Karl, 430
Whitaker, Carl, 377,
    394–395
White, Leonard D., 416–417
White Collar (Mills), 418
Whyte, William H., 417
Whytt, R., 47
Wilkins, Maurice, 265, 266
Wolf, Alexander, 333
Wolf, Montrose, 85
Women's issues. See Gender
    issues
World Health Organization,
    167

Yalom, Irving D., 344, 347–350,
    361
Young Man Luther (Erikson),
    197, 209
Youth. See Children and
    adolescents